COUNSEL MISCONDUCT BEFORE THE INTERNATIONAL CRIMINAL COURT

This is the first comprehensive study of the law governing professional misconduct by defence lawyers before the International Criminal Court. The ICC's regulatory regime was introduced in response to instances of misconduct experienced by other international and domestic criminal courts. The book first turns to how the ICC's forerunners – the International Criminal Tribunals for the former Yugoslavia and Rwanda and the Special Court for Sierra Leone – coped with misconduct, often resulting in controversy. The book also looks at the approaches that have evolved in Germany and the United States, reflecting the different role of defence lawyers in the civil and common law criminal justice traditions.

The book offers a unique insight into the professional responsibilities of defence lawyers within the various international and national regimes. Offering practical guidance on disciplinary systems and other sanctioning mechanisms, it also explores the inherent tension at the heart of the defence lawyer's role: to ensure the human right to a fair trial we want them to be zealous advocates for their clients; at the same time we ask them to commit themselves as officers of the court.

Studies in International and Comparative Criminal Law: Volume 11

Studies in International and Comparative Criminal Law
General Editor: Michael Bohlander

Criminal law had long been regarded as the preserve of national legal systems, and comparative research in criminal law for a long time had something of an academic ivory tower quality. However, in the past 15 years it has been transformed into an increasingly, and moreover practically, relevant subject of study for international and comparative lawyers. This can be attributed to numerous factors, such as the establishment of ad hoc international criminal tribunals and the International Criminal Court, as well as to developments within the EU, the UN and other international organisations. There is a myriad of initiatives related to tackling terrorism, money laundering, organised crime, people trafficking and the drugs trade, and the international 'war' on terror. Criminal law is being used to address global or regional problems, often across the borders of fundamentally different legal systems, only one of which is the traditional divide between common and civil law approaches. It is therefore no longer solely a matter for domestic lawyers. The need exists for a global approach which encompasses comparative and international law.

Responding to this development this new series will include books on a wide range of topics, including studies of international law, EU law, the work of specific international tribunals, and comparative studies of national systems of criminal law. Given that the different systems to a large extent operate based on the idiosyncracies of the peoples and states that have created them, the series will also welcome pertinent historical, criminological and socio-legal research into these issues.

Volume 1: The German Criminal Code: A Modern English Translation
Michael Bohlander

Volume 2: Principles of German Criminal Law
Michael Bohlander

Volume 3: Crime, Procedure and Evidence in a Comparative and International Context: Essays in Honour of Professor Mirjan Damaska
Edited by John Jackson, Maximo Langer and Peter Tillers

Volume 4: The Criminal Responsibility of Senior Political and Military Leaders as Principals to International Crimes
Hector Olasolo

Volume 5: Transnational Organised Crime in International Law
Tom Obokata

Volume 6: Sentencing in International Criminal Law: The Approach of the Two ad hoc Tribunals and Future Perspectives for the International Criminal Court
Silvia D'Ascoli

Volume 7: OLAF at the Crossroads
Constantin Stefanou, Simone White and Helen Xanthaki

Volume 8: Principles of German Criminal Procedure
Michael Bohlander

Volume 9: Hybrid and Internationalised Criminal Tribunals
Sarah Williams

Volume 10: The Defendant in International Criminal Proceedings: Between Law and Historiography
Björn Elberling

Counsel Misconduct before the International Criminal Court

Professional Responsibility in International Criminal Defence

Till Gut

·HART·
PUBLISHING

OXFORD AND PORTLAND, OREGON
2012

Published in the United Kingdom by Hart Publishing Ltd
16C Worcester Place, Oxford, OX1 2JW
Telephone: +44 (0)1865 517530
Fax: +44 (0)1865 510710
E-mail: mail@hartpub.co.uk
Website: http://www.hartpub.co.uk

Published in North America (US and Canada) by
Hart Publishing
c/o International Specialized Book Services
920 NE 58th Avenue, Suite 300
Portland, OR 97213-3786
USA
Tel: +1 503 287 3093 or toll-free: (1) 800 944 6190
Fax: +1 503 280 8832
E-mail: orders@isbs.com
Website: http://www.isbs.com

British Library Cataloguing in Publication Data
Data Available

ISBN: 978-1-84946-317-1

Typeset by Hope Services, Abingdon
Printed and bound in Great Britain by
Lightning Source UK Ltd

For my queen, Regina

PREFACE

> Membership in the Bar is a privilege burdened with conditions.
>
> Justice Benjamin N Cardozo, *In re Rouss*, 221 N.Y. 81, 116 N.E. 782 (Court of Appeals of New York, 1917).
>
> That government hires lawyers to prosecute and defendants who have the money hire lawyers to defend are the strongest indications of the wide-spread belief that lawyers in criminal courts are necessities, not luxuries. The right of one charged with crime to counsel may not be deemed fundamental and essential to fair trials in some countries, but it is in ours.
>
> Justice Hugo L Black, *Gideon v Wainwright*, 372 U.S. 335 (Supreme Court of the United States, 1963).
>
> [A] jury trial is a fight and not an afternoon tea.
>
> Justice William R Riddell, *Dale v Toronto R.W. Co.*, 34 Ont. L.R. 104 (Supreme Court of Ontario, 1915).

These three quotes may be no more than a rather random and moreover quite one-sided selection from three jurisdictions, out of the many more in existence. As is plain to see from the citations, the first two are from the United States of America, and the third hails from the province of Ontario in Canada. They thus represent merely one dominating legal tradition – the Anglo-Saxon common law tradition. It is readily conceded that this leaves out all the other eminent legal systems of the world. But the common law is very distinctive in that it has produced a wealth of jurisprudence and case law that is notable and important for international trials, and it knows how to put into words the essential beliefs underlying the system. Among this is a trial culture that expressly recognises the right to defence and equality of arms as core values of the law.

The idea behind this transcends the common law, though. Of course, other legal systems emphasise their commitment to the idea of a fair trial and the right to counsel quintessentially to the same effect. Likewise do the international courts. One feature setting apart the common law courts of this world from others, though, is the way that judicial rulings are associated with their makers. It illustrates fittingly how persons and their respective individualities create and shape the law. More specifically, it can be grasped how they are one out of different actors in the administration of justice. Each of these actors is a human person who exercises a role, and as such they represent different tasks and interests. Defence lawyers serve very specific interests, among them are chiefly those of criminal suspects and accused. The famous quote by Justice Black in *Gideon v Wainwright* most aptly conveys that representation by a lawyer is indeed also one of our common interests on which modern justice builds, namely affording any suspect or accused a fair trial.

Justice Black does not fail to hint at another point. The government's effort is to effectively prosecute crime. It thus pursues a fundamental interest of society. Pitting the common interest of holding someone accountable against his or her fundamental liberty interests, however, can make a trial quite messy and unruly. Trials are prone to suffer from human inadequacies, unfortunate slips and calculated punches. Justice Riddell in *Dale v Toronto R.W. Co.* wittily observes how the stakes in this are typically higher than in more ordinary social events.

Although trials may be fights, they are societal events and not without rules. As actors within the system, lawyers need to commit to playing along the fundamental rules. They are allowed to fight for a cause, for whichever interest they legitimately take a stand. Justice Cardozo spells out very succinctly in *Rouss* how this comes in exchange for being bound by the rules. For defence lawyers as members of the Bar, these conditions, as Justice Cardozo calls them, result in professional ethics. The consequence which lawyers have to bear is professional responsibility.

ACKNOWLEDGEMENTS

This book is the published version of my thesis for the *Doctor iuris* degree awarded by the Faculty of Law of the University of Cologne. This thesis entitled 'Reacting to Counsel Misconduct before the International Criminal Court' was supervised by Professor Claus Kreß and defended in January 2011.

Since coming to Cologne in late 2005, and throughout my thesis, I had the privilege of working as a research associate to Professor Kreß. I owe him beyond words for years of faith in my work and his spirited mentorship.

Being part of his *Lehrstuhl* was always an extraordinary joy and inspiration to me – and it still is. All those people who shared their time and their thoughts with me, some of them their offices, but all of them their friendship, who joined on *Mensa* trips and other legal as well as distinctly non-legal functions: thank you.

Professor Thomas Weigend is an eminent scholar of international criminal law and a great personality. I am very glad and thankful for having had him as the co-referee for my thesis.

Indispensable research on the United States, in particular in chapter two, was done during a visit to Dallas, Texas, and to Washington, DC, in the spring of 2008. I am very much indebted to Associate Professor Jenia Iontcheva Turner of the Dedman School of Law of Southern Methodist University, and to Professor David Luban of the Georgetown University Law Center for hosting me. I am grateful to the German Academic Exchange Service (DAAD) for funding this.

I am honoured that my thesis is a co-winner of the 2012 faculty prize, under the generous sponsorship of the law firm of Cornelius Bartenbach Haesemann & Partner.

It is my great pleasure to thank my dear parents for their perennial support. Note to my brothers: 1. No zebrafish were harmed during the making of this book; 2. Computers are very fine typewriters.

This is an entire book on the worthy topic of misconduct by lawyers and their professional responsibility. Much more remains to be said on a more general theme: 'Dealing with Neglect by PhD Student Fiancé – Personal Responsibility beyond Thesis Writing'. I'm only starting to make up on this one but I guess I know the gist. It would have to be: thank you for everything, Regina.

TG

Cologne, June 2012

PS Hello, Carlo

CONTENTS

Introduction

I Common Professional Standards for Defence Lawyers before the ICC

Rules of professional conduct are a universal phenomenon established well before the inception of the international criminal courts.[1] The regulation of professional conduct is an essential feature of legal orders, although it may, of course, differ in detail.[2] Most jurisdictions provide for rules which either directly or indirectly mandate or otherwise address conduct by legal professionals. It is a general phenomenon intrinsically linked to legal systems. Every court has its ordinary laws of procedure that prescribe the rights and duties of counsel participating in proceedings. Professional rules add another layer of regulation, on top of the first layer which is applied by the courts in the course of legal proceedings.[3]

It is understood that a lawyer has duties arising from the fact that he or she is representing a client, and therefore is in a position of trust where he or she is expected to safeguard the client's interests. On the other hand, professional rules are necessary for the functioning of the system of the administration of justice as a whole. This does not concern individual cases but rather the balance of the overall system.

This book examines the evolving regime on the professional conduct of lawyers acting before the International Criminal Court (ICC), in particular counsel for the defence. The purpose is to further the understanding of such rules and their practical implications for the work of counsel, especially with regard to the disciplinary system and other measures in connection with misconduct.

The ICC regime itself is a response to the considered need for such rules. This need also existed for the other courts within the history of international criminal justice, such as the International Criminal Tribunals for the former Yugoslavia and Rwanda (ICTY and ICTR) and the Special Court for Sierra Leone (SCSL). Consequently, the study will also turn to other developments on the international level leading up to the status quo of the ICC. This will be complemented by a comparative survey of national systems.

[1] JT Tuinstra, *Defence Counsel in International Criminal Law* (Cambridge, Cambridge University Press, 2009) 195–201, 241–43.

[2] See ibid, 193–94, 272–73.

[3] S Kay and B Swart, 'The Role of the Defence' in A Cassese, P Gaeta and JRWD Jones (eds), *The Rome Statute of the International Criminal Court: A Commentary* (Oxford, Oxford University Press, 2002) 1432.

Beyond the ICC's primary legal source – its own statutory law – Article 21(1) of the Rome Statute itself also directs the Court to other sources of law:

> The Court shall apply:
>
> (a) In the first place, this Statute, Elements of Crime and its Rules of Procedure and Evidence;
> (b) In the second place, applicable treaties and the principles and rules of international law, . . . ;
> (c) Failing that, general principles of law derived by the Court from national laws of legal systems of the world including, as appropriate, the national laws of States that would normally exercise jurisdiction over the crime, provided that those principles are not inconsistent with this Statute and with international law and internationally recognized norms and standards.

With a view to the ICC, a closer examination of the UN tribunals in chapter one will help to identify the said 'principles and rules of international law' that may have been generated in the meantime.[4] The same can be said of chapter two on Germany and the United States for 'principles of law derived by the Court from national laws of legal systems of the world'. Furthermore, it seems advisable to delve into national jurisdictions as a matter of principle. Defence counsel hail from different countries where they have been trained and where they practise. Thus the respective backgrounds must be taken into consideration.

II Concepts of Professional Conduct, Professional Responsibility and Professional Ethics

The general subject of professional conduct raises a whole host of issues, which can certainly be approached from very different angles. The general concept of legal ethics would stretch far enough to also capture jurisprudential or wider philosophical reflections on law as an ethical system and on the moral obligations of individual lawyers, beyond the objective and commonly accepted standards of court and client-work in the context of international criminal courts.

Similarly, construing professional conduct as a general theory of the role and the position of the defence in international criminal proceedings appears to be a

[4] See, however, from a methodology perspective the qualifications made by Judge Kaul in *Situation in the Republic of Kenya*, ICC-01/09-19, Pre-Trial Chamber II, Decision Pursuant to Article 15 of the Rome Statute on the Authorization of an Investigation into the Situation in the Republic of Kenya, 31 March 2010, Dissenting Opinion of Judge Kaul, paras 28–30. Pre-Trial Chamber II of the ICC has held that 'the rules and practice of other jurisdictions, whether national or international, are not as such "applicable law" before the Court beyond the scope of article 21 of the Statute' (*The Prosecutor v Joseph Kony et al*, ICC-02/04-01/05-60, Pre-Trial Chamber II, Decision on the Prosecutor's Position on the Decision of Pre-Trial Chamber II to Redact Factual Descriptions of Crimes from Warrants of Arrest, Motion for Reconsideration and Motion for Clarification, 28 October 2005, para 19).

topic of its own.[5] It might prove rewarding in terms of understanding the functioning of the administration of international criminal justice and the interaction of the participants therein. However, it would not be exclusively concerned with the professional responsibility of the individual lawyer.

Therefore, focusing on the sanctioning and disciplining regime for misconduct seems the most promising approach. It deals with the immediately relevant implications for the practice of the ICC, as well as identifying the major categories of misconduct.

It is emphasised that this study is not going to engage in theoretical explanations that go beyond the legal framework of professional ethics, to which the analysis is confined throughout this book. Authors have suggested that character, personality and individual integrity may ultimately be the key to legal ethics.[6] There is no disputing this, but 'common moral principles'[7] will, first of all, constitute no firm lead in the international arena and thus fail to address the immediate need for regulation.

Secondly, it may principally be ill-fitted to contribute to regulation at all. Apart from the more or less external systems of enforcement,[8] there is clearly such a thing as non-legal regulation, going back to the time where 'reliable gossip' sufficed to single out black sheep from the profession.[9] Among the advantages of non-legal regulation may be its quickness and the low transaction costs, but it will invariably be non-transparent and offer no procedural regularity.[10] Professional regulation serves to reconcile the antagonisms underlying the role of the lawyer, in particular the advocate in litigation. If non-legal regulation takes the path of unorganised sanctions, it may still be effective but endangers the values of procedural transparency, accountability and evenhandedness which are at the core of the system of justice that the regulatory system itself seeks to preserve. It may be especially harmful in the international context. Lastly, non-legal regulation cannot or should not be engaged by the court or other institutions on purpose. If regulation is non-legal because it primarily relies on individual ethics or morals, it faces at the outset the same problem of non-transparency, and although it may be the ultimate key to professionalism, a serious problem of efficiency. Therefore, both these strands of non-legal regulation will be discarded for the purpose of this book.

[5] It justifies a separate book, see Tuinstra (n 1).

[6] L Griffin, 'The Lawyer's Dirty Hands' (1994–95) 8 *Georgetown Journal of Legal Ethics* 219, 263; MN Browne, CL Williamson and LL Barkacs, 'Purported Rigidity of an Attorney's Personality: Can Legal Ethics Be Acquired' (2005–06) 30 *Journal of the Legal Profession* 55; S Dolovich, 'Ethical Lawyering and the Possibility of Integrity' (2002) 70 *Fordham Law Review* 1629.

[7] Griffin (n 6) 282.

[8] DB Wilkins, 'Who Should Regulate Lawyers?' (1992) 105 *Harvard Law Review* 801, 803.

[9] GC Hazard and C Beard, 'A Lawyer's Privilege Against Self-Incrimination in Professional Disciplinary Proceedings' (1987) 96 *Yale Law Journal* 1060, 1074.

[10] See generally WB Wendel, 'Nonlegal Regulation of the Legal Profession: Social Norms in Professional Communities' (2001) 54 *Vanderbilt Journal of Transnational Law* 1955.

This study will stick to legal ethics as a 'closed system'.[11] This will largely be based on the rules as they stand. This may be very positivist or formalist but is a practical starting point.[12]

III The Various Types of Enforcement Mechanisms in Counsel Regulation

In the US context, David Wilkins has put forward a sophisticated model of how lawyers are regulated, describing four types of enforcement mechanisms: disciplinary controls, liability controls, institutional controls and legislative controls.[13] Disciplinary controls are handled by independent agencies which engage in a process resembling a criminal prosecution. As liability controls, lawyers are primarily sued by affected individuals. Institutional controls are those mechanisms which are used by the institutions themselves within which lawyers work. Finally, he describes legislative controls, being controls on the basis of state authority and legislation, regardless of whether they are applied by executive or legislative bodies, where 'authority and operation ultimately rest in the hands of the executive or the legislative branch rather than the courts'.[14] Wilkins himself stresses that '[e]ach of the four regulatory models is capable of producing efficient compliance, but only in certain quadrants'.[15]

No author has seriously disputed Wilkins' conclusion that the regulation of counsel is a multi-tiered system, whose model the analysis in this book will follow.

All of the described sub-sets within the overall system of 'regulation'[16] ultimately serve the same goal: safeguarding the profession as a free one, consistent with the ideal of the rule of law, while establishing checks on the behaviour of professionals for the common good, ie, societal interests, interests of the client and those of third parties. If only single sub-sets of regulation – such as codes of conduct – are examined and compared with each other, this fails to take into account that the sub-sets vary crucially: how and by whom they are created, how aspiring or binding the respective sub-set is, or whether it serves internal or external functions.[17]

[11] As it is called by Griffin (n 6) 234.

[12] See DB Wilkins, 'Legal Realism for Lawyers' (1990) 104 *Harvard Law Review* 468, 471.

[13] Wilkins (n 8). See also his 'afterword': DB Wilkins, 'Afterword: How Should We Determine Who Should Regulate Lawyers? – Managing Conflict and Context in Professional Regulation' (1996) 65 *Fordham Law Review* 465. See further CA Rogers, 'Context and Institutional Structure in Attorney Regulation: Constructing an Enforcement Regime for International Arbitration' (2003) 39 *Stanford Journal of International Law* 1.

[14] Wilkins (n 8) 809.

[15] ibid, 873.

[16] On the use of the term, see BH Barton, 'An Institutional Analysis of Lawyer Regulation: Who Should Control Lawyer Regulation – Courts, Legislatures or the Market?' (2003) 37 *Georgia Law Review* 1167, 1168, clarifying that none of various conceivable sub-sets are 'the only determinants of lawyer behavior'.

[17] LE De Groot-Van Leeuwen and WT De Groot, 'Studying Codes of Conduct: A Descriptive Framework for Comparative Research' (1998) 1 *Legal Ethics* 155, 159.

Many studies highlight only one of the sets of controls outlined by Wilkins, although they acknowledge that different authorities are involved, that public and private controls exist and that measures pursue different purposes.[18] Those who look at the bigger picture categorise the regulation of counsel around legally enforceable controls, sufficiently similar to Wilkins.[19]

The examination of how counsel are effectively regulated would be incomplete, however, without fully considering how these tools are applied which warrants a closer look at three issues. The first is the applicable procedure for each set of measures. Each single measure has, of course, its own governing set of rules. As will be shown, these vary greatly in detail. The more interesting issue is, however, the fundamental principles underlying the imposition of sanctions and the procedural safeguards for counsel. In this regard, the above-discussed measures can be grouped into three major categories. First, truly criminal proceedings traditionally come with particular due process requirements. Disciplinary sanctions are a second category and follow a procedure which sets it apart from criminal procedure but is also again distinguishable from other measures. Finally, the procedure for the remaining measures will be outlined. These are principally the institutional measures described above. The analysis of the measures and a comparison will allow them to be put into a relationship with each other.

[18] See, eg, GL Hampton, 'Toward an Expanded Use of the Model Rules of Professional Conduct' (1990–91) 4 *Georgetown Journal of Legal Ethics* 655, 656.

[19] TD Morgan, 'Sanctions and Remedies for Attorney Misconduct' (1994–95) 19 *Southern Illinois University Law Review* 343, 344; Barton (n 16) fns 6 *et seq*; BH Barton, 'Why Do We Regulate Lawyers: An Economic Analysis of the Justifications for Entry and Conduct Regulation' (2001) 33 *Arizona State Law Journal* 429, 432; M Kilian, 'Berufsrechtliche Verantwortlichkeit von Strafverteidigern' in T Weigend, S Walther and B Grunewald (eds), *Strafverteidigung vor neuen Herausforderungen – Denkanstöße aus sieben Rechtsordnungen* (Berlin, Duncker & Humblot, 2008) 113–56.

1

The UN International Criminal Tribunals: ICTY, ICTR and SCSL

I The UN Tribunals: Criminal Justice Steps onto the International Arena Again

The two United Nations ad hoc Tribunals, the United Nations International Criminal Tribunal for the former Yugoslavia (ICTY) and the International Criminal Tribunal for Rwanda (ICTR) were the first instances of modern international criminal courts in the 1990s. They were followed by another international tribunal with UN backing, the Special Court for Sierra Leone (SCSL). All three have in common that they are genuinely international courts with comprehensive jurisdiction over the international core crimes.[1] They are not entrenched in a domestic judiciary but all have had to develop their own, distinctly international procedure. This is also reflected in the regulation of counsel. That they had to come up with a new, truly international approach justifies placing particular emphasis on the three named Tribunals. Their truly international footing and their competence over the core crimes sets them apart from the other internationalised and hybrid courts with varying involvement from the UN, such as the Special Tribunal for Lebanon.[2]

The ICTY, the ICTR and the SCSL have thus become the seminal predecessors to the ICC. As they engaged in the adjudication of cases, it was considered there was a need to institute a regulatory scheme for defence counsel. The experience and the practice of the UN tribunals with regard to counsel misconduct is helpful when examining the ICC.[3]

[1] For a comparative general study of the named courts, see WA Schabas, *The UN International Criminal Tribunals: the former Yugoslavia, Rwanda and Sierra Leone* (Cambridge, Cambridge University Press, 2006). See also JT Tuinstra, *Defence Counsel in International Criminal Law* (Cambridge, Cambridge University Press, 2009) 9.

[2] Established by an Agreement between the UN and the Lebanese Republic, pursuant to Security Council Resolution 1664 (2006) of 29 March 2006. The Statute is contained in Security Council Resolution 1757 (2007) of 30 May 2007.

[3] See, however, the qualifications made in the ICC's jurisprudence on adopting case law and practice from the other international jurisdictions, in particular *The Prosecutor v Joseph Kony et al*, ICC-02/04-01/05-60, Pre-Trial Chamber II, Decision on the Prosecutor's Position on the Decision of Pre-Trial Chamber II to Redact Factual Descriptions of Crimes from Warrants of Arrest, Motion for

Most notably, the UN tribunals have relied on the concept of contempt which they recognised as an inherent power, rooted in international law. The ICTY, in particular, has used this as a sanctioning instrument and conducted a number of contempt proceedings in response to misconduct of defence lawyers.[4] It remains to be seen to what extent reliance on such powers still remains relevant for the ICC. However, the records of the ICTY and the ICTR feature certain facets of professional misconduct and regulation which transgress the specific institutional context.

A The General Context of the UN Tribunals

Following decades of chilled standstill during the Cold War, two international tribunals were set up by the United Nations' Security Council in the 1990s. The Security Council decided, in Resolution 808 (1993),[5] to establish an international tribunal 'for the prosecution of persons responsible for serious violations of international humanitarian law committed in the territory of the former Yugoslavia since 1991', and subsequently did so by Resolution 827 (1993).[6] Soon after that a sister court, the International Criminal Court for Rwanda, followed in Resolution 955 (1994).[7] This was complemented in 2000 by a third international court under the auspices of the UN – the Special Court for Sierra Leone. The Security Council requested the Secretary-General in Resolution 1315 (2000)[8] to negotiate an agreement with the Government of Sierra Leone. This agreement subsequently created the SCSL's Statute.

The UN Resolutions and the Agreement, respectively, were the founding acts but provided little more than the basis on which these tribunals still operate. The statutes of the named courts contain prescriptions of the penalised offences, general principles of substantive criminal law and a rough outline of the general procedure, including safeguards for the rights of the accused. Thus, they only provide a limited statutory framework. Most procedural issues are governed by the Rules of Procedure and Evidence (the RPE). Over the years, the RPE have had various amendments and have thus grown to accommodate many issues arising from the proceedings before both tribunals. They depart from each other on a number of issues but feature, by and large, overwhelming commonalities.

According to Rule 6 of the respective RPE, they are amended by the plenary of the respective judges. In many cases, amendments for one tribunal may simply

Reconsideration and Motion for Clarification, 28 October 2005, para 19; *Situation in the Republic of Kenya*, ICC-01/09-19, Pre-Trial Chamber II, Decision Pursuant to Article 15 of the Rome Statute on the Authorization of an Investigation into the Situation in the Republic of Kenya, 31 March 2010, Dissenting Opinion of Judge Kaul, paras 28–30, see above, Introduction (n 4).

[4] See below, II.B.ii at 16–25.

[5] Adopted 22 February 1993.

[6] Adopted 25 May 1993.

[7] Adopted 8 November 1994.

[8] Adopted 14 August 2000.

have been deemed equally useful for the other one, as the problems before one are mirrored in the practice of the sister court. It may also have contributed that the ICTY and the ICTR share a rota of permanent judges, ie, the ones sitting on the bench of the common ICTY/ICTR Appeals Chamber. Moreover, the ICTR RPE expressly constituted the starting point for the SCSL RPE.[9]

The major if not exclusive role of the judges in the evolution of the RPE has encountered criticism. The RPE substantially shape the administration of justice before both courts. They do not simply organise the tribunals' business but determine fundamental principles underlying the system as a whole. To name just a few examples, the sentencing process, the admissibility of evidence and remedies against the decisions of organs of the tribunals are briefly mentioned in the statutes but only fully developed in the RPE. All these subjects concern essential tenets of the tribunals' law. It has been questioned how these wide-ranging powers of the judges can be reconciled with the role of the judges as neutral arbiters.

Beyond the RPE, a range of other rules bearing relevance to the defence have been enacted. Many have been promulgated by the Registrar within his own authority, others required involvement of the President or the judges. The principal issue here seems to be, however – and the RPE simply serve as the prime example – that organs of the tribunals are vested with broad legislative powers. Most strikingly, this can be said of the judges who, according to a theory of strict separation of powers, should not be part of the rule-making process but rather be impartial adjudicators while bound by those rules.[10] This constitutes a major difference from national systems where rules are either enacted by parliament or at least form part of a self-regulatory regime which draws its legitimacy from the involvement of the body's members.

Notwithstanding these questions, it needs to be underscored that the tribunals were faced with the challenge of adjudicating the pending cases in a fair and expeditious manner. The tribunals' jurisprudence was to not fall back behind the standards afforded by national judiciaries and internationally recognised requirements.[11] Accordingly, they evolved into fully-fledged criminal courts, along with the necessary accompanying statutory framework.

[9] See below, IV.A at 46, on the legal bases of the SCSL.

[10] It needs only brief mention that, of course, quite different notions underlie the role of judges and their part in the creation of law in the different domestic systems. The comprehensive powers afforded to the judges of the international tribunals (see Art 15 of the ICTY Statute, and Art 14 of the ICTR Statute) are by any means unique. Even where the judiciary has the principal power to prescribe rules, these are still (partially or wholly) subject to legislative review. See, eg, for US federal courts the Rules Enabling Act, 28 U.S. Code §§ 2071–2077.

[11] In the meantime, a weighty argument has been made of how some of the objectives behind international criminal justice, inter alia, that of enforcing humanitarian international law and human rights, may pose a challenge to the classic notion of the criminal process: D Robinson, 'The Identity Crisis of International Criminal Law' (2008) 21 *Leiden Journal of International Law* 925, 926.

B The Defence before the UN Tribunals

From their very inception, it was a principal objective of the UN tribunals to ensure the respect of due process guarantees to the highest possible degree. It goes without saying that all suspects and accused before the tribunals are entitled to effective legal assistance and representation.[12] This principle is enshrined in nearly all national criminal justice systems and is furthermore mandated by various international human rights treaties.[13] Given the average charges before the international courts, the importance of effective assistance is obvious.

Such assistance was and is still being provided by a diverse list of lawyers. As the UN tribunals thrived, a community of international defence lawyers developed. This community is by no way homogenous. Their varied professional backgrounds hint at their equally diverse national disciplinary regimes. The defence lawyers before the ICTY and the ICTY provide ample evidence for this. Whereas the majority of indictees relied on lawyers from their own ethnicity (in the case of the ICTY) or of their own language (francophone for the ICTR), lawyers from all over the world took up the job of defending individuals accused of genocide, war crimes and crimes against humanity. By the end of 2002, approximately 135 defence counsel had acted as lead or co-counsel before the ICTY.[14] Of those, 84 came from the former Yugoslavia, 34 from the United States, Canada or the United Kingdom and 17 from the rest of the world, save one all from European civil law countries. Figures from 2005 state the total number of lawyers assigned to ICTY indictees as 131.[15] Of these, 76 were from the former Yugoslavia, 43 from the major common law jurisdictions (the United States, the United Kingdom, Australia and Canada) and 12 from the rest of the world, mostly European countries of the civil law tradition. In contrast, the distribution as of October 2000 was 32 lawyers from the former Yugoslavia, 19 US/Canadian/British lawyers and one Frenchman, making a total of 52.[16] This shows that the group of international criminal defence lawyers has become more diverse, although it is still dominated

[12] Art 21(4)(d) ICTY Statute, Art 20(4)(d) ICTR Statute. See also Art 67(1)(d) ICC Statute.

[13] Art 14(3)(d) of the International Covenant on Civil and Political Rights, UN Doc. A/6316 (1966), 999 UNTS 171, Art 6(3)(c) of the European Convention for the Protection of Human Rights and Fundamental Freedoms (CETS No.: 005). See further Tuinstra (n 1) 4, 13–72; RJ Wilson, 'Procedural Safeguards For The Defense In International Human Rights Law' in M Bohlander, R Boed and RJ Wilson (eds), *Defense in International Criminal Proceedings* (Ardsley, NY, Transnational Publishers, 2006) 7–30; JE Kastenberg, 'The Right to Assistance of Counsel in Military and War Crimes Tribunals: An International and Domestic Law Analysis' (2003) 14 *Indiana International & Comparative Law Review* 175.

[14] C Rohde, 'Legal Aid and Defence Counsel Matter' in R Dixon and KAA Khan (eds), *Archbold International Criminal Courts*, 1st edn (London, Sweet & Maxwell, 2003) § 20–59. See also JG Cedarbaum, 'Restrictions on U.S. Attorneys Practicing before International Criminal Tribunals' (2004) 98 *American Journal of International Law* 141.

[15] S Van Der Vliet, 'Legal Aid and Defence Counsel Matter' in R Dixon and KAA Khan (eds), *Archbold International Criminal Courts*, 2nd edn (London, Sweet & Maxwell, 2005) § 20–82.

[16] M Bohlander, *Gerichtliche Sanktionen gegen Anwälte wegen Mißbrauchs von Verfahrensrechten* (Aachen, Shaker, 2001) 80 (citing as source the ICTY's Office of Legal Aid and Detention).

by lawyers from the region connected with the indictees, and the common law world. This finding is somewhat corroborated by the figures for the ICTR. The 2000 annual report listed 60 counsel assigned so far, of whom 21 are from Europe, 15 from Africa and 24 from North America.[17] Out of 91 counsel assigned as of 15 May 2005, 37 come from North America, 26 from Europe and 29 from Africa.[18]

It thus seems safe to conclude that the community of active defence lawyers before the international tribunals is typically composed of a majority of lawyers connected with the indictees through regional origin and/or language, a considerable portion, ie, up to a third, of common law-trained defence counsel and a fairly small number of continental European lawyers. This distribution comes as no surprise and is readily explained by the assignment policies of the international tribunals. The Registrars of both international tribunals attempt to respect the preferences of the suspects or accused who tend to choose lawyers from the same ethnic or linguistic background.[19] However, due to the adversarial slant of both tribunals, these lawyers often team up with lawyers more accustomed to the common law style, procedural and evidentiary regimes of the tribunals to take over representation in court.[20]

What are the implications of this for the issue at stake, that of professional misconduct? It should be stressed that the overwhelming majority of counsel working before the international tribunals are experienced criminal defence lawyers who categorically adhere to high ethical standards when practising in their home jurisdictions. Appearing before the tribunals, however, they are placed into a unique context which may play a role in creating new challenges to professional conduct.[21] These courts face the discrepancy between offering, on the one hand, a broad selection of lawyers in order to provide defendants with counsel they can trust and, on the other, providing counsel capable of efficiently handling cases within the narrow specialty of complex international criminal cases. The Registrar thus, at the same time, faces the dilemma between the responsibility of choosing and assigning counsel to ensure fair representation of the accused, while also ensuring the smooth running of proceedings in court.

Although the importance of the defence is frequently emphasised, the relationship of counsel with the ICTY has been termed a troubled one, and poor performance by some counsel has been cited as a problem.[22] The approach of some defence lawyers has caused friction, although any intentional disturbances have

[17] ICTR, *Fifth Annual Report of the ICTR* (UN Doc. A/55/435-S/2000/927, 2 October 2000), para 88.

[18] MM Niang, 'ICTR' in M Bohlander, R Boed and RJ Wilson (eds), *Defense in International Criminal Proceedings* (Ardsley, NY, Transnational Publishers, 2006) 205. For the exact current distribution, see the ICTR's 'Status of Detainees' webpage.

[19] Van Der Vliet (n 15) § 20–27.

[20] See MS Ellis, 'Achieving Justice before the International War Crimes Tribunal: Challenges for the Defense Counsel' (1997) 7 *Duke Journal of Comparative & International Law* 519, 526 and fn 38.

[21] See also Tuinstra (n 1) 104 (putting forward as a question of theory for her ch IV whether there may be a link between the nature of international criminal proceedings and the challenges to defence counsel).

[22] D Tolbert, 'The ICTY and Defense Counsel: A Troubled Relationship' (2003) 37 *New England Law Review* 975, II.

been isolated events. The work of defence counsel has probably not always been valued appropriately, at least financially.[23] Whereas in some cases this may have compromised quality standards in respect of legal skills or legal ethics, the overall evidence points to the conclusion that it is not only the remuneration of counsel which is sufficient to ensure a dedicated defence in compliance with all professional requirements; it leaves open what constitutes the root cause of professional misconduct, and how the relationship of the defence towards the other actors within the overall system fits into the picture.

II Misconduct before the International Criminal Tribunal for the former Yugoslavia

A The Legal Sources of the ICTY on Counsel Misconduct

The primary source of the ICTY is the Tribunal's Statute. As far as the defence is concerned, it remains largely silent. Article 11 lists the Chambers, the Prosecutor and the Registrar as the Tribunal's organs. It does not specifically mention the defence. Of course, the Statute enshrines the right of the accused to defence in Article 21(4)(d). The Statute does not expressly recognise the defence and its independence, but it is, of course, far from surprising that the Statute does not elaborate on the topic, being but the founding act.

With Rules 44–46 and Rules 77 and 77bis, the Rules of Procedure and Evidence[24] contain provisions that are immediately relevant for the issue of misconduct of counsel for the defence and the sanctioning thereof.

In Section 2 of Part 4, Rules 44–46 specifically address defence counsel.[25] Rule 44 specifies the qualifications and duties of counsel. Potential counsel have to produce their prior disciplinary and criminal records.[26] It seems notable that Rule 44(A) has been amended considerably.[27] Rule 44(A) further specifies that counsel have to be members of the officially recognised association of counsel – the Association of Defence Counsel Practising Before the International Criminal

[23] For an impression from the earlier days of the ICTY, see MS Ellis, 'The Evolution of Defense Counsel Appearing Before the International Criminal Tribunal for the Former Yugoslavia' (2003) 37 *New England Law Review* 949, 950: the hourly rate for Michail Wladimiroff, one of the most eminent defence counsel of the Netherlands, came out to be US$26. For an evaluation of the ICTY's counsel remuneration system, see D Wippman, 'The Costs of International Justice' (2006) 100 *American Journal of International Law* 861, 871. For a general overview on counsel remuneration by the international courts see Tuinstra (n 1) 33–38.

[24] First adopted on 11 February 1994. The latest version is IT/32/Rev.47, 28 August 2012.

[25] Counsel for the ICTY's Office of the Prosecutor are not covered. See below, II.B at 14 (n 42).

[26] See M Martínez, 'ICTY' in M Bohlander, R Boed and RJ Wilson (eds), *Defense in International Criminal Proceedings* (Ardsley, NY, Transnational Publishers, 2006) 96. See also Rohde (n 14) § 20–40, 56, 57, on prior record and good standing.

[27] Most recently by revision IT/32/Rev.32, 28 July 2004.

Tribunal for the Former Yugoslavia (ADC-ICTY) – which has disciplinary rules forming part of its own constitution.[28] Rule 44(C) obliges counsel to comply with all pertinent ICTY law. Rule 45 ICTY RPE specifies the assignment of counsel, including the so-called Rule 45 List of Counsel. Counsel may be removed from this list by the Registrar and thus become ineligible to represent before the Tribunal, irrespective of whether they are privately retained or court-assigned.[29] Finally, Rule 46 addresses misconduct of defence counsel and provides for the enactment of a code. This regulates primarily counsel's conduct during sessions and other aspects of handling the proceedings.

On 12 June 1997, the Registrar issued the initial version of the Code of Conduct for ICTY counsel[30] stipulated for in Rule 46(D). The Registrar's *travaux préparatoires* were confidential;[31] however, they are said to bear a certain kinship to the Model Rules of the American Bar Association.[32] The Code was essentially drafted by judges.[33] It has been revised three times and was accordingly amended on 12 July 2002 (introducing a disciplinary regime in Arts 37–50), on 29 June 2006 and on 6 April 2009.[34]

It is the contempt powers under Rule 77 RPE which provide for criminal sanctions: any person, including but not limited to counsel, who knowingly and wilfully interferes with the administration of justice by the ICTY may be punished in accordance with paragraph (G) of the current version.[35]

Rule 77 has undergone quite a number of changes along with the revisions of the RPE.[36] Failing to answer a question as a witness was the starting point for Rule

[28] Part V, Arts 15–19. The mandatory membership is quite unique, and 'distinguishes the relationship between the defense and the organs of the International Tribunal from that which exists before all other existing international courts': S Bourgon, 'Associations Of Defense Counsel – Development And Role' in M Bohlander, R Boed and RJ Wilson (eds), *Defense in International Criminal Proceedings* (Ardsley, NY, Transnational Publishers, 2006) 483. On the ADC-ICTY in detail, see below, II.B.v at 27.

[29] See Martínez (n 26) 97.

[30] Code of Professional Conduct, Initial document, 12 June 1997. See further Martínez, ibid, 124–27; M Bohlander, 'The Defence' in G Boas and WA Schabas (eds), *International Criminal Law Developments in the Case Law of the ICTY* (Leiden, Martinus Nijhoff, 2003) 54–74; M Bohlander, 'International Criminal Defence Ethics: The Law of Professional Conduct for Defence Counsel Appearing before International Criminal Tribunals' (2000) 1 *San Diego International Law Journal* 75, 91–96; Tuinstra (n 1) 217–19. With regard to OTP counsel, see Prosecutor's Regulation No 2 (1999), Standards of Professional Conduct – Prosecution Counsel, and below at 37 (fn 197).

[31] Bohlander, 'The Defence' (n 30) 54.

[32] Bohlander (n 16) 82–83; Bohlander, 'International Criminal Defence Ethics' (n 30) 96; Ellis (n 23) 949, fns 135 and 136.

[33] S Kay and B Swart 'The Role of the Defence' in A Cassese, P Gaeta and JRWD Jones (eds), *The Rome Statute of the International Criminal Court: A Commentary* (Oxford, Oxford University Press, 2002) 1434.

[34] Code of Professional Conduct for Counsel Appearing before the International Criminal Tribunal (as amended on 12 July 2002, IT/125 Rev 1, on 29 June 2006, IT/125 Rev 2, and on 6 April 2009, IT/125 Rev 3).

[35] It provides for imprisonment of up to seven years or a fine not exceeding €100,000, or both. The latest revision of Rule 77 is Rev 43, 22 July 2009.

[36] It was adopted 11 February 1994, revised 30 January 1995, amended 25 July 1997, revised 12 November 1997, amended 13 December 2001 and 22 July 2009. Some of the history of the Rule is recounted briefly by the Appeals Chamber in *Prosecutor v Duško Tadić*, IT-94-1-A-R77, Appeals Chamber, Judgment on Allegations of Contempt against Prior Counsel, Milan Vujin, 31 January 2000,

77. As of Revision 3, 30 January 1995, interfering with witnesses was added, and the title was changed from 'Contempt of Court' to 'Contempt of the Tribunal'. Revision 11, 25 July 1997, brought with it the category of disclosing protected information by 'a person participating in proceedings'. Revision 12, 20 October and 12 November 1997, introduced the failure to comply with orders or to attend or to produce documents. Furthermore, a catch-all clause was added, as paragraph (F).[37] Lastly, the applicable fine of up to US$10,000 plus up to six months' imprisonment was now changed to a fine of Dfl 15,000 (Dutch Guilders). Revision 13, 9–10 July 1998, increased the maximum fine to Dfl 20,000; the maximum imprisonment term was left at six months. With Revision 14, 4 December 1998, the maximum imprisonment doubled for some forms of contempt to 12 months, the maximum fine to not exceeding Dfl 40,000, or both. For the more serious categories of contempt, the maximum penalties went up drastically to seven years' imprisonment, and/or a fine of Dfl 200,000. Revision 19, 1 and 13 December 2000, removed different maximum sentences for different kinds of contempt and provided for a uniform ceiling of seven years' imprisonment, and/or a fine of Dfl 200,000[38]. Furthermore, paragraph (I) was inserted, providing for measures in addition to the mentioned penalties: declaring the ineligibility of counsel to represent persons before the Tribunal, and declaring that counsel committed misconduct in terms of Rule 46. Revision 23, 12 July 2002, amended the appeals regime, supposedly in response to the Vujin appeal judgment.[39]

In conclusion, Rule 77 has been constantly amended to list an ever greater number of categories of contempt. Although it is not primarily addressed at counsel, they are subject to it in their work. As will be shown,[40] one could claim, however, that the exact wording of the provision is blatantly irrelevant for the punishment of contempt by Chambers of the ICTY. At first glance, the amendments to Rule 77 constitute a step-by-step enlargement of criminal liability for contempt. Such a process of broadening the criminal law of contempt would, of course, be the undisputed right of any legitimised, competent legislative body if it felt the need to do so, and if it succeeded in fielding a majority of votes for this. As can be seen later,[41] the problem with Rule 77 is slightly different: it is the judges who deduce criminal liability, by entrenching it in the RPE, an instrument which holds a rank inferior to the Statute, where the other criminal offences within the jurisdiction of the Tribunal are prescribed.

paras 19–23, see below, II.B.ii. It is also summarised by Bohlander (n 16) 88–90; T Spronken, 'Commentary' in A Klip and G Sluiter (eds), *Annotated Leading Cases of International Criminal Tribunals, vol 7, The International Criminal Tribunal for the former Yugoslavia 2001* (Antwerp, Intersentia, 2005) 228, and by S D'Ascoli, 'Sentencing Contempt of Court in International Criminal Justice' (2007) 5 *Journal of International Criminal Justice* 735, 739.

[37] 'Nothing in this Rule affects the inherent power of the Tribunal to hold in contempt those who knowingly and wilfully interfere with its administration of justice'.

[38] Changed to €100,000 by Rev 22, 13 December 2001.

[39] See below, II.B.ii.a at 16–19.

[40] See in detail below, II.B.ii, in particular at 17 (n 64).

[41] Below, II.B.ii from 16.

Rule 73(D) provides that Chambers may, notwithstanding the sanctions under Rule 46, find a motion to be frivolous or abusive. As a consequence, the Registrar will withhold the payment of fees associated with the production of that motion and/or costs thereof.

B The ICTY's Practice

The Tribunal has, to a varying degree, made use of the different tools. This has resulted in a considerable body of case law which includes contempt proceedings against counsel, ensuing issues of legal representation and allegations against the prosecution. The Trial Chamber in *Prosecutor v Furundžija*[42] held in an early decision that Chambers did not have disciplining power over counsel for the prosecution, who had repeatedly failed to comply with orders. It therefore left it at expressing its 'dismay at the conduct of the Prosecution' and referring a complaint to the Prosecutor to deal with the matter.

i *Disciplinary Proceedings*

No disciplinary proceedings had been instituted by October 2002,[43] which is not too surprising, as the necessary amendments had only been passed earlier that year.[44] By mid-2003, two disciplinary complaints of one counsel against another one were before the Disciplinary Panel.[45] By mid-2005, four complaints had been brought against counsel.[46] In comparison with the number of the reported instances of misconduct through the other avenues, the number of actually pending cases seems rather small.

a The Appeals Decision in the Case of Slaviša Prodanović

After the disciplinary procedure had been introduced, the issue arose whether a retroactive application to cases was permissible. Disciplined counsel Slaviša Prodanović, who was accused of not performing any investigative work for his client, argued to the negative. However, the Disciplinary Panel held that the 1997

[42] *Prosecutor v Anto Furundžija*, IT-95-17/1-PT, The Trial Chamber's Formal Complaint to the Prosecutor Concerning the Conduct of the Prosecution, 5 June 1998. On this case, see L Arbour, 'Legal Professionalism and International Criminal Proceedings' (2006) 4 *Journal of International Criminal Justice* 674.

[43] Rohde (n 14) § 20–144.

[44] 12 July 2002, IT/125 Rev 1.

[45] ICTY, *Comprehensive report on the progress made by the ICTY in reforming its legal aid system* (UN Doc. A/58/288, 12 August 2003) para 46.

[46] Van Der Vliet, 'Legal Aid and Defence Counsel Matter' in R Dixon and KAA Khan (eds), *Archbold International Criminal Courts*, 1st edn (London, Sweet & Maxwell, 2003) § 20–82. Martínez refers to three complaints (on financial misconduct and conflict of interest) and two rendered decisions, with one appealed to the Disciplinary Board, by 2005 (Martínez (n 26) 122).

Code sufficed. This was confirmed on appeal by the President.[47] Counsel were found to be bound by Rule 44 RPE. The Code of 1997 was said to have established the necessary substantive jurisdiction, and it apparently sufficed that it had indicated that an enforcement procedure would be set up.[48]

The two other grounds of appeal by Prodanović were an alleged lapse of time for filing the complaint and an unjust delay of proceedings. The President found that the 12-month submission period for the complaint did not start on the Tribunal's authorities becoming aware of an allegation; instead, sufficient information to establish reasonable knowledge is required. This may entail first undergoing verification measures.[49] Bringing the case before the disciplinary body within one year subsequently did not constitute an unjust delay, contrary to the appellant's claim.[50] In conclusion, the Disciplinary Panel's decision to suspend Prodanović from practising before the Tribunal was upheld.

b The Appeals Decision in the Case of Deyan Ranko Brashich

In 2007, a rather hefty fine was handed down in another case on appeal – that against Deyan Ranko Brashich.[51] Acting under then enacted Revision 2 of the ICTY Code, the Disciplinary Board ordered him to pay €10,000, along with issuing a reprimand. The Disciplinary Panel had first dismissed the complaint against him, against which the Registrar appealed. The Disciplinary Board found Brashich in misconduct for failing to disclose relevant prior disciplinary proceedings in the New York Supreme Court[52] which would have made him ineligible to practise before the Tribunal. The Board reiterated that the standard of proof in disciplinary procedures was one of beyond reasonable doubt. It thus made clear that professional discipline in the ICTY extends to more than an administrative nature.[53] While considering it commendable to adopt a sanction of *restitutio in integrum* under the Code, the Board stressed that it was not available under the current legal framework.[54] Brashich could therefore not be ordered, contrary to the Registrar's appeal, to repay funds he had received from the Tribunal because he had engaged in unlawful representation.

[47] *Prosecutor v Mitar Rašević*, IT-97-25/1-PT, President, Decision on Appeal Against Disciplinary Panel Decision, 5 November 2003, para 3.

[48] See the initial version of the Code, IT/125, 12 June 1997: 'Article 22. Enforcement. Counsel must abide by and voluntarily submit to any enforcement and disciplinary procedures as may be established by the Tribunal in accordance with the Rules'.

[49] *Prosecutor v Mitar Rašević* (n 47) para 4.

[50] ibid, para 6.

[51] *Prosecutor v Momčilo Krajišnik*, IT-00-39-A, Disciplinary Board, Decision in the Appeal by the Disciplinary Board in the Matter of Mr Deyan Ranko Brashich, Attorney at Law from the United States, 22 May 2007.

[52] ibid, paras 21–24, 32, in violation of Art 35 (v) ICTY Code.

[53] ibid, paras 18–19.

[54] ibid, paras 44–48. See for Rev 3 of the Code above, II.A (n 34), and new Art 47(D), allowing for restitution orders.

ii Contempt of the Tribunal

The bulk of misconduct by counsel or other members of the defence[55] has, nevertheless, been tackled via the avenue of contempt of the Tribunal.[56] Among the most controversial cases in the record of the ICTY have been convictions under this doctrine. Broadly, it can be said that the concept of criminal contempt is mainly derived from the common law tradition.[57] It should be noted that not only defence counsel were held to have been in contempt, but that the scope of contempt is universal and applies to witnesses and external persons as well.[58] Other measures against counsel misconduct have been resorted to, but contempt seems still to remain the weapon of choice for the most serious cases.

Up until today, the ICTY has handled about 20 contempt cases under Rule 77 of its RPE. Among those indicted for contempt before the ICTY were four defence counsel: attorneys Vujin, Nobilo, Avramović and Maglov. Vujin was convicted; Nobilo was initially convicted but his appeal was allowed; Avramović was acquitted; the charges against Maglov were eventually dropped. In a fifth case, a complaint was brought against lawyers Residović and O'Sullivan, but it was decided not to proceed with any investigation. Although five cases in over ten years[59] may not seem a very authoritative record, it nevertheless seems good for identifying some fundamental issues of criminal sanctions against counsel.

a The Case of Milan Vujin

The most intriguing contempt case is arguably the conviction of Milan Vujin.[60] He was found guilty and fined Dfl 15,000 for submitting false documents and

[55] See, eg, *Prosecutor v Jelena Rašić*, IT-98-32/1-R77.2, Office of the Prosecutor, Indictment, 8 July 2010. She is alleged to have bribed witnesses and otherwise meddled with their statements in the *Lukić & Lukić* case.

[56] See Tuinstra (n 1) 226–31.

[57] Spronken (n 36) 225. Within the history of international criminal law, it can be traced to the era of the International Military Tribunal at Nuremberg and the *Folgeprozesse*, see R Dixon and KAA Khan (eds), *Archbold International Criminal Courts*, 1st edn (London, Sweet & Maxwell, 2003) § 16–32 to 43, who refer to the cases of *US v Karl Brandt*; *US v Altstoetter* (defence counsel trying to influence expert testimony); *US v Krupp* (defence counsel walking out, later dealt with on a disciplinary basis), all of them part of the *Folgeprozesse*. For the IMTs see M Bohlander, 'International Criminal Tribunals and their Power to Punish Contempt and False Testimony' (2001) 12 *Criminal Law Forum* 91, 108.

[58] C Brants, 'Commentary' in A Klip and G Sluiter (eds), *Annotated Leading Cases of International Criminal Tribunals, vol 6, The International Criminal Tribunal for Rwanda 2000–2001* (Antwerp, Intersentia, 2003) 459–60. She lays out different categories of contempt, and speaks of a 'separate category' of contempt by those 'professionally involved'.

[59] O Triffterer in O Triffterer (ed), *Commentary on the Rome Statute of the International Criminal Court*, 2nd edn (Munich, Beck, 2008) art 71, mn 16, only mentions the cases of *Vujin*, *Nobilo* and *Avramović*.

[60] *Prosecutor v Duško Tadić*, IT-94-1-A-R77, Appeals Chamber, Judgment (n 36). For case notes, see J Cockayne, 'Commentary' in A Klip and G Sluiter (eds), *Annotated Leading Cases of International Criminal Tribunals, vol 4, The International Criminal Tribunal for the former Yugoslavia 1999–2000* (Antwerp, Intersentia, 2002) 191–200, and Spronken (n 36) 225–33.

manipulating witnesses. On appeal, this conviction was upheld.[61] It seems beyond question that the misconduct at stake was very serious.[62] Furthermore, it was not submitted at trial that the allegations, if proven, would not constitute contempt as prescribed by Rule 77.[63] However, the decisions merit closer attention with respect to disciplining mechanisms in general, as they were the first decisions to explain and expressly affirm the largely unwritten powers of the Tribunal to impose criminal penalties for contempt. The issue at stake was not so much the scope of Rule 77[64] but the legitimacy of prescribing such powers in the RPE, whereas the Statute is silent on such sanctions. Furthermore, the procedural framing revealed how fragmentary the Tribunal's overall mechanism was.

As to this first point of a legitimate basis for criminal contempt in the Tribunal's law, the Chamber held that

> 13. [t]here is no mention in the Tribunal's Statute of its power to deal with contempt. The Tribunal does, however, possess an inherent jurisdiction, deriving from its judicial function, to ensure that its exercise of the jurisdiction which is expressly given to it by that Statute is not frustrated and that its basic judicial functions are safeguarded. As an international criminal court, the Tribunal must therefore possess the inherent power to deal with conduct which interferes with its administration of justice. The content of that inherent power may be discerned by reference to the usual sources of international law.

The Chamber turned to what it deemed the applicable sources, namely the example of the Nuremberg Tribunal[65] and the example of inherent powers of

[61] *Prosecutor v Duško Tadić*, IT-94-1-A-AR77, Appeals Chamber, Appeal Judgement on Allegations of Contempt Against Prior Counsel, Milan Vujin, 27 February 2001.

[62] The allegations which were proven and for which he was convicted (see para 160) were the tendering into evidence two witness statements that he knew to be false (paras 44, 132–34 and 46–51, 135–38, respectively), and the manipulation of two witnesses whom he had instructed to withhold the identification of other witnesses from co-counsel (paras 142, 146, 150). The allegations not proven were the manipulation of witnesses by instructing three other witnesses to withhold the identification of other witnesses from co-counsel (paras 147–49), and instructing witnesses to answer according to gestures during interviews in Prijedor (paras 151–54) and bribing another witness by giving him DM 100 after an interview (paras 155–59).

[63] *Prosecutor v Duško Tadić*, IT-94-1-A-R77, Appeals Chamber, Judgment (n 36) paras 12, 29.

[64] As far as the substantive foundation is concerned, the Chamber expressly cited (see para 23: 'Rule 77, so far as it is relevant, is now in the following terms') Rule 77 as it stood after Rev 14 of 4 December 1998. It made it clear, though, in para 26, that it relied on the concept of contempt *in general*, as formulated by the catch-all clause in the new para (F) added by Rev 12 of 20 October/12 November 1997 (not contained in Rev 11 of 25 July 1997). It emphasised, in para 24, that the statutory entrenchment of different categories of contempt in Rule 77 did not mean the introduction of new ex post facto/retroactive offences. These categories, in the Chamber's opinion, just spell out what is an unwritten authority of the Tribunal: they are of a declarative character, not constitutive. Thus, it was of no relevance that the wording of the Rule throughout the time of the accused's conduct (para 2 of the judgment: September 1997 to April 1998; applicable versions thus seem to have been Rev 11 and 12) did not specifically penalise these acts. For punishment, however, the Chamber relied on Rev 12 of 20 October and 12 November 1997 (see para 165). It only provided for 'a fine not exceeding Dfl 20,000 or a term of imprisonment not exceeding six months', whereas the punishment for threatening, intimidation or bribing had been sharply increased to 'a term of imprisonment not exceeding seven years, or a fine not exceeding Dfl 200,000, or both' by Rev 14.

[65] *Prosecutor v Duško Tadić*, IT-94-1-A-R77, Appeals Chamber, Judgment (n 36) para 14.

the International Court of Justice.[66] It further resorted to comparative law and stated:

> 15. It is otherwise of assistance to look to the general principles of law common to the major legal systems of the world, as developed and refined (where applicable) in international jurisprudence. Historically, the law of contempt originated as, and has remained, a creature of the common law. The general concept of contempt is said to be unknown to the civil law, but many civil law systems have legislated to provide offences which produce a similar result.

The Chamber went on to stress that the judges of the Tribunal are not empowered to produce new offences. Rule 77, however, was said to be a rule of procedure and evidence only, which discerns the content of the inherent powers[67] the Tribunal has held since its creation.[68] The Chamber emphasised that the statutory phrasing of the Rule does not displace the underlying law but then affirmed that sub-rules (A) to (D) were statements reflecting the applicable law. In the Chamber's own words:

> (a) [T]he inherent power of the Tribunal as an international criminal court to deal with contempt is for present purposes adequately encompassed by the wording of the reservation inserted in Rule 77 in November 1997 – that the Tribunal has the power 'to hold in contempt those who knowingly and wilfully interfere with its administration of justice' – as such conduct would necessarily fall within the general concept of contempt, being 'conduct which tends to obstruct, prejudice or abuse the administration of justice'; and
>
> (b) each of the formulations in the current Rules 77(A) to (D), when interpreted in the light of that statement of the Tribunal's inherent power, falls within – but does not limit – that inherent power, as each clearly amounts to knowingly and wilfully interfering with the Tribunal's administration of justice.[69]

In conclusion, the Tribunal did not require statutory authorisation to regulate and even to impose criminal penalties on counsel. On appeal, another bench of the Appeals Chamber endorsed the findings of the first bench in a rather succinct fashion:

> [C]onsidering paragraphs 12 to 29 of the Judgement in which the basis of the International Tribunal's power to prosecute and punish matters of contempt is clearly set out;
>
> considering that Article 15 of the Tribunal's Statute instructs the Judges of the International Tribunal to 'adopt rules of procedure and evidence for the conduct of the pre-trial phase of the proceedings, trials and appeals, the admission of evidence, the protection of victims and witnesses and **other appropriate matters**'(emphasis added);
>
> considering that in order to function effectively and fairly, the International Tribunal must have the power to prosecute and punish contempt;

[66] ibid, para 13, fn 1.
[67] ibid, para 24.
[68] ibid, para 28.
[69] ibid, para 26.

> considering that the adoption of rules to prosecute and punish contempt falls within the purview of 'other appropriate matters' as required by Article 15 of the Statute; decides that the Appellant's submission regarding the International Tribunal's lack of power to prosecute and punish contempt is without merit.[70]

As part of the sentencing, the first bench had also considered the other consequences for counsel.[71] It declared Vujin 'guilty of professional misconduct' in violation of Articles 13 and 20[72] of the ICTY Code of Professional Conduct.[73] The Chamber briefly considered Rule 46 RPE ('Misconduct of Counsel') but held that it is only applicable where counsel is still appearing before the Tribunal.[74] It further directed the Registrar to strike Vujin off the list of eligible counsel and notify his Bar association. Finally, it imposed a substantial fine of Dfl 15,000 (out of a possible Dfl 20,000).[75]

In particular it is the legal basis as laid out by the Chambers which has drawn a lot of criticism.[76] At this point, it should suffice to say that these judgments were simply groundbreaking in vesting the Tribunal with such far-reaching powers. Secondly, it illustrates that the procedural framework for contempt was inchoate. The phrasing of Rule 77(J) at that time did not foresee the possibility that an Appeals Chamber would enter a conviction in first instance,[77] and thus remained silent on remedies against such judgments.[78] The jurisdictional dissent of Judge Wald[79] merely related to this aspect of appellate jurisdiction of the Chamber but did not question the general jurisdiction to entertain contempt proceedings.

[70] ibid (emphasis in quote is the one added by the Appeal Chamber in the original). Some authors conclude from this passage a difference in reasoning between the first and second *Vujin* judgments and argue that the latter assumes a more direct rooting in the Statute: Bohlander (n 57) 101; Spronken (n 36) 227–28. See also below, II.C at 28–33.

[71] *Prosecutor v Duško Tadić*, IT-94-1-A-R77, Appeals Chamber, Judgment (n 36) paras 168–72.

[72] Then: '(2) Counsel must not knowingly: (a) make an incorrect statement of material fact to the Tribunal; or (b) offer evidence which the Counsel knows to be incorrect'. (Art 13), '(2) Counsel must not knowingly: . . . (c) engage in conduct involving dishonesty, fraud, deceit or misrepresentation; (d) engage in conduct which is prejudicial to the proper administration of justice before the Tribunal' (Art 20).

[73] Initial document, 12 June 1997 (IT/125). At that point, the Code did not provide for sanctions of its own, see above, II.A at 12, 14 (ns 34 and 44).

[74] Vujin had acted in various capacities for Tadić until November 1998; *Prosecutor v Duško Tadić*, IT-94-1-A-R77, Appeals Chamber, Judgment (n 36) para 2.

[75] ibid, para 165.

[76] See below, II.C at 28–33.

[77] See Rule 77(J), Rev 17, 17 November 1999: 'Any decision rendered by a *Trial* Chamber under this Rule shall be subject to appeal' (emphasis added).

[78] See now Rule 77(K), as amended by Rev 23, 12 July 2002: 'In the case of decisions under this Rule by the Appeals Chamber sitting as a Chamber of first instance, an appeal may be submitted in writing to the President within fifteen days of the filing of the impugned decision. Such appeal shall be decided by five different Judges as assigned by the President'.

[79] *Prosecutor v Duško Tadić*, IT-94-1-A-R77, Separate Opinion of Judge Wald Dissenting from the Finding of Jurisdiction, 27 February 2001.

b The Case of Anto Nobilo

Although the trial of Anto Nobilo[80] was held before that of Vujin, the appeal judgment was only rendered after.[81] During cross-examination, Nobilo had mentioned the full name and the occupation of a witness. As this witness was under protection, all parties should have refrained from disclosing such details.[82] Nobilo was first fined Dfl 10,000 (of which 6,000 was suspended) and a one-year probation period. His appeal was allowed, however, and repayment of the Dfl 4,000 ordered.

The essence at appeal was not whether the Tribunal possessed or lacked contempt powers and the judgment is rather instructive on the subjective elements of contempt. The key issue was whether he acted 'knowingly'. The Trial Chamber specifically referred to the professional duties of counsel and extended the definition of 'knowing' as including the 'deliberate failure to ascertain the circumstances under which a witness testifie[s]'.[83] The Appeal Chamber's reasoning is relevant to the subject of disciplining counsel in several regards. First, it deals with the mental threshold in misconduct which amounts to a criminally punishable act:

> 45. Mere negligence in failing to ascertain whether an order had been made granting protective measures to a particular witness could never amount to such conduct. It is unnecessary in this appeal to determine whether any greater degree of negligence could constitute contempt. Negligent conduct could be dealt with sufficiently, and more appropriately, by way of disciplinary action, but it could never justify imprisonment or a substantial fine even though the unintended consequence of such negligence was an interference with the Tribunal's administration of justice. At the other end of the spectrum, wilful blindness to the existence of the order in the sense defined is, in the opinion of the Appeals Chamber, sufficiently culpable conduct to be more appropriately dealt with as contempt. Whether other states of mind, such as reckless indifference to the existence of the order, constitute contempt by a knowing violation of the order can be left to the cases in which they arise for determination.

Building on this, the Appeals Chamber interpreted the Trial Chamber's statements to have held counsel culpable for deliberately omitting to gather all the relevant circumstances. Since the evidence was, in the Appeals Chamber's view, not sufficient to indicate a suspicion, or a realisation that the order existed, there could be no wilful blindness to that effect.[84] It went on to hold that

[80] *Prosecutor v Zlatko Aleksovski*, IT-95-14/1-T, Trial Chamber, Finding of Contempt of the Tribunal, 11 December 1998. Case notes by M Veldt, 'Commentary' in A Klip and G Sluiter (eds), *Annotated Leading Cases of International Criminal Tribunals, vol 3, The International Criminal Tribunal for the former Yugoslavia 1997–1999* (Antwerp, Intersentia, 2001) 357–62, and Spronken (n 36) 225–33.

[81] *Prosecutor v Zlatko Aleksovski*, IT-95-14/1-AR77, Appeals Chamber, Judgment on Appeal by Anto Nobilo Against Finding of Contempt, 30 May 2001.

[82] See Rule 77(A)(iii) RPE (disclosing information in violation of order).

[83] *Prosecutor v Zlatko Aleksovski*, IT-95-14/1-T, Trial Chamber, Finding of Contempt (n 80) 3.

[84] *Prosecutor v Zlatko Aleksovski*, IT-95-14/1-AR77, Appeals Chamber, Judgement (n 81) para 51.

> 53. [i]n the light of these conclusions, it is strictly unnecessary for the Appeals Chamber to determine whether it is necessary for the prosecution also to establish an intention to violate or disregard the order which was violated, but the issue is an important one for future prosecutions for contempt and the matter has been fully argued. The Appeals Chamber accordingly proposes to express its opinion upon that issue.
> 54. In most cases where it has been established that the alleged contemnor had knowledge of the existence of the order (either actual knowledge or a wilful blindness of its existence), a finding that he intended to violate it would almost necessarily follow. There may, however, be cases where such an alleged contemnor acted with reckless indifference as to whether his act was in violation of the order. In the opinion of the Appeals Chamber, such conduct is sufficiently culpable to warrant punishment as contempt, even though it does not establish a specific intention to violate the order. The Appeals Chamber agrees with the prosecution that it is sufficient to establish that the act which constituted the violation was deliberate and not accidental. It was therefore unnecessary for the Trial Chamber to have found that the result which Mr Nobilo sought to achieve was a violation of the order.

This just illustrates that the fate of criminal sanctions, as opposed to mere disciplinary measures, will often hinge on the classification of the mental state of counsel.[85] It should be noted that Rule 77 ICTY RPE is restricted to 'knowing' violations, whereas other provisions may operate on the basis of 'intentional' ones. However the exact delineation goes, the Chamber seems to have acknowledged that the use of criminal offences in sanctioning misconduct should be restricted:

> (1) Both the purpose and the scope of the law of contempt to be applied by this Tribunal is to punish conduct which tends to obstruct, prejudice or abuse its administration of justice in order to ensure that its exercise of the jurisdiction which is expressly given to it by its Statute is not frustrated and that its basic judicial functions are safeguarded.
> (2) The law of contempt is not designed to buttress the dignity of the judges or to punish mere affronts or insults to a court or tribunal; rather, it is justice itself which is flouted by a contempt of court, not the individual court or judge who is attempting to administer justice.[86]

The intricate question of the appropriate role of criminal prosecutions for safeguarding ongoing trials is all the more highlighted by the Separate Opinion of Judge Robinson who also speaks out in favour of a narrower approach:

> 4. The matter should have ended with that explanation, unless there was a substantial basis for attributing mala fides to Mr Nobilo. I say this, well aware that Mr Nobilo's later explanation – that he revealed the identity of the witness in order to give added weight to the facts marked on the map – shows that he had a motive in making the

[85] Intent distinguishes the criminal offence of contempt from other measures. It is noted that the offence under Art 70 of the ICC Statute also requires intent. The understanding of intent thus could turn out to be decisive for distinguishing criminal acts from other disciplinable conduct. See on the ICC ch 3, II.B.i at 239.

[86] *Prosecutor v Zlatko Aleksovski*, IT-95-14/1-AR77, Appeals Chamber, Judgement on Appeal (n 81) para 36.

> revelation. However, in my view, it is not a motive such as would warrant the attribution of mala fides to him. His motive was that of any lawyer, that is, to present his evidence in the most advantageous way. In making this comment I am well aware that there have been cases of misconduct by counsel appearing before the Tribunal. However, unless there is evidence of mala fides, counsel should be given the benefit of the doubt, and the prosecutorial discretion should be exercised in his favour.[87]

This statement expressly recognises that cracking down on misconduct by means of criminal sanctions is just one part of the picture. A balance has to be struck with rights of the defence.[88] Moreover, the Appeals Chamber pointed out one of the central procedural flaws in the ICTY's existing regime, namely the 'danger of a Chamber being both the prosecutor and the judge in relation to a charge of contempt, and the possibility in such a case that the ordinary procedures and protections for the parties are overlooked'.[89] In conclusion, the procedural framework left a lot to be desired.

c The Case of Branislav Avramović

The contempt trial in this case, where counsel was charged with having intimidated a witness together with an accused, ended in an acquittal.[90] The Trial Chamber endorsed the Vujin appeal judgment with regard to the jurisdiction for contempt, and stated that the alleged conduct as such 'was not argued, nor could it be, that the allegations . . . would not constitute contempt'.[91] The key issue at hand was the required proof beyond reasonable doubt. In this regard, the Chamber concluded that

> [i]n the end, although the uncorroborated evidence of Witness Agnes raised grave suspicions in relation to the conduct of Mr Avramovic, it did no more. Not even the gravest of suspicions can establish proof beyond reasonable doubt, and far more substantial evidence would be required before Mr Avramovic could be found guilty.[92]

This illustrates once more that, as criminal prosecutions carry grave charges and therefore have to meet high standards of proof, it may be advisable to have a disciplinary system in place to cater for all other cases, and to align both.

[87] ibid, Separate Opinion of Judge Patrick Robinson.

[88] See, with an emphasis of the 'position of defence counsel', Spronken (n 36) 231. Quite instructive (and referring to the English case of *Erskine*) Brants (n 58) 465.

[89] *Prosecutor v Zlatko Aleksovski*, IT-95-14/1-AR77, Appeals Chamber, Judgement (n 81) para 56.

[90] *Prosecutor v Blagoje Simić et al*, IT-95-9-R77, Trial Chamber, Judgement in the Matter of Contempt Allegations Against an Accused and his Counsel, 30 June 2000. This was not appealed by the Prosecutor. See the case note by C Gane, 'Commentary' in A Klip and G Sluiter (eds), *Annotated Leading Cases of International Criminal Tribunals, vol 5, The International Criminal Tribunal for the former Yugoslavia 2000–2001* (Antwerp, Intersentia, 2003) 240–42.

[91] *Prosecutor v Blagoje Simić et al*, IT-95-9-R77, Trial Chamber, Judgement (n 90) para 92.

[92] ibid, para 99.

d The Case of Milka Maglov

Similar problems are, again, demonstrated by the fourth case. The proceedings in *Prosecutor v Radoslav Brđanin, Concerning Allegations against Milka Maglov*[93] commenced in early 2003 on the Trial Chamber's initiative. The allegations were that Maglov, co-counsel for Brđanin, had intimidated a witness and revealed the identity of a witness to a member of the public and that his role in the trial was in violation of an order of the Chamber. The case finished in late 2004 when the Chamber granted the Prosecutor's motion to end proceedings.[94] The witnesses had been very reluctant to come forward because of their concerns for security and privacy.[95] The Prosecutor therefore suggested dealing with the case administratively rather than continuing the criminal procedure.

The case is also noteworthy insofar as the Chamber opted for prosecution by amicus curiae as external prosecutor.[96] This illustrates once more how the ICTY regime had not evolved into a coherent system after almost ten years.[97] Nevertheless, the case produced contains findings on the substantive law, in a Rule 98bis decision of 2004.[98] The Trial Chamber spells out very thoroughly the material elements of different kinds of misconduct, notably 'intimidation of a witness',[99] 'otherwise interfering with a witness'[100] and 'disclosing the identity of a witness'.[101] The criminal contempt orders were eventually vacated on recommendation by the amicus curiae prosecutor because of the reluctance of the witnesses to testify again.[102]

e The Case of Edina Residović and Eugene O'Sullivan

As early as 1999, it was alleged by the Prosecution that counsels Edina Residović and Eugene O'Sullivan were involved in leaking a confidential witness list to a

[93] *Prosecutor v Radoslav Brđanin, Concerning Allegations Against Milka Maglov*, IT-99-36-R77, Order Instigating Proceedings Against Milka Maglov, 8 May 2003.

[94] *Prosecutor v Radoslav Brđanin, Concerning Allegations Against Milka Maglov*, IT-99-36-R77, Decision Confirming Vacation of Prior Orders and Termination of Proceedings, 17 December 2004.

[95] Transcript, 13 December 2004, at 323–24, 330.

[96] Brenda J Hollis was appointed by the Registrar, *Prosecutor v Radoslav Brđanin, Concerning Allegations Against Milka Maglov*, IT-99-36-R77, Registry, Decision, 29 October 2003.

[97] In the meantime, however, a Practice Direction on Procedure for the Investigation and Prosecution of Contempt before the International Tribunal had been issued by the President (IT/227, 6 May 2004), which gives guidance on the appointment of and prosecution by such an external prosecutor.

[98] *Prosecutor v Radoslav Brđanin, Concerning Allegations against Milka Maglov*, IT-99-36-R77, Decision on Motion for Acquittal pursuant to Rule 98 bis, 19 March 2004.

[99] ibid, paras 21–24.

[100] ibid, paras 27–29.

[101] ibid, paras 36–41.

[102] *Prosecutor v Radoslav Brđanin, Concerning Allegations against Milka Maglov*, IT-99-36-R77, Decision (n 94). On the oral decision, see the transcript of 13 December 2004, at 323–24, 331–34. The suggestion of dealing with the matter administratively in essence not to have Maglov appearing before the ICTY in the future, and to establish tighter protective measures for the benefit of witnesses.

Sarajevo newspaper.[103] The Trial Chamber requested that the President of the Tribunal should conduct a judicial investigation into the case.[104] Since the report of the President concluded that it was likely that the accused had himself revealed a witness name in a telephone interview, the Trial Chamber decided to discontinue the investigation and declared the matter closed in respect of the counsel. It shows, however, that counsel are vulnerable to being associated with any abusive conduct by their clients.

Most of the above cases occurred before or around 2000. Since then, the targets have shifted. More recently, contempt proceedings have mainly been directed at witnesses and other people who have obstructed the giving of testimony. Among them have been a number of journalists.[105] By and large, the contempt convictions were mostly punishable by fines. [106]

In conclusion, only a minority of contempt cases concerned defence lawyers. They nevertheless deserve attention as the ICTY Chambers have explicitly opted for contempt as the sanction mechanism for the most serious cases. Contempt proceedings have not, however, been conducted in a uniform manner. Sometimes, cases have been prosecuted by the Office of the Prosecutor (OTP), sometimes by the Chamber itself and once by an independent amicus curiae prosecutor and, earlier on, investigated by the President of the Tribunal. This has also shown that prosecutions for contempt are criminal proceedings: they can be lengthy and time-consuming, and prosecution efforts may thus be frustrated.[107] At the same time, these cases yielded fundamental rifts between different legal systems, most notably with regard to the legitimacy of contempt powers. Statutory authorisation is not strictly needed to punish misconduct. The Tribunal's jurisdiction has

[103] *Prosecutor v Zejnil Delalić et al*, IT-96-21, Trial Chamber II, Order on Complaint brought by the Prosecution, 2 June 1997. It demonstrates that the confidentiality of proceedings is a touchy area. This case supposedly caused the amendment by Rev 11 of 25 July 1997 RPE, namely adding the disclosure of protected information.

[104] *Prosecutor v Zejnil Delalić et al*, IT-96-21, Report of the President in the Matter of the Referral of Complaint, 27 May 1997.

[105] See, inter alia, *Prosecutor v Josip Jović*, IT-95-14 and IT-95-14/2-R77, Trial Chamber III, Judgement, 30 August 2006 (€15,000 fine each), and *Prosecutor v Josip Jović*, IT-95-14 and IT-95-14/2-R77, Trial Chamber III, Judgement, 30 August 2006 (conviction confirmed); *Prosecutor v Stjepan Šešelj, Domagoj Margetić and Marijan Križic*, IT-95-14-R77.5, Trial Chamber, Decision on the Prosecution Motion to Withdraw the Indictment, 20 June 2006; *Prosecutor v Josip Jović*, IT-95-14 and IT-95-14/2-R77, Trial Chamber III, Judgement, 30 August 2006 (fine of €20,000); *Prosecutor v Domagoj Margetić*, IT-95-14-R77.6, Trial Chamber I, Judgement on Allegations of Contempt, 7 February 2007; and *Prosecutor v Vidoje Blagojević and Dragan Jokić*, IT-02-60-A, Appeals Chamber, Judgement, 9 May 2007; *Prosecutor v Baton Haxhiu*, IT-04-84-77.5-T, Trial Chamber I, Judgement on Allegations of Contempt, 24 July 2008 (sentenced to €7,000); the appeal notice was held inadmissible by *Prosecutor v Baton Haxhiu*, IT-04-84-77.5-A, Appeals Chamber, Decision on Admissibility of Notice of Appeal against Trial Judgement, 4 September 2008, for missing the deadline.

[106] The payment of which is now usually stayed until the judgment is final, see *Prosecutor v Ivica Marijačić and Markica Rebić*, IT-95-14-R77.2-A, Appeals Chamber, Decision on Payment of Fines, 7 April 2006; *Prosecutor v Josip Jović*, IT-95-14 and 14/2-R77, Appeals Chamber, Decision on Motion of Josip Jović for Suspension of the Order on Payment of Fines, 29 September 2006.

[107] See the criticism of Judge Bonomy in his Separate Opinion in *Prosecutor v Stjepan Šešelj, Domagoj Margetić and Marijan Križic*, IT-95-14-R77.5, Trial Chamber, Decision on the Prosecution Motion to Withdraw the Indictment, 20 June 2006.

been upheld throughout. Neither is the Tribunal's range of measures limited to those expressly foreseen in the Rules. For instance, a cessation order was issued by a Chamber.[108]

iii Other Decisions by the Chambers

It is, in general, the chambers' responsibility to ensure the integrity of the proceedings before the ICTY. Of course, the chambers did not limit themselves to contempt proceedings in discharging this task. Other decisions do touch actual or potential misconduct, or they implement countermeasures although not addressing them in terms of contempt. The Appeals Chamber has, for example, declared void an appeals brief that did not meet the page limits.[109] Although technically a reaction to misconduct but, more accurately, a preventive trial management measure, Chambers have also adopted sets of trial guidelines[110] and ordered the parties to submit a detailed and specific agenda regarding the issues raised by them at least two days in advance of impending hearings, without permission to then raise any issue not previously made known to the Chamber.[111]

As far as the quite pertinent Rule 46[112] is concerned, it has to be noted that it had not been enforced against any lawyer by 2000.[113] This rule initially concerned the conduct of proceedings during sessions, in particular the maintenance of the court's dignity, the so-called courtroom decorum.[114] In particular, paragraph (A) has been amended to cover a lot more.

It is, however, not conclusive as to the potential sanctions. The Tribunal viewed itself empowered to strike counsel off the Rule 44 list.[115] Further, it expressly held that audience could be refused in cases beyond Rule 46. By relying again on the notion of inherent powers, the regulatory options of Chambers were held to encompass a broad range of measures against counsel:

> Although none of the express provisions of the Tribunal's law apply, the Trial Chamber is of the opinion that the inherent power now long recognised by the Chambers is a

[108] For cessation orders, see *Prosecutor v Tihomir Blaškić*, IT-95-14-T, Trial Chamber, Order for the Immediate Cessation of Violations of Protective Measures for Witnesses, 1 December 2000; *Prosecutor v Tihomir Blaškić*, IT-95-14-A, Order for the Immediate Cessation of Violations of Protective Measures for Witnesses, 2 December 2004.

[109] *Prosecutor v Enver Hadžihasanović and Amir Kubura*, IT-01-47-A, Appeals Chamber, Decision on Appeal Brief Annexes, 20 February 2007.

[110] See, eg, *Prosecutor v Rasim Delić*, IT-04-83-T, Trial Chamber I, Decision Adopting Guidelines on the Admission and Presentation of Evidence and Conduct of Counsel in Court, 24 July 2007; *Prosecutor v Momčilo Perišić*, IT-04-81-T, Trial Chamber I, Order for Guidelines on the Admission and Presentation of Evidence and Conduct of Counsel in Court, 29 October 2008.

[111] *Prosecutor v Vojislav Šešelj*, IT-03-67-T, Trial Chamber III, Order regarding the Organization of Upcoming Hearings, 15 November 2010. On setting deadlines for the presentation of evidence in Germany, see ch 2, II.iii.a at 76.

[112] See Tuinstra (n 1) 223–26.

[113] Bohlander (n 16) 84.

[114] Bohlander, 'International Criminal Defence Ethics' (n 30) 83.

[115] *Prosecutor v Duško Tadić*, Appeals Chamber, Appeal Judgement (n 61).

> sufficient foundation on which to proceed in this matter. The Trial Chamber considers the inherent power by necessity to include the power to refuse audience to counsel, notwithstanding that he may be otherwise qualified under Rule 44 (A) of the Rules of Procedure and Evidence, but who is for other reasons not a fit and proper person to appear before the Tribunal.[116]

ICTY Chambers did resort to 'warnings' under Rule 46[117] and disqualified counsel from the case at hand for misconduct.[118] Most of these decisions have not been as prominent as cases concerning the conduct underlying contempt charges. At first glance, however, they seem to stand in contrast to the frequency with which warnings have been issued by the ICTR.[119] The same can be said of the non-payment of fees for frivolous or otherwise abusive motions.[120] The benefit (to Chambers, that is) of Rules 46 and 73(D) should not be underestimated. Compared with contempt, it offers the advantage of simple and quick reactions, which are final and cannot be reviewed.

iv The Registrar

Another important actor in the regulation of the activities of counsel has been the Registrar. In practice, the Registry is vested with broad powers to assign defence lawyers and to deal with any other issue related to the conduct of counsel.[121] Not

[116] *Prosecutor v Dragoljub Kunarac et al*, IT-96-23-PT and IT-96-23/1-PT, Trial Chamber, Decision on the Request of the Accused Radomir Kovać to allow Mr Milan Vujin to appear as co-counsel acting pro bono, 14 March 2000, para 13. See also the Separate Opinion of Judge Hunt on Request by Radomir Kovać to allow Milan Vujin to appear as counsel acting without payment by the Tribunal, 24 March 2000, paras 7–11.

[117] See Tuinstra (n 1) 223–24. See, eg, *Prosecutor v Zejnil Delalić et al*, IT-96-21, Trial Chamber II, Order, 16 June 1998, or the call to order in *Prosecutor v Jadranko Prlić et al*, IT-04-74-T, Trial Chamber III, Ordonnance portant rappel à l'ordre à l'encontre de maître Karnavas, 15 June 2009, and *Prosecutor v Jadranko Prlić et al*, IT-04-74-T, Submission pursuant to the Ordonnance portant rappel à l'ordre à l'encontre de maître Karnavas, 15 June 2009.

[118] eg, *Prosecutor v Gotovina et al*, IT-06-90-PT, Trial Chamber I, Decision on Finding of Misconduct of Attorney Miroslav Separović, 6 March 2007, in furtherance of previous decision *Prosecutor v Gotovina et al*, IT-06-90, Trial Chamber I, Decision on Conflict of Interest of Attorney Miroslav Separović, 27 February 2007; upheld by Appeals Chamber, *Prosecutor v Gotovina et al*, IT-06-90-AR7.1, Appeals Chamber, Decision on Miroslav Šeparović's interlocutory appeal against Trial Chamber's decisions on conflict of interest and finding of misconduct, 4 May 2007. Related to this, see *Prosecutor v Gotovina et al*, IT-06-90-PT, Trial Chamber, Decision on conflict of interest of attorneys Čedo Prodanović and Jadranka Sloković, 5 April 2007 and *Prosecutor v Gotovina et al*, IT-06-90-AR73.2, Appeals Chamber, Decision on Ivan Čermak's interlocutory appeal against Trial Chamber's decision on conflict of interest of attorneys Čedo Prodanović and Jadranka Sloković, 29 June 2007.

[119] See below III.B.iii at 40–41.

[120] See Tuinstra (n 1) 225; *Prosecutor v Miroslav Kvočka et al*, IT-98-30/1-A, Appeals Chamber, Decision on Motion by Zoran Žigić for Issuing a Binding Order to the Prosecution, 7 March 2002. See case note by DDN Nsereko, 'Commentary' in A Klip and G Sluiter (eds), *Annotated Leading Cases of International Criminal Tribunals, vol 8, The International Criminal Tribunal for the former Yugoslavia 2001–2002* (Antwerp, Intersentia, 2005) 386.

[121] See Nsereko (n 120) 376–81. For example, *Prosecutor v Milan Martić*, IT-95-11-T, Deputy Registrar, Decision, 20 February 2006, where counsel was assigned despite the usual language requirements. On judicial review of the Registrar, see: C Rohde, 'Are Administrative Decisions from the Registry Appealable?' in R May et al (eds), *Essays on ICTY Procedure and Evidence in Honour of*

all are in response to misconduct. Probably the largest portion of Registry decisions is on the determination of total or partial indigence. The latter case law is highly relevant in the Tribunal's practice but of no particular benefit to the present study. The Registry, however, decides on the workload and on conflicts of interest,[122] and thus exercises some kind of preventive control.

As can be seen from Registry decisions, counsel have been withdrawn for poor work.[123] Counsel Nikola Kostich had been admonished before, based on Article 20(A)(i) of the Directive on Assignment of Defence Counsel, and a Chamber had ruled 'that any further Defence motion that so blatantly ignores the general rules and procedures governing the proceedings before the International Tribunal shall be considered a major failure of counsel for the Defence to perform his obligations'.[124] Similarly, counsel Željko Olujić was withdrawn for poor work.[125] He, too, had been warned for misconduct before, albeit in an unrelated case.[126]

It is conceded that the listed practice is not exhaustive. It should suffice to illustrate, however, that there has been misconduct of various kinds. Furthermore, it is discernible that both Chambers as well as the Registrar have made use of their authority.

v *The Association of Defence Counsel Practising before the ICTY*

The Association of Defence Counsel Practising before the International Criminal Tribunal for the Former Yugoslavia (ADC-ICTY) has been increasingly involved in the Tribunal's activities,[127] inter alia, in training activities[128] and in advisory opinions on the Code of Conduct.[129] The defence is otherwise involved through the Advisory Panel pursuant to Article 32 of the Directive on Assignment of Defence Counsel.[130] Furthermore, the ADC-ICTY appoints two members of the Disciplinary Board.[131]

Gabrielle Kirk McDonald (The Hague, Kluwer, 2001), 509–29; *Prosecutor v Milan Martić*, IT-95-11-PT, Trial Chamber, Decision on Appeal Against Decision of Registry, 2 August 2002, at 6–7, and below at 43. See also Tuinstra (n 1) 32–33 for an overview of the ICTY's list counsel system and Tuinstra, ibid, 49–52 and 78–82 on the Registrar's powers to address counsel incompetence and general oversight powers.

122 See, eg, *Prosecutor v Jovica Stanišić and Franko Simatović*, IT-03-69, Registry, Decision, 27 February 2008.

123 *Prosecutor v Stanislav Galić and Prosecutor v Dragoljub Kunarac*, IT-98-29-PT and IT-96-23-T and IT-96-23/1-T, Registrar, Decision, 22 November 2000.

124 *Prosecutor v Stanislav Galić*, IT-98-29, Order on the Defence Motion for Discovery, 11 May 2000.

125 *Prosecutor v Ivica Rajić*, IT-95-12-S, Registrar, Decision, 2 December 2005.

126 *Prosecutor v Zejnil Delalić et al*, IT-96-21, Trial Chamber II, Order (n 117).

127 On the history of ADC-ICTY, including their achievements, see Bourgon (n 28) 483–87 and Martínez (n 26) 97. See also Tuinstra (n 1) 88–99, 219.

128 Ellis (n 23) 970.

129 *Prosecutor v Jadranko Prlić et al*, IT-04-74-T, Trial Chamber III, Second Order Appointing an Amicus Curiae, 25 August 2009; *Prosecutor v Jadranko Prlić et al.*, IT-04-74-T, Trial Chamber III, Order Appointing an Amicus Curiae, 3 July 2009; *Prosecutor v Jadranko Prlić et al.*, IT-04-74-T, Trial Chamber III, Decision Subsequent to the *Amicus Curiae* Report, 3 November 2009.

130 IT/73/Rev.7, 22 July 1999. See Tuinstra (n 1) 87–88.

131 Art 46(C)(ii.) ICTY Code.

As far as sanctioning possibilities are concerned, the disciplinary regime established by the ADC-ICTY deserves attention.[132] Rule 44(A)(iii) RPE provides that counsel has to be a member of an association of counsel officially recognised by the Registrar. Since the ADC-ICTY is the only such association, membership is virtually compulsory. The ADC-ICTY may ultimately terminate the membership of counsel,[133] which effectively means disbarment from the ICTY. In this respect, the status of the ADC may be that of a private association under Dutch domestic law,[134] but membership of it is as determinative for counsel as being on the formal ICTY counsel list or other Tribunal requirements.

As far as the practice goes, the ADC-ICTY has suspended one lawyer's membership.[135] The other available measures are not as far-reaching:[136] the Disciplinary Council can mediate, issue a formal warning or refer the complaint to the Disciplinary Panel of the ICTY. Fines are not an option. Decisions can be appealed to the Executive Committee.[137]

The discrepancy in figures compared with the numbers reported by the Tribunal as such indeed suggest that the ADC-ICTY and the Tribunal are 'two separately existing systems' which can potentially 'merge or coordinate'[138] but have not. This is indeed the question for any two systems which are, in one way or another, intended to supplement each other. However, as far as the ADC-ICTY is concerned, it seems as though its input has been – and will remain – somewhat limited.[139]

C The Assessment of the ICTY's Regime in Scholarship

i Critique of Contempt in Particular

It is the inherent powers under the doctrine of contempt and, more specifically, the 'open-ended nature of the Tribunal's contempt jurisdiction'[140] that has drawn the harshest criticism from scholarship, although authors consent in principle that some form of regulation of counsel is advisable. The lack of pertinent provisions in the Statute is said to be a distinct lacuna which makes the 'Statute . . . manifestly deficient'; the drafters are presumed to have simply overlooked the

[132] The Constitution of the ADC-ICTY contains Part V (Arts 15–18), addressing the Association's powers to respond to alleged misconduct. See Bourgon (n 28) 489–501.

[133] See Art 18(8)(d) ADC-ICTY Constitution.

[134] Tuinstra (n 1) 88, fn 122.

[135] ICTY, *Comprehensive report* (n 45) para 45. Disciplinary decisions of the ADC ICTY are confidential, see Art 18(11).

[136] See Art 18(8)(a)–(d) ADC-ICTY Constitution.

[137] Art 18(10).

[138] Van Der Vliet (n 15) in R Dixon and KAA Khan (eds), *Archbold International Criminal Courts*, 1st edn (London, Sweet & Maxwell, 2003) § 20–229.

[139] Stéphane Bourgon, a past president of the ADC-ICTY, can be read to allege a lack of belief in the defence's function on the Tribunal's part. See Bourgon (n 28) 488–89.

[140] Gane (n 90) 239.

possibility of contemptuous behaviour.[141] Authors have warned that primary reliance on contempt could turn out as a rather symbolic approach that may ultimately be damaging.[142] In this context, it is argued that judicial contempt powers yielded the risk of potential abuse by judges, caused tension with the position of counsel and disallowed an unfettered representation of the client.[143] Counsel enjoy a special status where they are supposed to be – at the same time – loyal to their clients and dedicated to the court's objective while remaining independent when discharging their duties.[144] It appears an ever recurring dilemma between reconciling restraints on counsel's conduct with his or her institutional role of confidant, assistant and representative of the suspect or accused. As such, it is a very sensitive issue, and it has been suggested that it is preferable to rely on disciplinary measures rather than criminal prosecutions.[145]

At the very core of the criticism was that the ICTY had no valid source for the self-prescribed power to impose criminal sanctions for contempt.[146] Contempt pursuant to Rule 77 is without a doubt a criminal offence.[147] Since the Tribunal is bound by the rule of law and the principle of legality, it can only exercise criminal powers in accordance with the substantive jurisdiction with which it has been entrusted by the Statute. This jurisdiction, it is argued, is limited to the core crimes listed there.[148] The Appeals Chamber's understanding of Rule 77 RPE, which construed it either as procedural aspects of unwritten powers,[149] or alternatively as being covered by the 'other appropriate matters' clause of Article 15 of the Statute,[150] is viewed as highly problematic.[151] It seems unclear as to how to categorise these powers, whether they are inherent, implied or ancillary.[152]

It is another common criticism that the comparative legal analysis by the Appeals Chamber in Vujin was unconvincing. The Tribunal principally relied on common law precedents and then attempted to buttress this by referring to practice from other jurisdictions. It stated that such acts would also be punishable

[141] ibid, 236. See also Spronken (n 36) 228.

[142] Bohlander (n 57) 118.

[143] See Bohlander (n 16) 106.

[144] Spronken (n 36) 231.

[145] ibid.

[146] A summary is given ibid, 227. For other examples where Chambers drew on unwritten powers, see GH Oosthuizen, 'Of Misconduct, Contempt, False Testimony, Rule Mutations and other Interesting Powers: A Potpourri of Questions and Notes' in R May et al (eds), *Essays on ICTY Procedure and Evidence in Honour of Gabrielle Kirk McDonald* (The Hague, Kluwer, 2001); GP Lombardi, 'Legitimacy and the Expanding Power of the ICTY' (2003) 37 *New England Law Review* 887.

[147] Bohlander (n 57) 92; Cockayne (n 60) 199; Spronken (n 36) 225.

[148] Bohlander, 'International Criminal Defence Ethics' (n 30) 88.

[149] See the first *Vujin* Judgment (*Prosecutor v Duško Tadić*, IT-94-1-A-R77, Appeals Chamber, Judgment (n 36) above, II.B.ii at 16–17.

[150] See the *Vujin* Appeal (*Prosecutor v Duško Tadić*, IT-94-1-A-AR77, Appeals Chamber, Appeal Judgement (n 61), above, II.B.ii at 17–19, also n 70.

[151] Cockayne (n 60) 191–92.

[152] See L Symons, 'The Inherent Powers of the ICTY and ICTR' (2003) 3 *International Criminal Law Review* 369. More generally, see J Klabbers, *An Introduction to International Institutional Law* (Cambridge, Cambridge University Press, 2002) 67–81; JE Alvarez, *International Organizations as Law-Makers* (Oxford, Oxford University Press, 2006) 92–145.

under statutory criminal offences in many countries from the civil law tradition.[153] In doing this, it may have overestimated the factual criminality in continental legal orders. The comparison to civil law may even argue for the need for express statutory authorisation.[154] Moreover, some of the acts swiftly dealt with by the Tribunal as inherent powers in common law doctrine would not necessarily fall under the analogous notion of contempt in some common law jurisdictions. In Scottish practice, for example, contempt is restricted to 'contempt in the face of the court', whereas many of the pertinent allegations before the Tribunal would have been treated as genuine criminal offences, requiring the necessary jurisdiction.[155] The scope of contempt is potentially broad in US doctrine but is reined in by the crucial element of a prior order; the concept of non-criminal contempt and limited punishment under summary procedures further blur the picture.[156] General reference to the common law is therefore misplaced in order to explain Rule 77's rationale and thrust.

Among international precedents, the ICTY relied on the *Nuclear Tests* case of the International Court of Justice (ICJ).[157] This, however, seems to be a rather unsound footing since the ICJ did not even remotely pronounce on criminal sanctions.[158] Moreover, it is argued that such centralised contempt powers may be conceivable for a criminal court vested with a paramount rank and accordingly wide jurisdiction analogous to the ICJ. The ICTY, in contrast, it is contended, should confine itself to what it is, a subsidiary organ of the Security Council. Therefore, it should leave sanctioning measures to states or the Council itself.[159] Lastly, the ICTY disregarded the practice of the court that resembles itself most: the ICTR. The ICTR example, with its more lenient sanctions and narrower scope, argued against the compelling assumption of such drastic powers.[160]

Although most authors have been quite critical of all of those methodological blemishes, they do put forward justifications for the use of criminal penalties in sanctioning misconduct or perjury. Quite pragmatically, overall credibility is invoked: '[A] tribunal that does not have the power to deal with contempt or per-

[153] D'Ascoli (n 36) 750.

[154] Cockayne (n 60) 193; Gane (n 90) 237. Even if some parallels exist in examined national offences, the sentencing range was not remotely addressed, see Bohlander (n 57) 99.

[155] Gane (n 90) 238. See also, from a common law perspective, Symons (n 152) 403. D'Ascoli (n 36) 753, points out that the SCSL distinguishes summary contempt from a full criminal prosecution for contempt.

[156] See ch 2, III.B.iii.a at 132. Given this, the common law concept of contempt may not be as vague as D'Ascoli (n 36) 750, seems to assume.

[157] *Prosecutor v Duško Tadić*, IT-94-1-A-R77, Appeals Chamber, Judgment (n 36) para 13, fn 11.

[158] Gane (n 90) 237. The ICJ was confronted with clarifying issues that would be decisive for affirming its jurisdiction and the admissibility of the pending case. It held that it may for this purpose 'go into other questions which may not be strictly capable of classification as matters of jurisdiction or admissibility but are of such a nature as to require examination in priority to those matters.' (*Nuclear Tests Case (Australia v France)*, Judgment, 20 December 1974, para 22). This is hardly akin to assuming distinct criminal powers.

[159] Cockayne (n 60) 193.

[160] D'Ascoli (n 36) 752.

jury committed in the course of proceedings before it, lacks credibility'.[161] It is emphasised that centralised proceedings are particularly necessary to protect the integrity of international criminal courts when a decentralised approach has turned out to be unpromising. International justice should not be allowed to be frustrated because neither the offender's home country nor third countries take appropriate action. Political opposition to the international court in the home country will often result in leniency or even benevolence towards obstructive behaviour. There is also no reliable net of national laws which would allow for domestic prosecutions of offences against the ICTY's administration of justice, based on extraterritorial jurisdiction.[162] In addition, Cockayne offers a theoretical justification expressly acknowledging the ICTY's somewhat awkward nature as a criminal court and international organisation of a new kind at the same time. Relying on Seyerstad,[163] he argues that international organisations should be viewed as inherently empowered to perform any sovereign act in accordance with their constitutive instruments to attain the aims set out in these instruments. Such sovereign acts could also be criminal sanctions, as long as they respect the sovereignty of states and human rights standards.

It is not only the source of the Tribunal's contempt powers, but their scope which has drawn criticism. In particular, the open-ended nature of contempt has been said to run counter to the principle of legality.[164] Rule 77(F), added on 12 November 1997, reads that '[n]othing in this Rule affects the inherent power of the Tribunal to hold in contempt those who knowingly and wilfully interfere with its administration of justice'.[165] The only limitation is that of knowing and wilful behaviour. Apart from that, every particular charge of contempt may thus carry a new interpretation of contempt, without the accused knowing the exact elements beforehand.[166] Cockayne argues, though, that the case law, especially the Vujin judgment, and the obligations under the Code of Conduct give some guidance. Moreover, the offender would typically know that he or she interferes with the Tribunal's administration of justice, regardless of the existence of a specific prohibition.[167] Finally, the open-ended scope also creates uncertainty as to the possible measures.[168] The maximum punishment under Rule 77 can be quite drastic.[169]

[161] JJE Schutte, 'Legal and Practical Implications, from the Perspective of the Host Country, Relating to the Establishment of the International Tribunal for the Former Yugoslavia' (1994) 5 *Criminal Law Forum* 423, 433. With essentially the same point D'Ascoli (n 36) 755.

[162] Cockayne (n 60) 196.

[163] F Seyersted, *United Nations Forces in the Law of Peace and War* (Leiden, Sijthoff, 1966) 155.

[164] Cockayne (n 60) 196–99; Spronken (n 36) 228–29; D'Ascoli (n 36) 753.

[165] This catch-all clause is now contained in para (A). The Appeals Chamber, in the first Vujin judgment (*Prosecutor v Duško Tadić*, IT-94-1-A-R77, Appeals Chamber, Judgment (n 36)) emphasised that the base for contempt proceedings were the unwritten powers of the Tribunal, not the wording of Rule 77, see above at 19, (n 70). In light of this, one could even argue that the wording is totally irrelevant.

[166] Spronken (n 36) 229.

[167] Cockayne (n 60) 197; D'Ascoli (n 36) 752. I find it doubtful whether this is satisfactory. It could have a point, though, in stressing the principal requirement of counsel: at the very core, it is not to interfere with or obstruct the administration of justice.

[168] Cockayne (n 60) 198.

[169] On guiding sentencing principles, see D'Ascoli (n 36).

All the foregoing criticism has focused on the substantive law of contempt. However, criticism has also been voiced in respect of the procedure. In particular, many authors have questioned whether accused are afforded all necessary due process rights appropriate for criminal proceedings. The internationally recognised standards for criminal trials provide for, inter alia, timely and precise information on the charges and impartial judges. Initially, contempt charges were not necessarily accompanied by a formal indictment, and the formulation of the charges was not very specific.[170] Other shortcomings were that trials *in absentia* were theoretically possible,[171] and that it was not clear whether and how convictions could be appealed.[172]

As far as the current law is concerned, it is further argued in favour of revising the roles of the parties in contempt proceedings, which are not at all clear-cut, and rather establish a truly independent prosecutor.[173] Instead, chambers continue to indict and prosecute cases themselves.[174] Gane has summed up these points in three theses,[175] ie, the chambers should be relieved of any prosecutorial function, that a case must be remitted to another chamber,[176] and that no involvement shall occur of the same person in merit proceedings and related contempt proceedings.[177]

ii Comments on the Code of Conduct and the other Aspects of the Disciplinary Regime

It has just been explained in the foregoing that the sanctioning of counsels with criminal punishment has drawn most of the scholarly attention. Comments on the ICTY Code of Conduct and disciplinary regime as such, on the other hand, are scarce.[178] They usually give overviews but do not discuss the disciplinary

[170] Spronken (n 36) 230.

[171] Bohlander, 'International Criminal Defence Ethics' (n 30) 85; Bohlander (n 57) 106; Cockayne (n 60) 199.

[172] Cockayne (n 60) 199.

[173] ibid, 198–99.

[174] Inter alia in *Prosecutor v Milan Milutinović et al (Protić Contempt)*, IT-05-87-R77.1, Trial Chamber, Order to Vacate Warrant of Arrest and Order In Lieu of Indictment, 9 March 2007 (witnesses first not bowing to a *subpoena ad testificandum*); *Proscutor v Momčilo Krajišnik*, IT-00-39-R77.1, Trial Chamber I, Order in Lieu of Indictment on Contempt concerning Branko Đerić, 27 June 2006; *Prosecutor v Ramush Haradinaj et al (Kabashi Contempt)*, IT-04-84-R77.1, Trial Chamber, Order In Lieu of Indictment for Contempt Concerning Shefqet Kabashi, 5 June 2007; *Prosecutor v Vojislav Šešelj*, IT-03-67-T, Trial Chamber III, Order in Lieu of an Indictment for Contempt against Ljubiša Petković, 13 May 2008 (both, again, *subpoena ad testificandum*).

[175] Gane (n 90) 241–42.

[176] The Practice Direction on Procedure for the Investigation and Prosecution of Contempt (see above, IIB.ii.d (n 97) prescribes this as the default case. See also *Prosecutor v Slobodan Milošević, Contempt Proceedings Against Kosta Bulatović*, IT-02-54-R77.4, Trial Chamber, Decision on Contempt of the Tribunal, 13 May 2005, paras 4–11.

[177] See also Spronken (n 36) 231 *ad finem*. Interestingly enough, Rule 91(F) ICTY RPE provides for the exclusion of the judge before whom perjury was committed, whereas such an exclusion is unbeknown to the ICTR RPE; see Bohlander (n 57) 95.

[178] Among the most exhaustive are Bohlander, 'The Defence' (n 30) 54–59, and Martínez (n 26) 120–27.

regime in detail. It has been maintained that the Code takes into account the unique environment of the ICTY and attempts to establish the highest professional standards.[179] A lacuna has been detected in the counsel's responsibility for team members:[180] counsel cannot be held responsible if he or she did not order or approve the misconduct, or if he or she does not have direct supervisory authority over the team member.

On the disciplinary procedure, it was noted that the Registry's neutral position has been challenged by the new independent Disciplinary Panel. The disciplinary body is still said to be not as independent as it could or should be since it is intrinsically linked with the Registry.[181] Some authors have suggested a stronger use of the disciplinary procedure.[182]

D Analysis of the ICTY Regime

Put briefly, the ICTY has encountered instances of counsel misconduct and reacted to them in various ways. Holding in contempt has not been used as an instrument to specifically regulate the behaviour of counsel, but has rather stretched to cover a larger spectrum of interference with the administration of justice. Not all contempt cases have been adjudicated swiftly, though. This illustrates once more that, as criminal prosecutions carry grave charges and therefore have to meet high standards of proof, it may be advisable to have a disciplinary system in place to cater for all other cases, and to align both. In addition to the contempt cases, misconduct of counsel has occasionally been addressed.

Contempt has not been the exclusive tool used to regulate defence misconduct. It has been applied with a more general scope, even though it is restricted to instances of wilful interference. Defence-specific mechanisms have been employed but have not been the weapon of choice in the most serious cases. The disciplinary procedures against Prodanović and Brashich targeted unrelated instances. While they are proof that a disciplinary scheme can appropriately capture some forms of misconduct, the evidence of a rather small number of cases litigated in the disciplinary system is a first indicator of how relatively little weight is placed on it.

The issue of a legitimate base for contempt and the question of inherent powers may be obsolete now, given that the jurisprudence of the ICTY is settled, and in light of the much sounder statutory basis of the Statute and the RPE of the ICC. The problem should thus not be the statutory backing anymore. Nevertheless, it has been interesting to map out how much power the Chambers of the ICTY have been vested with.

In conclusion, the ICTY has mainly relied on contempt proceedings to sanction misconduct. In theory, counsel face severe criminal sanctions of fines up to

[179] Martínez (n 26) 124.
[180] ibid, 125.
[181] ibid, 125–26.
[182] Spronken (n 36) 231.

€100,000, or imprisonment of up to seven years. Imprisonment has never been imposed on counsel; the fine in the case of Vujin was Dfl 15,000. Among other possible consequences of contempt are striking off the list of counsel, a finding of ineligibility to represent a suspect or an accused, or a finding of confirmed misconduct in terms of Rule 46(A). The latter Rule provides for related sanctions, which are a refusal of audience, and again, ineligibility to represent. Neither Rule 77 nor Rule 46 is conclusive, however. Ordering the Registrar to exercise his discretion towards striking off the list of counsel, warning and the non-payment of fees are still not expressly listed in these provision, but have been ordered in practice.

The Registrar's powers stand back behind these, which seems justified as the Registrar's tasks are generally of an administrative nature, and they are subject to review by the President of the Tribunal. In practice, however, the powers of the Registrar are nevertheless considerable. Since almost all counsel are assigned by the Tribunal, the Registrar's decision to withdraw counsel, or not to admit to the list of counsel, can be far-reaching. On the other hand, it is noted that the Registrar may be in the best position to prevent 'cronyism among a small clique of international defense lawyers'.[183]

This is complemented by the disciplinary regime of the Code of Professional Conduct. The Disciplinary Panel can admonish counsel, give advice as to future conduct, give a public reprimand, impose a fine of up to €50,000, suspend for a fixed time of up to two years, or issue a permanent ban. Although they are not criminal sanctions *strictu sensu*, the practical consequences for counsel can be equally harsh. The fines, for example, that of €10,000 for Brashich,[184] can amount to a quite substantial sum, and bans to practice before the Tribunal carry the same results for counsel and accused as those issued by judges or the Registry. The purpose and nature of the ICTY professional discipline procedure is clearly punitive.[185]

All the described mechanisms are procedures administered by the Tribunal itself. Self-regulation of counsel, in contrast, has not played a major role. The ADC-ICTY has a number of disciplining measures within its powers which may be invoked of cases of misconduct. Discontinuation of membership even equals disbarment. Mediating and the issuance of a formal warning are to some extent internal sanctions, but referral of a complaint to the Disciplinary Panel of the ICTY may result in the abovementioned sanctions.[186] It needs to be noted, though, that proceedings by the ADC-ICTY depend on the concerned counsel's consent, and can even then be referred to the Tribunal.[187]

[183] See Tolbert (n 22) II.C.

[184] See above at 15.

[185] The Code, in Art 47, speaks of sanctions and that they constitute a sentence, as the wording of Art 47(C), (D), and (G), and Art 50(A) intimates. See also ch 3, II.A.v.f at 226, and vi at 236.

[186] Tuinstra (n 1) 223–24. See, eg, *Prosecutor v Zejnil Delalić et al*, IT-96-21, Trial Chamber II, Order (n 117) or the call to order in *Prosecutor v Jadranko Prlić et al*, Trial Chamber III, Ordonnance (n 117) and *Prosecutor v Jadranko Prlić et al*, Submission (n 117).

[187] If counsel does not consent, the matter shall be referred to the Tribunal's disciplinary regime (Art 18(5) of the Constitution).

It can be seen from the above that the ICTY's system rests on four pillars: the Chambers, the Registry, the disciplinary bodies and the ADC-ICTY. The practical emphasis is on the Chambers and the Registry. The disciplinary regime is not formally subordinated to proceedings by the Chambers; the latter prevails in any event. Article 38 ICTY Code provides on its disciplinary regime that '[it] shall not affect the inherent powers of the Tribunal to deal with conduct which interferes with the administration of justice under the Statute, the Rules or any other applicable law'. As can be seen, self-regulation of counsel is not fully independent from the Tribunal – cases go before the ICTY Disciplinary Panel if counsel does not consent, and may be referred to it as well where counsel does consent.

Despite the clear focus on Chambers' measures and the Registry, the relationship of the four pillars is not conclusively settled. The alignment of the parallel systems, ie, the priority of direct Chamber regulation and the role of the Registry, seems rather due to the fact that the other two – the disciplinary bodies and the ADC-ICTY – are under-used and that their powers are negligible in comparison. Even if the judges' and the Registry's powers are similar on paper, this does not hold true for their practical role. It could be argued that it is only the President reviewing Registry decisions on application of the defendant. The Registry is, however, under the general authority of the President, as Rules 30–33 RPE set forth. To be fair, it should be noted with regard to the disciplinary procedure that the ADC-ICTY and the Registrar appoint one member each to the Disciplinary Panel. The ADC-ICTY also appoints two members of the reviewing Disciplinary Board. The other three members, though, are judges of the Tribunal itself. The final verdict, therefore, in particular those cases of any significant importance, lies with a full bench of ICTY judges.

In conclusion, it needs to be stressed that the ICTY has succeeded in establishing a working regime to sanction and otherwise maintain discipline among counsel. The need for criminal sanctions in this should be acknowledged. A lack of such regulations would indeed constitute a 'serious lacuna' since 'a tribunal that does not have the power to deal with contempt or perjury committed in the course of proceedings before it, lacks credibility'.[188] The same concerns can be raised with regard to Rule 91, 'False Testimony under Solemn Declaration', in particular as going beyond the Tribunal's jurisdiction.[189] Some authors argue that the mandate with which the Tribunal was originally vested by the Security Council was that of trying war crimes and the like. Stretching this mandate to also encompass other offences would consequently be ultra vires. Some domestic laws would probably not recognise contempt as a crime under the Statute, and therefore

[188] Schutte (n 161) 433.

[189] ibid, 432; HJ Brady and JC Nemitz, 'The Offence of Perjury under International Law: The False Testimony of Witness L' (1998) 11 *Journal of International Law of Peace and Armed Conflict/Humanitäres Völkerrecht – Informationsschriften* 162; A Klip, 'Commentary' in A Klip and G Sluiter (eds), *Annotated Leading Cases of International Criminal Tribunals, vol 1, The International Criminal Tribunal for the former Yugoslavia 1993–1998* (Antwerp, Intersentia, 1999) 214.

cooperation by those states could be uncertain.[190] However, it was also hinted at the fact that the states had, on the other hand, not objected to entrusting the judges with broad rule-making powers, and that ancillary powers could be invoked by the judges.[191]

It is also argued that sanctions against perjury are an essential part of the criminal trial.[192] If ordinary criminal courts have criminal sanctions at their hands, why should international criminal courts be left without them? At the end of the day, they deal with criminal trials as do their national counterparts. The ICTY invoked the same justificatory rationale that presumably national courts rely on, safeguarding the administration of justice before the Tribunal.

Beyond this pragmatic rationale, other justifications have been advanced, taking into consideration the unique circumstances of the ICTY. The most persuasive approach is Cockayne's interpretation of Seyerstad.[193] According to it, international organisations are held empowered to perform any acts necessary for exercising their functions, as long as they do not contravene their own constitutive instruments, states' sovereignty or human rights. Consequently, this includes criminal offences. This may not be consonant with a strict principle of legality. A strictly construed principle of legality would require explicit statutory authorisation. Although the international legislator, ie, the Security Council, has not explicitly endowed the Tribunal with criminal powers in the Statute as the founding act, this does compel ruling them out entirely. The prosecution of criminal acts under the umbrella of the RPE is therefore possible since it does not contravene the Tribunal's own constitutive instruments in this respect. Nor does it a priori disrespect state sovereignty or basic human rights.

It has to be conceded that the offences concerned are not core crimes which are as manifestly illegal as to assume knowledge thereof by every person. The administration of justice, on the other hand, is universally recognised as a fundamental legal interest, and links offences against it to the court's objective. Professional conduct by counsel which respects the basic tenets of the court's procedure is part of any criminal trial. Counsel do not have unfettered freedom in discharging their duties. This does not change in the international arena. Therefore, creating a regulatory framework for counsel is within the ambit of the Tribunal. This certainly justifies an administrative and a disciplinary regime as implied within the Tribunal's mandate to enforce these duties. But does this equally hold true for

[190] Bohlander, 'International Criminal Defence Ethics' (n 30) 88; Bohlander (n 57) 107; Gane (n 90) 234–44. For the ICC and Art 70 offences, see ch 4, III.B at 302.

[191] WA Schabas, 'Le Règlement de preuve et de procédure du Tribunal international chargé de poursuivre les personnes présumées responsables de violations graves du droit international humanitaire commises sur le territoire de l'ex-Yougoslavie depuis 1991' (1993–94) 8.1 *Revue québécoise de droit international* 112, 113, 114. He eventually holds Rule 91 to be 'attaquable comme un excès de pouvoir, en dehors du mandat accordé par la Conseil de sécurité au Tribunal' and concludes that '[i]l s'agit, en effet, d'un Règlement adopté par onze juge et non pas de la *Charte* elle-même'. Brady and Nemitz (n 189) argue in favour of the rule.

[192] See Brady and Nemitz (n 189).

[193] See above, II.C.i at 31. See also DF Vagts, 'The International Legal Profession: A Need for More Governance?' (1996) 90 *American Journal of International Law* 250, 251 ff.

criminal sanctions against counsel? As a means of last resort, this seems tenable, in particular taking into consideration the oddity of the international setting. The use of criminal sanctions to achieve compliance with the most basic norms, as well as the stigma associated with it, however, argue compellingly against inherent powers to the extent in which they were assumed by the ICTY. That many sentences handed down so far are said to be relatively symbolic[194] does not change their criminal nature. In conclusion, it seems sound that the judges as the Tribunal's governing body could, therefore, provide for criminal offences in order to serve its primary mandate, as long as the scope is foreseeable and if due process rights are afforded. However, assuming open-ended inherent powers as is the case under Rule 77, is transgressing these powers.

III Misconduct before the International Criminal Tribunal for Rwanda

A The Legal Sources of the ICTR on Counsel Misconduct

It seems fair to say that the ICTR rules are in general quite similar to those of the ICTY.[195] Rules 44–46 ICTR RPE govern counsel issues. Professional ethics are again not expressly addressed in the Statute.[196] Unlike Rule 44(A) ICTY RPE, counsel need not be members of an association before this Tribunal. Rules 46(A) and 45ter(B) provide for the sanctioning, including forfeiture of fees in the case of counsel's failure to perform. In contrast to the ICTY RPE, Rule 46 also applies to counsel for the prosecution.[197]

Rule 46 vests the Registrar with the power to enact a Code of Conduct. The ICTR 'Code of Professional Conduct for Defence Counsel' was issued by the Registrar on 8 June 1998.[198] It resembles very closely the ICTY Code,[199] for example, the definition of misconduct in Article 20. The Code does not contain a disciplinary regime of its own. It only mentions the laying of information to judges or Chambers, or communicating misconduct to domestic bodies. Article 22, however, as the same Article of the ICTY Code of 1997, refers to a

[194] D'Ascoli (n 36).

[195] Brants (n 58) 461. See on the ICTY Rules above, II.A at 11–14.

[196] R Boed, 'ICTR' in M Bohlander, R Boed and RJ Wilson (eds), *Defense in International Criminal Proceedings* (Ardsley, NY, Transnational Publishers, 2006) 229. See for the ICTY above, II.A at 11.

[197] Regarding the OTP, the ICTR has in common with the ICTY the Prosecutor's Regulation No 2 (1999). See above (n 30).

[198] ICTR, *Code of Professional Conduct for Defence Counsel* (8 June 1998) republished in the ICTR's Basic Documents, 14 March 2008. See also on the Code and discipline under the ICTR regime, Tuinstra (n 1) 220–21.

[199] Above, II.A at 12.

disciplinary procedure.[200] Predictably, this should suffice to justify later disciplinary measures, if the ICTR adheres to the ICTY case law.

Rule 77 RPE, again, confers contempt powers the Tribunal. Initially, it differed from Rule 77 ICTY RPE and was, in particular, much narrower in scope and more lenient in terms of punishment.[201] Effectively, it only penalised the refusal to testify and intimidating witnesses. It did not contain a catch-all reference to inherent powers of the Tribunal. It was perhaps not deemed necessary; however, this is mere speculation as the consultations are confidential.[202] In the meantime, Rule 77 ICTR RPE has been likened, almost but not completely, to the phrasing of its ICTY counterpart.[203] A reference to inherent powers was inserted on 27 May 2003. The penalties constitute the most discernible difference.[204] The maximum term of imprisonment has risen to five years but the maximum monetary fine was left at US$10,000.

With regard to motions, Rule 73(F) ICTR Rules is again a parallel to the ICTY RPE, as it allows for withholding fees.

B The ICTR's Practice

The ICTR has also seen its share of proceedings concerning misconduct by counsel, relating to various kinds of misconduct.[205] Rule 46 ICTR RPE has also been applied variously. The misappropriation of funds has been a recurring issue,[206] as well as the filing of frivolous motions.

i Disciplinary Proceedings

Disciplinary proceedings are unaccounted for. This is explained by the absence of a disciplinary procedure in the ICTR Code. However, it seems conceivable that misconduct from before the formal inception of such a procedure may be thus addressed if the future disciplinary body decides to follow the ICTY lead.[207]

[200] For the ICTY, see above, II.B.i.a at 15. It is quite a paradox that counsel 'must . . . voluntarily submit' to the procedure.

[201] See Bohlander, 'International Criminal Defence Ethics' (n 30) 88; Boed (n 196) 273–76; R Dixon and KAA Khan (eds), *Archbold International Criminal Courts*, 2nd edn (London, Sweet & Maxwell, 2005) §16–61.

[202] Bohlander (n 16) 91–92.

[203] See amendment of 27 May 2003. The most current version of the ICTR RPE is of 9 February 2010. Revisions are not numbered.

[204] Which cannot be explained easily, see D'Ascoli (n 36) 742.

[205] See Brants (n 58) 463; Bohlander (n 16) 86–88.

[206] See Niang (n 18) 224–29.

[207] See above, IIB.i.a at 15.

ii Contempt of the Tribunal

The findings for the ICTR in that regard differ somewhat from the ICTY. In principle, the contempt powers of the ICTR are the same as those held by the ICTY. Similar to the ICTY, contempt proceedings have been undertaken against witnesses. Some of them were unsuccessful,[208] others resulted in convictions.[209] With particular regard to the defence, four defence team members were alleged to have presented themselves as OTP investigators, intimidating witnesses, and attempting to tamper with evidence.[210] Furthermore, one defence investigator was indicted on charges of fabricating evidence.[211]

In quite a number of further cases, misconduct allegations against defence counsel have arisen. Among these were violating disclosure rules as well as witness protection orders, tampering otherwise with witnesses and evidence and generally frivolous litigation. Interestingly enough, not all of the allegations were raised by the Chamber. A considerable number have been brought as motions to a Chamber to hold the other side in contempt. These were, on the one hand, motions directed at the defence but subsequently all declined. This has happened twice in *Bagosora et al*[212] and also in *Karemera et al*,[213] *Nahimana*,[214] *Nyiramasuhuko et al*,[215] *Zigiranyirazo* and *Kayishema and Ruzindana*.[216]

On the other hand, defence counsel motioned for holding in contempt the OTP as well in the cases of *Bagosora et al*,[217] *Nahimana*,[218] *Elizaphan and Gérard*

[208] *Prosecutor v Théoneste Bagosora et al*, ICTR-98-41-T, Decision on Motion to Hold Witness XAP in Contempt, 17 December 2003.

[209] *The Prosecutor v GAA*, ICTR-07-90-R77-I, Trial Chamber III, Judgement and Sentence, 4 December 2007 (9 months' sentence for giving false testimony).

[210] *Prosecutor v Pauline Nyiramasuhuko et al*, ICTR-97-21-T and ICTR-97-29-T and ICTR-96-15-T and ICTR-96-8-T, Decision on the Prosecutor's Allegations of Contempt, the Harmonization of the Witness Protection Measures and Warning to the Prosecutor's Counsel, 10 July 2001; Tuinstra (n 1) 231–32.

[211] *The Prosecutor v Léonidas Nshogoza*, ICTR-07-91-I, Indictment, 7 January 2008. No superior responsibility for counsel is contained in Art 20 ICTR Code. See in contrast, Art 34 ICTY Code and Art 7(4) and 32 ICC Code. It is noted, though, that Art 20 ICTR Code only lists instances of misconduct, inter alia, and is therefore not conclusive. See ch 3, II.A.iv at 193.

[212] *Prosecutor v Théoneste Bagosora et al*, ICTR-98-41-T, Decision on the Prosecution Motion ex parte in the Matter of Violation of the Chamber's Witness Protection Orders, and Contempt of Court, 5 July 2002; *Prosecutor v Théoneste Bagosora et al*, ICTR-98-41-T, Decision on Prosecution Motion for Sanctions, 25 April 2005.

[213] *Prosecutor v Édouard Karemera et al*, ICTR-98-44-R46, Decision on Prosecution Motion for Sanctions against Counsel for Nzirorera for Violation of Witness Protection Order and for an Injunction Against Further Violations, 19 April 2005.

[214] *Prosecutor v Ferdinand Nahimana*, ICTR-99-50-I, Decision (Interlocutory Appeal of the Decision of Trial Chamber I Rendered on 5 July 2001), 11 February 2001.

[215] *Prosecutor v Pauline Nyiramasuhuko et al*, ICTR-97-21-T and ICTR-97-29-T and ICTR-96-15-T and ICTR-96-8-T, Decision on the Prosecutor's Further Allegations of Contempt, 30 November 2001.

[216] *Prosecutor v Clément Kayishema and Obed Ruzindana*, ICTR-95-1-T, Trial Chamber II, Decision on the Prosecution Motion for an Ruling on the Defence continued Non Compliance with Rule 67(A) (ii) and with the Written and Oral Orders of the Trial Chamber, 3 September 1998.

[217] *Prosecutor v Théoneste Bagosora et al*, ICTR-98-41-T, Decision on Reconsideration of Order to Reduce Witness List and on Motion for Contempt for Violation of that Order, 1 March 2004.

[218] *Prosecutor v Ferdinand Nahimana*, Decision (n 214).

Ntakirutimana[219] and twice in *Nyiramasuhuko et al.*[220] The outcome of some of the defence motions even had the opposite result and ended in sanctions against counsel – ie, non-payment of fees for the motion.[221]

The only cases where contempt proceedings were actually initiated in response to alleged counsel misconduct were those of Peter Robinson, counsel for Nzirorera in *Karemera*, and of Peter Erlinder. Trial Chamber III, presided by Judge Byron, ordered Robinson to 'submit an affidavit showing cause why he should not be held in contempt of court' and to appear in court thereafter.[222]

iii Other Decisions by the Chambers

Instead of contempt, Chambers have made use of other measures.[223]They have issued warnings against the defence in the cases of *Akayesu*,[224] *Bicamumpaka*,[225] *Musema*,[226] *Ndindiliyimana et al*[227] and *Karemera*,[228] and denied a motion in

[219] *Prosecutor v Elizaphan and Gérard Ntakirutimana*, ICTR-96-10-T and ICTR-96-17-T, Decision on Prosecution Motion for Contempt of Court and two Defence Motion for Disclosure etc, 16 July 2001.

[220] *Prosecutor v Pauline Nyiramasuhuko et al*, Decision on the Prosecutor's Allegations of Contempt (n 210); *Prosecutor v Pauline Nyiramasuhuko et al*, ICTR-97-21-T and ICTR-97-29-T and ICTR-96-15-T and ICTR-96-8-T, Decision on the Full Disclosure of the Identity and Unredacted Statements of the Protected Witnesses, 8 June 2001.

[221] *Prosecutor v Laurent Semanza*, ICTR-97-20-I, Decision on the Defence Motion for Dismissal of the entire Proceedings due to persistent and continuing Violations of the Rights of the Accused, Rules of Procedure and Evidence and the Statute of the Tribunal and Abuse of Process, 11 September 2000; *Prosecutor v Laurent Semanza*, ICTR-97-20-I, Decision on the Defence Motion for the Adjournment of the Trial Proceedings, 30 October 2000; *Prosecutor v Laurent Semanza*, ICTR-97-20-I, Decision Pursuant to Rule 73(E) in Relation to the Defence extremely urgent Motion for Review of the Oral Decision of 14 November 2001, 13 December 2001.

[222] *Prosecutor v Édouard Karemera et al*, ICTR-98-44-T, Trial Chamber III, Decision Initiating Contempt Proceedings Against Peter Robinson, 8 June 2010. See ch 2, III.C.iii at 147, for the resemblance to US contempt orders. For Erlinder see n 233.

[223] Tuinstra (n 1) 223–26. See, eg, *Prosecutor v Zejnil Delalić et al*, IT-96-21, Trial Chamber II, Order (n 117) or the call to order in *Prosecutor v Jadranko Prlić et al*, Trial Chamber III, Ordonnance (n 117) and *Prosecutor v Jadranko Prlić et al*, IT-04-74-T, Submission (n 117).

[224] *Prosecutor v Jean-Paul Akayesu*, ICTR-96-4-T, Issuance of Warning against Defence Counsels, 19 March 1998.

[225] *Prosecutor v Jérôme Clément Bicamumpaka*, ICTR-99-50-I, Decision on the Defence Motion on a Point of Law (Rule 73), 8 April 2003.

[226] *Prosecutor v Alfred Musema*, ICTR-96-13-I, Warning and Notice to Counsel in Terms of Rule 46A of the Rules of Procedure and Evidence, 31 October 1997.

[227] *Prosecutor v Augustin Ndindiliyimana et al*, ICTR-2000-56-T, Decision on Request for Certification of Appeal From the Decision of Trial Chamber dated 13June 2004 (sic) Dismissing Applicant's Request for a Citation of Contempt of the Journalist Gatare of Radio Rwanda for Publishing the Names of Protected Witnesses, 1 July 2005.

[228] *Procureur c Édouard Karemera et al*, ICTR-98-44-T, Avertissement à la défense d'Édouard Karemera pour refus de se conformer aux ordonnances de la Chambre, Article 46 du Règlement de procédure et de preuve, 27 juin 2008; *Procureur c Édouard Karemera et al*, ICTR-98-44-T, Décision enjoignant à la défense d'Édouard Karemera de déposer immédiatement l'ordre de comparution de ses témoins, Articles 46 et 54 du Règlement de procédure et de preuve, 25 juin 2008.

Ntakirutimana.[229] In one case, *Ntagerura*, a warning was lifted.[230] These warnings constitute the majority of instances of formal judicial disciplining,[231] again for similar allegations as underlay the contempt motions mentioned above. Consequently, the withdrawal of defence counsel was sometimes ordered.[232] Marie-Paule Honegger, counsel for Musema, and Peter Erlinder, counsel for Ntabakuze, were refused audience for good by a Chamber.[233]

What seems to have happened as well on numerous occasions is the non-payment of fees for motions that Chambers have deemed abusive.[234] Such decisions are apparently the most frequent disciplinary tool used by Chambers, without being subject to appeal.[235] The sanction of fee-denial cannot be imposed on the prosecution, putting counsel at another disadvantage. This happened, for example, four times within three months in the case of *Semanza.*[236]

In the contempt case of aforementioned defence investigator Nshogoza,[237] Trial Chamber III imposed fines of US$5,000 and US$500 under Rule 46 RPE on his counsel Turner for not reducing the witness list according to the Chamber's orders, for obstructive conduct – including comportment in the courtroom – and for her refusal to commence her case.[238] The Appeals Chamber, however, contrasted Rule 46 with Rule 77 and allowed the appeal:

> [P]ecuniary sanctions are not within the permitted scope of penalties that may be applied under Rule 46 of the Rules. The text of the rule itself does not refer to pecuniary sanctions, while provisions such as Rule 77(G) of the Rules provide the means for punishing an attorney's misconduct through fines where that is deemed appropriate. Given

[229] *Prosecutor v Elizaphan and Gérard Ntakirutimana*, ICTR-96-10-T and ICTR-96-17-T, Decision on the Defence's Motion on Prosecutorial Misconduct and on the Prosecutor's Counterclaim, 12 September 2002 (denied, including counterclaim).

[230] *Prosecutor v André Ntagerura*, ICTR-96-10A-I, Decision on the Defence Motion Requesting for the Withdraw of the Warning Issued against the Defence, 21 May 1999.

[231] Boed (n 196) 274. Many of the decisions with formal warnings are reprinted there, 241–67.

[232] *Prosecutor v Théoneste Bagosora*, ICTR-96-7-T, Decision on the Request by the Accused for Change of Assigned Counsel, 26 June 1997; *Prosecutor v Georges Rutaganda*, ICTR-96-3-T, Trial Chamber I, Decision on the Accused's Motion for Withdrawal of his Lead Counsel, 31 October 1997; *Prosecutor v Jean-Bosco Barayagwiza*, ICTR-97-19-T, Decision on Defence Counsel Motion to Withdraw, 2 November 2000; *Prosecutor v Alfred Musema*, ICTR-96-13-I, Decision to Withdraw Assigned Counsel and to Allow the Prosecutor Temporarily to Redact Identifying Information of Her Witnesses, 18 November 1997.

[233] *Prosecutor v Alfred Musema*, Decision (n 233); *Aloys Ntabakuze v The Prosecutor*, ICTR-98-41A-A, Appeals Chamber, Order Imposing Sanctions on Ntabakuze's Lead Counsel, 21 April 2011. On Erlinder, see ch 4, III.C at 307.

[234] See Tuinstra (n 1) 225–26.

[235] Brants (n 58) 458, 464–67; Boed (n 196) 275. See also the listing by K Ogetto, 'Associations Of Defense Counsel – Development And Role' in M Bohlander, R Boed and RJ Wilson (eds), *Defense in International Criminal Proceedings* (Ardsley, NY, Transnational Publishers, 2006) 422, fn 193.

[236] See above (n 222), and *Prosecutor v Laurent Semanza*, ICTR-97-20-I, Decision on the Defence Motion for the Interpretation of Rules 89(A), (B), (C), (D), and 90(F) of the Rules of Procedure and Evidence and for the Recall of a Witness, 1 December 2000. See also the case note by Brants (n 58) 464.

[237] Above, III.B.ii at 39 (n 211).

[238] *Prosecutor v Léonidas Nshogoza*, ICTR-2007-91-T, Trial Chamber III, Decision to Sanction the Defence for Failure to Comply with the Chamber's Orders, 11 March 2009, and *Prosecutor v Léonidas Nshogoza*, ICTR-07-91-T, Trial Chamber III, Further Decision to Sanction Defence Counsel for Misconduct, 17 March 2009.

> the absence of clear parameters regarding the scope of sanctions permitted under Rule 46, and the context of the Rules, the Appeals Chamber finds that the Trial Chamber acted outside its jurisdiction in imposing pecuniary sanctions on the Counsel pursuant to Rule 46(A) of the Rules.[239]

There is little to add to this sound analysis of the scope of Rule 46(A) in light of the law of contempt. It would indeed be at odds with Rule 77 to allow punitive monetary fines even more easily, exacerbating the existing problems of due process. Among the latter is the lack of an appeal from Rule 46 sanctions.[240] The Appeals Chamber considered the appeal only as extraordinary, going to jurisdiction.[241] This does not offer the required remedy for routine cases.

The case also aptly highlights how disciplining counsel is intertwined with defence rights. Counsel Turner asserted on appeal that she was 'acting to preserve the rights of her client', that the Trial Chamber had mischaracterised and misrepresented her conduct, and that the fines were 'manifestly excessive assessed against [her] alleged infractions'.[242] As it struck down the Trial Chamber's ruling for lack of jurisdiction, there was no need for the Appeals Chamber to delve further into this. It is noted at this point that ignoring court orders is certainly no option to counsel and may ultimately be to the detriment of the client.

iv The Registrar

Of course, the Registrar also acted in the face of misconduct, or on Chamber's instruction.[243] This includes the assignment or withdrawal of counsel.[244] One counsel, Jean Yaovi Dégli, was withdrawn because of financial irregularities. He was declared ineligible for legal aid assignments and removed from the list.[245] Another counsel, Richard Harvey, was withdrawn due to his unavailability caused

[239] *Prosecutor v Léonidas Nshogoza*, ICTR-2007-91-A, Appeals Chamber, Decision on Appeal Concerning Sanctions, 26 June 2009, para 29.

[240] ibid, para 15. See also below, III.C at 44, for more scholarly critique of Art 46 sanctions in this vein.

[241] ibid, para 26.

[242] ibid, para 17.

[243] Tuinstra (n 1) 221–22. From the case law see, eg, *Prosecutor v Jean-Paul Akayesu*, ICTR-96-4-T, Decision Concerning a Replacement of an Assigned Defence Counsel and Postponement of Trial, 31 October 1996; *Prosecutor v Joseph Nzirorera*, ICTR-98-44-T, Decision of Withdrawal of Mr Andrew McCartan as Lead Counsel and Mr Martin Bauwens as Co-Counsel of the Accused Joseph Nzirorera, 5 February 2002, reviewed by *Prosecutor v Joseph Nzirorera*, ICTR-98-44-T, The President's Decision on Review of the Decision of the Registrar Withdrawing Mr Andrew McCartan as Lead Counsel of the Accused Joseph Nzirorera, 13 May 2002.

[244] See ICTR, *Directive on the Assignment of Defence Counsel/Directive relative à la commission d'office de Conseils de la défense* (approved 9 January 1996, last amended 15 June 2007) and further on assignment by the ICTR Registrar Niang (n 18) 163–229. See Tuinstra (n 1) 32–33 on the ICTR list counsel system, and Tuinstra, ibid, 49–52 and 78–82 on the Registrar's powers to address counsel incompetence and many other counsel issues.

[245] *Prosecutor v Théoneste Bagosora et al*, ICTR-98-7-T, Registry, Decision to Withdraw the Assignment of Mr Jean Yaovi Degli as Defense Counsel for Gratien Kabiligi, 26 October 2004; for critique see Tuinstra (n 1) 221.

by non-Tribunal commitments. He was declared ineligible for assignment to suspects and accused of the ICTR, and the State Bar of New York was notified.[246]

The Registrar may report matters to other bodies of the Tribunal but is not obliged to do so. Thus, both Rule 46(D) of the Rules and Article 20(B)(ii) of the Directive give the Registrar a discretion as to how to proceed in the event of a finding of serious breach of the Code of Professional Conduct. Furthermore, it was held in the same decision that action by the Registrar was of an administrative nature. Therefore, the due process rights accorded a suspect or accused facing criminal investigation or prosecution cannot be invoked by counsel.[247]

v The Defence Lawyers' Association at the ICTR

Defence lawyers before the ICTR founded an association to represent their interests, the Association des avocats de la défense (ADAD), in 1997.[248] It operated without official recognition by the full Tribunal until at least 2005, although it was recognised by the Registry by 2004.[249] It was for the first time represented in the 14th Plenary Session on 23 and 24 April 2004.[250] The defence is otherwise involved through the Tribunal's Advisory Panel pursuant to Article 29 of the Directive.[251] By mid-2004,[252] the ADAD had 65 members out of a total of over a hundred acting counsel, notably on a voluntary basis. In practice, however, the ADAD as the only such organisation seems to enjoy a de facto status as the representative association of counsel.[253] As far as the work of the ADAD is concerned, it has particularly engaged in amicus curiae and advocacy activities for accused and defence rights.[254]

It seems that the ADAD does not possess self-regulation of its own. At least a former president of the association, Kennedy Ogetto, has argued in favour of self-regulation of the defence in disciplinary matters, in spite of the absence of such a regime.[255] Judging from the experience of the ADC of the ICTY, it seems fair to conclude that the ADAD would also be limited in its ability to fully govern and

[246] *Prosecutor v Juvénal Kajelijeli*, ICTR-98-44A-T, Decision on Withdrawal of Mr Richard Harvey as Co-Counsel of Mr Juvénal Kajelijeli, 2 April 2001.

[247] *Prosecutor v Joseph Nzirorera*, The President's Decision (n 244). See for the ICTY, Rohde (n 121).

[248] Ogetto (n 235) 505–09. See also Tuinstra (n 1) 88–99.

[249] See on the one hand, *Prosecutor v Théoneste Bagosora et al*, ICTR-98-7-T, Decision on the Defence Motions for the Reinstatement of Jean Yaovi Dégli as Lead Counsel for Gratien Kabiligi, 19 January 2005, para 26, and on the other, ICTR, ICTR/INFO-9-3-15.EN, Registry's Response to the Allegations of Serious and Repeated Violations of the Rights of the Defence, 29 January 2004.

[250] ICTR, *Newsletter*, February–April 2004, 13.

[251] Tuinstra (n 1) 87–88.

[252] Ogetto (n 235) 516.

[253] ibid, 508.

[254] ibid, 509–16. See, eg, *Prosecutor v Théoneste Bagosora et al*, ICTR-98-7-T, Decision on the Defence Motions for the Reinstatement of Jean Yaovi Dégli as Lead Counsel for Gratien Kabiligi, 19 January 2005 (standing granted); *Procureur c Athanase Seromba*, TPIR-2001-66-T, Décision sur les requêtes en annulation de sanction et en intervention en qualité d'amicus curiae, 22 octobre 2004 (standing denied).

[255] Ogetto (n 235) 526.

sanction counsel misconduct. Moreover, termination of ADAD membership does not equal ineligibility before the Tribunal, as is the case for the ADC-ICTY. All in all, the impact of the ADAD on the regulation of counsel appears rather peripheral.

C Assessment of the ICTR's Regime in Scholarship

The ICTR has drawn less scholarly attention than its sister court. This may be explained by the smaller overall number of cases, and primarily because the ICTR has had less coverage in general. The main issues identified in scholarship are similar to those on the ICTY. Brants holds the lack of provisions on contempt to be 'a serious oversight' rather than 'a deliberate omission and therefore not curtailment of power'.[256]

With regard to the non-payment of fees for certain motions, a much more frequent measure, there has been criticism that counsel are not afforded appropriate guarantees, such as timely notice, the right to be heard or to lodge an appeal, even though the consequences can be harsh.[257] Chambers have been innovative, for example, by ordering the payment of costs to other participants, but this has been held to be questionable.[258] There seems to be a point in this. If formally tried for contempt, counsel faces a maximum fine of US$10,000, and most ordinary cases will draw a much lesser sentence. If a similarly high sentence can be reached by fee denial, why should the Tribunal bother with onerous contempt proceedings? The Trial Chamber's reliance on Rule 46 RPE for pecuniary sanctions against counsel Turner[259] instead of under Rule 77 serves as a good example. Given the potential sanctioning effect of the non-payment of fees, a review opportunity and a more formalised and stricter procedure seem desirable. The point of legal guarantees has also been raised in respect to the Registrar, ie, that judicial control of the Registrar is restricted to few cases.[260]

D Analysis of the ICTR Regime

The smaller number of cases and the lesser attention devoted to the ICTR in legal writing make it somewhat more difficult to make out clear findings on the Tribunal's sanctioning regime. It seems safe to say the ICTR has produced, with a regulatory framework that is fairly similar to that of the ICTY, different case law. Although both Tribunals have experienced patterns of misconduct, the ICTR's overall approach to misconduct tends to appear more lenient than that of the

256 Brants (n 58) 459.

257 ibid, 465–67; Ogetto (n 235) 522–23. For a general overview on counsel remuneration by the international courts, see Tuinstra (n 1) 33–38.

258 Brants (n 58) 465.

259 Above, III.B.iii at 41.

260 Ogetto (n 235) 505. See also above, III.B.iv, at 43, in particular n 247.

ICTY. The ICTR readily recognised the concept of contempt as broad inherent powers,[261] but only in one case embarked on criminal prosecutions, for which it set a high threshold. It mostly relied on the minor forms of contempt, especially warnings and the non-payment of fees.

Of course, it needs to be taken into account that for a long period the ICTR did not have the same instruments available to it as the ICTY. First, the contempt powers were only broadened to apply to counsel in 2003. Secondly, the ICTR does not have, even now, a disciplinary procedure in place. However, Chambers could rely on Rule 46 of the ICTR RPE to issue warnings, refuse audience and notify domestic regulatory bodies. The Registrar could address misconduct through his assignment powers. The Registrar, on his part, has done so. As far as contemptuous conduct before Chambers is concerned, they have continuously refused to sanction for contempt. The sole exception, where contempt proceedings were actually initiated orally, was the case of counsel Robinson in *Karemera*.[262] ICTR Chambers have rather resorted to warnings and non-payment of fees.

It may be argued that the ICTR has not seen instances of contempt as grave as the ICTY cases. The allegations in the abovementioned ICTY cases revolved mostly around interfering with witnesses and violating protective measures. However, at least the latter have also been the subject of contempt motions before the ICTR. Nevertheless, the ICTR seems considerably more hesitant to launch contempt proceedings. Boed cites as 'representative' a passage from *Nyiramasuhuko et al*[263] to establish a prima facie standard as threshold to contempt proceedings:

> 5. However, the Chamber bears in mind the gravity of such allegations and the fact that, should the Chamber decide to proceed with the Prosecutor's request for investigations on these issues, a trial would commence within the Trial, at the conclusion of which these allegations could result, if proven, notably, in a verdict of Contempt of the Tribunal and the imposition of a 'fine (. . .) or a term of imprisonment (. . .),' pursuant to Rule 77(C) of the Rule.
> 6. For this reason, and bearing in mind the principle of innocence, any allegations of contempt are to be handled with due care. Consequently, the Prosecution is to justify its request for investigations by prima facie satisfying the Trial Chamber that there are reasonable grounds to believe that contemptuous conduct may have taken place, which may be attributable to the alleged contemnor.

Therefore, 'the primary judicial vehicle for disciplining counsel is Rule 46 of the Rules of Procedure and Evidence'. [264] Relative to the ICTY, this factually deprives the ICTR regime of one regulatory level. The disciplinary options appear underused as well. Moreover, since membership in an officially ICTR recognised Bar association is not mandatory, counsel may not be subject to intra-professional

[261] See, eg, *Prosecutor v Pauline Nyiramasuhuko et al*, Decision on the Prosecutor's Further Allegations of Contempt (n 215) para 8.

[262] Above, III.B.ii at 40.

[263] Above n 263.

[264] Boed (n 196) 273.

discipline. By and large, this shows that the ICTR has arrived at a different approach to sanctioning and disciplining counsel misconduct despite a framework that seems, at first glance, so similar to that of the ICTY.

IV Misconduct before the Special Court for Sierra Leone

A The Legal Sources of the SCSL on Counsel

Like the two ad hoc Tribunals, the SCSL builds on a statute.[265] Likewise, the legal basis for the regulation of counsel at the SCSL has its roots in the RPE.[266] Again, Rules 44–46 RPE govern counsel issues. Rule 46 on misconduct contains basically what its ICTY and ICTR counterparts encompass, with some differences as to the personal scope, which includes prosecution counsel and amicus curiae, and the possibility of appealing decisions.

Rule 46(G) provides for the Code of Professional Conduct for counsel, which was enacted in 2005.[267]

Furthermore, the SCSL relies on contempt powers modelled on the ICTR example. However, Rule 77(C) SCSL RPE is notable as it distinguishes summary convictions from a full trial.[268]

B The SCSL's Practice

i Disciplinary Proceedings

The Special Court's disciplinary bodies have handled cases under their disciplinary regime against both prosecution and defence counsel.[269]

[265] Signed on 16 January 2002. See also, 'The Special Court Agreement, 2002, (Ratification) Act', *Supplement of the Sierra Leone Gazette Vol CXXXIII, No 22* (2002). On the differences to the ICTY and the ICTR set-up and the status of the SCSL as an international court, see Schabas (n 1) 39, 53–60, 79, 595–96; C Kreß, 'Commentary' in A Klip and G Sluiter (eds), *Annotated Leading Cases of International Criminal Tribunals, vol 9, The Special Court for Sierra Leone 2003–2004* (Antwerp, Intersentia, 2006) 202–08.

[266] Art 14 SCSL Statute as well as Section 10 Ratification Act expressly point to the ICTR RPE as the mother rules. On the ICTR, see above, III.A.

[267] *Code of Professional Conduct for Counsel with the Right of Audience before the Special Court for Sierra Leone* (Amended on 13 May 2006, adopted 14 May 2005).

[268] See Rule 77(G) thereof, and D'Ascoli (n 36) 742.

[269] On the prosecution, see *Prosecutor v Issa Hassan Sesay*, SCSL-04-15-T-CCC32-485, President, Decision on complaint pursuant to Article 32 of the Code of Professional Conduct for Counsel With the Right of Audience Before the Special Court for Sierra Leone, 20 February 2006; G Boas, 'Commentary' in A Klip and G Sluiter (eds), *Annotated Leading Cases of International Criminal Tribunals, vol 21, The Special Court for Sierra Leone 2004–2006* (Antwerp, Intersentia, 2010) 679–80.

A disciplinary hearing was held against defence lawyers Yada Williams and Ibrahim Yillah.[270] Yada Williams was publicly reprimanded and fined one million leones (about €250), out of the possible maximum of two million, for pushing and slapping a staff member of the Court and behaving aggressively towards another one. For Ibrahim Yillah, the evidence was held insufficient to establish that he had made false statements in relation these incidents.

In a disciplinary hearing for counsel Courtenay Griffiths, the Trial Chamber did not constitute and the matter was adjourned. The matter was declared closed after counsel apologised for misconduct (see below, iii).[271]

ii Contempt of the Special Court

Furthermore, the SCSL has litigated cases under the doctrine of contempt, some of them in connection with the defence.

Defence investigator Brima Samura was found not guilty of revealing the identity of a protected witness due to a lack of wilfulness.[272] In the related case, the wives and friends of three accused were sentenced to a 'conditional discharge' for threatening that protected witness.[273]

During the opening statements of the *Taylor* case, the presiding judge discussed the possibility of holding counsel Karim Khan in contempt but abstained.[274] Counsel argued that he was bound by the instructions of the accused not to represent him any more. He consequently withdrew from the court room despite a court order to continue representation. The issue was eventually resolved by directing the attending duty counsel to take charge of Taylor's opening statements instead of Khan.

iii Other Measures by the Chambers

As to the general judicial powers to sanction specifically counsel misconduct, Rule 46 has been used at least once. During the examination-in-chief in the Taylor case, counsel Courtenay Griffiths had called one prosecution counsel a 'boy'.[275]

[270] *Re Williams and Yillah*, Code of Conduct Hearing, 10 November 2005. See on this, Boas (n 269) 681–82.

[271] *Trial Chamber II*, SCSL-03-01-T, Order re: Defence Motion Seeking Termination of the Disciplinary Hearing of Failure to Properly Constitute the Trial Chamber and/or Leave to Appeal the Remaining Judges' Decision to Adjourn the Disciplinary Hearing, 18 March 2011.

[272] *Independent Counsel v Brima Samura*, SCSL-2005-01, Trial Chamber I, Judgement in Contempt Proceedings, 26 October 2005. See on this case, Boas (n 269) 676–79.

[273] *Independent Counsel v Margaret Fomba Brima, Neneh Bah Jalloh, Esther Kamara, Anifa Kamara*, SCSL-2005-02 and SCSL-2005-03, Trial Chamber I, Sentencing Judgement in Contempt Proceedings, 21 September 2005. On this case, see G Azarnia, 'Commentary' in A Klip and G Sluiter (eds), *Annotated Leading Cases of International Criminal Tribunals, vol 21, The Special Court for Sierra Leone 2004–2006* (Antwerp, Intersentia, 2010) 638–46.

[274] *Prosecutor v Charles Ghankay Taylor*, SCSL-2003-01-T, Trial Chamber II, Transcript, 4 June 2007, 22–26.

[275] *Prosecutor v Charles Ghankay Taylor*, SCSL-2003-01-T, Trial Chamber II, Transcript, 12 August 2010, 46093.

The presiding judge ordered him to apologise to the Court and to opposing counsel personally. When counsel Griffiths apologised to the Court but refused to apologise to opposing counsel, the judge cited Article 7 of the Code of Conduct and gave a formal warning under Rule 46.[276] The accused then instructed one of his co-counsel to apologise fully to the OTP members.[277] As this did not suffice either in the eyes of the presiding judge, counsel was warned again and then refused audience.[278] Eventually, twenty minutes later, counsel Griffiths did apologise to the concerned OTP counsel and was allowed to resume the examination-in-chief which he had prepared.[279] Again, this demonstrates how sanction of counsel can affect the defence of the accused who will usually hold a vital interest in the effective examinations of witnesses, and thereby prefer counsel who prepared the case to conduct the case.

iv Appointment and Withdrawal of Counsel

The powers regarding the appointment and the withdrawal of counsel within the SCSL have been handled in a similar fashion to that of the ad hoc Tribunals.[280] A notable difference would be that it is the Principal Defender within the Registry's Defence Office, not the Registrar, who manages the assignment of counsel by the Court. As with Registry decisions, judicial review is in place.[281]

C Analysis of the SCSL Regime

Overall, the SCSL's approach is therefore similar to the ICTY and the ICTR. The SCSL has used all options available to it for incidents of misconduct, including contempt and disciplinary proceedings. However, the relatively small number of cases and the lack of specific scholarship on the SCSL in this area make it harder to draw conclusive findings.

In comparison to the ICTY and the ICTR, it could be noted that the SCSL has been somewhat more counsel-friendly. All of the examined cases, be it the allegations of prosecution misconduct in Sessay, the disciplinary findings for Williams and Yillah, or Khan walking-out, show clear awareness of the roles of counsel and moderation in sanctioning. Moreover, Rules 46 and 77 are more sophisticated and arguably fairer to counsel than their ICTY and ICTR counterparts. Rule

[276] ibid, 46096–97.

[277] ibid, 46097–98.

[278] ibid, 46098.

[279] ibid, 46101.

[280] G Mettraux, 'Commentary' in A Klip and G Sluiter (eds), *Annotated Leading Cases of International Criminal Tribunals, vol 9, The Special Court for Sierra Leone 2003–2004* (Antwerp, Intersentia, 2006) 572–74.

[281] See, eg, the non-assignment of counsel Terrence Michael Terry, *The Prosecutor v. Alex Tamba Brima et al*, SCSL-2004-06-PT, Trial Chamber, Decision on applicant's motion against denial by the Acting Principal Defender to enter a legal service contract for the assignment of counsel, 6 May 2004.

46(H) SCSL RPE very commendably provides for judicial review of Rule 46 sanctions which constitutes a clear improvement over the ICTY and ICTR rules. Rule 77(C) differentiates between three options to conduct contempt proceedings: summarily by the bench, by the authorities of Sierra Leone, or by prosecution by an independent counsel. In principle, this offers much more tailored-to-the-case solutions. Moreover, using independent counsel laudably allows for a prosecution at arm's length, unlike indictments by the OTP or orders *in lieu* by Chambers.

These varying findings on the SCSL should not be overestimated, though, as far as the overall scheme of disciplining counsel is concerned. The SCSL may seem more advanced, in some respects, than the ICTY and the ICTR in the field of counsel regulation. It has dealt with prosecution misconduct alike and has endeavoured to strengthen the defence by an independent Defence Office. From the institutional perspective, however, this has not brought fundamental changes to the two larger Tribunals. The Defence Office headed by the Principal Defender has not grown into an entity independent from the Registry,[282] let alone become a decisive factor in defence management or counsel discipline. The SCLS's practice may feature differences in detail, but they only reflect the marginally different law of the SCSL. Therefore, the SCSL does follow the methods of the ICTY and the ICTR when considering counsel misconduct.

V Conclusion on the UN Tribunals: Lessons to Learn

The above examination indicates how the ICTY, the ICTR and the SCSL can serve as models for counsel regulation. All of them aim at a comprehensive regime of regulating professional conduct but have generated slightly different results. It becomes clear from the practice of these courts that instances of professional misconduct do occur in significant numbers. Among the forms that they have encountered most frequently are, in particular, breaches of protective measures and of confidentiality obligations, financial irregularities and abusive motions. Most misconduct occurs through negligence or with disregard to obligations, although not quite with intent. Purposive disturbances are hence not a common problem. There apparently is a need, though, to retain criminal offences to curb the most serious instances of misconduct. Nevertheless, these criminal offences seem, by their nature, to only apply to a small section of overall misconduct.

The overwhelming majority of counsel misconduct is dealt with by measures other than contempt. These further measures have evolved as flexible and suitable tools. It needs to be noted, however, that the ad hoc Tribunals' and the SCSL's Statutes, Rules or other documents do not always provide a clear legal basis. The Tribunals, as well as the SCSL, resorted to the concept of inherent powers to regulate and safeguard their own proceedings in these cases. Even if the legitimacy

282 Schabas (n 1) 615–16; Tuinstra (n 1) 83–86. See on the Defence Office Rules 2(A) and 45 SCSL RPE.

of the various regulatory and disciplining measures is acknowledged, certain due process issues remain. Counsel have had little part in regulating and disciplining their colleagues. This has been the Tribunals' and the SCSL's very own domain.

It can be concluded from all this for other courts, namely the ICC, that no criminal court will ever be safe from misconduct. The challenge thus is to devise a multi-layered and flexible system. Any regime should discourage misconduct in first place and seek to ensure high principles from counsel practising before a court. A range of suitable measures should be available to the court and its organs when misconduct has occurred and reacting to the most serious cases of misconduct may necessitate criminal sanctions. Going one step further, things become less clear, and choices have to be made.

How is truly criminal contempt going to be delineated from simple regulation and discipline? A criminal prosecution for contempt in particular requires reasonable grounds to act upon. Professional discipline and other types of administrative prosecution have a much lower threshold and are administered rather before misconduct occurs.

If criminal sanctions are a reality, are they soundly based in the court's governing laws?

Which guarantees apply to the various measures? In particular, are criminal proceedings accompanied by corresponding rights?

Are measures against counsel and, in particular, any consequences proportional? Which constraints apply herein?

Who launches proceedings and investigates allegations?

To what extent should concerned judges be involved in proceedings?

How can the need for an effective sanction against counsel be balanced with the impact on the accused and the rights of counsel?

What is the importance of a criminal Bar? Is self-regulation a viable model in a particular setting? Should it be used in addition?

It would be preferable if those points are clearly addressed, entrenched and clarified in the statutory law of the court. This will not always be the case. It is a legal reality that statutory law contains lacunae. As a consequence, in practice, it frequently becomes important to probe the permissibility and suitability of individual legal measures. This may raise the issue of inherent powers. As has been seen, claims of inherent powers can be problematic in international courts. It has been pointed out that the principal legitimacy of the pertinent powers of the ICC are likely to be less contestable.[283] They are provided for in the Statute itself and the RPE and both were adopted by the state parties at the Rome Conference in 1998. Arguably, these provisions thus have a sound foundation, and are conclusive as to allow no further inherent powers of the Court. Since Articles 70 and 71 of the ICC Statute are narrower in scope than the catch-all clause of contempt, it seems safe to claim that the ICC will have to rely on a multi-layered system to address misconduct by counsel.

[283] See Spronken (n 36) 225–26; Cockayne (n 60) 199–200.

2

The National Models: Germany and the United States

I The Two National Models: Commonalities and Differences

In the previous chapter, it was shown how the UN tribunals have developed a fully-fledged regime on the regulation of counsel, including sanctioning mechanisms. The UN tribunals arrived at a functional system but due to their relative novelty and the limited number of cases it does not benefit from the solid body of scholarship that can be found on the national level.

International courts have faced issues that are well known to national judiciaries. Chapter one demonstrated that criminal liability should attach to grave forms of misconduct. This raises the question of the role of criminal law, and how truly criminal acts are going to be delineated from simple regulation and discipline. It also entails a discussion of the nature of the different measures used in Germany and the United States, and which guarantees apply to them. In a related vein, the applicable constraints before the respective constitutional backgrounds require closer examination in order to resolve the issue of how the need for an effective sanction against counsel can be balanced with the impact on the accused and the rights of counsel. This also extends to the procedure, ie, who launches proceedings and investigates allegations and what the involvement of judges is in such proceedings. Finally, it will be demonstrated that systems tend to be multi-tiered, and what the relationships are between the available measures.

Whereas the commonalities and the differences between the US and Germany remain to be mapped out in detail, both can contribute to the overall endeavour. From a practical stance, it is noted that many American lawyers have defended before international tribunals. Moreover, US scholarship in the field of professional responsibility is vast and arguably unmatched worldwide. Recurring topics such as the inherent power of courts and multi-jurisdictional practice resurface in the international arena. It is, furthermore, a common law jurisdiction representing a major legal system as envisaged by the ICC Statute. As such it also stands for the adversary model embodying the often reiterated ideal of zealous advocacy. Germany, on the other hand, is grounded in a different, more inquisitorial procedural model and thus represents the civil law tradition.[1] Together, they are a starting point to fulfil the mandate of Article 21(1)(c) of the ICC Statute, ie, to apply as law the 'general principles of law derived by the Court from national laws of legal systems of the world including, as appropriate, the national laws of states that would normally exercise jurisdiction over the crime'.

A Criminal Defence in Germany

Defence lawyers have a key role in criminal proceedings in Germany. While this seems a simple truth, another simple truth is that defence lawyers, due to this role, contribute to expediting or delaying the trial. A third truth is that criminal trials in Germany sometimes do not run as smoothly as they could. What this adds up to is that defence counsel have occasionally been blamed of standing in the way of justice. In particular, the delay of proceedings has sometimes been credited to counsel and likened to misconduct.[2] However, it can be argued that the root causes of delay can be tackled without curtailing substantial rights of the defence.[3]

As a starting point, it has to be noted that participation of counsel is accorded a high priority under German criminal procedure.[4] An accused person or suspect may seek legal assistance at any stage of the proceedings and elect up to three counsel.[5] Any lawyer called to the German Bar – and any law professor – may act as defence counsel in criminal cases.[6] Practising lawyers in the field may be recognised as Certified Specialist in Criminal Law.[7] This does not have express implications, however, with respect to regulatory purposes or discipline.[8] Section 140 of the Code of Criminal Procedure lists many cases where the participation of

[1] From a comparative perspective, see J Hodgson, 'The Role of the Criminal Defence Lawyer in an Inquisitorial Procedure: Legal and Ethical Constraints' (2006) 9 *Legal Ethics* 125; J Hodgson, 'The Role of the Criminal Defence Lawyer in Adversarial and Inquisitorial Procedure' in T Weigend, S Walther and B Grunewald (eds), *Strafverteidigung vor neuen Herausforderungen – Denkanstöße aus sieben Rechtsordnungen* (Berlin, Duncker & Humblot, 2008) 45–59.

[2] It appears, however, to be seen to be linked to a combination of several factors. See, eg, M Bohlander, *Gerichtliche Sanktionen gegen Anwälte wegen Mißbrauchs von Verfahrensrechten* (Aachen, Shaker, 2001) 57–59, 71–72.

[3] K Nehm and L Senge, 'Ursachen langer Hauptverhandlungen – dargestellt am Beispiel von 3 Strafverfahren' (1998) *Neue Zeitschrift für Strafrecht* 377, 389.

[4] On German criminal procedure in general, see T Weigend, 'Germany' in CM Bradley (ed), *Criminal Procedure A Worldwide Study*, 2nd edn (Durham, Carolina Academic Press, 2007). For more recent case law on effective defence, see *Bundesgerichtshof*, 2 December 2008, 3 StR 203/08, Neue Zeitschrift für Strafrecht 2009, 692, with a case note by K Gaede, 'Schlechtverteidigung – Tabus und Präklusionen zum Schutz vor dem Recht auf wirksame Verteidigung?' (2007) *Höchstrichterliche Rechtsprechung im Strafrecht* 402.

[5] Section 137 Code of Criminal Procedure (StPO).

[6] Section 138 StPO. See also Section 139.

[7] See the *Fachanwaltsordnung* (Certified Experts' Act), below II.A (n 46).

[8] See also A Jungk, 'Gesteigerte Haftung des Fachanwalts?' (2007) *Anwaltsblatt* 227 (with a focus on civil liability; arguing that a Certified Expert may be held to a higher standard under contract law if hired in his or her special practice area).

counsel is mandatory.[9] Counsel will then be assigned by the court pursuant to Section 141 if the accused has not retained counsel of his or her own choice. The financial conditions of the accused are of no relevance. The presiding judge will choose counsel in accordance with Section 142, usually respecting the choice of the accused.

Counsel are therefore in place to represent defendants in all cases of sufficient gravity. Even those wishing to argue *pro se* are assigned counsel. This can be understood as a duty of the court to safeguard the rights of the accused in all eventualities. In some cases, counsel are assigned even though the accused has retained counsel of choice. German courts have argued in favour of the necessity of such assignments to ensure the smooth conduct of proceedings in the interest of justice, and more generally, that it was necessary for ensuring effective legal assistance and defence.[10] Courts have also stressed, however, that priority must be given to the relationship between the accused and his or her counsel of trust.[11]

It already resonates from this that the participation of counsel has not always been free of tension. Obstructionist techniques have been used by counsel, for example, in political cases. The experience of trials against members of the terrorist group *Rote Armee Fraktion* (Red Army Faction) even prompted Parliament to amend the Code of Criminal Procedure with provisions allowing for the exclusion of defence counsel.[12]

[9] German legislation can be found online at www.gesetze-im-internet.de, including translations into English. In the following, most quotations use the translations endorsed by the German Federal Ministry of Justice. The English versions are, however, not authoritative, and may sometimes be misleading in some parts. The Code of Criminal Procedure, translated by Brian Duffett and Monika Ebinger, is available from the above-mentioned website at www.gesetze-im-internet.de/englisch_stpo/. The German Criminal Code (StGB) has been translated and published as a book by M Bohlander, *The German Criminal Code, A Modern English Translation* (Oxford, Hart Publishing, 2008), but is also available online from the same source at www.gesetze-im-internet.de/englisch_stgb. Professional rules including some translations are available at www.brak.de/fuer-anwaelte/berufsrecht, from the website of the German Federal Bar (see below, II.A at 59). See Bohlander, ibid, 13, on citation and style of German legislation. German court names in this book follow the official translation list of the German Federal Foreign Office, see www.auswaertiges-amt.de/cae/servlet/contentblob/373544/publicationFile/157642/Gerichtsbezeichnungen.pdf.

[10] *Bundesgerichtshof*, 24 January 1961, 1 StR 132/60, BGHSt 15, 306, 309; *Bundesverfassungsgericht*, 8 April 1975, 2 BvR 207/75, BVerfGE 39, 238 (*Stammheim*) 246–47; F Schellenberg, 'Notwendige Verteidigung' (1996) *Strafverteidiger* 641; I Müller, 'Pflichtverteidiger – Verteidiger wessen Vertrauens?' (1981) *Strafverteidiger* 570; L Meyer-Goßner, *Strafprozessordnung*, 53rd edn (Munich, Beck, 2010) §141; mn 1a. This was held to be compatible with the Convention by the European Court of Human Rights, see *Croissant v Germany*, application no 13611/88, Judgment, 25 September 1992. See also *Prosecutor v Momčilo Krajišnik*, IT-00-39-A, Appeals Chamber, Decision on Momčilo Krajišnik's Request to Self-Represent, on Counsel's Motion in Relation to Appointment of *Amicus Curiae*, and on the Prosecution Motion of 16 February 2007, 11 May 2007, paras 66–70 of Judge Schomburg's Fundamentally Dissenting Opinion. There has been criticism of many different kinds in German scholarship; see J Bockemühl, 'Anmerkung zu OLG Düsseldorf StV 2004, 62' (2004) *Strafverteidiger* 63; T Weigend, 'Anmerkung zu BGH NStZ 1997, 46' (1997) *Neue Zeitschrift für Strafrecht* 47; B Schneider, 'Probleme der Auswahl des Pflichtverteidigers und sog. Ersatzverteidigers' (1985) *Zeitschrift für Rechtspolitik* 209; M Künzel, 'Erfahrungen eines Zwangsverteidigers' (1981) *Strafverteidiger* 464.

[11] See, eg, *Oberlandesgericht Frankfurt*, 9 October 1985, 3 Ws 867/85, StV 1986, 144.

[12] Sections 138a ff. On the Red Army Faction, see also the ECHR case of *Ensslin, Baader and Raspe v Federal Republic of Germany*, application nos 7572/76, 7586/76, 7587/76, 1978, Decision on the admissibility of the applications, 8 July 1978, and generally H Breucker, *Verteidigungsfremdes Verhalten*

B The German Approach to the Regulation of Counsel

It has been mentioned above that the criminal trial in Germany has at times confronted difficulties. In respect of counsel, a comprehensive system is in place to maintain general discipline, and a number of tools have been developed and used within the German framework to curb genuine misconduct. As a starting point, German doctrine holds lawyers to be an *Organ der Rechtspflege.*[13] Section 1 of the Federal Lawyers' Act (*Bundesrechtsanwaltsordnung*, or BRAO) stipulates that 'Der Rechtsanwalt ist ein unabhängiges Organ der Rechtspflege'. This is translated in an official English version[14] as 'A *Rechtsanwalt* is an independent agent in the administration of justice'. This wording is probably a bit misleading. It is not meant to declare German lawyers primarily as independent agents for their clients. At least to the same degree – and arguably even stronger – Section 1 stresses that a *Rechtsanwalt* is an agent within the overall process of the administration of justice. This bears resemblance to the concept of the lawyer as an 'officer of the court' in the Anglo-American legal traditions.[15] The view that lawyers only have private duties vis-a-vis their clients has been advocated in German scholarship,[16] but does not reflect the general opinion.

Major differences can be made out as well, notably in the UN tribunals, as were discussed in chapter one. As far as 'contempt of the court' is concerned, such a concept is unknown in German law.[17] Some authors have even gone so far as to assign immunity from such sanctions to counsel. It has been alleged that courts have no power to force lawyers bent on conflict to conduct themselves professionally and ethically. Admonition in open court can even provide a reason for a

(Berlin, Duncker & Humblot, 1993). For commentary on Section 138, see E Müller and K Gussmann, *Berufsrisiken des Strafverteidigers* (Munich, Beck, 2007) 123–34.

[13] On the role of counsel, see F Salditt, 'Zur Stellung des Strafverteidigers' in G Widmaier (ed), *Münchener Anwaltshandbuch Strafverteidigung* (Munich, Beck, 2006) 2–22, and F Edelkötter, *Der Anwalt in Deutschland und in England* (Münster, Lit, 2005) 24–27; M Kleine-Cosack, *Bundesrechtsanwaltsordnung*, 6th edn (Munich, Beck, 2009) § 1, mns 21–22; W Hartung in W Hartung and V Römermann (eds), *Berufs- und Fachanwaltsordnung*, 4th edn (Munich, Beck, 2008) § 1 BerufsO, mns 60–63, 71–72; C Wolf in R Gaier, C Wolf and S Göcken (eds), *Anwaltliches Berufsrecht* (Cologne, Heymanns, 2010) § 1 BRAO, mns 83–96; WE Feuerich in WE Feuerich and D Weyland (eds), *Bundesrechtsanwaltsordnung*, 7th edn (Munich, Vahlen, 2008) § 1 BRAO, mns 1–8; L Koch in M Henssler and H Prütting (eds), *Bundesrechtsanwaltsordnung*, 3rd edn (Munich, Beck, 2010) § 1, mns 66–81.

[14] Translation as of 1 June 2011, available from the German Federal Bar's homepage at www.brak.de/w/files/02_fuer_anwaelte/berufsrecht/brao_stand_1.6.2011_englisch.pdf. See also above at 53 (n 9) on translations of German legislation.

[15] See Edelkötter (n 13) 32–37, for England, and below D at 56, for the United States. For a defence perspective on the role of counsel, see E Müller, 'Berufsbild und Berufsethos des Strafverteidigers' (2009) *Neue Juristische Wochenschrift* 3745; E Müller, 'Von der Verantwortung des Verteidigers – Ein Bericht – III' in F Herzog and U Neumann (eds), *Festschrift für Winfried Hassemer* (Heidelberg, CF Müller, 2010) 1089–101.

[16] See, eg, H-J Wassmann, *Strafverteidigung und Strafvereitelung* (University of Hamburg, unpublished doctoral thesis, 1982) 73, 88.

[17] M Jahn, 'Sitzungspolizei contra "Konfliktverteidigung"? Zur Anwendbarkeit der §§ 176ff. GVG auf den Strafverteidiger' (1998) *Neue Zeitschrift für Strafrecht* 389, 393.

recusal motion.[18] As a general statement, it seems safe to say that there is no systematic direct regulation by courts. Some writers have suggested introducing more direct measures – principally excluding lawyers from the trial – but also fines to deal with contempt.[19] The focus has clearly been on indirect sanctioning, ie, roughly speaking on *ex post* controls. This means principally *Standesrecht* (professional ethics), or more accurately *Berufsrecht* (professional rules).[20] Nevertheless, other enforcement mechanisms exist.

C Criminal Defence in the United States

Defence lawyers also play a fundamental role in the United States. The Sixth Amendment of the United States Constitution provides that '[i]n all criminal prosecutions, the accused shall enjoy the right to . . . have the Assistance of Counsel for his defence'. This right to counsel was bolstered in pivotal cases, most notably *Gideon v Wainwright*[21] in 1963, where the Supreme Court held that indigent accused hold a general constitutional right to have counsel appointed, in state prosecutions as well as federal prosecutions. All across the board, the 1960s brought about a string of cases strengthening defence rights, amounting to what has been called a 'due process revolution'.[22] The right to counsel was materialised in *Strickland v Washington* where the Court required 'effective assistance' to satisfy the right to counsel.[23]

For felonies, virtually all accused are represented by counsel, although substantially more self-representation takes place for misdemeanours. Counsel are often publicly funded lawyers such as public defenders or other court-assigned lawyers.[24]

[18] M Bohlander, 'A Silly Question? Court Sanctions Against Defence Counsel for Trial Misconduct' (1999) 10 *Criminal Law Forum* 467, 476 and 478.

[19] See J Herrmann, 'Die Strafprozeßreform vom 1.1.1975' (1976) *Juristische Schulung* 413, 418, and other authors cited by Jahn (n 17) 393. See also W Dueren, *Contempt – das Rechtsinstitut des Contempt in der politischen Realität der USA* (Munich, de Smet, 1974); H Lienert, *Der Contempt of Court im anglo-amerikanischen Recht* (University of Freiburg, unpublished doctoral thesis, 1956).

[20] Bohlander (n 18) 488.

[21] *Gideon v Wainwright*, 372 US 335, 83 SCt 792, 93 ALR2d 733, 9 LEd2d 799, 23 OO2d 258 (Supreme Court of the United States, 1963). See also *Argersinger v Hamlin*, 407 US 25, 92 SCt 2006 (Supreme Court of the United States, 1972); *Scott v Illinois*, 440 US 367 (Supreme Court of the United States, 1979).

[22] D Luban, 'Are Criminal Defenders Different?' (1992–93) 91 *Michigan Law Review* 1729, 1736. See also JH Israel, 'Free-Standing Due Process and Criminal Procedure: The Supreme Court's Search for Interpretive Guidelines' (2001) 34 *Saint Louis University Law Journal* 303.

[23] *Strickland v Washington*, 466 US 668, 104 SCt 2052, 80 LEd2d 674 (Supreme Court of the United States, 1984), but see, eg, the criticism by JW Hall, *Professional Responsibility in Criminal Defense Practice*, 3rd edn (St Paul, Minn, Thomson/West, 2005) § 10:7; *United States ex rel. Thomas v O'Leary*, 856 F2d 1011 (United States Court of Appeals, Seventh Circuit, 1988) ('The Sixth Amendment right to counsel, of course, guarantees more than just a warm body to stand next to the accused during critical stages of the proceedings; an accused is entitled to an attorney who plays a role necessary to ensure that the proceedings are fair') and below, III.B.iii.b at (n 486).

[24] See CW Harlow, *Defense Counsel in Criminal Cases* (Bureau of Justice Statistics, NCJ 179023, 2000) 1 (1996 state/1998 federal figures): over 80% court-assigned/financed defence counsel in state cases (68% public defenders), about 66% publicly financed lawyers in federal cases (30% Federal Defender Organization and 36% panel attorneys).

The defence counsel corps is by no way a homogenous group, though, and wide gaps among practices exist. Some lawyers may have the resources and circumstances underlying their cases to drive strong bargains for their clients, whereas others resort to bargaining to cope with their caseload.[25]

This may bear some influence on the litigation style but allegations of misconduct have come from all kinds of lawyers, whether civil or criminal. Arguably any serious lawyer, and especially defence counsel, will invoke the duty of zealous advocacy under the adversarial model of procedure.[26] Misconduct occurs on both sides. Prosecutors fail to discharge their procedural duties, for example, by committing disclosure violations, and thus breach their professional duties, or they may not live up to their appropriate ethical standards in the treatment and addressing of accused.[27] Prosecutor misconduct may be under-reported, and doubts are justified as to whether the system works in the same way as for defence lawyers. Some of those, in turn, do use abusive litigation strategies. Tactics range from the unfair to the criminal,[28] such as the coaching of witnesses, cross-examination with the purpose of degrading and harassing, suborning perjury, concealing or destroying evidence or interfering or tampering with witnesses.

D The US Approach to the Regulation of Counsel

The prevalence of the adversarial system, where the parties seem more pitted against each other than in the inquisitorial system, with presumably stronger case controlling powers by the judge, goes hand in hand with the goal of zealous representation of clients. Zealous advocacy has been a recurring ideal for lawyers under adversarial procedure.[29] As a professional duty, zealous advocacy can be traced back to the very first codification of professional rules in the United States – the 1908 ABA Canon of Professional Ethics – and it was taken up again in the subsequent codification – the 1969 ABA Model Code of Responsibility.[30] As a concept,

[25] See Luban (n 22) 1731, who speaks of 'two criminal justice systems, two criminal populations, and two criminal defense bars. . . . The former are the public defenders and panel attorneys working for $40 an hour; the latter are . . . white collar defense lawyers, the mob lawyers, the Miami drug bar'.

[26] See MH Freedman, 'Professionalism in the American Adversary System' (1992) 41 *Emory Law Journal* 467, 470; MH Freedman, 'Henry Lord Brougham and Zeal' (2006) 34 *Hofstra Law Review* 1319. For a critique of the adversarial model and 'hardball litigation', see D Luban, *The Good Lawyer: Lawyers' Roles and Lawyers' Ethics* (Totowa, Rowman & Allanheld, 1983); D Luban, *Lawyers and Justice, An Ethical Study* (Princeton, Princeton University Press, 1988); HL Feldman, 'Beyond the Model Rules: The Place of Examples in Legal Ethics' (1998–99) 12 *Georgetown Journal of Legal Ethics* 409, 410; Hall (n 23) § 3:20; EE Sward, 'Values, Ideology, and the Evolution of the Adversary System' (1989) 64 *Indiana Law Journal* 301.

[27] K Gier, 'Prosecuting Injustice: Consequences of Misconduct' (2006) 33 *American Journal of Criminal Law* 191.

[28] See Hall (n 23) § 3:17.

[29] See above (n 26).

[30] See ER Gaetke, 'Lawyers as Officers of the Court' (1989) 42 *Vanderbilt Law Review* 39, 40. American Bar Association, *Canons of Professional Ethics*, Appendix B of the 1907 Report of the Association's Committee on Canons of Ethics (A.B.A. Reports XXXI, 685–713): 'Canon 15. How Far a Lawyer May Go in Supporting a Client's Cause. . . . The lawyer owes entire devotion to the interest of

it goes even further back into the English common law tradition.[31] This has been softened by Rules 1.3 and 3.1 to 3.5 of the Model Rules of Professional Conduct of 1983; it has remained unchanged and is included the revised 2000 version. The same or similar phrasing to the Model Code of Responsibility is still found in many codes, either in direct reliance on the words of Canon 7 or in their own words.[32]

All of these, however, also reflect the tension between representing a client's cause on the one hand, and the duty to respect the legal system, ie, the 'bounds of law' on the other. The codes themselves make clear that the ideal of zealous advocacy does not relieve lawyers from obeying the general law and/or the disciplinary rules, such fundamental prohibitions as making false statements to the court or to other persons and to refrain from other conduct which is dishonest, fraudulous, deceptive, or misrepresentative.[33] This is also reflected in assigning a second role to counsel, other than that of the advocate: the role as officer of the court.[34] Scholars, on the one hand, have argued that it should be more than just a label and have criticised the adversary model.[35] It has been defended to the same vigour, though, and the primacy of the role of officer of the court has thus been rejected.[36]

the client, warm zeal in the maintenance and defense of his rights and the exertion of his utmost learning and ability, to the end that nothing be taken or be withheld from him, save by the rules of law, legally applied'; American Bar Association, *Model Code of Professional Responsibility* (adopted by the House of Delegates of the American Bar Association on 12 August 1969) 'Canon 7. A Lawyer Should Represent a Client Zealously Within the Bounds of the Law'.

[31] See on this 'sacred duty', as put by Henry Lord Brougham: Freedman, 'Henry Lord Brougham and Zeal' (n 26); MH Freedman, 'Henry Lord Brougham, Written by Himself' (2006) 19 *Georgetown Journal of Legal Ethics* 1213; FC Zacharias and BA Green, '"Anything Rather than a Deliberate and Well-Considered Opinion" – Henry Lord Brougham, Written by Himself' (2006) 19 *Georgetown Journal of Legal Ethics* 1221.

[32] See District of Columbia Court of Appeals, *District of Columbia Rules of Professional Conduct* (1 February 2007): 'Rule 1.3 – Diligence and Zeal: (a) A lawyer shall represent a client zealously and diligently within the bounds of the law'; Supreme Judicial Court of Massachusetts, *Court Rule 3:07, Massachusetts Rules of Professional Conduct* (Promulgated 426 Mass. 1301, As Amended Effective 1 January 2008): 'Rule 1.3 Diligence:. . . The lawyer should represent a client zealously within the bounds of the law'; Appellate Divisions of the Supreme Court of New York, *New York Lawyer's Code of Professional Responsibility* (New York Codes, Rules and Regulations, Title 22, Part 1200, updated through 28 December 2007), features as disciplinable rules DR 7-101 [1200.32] 'Representing a Client Zealously', and DR 7-102 [1200.33] 'Representing a Client Within the Bounds of the Law', and makes further reference to Canon 7 as part of the Ethical Considerations.

[33] MH Freedman, 'In Praise of Overzealous Representation – Lying to Judges, Deceiving Third Parties, and Other Ethical Conduct' (2006) 34 *Hofstra Law Review* 771.

[34] *In re Snyder*, 472 US 634, 105 SCt 2874, 86 LEd2d 504 (Supreme Court of the United States, 1985); *People ex rel. Karlinv Culkin*, 248 NY 465, 162 NE 487, 60 ALR 851 (Court of Appeals of New York, 1928); LR Patterson and TB Metzloff, *Legal Ethics: The Law of Professional Responsibility*, 3rd edn (New York, Matthew Bender & Co, 1989) 27–43.

[35] RJ Martineau, 'The Attorney as an Officer of the Court: Time to take the Gown off the Bar' (1984) 35 *South Carolina Law Review* 541; Gaetke (n 30) 39. For a fundamental critique, see Luban, *Lawyers and Justice* (n 26) 50–147; D Luban, *Legal Ethics and Human Dignity* (Cambridge, Cambridge University Press, 2007) 19–64.

[36] MH Freedman, 'Are the Model Rules Unconstitutional?' (1981) 35 *University of Miami Law Review* 685; Freedman, 'Professionalism in the American Adversary System' (n 26) 467; RJ Uphoff, 'The Role of the Criminal Defense Lawyer in Representing the Mentally Impaired Defendant: Zealous Advocate or Officer of the Court?' (1988) 1988 *Wisconsin Law Review* 65; S Ellmann, 'Lawyers and Clients' (1987) 34 *University of California at Los Angeles Law Review* 717.

The tension between both means that counsel is subject to numerous kinds of regulation. Ethics codes exist, which usually do not distinguish criminal from other legal practices.[37] On the basis of these codes, the Bars and the courts exercise professional discipline.

More specifically and most notably, the regulation of counsel was originally within the realm of the courts. Courts prescribe rules of procedure and evidence as well as local rules. All are nevertheless subject to review by Congress or state legislature. Moreover, it is of course the legislative which sets forth law such as that dealing with criminal offences. But the powers of the courts are arguably the most characteristic and most forceful kind of regulation. The study of the International Criminal Tribunal for the former Yugoslavia (ICTY) and the International Criminal Tribunal for Rwanda (ICTR) has already briefly dealt with the concept of contempt given to courts.[38] The use of contempt powers is probably the most important in practical terms in the United States. What is even more characteristic for the US approach, and in respect of the fundamental structures more important, is that regulatory powers largely originate from the courts. Courts avail themselves of inherent powers to regulate lawyers appearing before them, be it through the rules of procedure, the law of contempt, or simply by inherent powers as such.[39] Most measures are traceable to this grander concept of inherent powers. It helps to understand the concept of contempt better, but it essentially explains the origin of many other measures and sanctions and also why courts ultimately play the greatest role in sanctioning counsel for misconduct. Courts can, of course, make use of procedure to remedy or sanction misconduct, for example, by disqualifying a lawyer, excluding evidence, or dismissing a claim or a defence.[40] Aside from procedural options and contempt in general, state and federal courts can respond specifically to litigation-related misconduct by imposing fines or costs, if it is considered 'frivolous', 'unreasonable', 'vexatious', or otherwise abusive.[41] The model rule for this under civil procedure would be Rule

[37] FC Zacharias, 'Reconceptualizing Ethical Roles' (1997) 65 *George Washington Law Review* 169, 170; A Smith, 'The Difference in Criminal Defense and the Difference it Makes' (2003) 11 *Washington University Journal of Law and Policy* 83, 135. The ABA promulgates 'Standards for Criminal Justice', in order to take into account the particularities of criminal proceedings. See Hall (n 23) § 1:9; A Harting, *Berufspflichten des Strafverteidigers und Sanktionierung pflichtwidrigen Verhaltens* (Bonn, Deutscher Anwaltverlag, 2008) 250–60. They are not binding regulation, though.

[38] See ch 1, II.B.ii at 16–25, C.i at 28–32 and III.B.ii at 39–40, D at 44–45.

[39] *Ex parte Secombe*, 60 US 9, 19 How 9, 1856 WL 8736 (Supreme Court of the United States, 1856); *People ex rel. Karlinv Culkin* (n 34); *Flaksa v Little River Marine Const. Co*, 389 F2d 885 (United States Court of Appeals, Fifth Circuit, 1968); *In re Quaid*, 646 So2d 343 (Supreme Court of Louisiana, 1994) (per constitution, Bar disciplinary matters come within the courts' original jurisdiction of the Supreme Court); *In re Snyder* (n 34); *Theard v U.S.*, 354 US 278, 77 SCt 1274, 1 LEd2d 1342 (Supreme Court of the United States, 1957); *Richardson v Hamilton International Corporation*, 469 F2d 1382 (United States Court of Appeals, Third Circuit, 1972); *Maryland State Bar Ass'n, Inc.v Agnew*, 318 A2d 811, 271 Md 543 (Court of Appeals of Maryland, 1974).

[40] 'Restatement of the Law, Third, The Law Governing Lawyers' in American Law Institute (ed), (2000) §6, Comment i. to m.; *Flaksa v Little River Marine Const. Co* (n 39).

[41] 'Restatement of the Law' (n 40) § 110, at 181; RD Rotunda and JS Dzienkowski, *Legal Ethics: The Lawyer's Deskbook on Professional Responsibility*, 2007–08 edn (St Paul, Thomson/West, 2007) § 3.1.-2(c).

11 of the Federal Rules of Procedure and Evidence. A string of equivalent rules or ones with similar effects which do not distinguish civil and criminal cases do exist, such as Rule 38 of the Federal Rules of Appellate Procedure, or 28 US Code § 1927. The effect is that courts have an arsenal of sanctions available to them.

II Legal Responses to Misconduct: Germany

A The General Layout of the German System

Various sources of law become relevant for counsel discipline. These are on the one hand the ordinary laws applying to any person which may gain special relevance since they cover also counsel's work. On the other hand, counsel in Germany are subject to a counsel-specific regime.

The Criminal Code is applicable to the work of all lawyers and contains offences covering some cases of misconduct.[42] As a separate system, professional rules are in place. German licensed lawyers (*Rechtsanwälte*) are mandatory members of one of the 28 Bars (*Rechtsanwaltskammern*) in Germany.[43] They qualify for membership by obtaining a law degree from a German law school followed by spending two years in mandatory practical training.[44] The *Bundesrechtsanwaltskammer* (BRAK, the German Federal Bar) acts as the umbrella organisation of all the Bars.[45] As members of a Bar, German lawyers are subject to the *Bundesrechtsanwaltsordnung* (BRAO, the Federal Lawyers' Act) and the *Berufsordnung für Rechtsanwälte* (BORA, the Rules of Professional Practice).[46] The disciplinary parts of the BRAO apply to foreign lawyers who may practise in Germany as European lawyers in accordance with the *Gesetz über die Tätigkeit europäischer Rechtsanwälte in Deutschland* (EuRAG, the Law Regulating the Activity of European Lawyers in Germany).[47] Law professors and other persons eligible to practise do not fall under this regime.[48] [49]

[42] See above at 53 (n 9) on translations of German legislation, including the Criminal Code and other Acts.

[43] Most of those regional Bars cover the judicial district of one of the 24 Higher Regional Courts, see Section 60 BRAO, plus three regional Bars for defunct judicial districts. In addition, the Federal Court of Justice requires special admission in civil matters. It therefore has its own Bar, Sections 162, 164 BRAO, for lawyers exclusively pleading these civil appeals. With the latter exception, membership follows from the location of the lawyer's office, Section 27 BRAO.

[44] For a comprehensive account, see I von Münch, *Legal Education and the Legal Profession in Germany* (Baden-Baden, Nomos, 2002).

[45] Section 175(1) BRAO.

[46] Further regulation is, inter alia, provided by the *Fachanwaltsordnung* (FAO, the Certified Experts' Act) and the *Rechtsanwaltsvergütungsgesetz* (RVG, the Lawyers' Fees Act). All documents are available from the Bundesrechtsanwaltkammer's homepage at www.brak.de/fuer-anwaelte/berufsrecht. The translations used here are those available from that homepage.

[47] See Section 6 EuRAG. See also below, II.D.ii at 97–100.

[48] Kleine-Cosack, *Bundesrechtsanwaltsordnung*, 6th edn (n 13) 113, mn 1.

[49] See Sections 138 and 139 StPO.

Uniform professional rules have existed at the federal level since 1878.[50] It had been the tradition since the *Reichsrechtsanwaltsordnung* of 1878 to rely on self-governed courts composed of honorary judges recruited from among the members of the Bar, instead of disciplinary powers administered by state courts.[51] In 1987, the *Bundesverfassungsgericht* (Federal Constitutional Court) struck down the traditional system of professional standards decreed by the Federal German Bar.[52] The Court held that they must be democratically enacted by Parliament within a legislated framework. The *Standesrecht* from before 1987 was thus demystified and there was a general trend towards 'a statutory codification of attorneys' professional rules'.[53]

The BRAO underwent substantial reform in 1994. Professional standards are now entrenched in the *Berufsordnung* (BORA, the Rules of Professional Practice) which are adopted and amended by the Federal Bar's elected Statutory Assembly (*Satzungsversammlung*). Amendments of the BORA must be communicated to the German Federal Ministry of Justice before they enter into force. The Ministry acts as the Supervisory Authority (*Aufsichtsbehörde*) to regulate these bye-laws. Pursuant to Section 191e BRAO, the Ministry is vested with the power to strike down the Rules, or parts thereof. The Bar is thus now bound by a legislative framework.[54] It still seems appropriate to speak of autonomous regulation since the Ministry does not have full discretion to strike down rules and substitute its own judgment (*Fachaufsicht*). Control of the actual content of the Rules is restricted to remedying breaches of existing law (*Rechtsaufsicht*).[55]

[50] T Krach, '130 Jahre "Grundgesetz der Anwaltschaft"' (2008) *Neue Juristische Online Zeitschrift* 2628, 2628; Wolf (n 13) Einleitung, mns 64–101; Koch (n 13) Einleitung, mns 1–26; Hartung (n 13) Einführung, mns 1–12.

[51] V Römermann and W Hartung, *Anwaltliches Berufsrecht* (Munich, Beck, 2002) 12; F Ostler, '100 Jahre Rechtsanwaltsordnung' (1979) *Neue Juristische Wochenschrift* 1959, 1960. For a historical account of the profession and professional rules of West and East Germany, see F Busse, *Deutsche Anwälte. Geschichte der deutschen Anwaltschaft 1945–2009, Entwicklungen in West und Ost* (Bonn, Deutscher Anwaltverlag, 2010). See further on the profession in Germany, E Blankenburg and U Schultz, 'German Advocates: A Highly Regulated Profession' in R Abel and P Lewis (eds), *Lawyers in Society* (Berkeley, University of California Press, 1995); D Rueschemeyer, *Lawyers and their Society, A Comparative Study of the Legal Profession in Germany and in the United States* (Cambridge, Mass, Harvard University Press, 1973).

[52] *Bundesverfassungsgericht*, 14 July 1987, 1 BvR 537/81 and 1 BvR 195/87, BVerfGE 76, 171-196 = NJW 1988, 191 (*Standesrichtlinien*); *Bundesverfassungsgericht*, 14 July 1987, 1 BvR 362/79, BVerfGE 76, 196-210 = NJW 1988, 194 (*Werbeverbot für Rechtsanwalt*); *Bundesverfassungsgericht*, 21 October 1987, 1 BvR 651/86 et al, BVerfGE 77, 125–29. See Edelkötter (n 13) 8–10; Römermann and Hartung (n 51) 6–9; M Kleine-Cosack, 'Verfassungswidriges Standesrecht – Notwendigkeit einer Ersetzung der Standesrichtlinien durch ein grundgesetzkonformes Berufsrecht' (1988) *Neue Juristische Wochenschrift* 164; R Zuck, 'Die notwendige Reform des anwaltlichen Berufs- und Standesrechts' (1988) *Neue Juristische Wochenschrift* 175; C Knauer and C Wolf, '20 Jahre "Bastille-Entscheidungen" des Bundesverfassungsgerichts – Von der Liberalisierung und Kommerzialisierung des Anwaltsberufs' (2007) *BRAK-Mitteilungen* 142. For a comparative account of the pre-1987 situation, see D Luban, 'The Sources of Legal Ethics: A German–American Comparison of Lawyers' Professional Duties' (1984) 48 *Rabels Zeitschrift für ausländisches und internationales Privatrecht* 245.

[53] Römermann and Hartung (n 51) V, 6.

[54] M Wirtz, *Die Regelungskompetenz der Satzungsversammlung* (Bonn, Deutscher Anwaltverlag, 2004) 298–99.

[55] Kleine-Cosack, *Bundesrechtsanwaltsordnung*, 6th edn (n 13) § 176, mns 2–4, § 191e, mn 1;

The procedure in cases of alleged misconduct is in principle that complaints are brought before the executive committee of the Regional Bar. The Council of the respective Bar holds the discretion to, inter alia, reprimand lawyers. However, substantial cases go before Lawyers' Disciplinary Courts (*Anwaltsgericht*). In the first instance, they are composed of three lawyers.[56] The Higher Lawyers' Courts (*Anwaltsgerichtshof*) considering appeals have a mixed composition: out of five judges, two are judges of the Higher Regional Court,[57] a state court of appeals and the presiding judge is a lawyer. These Higher Disciplinary Courts are formally part of the respective Higher Regional Court. Finally, appeals on legal grounds are considered by a *Senat für Anwaltssachen* (Senate for Matters concerning the Legal Profession), a division of the Federal Court of Justice.[58] Here, the bench is then composed of four judges of the Federal Court of Justice and three lawyers appointed by the Federal Ministry of Justice.

B Specific Measures against Counsel Misconduct

i *Professional Discipline*

As has been explained above, German lawyers in private practice are, as mandatory members of the Federal German Bar, subject to the Federal Lawyers' Act (BRAO) and the Rules of Professional Practice (BORA).[59] The BRAO lays down the most fundamental duties of lawyers and contains rules on the disciplinary measures and procedure. The BORA further spells out the professional obligations. It is therefore the BRAO and the BORA which essentially form the foundation for disciplining counsel in Germany.

The BRAO and the BORA provide attorneys with a federal, uniform set of professional rules. No specific statutory acts on criminal defence exist, and within the mentioned acts, no explicit rules governing criminal defence lawyers exist.[60] Practically speaking, the overall relevance of the disciplinary regime has often been held to be limited. Although the number of lawyers has been increasing during the past years, the number of actual cases remains small.[61]

Feuerich (n 13) § 176, mns 5–7, § 191e, mn 2; Hartung (n 13) § 176, mn 2, § 191e, mns 3–5; S Göcken in R Gaier, C Wolf and S Göcken (eds), *Anwaltliches Berufsrecht* (Cologne, Heymanns, 2010) § 176, mn 7; C Dahns in R Gaier, C Wolf and S Göcken (eds), *Anwaltliches Berufsrecht* (Cologne, Heymanns, 2010) 191e, mns 1–5.

[56] Sections 94–96 BRAO. These attorneys are nominated by the regional Bar but appointed by the respective Ministry of Justice.

[57] *Oberlandesgericht*, Section 104 BRAO.

[58] Sections 106, 107 BRAO.

[59] See above, II.A at 56.

[60] M Kleine-Cosack, 'Berufsrechtliche Risiken' in G Widmaier (ed), *Münchener Anwaltshandbuch Strafverteidigung* (Munich, Beck, 2006) 2079; Harting (n 37) 69, 385–88.

[61] M Kleine-Cosack, *Bundesrechtsanwaltsordnung*, 3rd edn (Munich, Beck, 1997) Vorbemerkung vor § 92, and Kleine-Cosack, *Bundesrechtsanwaltsordnung*, 6th edn (n 13) Vorbemerkung vor 92. See also for figures, T Dittmann in M Henssler and H Prütting (eds), *Bundesrechtsanwaltsordnung*, 1st edn (Munich, Beck, 1997) Vor § 92, mns 20, 21; T Dittmann in M Henssler and H Prütting (eds),

Although the BRAO and the BORA stipulate specific duties, they do not contain distinct offences. Instead, Section 113 BRAO provides that:

> (1) The Lawyers' Disciplinary Court shall impose sanctions on a Rechtsanwalt who is in negligent breach of the duties under this Act or set out in the professional code of conduct.
> (2) Conduct on the part of a Rechtsanwalt outside his/her field of professional duties which represents an unlawful act or an act likely to incur a fine shall be considered a breach of duty subject to sanctions by the Lawyers' Disciplinary Court if, in the circumstances of the individual case, it is particularly likely to undermine the respect and trust of persons seeking access to justice in a way that is significant for a Rechtsanwalt's professional practice.

This leaves the need to determine on a case-by-case basis whether a disciplinable duty has been breached.

The provision spells out a general fault requirement.[62] Furthermore, it can be seen from sub-section (2) that private misconduct only draws professional discipline for certain acts. Again, the translation of *rechtswidrige Tat oder eine mit Geldbuße bedrohte Handlung* as 'unlawful act or an act likely to incur a fine' is unfortunate. The first term denotes unlawful acts under criminal law,[63] the second term an act for which an administrative fine can be imposed.[64] What is therefore actually meant is that private misconduct has to come within the scope of a criminal or administrative offence in order to become a breach of professional discipline.

a Sanctionable Breaches of Professional Standards

The BRAO and its disciplinary procedure exist alongside criminal offences. The scope of this reaches further than the criminal regime, and it ostensibly aims at fully covering the professional conduct of counsel. In particular, it features a general clause in Section 43 of the BRAO, entitled 'General professional duties' which provides that

Bundesrechtsanwaltsordnung, 3rd edn (Munich, Beck, 2010) Vor § 92, mn 20, fn 24); and U Schultz, 'Legal Ethics in Germany' (1997) 4 *International Journal of the Legal Profession* 55, 76, for figures (under 1000 cases a year) and 79–82 for case summaries.

[62] M Kleine-Cosack, *Bundesrechtsanwaltsordnung*, 5th edn (Munich, Beck, 2008) § 113, mn 17; R Zuck in R Gaier, C Wolf and S Göcken (eds), *Anwaltliches Berufsrecht* (Cologne, Heymanns, 2010) § 113, mn 46. It is noted that the translation of *schuldhaft* as 'negligent' seems misleading. As intentional behaviour fulfils this fault requirement as well, 'culpable' would be correct.

[63] See Section 11(1) Criminal Code ('Definitions'): '5. 'unlawful act' exclusively means an act that fulfils all the elements of a criminal provision'.

[64] See Section 1 Administrative Offences Act ('Definitions') (author's translation):

> (1) An administrative offence is an unlawful and blameworthy act that fulfils all the elements of an administrative provision that allows the imposition of an admistrative fine.
> (2) An act for which an administrative fine may be imposed is an unlawful act that fulfils all the elements of a provision within the meaning of sub-section (1), even though it has not been committed in a state of blameworthiness.

> [a] Rechtsanwalt must practise his/her profession conscientiously. A Rechtsanwalt must show that he/she is worthy of the respect and the trust that his/her status as Rechtsanwalt demands, both when practising and when not practising his/her profession.

No resort to this general clause of Section 43 BRAO clause is needed, of course, if particular professional duties can be identified from statutory law. Section 43a BRAO lists the most fundamental duties. Among those explicitly listed are counsel's duty to ensure his or her independence, to protect the confidentiality of clients, objectivity, to prevent conflicts of interests, financial honesty and diligence and to pursue continuing education.[65] Further sections in the BRAO provide for limited advertising, stipulate a duty for lawyers to perform and render their services professionally once they have accepted a client, or otherwise to decline the representation promptly, provide for fee regulations, oblige counsel to document his or her services, to retain professional liability insurance and to cooperate with the Bar Council in regulatory matters. This body of rules is further elaborated in the Rules of Professional Practice (*Berufsordnung*), as provided for in Section 59b BRAO.

According to one view – including that of the majority of the disciplinary courts – even if professional duties are not to be found in the BRAO or the BORA but elsewhere in statute, discipline can still be based on them in conjunction with Section 43 BRAO. Moreover, disciplinary courts have held that sanctions can be based on this section alone as a catch-all provision if no specifically spelled-out statutory duty exists.[66] Following this lead, Kleine-Cosack argues that its purpose is to fill lacunae only, and that this is legitimate. It would be wrong to fall back on Section 43 if other statutes deliberately remain silent on a certain matter and thus decidedly refrain from entrenching a professional duty. He further points to the fact that such a general clause is used and accepted in the regulation of other free professions.

Critics of this, quintessentially the domininant view in scholarship, argue that the general clause should not be interpreted to generate distinct professional duties, let alone sanctionable ones.[67] This is held unconstitutional by the critics

[65] See for details, Harting (n 37) 110–83.

[66] Kleine-Cosack, *Bundesrechtsanwaltsordnung*, 6th edn (n 13) § 43, mns 9–15; Dittmann in Henssler and Prütting (eds), *Bundesrechtsanwaltsordnung*, 3rd edn (n 61) § 113, mn 11; Zuck (n 62) § 113, mn 26. The Federal Constitutional Court has upheld the general clause as constitutional, *Bundesverfassungsgericht*, 4 April 1984, 1 BvR 1287/83, BVerfGE 66, 337, paras 52–53. From the BGH's case law, see *Bundesgerichtshof*, 17 December 1990, AnwSt (R) 17/90, para 6; *Bundesgerichtshof*, 7 October 1991, AnwZ (B) 25/91, NJW 1992, 45, para 4, *Bundesgerichtshof*, 17 December 1990, AnwSt (R) 17/90, para 6; *Bundesgerichtshof*, 7 October 1991, AnwZ (B) 25/91, NJW 1992, 45, para 4.

[67] H Prütting, 'Bundesrechtsanwaltsordnung' in M Henssler and H Prütting (eds) *Bundesrechtsanwaltsordnung*, 3rd edn (Munich, Beck, 2010) § 43, mn 23; Feuerich (n 13) § 113, mn 10; B Grunewald and K Piepenstock, 'Anwaltliche Berufspflichten – Verstöße gegen § 43 BRAO und anwaltsgerichtliche Maßnahmen' (2000) *Monatschrift für Deutsches Recht* 869; R Zuck, 'Standesrecht und Verfassungsrecht' in OF von Gamm, P Raisch and K Tiedemann (eds), *Festschrift für Gerd Pfeiffer* (Cologne, Heymanns, 1988) 1014–115; JH Husmann, *Freie Advokatur im Zwangsverband? Eine Untersuchung über die Erziehungsbedürftigkeit des Rechtsanwalts* (Würzburg, Libertas, 1970) 38–41; Harting (n 37) 107–10, with further references.

because it allegedly violates the principles of legality in two respects. From the perspective of German constitutional law, it is firstly emphasised that state acts impinging on citizens' rights are understood to require a statutorily entrenched legal basis (*Vorbehalt des Gesetzes*). Formerly, the Federal Bar's ethical guidelines (*Standesrichtlinien*) refined the general clause. The Federal Constitutional Court struck them down for the very reason that it did not constitute such democratically enacted statutory law.[68] It was only held acceptable to rely on these guidelines for a transitory period. Not requiring explicit provisions at all, of whichever character, it is argued, would now be at odds with this jurisprudence and even fall back behind the previous state. The second branch of the criticism is aimed at the fundamental concern of vagueness. It is conceded that lawyers are professionals who should always stay abreast of the current law, including their own professional rules. This should heighten their sensitivity towards objectionable conduct. On the other hand, a general clause simply does not afford fair notice in light of the sanctions it may entail.

However, it needs to be stressed that professional best practice may sometimes be best described along general guidelines.[69] This justifies relaxing the principle of legality to some degree. The first point, ie, the constitutional characterisation of the rules, may be a problem due to the rather specific constitutional setting in Germany. No compelling implications for other legal orders should be drawn from this fact alone.[70] Apart from this, certainty and vagueness are separate problems. If grave sanctions of a punitive nature attach to misconduct, the flexibility of a general clause needs to be sacrificed in favour of clear guidance for potential defendants. Several things assist in resolving this. Official warnings and reprimands based on Section 43 alone could be allowed but not fines or bans.[71] Moreover, it should be mandatory to reflect as mitigating in sentencing if no specifically identifiable duty existed in statute.

Since reprimands are clearly a means of castigating counsel and consequences attach to them,[72] they should fall within those measures that cannot be based on unwritten duties. As far as warnings are concerned, they are the lightest available measure.[73] It should be permissible to base them on the general clause of Section 43 BRAO, in spite of the majority scholarly view. Treating warnings as sanctions because they are listed as measures in Section 114(1) BRAO, and for this mere

[68] See above, II.A (n 52).

[69] See also below, III.B.i.b on the US, at 119–21, and ch 3, II.A.iv.b on the ICC, at 195–201.

[70] The example of the ICTY, however, has shown that the prohibited conduct may be expressly laid down in a provision whereas it is the foundation that may still be questionable. Rule 77 RPE illustrated that it is rather the prescription of these provisions in the first place which may raise concerns (ch 1, I.B.i at 13).

[71] I Sue, *Rechtsstaatliche Probleme des anwaltlichen Standesrechts* (University of Göttingen, unpublished doctoral thesis, 1986) 113–33. This is strengthened by a cost-benefit analysis; see DB Wilkins, 'Who Should Regulate Lawyers?' (1992) 105 *Harvard Law Review* 801, 821.

[72] Kleine-Cosack, *Bundesrechtsanwaltsordnung*, 6th edn (n 13) § 114, mn 10; Dittmann in Henssler and Prütting (eds), *Bundesrechtsanwaltsordnung*, 3rd edn (n 61) § 114, mn 8.

[73] See Zuck (n 62) § 114, mn 7 (pointing out that warnings as a formal measure have been struck from the disciplinary codes for civil servants).

reason concluding to the same impermissibility as for reprimands, would be circular. Furthermore, the listing under Section 114(1) BRAO does not compel treating all these measures alike, for example, equating all of them to criminal sanctions. Professional discipline as a whole may be a quasi-criminal regime. It emulates the criminal law but is still clearly distinguishable from it. In particular, it has a wider scope than the criminal law. Consequently, it makes sense to reflect the various facets of this in sanctioning as well.

The crucial question should be what is the purpose and impact of a warning. A warning signals that there has been or that there will be something to disapprove of. It cautions against doing something or repeating it but does not go farther than stating this. It should be possible to do this and make an official finding on the given case. Of course, this is not neutral, and it will be entered onto counsel's record. On the other hand, it does not have further consequences. It thus very closely resembles executive-style measures such as statements by the Bar Council which may subsequently be ruled on by a court pursuant to Sections 74a or 112a BRAO. Given this, no compelling reasons argue that these two should be treated differently. As the lightest official measure with no further consequence, warnings under Section 114 BRAO should be allowed, even if they are based on the general clause of Section 43 BRAO as last resort.

In conclusion, the disciplinary regime is comprehensive in substance.[74] The rules of professional conduct are capable of capturing all instances of misconduct due to the general clause of Section 43 BRAO.

b The Administration of Sanctions

The applicable sanctions are not discriminated according to the precise kind of misconduct. The measures available to local Bar Councils and the sanctions by the disciplinary courts in responding to misconduct are laid down in Section 73, Section 74 and Section 114 respectively while others are unwritten powers. Counsel cannot be sanctioned, though, if he or she withdraws from the Bar (Section 113(3)). Should counsel ever be readmitted, proceedings can be reinstated.[75]

It is the regional Bar Council under the BRAO which is to 'advise and instruct the members of the Bar in matters of professional ethics'.[76] The Council may also issue a formal opinion on a specific case, although the BRAO does not expressly provide for this.[77] Also into the same category would fall advice and instructions which are not strictly neutral but of an admonitory nature. Finally, the Council

[74] See for details, Harting (n 37).

[75] Kleine-Cosack, *Bundesrechtsanwaltsordnung*, 6th edn (n 13) § 113, mn 2; Dittmann in Henssler and Prütting (eds), *Bundesrechtsanwaltsordnung*, 3rd edn (n 61) § 113, mn 16.

[76] Section 73 (2) BRAO: 'Dem Kammervorstand obliegt insbesondere, 1. die Mitglieder der Kammer in Fragen der Berufspflichten zu beraten und zu belehren'. See on the Bar Council's powers, Harting (n 37) 285–88; R Lauda in R Gaier, C Wolf and S Göcken (eds), *Anwaltliches Berufsrecht* (Cologne, Heymanns, 2010) § 74, mns 1, 3–10.

[77] *Bescheid*, see Kleine-Cosack (n 60) 2093.

may issue official reprimands[78] under the conditions set out in Section 74 BRAO. Simple advice (*Rat*) and neutral instruction (*Belehrung*) on a certain issue cannot be challenged. It has been emphasised that it should be the main purpose of this supervisory function of the Council to inform counsel in advance and thus prevent misconduct at the very outset. Its goal should not be a binding order to counsel but neutral advice, which counsel uses to guide his or her prospective conduct, and which he or she may invoke to exonerate him or herself later.[79] Decisions other than informal neutral advice can be challenged before the disciplinary courts (Section 112a BRAO).[80] Similarly, counsel can lodge a complaint against an official reprimand with the Council (Section 74(5) BRAO). If this is dismissed, counsel can bring the case before the Disciplinary Court pursuant to Section 74a BRAO.

Significant breaches of professional duties are ruled on by the Disciplinary Courts.[81] The measures available to these courts cover a wide range of sanctions, set out in Section 114 BRAO.[82] It essentially comprises warnings, reprimands, fines, prohibiting an attorney from practising in a certain field of law for a fixed term and exclusion from the Bar. The maximum monetary fine is €25,000.[83] A provisional ban can be ordered under Section 161a, '[i]f there are pressing grounds to believe that a sanction will be imposed on a Rechtsanwalt under Section 114 para 1 no 4'. Disbarred counsel can apply to be reinstated.[84]

Proceedings before the Disciplinary Courts (*Anwaltsgericht*) take precedence over the measures taken by the Bar Council, in particular the right to reprimand counsel. Cases before the Disciplinary Courts are prosecuted by the Public

[78] *Rüge*. In particular if 'the *Rechtsanwalt* bears only little blame and an application for the institution of disciplinary proceedings does not seem necessary'. Section 74(1). See ibid, 2093–94.

[79] See F Hülk, *Chancen und Grenzen einer unmittelbaren Sanktionierung anwaltlichen Fehlverhaltens in den USA und Deutschland* (Osnabrück, Rasch, 2001) 74.

[80] '(1) Administrative acts performed under this Act or under a statutory order passed under this Act may be challenged by applying for a ruling from a Laywers' Disciplinary Court, even if this is not expressly provided for'.

[81] See Kleine-Cosack (n 60) 2094–97; Harting (n 37) 289–301.

[82] Section 114 (Sanctions that may be imposed by a Lawyers' Disciplinary Court):

(1) Sanctions that may be imposed by a Lawyers' Disciplinary Court are
1. a warning,
2. a caution,
3. a fine of up to twenty-five thousand euros,
4. a ban on acting as representative and counsel in certain fields of law for a period of between one and five years,
5. exclusion from the legal profession.

(2) A caution and a fine may be imposed in conjunction.

See G Gribbohm, 'Die ehrengerichtlichen Berufs- und Vertretungsverbote in der Rechtsprechung des Senats für Anwaltssachen des Bundesgerichtshofs' in OF von Gamm, P Raisch and K Tiedemann (eds), Festschrift für Gerd Pfeiffer (Cologne, Heymanns, 1988) 911–27.

[83] A fine of €25,000 was actually imposed on a German lawyer who had agreed on a contingent fee. On appeal, this was reduced to €5,000. See *Bundesverfassungsgericht*, 12 December 2006, 1 BvR 2576/04, BVerfGE 117, 163–202 (*Erfolgshonorar*), paras 20, 21.

[84] See *Anwaltsgerichtshof Frankfurt*, 5 November 2007, 2 AGH 9/07, BRAK-Mitt 2008, 140, though, for the necessary period of rehabilitation.

Prosecutor (Section 120). The Disciplinary Court can enter a conviction, an acquittal, or may close the proceedings (Section 139(2) BRAO). Judgments and other decisions by the Disciplinary Court can be appealed to the Higher Lawyers' Court (*Anwaltsgerichtshof*). An appeal on legal grounds against judgments of this court can be filed with the Federal Court of Justice if it involves the prohibition to act as counsel in a certain field of law or the exclusion from the Bar, or if the Higher Lawyers' Court has granted leave to appeal.

While the procedure for disciplinary proceedings as well as their relationship to other measures remains to be discussed in detail, it seems important at this point to emphasise that the disciplinary regime is, by and large, governed by a judicial procedure. The BRAO contains a number of procedural rules in Sections 117–161a. In its first sentence, Section 116 points to those rules, and declares, failing that, the Court Constitution Act and the Code of Criminal Procedure are applicable mutatis mutandis.[85]

Most authors stress that it is just a limited number of cases which are handled under the disciplinary regime. Sometimes, the overall utility and effectiveness of this disciplinary regime has been questioned.[86] While the question whether disciplinary sanctions are an effective and efficient mean of countering misconduct is valid as such, it should not be looked at in isolation; it needs to be considered in relation to other forms of controls and sanctioning mechanisms.[87] It may very well be that the main role of disciplinary controls is to supplement other enforcement mechanisms. Furthermore, a limited number of cases may be an indicator of a very high level of ethics. It may thus suffice to have enforceable rules in place without them being necessarily enforced in a great number of cases. It seems therefore fair to stress the qualitative relevance of a disciplinary regime.[88] Even though actual proceedings may not figure prominently in the public perception of the legal community, it is underpinned by a binding code of conduct which gives the community, most importantly, normative guidance. It may not be possible to achieve this as conclusively and as efficiently by other means.

ii Criminal Law

During the course of their work, defence lawyers in Germany potentially face a number of criminal sanctions.[89] It is, of course, a criminal offence for counsel to associate with the crime of his or her client, ie, by aiding and abetting.

[85] See below, II.C.i at 87 (n 189).

[86] See Bohlander (n 2) 67–70.

[87] See above, Introduction, III at 4–5.

[88] T Wagner, *Die Konkurrenz zwischen dem Strafverfahren und dem anwaltsgerichtlichen Verfahren in gleicher Sache* (Berlin, Duncker & Humblot, 2005) 15.

[89] See E Müller, 'Strafrechtliche Risiken' in G Widmaier (ed), *Münchener Anwaltshandbuch Strafverteidigung* (Munich, Beck, 2006) 2041–77 (§ 55); Müller and Gussmann (n 12) 5–106; W Beulke and F Ruhmannseder, *Die Strafbarkeit des Verteidigers*, 2nd edn (Heidelberg, CF Müller, 2010); W Krekeler, 'Strafrechtliche Risiken des anwaltlichen Berufs' in B Binnewies and R Spatscheck (eds), *Festschrift für Michael Streck* (Cologne, Otto Schmidt, 2011).

Much of the misconduct that has occurred in the context of the ad hoc Tribunals, and which was prosecuted as contempt, would not be covered by criminal laws in Germany. Only a few offences exist concerning very select professional duties.[90] In comparison, general offences such as fraud and money laundering or obstruction of punishment are generally applicable.[91] As far as their relevance for counsel is concerned, they critically intertwine with counsel conduct. 'Obstruction of punishment' (Section 258 Criminal Code), for example, is not a self-explanatory concept.

a Offences in Connection with the Criminal Trial as such

It is noted that some of these offences are held to have the administration of justice as the protected legal interest. This is usually understood to mean the administration of justice by German authorities.[92] The administration of justice by international courts, such as the ICC, is thus not per se protected. Statutory amendments are needed in this regard to discharge Germany's duties as a state party under the Rome Statute. They have only been enacted with regard to bribing judges and other officials as well as the perjury offences under Sections 153–61.[93]

A threat intrinsically linked to any kind of criminal defence activity under German law is Section 258 of the StGB (*Strafvereitelung*, Assistance in avoiding prosecution or punishment).[94] It provides for imprisonment for up to five years' imprisonment or a fine.[95] Any defence activity has by definition the potential to

[90] See Section 203 Criminal Code, addressing confidentiality obligations, and Section 356 Criminal Code on conflict of interests below, b at 71.

[91] See below, c at 71–72.

[92] P Cramer in W Joecks and K Miebach (eds), *Münchener Kommentar zum StGB*, vol 3 [§§ 185–262] (Munich, Beck, 2003) § 258, mn 4.

[93] See Section 2 of the *Gesetz über das Ruhen der Verfolgungsverjährung und die Gleichstellung der Richter und Bediensteten des Internationalen Strafgerichtshofs* (BGBl. I 2002, 2144, 2162), declaring judges and other officials of the ICC equivalent to German judges and officials for the purposes of Sections 331–36 and 338 Criminal Code. No such provision has been enacted for Section 258. For perjury offences, see Art 1 of the *Gesetz zur Umsetzung des Rahmenbeschlusses des Rates der Europäischen Union zur Bekämpfung der sexuellen Ausbeutung von Kindern und der Kinderpornographie* (published in BGBl. I 2008, 2149); A Sinn, 'Die Einbeziehung der internationalen Rechtspflege in den Anwendungsbereich der Aussagedelikte' (2008) *Neue Juristische Wochenschrift* 3526.

[94] See Harting (n 37) 346–52.

[95] Section 258 (Assistance in avoiding prosecution or punishment):

(1) Whosoever intentionally or knowingly obstructs in whole or in part the punishment of another in accordance with the criminal law because of an unlawful act or his being subjected to a measure (section 11 (1) No 8) shall be liable to imprisonment of not more than five years or a fine.
(2) Whosoever intentionally or knowingly obstructs in whole or in part the enforcement of a sentence or measure imposed on another shall incur the same penalty.
(3) The penalty must not be more severe than that for the act.
(4) An attempt shall be punishable.
(5) Whosoever by the offence simultaneously intends to avoid, in whole or in part, his own punishment or being subjected to a measure or that a sentence or measure imposed on him be enforced shall not be liable under this provision.
(6) Whosoever commits the offence for the benefit of a relative shall be exempt from liability.

slow down and thus obstruct the process. It has therefore been held by courts and scholarship alike as obvious that criminal defence as such does not fulfil the elements of the offence. The question whether punishment has been obstructed or not rather depends on the permissibility of counsel's actions in terms of procedure.[96] A mere breach of ethical duties will not constitute the criminal offence of *Strafvereitelung*.[97] It is argued in that regard that conduct which is permissible in respect to the generally governing criminal procedure should not draw sanctions via other avenues, such as professional discipline.[98]

As far as the substantive elements are concerned, it needs to be noted that the offence does not generally cover any behaviour which is obstructive to justice but, more precisely, the obstruction of punishment (or enforcement thereof). A causal requirement exists to the effect that only acts are covered which are capable of achieving this.[99] However, significantly delaying investigations or proceedings has been held to suffice for obstruction.[100] The mental element requires *Absicht* (purpose) or *Wissentlichkeit* (knowledge).[101] Some scholars have interpreted this as requiring an even higher form of special intent.[102] All in all, these are two reasons leading to a high threshold for criminal liability for the bulk of professional misconduct, first because of the high mental requirement, and secondly, because obstruction is a consequence crime, not a mere conduct crime.

The delineation of what is still permissible under the laws of criminal procedure is quite difficult. Since no general principle to distinguish procedurally permissible and impermissible defence has been developed, the assessment is usually made on a case-by-case basis.[103] It also becomes crucially relevant for – on the one hand – defining criminal conduct, but further for distinguishing good practice

[96] *Bundesgerichtshof*, 9 May 2000, 1 StR 106/00, BGHSt 46, 53–61, 54; Cramer (n 92) § 258, mn 10; W Stree and B Hecker in A Schönke and H Schröder (eds), *Strafgesetzbuch, Kommentar*, 28th edn (Munich, Beck, 2010) § 258, mns 19–20; T Fischer, *Strafgesetzbuch und Nebengesetze*, 58th edn (Munich, Beck, 2011) § 258, mns 67–20; Müller (n 89) 2045, 2052–53; T Kappelmann, *Die Strafbarkeit des Strafverteidigers. Zur Abgrenzung von strafbewehrten und straffreien Prozesshandlungen durch zweckorientierte Auslegung prozessualer Befugnisse* (Baden-Baden, Nomos, 2006) 18–29, 35–67, 121–23; W Kargl, 'Das Unrecht der Strafvereitelung – insbesondere zu den strafrechtlichen Grenzen der Strafverteidigung' in R Michalke et al (eds), *Festschrift für Rainer Hamm* (Berlin, De Gruyter, 2008) 235–54; W Schautz, *Strafrechtliche Grenzen des Verteidigerhandelns, insbesondere im Hinblick auf die Strafvereitelung, § 258 StGB* (University of Würzburg, unpublished doctoral thesis, 1988)131; Wassmann (n 16) 238–39; see Harting (n 37) 347, fn 1615 for further references. G Waldhorn, *Das Verhältnis von Strafverteidigung und Begünstigung* (University of Würzburg, unpublished doctoral thesis, 1967), 85, assesses counsel's conduct as justified, albeit constituting the element of obstruction.

[97] *Oberlandesgericht Nürnberg*, 12 March 2012, 1 St OLG Ss 274/11; Cramer (n 92) § 258, mn 30; Fischer (n 96) § 258, mn 22.

[98] M Kleine-Cosack, *Bundesrechtsanwaltsordnung*, 4th edn (Munich, Beck, 2003) § 43, mn 6; see also V Mehle, 'Einschränkung der Strafverteidigung durch das Berufsrecht?' in E-W Hanack et al (eds), *Festschrift für Peter Rieß* (Berlin, de Gruyter, 2002) 317–29.

[99] Cramer (n 92) § 258, mns 23–28; M Jahn, 'Anmerkung zu BGH NJW 2006, 2421' (2006) *Juristenzeitung* 1134, 1136.

[100] *Bundesgerichtshof*, 19 May 1999, 2 StR 86/99, BGHSt 45, 97–103, 100; Stree and Hecker (n 96) § 258, mn 14; Fischer (n 96) § 258, mn 8.

[101] See Cramer (n 92) § 258, mns 36–40; Müller (n 89) 2055.

[102] Kappelmann (n 96) 67.

[103] Harting (n 37) 347–52.

from unprofessional and thus disciplinable conduct on the other. Much scholarly attention has been devoted to this topic, in particular in criminal doctrine. Among the debated issues, but certainly not limited to this, are whether counsel can try freely to influence participants, whether counsel has a right to his or her own investigations, whether documents may be freely communicated to the client, the scope of confidentiality, whether counsel may present evidence of points of law falsely, or whether counsel may pay a fine for the client.

Section 257 (*Begünstigung*, Securing Benefits) also attaches to the original crime.[104] Similar to *Strafvereitelung*, counsel will not commit the offence if acting within the confines of permissible defence[105]. It requires special intent to benefit the perpetrator of the principal crime. It thus has a quite narrow scope and also features a high subjective threshold.

The central point in resolving these issues is foremost the understanding of the role of counsel. It follows that the substantive law can thus not be determined finitely. This being said, it appears that most of the substantive criminal law on counsel misconduct can be identified relatively easily. 'Obstruction of punishment' (Section 258 Criminal Code), and along with it 'securing benefits of a crime' (Section 257 Criminal Code) are the exceptions. Criminal conduct will often qualify as unprofessional conduct. If offences on the administration of justice are concerned, this will assumedly automatically be the case. Conversely, unprofessional conduct may amount to obstruction, but may not necessarily do so. It is argued that the mere breach of professional ethics does not establish criminal liability for obstruction of punishment.[106]

Beyond that, more guidance can be drawn from the recent case of Sylvia Stolz, defence lawyer for Holocaust denier Ernst Zündel.[107] This case has emerged as one of the newer leading cases on obstructionist tactics by the defence.

With regard to documents and other evidence, offences under chapter 23 of the Criminal Code (*Urkundenfälschung*, Falsification of Documents) are of relevance, in particular Section 267 and Section 274.[108] These offences would presumably cover many instances of tampering with physical evidence. Again, they feature a particular mental requirement, ie, the specific purpose of causing legal prejudice.

If an attorney coerces another person into an act under no colour of right, this may attract liability under Section 240 (*Nötigung*, Coercion). This may, for example, become relevant in respect of witnesses or victims. Again, the conceivable relevance should be limited, as it must be committed by force or threat, and procedurally permissible conduct would not fall under this section.

Lastly, filings and pleadings may be deemed offensive in a way which constitutes offences under Sections 185–87 (*Beleidigung*, *Üble Nachrede*, *Verleumdung*,

[104] Section 257 (Assistance after the fact): '(1) Whosoever renders assistance to another who has committed an unlawful act, with the intent of securing for him the benefits of that act, shall be liable to imprisonment of not more than five years or a fine'.

[105] Waldhorn (n 96) 85.

[106] See above n 97.

[107] See on this case later in this ch below, E at 102–05.

[108] See generally, Harting (n 37) 352–55.

Insult, Defamation, and Intentional Defamation).[109] Whereas it may be desirable to have rules in place to prevent such conduct, it again seems clear that this only captures one isolated aspect of unprofessional behaviour.

Summing up, it seems safe to stress that the abovementioned offences cover a wide range of conceivable misconduct. However, no general criminal offence exists in German law to curb unprofessional conduct which puts the administration of criminal proceedings in danger.

b Offences on Specific Professional Duties

Moreover, the German Criminal Code contains offences which aim at specific professional duties. In addition to vesting the lawyer with a privilege in the lawyer–client relationship, it may even be criminal for a lawyer to disclose facts which have come to his or her knowledge within this context (Section 203, *Verletzung von Privatgeheimnissen*, Violation of Private Secrets), or to abuse such inside knowledge for financial gains (Section 204, *Verwertung fremder Geheimnisse*, Exploitation of the Secrets of Another).[110] Another offence under Section 356 (*Parteiverrat*, Violating the attorney–client relationship) provides for a sentence of up to five years' imprisonment for lawyers who serve clients with adverse interests.[111] As becomes apparent from this, some offences exist which correspond with genuine professional duties, such as preventing conflicts of interest and the confidentiality of the lawyer–client relationship. On the other hand, it seems obvious that these are just two out of many professional duties. German criminal law does not therefore systematically cover professional duties of lawyers.

c Offence Pertaining to Financial Irregularities

The business of lawyers regularly involves the handling of money or other responsibilities of a fiscal nature. This is reflected in the canon of professional duties and in the criminal law. The German Criminal Code contains, in Section 352, the offence of *Gebührenüberhebung* (Demanding Excessive Fees), a fraud-related crime. Excessive billing by a German lawyer based on a valid fee agreement, however, is not covered by this section.[112] It may in that case, as in many other scenarios, constitute plain fraud (Section 263, *Betrug*, Fraud).[113]

Given that oftentimes a fiduciary relationship exists between the lawyer and the client or any other principal, the rather wide reach of Section 266 (*Untreue*,

[109] See generally ibid, 355–56. See also R Kölbel, 'Strafrechtliche Haftung für prozessbedingte sekundäre Viktimisierung' (2007) 119 *Zeitschrift für die gesamte Strafrechtswissenschaft* 334, 343.

[110] See Harting (n 37) 360–61.

[111] See C Deckenbrock, *Strafrechtlicher Parteiverrat und berufsrechtliches Verbot der Vertretung widerstreitender Interessen* (Bonn, Deutscher Anwaltverlag, 2009) 31–146, 225–38; Harting (n 37) 368–70.

[112] *Bundesgerichtshof*, 6 September 2006, 5 StR 64/06, Strafverteidiger 2007, 462.

[113] See Harting (n 37) 361–62.

Embezzlement) should cover many other conceivable scenarios. Furthermore, the German Criminal Code contains a provision on money laundering (Section 261, *Geldwäsche*).[114] This section applies to counsel handling proceeds of crime. This may include receiving fees for legal services, and lesser forms of mens rea on the lawyer's part and even cases of negligence, may suffice.[115]

In conclusion, most misconduct by counsel involving financial irregularities will be criminal under the Criminal Code. This is the consequence, though, of general offences rather than ones aimed specifically at counsel.

d Legal Consequences of Criminal Offences

As far as the practical implications are concerned, it is not only the existence and scope of the criminal offences that are of relevance for practising counsel, but rather the legal consequences for counsel. All the abovementioned criminal offences carry sentences of imprisonment and fines. Most of the offences listed above provide for a maximum sentence of five years or a fine. Of the offences directly involving professional duties, Section 203 (*Verletzung von Privatgeheimnissen*, Violation of Private Secrets) and Section 352 (*Gebührenüberhebung*, Demanding Excessive Fees) provide for a considerably lesser sentence of up to one year, while Section 356 (*Parteiverrat*, Violating the Attorney–Client Relationship) also carries the maximum of five years' imprisonment.

In addition, other legal consequences may attach to allegations of criminal conduct within a professional setting. Section 70 of the German Criminal Code[116]

[114] See ibid, 356.

[115] *Bundesgerichtshof*, 12 February 2001, AnwSt (R) 15/00, and subsequently *Bundesverfassungsgericht*, 30 March 2004, 2 BvR 1520/01, 2 BvR 1521/01, BVerfGE 110, 226. See generally K Winkler, *Die Strafbarkeit des Strafverteidigers jenseits der Strafvereitelung – zugleich ein Beitrag zur Auslegung des § 261 StGB* (Hamburg, Kovač, 2005); A Bussenius, *Geldwäsche und Strafverteidigerhonorar* (Baden-Baden, Nomos, 2004).

[116] Section 70 (Order for professional disqualification):

(1) If a person has been convicted of an unlawful act he committed in abuse of his profession or trade or in gross violation of the attendant duties, or has not been convicted merely because he was proven to have acted in a state of insanity or his having so acted could not be excluded the court may make an order disqualifying him from engaging in that profession, branch of profession, trade or branch of trade, for a period from one year to five years, if a comprehensive evaluation of the offender and the offence shows that by further engagement in the profession, branch of profession, trade or branch of trade there is a danger that he will commit serious unlawful acts of the kind indicated above. The disqualification order may be made in permanence if there is reason to believe that the statutory maximum period will not suffice to avert the danger posed by the offender.

(2) If the offender had been provisionally disqualified from engaging in a profession, branch of profession, trade or branch of trade (section 132a of the Code of Criminal Procedure), the minimum term of disqualification shall be reduced by the time during which the provisional disqualification was in effect. In no case may it be less than three months.

(3) For the duration of the disqualification the offender must neither engage in the profession, branch of profession, trade or branch of trade on behalf of another nor have a person who is subject to his instructions engage in it on his behalf.

(4) The disqualification shall commence when the judgment becomes final. Any period of a provisional disqualification imposed because of the act shall be credited to the disqualification

makes it possible for courts, as part of the judgment, to ban an accused lawyer from practising for a period of between one and five years, or even for life.[117] A conviction carrying a sentence of a year or more leads to losing the ability to hold public office (Section 45(1) Criminal Code). Since membership of the Bar is considered a public office by the law, this effectively means automatic disbarment.[118]

A provisional ban can be issued pursuant to Section 132a Code of Criminal Procedure if there are 'cogent reasons for assuming' that such a disposition will be made in a judgment. Finally, Section 145c Criminal Code makes the contravention of such court ordered bans criminal and provides for up to one year's imprisonment or a fine.

All of this shows that the German criminal law covers a wide range of conceivable misconduct, although it does not feature a general criminal offence aimed at misconduct of counsel. German law also offers flexible sanctioning tools. Section 258 of the Criminal Code comes closest to a catch-all provision, but its scope is limited in several ways. In that respect, the German approach is more similar to that of the ICC Statute than that of Rule 77 of the Rules of Procedure and Evidence (RPE) of the ad hoc Tribunals. Whereas Rule 77 obviously also lists specific offences, its listing is not exhaustive and contains the explicit reference to the inherent powers, from which the powers of the Tribunals to punish misconduct are derived.

iii Other Measures as Institutional Controls

a Direct Measures by Courts

All of the measures which have been discussed above are indirect measures. That is to say they are not administered by courts as part of proceedings in which counsel is representing a client. Moreover, these measures are typically applied *ex post.* They may be suited to sanctioning misconduct from the past. However, this leaves unanswered the question of how to react to misconduct before it occurs or while it is occurring. It was mentioned that the Bar Councils can issue advisory opinions and reprimands. With regard to the notification and cooperation duties under Section 56 BRAO, it may further impose a fee on counsel for violating those duties (Section 57 BRAO). This only concerns a minor issue, though. The more pressing question is certainly the powers of courts.

Sections 176–83 of the *Gerichtsverfassungsgesetz* (the Courts Constitution Act)[119] vest judges with powers to safeguard the orderly conduct of proceedings

period to the extent it has run following the date on which the judgment in those proceedings in which the factual findings underlying the measure could last have been examined was pronounced. Any period during which the offender was kept in detention by order of a public authority shall not be so credited.

[117] For details, see Müller and Gussmann (n 12) 113–33.

[118] See Section 14(2), no 2 BRAO, reprinted below at 82.

[119] See above at 53 (n 9) on translations of German legislation.

(*Sitzungspolizei*). It could be asserted that they bear some resemblance, or at least aim at something similar to Article 71 ICC Statute.[120] However, these sections of the Courts Constitution Act do not apply to counsel.[121] This is undisputed, although some scholars have argued to extend it statutorily to cover counsel as well.[122] In any event, such measures would be reviewable under German law, all the more since they would have to be done, and have been done, *contra legem*.[123]

The existence of the disciplinary regime or of criminal offences does not rule out the need or the possibility for such provisions. Criminal and disciplinary sanctions may not be applicable, or they may not fulfil the same purpose.[124] It has also been argued that such direct sanctions are probably not necessarily incompatible with the role and position of counsel.[125] In conclusion, direct sanctioning cannot be pursued through Sections 176–83 Courts Constitution Act in practice, and the legal community is reluctant in effect to amend these sections to allow this. However, judges may very well express their dismay at defence counsel and, for example, adjourn the court, give advice or admonish counsel.[126]

Other instances of direct sanctioning can be found in various statutes. They seem to constitute isolated examples rather than a systematic approach to discourage lawyers from wasting court time.[127] For example, pursuant to Section 102 of the German Code of Civil Procedure from 1898 to 1964, courts could impose litigation expenses on counsel which had been caused by gross negligence. The Federal Constitutional Court, with its immense case load, can fine persons who lodge frivolous constitutional complaints or injunctions with fines of up to €2,600, according to Section 34 of the *Bundesverfassungsgerichtsgesetz* (Act on the Federal Constitutional Court). Section 38 of the *Gerichtskostengesetz* (Court Fees Act) which authorises courts to impose a fee on parties who cause a re-scheduling of court sessions or who withhold or fail to tender evidence in a due manner and thus delay the termination of the case.[128] Section 145(4) of the Code of Criminal Procedure, too, provides for expenses to be borne by defence counsel if counsel is

[120] On Art 71 ICC Statute, see ch 3, II.C.ii at 256–63.

[121] Jahn (n 17) 391; K Gröner, *Strafverteidiger und Sitzungspolizei* (Berlin, Duncker & Humblot, 1998) 93–94; *Oberlandesgericht Hamm*, 9 May 2000, 2 Ws 122/03, Strafverteidiger 2004, 69, with a case note by M Jahn, 'Keine Anwendung der sitzungspolizeilichen Vorschriften auf Strafverteidiger' (2004) *Juristenzeitung* 207. See also W Beulke, 'Kleider machen Strafverteidiger!?, – oder: sitzungspolizeiliche Maßnahmen und die Mär vom "T-Shirt-Verteidiger"' in R Michalke et al (eds), *Festschrift für Rainer Hamm* (Berlin, De Gruyter, 2008) 21–40.

[122] eg, Gröner (n 121) 195–207. A majority of German defence counsel as well as prosecutors spoke out against this in a study by Bohlander (n 2) 63–65. The interviewees were most critical of the fact that judges involved in the same trial would exercise such powers. Some expressed concerns that judges might abuse such a tool to chastise counsel they simply dislike or deem troublesome.

[123] See Gröner (n 121) 140–88.

[124] See, eg, *Bundesverfassungsgericht*, 10 July 1996, 1 BvR 873/94, NStZ 1997, 35. with a case note by E Foth, 'Zur ehrengerichtlichen Ahndung des Ungehorsams eines Rechtsanwalts gegenüber einer die Ordnung in der Sitzung betreffenden Anordnung des Vorsitzenden' (1997) *Neue Zeitschrift für Strafrecht* 36.

[125] Gröner (n 121) 94, 204.

[126] ibid, 112.

[127] Hülk (n 79) 71.

[128] ibid, 89.

absent or refuses to participate and court sessions need to be adjourned as a result.

Taken altogether, however, it becomes clear that not all of these examples are relevant to German criminal proceedings. Moreover, they are far from a systematic sanctioning regime. It may be taken as an indication that fines and the responsibility for expenses can be used as sanctions. Generally, courts have not systematically denied fees to counsel for delaying or otherwise abusing the trial.[129]

A more general approach has been attempted under the doctrine of *Rechtsmissbrauch im Strafverfahren*, or literally 'abuse of process rights'. It has been held abusive if the defence is mounted in a way which makes it, on the one hand, formally permissible and falling within the confines of the procedural rules,[130] but at the same time the overall conduct intimates that the accused or counsel does not subscribe to the principal objectives of the criminal trial. There are few cases however where the doctrine of *Rechtsmissbrauch* has actually been applied. The consequences are usually the dismissal of the motion at stake, the restriction of evidence, or other curtailments of defence rights.

In what has become the first leading case on the subject,[131] the accused had filed about 300 motions to procure and hear evidence (*Beweisanträge*)[132] during a year of trial but subsequently withdrew them after confessing to the charges. He then renounced this confession a few weeks later and announced 200 further evidence motions. The trial court was forced to spend the following 30 trial days (or seven months) almost exclusively discussing and ruling on the accused's evidence motions. The Federal Court of Justice condoned on appeal that the trial court had dismissed 106 of the motions and had then barred the accused from filing further motions himself and limited the accused to doing so through counsel. This is contrary to regular procedure which generally allows the represented accused to act along with counsel, including, for example, filing motions or examining

[129] Isolated examples for some kind of fee-denial would be *Oberlandesgericht Schleswig*, 22 February 1996, 1 StR 35/96, 1 StR 192/95, NStZ 1996, 443, or *Oberlandesgericht Hamm*, 28 November 2000, 2 (s) Sbd. 6-202/2000, NStZ-RR 2002, 95. See ch 1, III.B.iii at 40–41, for fee-denial by the ICTR.

[130] One could quibble about saying it 'appears to fall with the confines of the procedural rules'. However, this would beg the question. The issue of abuse only arises because the conduct is indeed fully covered by the rule. The point is that it may contravene the spirit of the law. See L Senge, 'Missbräuchliche Inanspruchnahme verfahrensrechtlicher Gestaltungsmöglichkeiten – wesentliches Merkmal der Konfliktverteidigung? Abwehr der Konfliktverteidigung' (2002) *Neue Zeitschrift für Strafrecht* 225, 226, and E Kempf, 'Missbrauch im Strafprozess – Peccatur intra et extra muros' in F Herzog and U Neumann (eds), *Festschrift für Winfried Hassemer* (Heidelberg, CF Müller, 2010) 1042, both citing to H-H Kühne, 'Rechtsmißbrauch des Strafverteidigers?' (1998) *Neue Juristische Wochenschrift* 3027, 3027.

[131] *Bundesgerichtshof*, 7 November 1991, 4 StR 252/91, BGHSt 38, 111 (*Ausschluß des Angeklagten vom Beweisantragsrecht*), referring to *Bundesgerichtshof*, 22 August 1990, 3 StR 406/89, StV 1991, 99. See on this case W Beulke, 'Missbrauch von Verteidigerrechten – eine kritische Würdigung der jüngsten Rechtsprechung' in M Böse and D Sternberg-Lieben (eds), *Grundlagen des Straf- und Strafverfahrens-rechts, Festschrift für Knut Amelung zum 70. Geburtstag* (Berlin, Duncker & Humblot, 2009) 548–49.

[132] In Germany, parties generally introduce evidence by such motions to the court. See S Kirsch, 'The Trial Proceedings before the ICC' (2006) 6 *International Criminal Law Review* 275, 289; Bohlander (n 18) 469. See on the excessive use, M Niemöller, 'Zum exzessiven Gebrauch des Beweisantragsrechts' (2010) *Juristische Rundschau* 332.

witnesses. The Federal Court stressed that using procedural rights to achieve illegitimate objectives was prohibited in the criminal trial, as in any other kind of formalised legal process. This was said to be the case where a participant in the proceedings exercised his or her rights under the Code of Criminal Procedure to intently pursue goals alien or contrary to the proceedings. In particular, it was argued to amount to abuse of procedure where motions were purportedly filed in search of the truth[133] but were actually aimed at pursuing goals alien to the proceedings, such as delaying the trial.

Restrictions on evidence motions for abuse of process were also imposed on counsel, although the Federal Court of Justice expressly stressed the exceptional character of the case.[134] In a murder trial, counsel had tried to delay the proceedings, again by excessive evidence motions (over 320 during almost two years). The trial court eventually set a deadline within which counsel could move for further evidence. It ruled that it would deal with later evidence motions summarily in the judgment and not rule on each of them separately beforehand, as German criminal procedure would normally require. The Federal Court of Justice upheld this practice in subsequent cases, as did the Federal Constitutional Court.[135]

Motions as such have been dismissed as abusive where the trial court held that counsel primarily intended to use them to delay the trial.[136] Pertinent filings late into the trial were said to be an indication of this motive. More recently, the Federal Court has even gone so far as to hold that no significant actual delay of the

[133] On the search of the truth as an objective of the criminal trial in Germany, see *Bundesgerichtshof*, 28 August 1997, 4 StR 240/97, BGHSt 43, 195, para 26; *Bundesgerichtshof*, 3 March 2005, GSSt 1/04, BGHSt 50, 40, para 47 (excerpts translated by JI Turner, *Plea Bargaining Across Borders* (New York, Aspen Publishers, 2010) 84–97); *Bundesgerichtshof*, 11 August 2006, 3 StR 284/05, BGHSt 51, 88 (*Unzulässigkeit unwahrer Protokollrüge*), para 25; *Bundesverfassungsgericht*, 6 October 2009, 2 BvR 2580/08, NJW 2010, 592 (*Ablehnung von Beweisanträgen wegen Verschleppungsabsicht*), para 18; Meyer-Goßner (n 10) Einleitung, mn 10; H Kudlich, *Strafprozeß und allgemeines Mißbrauchsverbot. Anwendbarkeit und Konsequenzen eines ungeschriebenen Mißbrauchsverbots für die Ausübung strafprozessualer Verteidigungsbefugnisse* (Berlin, Duncker & Humblot, 1998) 209–13. In English, see Turner (n 133) 72–78, 84–97; see T Abdallah, *Die Problematik des Rechtsmißbrauchs im Strafverfahren. Eine Untersuchung unter besonderer Berücksichtigung der verfassungsrechtlichen Bezüge des Strafprozeßrechts* (Berlin, Duncker & Humblot, 2002) 99–108, 145–46, for a critical stance.

[134] *Bundesgerichtshof*, 14 June 2005, 5 StR 129/05, NJW 2005, 2466 (*Frist für Beweisanträge*). See Beulke (n 131) 551–52.

[135] *Bundesgerichtshof*, 6 October 2009, 3 StR 375/09, paras 22–34; *Bundesverfassungsgericht*, 6 October 2009, 2 BvR 2580/08, NJW 2010, 592 (*Ablehnung von Beweisanträgen wegen Verschleppungsabsicht*), but see now also *Bundesgerichtshof*, 20 July 2011, 3 StR 44/11, NJW 2011, 2821, para 9. From a defence counsel perspective, see E Kempf, 'Der zu (späte) Beweisantrag' (2010) *Strafverteidiger Forum* 316; R Hamm, 'Fristenregelung für Beweisanträge?' in F Herzog and U Neumann (eds), *Festschrift für Winfried Hassemer* (Heidelberg, CF Müller, 2010) 1017–28. See also ch 1, B.iii at 24 (n 111), on an order by an ICTY Trial Chamber regarding the organisation of the proceedings in the *Šešelj* case.

[136] See the case notes by W Beulke and F Ruhmannseder, 'Beweisantrag in Prozessverschleppungsabsicht, Anmerkung zu BGH, Beschl.v 9.5.2007 – 1 StR 32/07' (2008) *Neue Zeitschrift für Strafrecht* 300; Beulke (n 131) 554–56; R Michalke, 'Anmerkung zu BGH, Beschl.v 9.5.2007 –1 StR 32/07' (2008) *Strafverteidiger* 228; M Niemöller, 'Prozessverschleppung – die Absicht genügt' (2008) *Neue Zeitschrift für Strafrecht* 181; W Bauer, 'Der Ablehnungsgrund der Prozessverschleppungsabsicht' (2008) *Neue Zeitschrift für Strafrecht* 542; M Niemöller, 'Nochmals: Prozessverschleppung – Entgegnung auf Bauer' (2009) *Neue Zeitschrift für Strafrecht* 129.

proceedings may be required,[137] although this has remained controversial. Another bench of the Federal Court asserted that there was still the objective requirement that counsel's conduct may delay the trial significantly and stressed that motions very late in the trial did as such not prove counsel's intention to obstruct the proceedings.[138]

The notion of abuse of procedure has also been decisive for the dismissal of defence appeals contending procedural errors. In two cases, the defence alleged procedural errors by the trial court, citing the trial transcripts (which are part of the formal trial record for the purpose of the appeal). According to the transcripts, the accused had not been represented by counsel, although assignment throughout the trial was statutorily mandated under the Code of Criminal Procedure in the first case,[139] and the charges had not been read at the beginning of the trial in the second case[140] respectively. However, appealing counsel knew the transcripts were incorrect in these two regards. The Federal Court of Justice ruled it abusive of the defence counsel to allege these apparent errors as grounds of appeal. This was affirmed by the Federal Constitutional Court.[141]

It seems fair to draw the conclusion that the abuse of defence rights is acknowledged as an established doctrine by the courts.[142] It is accepted increasingly in scholarship,[143] though the latter tends to remain critical. The most crucial point about the doctrine would be, however, that it should not be used to justify measures that merely enhance the efficiency of the trial while compromising defence rights. The cited jurisprudence deals with extreme cases, as is emphasised by the

[137] *Bundesgerichtshof*, 9 May 2007, 1 StR 32/07, BGHSt 51, 333 (*Absicht der Prozessverschleppung*); cited again by the same bench in *Bundesgerichtshof*, 23 September 2008, 1 StR 484/08, BGHSt 52, 355 (*Verschleppungsabsicht*), this was upheld by the Federal Constitutional Court, *Bundesverfassungsgericht*, 6 October 2009, 2 BvR 2580/08, NJW 2010, 392 (*Ablehnung von Beweisanträgen wegen Verschleppungsabsicht*) (the latter stressing, however, para 24, that the timing of the motion cannot be cited as the sole reason by a trial court but needs to be assessed before the background of the overall conduct in the proceedings). See also on the role of counsel *Bundesgerichtshof*, 2 November 2010, 1 StR 544/09, NStZ 2011, 294, para 66.

[138] *Bundesgerichtshof*, 18 September 2008, 4 StR 353/08, NStZ-RR 2009, 21*Bundesgerichtshof*, 2 December 2008, 3 StR 203/08, Neue Zeitschrift für Strafrecht 2009, 692. See also *Bundesgerichtshof*, 28 October 2010, 4 StR 359/10, StV 2011, 397 (*Ablehnung eines Beweisantrages wegen Prozessverschleppungsabsicht*).

[139] *Bundesgerichtshof*, 11 August 2006, 3 StR 284/05, BGHSt 51, 88 (*Unzulässigkeit unwahrer Protokollrüge*).

[140] *Bundesgerichtshof*, 23 August 2006, 1 StR 466/05, NJW 2006, 3582 = NStZ 2007, 51 (*Vorlagebeschluss Rügeverkümmerung*); *Bundesgerichtshof*, 23 April 2007, GSSt 1/06, BGHSt 51, 298 = NJW 2007, 2419 (*Rügeverkümmerung*).

[141] *Bundesverfassungsgericht*, 15 January 2009, 2 BvR 2044/07, BVerfGE 122, 248 = NJW 2009, 1469 (*Rügeverkümmerung*).

[142] On the history see Abdallah (n 133) 27–87; on abuse of process in non-criminal proceedings see C Fahl, *Rechtsmißbrauch im Strafprozeß* (Heidelberg, CF Müller 2003) 15–42.

[143] See Beulke (n 131) 563; Kudlich (n 133) 248–56 (requiring the subjective awareness of pursuing goals extraneous to the criminal trial and furthermore priority of the statutory criminal procedure, including the sanctions and reaction mechanisms provided by it), with a proposal for a general clause at 360; Abdallah (n 133) 185–99, 209 (favouring the use of the judicial power to preside over the conduct of the proceedings, Section 238 StPO, and to disqualify counsel under Section 138a StPO); Fahl (n 142) 722–837 (assuming a lacuna in the Code of Criminal Procedure, 727–28, but acknowledging the existence of a general principle, 729–33; arguing against codifying it, 733–34).

Federal Court itself in the rulings. The ensuing problem would be that these cases are used as precedents and falsely used to draw general conclusions about abuse of process, and in view of their exceptional character courts should be reluctant to rely on them. What is needed is a common effort from all actors towards a genuine fair trial.[144] It is reiterated that allegations of abuse target formally permissible defence strategies. The latter must be distinguished from illegal and even criminal conduct. It results from the nature of many defence rights that their exercise may cross the line from the permissible to the abusive. As far as their material content is concerned, some defence rights under the Code of Criminal Procedure are simply phrased as absolute. Others contain general clauses or only malleable qualifications. They thus fail, by their nature, to prescribe a precise limit of where counsel ventures from the permissible to the abusive. The potential for abuse is therefore inevitable.

Morover, the special task of defence lawyers needs to be recognised.[145] Lawyers act as officers of the court, or *Organ der Rechtspflege*, to use the German counterpart.[146] This special professional role commits counsel to accepting the principal goals of the criminal trial.[147] Given this, the definition of abuse offered by the Federal Court of Justice in the leading case of BGHSt 38, 111 deserves merit as a general principle.[148] The participants in the proceedings cannot be allowed to use the rights endowed to them under the Code of Criminal Procedure to intently pursue goals alien or contrary to the proceedings. Nonetheless, the vital question would be to identify the necessary threshold of abuse, which again can only be described by indeterminate clauses.[149] It is noted that the notion of the defence lawyer abusing the process raises general issues of delineating permissible from impermissible defence conduct (as illustrated by the case of *Zündel*).[150] This remains to be tackled from a more fundamental perspective. With particular regard to abuse of process rights by defence lawyers, it must be emphasised that they are vested with special privileges.[151] They represent solely their client and for this purpose they are tasked to advocate the client's case and to question the charges. This must include the use of all available means not actually prohibited. It is not the job of defence counsel to manage and expedite the trial.[152]

Rather, the key to resolving unwieldy trials should be by the management and guidance of the court,[153] in particular through scheduling and orders. The

[144] Kempf (n 130) 1053.

[145] See above, I.A at 52–53, and below II.E at 100–01.

[146] Above, I.B at 54.

[147] Senge (n 130) 227. See also Abdallah (n 133) 147–58, on the administration of justice as a factor in determining abuse.

[148] Likewise Kudlich (n 133) 289–90.

[149] Senge (n 130) 226.

[150] Below, II.E.ii at 102–05.

[151] Beulke (n 131) 563; Abdallah (n 133) 120–28.

[152] Senge (n 130) 227.

[153] See ibid, 229; Nehm and Senge (n 3) 377; B Malmendier, '"Konfliktverteidigung" – ein neues Prozeßhindernis?' (1997) *Neue Juristische Wochenschrift* 227, 228.

doctrine of abuse should be resorted to only where needed to curb actual obstruction in cases where counsel is bent on boycotting or perverting the trial as such.[154] Thus, it will not justify dismissing separate filings or forfeiting just one specific right. What is needed is an overall effect on the trial, along with an assessment of the conduct of counsel. As to the cases discussed in the foregoing, the abuse doctrine, for example, does not per se warrant denying the right to appeal procedural errors as argued in BGSt 51, 88 and BGHSt 51, 298.[155] (The Federal Court's other argument is more persuasive in this regard: an appeal based on incorrect trial transcripts does ultimately not further the search for the material truth; this will not be achieved by a retrial.) Dismissing motions as abusive (as in BGHSt 51, 333 and BGHSt 52, 355) should only have been done if they created significant delay and there is proof from the prior trial conduct by counsel that this is the specific motive (as held by BGH NStZ-RR 2009, 21). Imposing a deadline for motions (as in BGH NJW 2005, 2466) seems tolerable if it follows exhaustive evidence taking and the proceedings threaten to unravel otherwise. The rationale here, however, cannot be trial efficiency.

All of above specific sanctioning mechanisms, as well as the more general abuse doctrine, may be suitable responses to a frivolous defence strategy. On the other hand, they will not always address counsel misconduct adequately. First, misconduct by counsel is a personal issue. The curtailment of defence rights does not address counsel in his or her private capacity. This will not be too helpful in criminal cases. In civil cases, damages may be recovered by the client from counsel. This is not a feasible option in criminal cases. Secondly, a doctrine of abuse of process to establish misconduct and respond to it is intrinsically linked to the procedure before the court. More importantly, this would only cover misconduct which arises from procedure. This leaves large areas of conceivable misconduct uncovered. It may nevertheless be important to keep such a doctrine in mind to have an additional and diversified response to misconduct.

The only universal tool for judges to be able to respond to misconduct under German criminal procedure is therefore the exclusion of counsel from a running trial. For counsel retained by the accused, this can only be achieved in accordance with Sections 138a to 138d of the Code of Criminal Procedure.[156] These provisions allow for the exclusion of counsel where there are strong suspicions leading to the belief that counsel is a party to the offence which is tried; abuses communication privileges; is an accessory to the case; obstructs justice in the given case; handles goods from the offence at stake; or if counsel's participation would pose a

[154] Beulke (n 131) 563–64; Senge (n 130) 228.

[155] See also Fahl (n 142) 700–05.

[156] See in detail, M Remagen-Kemmerling, *Der Ausschluß des Strafverteidigers in Theorie und Praxis* (Berlin, Duncker & Humblot, 1992); on the history of the exclusion of counsel, Fahl (n 142) 318–24. It is professional misconduct for the disqualified lawyer to represent his or her client in other proceedings, *Anwaltsgerichtshof Celle*, 10 July 2006, AGH 13/05, BRAK-Mitt 2006, 283.

danger to German national security.[157] In principle, Sections 138a to 138d applies to court-assigned counsel as well.[158] He or she can be withdrawn by the presiding judge pursuant to Section 141 and Section 143, affording a certain discretionary margin.[159]

One of the more recent cases from German jurisprudence on the exclusion of chosen counsel was against Ernst Zündel.[160] Aside from the fact that one of Zündel's defence lawyers, Sylvia Stolz, eventually being prosecuted and convicted separately,[161] the prosecution moved to the Higher Regional Court pursuant to Section 138c(1) of the Code of Criminal Procedure to disqualify her from acting as counsel for Zündel in the running trial on grounds of Section 138a(1), no 3 (obstruction of justice). The Higher Regional Court, the *Oberlandesgericht* Karlsruhe, ordered her exclusion, which she appealed to no avail to the Federal Court of Justice, the *Bundesgerichtshof.*

This disqualification of counsel in the Zündel case is illustrative in two regards.

First, more generally and irrespective of Zündel, it has been voiced that judges may be lured by the temptation of light-handedly and even wrongly alleging counsel to be party to the crime, and to exclude him or her from the trial on these

[157] Section 138a (Exclusion of Defence Counsel):

(1) Defence counsel shall be excluded from participation in proceedings if he is strongly suspected, or suspected to a degree justifying the opening of the main proceedings,
   1. of being involved in the offence which constitutes the subject of investigation,
   2. of abusing communication with an accused who is not at liberty for the purpose of committing criminal offences or substantially endangering the security of a prison, or
   3. of having committed an offence which in the case of the conviction of the accused would constitute accessoryship after the fact, obstruction of justice, or handling stolen goods.

. . .

Section 138b (Exclusion of Defence Counsel for Endangering National Security):
Defence counsel shall also be excluded from participating in proceedings the subject of which is one of the criminal offences designated under section 74a subsection (1), number 3, section 120 subsection (1), number 3, of the Courts Constitution Act, or non-performance of the duties pursuant to section 138 of the Criminal Code concerning criminal offences of high treason or endangering external security pursuant to sections 94 to 96, 97a, 100 of the Criminal Code, if in view of certain facts there is reason to assume that his participation would endanger the security of the Federal Republic of Germany. Section 138a subsection (3), first sentence, number 1, shall apply mutatis mutandis.

[158] *Bundesgerichtshof,* 20 March 1996, 2 ARs 20/96, BGHSt 42, 94.

[159] *Bundesverfassungsgericht,* 8 April 1975, 2 BvR 207/75, BVerfGE 39, 238 (*Stammheim*), 246; Meyer-Goßner (n 10) § 141, mn 6, § 143, mns 3–6. Weigend (n 10) rightly points out some of the contradictions of this jurisprudence.

[160] *Bundesgerichtshof,* 24 May 2006, 2 ARs 199/06, 2 AR 102/06, NJW 2006, 2421 (the Federal Court's decision on the disqualification motions); see *Bundesgerichtshof,* 12 September 2007, 1 StR 337/07, Neue Zeitschrift für Strafrecht-Rechtsprechungs-Report 2008, 48*Bundesgerichtshof,* 12 September 2007, 1 StR 337/07, NStZ-RR 2008, 48, for the conviction in the underlying case. See on more details of this case later in this ch below, E at 102–05.

[161] The charges were, inter alia, defamation, coercion, attempted obstruction of justice, the use of symbols of unconstitutional organisations and denying the Holocaust. She partially succeeded on a first appeal, *Bundesgerichtshof,* 2 December 2008, 3 StR 203/08, Neue Zeitschrift für Strafrecht 2009, 692, the new sentencing to 3 years and 6 months after the subsequent rehearing was later upheld, *Bundesgerichtshof,* 6 October 2009, 3 StR 375/09, on her second appeal. In addition to imprisonment, she was banned by the trial court from practising as an attorney for the ordinary statutory maximum of five years pursuant to Section 70 Criminal Code (see above, II.B.ii.d at 72–73).

grounds. This infringes on counsel's rights as well as the right to legal assistance of the accused. Summing up thus, there may be a dire need for the exclusion of counsel, but, once again, this is not appropriate as a general instrument.

Secondly, the specific case raises intriguing question about how to delineate permissible from impermissible defence conduct. However, this is a more general issue and does not necessarily further the understanding of the specific provison of Section 138a of the Code of Criminal Procedure.[162]

The disciplinary procedure and other indirect measures have already been described above. In addition to these two tiers, other indirect responses may attach to misconduct. The fitness to practice can also be addressed in terms of administrative measures. In addition, lawyers may be sued for misconduct under private law.

b Admission to the Bar as an Indirect Measure

The disciplinary regime provides for specific sanctions, inter alia, a ban from the profession. The disciplinary procedure is in principle governed by the Bar Council and the Lawyers' Courts. Notwithstanding this, admission to the Bar is, of course, a necessary prerequisite to practice. The admission to the Bar itself is now handled by the Regional Bars (*Rechtsanwaltskammern*).[163] Admission can be refused, withdrawn or revoked pursuant to Section 7 and Section 14 BRAO, as well as provisions in other statutory Acts.[164] Sections 7 and 14 BRAO read:

> § 7 (Rejection of an application for admission to the legal profession):
> An application for admission to the legal profession shall be rejected,
>
> 1. if the applicant has forfeited a basic right by virtue of a decision of the Federal Constitutional Court (Bundesverfassungsgericht);
> 2. if the applicant does not have the right to take public office on grounds of a criminal conviction;
> 3. if the applicant has been excluded from the legal profession by virtue of a final judgment and less than eight years have elapsed since such a judgment became final; this shall have no bearing on number 5;
> 4. if a final judicial decision has been taken against the applicant in impeachment proceedings against a judge or in disciplinary proceedings for removal from an office in the administration of justice;
> 5. if the applicant is guilty of behaviour which makes him/her appear unworthy to practise as a Rechtsanwalt;
> 6. if the applicant opposes the Free, Democratic Basic Order in a way that is punishable by law;

[162] On the underlying issue in detail see below, II.E at 100–05.

[163] See C Dahns, 'Die kleine BRAO-Reform – Änderungen durch das Gesetz zur Stärkung der Selbstverwaltung der Rechtsanwaltschaft' (2007) *Neue Juristische Wochenschrift* 1553, 1553.

[164] See M Vogel, *Versagung, Rücknahme und Widerruf der Anwaltszulassung wegen Unwürdigkeit der Person* (Bonn, Deutscher Anwaltverlag, 1995) 21–44, 52–66, 71–131.

7. if the applicant, for reasons of health, is incapable of properly practising as a Rechtsanwalt for more than merely a temporary period;
8. if the applicant engages in an occupation which is inconsistent with the profession of a Rechtsanwalt, particularly his/her status as an independent agent in the administration of justice, or which is likely to undermine confidence in the Rechtsanwalt's independence;
9. if the applicant's finances are in a state of deterioration; this shall be suspected to be the case if insolvency proceedings have been instituted against the applicant or if the applicant is entered in the register to be kept by the Insolvency Court or the Enforcement Court (§ 26 para. 2 of the Insolvency Code [Insolvenzordnung]), § 915 of the Code of Civil Procedure [Zivilprozeßordnung]);
10. if the applicant is a judge, a civil servant, a regular solider or a soldier in short-term service unless the applicant is performing his/her tasks in an honorary capacity or unless the applicant's rights and duties derive from §§ 5, 6, 8 and 36 of the Members of Parliament Act (Abgeordnetengesetz) of 18 February 1977 (Federal Gazette I p. 297) or from equivalent legislation.

§ 14 (Withdrawal and revocation of admission to the legal profession):

(1) Admission to the legal profession shall be withdrawn with effect for the future if facts subsequently become known which mean that admission would have had to be refused had such facts been known at the time.

(2) Admission to the legal profession shall be revoked,

1. if a Rechtsanwalt has forfeited a fundamental right by virtue of a decision of the Federal Constitutional Court;
2. if a Rechtsanwalt has become unfit to take public office on grounds of a criminal conviction;
3. if a Rechtsanwalt, for reasons of health, is incapable of properly practising the profession of Rechtsanwalt for longer than merely a temporary period unless it does not unduly obstruct the administration of justice for the Rechtsanwalt to remain in the legal profession;
4. if a Rechtsanwalt has renounced the rights conferred through his/her admission to the legal profession in a written notice sent to the Regional Judicial Administration;
5. if a Rechtsanwalt has been appointed as a judge or a lifelong civil servant, has been enlisted to serve as a regular solider or has been reinstated in his/her former appointment as a judge or lifelong civil servant or as a regular soldier under § 6 of the Members of Parliament Act (Abgeordnetengesetz) or under equivalent legislation and theRechtsanwalt does not renounce the rights conferred through his/her admission to the legal profession;
6. if a Rechtsanwalt's admission before a court is revoked under § 35 para. 1;
7. if a Rechtsanwalt's finances have fallen into a state of deterioration, unless this does not put the interests of the client at risk; a state of financial deterioration shall be assumed if insolvency proceedings have been instituted against the Rechtsanwalt or the Rechtsanwalt has been entered in the register to be kept by the Insolvency Court or the Enforcement Court (§ 26 para. 2 of the Insolvency Code, § 915 of the Code of Civil Procedure);
8. if a Rechtsanwalt engages in an occupation which is inconsistent with the Rechtsanwalt's profession, in particular with the Rechtsanwalt's status as an

independent agent in the administration of justice, or which may undermine confidence in the Rechtanwalt's independence; this shall not be the case if the revocation would be an unreasonably harsh measure for the person in question;

9. if a Rechtsanwalt does not maintain the mandatory professional indemnity insurance (§ 51).

(3) After hearing the opinion of the Council of the Bar a dispensation may be granted so that admission to the legal profession is not revoked if the reasons for refusing admission no longer exist.

All of these provisions list more or less specific grounds on which this can be based. They address and safeguard in some way issues of professional integrity and fitness to practice.

Some of the above grounds result in automatic non-admission or disbarment. In these cases, the decision by the bar to revoke or refuse admission is rather technical. Other paragraphs leave a considerable margin of interpretation to the Bar, however.[165]

The latter can be said in particular of Section 7(5) which provides for the non-admission of anyone 'guilty of behaviour which makes him/her appear unworthy to practise'. Crimes committed in a professional context may justify the refusal, in particular if directed against the citizens' interest in the integrity of legal services or against the administration of justice.[166] Further categories where admission was denied include dishonesty, in particular making false statements when applying to the Bar, and unprofessional behaviour.[167] Furthermore, applicants have been denied in the past due to their private lifestyles. Contemporary commentators challenge the individual constitutional liberties and changed mores, thus calling for reluctance in this respect.[168] In any event, general opinion has it that the indignity clause in no 5 must not be utilised in a way to circumvent the other more specific statutory grounds for refusal. This concerns in particular the relationship of no 5 to no 6 (refusal for political views), (health, for example, substance abuse) and no 9 (debt).[169] In any event, a balance must be struck on a case-by-case basis between the behaviour on the one hand and the mitigating factors on the other,[170] such as lapse of time, gravity and frequency of the incriminated acts and the applicant's attitude in regard to them.

For withdrawals under Section 14(1) and revocation under Section 14(2) BRAO, a formal decision by a disciplinary court is needed. Revocation (*Widerruf*) essentially follows from a change of pertinent circumstances, as listed in

[165] See Feuerich (n 13) § 14, mn 10.

[166] *Bundesgerichtshof*, 12 September 2007, 1 StR 337/07, Neue Zeitschrift für Strafrecht-Rechtsprechungs-Report 2008, 48, paras 7–10; Vogel (n 164) 30–34.

[167] Vogel (n 164) 34–35, also with a critique as to the latter; M Henssler in M Henssler and H Prütting (eds), *Bundesrechtsanwaltsordnung*, 3rd edn (Munich, Beck, 2010) § 7, mns 49–57.

[168] J Schmidt-Räntsch in R Gaier, C Wolf and S Göcken (eds), *Anwaltliches Berufsrecht* (Cologne, Heymanns, 2010) § 7, mn 41; Henssler (n 167) § 7, mn 56; Kleine-Cosack, *Bundesrechtsanwaltsordnung*, 6th edn (n 13) § 7, mn 10; Vogel (n 164) 36–37.

[169] Schmidt-Räntsch (n 168) § 7, mns 42–44, 47–49; Vogel (n 164) 37–45.

[170] Kleine-Cosack *Bundesrechtsanwaltsordnung*, 6th edn (n 13) § 7, mns 11–17; Schmidt-Räntsch (n 168) § 7, mns 44–46; M Vogel (n 164) 52–58.

paragraph 2, after admission. Withdrawal (*Rücknahme*) follows ineligibility for admission under Section 7 BRAO in first place, ie, if pre-admission facts surface later. Whether after withdrawal or revocation, readmission is possible – after eight years at the earliest. All of these decisions can be challenged before the Higher Lawyers' Court, Section 9(2) and Section16(5) BRAO.

The Regional Bar is bound to withdraw admission, under Section 14(1) if facts from prior to admission come to light after admission. It is noted that indignity to the profession is not listed in Section 14(2) as a ground for revoking an existing admission after it has been lawfully granted. Therefore, later offensive conduct of a once admitted attorney is as such no basis for revocation.[171] Section 14 thereby deviates from the admission scheme under Section 7. This deviation has been called erratic by some authors arguing in favour of amending an indignity clause as contained in Section 7.[172] There is, however, practically little need for it as any admitted attorney is subject to the regime of disciplinary measures by the Bar Council and the disciplinary courts.[173] This may include disbarment under Section 114(2), no 5 BRAO.[174] If reaching the appropriate high threshold, disbarment may be imposed for misconduct not related to counsel's work.[175] The indignity clause in Section 7(5) BRAO can be invoked against readmission after revocation for one of the other grounds under Section 14(2) BRAO.[176] Given the harsh consequences of disbarment, an argument can be made that the judicial procedure for formal disciplinary sanctions is better suited and affords the necessary due process. On the other hand, the administrative revocation by the Bar Council is subject to judicial review which follows according to Section 112a BRAO. However, counsel can be said to gain some reasonable expectations through admission in accordance with the rule of law, despite the wording of Section 14(1) BRAO.[177] This would be undermined by allowing disbarment through the easier path of administrative revocation of the licence to practice.

iv Liability Controls as an Indirect Measure

It is in principle conceivable that German lawyers are held liable under general laws of civil liability.[178] Assigned counsel may also incur such liability.[179] For a

[171] Schmidt-Räntsch (n 168) § 14 BRAO, mn 12; Henssler (n 167) § 14, mn 8.

[172] Vogel (n 164) 64–65.

[173] Schmidt-Räntsch (n 168) § 14 BRAO, mn 12. See above, II.B.i at 61–67, for the available measures.

[174] See Feuerich (n 13) § 114, mns 35–42.

[175] Henssler (n 167) § 14, mn 8.

[176] Dittmann in Henssler and Prütting (eds), *Bundesrechtsanwaltsordnung*, 3rd edn (n 61) § 114, mn 15.

[177] See Kleine-Cosack, *Bundesrechtsanwaltsordnung*, 6th edn (n 13) § 14, mns 3–4.

[178] In detail M Schultz, 'Die zivilrechtliche Haftung des Rechtsanwalts' in R Gaier, C Wolf and S Göcken (eds), *Anwaltliches Berufsrecht* (Cologne, Heymanns, 2010) 1935–2074; with a focus on criminal defence lawyers, K Schlecht, *Die zivilrechtliche Haftung des Strafverteidigers. Zugleich eine Darstellung seines Pflichtprogramms* (Tübingen, Mohr Siebeck, 2006).

[179] Schlecht (n 178) 15–37.

number of reasons, however, it has at no point developed into a practically relevant sanctioning instrument for criminal defence lawyers.[180] Among these reasons are that accused or suspects are much less likely to sue their lawyers than corporate clients, that professional malpractice may not directly burden the client or that damages are immaterial, can typically not be proven or are for other reasons not recoverable.

v Conclusion

Summing up, a whole range of measures can be taken against counsel who have committed or are suspected of misconduct. The emphasis under the German system is on the criminal law and the disciplinary regime. Among those two, criminal proceedings prevail over disciplinary proceedings, although details remain to be examined later.[181] In addition to those main pillars, all other forms of controls identified by Wilkins[182] exist as well. The legal profession is further bound by other regimes which address particular concerns, such as the German Anti-Money Laundering Act (*Geldwäschebekämpfungsgesetz*).[183] This all leads to a high degree of regulation. It is noted that such complex regulation cannot be achieved by the ICC alone. A point could thus be made that this is better left to domestic jurisdictions which are the best placed to know exactly what is necessary for domestic lawyers.

In the foregoing, the applicable regimes have been identified and described. The disciplinary regime does not discriminate between different legal specialsations. It seems to be fair to claim that, in general, German lawyers are subject to a uniform set of rules. Of course, the field of law in which a lawyer handles a case factually determines the specifically applicable rules. A defence counsel representing an accused in a criminal trial may be charged with *Strafvereitelung* if his or her defence is obstructive, whereas this is of little or no relevance to divorce lawyers. On the other hand, civil liability may play a lesser role and thus not matter as much. Among the arguments in favour of a uniform set of rules are that this would help to entrench common – and thus maybe stronger – ethics. Criminal lawyers share with their colleagues a common heritage of values. On the other hand, rules may have to be adapted to do justice to the fact that a lawyer acts as

[180] See Harting (n 37) 363–82; M Kilian, 'Berufsrechtliche Verantwortlichkeit von Strafverteidigern' in T Weigend, S Walther and B Grunewald (eds), *Strafverteidigung vor neuen Herausforderungen – Denkanstöße aus sieben Rechtsordnungen* (Berlin, Duncker & Humblot, 2008) 132–34; S Barton, 'Zivilrechtliche Risiken' in G Widmaier (ed), *Münchener Anwaltshandbuch Strafverteidigung* (Munich, Beck, 2006) 2098–115; TC Knierim, 'Die zivilrechtliche Haftung des Strafverteidigers' in W Beulke and E Müller (eds), *Festschrift zu Ehren des Strafrechtsauschusses der Bundesrechtsanwaltskammer* (Neuwied, Luchterhand, 2006) 115–48; G Zwiehoff, 'Haftung des Strafverteidigers?' (1999) *Strafverteidiger* 555. On the liability in international cases, see C Louven, 'Die Haftung des deutschen Rechtsanwalts im internationalen Mandat' (1997) *Versicherungsrecht* 1050.

[181] See in particular Section 118 BRAO, below II.D.i at 95.

[182] Above Introduction, III at 4, n 13.

[183] See Müller and Gussmann (n 12) mns 214–22.

defence counsel in criminal matters. As far as a preliminary analysis is concerned, Germany has a universal approach. Particularities for defence counsel have been taken into consideration, however, by the courts.[184] Rights of the accused may also be a factor to be taken into account when considering a fit response to counsel misconduct.

C The Procedure for the Various Measures

i Disciplinary Procedure

Proceedings under the disciplinary regime are of a quasi-criminal nature.[185] Notwithstanding more specific provisions in the *Bundesrechtsanwaltsordnung*, the rules of criminal procedure and evidence apply (Section 116 BRAO).[186] Allegations of breaches of professional rules are investigated and prosecuted by public prosecutors (Section 120 BRAO). Lawyers themselves may apply for the initiation of proceedings under Section 123 to purge themselves of allegations. Prosecutors as well as the local Bar are under duty to notify each other of any suspicions of breaches of professional duties (Section 120a). Proceedings can only be formally launched by the prosecution submitting accusations to the Disciplinary Court (Section 121). In accordance with regular criminal procedure, the prosecution is generally bound to investigate by the principle of legality.[187] However, it is clear from Sections 122 and 123 that the prosecution may close proceedings, in which case it submits a reasoned notification to the Bar and/or the concerned attorney. The Bar as well as the concerned lawyer can press for disciplinary proceedings. The BRAO does provide reasons for which a case may be closed by the prosecution. Thus, although the principle of legality obliges the prosecution to open a case, it is also vested with full discretion to close the case. The prosecution is not bound by the narrower provisions of the Code of Criminal Procedure, which only allow dropping a case under certain conditions.[188] Lawyers enjoy the right to remain silent, by virtue of Section 136 of the Code of Criminal Procedure, mutatis mutandis. The lawyer is furthermore presumed to be innocent until actually convicted, and has a right to expeditious proceedings. As noted before, the rules of

[184] eg, the Federal Constitutional Court stressed how money laundering charges affect criminal defence lawyers und therefore require caution in proceeding with investigations. Criminal defence lawyers are, however, not per se exempt of these generally applicable laws. See *Bundesverfassungsgericht*, 30 March 2004, 2 BvR 1520/01, 2 BvR 1521/01, BVerfGE 110, 226, paras 86, 153–56.

[185] See for a general overview, H Dahs, 'Berufsgerichtliche Verfahren' in G Widmaier (ed), *Münchener Anwaltshandbuch Strafverteidigung* (Munich, Beck, 2006) 1986–88; H Elbs and O Klemke, 'Leitfaden zum anwaltsgerichtlichen Verfahren' (2005) *Anwaltsblatt* 56.

[186] See above, II.Bi.b at 67.

[187] Dittmann in Henssler and Prütting (eds), *Bundesrechtsanwaltsordnung*, 3rd edn (n 61) § 120, mn 1; F Johnigk in R Gaier, C Wolf and S Göcken (eds), *Anwaltliches Berufsrecht* (Cologne, Heymanns, 2010) § 120a, mn 1.

[188] Dittmann in Henssler and Prütting (eds), *Bundesrechtsanwaltsordnung*, 3rd edn (n 61) § 122, mns 3–5.

evidence are generally those of criminal procedure.[189] The principle of in *dubio pro reo* applies.[190] Accordingly, facts underlying a sanction under Section 114 BRAO must be proven beyond a reasonable doubt. Convictions and other decisions can be appealed (Sections 142 ff), similar to criminal proceedings. Misconduct not justifying disbarment or a temporary ban is subject to a limitation period of five years (Section 115).

The procedure thus largely follows what would be done in a criminal trial. It differs insofar as hearings are not public, can be held in absence of the lawyer and that a lawyer cannot be arrested or otherwise detained for the purpose of the disciplinary proceedings (Section 117). Hearings are generally not open to the wider public (Section 135). They must be opened, however, on request of the lawyer, and may be opened on request of the prosecutor. Lawyers of the local Bar und certain officials have access to non-public hearings, though. Hearings can be conducted *in absentia* if the lawyer has been properly summoned (Section 134).

It has already been pointed out above that the regional Bar Council has autonomous, ie, rather executive disciplinary powers.[191] It may issue advice, instructions, formal opinions and official reprimands. In respect to official reprimands, the lawyer enjoys procedural safeguards as set out in Section 74. They have to be reasoned, the lawyer has to be heard beforehand and a limitation period of three years applies. Lawyers can lodge a complaint against official reprimands with the Council and eventually have the complaint reviewed by the Disciplinary Court.

Simple advice and neutral instructions are not reviewable by the Disciplinary Court. Section 112a(1), however, provides that

> [t]he Higher Lawyers' Court shall adjudicate . . . on all public-law disputes in accordance with the present Act, on the basis of a statutory order adopted on the basis of the present Act, or in accordance with the by-laws of a Bar . . . insofar as the disputes do not by their very nature fall into the jurisdiction of a Lawyers' Disciplinary Court, or they are not explicitly allocated to another court (administrative law matters concerning the legal profession).

Thus, not all measures concerning counsel are necessarily handled as disciplinary matters, or under the disciplinary regime. For a number of matters, the BRAO contains special procedural rules. For example, for administrative matters, Sections 112b–112g govern the proceedings. Section 112a with its general catch-all clause ensures, however, that all counsel matters are eventually subject to judicial review.

Summing up, the disciplinary procedure features strong parallels with criminal procedure. The differences are few, such as the possibility of a hearing *in absentia*; that they are as default held in closed sessions; and that counsel cannot be summoned or arrested. Some of these deviations illustrate that the procedure may need to be adapted to counsel's special situation. In other instances, it just makes sense

189 See Kleine-Cosack, *Bundesrechtsanwaltsordnung*, 6th edn (n 13) § 116, mns 3–4; Dittmann in Henssler and Prütting (eds), *Bundesrechtsanwaltsordnung*, 3rd edn (n 61) § 116, mns 2–33; Johnigk (n 187) § 116, mns 7–37; Feuerich (n 13) § 116, mns 6–82.

190 Johnigk (n 187) § 116, mn 24, fn 121; Feuerich (n 13) § 116, mn 50; Gribbohm (n 82) 925.

191 See above, B.i.b at 65–66.

that principles of the stricter criminal procedure may be sacrificed in favour of a more flexible and simplified regime because of the lesser gravity of the sanctions. The possibility of a trial *in absentia* and the non-public trial come to mind. The core principles of criminal procedure are incorporated in the disciplinary regime.[192] On the other hand, it becomes apparent from measures such as advice and neutral instruction, the admission to the Bar and in particular Section 112a(1), that a number of acts are of an administrative nature requiring or allowing a different procedure.

As has been shown, counsel enjoys a high level of procedural guarantees under the regular disciplinary regime. The character of the disciplinary regime is quasi-criminal.[193]

ii Criminal Procedure

All the criminal offences attaching to misconduct are handled under normal criminal procedure. They are prosecuted by public prosecutors before ordinary criminal courts. Cases are thus typically not brought before the judges before whom misconduct has occurred. The prosecution has no discretion to initiate proceedings but is obliged to do so if there are sufficient factual grounds (Section 152 Code of Criminal Procedure). No trial can be held in the absence of the accused (Section 230 Code of Criminal Procedure). A conviction can only be entered if the court considers no reasonable doubt.[194] Convictions and other decisions can be appealed in accordance with Sections 296–358. Put briefly, the procedure under the German criminal law regime provides for high standards just as in other cases.

iii The Procedure for Other Measures

The criminal law and the disciplinary system may be the main instruments in response to counsel misconduct. The practice of criminal courts has shown, however, that direct measures, or institutional controls, to use the words of Wilkins, are needed to address specific issues. Oftentimes, they are just much more effective. On the other hand, they harbour the potential to infringe counsel rights and those of the accused to effective assistance. This should reflect in the respective procedure.

[192] K Rogall, 'Die Vorkolloquien und Resolutionsentwürfe zur Vorbereitung des XVII. Internationalen Strafrechtskongresses der AIDP vom 12–19. September 2004 in Peking, Thema III: Die Prinzipien des Strafprozesses und ihre Anwendung im Disziplinarverfahren (Santiago de Chile, 21–26.9.2003)' (2004) 116 *Zeitschrift für die gesamte Strafrechtswissenschaft* 251, 252.

[193] Whether a quasi-criminal nature is necessarily warranted, has been disputed. It has been argued that the German Parliament would be free to adopt a different regime, eg, a rather administrative procedure. K Rogall, 'Germany: Principles of Criminal Procedure and their Application in Disciplinary Procedures' (2003) 74 *Revue internationale de droit pénal* 925. This is probably not consented worldwide, see Rogall (n 192) 253.

[194] *Bundesgerichtshof*, 26 May 1992, 5 StR 122/92, BGHSt 38, 302; Meyer-Goßner (n 10) § 261, mns 2, 26.

The relevant instruments have already been described above.[195] Counsel can be fined for frivolous filings, can be ordered to bear expenses if causing a delay in proceedings, or he or she may be withdrawn from the case. Of course, these instruments do not systematically apply to all conceivable criminal proceedings. It is at this point that procedure matters, though. The question is what are the core requirements needed to safeguard the rights of the concerned lawyer and of the client on the one hand, while helping to hold an expeditious and effective trial on the other. Within the national context, the German Constitution (*Grundgesetz*, the Basic Law) has, of course, to be taken into account. It guarantees general access to the judiciary to have acts by state authorities reviewed.[196]

As has been discussed, the criminal as well as the disciplinary procedure provides for very specific safeguards, as is appropriate in light of the sanctions. The other conceivable measures are usually not accompanied by a wealth of procedural provisions. It has been pointed out before, however, that these measures can have quite an impact on counsel. It goes without saying that this thus necessitates adequate procedural rules. Sometimes, they may be provided for specifically; in other cases, they may flow from the general rules of procedure. Which of those models is followed is actually of secondary importance. The important thing seems to be that the core principles of due process also apply to these measures. Among the main requirements that come to mind for this are the principle of legality; the requirement of a prior warning; the right of counsel to be heard and thus defend him or herself; the right to a reasoned decision; proportionality between the kind and nature of the misconduct and the legal consequence; and the right to a review by impartial judges.[197]

Direct sanctioning has been discussed above.[198] Examples of direct sanctioning are orders for fines or imposing expenses on counsel by the judge or the bench concerned. Another instance of direct sanctioning may be the exclusion of counsel from a case. Finally, the Court Constitution Act explicitly provides for contempt-like powers, although they do not apply to counsel.[199] If the trial outcome is affected, decisions of the court can typically be challenged by appealing the final verdict.

All these measures are taken by the same judge or bench concerned who may not be impartial. More often than not counsel must be heard beforehand and can appeal these orders to a new bench.[200] Fees or expenses which are to be appealed

[195] Above, B.iii at 73–85.

[196] *Grundgesetz* (Basic Law) Art 19(4): 'Should any person's rights be violated by public authority, he may have recourse to the courts. If no other jurisdiction has been established, recourse shall be to the ordinary courts'.

[197] C Brants, 'Commentary' in A Klip and G Sluiter (eds), *Annotated Leading Cases of International Criminal Tribunals, vol 6, The International Criminal Tribunal for Rwanda 2000–2001* (Antwerp, Intersentia, 2003) 464–67, develops guiding ideas in the ICTR context.

[198] See above, B.iii at 73–81.

[199] See above, B.iii at 74.

[200] See Section 145(4) Code of Criminal Procedure, and Section 304(2) for the appeal; Meyer-Goßner (n 10) § 145, mn 23. For Section 176 ff of the Court Constitution Act, Section 181 mutatis mutandis, Section 238(2) and Section 304 Code of Criminal Procedure provide remedies, Gröner (n 121) 152.

sometimes have to exceed a certain amount, or leave is needed.[201] Section 34 Federal Constitutional Court Act is one of the few examples, and probably the only one, where an order cannot be appealed. It empowers the court to impose a fine for frivolous constitutional complaints and other kinds of motions before it. However, the court usually has to give a warning before making such an order.[202]

The procedure if counsel has taken up a job and is subsequently refused part of the fees is governed by the *Rechtsanwaltsvergütungsgesetz* (Lawyer's Fees Act). Section 55 thereof is the central provision for fee claims. Court-assigned counsel has to claim fees and expenses from the registry of the court, even if in some cases the amount of a fee is determined by the bench.[203] If a judge, or a bench, has determined a fee, the court's registry is bound by this. The determination by the bench may in some cases not be immediately reviewable.[204] However, by virtue of Sections 56 and 33 of the Lawyer's Fees Act, counsel can move for a review of the registry's decision by the same judge or bench, and may typically appeal this decision to a higher court.[205]

As can be gathered from the foregoing, counsel enjoys wide rights to have measures affecting him or her reviewed by impartial judges. Where there is no right to appeal, counsel has to be warned. A general right to be heard before a court decision is issued flows from Section 33 Code of Criminal Procedure and is mandated constitutionally.[206] Similarly, Section 34 sets out as a principle that appealable court decisions and those dismissing a motion shall be issued with reasons. In virtually all cases, counsel will thus receive a reasoned opinion.

The scope of the principle of legality is not explicitly clear from the aforementioned examples. Constitutional jurisprudence has taken a strict approach, though. It requires a statutory provision as the legal base (*Ermächtigungsgrundlage*) for any act restricting the liberty of citizens. In the case of defence counsel, the yardstick is in particular the freedom to choose and exercise an occupation under Article 12 Basic Law.[207] A prominent example is the exclusion of a counsel from a case.[208] Whereas the Federal Court of Justice has relied on inherent powers and also argued on the basis of customary law, the Federal Constitutional Court rejected this notion. The Constitutional Court left room for the application of

[201] For orders under Section 38 of the Court Fees Act, see § 69. For the exclusion of counsel from a case under Section 138a *et seq* see 138d(6).

[202] *Bundesverfassungsgericht*, 19 December 2006, 2 BvR 2357/06, 2 BvR 2389/06, paras 12–15.

[203] K Leipold, *Anwaltsvergütung in Strafsachen* (Munich, Beck, 2004), mns 333–34, 344, 348.

[204] eg, the determination of the *Pauschgebühr*, a lump sum for complex cases, Section 42 RVG, in which case counsel has to be heard, though (ibid, mns 175–76).

[205] See, eg, *Oberlandesgericht Stuttgart*, 8 August 2005, 4 Ws 118/05, Strafverteidiger 2006, 200. If a fundamental question of law is involved and leave is granted, the higher court's decision can be appealed again, see, eg, *Oberlandesgericht Frankfurt*, 15 November 2006, 2 Ws 137/06, RVGreport 2007, 71.

[206] See C Krehl, 'Der verfassungsrechtliche Schutz rechtlichen Gehörs im Strafverfahren' in F Herzog and U Neumann (eds), *Festschrift für Winfried Hassemer* (Heidelberg, CF Müller, 2010) 1055–71.

[207] See, eg, *Bundesverfassungsgericht*, 12 April 2005, 2 BvR 1027/02, BVerfGE 113, 29, para 86.

[208] *Bundesverfassungsgericht*, 14 February 1973, 2 BvR 667/72, BVerfGE 34, 293 (*Schily*); *Bundesverfassungsgericht*, 19 December 1962, 1 BvR 163/56, BVerfGE 15, 226 (*Vorkonstitutionelles Gewohnheitsrecht*).

customary law which predates the enactment of the Basic Law. Newer customary law does not suffice, though, and statutory codification is needed to regulate counsel. This even extends to formalities such as the perennial debate on professional obligations of German lawyers to wear robe and tie in the court room.[209]

Finally, proportionality between misconduct and the attaching legal consequences is a crucial criterion for judging the equitableness of a regulatory regime. This is not expressly addressed in any of the examined provisions. Constitutional jurisprudence, however, has continuously held this to be a general principle to be respected by the courts and any other state bodies.[210] Therefore, its application in criminal proceedings, including the criminal trial, is ensured in principle.[211]

As a further measure with an indirect nature, the refusal of membership to the Bar or termination thereof may also become a relevant tool in practice. Since Bar membership is usually a general prerequisite to practise, the impact on counsel and his or her work is considerable. Revoking admission under Section 14(2) BRAO seems to be of a rather technical nature. Section 7, in particular no 5 thereof, and its equivalent in Section 14(1), however, vest the Bar with a considerable margin of appreciation. Hence, the possibility of a review and other procedural guarantees are warranted. However, any issue related to the admission to the Bar which can be brought before the Higher Lawyers' Court is an administrative measure within the confines of Section 32 and Section 112a BRAO.[212] Pursuant to these, among further amendments in 2007 and 2009,[213] the procedure for such administrative measures and the pertinent judicial review now follows the rules of general administrative procedure, Sections 32 and 112c BRAO, respectively.[214] Under the pertinent regime, the Bar acts *proprio motu*.[215] Until 2009, now repealed Section 36a(2) provided that the failure of the attorney to cooperate could result in a finding against him or her if the necessary elements remained unproven.[216] Of course, lawyers have to substantiate their claims when applying to be granted legal privileges, such as admission to the Bar. This now flows from general principles of German administrative procedure.[217] The attorney is not precluded from introducing facts anew during later review in the

[209] See from the more recent case law, *Landesarbeitsgericht Niedersachsen*, 29 September 2008, 16 Ta 333/08, Anwaltsblatt 2008, 883; *Landgericht Mannheim*, 27 January 2009, 4 Qs 52/08, NJW 2009, 1094, with the case note by W Leitner, 'Anmerkung zu LG Mannheim NJW 2009, 1096' (2009) *Neue Juristische Wochenschrift* 1096. On attire requirements before US courts see below, III.A (n 343).

[210] See *Bundesverfassungsgericht*, 13 April 2007, 1 BvR 3174/06, NJW 2007, 2839, where the Federal Constitutional Court reversed a ruling by a trial judge as excessive, where the trial judge had imposed a fine of €250 under Section 178 GVG on a party for insulting the judge and disrupting the proceedings.

[211] See Meyer-Goßner (n 10) Einleitung, mns 20–22; Rogall (n 193) 937.

[212] Kleine-Cosack, *Bundesrechtsanwaltsordnung*, 6th edn (n 13) § 7, mns 99–106, § 14, mns 36–47.

[213] See Prütting (n 67) § 32, mns 1–6.

[214] Kleine-Cosack , *Bundesrechtsanwaltsordnung*, 6th edn (n 13) § 112a, mns 1–19; A Siegmund in R Gaier, C Wolf and S Göcken (eds), *Anwaltliches Berufsrecht* (Cologne, Heymanns, 2010) § 32, mns 1–15; Schmidt-Räntsch (n 168) § 112c, mns 1–2.

[215] Siegmund (n 214) § 32, mns 41–45.

[216] See Feuerich (n 13) § 36a, mns 4–8; Siegmund (n 214) § 32, mns 50–51.

[217] Siegmund (n 214) § 32, mns 52–56; Kleine-Cosack, *Bundesrechtsanwaltsordnung*, 6th edn (n 13) § 36, mns 5–7.

court.[218] If counsel on the other hand challenges a measure directed against him or her, no duty to incriminate oneself should be assumed.[219] As far as fees for breaches of notification and cooperation duties under Article 56 are concerned, counsel has to be warned and can appeal the imposition of such a fee (Section 57 BRAO). Similarly with admission issues, the public prosecutor is not involved.

In spite of those differences in the criminal and disciplinary regime, counsel is afforded fundamental due process guarantees. All measures can be brought before courts for an independent review and counsel can be heard prior to any review. In addition, decisions in relation to admission as an attorney are made by the responsible Bar. The autonomy of the profession in this may also count as a factor in guaranteeing fair proceedings.

Finally, liability controls were discussed above. It appears that civil liability is less relevant to criminal defence counsel than the other forms of control. The procedure simply follows that of any civil law suit in Germany and thus adequate rules are guaranteed.

iv Analysis of the Applicable Procedures

The procedure for conceivable measures has been outlined. German scholars stress that the disciplinary regime and the criminal regime are distinct.[220] This shows in the applicable procedure. What the exact difference between the two regimes is has not been explained authoritatively. By and large, the view prevails that the disciplinary regime is an *aliud*, of which the purpose is held to be that of prevention. In respect of the individual, it is supposed to deter from repeat breaches in the future. Members of the profession should also be deterred and have their sense of legal ethics reinforced. Retribution is allegedly not a goal. All of this helps to explain and justify some of the differences between the criminal and the disciplinary procedures and despite these differences, both procedures are still close. The disciplinary procedure is eventually a quasi-criminal procedure. This is to say, it is a criminal procedure with some relaxations. The fundamental tenets are the same. As Rogall emphasises, what criminal and disciplinary sanctions have in common is that they are used to investigate allegations of human wrongdoing.[221] More precisely, it could be added that this is done by state authorities and by claiming sovereign state powers. Individuals are singled out, and a stigma attaches. This argues for applying in principle rules of criminal procedure.

However, the rules of procedure and evidence are relaxed in some regard. In addition, some of the substantive rules are relaxed as well. The general principles of criminal liability are not spelled out as detailed as is the case in substantive

[218] Siegmund (n 214) § 32, mn 55.

[219] See Kleine-Cosack, *Bundesrechtsanwaltsordnung*, 4th edn (n 98) § 36a, mn 2, and Kleine-Cosack, *Bundesrechtsanwaltsordnung*, 5th edn (n 62) § 36a, mns 2, 4.

[220] See below (nn 226 and 227).

[221] Rogall (n 193) 934. See also *Bundesverfassungsgericht*, 11 June 1969, 2 BvR 518/66, BVerfGE 26, 186 = NJW 1969, 2192 (*Ehrengerichte*), para 50.

criminal law. No distinction is made between different degrees of participation. Attempts are not punished. The requisite 'elements of crime', or the infraction, are usually not spelt out as rigorously. Further, the Rules of Professional Practice operate on a number of general clauses. Rogall concludes that this is a consequence of granting the responsible supervisory organs powers broad enough to effectively guard the functioning of the institutions and their public perception.[222]

Summing up, different procedural models are conceivable. It could be argued that the legislator's choice narrows down once a regime has really taken on a criminal character. This is principally determined by the accusation and by the sanctions. Procedure then follows. Even though it makes a system identifiable and shapes it, it is not as determinative as the sanctions. Going from this finding, the procedure for discipline seems not predetermined. Rogall has argued that there is a margin of legislative discretion to make the procedure more administrative or leave it criminal.[223] Nonetheless, it must meet general procedural standards. He counts among these the principle of legality, procedural safeguards and impartial courts. This is also the case for the more administrative issues and procedures for lawyers. An immediate review can also be achieved in the other instances of direct sanctioning.

D The Relationship of the Various Measures

i Multiple Proceedings for the Same Facts

As the different characters of the conceivable measures have become clear, the question remains how they relate to each other. More precisely, different kinds of relations can be distinguished.[224] They could be called vertical insofar as, within the same jurisdiction, several regimes of a distinct nature may be applicable at the same time and thus be stacked upon each other. If similar mechanisms from different jurisdictions compete, this could be called horizontal. Moreover, general connections exist among the controls in terms of substance.[225]

Both horizontal and vertical competition raise the issue of *ne bis in idem* if legal responses attach to the same facts. The fact that different measures serve different purposes and result in different legal consequences helps to reconcile their parallel application with the concept of *ne bis in idem*. Under German law, criminal sanctions do not preclude disciplinary action; they are held to have different aims.[226] It has been disputed whether this is enough to just whisk away the bar of double jeopardy. Authors have suggested that it seems rather a question of

[222] Rogall (n 193) 934.
[223] ibid, 946.
[224] Ch 4, I.A at 286–87.
[225] Wolf (n 50) Einleitung, mns 29–31.
[226] Rogall (n 193) 930; Müller (n 89) 2075; P Paepcke, 'Die Grenzen anwaltschaftlicher Ehrengerichtsbarkeit' in OF von Gamm, P Raisch and K Tiedemann (eds), *Festschrift für Gerd Pfeiffer* (Cologne, Heymanns, 1988) 987–88.

balancing whether both the criminal and the disciplinary sanction amount to the same or not.[227] A factor may be whether the professional status of the lawyer is already an integral part of the criminal sanction, be it as an element of the criminal offence or as consideration in the sentencing process.

Different solutions are conceivable.[228] Two sanctions can be reconciled by differentiating and thus avoiding any overlap. This can be addressed in terms of factual overlap and legal overlap. First, this can be achieved by declaring criminal punishment and disciplinary sanctions distinct in nature and thus simply not overlapping. Factual overlap can be minimised by declaring disciplinary breaches to be subsidiary in substance to criminal provisions, or drafting disciplinary rules accordingly. Of course, this also prevents legal overlap. Another solution would be to disallow any disciplinary proceedings as a matter of procedure if a criminal case arises. Or, simultaneous proceedings may be permissible but sanctions under one regime would need to be taken into account and to be offset by the other.

It has to be noted that there may be no factual overlap, and therefore no legal overlap at all in many cases: although German criminal law covers a wide range, it does not cover every conceivable type of misconduct. The legal interest at stake may not be prominent enough for the misconduct to amount to a crime. In other cases, the counsel's misconduct may not have been intentional and thus fail to meet the mental threshold of the relevant offences under German criminal law. In many other instances, though, both regimes apply. Counsel is thus potentially in double jeopardy, unless the two systems were truly distinct.[229]

However, this does clearly not apply to the pairing of German criminal law and the disciplinary procedure under the auspices of the BRAK. On the one hand, the substantive professional standards are decided by the *Satzungsversammlung* (the Statutory Assembly), and lawyers participate in the disciplinary procedure as judges. On the other hand, the Rules of Professional Practice are subject to the approval of the Federal Ministry of Justice.[230] The Ministry also acts as the general review body of the Federal Bar as a public institution (Section 176 BRAO). These review powers do not extend to substituting discretionary decisions by the Bar. However, they are still highly regulatory. Moreover, in the course of these disciplinary proceedings, state prosecutors act as prosecutors, the adjudicating bodies are dominated by state judges and the disciplinary regime has sanctions which are very similar to the criminal system. Lastly, it is reiterated that membership is mandatory. Counsel cannot be sanctioned if he or she withdraws from the Bar (Section 113(3)). Proceedings can be reinstated when counsel is readmitted.[231] All

[227] U Lambrecht, *Strafrecht und Disziplinarrecht* (Frankfurt a.M., Lang, 1997) 55.

[228] ibid, 121–50.

[229] eg, voluntary membership in private lawyers' organisations. See J Taupitz, *Die Standesordnungen der freien Berufe: geschichtliche Entwicklung, Funktionen, Stellung im Rechtssystem* (Berlin, de Gruyter, 1991) 470–71, 699–703.

[230] See above, II.B.i at 60. Moreover, it has been stressed by critics that the relevance of the Statutory Assembly is virtually negligible, M Kleine-Cosack, 'Anfang von Ende der Satzungsversammlung' (2007) *Anwaltsblatt* 409.

[231] Above, II.B.i.b at 65 (n 75).

in all, the disciplinary regime should be viewed as a supplementary state system rather than a fully autonomous regime.

For these reasons, it seems well justified that the criminal and the disciplinary regime are not handled independently from each other. Measures under both systems are not fully permissible in a simultaneous manner and simply offset. Instead, the BRAO provides in Section 118(1) for a primacy of the criminal procedure from the point that an indictment is filed. The disciplinary case against counsel may be further investigated but the procedure may not go forward otherwise. If counsel is acquitted in a criminal court, he or she can only be disciplined for conduct that does not constitute a criminal offence. If a sanction has actually been imposed on counsel by a court or other authority – be it punishment, a disciplinary measure or other sanction – an additional disciplinary measure is only permissible if necessary 'in order to compel the Rechtsanwalt to perform his/her duties and to protect the standing of the legal profession' (Section 115b).[232] However, a finding of ineligibility to represent in a certain field of law for a fixed time or permanent disbarment remains possible in any case.[233]

Therefore, a mechanism is in place to prevent double jeopardy in principle.[234] The notion underlying Section 115b BRAO would be that the imposition of the first sanction will typically suffice.[235] It only allows for a second sanction if warranted as a disciplinary *addendum*.[236] This may be a disciplinary sanction on top of a first sanction (*positiver Überhang*), or a disciplinary sanction in spite of an acquittal in criminal proceedings (*negativer Überhang*). It should thus boil down to a primacy of the criminal law while leaving open the exact criteria to assume a necessity for a disciplinary *addendum*. In this respect, Section 115b lists as requirements that an additional disciplinary sanction must be necessary to ensure individual compliance with professional rules and safeguard the integrity of the profession at large.

There has, however, been some critical analysis. Kleine-Cosack notes that the standing of the profession is often invoked too hastily to justify disciplinary sanctions.[237] Zuck questions the legitimacy of 'standing of the profession' as a criterion should it be understood only as safeguarding the reputation of lawyers.[238] Among the less controversial cases will be where the first sanction did not take into account that the attorney in question breached professional rules with his or her conduct. For example, some criminal offences and some criminal sanctions explicitly pertain to the offender's capacity as a lawyer, whereas other, more

[232] On Section 115b, see Paepcke (n 226) 992–96. See also *Anwaltsgerichtshof München*, 25 April 2006, BayAGH II – 2/06, BRAK-Mitt 2006, 176.

[233] This may be explained by the fact that the previous sanction is typically a monetary fine and does not comprise professional bans. See Wagner (n 88) 120–21.

[234] See L Koch and M Kilian, *Anwaltliches Berufsrecht* (Munich, Beck, 2007) 309–13; Feuerich (n 13) § 115b, mn 30.

[235] Dittmann in Henssler and Prütting (eds), *Bundesrechtsanwaltsordnung*, 3rd edn (n 61) § 115b, mn 3.

[236] Zuck (n 62) § 115b, mn 19.

[237] Kleine-Cosack, *Bundesrechtsanwaltsordnung*, 6th edn (n 13) § 115b, mn 8.

[238] Zuck (n 62) § 115b BRAO, mn 13.

general ones in particular do not.[239] If the sentencing for a criminal conviction reflects the position of counsel, though, no second, specifically professional sanction will be needed.[240] Essentially, both prongs of the test under Section 115b BRAO will be safely met if focusing on the person of sanctioned counsel and his or her attitude towards the first sanction. In this, the individual effect of the first measure on the attorney in question will have to be assessed, rather than what the disciplinary bodies see fit for the average attorney.[241]

A disciplinary sanction is not affected by court orders and any other measures which are not of a sanctioning character.[242] Most authors include herein measures according to Section 176 ff of the Court Organisation Act as well as other warnings or orders, whether they carry a fee or not. Of course, criminal or disciplinary proceedings are neither affected by civil suits and administrative measures taken by the Bar or other admission-related measures. This may be explained by the fact that the inquiry into guilt indicates that blame is the purpose of the sanction and therefore requires an element of culpability. Thus, these sanctions are aimed directly at counsel personally. Of course, personal fault may also be an element in the determination of other measures. However, most of these measures are oriented towards compensating directly. Criminal sanctions and disciplinary measures are directed more to the future and can be handed down even though no appreciable harm occurs.

Wagner argues for a wider catalogue of measures that need to be taken into account when considering whether additional sanctioning is required. In his opinion, the criterion should be whether deterrence has been achieved and whether additional sanctioning is truly needed.[243] Those are still somewhat malleable criteria but it may indeed help to prevent unproportional outcomes. Proportionality seems a general applicable concept.[244] It is in particular the similarity of sanctions that can raise excessiveness concerns and thus a kind of double jeopardy. If counsel is made to answer a case before a criminal as well as a disciplinary court, this can be explained by the two different kinds of responsibility that counsel carries. As to the first, he or she is criminally liable as an ordinary citizen; as to the second, this should be restricted to what is needed to restore professional integrity and should not be used to punish counsel twice.[245]

[239] See above, B.ii.a–c at 68–72, and B.ii.d at 72–73, respectively.

[240] See Dittmann in Henssler and Prütting (eds), *Bundesrechtsanwaltsordnung*, 3rd edn (n 61) § 115b, mn 10; Feuerich (n 13) § 115b, mns 35–73.

[241] Zuck (n 62) § 115b BRAO, mn 12; Feuerich (n 13) § 115b, mns 31–33.

[242] Kleine-Cosack, *Bundesrechtsanwaltsordnung*, 6th edn (n 13) § 115 b, mn 5; Dittmann in Henssler and Prütting (eds), *Bundesrechtsanwaltsordnung*, 3rd edn (n 61) § 115 b, mn 7; Paepcke (n 226) 992.

[243] Wagner (n 88) 174–75.

[244] Zuck (n 62) § 115b BRAO, mns 14–19.

[245] See *Bundesverfassungsgericht*, 2 May 1967, 2 BvR 391/64 and 263/66, BVerfGE 21, 378 (*Wehrdisziplin*), where the Federal Constitutional Court held that military discipline alongside the criminal trial did not trigger constitutional double jeopardy. Disciplinary incarceration would need to be taken into account by the criminal court in sentencing to imprisonment. See also Mehle (n 98) 317–18.

Summing up, disciplinary proceedings are subsidiary to criminal proceedings. They are nevertheless possible in spite of those criminal proceedings. It remains to be seen whether the arguments in favour of this model are persuasive in the ICC setting. Among the reasons advanced in the German context are that it is more efficient to concentrate on only one procedure in order to prevent the need to examine the same evidence twice. Furthermore, the potential of contradictory findings is diminished by according a clear priority to one procedure. Out of the two, the criminal procedure is said to provide more effective and powerful tools to try a case. Wagner rightly points out that the first two arguments explain the primacy of one of the two co-existing regimes but are not compelling reasons to accord this primacy to the criminal procedure. Notwithstanding this, he acknowledges that criminal charges are of greater gravity and should therefore be given priority. Secondly, he describes the criminal procedure as the more general procedure of the two. As a specialised regime with its own, more intricate issues, the disciplinary procedure should follow.[246]

Based on this, it has become clear that disciplinary proceedings are permissible for the same conduct. They can be instituted at any time but need to be suspended as soon as an indictment is filed with a criminal court. If counsel is acquitted in a criminal court, a disciplinary finding is barred, even in the case of an erroneous acquittal.[247] In all other cases, Section 115b BRAO allows for supplementary disciplinary proceedings. General criteria do exist; nevertheless, a determination needs to be made on case-by-case basis.[248] It is possible for a disciplinary sanction to be handed down and subsequently be followed by criminal proceedings. The disciplinary sanction may be taken into account by the criminal court. Of course, this may sometimes prove difficult. If the criminal proceedings result in an acquittal, it is not even possible to factor in the disciplinary sanction or provide a specific remedy. For these reasons, Wagner argues for an option to review the disciplinary case.[249]

As far as other measures than criminal or disciplinary sanctions have been taken, such findings can be taken into consideration by the court in the criminal or disciplinary case. It is stressed again that there is no need to do so as they constitute no bar whatsoever to a criminal or disciplinary sanction. Ultimately, the constitutionally recognised principle of proportionality is the only bar. Strict rules preventing a different assessment or different outcome under one proceedings or another are not in place.

ii Proceedings in Other Jurisdictions and Transnational Work

So far, the relationship of measures within one jurisdiction has been discussed. As far as the horizontal relationship of measures from different jurisdictions is

246 See Wagner (n 88) 39–43.
247 ibid, 177.
248 ibid, 175–76.
249 ibid, 176.

concerned, it needs to be noted that foreign measures do not prevent sanctioning by German authorities. They may be taken into account if handed down under the rule of law.[250] Accordingly, no clear *ne bis in idem* would exist for transnational disciplinary proceedings. This is not a peculiarity of the disciplinary system, though. German criminal law does not recognise a general international *ne bis in idem* either.[251] Foreign judgments are taken into account for sentencing.[252] Furthermore, special provisions have been enacted to implement the obligations flowing from the statutes of the international courts, the ICC, the ICTY and the ICTR. As far as the ICC is concerned, Section 69 of the German ICC Act provides for *ne bis in idem* in respect of the core crimes, but also for crimes under Article 70(1) of the Statute. This leaves room for double proceedings regarding measures other than just the named criminal offences.[253]

Furthermore, no guiding rule settling conflicts of laws exists for professional discipline.[254] In principle, courts have found that the professional rules of Germany govern the conduct of lawyers admitted to the German Bar, irrespective of Bar membership in other jurisdictions.[255] Section 31(1) to 31(3) BORA addresses the practice of European foreign lawyers, pursuant to which they are held to German professional rules as well.[256] However, imposing domestic rules on those who are resident professionally goes without saying.[257] In relation to the critical issue of resolving conflicts, Section 31(1) to 31(3) BORA is not helpful. It will only lead to an accumulation of duties. Ironically, it is just this accumulation of duties arising from diverging rules that creates the need for a clear rule on conflicts.

A limited version of a necessary conflicts rule can be found in Section 29(1) BORA. It points to the Code of Conduct of the Council of Bars and Law Societies of Europe (CCBE) in its paragraph (1) for a lawyer's activities within the European

[250] Kleine-Cosack, *Bundesrechtsanwaltsordnung*, 6th edn (n 13) § 115b, mn 5.

[251] *Bundesverfassungsgericht*, 13 April 2007, 1 BvR 3174/06, NJW 2007, 2839*Bundesverfassungsgericht*, 4 December 2007, 2 BvR 38/06, StraFo 2008, 151.

[252] See Section 51(3) Criminal Code and U Franke in W Joecks and K Miebach (eds), *Münchener Kommentar zum StGB*, vol 1 [§§ 1–51] (Munich, Beck, 2003) § 51, mns 18–19. This general approach has started to crumble, even though it is far from being recognised as customary; H Kreicker, 'Deutschland' in A Eser and H Kreicker (eds), *National Prosecution of International Crimes*, vol 1 (Freiburg, edition iuscrim, 2003) 395–98.

[253] It is noted that the same seems to be possible before the ICC, see Rule 168 RPE. See on Rule 168 ch 4, II.A at 302.

[254] OL Knöfel, 'Anwalts-Kollisionsrecht' (2003) *Anwaltsblatt* 3, 4; OL Knöfel, *Grundfragen der internationalen Berufsausübung von Rechtsanwälten* (Bonn, Deutscher Anwaltverlag, 2005) 443–54; S Offermann-Burckart in M Henssler and H Prütting (eds), *Bundesrechtsanwaltsordnung*, 3rd edn (Munich, Beck, 2010) § 29 BORA, 81–84, 87 (arguing for the state where the attorney perfoms services). See also ch 4, I.B at 287–89.

[255] *Anwaltsgerichtshof Hamm*, 3 November 2000, 2 ZU 21/00, NJW 2001, 2555, 2556; *Bundesgerichtshof*, 12 February 2001, AnwSt (R) 15/00, 1421. See also Offermann-Burckart (n 254) § 29 BORA, mns 31–40.

[256] On the Law Regulating the Activity of European Lawyers in Germany (*Gesetz über die Tätigkeit europäischer Rechtsanwälte in Deutschland*, EuRAG), see above, A at 59.

[257] Knöfel, *Grundfragen* (n 254) 436–43, and with an overview and criticism of the existing approaches at 457–82.

Union or the European Economic Area.[258] It firstly contains the qualifier 'unless European Community law or German constitutional law, statute law or subordinate legislation take precedence'. This leaves unclear which law does actually apply and is not a practical solution as the CCBE Code is not binding law in first place.[259] It also raises constitutional concerns as such a far reaching choice of laws provision is not within the remit of the Statutory Assembly of the German Bar which adopted the BORA.[260] Instead, authors have mostly favoured an approach that would give preference to where the attorney acts,[261] or where his or her conduct has the greatest impact,[262] in other words, a principle of territoriality. Eventually, the CCBE Code itself does not actually contribute to resolving conflicts of professional laws. Although the BORA's reference to the CCBE and its Rule 1.5 seems clear-cut, it would also bring into play Rule 2.4 ('Respect for the Rules of Other Bars and Law Societies'). Pursuant to that Rule and the official commentary thereon, counsel would again in effect be bound to honour the professional standards in all jurisdictions concerned. Consequently, commentators advise lawyers to heed the strictest of the applicable professional rules.[263] This is not much help, though, if there is not one stricter and one comparatively laxer rule, but if the two plainly contradict each other. Then, counsel will only be able to meet one rule and breach the other.[264] He or she will therefore be bound to commit misconduct.

Furthermore, Section 29(2) provides that the German BORA is applicable to any other professional conduct not encompassed by sub-section (1).[265] In effect, German lawyers remain bound to their domestic professional rules[266] wherever they travel and irrespective of the type of professional activity they perform. Foreign lawyers, on the other hand, who don't have an established practice or otherwise fall under the EuRAG, are exempt from German professional standards.[267]

[258] Rule 1.5 CCBE Code of Conduct provides that '[c]ross-border activities shall mean: (a) all professional contacts with lawyers of Member States other than the lawyer's own; (b) the professional activities of the lawyer in a Member State other than his or her own, whether or not the lawyer is physically present in that Member State'.

[259] Knöfel, *Grundfragen* (n 254) 546; Offermann-Burckart (n 254) § 29 BORA, mn 41.

[260] See the criticism by Kleine-Cosack, *Bundesrechtsanwaltsordnung*, 6th edn (n 13) Anh. I 1, § 29, mns 1–3, Anh. III 1, mn 44, and above, A at 59.

[261] ibid, Anh. III 1, mn 44.

[262] M Kilian, 'Organisationsformen internationaler Tätigkeit von Anwaltsgesellschaften 'in M Henssler and M Streck (eds), *Handbuch des Sozietätsrechts* (Cologne, Otto Schmidt, 2001) H, mn 183; A Federle and K Fried in M Henssler and H Prütting (eds), *Bundesrechtsanwaltsordnung*, vol 2 (Munich, Beck, 2004) § 29 BORA, mn 37. See also M Henssler, 'Der lange Weg zur EU-Niederlassungsrichtlinie für die Anwaltschaft' (1999) *Zeitschrift für Europäisches Privatrecht* 689, 709.

[263] Offermann-Burckart (n 254) § 29 BORA, mn 87.

[264] See Knöfel, 'Anwalts-Kollisionsrecht' (n 254) 18.

[265] See the criticism by Kleine-Cosack, *Bundesrechtsanwaltsordnung*, 5th edn (n 62) Anh. I 1, § 29, mns 1–3, Anh. III 1, mn 44.

[266] R Zuck, 'Internationales Anwaltsrecht' (1987) *Neue Juristische Wochenschrift* 3033, 3035; see the criticism by Kleine-Cosack, *Bundesrechtsanwaltsordnung*, 6th edn (n 13) Anh. III 1, mn 44, and Offermann-Burckart (n 254) § 29 BORA, mns 81–84.

[267] See Knöfel, *Grundfragen* (n 254) 466–70, and see also above, A at 59.

In conclusion, conflicts of law are not resolved under German professional rules. The contemporary approach comes closest to what could be described as a kind of territoriality principle for those foreign lawyers with an established office in Germany, and a kind of permanent personality principle, binding German lawyers wherever they act in whatever matter. All of this is, however, far from a sophisticated doctrine.[268]

E Defence Rights and their Impact on the Regulation of Counsel

i Constitutional Guarantees

As a general consideration, rights of the defence, in particular those of constitutional rank, need to be taken into account. Constitutional considerations are a vital factor in discussing counsel regulation.[269] It goes without saying that no strict framework of constitutional law exists at the international level. The ICC has its own methodology of identifying the applicable law, namely Article 21 of the Rome Statute. Nonetheless, fundamental tenets may be identifiable that closely reflect what would be constitutional standards within a national legal order.

First, the rights of counsel limit the available measures. Among the rights enshrined in German constitutional law are the right to choose and exercise a profession (Art 12 Basic Law)[270] and the freedom of expression (Art 5 Basic Law).[271] Article 12 grants counsel the status of a free profession. In principle, this allows state regulation but not full control over counsel's activities. The rule of law is further referred to as a constitutional principle underlying the role of counsel.[272] It is inferred from Article 20, Article 28, Article 103(1) and Article 19(4) of the Basic Law. All of these rights afford counsel a privileged position but are also balanced with public interests restricting them again. This accounts for, for example, restrictions on the freedom of communication, confidentiality obligations, or the mandatory membership of the Bar, to highlight just a few examples.

Within the wider context, other constitutional guarantees are of course applicable in proceedings involving counsel. These guarantees do not immediately attach to the status of counsel as an attorney.[273] Proportionality is recognised as a

[268] Knöfel, 'Anwalts-Kollisionsrecht' (n 254) 10. The said author also points to a concept of *berufsbezogenes Internationales Berufsverwaltungsrecht* (professional international administrative law). He concludes that applicable professional rules should apply concurrently, but should not prejudice an attorney if conduct is required by the law of the jurisdiction governing the representation agreement between the lawyer and the client. This appears to be the most feasible solution to date. On the primacy of the ICC Code via Art 4, see ch 3, II.A.iii.c at 191–92, and ch 4, I.B at 287–89, as well as II.A at 291–97 and B at 297–98.

[269] See Zuck (n 67) 985–96.

[270] See Kleine-Cosack (n 60) 2080; MB Rick, *Die verfassungsrechtliche Stellung des Rechtsanwalts* (Bonn, Deutscher Anwaltverlag, 1998) 107, 128–45, 149–85, 190–98, 211–16, 223, 229–30.

[271] Rick (n 270) 108–24, 131–36.

[272] ibid, 75–89; Kleine-Cosack, *Bundesrechtsanwaltsordnung*, 6th edn (n 13) Einleitung, mns 49–50.

[273] See ibid, mns 56–58.

paramount principle for state action. It thus also applies in the sanctioning of counsel.[274] Just as with any suspect or accused, counsel can invoke due process rights.[275] The principle of democracy, as understood by German constitutional doctrine, requires statutory law as the legal base for state acts restricting the freedom of citizens. Thus, rules have to meet certain legislative standards. They either need to be adopted as a parliamentary act, or such an act must provide for the enactment of such further rules and prescribe the fundamental tenets, otherwise, they are not binding laws.[276]

Rights of the accused also need be taken into account. Misconduct by counsel as well as counter-measures to it may affect the client or other participants. It would be at odds with the right to a fair trial to burden them with decisions directed against counsel. In particular, this may concern the client's right to effective legal assistance. This seems less likely in the case of disciplinary or liability control which are typically methods of indirect sanctioning. Most markedly among the institutional controls are a number of direct measures which have implications for the accused. The exclusion or the suspension of counsel from a pending case and the doctrine of *Rechtsmißbrauch* come to mind.[277] They have the potential to render effective assistance by counsel impossible with the disturbing possible effect of preventing counsel defending his or her client effectively. In the extreme, it has been argued that counsel should therefore only be excluded or suspended following a criminal conviction.[278] Whereas this might disregard the proper balance between the individual's rights and the public interest in the administration of justice, it certainly illustrates the need to reconcile both.

In achieving this, it is acknowledged that different standards may be needed for different regimes. The constitutional guarantees differ in detail as proceedings of a criminal nature, of a disciplinary nature, an administrative nature and such of a private nature can be distinguished. It has been argued that it is the responsibility of the legislator to create specific rules, and to decide on which rules are put in place.[279] The implications of constitutional rights for the respective procedure may vary accordingly.

ii Delineating the Permissible from the Impermissible

The difficulty of reconciling the exercise of defence rights with safeguarding the administration of justice shows in particular in regulating – and if necessary disciplining – counsel. It seems fair to stress that in spite of differing regimes the delineation of permissible defence conduct remains an overarching issue. Counsel

[274] Rogall (n 193) 937. See also *Bundesgerichtshof*, 30 November 1987, AnwSt (R) 9/87, BRAK-Mitt 1988, 150, paras 13–14.

[275] Above, II.C at 86–92.

[276] Taupitz (n 229) 758, 791.

[277] See above, II.B.iii.a at 75–79.

[278] See D Göddeke, *Die Einschränkung der Strafverteidigung* (Köln, Pahl-Rugenstein, 1980) 211–13.

[279] Rogall (n 193) 946.

may incur responsibility for overstepping the limits. The question whether punishment has been obstructed or not is said to depend on the permissibility of counsel's actions in terms of procedure.[280] No general principle to distinguish procedurally permissible and impermissible defence has been developed, however. For the criminal offence of *Strafvereitelung* under Section 258 of the Criminal Code, the assessment is to be made on a case-by-case basis.[281]

One of the more recent cases from German jurisprudence, that against Ernst Zündel,[282] seems particularly instructive on the delineation of permissible and impermissible conduct. Zündel, the accused, had been expelled from Canada and was subsequently tried in Germany by the Regional Court of Mannheim under Section 130 of the German Criminal Code for denying the Holocaust. One of Zündel's defence lawyers, Sylvia Stolz, spread hate propaganda during her pleadings and filings. This resulted in extensive presentations and other pleadings as well as addresses to the audience during the trial, including advising the lay judges that they committed the offence of *Volksverleumdung* (defamation of the people), punishable by death, under the laws of the Third Reich purportedy still in force by sitting as judges in the trial. Further, she rambled on in lengthy monologues to the audience about the so-called 'Nuremburg sham trials', the court being an 'inquisition tribunal' and by denying the Holocaust. In spite of court orders, she continued addressing the audience 'to spread the truth'.

The courts held this to constitute undue delay of the proceedings. The prosecution moved to the Higher Regional Court pursuant to Section 138c(1) to disqualify her from acting as counsel for Zündel in the running trial on grounds of Section 138a(1), no 3 (obstruction of justice). The Higher Regional Court, the *Oberlandesgericht* Karlsruhe, ordered her exclusion,[283] which she appealed to no avail to the Federal Court of Justice, the *Bundesgerichtshof*.[284] Counsel Stolz was eventually prosecuted and convicted in a separate trial on charges of, inter alia, defamation, coercion, attempted obstruction of justice, the use of symbols of unconstitutional organisations and denying the Holocaust.[285] In addition to imprisonment, she was banned by the trial court from practising as an attorney for the ordinary statutory maximum of five years pursuant to Section 70 Criminal Code.[286]

[280] Müller (n 89) 2045, 2052–53; Kappelmann (n 96) 18–29, 35–67, 121–23; Kargl (n 96) 235–54.

[281] Harting (n 37) 347–52.

[282] *Bundesgerichtshof*, 24 May 2006, 2 ARs 199/06, 2 AR 102/06, NJW 2006, 2421 (the Federal Court's decision on the disqualification motions); see *Bundesgerichtshof*, 12 September 2007, 1 StR 337/07, NStZ-RR 2008, 48, on the underlying case of Zündel (his conviction upheld by the German Federal Court of Justice).

[283] *Oberlandesgericht Karlsruhe*, 31 March 2006, 3 Ausschl 1/06, Juristenzeitung 2006, 1129.

[284] See n 282.

[285] She partially succeeded on a first appeal, *Bundesgerichtshof*, 2 December 2008, 3 StR 203/08, Neue Zeitschrift für Strafrecht 2009, 692, the new sentencing to 3 years and six months after the subsequent rehearing was upheld on her second appeal, *Bundesgerichtshof*, 6 October 2009, 3 StR 375/09.

[286] See above, II.B.ii.d at 72–73.

The disqualification decision by the Higher Regional Court of Karlsruhe[287] is noteworthy because it constitutes a highly commendable exemplar in identifying and explaining defence misconduct. In short, the Court assessed the overall conduct and demonstrated in detail that counsel had ignored virtually all kinds of guiding procedural orders.

As the theoretical starting point, the Court highlighted counsel's position as an *Organ der Rechtspflege*, the German counterpart to the 'officer of the court'.[288] It then emphasised the apposite high threshold for the mental element for obstruction by counsel.[289] What is remarkable, comes after: the court stressed that it disregarded the content of the defence tactics, such as the numerous motions, including those for the recusal of judges, counsel's stance to be acting as an agent for the Third Reich, or denying the legitimacy of the Federal Republic. Instead, the court conducted a meticulous analysis of the proceedings during the four court days.

During the first session, counsel continued with her pleadings in spite of warnings, having her words and acts put on the official trial record by the presiding judge with a view to submitting them to the Public Prosecutor for laying charges (pursuant to Section 183 of the Courts Constitution Act).[290] The Court eventually refused to hear her.

On the second day, counsel disregarded a court order to file a motion in writing instead of reading it in court (Section 257a Code of Criminal Procedure),[291] warnings and calls to order. Eventually, her microphone was switched off. When she interrupted the examination of the accused by the presiding judge and opened a 'parallel session' in the court room, the Court had to be adjourned.

On the third day, counsel again interrupted the judges and thus caused the Court to be adjourned.

On fourth day in court, counsel again disregarged Section 257a orders to file motions in writing. The Court eventually handed down the decision pursuant to Section 138 Code of Criminal Procedure to disqualify her from representing the accused in the trial. In particular, the Court pointed out the fact that counsel had announced that she would ignore court orders in the future.

Based on this thorough analysis of the facts, the Court concluded that counsel intended to sabotage the trial. Counsel was said to be venturing outside the confines of the permissible procedure because she ignored orders or circumvented them. Moreover, the Court emphasised that none of the alleged procedural errors would justify counsel's defence, and that she would consequently need to seek

[287] *Oberlandesgericht Karlsruhe*, 31 March 2006, 3 Ausschl 1/06, Juristenzeitung 2006, 1129.

[288] Above, I.B at 54.

[289] See above, II.B.ii.a at 69.

[290] Section 183: If a criminal offence is committed at the sitting, the court must establish the facts and communicate the record thereof to the competent authority. Where appropriate, the provisional arrest of the perpetrator shall be ordered.

[291] Section 257a (Written Form): The court may require participants in the proceedings to file applications and proposals regarding questions of procedure in written form. This shall not apply to the applications referred to in Section 258. Section 249 shall apply mutatis mutandis.

appeal as the appropriate remedy. The Higher Regional Court stressed that the doctrine of *Rechtsmißbrauch* (abuse of process) should not be invoked not hastily by a court. It also emphasised the need for proportionality.

With this, it is conceded that the Higher Regional Court yielded no different result from the subsequent appeal decision by the Federal Court of Justice. Whereas there is small wonder as counsel uncontroversially engaged in professional misconduct, it is rather the clear and fitting reasoning of the Higher Regional Court that sticks out.

The Federal Court of Justice affirmed the exclusion, confirming the analysis of the Higher Regional Court.[292] However, it added another element constructed on a markedly different reasoning. The Federal Court held, based on an overall assessment, that counsel's conduct was alien to defence purposes (*verteidigungsfremd*).[293] The Court ruled that the mere pretence of defence – while in fact not contributing to the trial – was not permissible. In essence, procrastination of the running trial through ineffective defence was thus held to be enough for the offence of attempted obstruction of justice justifying the exclusion of counsel under Section 138c(1) and (2), and Section 138a(1), no 3 Code of Criminal Procedure.

This summary approach of the Federal Court of Justice has been criticised. Jahn stresses the causal element underlying the offence of *Strafvereitelung*.[294] Counsel is certainly causing the obstruction when only using the forum of the trial in order to further extraneous purposes. He counts among those presentations to the audience which do not fall within the recognised dialogue between the bench, the prosecution and the defence. On the other hand, counsel's conduct cannot be said, according to Jahn, to be causing the obstruction where the Chamber's powers exist to counter counsel's conduct if the bench could have effectively prevented misconduct otherwise. Jahn therefore favours the approach of Higher Regional Court of Karlsruhe. Böhm also commends the approach taken by the latter. He criticises the Federal Court for its departure from the criterion of procedural permissibility. Instead, the Court now assesses counsel's strategy and judges it as not constituting effective defence. He rightly views labelling defence tactics as *verteidigungfremd* as unduly impinging on counsel's territory and opening floodgates.[295] The later judgment by the Federal Court of Justice sheds little further light. In essence, the Federal Court quashed Stolz's conviction for attempted coercion but upheld in principle the one of attempted obstruction of

[292] *Bundesgerichtshof*, 24 May 2006, 2 ARs 199/06, 2 AR 102/06, NJW 2006, 2421, paras 7, 11, 12 (the Federal Court's appeal decision on the disqualification motions).

[293] ibid, para 9.

[294] Jahn (n 99) 1134. Counsel's duty to follow instructions of the presiding judge during the proceedings flows from Section 176 of the Court Constitution Act and Section 238 Code of Criminal Procedure, according to *Bundesgerichtshof*, 14 March 1994, AnwSt (B) 18/93, para 1, although that judgment was later reversed because of the unreasonable assessment of the evidence, *Bundesverfassungsgericht*, 10 July 1996, 1 BvR 873/94, NStZ 1997, 35.

[295] KM Böhm, '"Verteidigerfremdes Verhalten" – Neue Wege zur Ausschließung lästiger Strafverteidiger?' (2006) *Neue Juristische Wochenschrift* 2371.

justice.[296] It only reduced the initial three counts of obstruction (one for each court session; *Tatmehrheit*) to one count (*Tateinheit*). Aside from this, the Federal Court implicitly again followed its reasoning found in the disqualification appeal.[297] The defence activities by counsel Stolz were assessed *verteidigungsfremd* (alien to defence purposes) and the '*Verteidigungskonzept*' ('defence case') was put in quotation marks, thus signalling the Court's clear doubts about its existence.

With a more general perspective on the issue of delineating the permissible from the impermissible, the *Zündel* case is instructive because it illustrates the problem of courts usurping defence tactics. The Federal Court pays lip service to the the creed that courts should be reluctant to interfere with defence tactics. The Court even emphasises that this holds true in particular for delineating permissible and impermissible defence tactics. Simply calling defence conduct *verteidigungsfremd* is not a convincing legal argument. As Böhm has pointed out, it is not up to the court to assess the effectiveness of a defence strategy.[298]

This problem arises again with the doctrine of abuse of process rights, or *Rechtsmißbrauch*.[299] It is another way of sanctioning through direct measures, pitting defence rights and the administration of justice against each other. Therefore, delineating the permissible from the impermissible again becomes crucial for identifying abuse. It is preferable to carve out the impermissible according to to clear criteria, such as continous and significant non-compliance with court orders. The curtailing of evidence and other excursions into material defence rights carry the danger of the court encroaching on the margins of the professional judgement of counsel. This risk is smaller if courts operate along more formalised measures such as the prior setting of deadlines for trial proceedings.

F Conclusion on the German Model

Summing up, it seems fair to claim that German law emphasises the need for the effective and expeditious administration of justice and has various tools in place to respond to misconduct. Counsel misconduct is principally addressed by a number of rules of criminal law and a disciplinary regime where the criminal procedure takes primacy over the disciplinary regime. Further measures of an administrative nature exist but these do not affect disciplinary findings and may also prove helpful in safeguarding the trial. It needs to be noted, though, that they are not applied very often. Direct sanctioning is an option to courts in some cases but it is not used widely and is not available on a systematic basis.

[296] *Bundesgerichtshof*, 2 December 2008, 3 StR 203/08, Neue Zeitschrift für Strafrecht 2009, 692, para 12: counsel alleging prospects of a death penalty for the lay judges was held to constitute 'warnings' in nature rather than actual 'threats'. Apart from them being surreal, German courts and scholars hold it to be a constituent element of the latter element to the offence that the offender purports to hold the powers to realise the threat.

[297] ibid, paras 14–17.

[298] Böhm (n 295) 2373.

[299] See above, II.B.iii.a at 75–79.

The procedure for all these measures varies accordingly. Whereas criminal and disciplinary proceedings are similar and provide for typical guarantees of the criminal trial, other measures follow a more party-driven model. All procedures contain fundamental rights of counsel, among which are the right to be heard before the imposition of measures and the right of appeal to an independent judicial bench.

The German experience has shown that criminal sanctions are a reality. They are, however, soundly based in the general law. The same safeguards apply as in any other criminal case. Criminal proceedings are accompanied by corresponding rights which are discernable from constitutional law and correspond to what is mandated by international law. In contrast, disciplinary regulations have a much wider scope. The pertinent procedure is modelled after the criminal trial and entails fundamental guarantees. Both are therefore distinct but similar regimes. Under both, allegations are investigated ex post facto by independent prosecutors and adjudicated before independent bodies. Concerned judges are not involved in the proceedings. This is different for the direct measures mentioned above: *Sitzungspolizei* and the imposition of fees. Whereas it is understood that there may be a need for direct sanctioning as means of reacting immediately, it is reiterated that the court's powers of *Sitzungspolizei* do not apply to counsel.

III Legal Responses to Misconduct: United States

A The General Layout of the US System

Whereas the Constitutions of both Germany and the United States provide for a federalist system, this has much larger repercussions on criminal law and professional ethics in the United States than in Germany. The regulation of counsel in the United States relies much more on original judiciary powers, and statutory law governing litigation as well as professional rules can be found at the US federal and state level. The laws of the 50 states by their nature vary greatly. Federal rules purportedly offer some more uniformity as far as substance and procedure is concerned, although ethics vary, again, between federal courts.[300] Moreover, federal jurisdiction is relatively narrow and the practise of attorneys is regulated and happens primarily at the state level.

All of this points to one methodological problem: which jurisdiction or authority to rely on? The approach in response is usually a transjurisdictional one, such as that exemplified by the Restatement of the Law Governing Lawyers by the American Law Institute[301] or the model codifications of the American Bar

[300] JA McMorrow, 'The (F)Utility of Rules: Regulating Attorney Conduct in Federal Court Practice' (2005) 58 *Southern Methodist University Law Review* 3, 5.

[301] 'Restatement of the Law' (n 40) § 1, at 6–9; CW Wolfram, 'The Concept of a Restatement of the Law Governing Lawyers' (1987) 1 *Georgetown Journal of Legal Ethics* 195, 202.

Association (ABA). Such transjurisdictional work is particularly helpful as it maps out the entire law regarding the practice, going beyond a certain jurisdiction or narrower field such as professional ethics. The assumption is, though, that the underlying authority is similar enough to carve out reliable comparative findings.

The importance of the Restatement is probably quite limited,[302] although contrary arguments have been made.[303] Similarly, the ABA codifications are only a semi-authoritative source. They are principally 'model rules' as is apparent from their title. However, they have been adopted in one form or another in all but six states, of whom five (Illinois, New York, North Carolina, Oregon and Virginia) combine the Model Rules of Professional Conduct and the prior Code with only California having a system of its own.[304] The Model Rules of Professional Conduct have also been cited by federal courts and states which have not adopted them.[305] Smaller states seem to be more likely to adopt the model codifications as they are, but larger states with more resources have their own committees to modify them. Since the Restatement mostly[306] focuses on the enforceable law and since the ABA has been emulated a great deal, both seem good enough for comparative purposes, such as identifying general principles. Analysing an individual case – including matters of choice of law and its content – definitely requires a furthe look.

Despite these remaining uncertainties about the concretely applicable law, the general layout can be summarised as follows. Liability controls are subject to the 'normal rules of practice and procedure that govern litigation in state and federal courts'.[307] Suits may therefore fall under state or federal jurisdiction.[308] Similarly, both at the federal and the state level, governments have enacted and enforce legislation which can be ascribed regulatory effects, primarily criminal offences.[309] This kind of legislative regulation is typically not counsel specific, and little true legislation beyond criminal offences exists.

Most profession-specific rules in the United States emanating from institutional and disciplinary controls are grounded in the authority of the judiciary, not the legislative. In this, institutional controls depend on the pertinent (federal or state) institution before which counsel appears or acts. Disciplinary controls stem

302 Rotunda and Dzienkowski (n 41) § 1-4(a); RD Rotunda, 'Gauging the Impact of the Proposed Restatement of the Law Governing Lawyers' (1998) 9 *Professional Lawyer* 2. Another caveat would be that those instances of judicial reliance mainly happen with regard to substantive law, but not on issues of enforcement of attorney compliance.

303 S Martyn, 'Judicial Reliance on the Restatement (3d) of the Law Governing Lawyers' (1995) 2 *Professional Lawyer* 8, 9; DC Little, 'The Potential Impact of the Restatement (Third) of the Law Governing Lawyers' (1996) 25 *Colorado Lawyer* 83.

304 See R Zitrin and CM Langford, *Legal Ethics in the Practice of Law*, 2nd edn (New York, Matthew Bender & Co, 2001) xiii–ix; Hall (n 23) §§1:5, 1:7, 1:8. On California, see American Bar Association, *California Report on the Lawyer Regulation System* (2001); on New York, see New York State Bar Association, *Proposed Rules of Professional Conduct* (1 February 2008), which adopt the Model Rules.

305 McMorrow (n 300) 12; Wilkins (n 71) 801, fn 36.

306 They do nudge the law into a certain direction in unsettled areas. See Rotunda (n 302).

307 Wilkins (n 71) 807.

308 See below, III.B.iv at 140.

309 See below, III.B.ii at 124–29.

from the highest state courts, which licence lawyers, with little say from federal organs or the legislative in general.[310] The other important characteristic of institutional and disciplinary controls is that they show that the ultimate authority for regulating counsel is with the courts.[311]

Professional discipline has seen a century of history in the United States.[312] The first codification of professional rules by the ABA occurred with the Canons of Professional Ethics in 1908, at a time when a number of states had already enacted some statutory law on lawyers' duties or ethics codes.[313] It was from the 1960s onwards that lawyers became more regulated.[314] The Model Code of Professional Responsibility was adopted by the ABA's House of Delegates in 1969.[315] From 1977, an ABA commission, the 'Kutak Commission', evaluated the standards of the legal profession again.[316] This resulted in the more comprehensive Model Rules of Professional Conduct.[317] They were adopted by the House of Delegates in 1983. After amendments throughout the years following, a more comprehensive revision occurred in 2002 based on the work of the 'Ethics 2000 Commission' and the 'Commission on Multijurisdictional Practice'.[318]

Similar to Germany, all these developments indicate a change of legal ethics from custom – the latter often reflecting the values of the elitist Bars – to a regulated profession.[319] The ABA and other Bar Associations have tended to argue that enforcement should be left to disciplinary bodies.[320] Critics have been quick to

[310] See below, III.B.i.a at 114–15. This is in marked contrast to Germany where the BRAO is an act of the federal legislative. See above, II.A at 59–60.

[311] California is the only jurisdiction where discipline is regulated by statutory act, the Business and Professions Code (Chapter 4, Sections 6000–238). See below (n 313) and American Bar Association, *California Report* (n 304) 19 (Recommendation 1). Even then, this does not seem to abolish the principal authority of the judiary to regulate attorneys, see Section 6087. See also *In re Attorney Discipline System*, 19 Cal4th 582, 967 P2d 49, 79 CalRptr2d 836 (Supreme Court of California, 1998).

[312] See MM Devlin, 'Development of Lawyer Disciplinary Procedures in the United States' (1993–1994) 7 *Georgetown Journal of Legal Ethics* 911; CW Wolfram, 'Toward a History of the Legalization of American Legal Ethics – I. Origins' (2001) 8 *University of Chicago Law School Roundtable* 469; CW Wolfram, 'Toward a History of the Legalization of American Legal Ethics – II. The Modern Era' (2001–02) 15 *Georgetown Journal of Legal Ethics* 205; Zitrin and Langford (n 304); RD Rotunda, *Legal Ethics in a Nutshell*, 3rd edn (Eagan, Minn, Thomson/West, 2007) 4–8.

[313] American Bar Association, *Canons of Professional Ethics* (n 30) 685–713.

[314] Wolfram, 'II. The Modern Era' (n 312).

[315] American Bar Association, *Model Code of Professional Responsibility* (n 30); Rotunda (n 312) 4–5. It was made a 'Model Code' in 1978 for antitrust considerations.

[316] RJ Kutak, *Model Rules of Professional Conduct, Proposed Final Draft of May 30, 1981* (Commission on Evaluation of Professional Standards, May 30, 1981).

[317] WH Simon, 'Who Needs the Bar?: Professionalism without Monopoly' (2003) 30 *Florida State University Law Review* 639, and on this WB Wendel, 'Busting the Professional Trust: A Comment on William Simon's Ladd Lecture' (2002–03) 30 *Florida State University Law Review* 659; RC Cramton, 'Furthering Justice by Improving the Adversary System and Making Lawyers More Accountable' (2001–02) 70 *Fordham Law Review* 1599.

[318] See MC Love, 'The Revised ABA Model Rules of Professional Conduct: Summary of the Work of Ethics 2000' (2002) 15 *Georgetown Journal of Legal Ethics* 441; American Bar Association, *Client Representation in the 21st Century. Report of the Commission on Multijurisdictional Practice* (12 August 2002); Zitrin and Langford (n 304) ix–x.

[319] Zitrin and Langford (n 304) xi.

[320] MJ Powell, 'Professional Divestiture: The Cession of Responsibility for Lawyer Discipline' (1986) *American Bar Foundation Research Journal* 31, 34.

point out the problems with giving the Bar the monopoly of regulation, and they have advanced convincing arguments in favour of external regulation.[321] The US system as a whole may be lawyer-controlled, but it is certainly not self-regulation by lawyers. Although Bar associations may still argue that the source of regulation should be the profession itself, and although they produce and influence rules, the source is technically the highest court of the state which admits the attorney to practise.[322] In particular, courts claim original competence on admission and discipline of lawyers. This builds primarily on the concept of their 'inherent powers' to do so.[323]

The clearest recent enunciation of the issue of inherent powers would be *Chambers v Nasco*[324] in which a federal court had sanctioned the initial defendant, Chambers, who had sold his television station to Nasco, Inc.[325] He breached the contract and Nasco sued for specific performance. For dilatory and obstructionist tactics by Chambers along with others, including his lawyers, the court later imposed attorney's fees and expenses of approximately one million dollars, which were the costs that the other party had incurred in the litigation of the case and sanctions for filing an appeal in the matter.[326] Four lawyers were reprimanded, suspended or disbarred. Whereas some of the underlying misconduct was covered by statute, these statutory provisions could not account for all the monetary sanctions. Those rules either covered 'filings' only (Rule 11 of the Federal Rules of Procedure and Evidence) or 'attorneys' only (28 U.S. Code § 1927), but they were not broad enough in other respects. The court saw a base in its own 'inherent powers'. The Supreme Court affirmed this. The majority held (citations omitted):

> It has long been understood that '[c]ertain implied powers must necessarily result to our Courts of justice from the nature of their institution,' powers 'which cannot be

[321] CJ Whelan, 'Ethics Beyond the Horizon: Why Regulate the Global Practice of Law?' (2001) 34 *Vanderbilt Journal of Transnational Law* 931; TD Morgan, 'The Evolving Concept of Professional Responsibility' (1976–77) 90 *Harvard Law Review* 702. See also BH Barton, 'Why Do We Regulate Lawyers?: An Economic Analysis of the Justifications for Entry and Conduct Regulation' (2001) 33 *Arizona State Law Journal* 429; BH Barton, 'An Institutional Analysis of Lawyer Regulation: Who Should Control Lawyer Regulation – Courts, Legislatures or the Market?' (2003) 37 *Georgia Law Review* 1167. Critics have argued that the system of lawyer regulation as a whole tends to favour lawyers per se. See DL Rhode, 'Moral Character as a Professional Credential' (1985) 94 *Yale Law Journal* 491, 507; DL Rhode, *In the Interests of Justice: Reforming the Legal Profession* (Oxford, Oxford University Press, 2000) 117–84.

[322] Patterson and Metzloff (n 34) 57–60; CW Wolfram, *Modern Legal Ethics* (St Paul, Minn, West, 1986) § 2.2.1 at 22–23; § 2.3 at 37–38; § 2.4.2 at 42–45. See also below, III.B.i.a at 114.

[323] CW Wolfram, 'Lawyer Turf and Lawyer Regulation – The Role of the Inherent-Powers Doctrine' (1989–90) 12 *University of Arkansas at Little Rock Law Journal* 1; McMorrow (n 300) 19. From the case law, see *Ex parte Secombe* (n 39); *In re Snyder* (n 34); *U.S. v Williams*, 504 US 36, 112 SCt 1735, 118 LEd2d 352 (Supreme Court of the United States, 1992); *People ex rel. Karlin v Culkin* (n 34) *Richardson v Hamilton International Corporation* (n 39); *Flaksa v Little River Marine Const. Co* (n 39); *In re Quaid* (n 39); *Maryland State Bar Ass'n, Inc.v Agnew* (n 39).

[324] *Chambers v Nasco*, 501 US 32, 111 SCt 2123, 115 LEd2d 27, 59 USLW 4595, 19 FedRServ3d 817 (Supreme Court of the United States, 1991).

[325] *Nasco, Inc. v Calcasieu Television and Radio, Inc.*, 623 FSupp 1372 (United States District Court, W.D. Louisiana, 1985).

[326] *Nasco, Inc. v Calcasieu Television and Radio, Inc.*, 124 FRD 120 (United States District Court, W.D. Louisiana, 1989).

> dispensed with in a Court, because they are necessary to the exercise of all others.' For this reason, 'Courts of justice are universally acknowledged to be vested, by their very creation, with power to impose silence, respect, and decorum, in their presence, and submission to their lawful mandates.' These powers are 'governed not by rule or statute but by the control necessarily vested in courts to manage their own affairs so as to achieve the orderly and expeditious disposition of cases.' Prior cases have outlined the scope of the inherent power of the federal courts. For example, the Court has held that a federal court has the power to control admission to its bar and to discipline attorneys who appear before it. While this power 'ought to be exercised with great caution,' it is nevertheless 'incidental to all Courts.'[327]
>
> We discern no basis for holding that the sanctioning scheme of the statute and the rules displaces the inherent power to impose sanctions for the bad-faith conduct described above. These other mechanisms, taken alone or together, are not substitutes for the inherent power, for that power is both broader and narrower than other means of imposing sanctions. First, whereas each of the other mechanisms reaches only certain individuals or conduct, the inherent power extends to a full range of litigation abuses. At the very least, the inherent power must continue to exist to fill in the interstices. Even Justice Kennedy's dissent so concedes. Second, while the narrow exceptions to the American Rule effectively limit a court's inherent power to impose attorney's fees as a sanction to cases in which a litigant has engaged in bad-faith conduct or willful disobedience of a court's orders, many of the other mechanisms permit a court to impose attorney's fees as a sanction for conduct which merely fails to meet a reasonableness standard.[328]
>
> There is, therefore, nothing in the other sanctioning mechanisms or prior cases interpreting them that warrants a conclusion that a federal court may not, as a matter of law, resort to its inherent power to impose attorney's fees as a sanction for bad-faith conduct. This is plainly the case where the conduct at issue is not covered by one of the other sanctioning provisions. But neither is a federal court forbidden to sanction bad-faith conduct by means of the inherent power simply because that conduct could also be sanctioned under the statute or the Rules. A court must, of course, exercise caution in invoking its inherent power, and it must comply with the mandates of due process, both in determining that the requisite bad faith exists and in assessing fees. Furthermore, when there is bad-faith conduct in the course of litigation that could be adequately sanctioned under the Rules, the court ordinarily should rely on the Rules rather than the inherent power. But if in the informed discretion of the court, neither the statute nor the Rules are up to the task, the court may safely rely on its inherent power.[329]

This was criticised by the three-justice minority (Justice Kennedy, inter alia) on the grounds that the Court had distorted the rule-exception relationship between written and unwritten powers:

> Today's decision effects a vast expansion of the power of federal courts, unauthorized by Rule or statute. I have no doubt petitioner engaged in sanctionable conduct that

[327] *Chambers v Nasco* (n 324).

[328] ibid, 2134. Justice Scalia, in his Dissenting Opinion, does not view inherent powers limited to bad faith, but would not extend them to out-of-court conduct (2140–41). The latter is in line with the Kennedy dissent.

[329] ibid, 2135–36.

> warrants severe corrective measures. But our outrage at his conduct should not obscure the boundaries of settled legal categories. . . . The Court's . . . error lies in its failure to require reliance, when possible, on the panoply of express sanctioning provisions provided by Congress. . . . While the details of the Court's rule remain obscure, its general approach is clear: When express Rules and statutes provided by Congress do not reach the entirety of a litigant's bad-faith conduct, including conduct occurring before litigation commenced, a district court may disregard the requirements of otherwise applicable Rules and statutes and instead exercise inherent power to impose sanctions. The only limitation on this sanctioning authority appears to be a finding at some point of 'bad faith,' a standard the Court fails to define. This explanation of the permitted sphere of inherent powers to shift fees as a sanction for badfaith litigation conduct is as illegitimate as it is unprecedented.[330]
>
> By allowing courts to ignore express Rules and statutes on point, however, the Court treats inherent powers as the norm and textual bases of authority as the exception. . . . The Court has the presumption backwards. Inherent powers are the exception, not the rule, and their assertion requires special justification in each case. Like all applications of inherent power, the authority to sanction bad-faith litigation practices can be exercised only when necessary to preserve the authority of the court.[331]

The majority is also said to have been in error when extending the inherent powers to conduct which was not strictly speaking part of the litigation before the Court (ie, Chambers' breach of contract by trying to frustrate the sale):

> Based on this premise, the Court appears to disclaim that its holding reaches prelitigation conduct. . . . A court's inherent authority extends only to remedy abuses of the judicial process. By contrast, awarding damages for a violation of a legal norm, here the binding obligation of a legal contract, is a matter of substantive law . . . which must be defined either by Congress . . . or by the States . . . By exercising inherent power to sanction prelitigation conduct, the District Court exercised authority where Congress gave it none.[332]
>
> My discussion should not be construed as approval of the behavior of petitioner and his attorneys in this case. Quite the opposite. Our Rules permit sanctions because much of the conduct of the sort encountered here degrades the profession and disserves justice. District courts must not permit this abuse and must not hesitate to give redress through the Rules and statutes prescribed. It may be that the District Court could have imposed the full million dollar sanction against petitioner through reliance on Federal Rules and statutes, as well as on a proper exercise of its inherent authority. But we should remand here because a federal court must decide cases based on legitimate sources of power. I would reverse the Court of Appeals with instructions to remand to the District Court for a reassessment of sanctions consistent with the principles here set forth.[333]

It flows from this that the minority did not speak out against the existence and availability of inherent powers per se. According to their view, importance had to

[330] ibid, 2141–42 (Justice Kennedy, Rehnquist, Souter dissenting).
[331] ibid, 2143.
[332] ibid, 2148.
[333] ibid, 2149.

be placed on two points: (i) statutory and other written provisions should not be circumvented by way of inherent powers and; (ii) the latter should be confined to the authority of the court over the immediate litigation before it. Nonetheless, it does not doubt the legitimacy of inherent powers.

Essentially, two lines of arguments have been advanced against original powers of courts. The first line of argument against 'inherent' judical powers warns against the discretionary element and the potential for abuse. Some form of discretion attaches to the most judicial functions, however, and even desirable in regulating conduct.[334] The second one, the potential for abuse, is hinted at by the first point of the Kennedy dissent in *Nasco v Chambers* that it should be on authorisation by the legislative that courts act. The assumption of broad inherent powers is bound to be at odds with this presumed institutional set-up under the separation of powers doctrine if it sweepingly covers procedural lawmaking, litigation management and sanctioning.[335] If the true and exclusive function of the judiciary is to adjudicate a case and to be independent from the other branches of government, this may imply indispensable powers for the courts 'relating to the efficiency and reliability of the judicial process'[336] which are necessary if they would otherwise be unable to perform this function. Powers should be viewed more critically if they are just generally beneficial because they are deemed to help courts in functioning effectively.

Courts are little awed by this scholarship. This becomes clear from the courts' approach towards the relationship of the judiciary and the legislative in the area of contempt. It is recalled that the basis of contempt lies exactly with the inherent powers to safeguard the administration of justice. That contempt powers only flow from statute (and thus declaring any common law base inapplicable) has definitely remained an exception.[337] In the exercise of their contempt powers, courts do recognise that they are bound by the limitations of the constitution, just like the other branches of government,[338] but they essentially see it as a power that cannot be taken away by the legislative. Contempt statutes are thus said to be only

[334] McMorrow (n 300) 45.

[335] RJ Pushaw, 'The Inherent Powers of Federal Courts and the Structural Constitution' (2001) 86 *Iowa Law Review* 735, 843 (with a historical analysis of English and American law, 799–843); FC Zacharias and BA Green, 'Federal Court Authority to Regulate Lawyers: A Practice in Search of a Theory' (2003) 56 *Vanderbilt Law Review* 1303, 1321. See also GP Joseph, *Sanctions: The Federal Law of Litigation Abuse*, 4th edn (Albany, NY, Matthew Bender, 2008) § 26(A)(1) at 395, on categories of inherent powers claimed by courts (core inherent powers; those powers 'necessary to the exercise of all others'; those reasonably useful to achieve justice).

[336] SS Beale, 'Reconsidering Supervisory Power in Criminal Cases: Constitutional and Statutory Limits on the Authority of the Federal Courts' (1984) 84 *Columbia Law Review* 1433, 1464.

[337] Tennessee seems to be this exception, *State v Turner*, 914 SW2d 951 (Court of Criminal Appeals of Tennessee, 1995), relying on *In re Hickey*, 149 Tenn 344, 258 SW 417 (Supreme Court of Tennessee, 1924); *Scott v State*, 1 Cates 390, 109 Tenn 390, 71 SW 824 (Supreme Court of Tennessee, 1902); *State v Galloway*, 45 Tenn 326, 1868 WL 2122 (Supreme Court of Tennessee, 1868).

[338] *Ex parte Hudgings*, 249 US 378, 39 SCt 337, 63 LEd 656 (Supreme Court of the United States, 1919); *Graham v Jones*, 200 La 137, 7 So2d 688 (Supreme Court of Louisiana, 1942); *47th & State Currency Exchange, Inc.v B. Coleman Corp.*, 371 NE2d 294 (Appellate Court of Illinois, 1978); *Carroll v State*, 350 So2d 723 (Court of Criminal Appeals of Alabama, 1977).

in recognition of prelegislative powers.[339] Although it is an inherent power of the courts, many judiciaries accept that contempt powers can be reasonably regulated by the legislative.[340] Some have held that legislative attempts are not binding on the courts, but that as an issue of comity, courts should accept them and only invoke inherent powers if the statute is inadequate.[341] Lastly, a number of courts firmly reject the idea that they can be bound by the legislative,[342] although it is sometimes conceded that the legislative can provide for rules of practice and procedure.

Thus, court powers exist, and the inherent powers to protect their administration of justice are arguably just one conceivable basis. With supervisory powers over the adjudication of criminal justice, courts can address misconduct through procedure. More controversially, the authority to admit lawyers may be used to prevent prospective misconduct. And finally, the use of local rules may be construed by the courts to use them as a 'general ethics authority'.[343]

[339] *Young v U.S. ex rel. Vuitton et Fils S.A.*, 481 US 787, 107 SCt 2124 (Supreme Court of the United States, 1987); *City of Gary v Major*, 822 NE2d 165 (Supreme Court of Indiana, 2005); *Walker v Bentley*, 678 So2d 1265 (Supreme Court of Florida, 1996); *In re Doe*, 96 Hawaii 73, 26 P3d 562 (Supreme Court of Hawaii, 2001); *Cross Co. v United Automobile, Aircraft and Agricultural Implement Workers of America, Local 155*, 377 Mich 202, 139 NW2d 694 (Supreme Court of Michigan, 1966); *Beach v Beach*, 79 Ohio App 397, 74 NE2d 130 (Court of Appeals of Ohio, 1946).

[340] *Frisch v Henrichs*, 304 Wis2d 1, 736 NW2d 85 (Supreme Court of Wisconsin, 2007); *LeMay v Leander*, 92 Hawaii 614, 994 P2d 546 (Supreme Court of Hawaii, 2000); *U.S.v Kouri-Perez*, 187 F3d 1 (United States Court of Appeals, First Circuit, 1999); *Christensen v Iowa District Court for Polk County*, 578 NW2d 675 (Supreme Court of Iowa, 1998); *Sommer v Sommer*, 947 P2d 512 (Supreme Court of Oklahoma, 1997); *In re McKinney*, 70 Cal2d 8, 447 P2d 972, 73 CalRptr 580 (Supreme Court of California, 1968); *Nicholas v Commonwealth*, 186 Va 315, 42 SE2d 306 (Supreme Court of Appeals of Virginia, 1947); *Burdett v Commonwealth*, 103 Va 838, 48 SE 878 (Supreme Court of Appeals of Virginia, 1904), *State v Cameron*, 140 Wash 101, 248 P 408 (Supreme Court of Washington, 1926) (but see *Deskins v Waldt*, 499 P2d 206 (Supreme Court of Washington, 1972)); *Sanders v Laird*, 865 So2d 649 (District Court of Appeal of Florida, 2004); *Frost v Lotspeich*, 30 P3d 1185 (Court of Appeals of Oregon, 2001); *Hiber v Creditors Collection Service of Lincoln County, Inc.*, 961 P2d 898 (Court of Appeals of Oregon, 1998).

[341] *Continental Ins. Companies v Bayless & Roberts, Inc.*, 548 P2d 398 (Supreme Court of Alaska, 1976); *In re M.B.*, 101 WashApp 425, 3 P3d 780 (Court of Appeals of Washington, 2000).

[342] *State v Price*, 672 A2d 893 (Supreme Court of Rhode Island, 1996); *In re Interest of Krystal P.*, 251 Neb 320, 557 NW2d 26 (Supreme Court of Nebraska, 1996); *Doe v Commonwealth*, 396 Mass 421, 486 NE2d 698 (Supreme Judicial Court of Massachusetts, 1985), citing *In re Opinions of the Justices*, 314 Mass 767, 49 NE2d 252 (Supreme Judicial Court of Massachusetts, 1943); *State v Local Union 5760, United Steelworkers of America*, 172 Ohio St 75, 173 NE2d 331 (Supreme Court of Ohio, 1961); *McDougallv Sheridan*, 23 Idaho 191, 128 P 954 (Supreme Court of Idaho, 1913); *State v Morrill* 16 Ark 384, 1855 WL 607 (Supreme Court of Arkansas, 1855).

[343] Zacharias and Green (n 335) 1310. Not even the supposedly casual pace of life in the South Pacific is spared. See United States District Court for the Northern Mariana Islands, *Civil Local Rules* (Rev. (01/04) (As Amended Through 10/07), 1 January 2004), 'LR 83.3 – Practice in this Court; Dress Code. . . . All attorneys appearing in open court shall be suitably dressed. Minimum acceptable dress for male practitioners shall consist of a dress shirt, necktie, dress slacks, socks and shoes. Minimum acceptable dress for female practitioners shall consist of a dress, slacks, or skirt and blouse and shoes. The court may refuse to hear attorneys whose appearance does not conform to this Rule'. The Criminal Local Rules do not provide specifics on attorney attire. An example where criminal proceedings succumb to a laxer procedural standard than in civil cases? On the long history of the debate on professional obligations of German attorneys to wear robe and tie in the courtroom, see above, II.C.iii at 91 (n 209).

Summing up this first attempt at introducing the general outline for the regulation of counsel, it seems fair to say that all the conceivable controls exist within the US context. Disciplinary controls build on codes often modelled after the ABA Model Rules.[344] Institutional controls are arguably the most important, in particular the inherent powers claimed by courts.[345] In addition to those, legislative controls, such as criminal offences, are in place. Finally, liability controls exist but are of little relevance.[346]

B Specific Measures against Counsel Misconduct

i Professional Discipline

a The Applicable Disciplinary Regimes and Competent Authorities

Discipline is principally the domain of the highest state courts, but federal courts have disciplinary powers as well.[347] These are, however, generally more limited to their own litigation process and defer the seminal powers to admit and regulate to the states.[348] In principle, federal courts and agencies have disciplinary powers in connection with their business which is independent from what other institutions, such as states or agencies, may have as well.[349] The primary responsibility is with the state (and their respective Bars).[350]

The backbone of professional discipline in the United States is therefore the state system. The systems between states vary widely in resources for, and intensity of, enforcing professional rules this way.[351] For example,Wyoming employs a

[344] See also below, III.B.i at 114–24.
[345] For more details see below, III.iii.B.a and b at 130–37.
[346] Below, III.B.iv at 139–41.
[347] *In re Snyder* (n 34).
[348] See *In re Ruffalo*, 390 US 544, 88 SCt 1222, 20 LEd2d 117 (Supreme Court of the United States, 1968); *Sanders v Laird* (n 340); Hall (n 23) § 32:4; Zacharias and Green (n 335) 1324. Federal court discipline may therefore be more important for federal prosecutors, ie, government lawyers. See also 'Restatement of the Law' (n 40) § 1 d.
[349] *Gadda v Ashcroft*, 377 F3d 934 (United States Court of Appeals, Ninth Circuit, 2004); *Theard v U.S.* (n 39); *In re Abrams*, 521 F2d 1094 (United States Court of Appeals, Third Circuit, 1975); *In re Surrick*, 338 F3d 224 (United States Court of Appeals, Third Circuit, 2003). Government lawyers may be subject to discipline by their employers such as the Department of Justice or the JAG corps. See, however, 28 U.S. Code 530(B) (the 'McDade Amendment'), and on it GB LeDonne, 'Revisiting the McDade Amendment: Finding the Appropriate Solution for the Federal Government Lawyer' (2007) 44 *Harvard Journal on Legislation* 231.
[350] *Middlesex County Ethics Committeev Garden State Bar Association*, 57 US 423, 102 SCt 2515, 73 LEd2d 116, 434 (Supreme Court of the United States, 1982); *Mississippi Bar v Shah*, 749 So2d 1047 (Supreme Court of Mississippi, 1999). The authority of state Bars beyond regulating the profession or improving the quality of legal services is limited. Since membership is mandatory, it violates the member attorneys' right to free speech under the First Amendment to lobby just any cause. See *Keller v State Bar of California*, 496 US 1, 110 SCt 2228, 110 LEd2d 1 (Supreme Court of the United States, 1990).
[351] For 2007 figures, see American Bar Association, *Standing Committee on Professional Discipline, Survey on Lawyer Discipline Systems* (2007), Chart VIII. In California, lawyers are regulated by the state, not the supreme court, see above, III.A at 107, 108 (n 311).

disciplinary counsel staff of two, Florida and the various sections in New York of between 140 and 150 and California boasts about 240 people. Critical accounts call the existing administration flawed and relative. Common points of criticism are that rules are under-enforced, that cases are held pending for a long time, that the outcome is lawyer-friendly, that quite disparate outcomes occur in different states and that plea bargaining, secrecy and too many due process rights affect the process.[352]

Efforts to uniformise and federalise have been suggested but discipline has been ferociously guarded by the states as their privilege.[353] It is not uncommon for attorneys to be either admitted in more than one state, or to be admitted to the Bar of one or more federal courts in addition to their home state Bar. If not permanently admitted, attorneys also appear in a foreign jurisdiction *pro hac vice* (for one particular occasion).[354] Otherwise, attorneys run the risk of unauthorised practice.[355] Foreign lawyers have been held accountable for unauthorised practice, though some courts may acknowledge a 'limited practice exception' and the supervision by a licensed lawyer.[356] The potential exposure to the professional standards of more than one jurisdiction can lead to disparities and even contradictions.[357] Two different questions arise in these multijurisdictional settings as becomes clear from the disctinction drawn on sub-rules (a) and (b) of Rule 8.5 ('Disciplinary Authority; Choice Of Law') of the Model Rules of Professional Conduct:[358]

[352] MS Frisch, 'No Stone Left Unturned: The Failure of Attorney Self-Regulation in the District of Columbia' (2004–05) 18 *Georgetown Journal of Legal Ethics* 325; J Leubsdorf, 'Legal Malpractice and Professional Responsibility' (1995) 84 *Rutgers Law Review* 101, 103; JM Kraus, 'Attorney Discipline Systems: Improving Public Perception and Increasing Efficacy' (2000–01) 84 *Marquette Law Review* 273, 285, LC Levin, 'The Case for Less Secrecy in Lawyer Discipline' (2007) 20 *The Georgetown Journal of Legal Ethics* 1, 1; LC Levin, 'The Emperor's Clothes and Other Tales about the Standards for Imposing Lawyer Discipline Sanctions' (1998–99) 48 *American University Law Review* 1, 1. See for statistics, American Bar Association, *Standing Committee on Professional Discipline* (n 351), in particular Chart V.

[353] FC Zacharias, 'Federalizing Legal Ethics' (1994) 73 *Texas Law Review* 335.

[354] Rotunda and Dzienkowski (n 41) § 5.5-2.

[355] See, eg, *Birbrower, Montalbano, Condon & Frank v Superior Court*, 17 Cal4th 119, 949 P2d 1, 70 CalRptr2d 304 (Supreme Court of California, 1998), see S Poser, 'Multijurisdictional Practice for a Multijurisdictional Profession' (2002–03) 81 *Nebraska Law Review* 1379, 1381; Knöfel, 'Anwalts-Kollisionsrecht' (n 254) 16.

[356] RA Brand, 'Professional Responsibility in a Transnational Transactions Practice' (1997–98) 17 *Journal of Law and Commerce* 301, 315.

[357] These two competing jurisdictions can be states, but also a state and a federal court, or a state and military jurisdiction. See CC Ward, 'Law of Choice: Implementation of ABA Model Rule 8.5' (2005–06) 30 *Journal of the Legal Profession* 173; Poser (n 355); GJ Ritts, 'Professional Responsibility and the Conflict of Laws' (1993) 18 *Journal of the Legal Profession* 17, 91; Zacharias and Green (n 335); AR Mashburn, 'A Clockwork Orange Approach to Legal Ethics: A Conflicts Perspective on the Regulation of Lawyers by Federal Courts' (1994–95) 8 *Georgetown Journal of Legal Ethics* 473; D Hricik and J Ellis, 'Disparities in Legal Ethical Standards between State and Federal Judicial Systems: An Analysis and a Critique' (1999–2000) 13 *Georgetown Journal of Legal Ethics* 577; LS Mullenix, 'Multiforum Federal Practice: Ethics and *Erie*' (1995–96) 9 *Georgetown Journal of Legal Ethics* 89; CP Dungan, 'Avoiding "Catch-22s": Approaches to Resolve Conflicts between Military and State Bar Rules of Professional Responsibility' (2005–06) 30 *Journal of the Legal Profession* 31.

[358] See for details MH Aultman, 'A Post Conference Reflection: Does Amended Model Rule 8.5 Help Anyone?' (1995) 36 *South Texas Law Review* 1055, 1060; MC Daly, 'Resolving Ethical Conflicts in

(a) Disciplinary Authority. A lawyer admitted to practice in this jurisdiction is subject to the disciplinary authority of this jurisdiction, regardless of where the lawyer's conduct occurs. A lawyer not admitted in this jurisdiction is also subject to the disciplinary authority of this jurisdiction if the lawyer provides or offers to provide any legal services in this jurisdiction. A lawyer may be subject to the disciplinary authority of both this jurisdiction and another jurisdiction for the same conduct.

(b) Choice of Law. In any exercise of the disciplinary authority of this jurisdiction, the rules of professional conduct to be applied shall be as follows:

(1) for conduct in connection with a matter pending before a tribunal, the rules of the jurisdiction in which the tribunal sits, unless the rules of the tribunal provide otherwise; and

(2) for any other conduct, the rules of the jurisdiction in which the lawyer's conduct occurred, or, if the predominant effect of the conduct is in a different jurisdiction, the rules of that jurisdiction shall be applied to the conduct. A lawyer shall not be subject to discipline if the lawyer's conduct conforms to the rules of a jurisdiction in which the lawyer reasonably believes the predominant effect of the lawyer's conduct will occur.

The prior issue under (a) is thus which state or court has the competence, ie, the jurisdiction, to discipline. If two or more have jurisdiction, the issue would be one of choice of laws since the respective rules may be in conflict.[359] As to the first issue, admitted counsel are always subject to the rules of their own Bar. Also covered are out-of-state attorneys because states may have an interest, although this makes it necessary to refine the concept of when do attorneys actually perform 'significant in-state activity'.[360]

The flexible regime under (b) is relatively new. A detailed choice-of-law section was ony added in 1993, loosening the static rule of forum law which existed prior to that.[361] According to the initial version, the rules of a court's jurisdiction gov-

Multijurisdictional Practice – Is Model Rule 8.5 the Answer, an Answer, or No Answer at All?' (1995) 36 *South Texas Law Review* 715, 787; Daly (ibid) 793; JL Rensberger, 'Jurisdiction, Choice of Law, and the Multistate Attorney' (1995) 36 *South Texas Law Review* 799, 802. See also the critcism of Daly and Rensberger by AE Roach, 'The Virtues of Clarity: The ABA's New Choice of Law Rule for Legal Ethics' (1995) 36 *South Texas Law Review* 907, 928 and FC Zacharias, 'A Nouveau Realist's View of Interjurisdictional Practice Rules' (1995) 36 *South Texas Law Review* 1037, 938.

[359] Enforcement cannot be extra-territorial. States can only reprimand or disbar for themselves; R Kane et al, *Corpus Juris Secundum, Attorney & Client* (St Paul, Minn, Thomson/West, 2008) § 122. Discipline can be reciprocal, though, and thus be based on foreign adjudication. See below, III.D.iii at 162–63, and on the ICC ch 4, II.C at 298–300.

[360] See CW Wolfram, 'Expanding State Jurisdiction to Regulate Out-of-State Lawyers' (2001–02) 30 *Hofstra Law Review* 1015.

[361] See American Bar Association, *Client Representation in the 21st Century* (n 318) 73 (Appendix C). Many states still subscribe to a strict forum rule. See Rule 8.05 of the *Texas Disciplinary Rules of Professional Conduct* (Tex. Govt Code Ann., tit. 2, subtit. G, app. (Vernon Supp. 1995)) and similarly Rule 4-8.5 of the *Rules Regulating The Florida Bar, Chapter 4. Rules Of Professional Conduct* (Supreme Court of Florida, 2008). Outlining the general problem of a forum law approach as well as discussing possible reform on state level: CA Needham, 'Multijurisdictional Practice Regulations Governing Attorneys Conducting a Transactional Practice' (2003) 2003 *University of Illinois Law Review* 1331. On the implications of strict adherence to forum rules (although disqualification and not disciplinary cases), see *Image Technical Services, Inc.v Eastman Kodak Co.*, 820 FSupp 1212 (United States District Court, N.D. California, 1993) and *In re Mortgage & Realty Trust*, 195 BR 740 (United States Bankruptcy

erned. For other conduct outside one's clear home jurisdiction, the 'admitting jurisdiction in which the lawyer principally practices' was given preference, but an exception was made if a 'predominant effect' occurred in a different licensor jurisdiction. This solution was unclear and maybe too narrow.[362] It was nevertheless an improvement on the previous static rule, although it did not solve the concurrent authority of federal courts and administrative authorities.[363] Giving priority to the specific set of rules of a certain court was meant to be limited to American courts.[364] In 2002, however, the use of counsel's principal jurisdiction was discontinued, arriving at the current use of conduct/effect criteria. Furthermore, Comment 7 to the current Models Rules makes it clear that transnational practice also allows for choice-of-law under sub-rule (b).[365]

In the absence of harmonisation of professional standards or conflicts rules, state-to-state as well as state-to-federal conflicts will be inevitable. Many American lawyers practice in more than one jurisdiction, a phenomenon that recurs for international lawyers.[366] Rule 8.5(b) of the Model Rules offers a good lead. It makes sense to point to an international tribunal if the attorney's conduct is chiefly in relation to litigation before it, but it is unclear to what extent this deference will be accepted by national states. Within the ICC framework there is some progress in formulating international rules and how to treat cases of misconduct before international courts, and Rule 8.5 has merit in pointing to the tribunal before which litigation takes place.[367]

Conflicts of laws are not unique to the United States or to professional discipline. They may not arise for criminal offences but again for legal malpractice.[368] Morever, it seems a general experience which European lawyers likewise face.[369]

Court, C.D. California, 1996) discussed by RM Jarvis, 'Cross-Border Legal Practice and Ethics Rule 4-8.5 Why Greater Guidance Is Needed' (1998) 72 *Florida Bar Journal* 59. In both cases, California judges applied California conflict-of-interest rules to foreign lawyers (from Hong Kong and otherwise internationally, and from Missouri/DC).

[362] Rensberger (n 358) 836; Aultman (n 358). For an attempt to refine the notion of predominant effect and against uniformity, see S Felleman, 'Ethical Dilemmas and the Multistate Lawyer: A Proposed Amendment to the Choice-of-Law Rule in the Model Rules of Professional Conduct' (1995) 95 *Columbia Law Review* 1500. See further EA Carr and A Van Fleet, 'Professional Responsibility Law in Multijurisdictional Litigation: Across the Country and across the Street' (1995) 36 *South Texas Law Review* 859; GB Adams, 'Reflections on the Reaction to Proposed Rule 8.5: Consensus of Failure' (1995) 36 *South Texas Law Review* 1101.

[363] Roach (n 358) 929 (on the 1993 rule).

[364] D Luban, 'Friendly Amendment to Model Rule 8.5' (1995) 36 *South Texas Law Review* 1015.

[365] See DF Vagts, 'Professional Responsibility in Transborder Practice: Conflict and Resolution' (1999–2000) 13 *Georgetown Journal of Legal Ethics* 677, 690, had already suggested an analogy in transborder cases. M Majumdar, 'Ethics in the International Arena: The Need for Clarification' (1995) 8 *Georgetown Journal of Legal Ethics* 439, fn 12, has also used international and transnational interchangeably (writing on the pre-2002 amendments).

[366] See ch 4, I.A and B at 286–89. See also JL Krystinik, 'The Complex Web of Conflicting Disciplinary Standards in International Litigation' (2003) 38 *Texas International Law Journal* 815.

[367] See ch 4, I.B at 287–89.

[368] Vagts (n 365) 694. Criminal law knows not conflict of laws doctrine, see above (n 405).

[369] See ch 4, I.B at 289.

Regardless of the applicable substantive law for setting professional standards, it will of course be the *lex fori* of the disciplinary body which governs the procedure before it. The Model Rules of Professional Conduct set out the substantive law, whereas the ABA model codification for procedure is the Model Rules of Disciplinary Enforcement.[370] As a rough generalisation, the Model Rules of Disciplinary Enforcement propose a model under which a disciplinary counsel handles complaint. The latter thus go through a screening process with the possibility of an informal resolution. Otherwise, counsel makes recommendations – including alternatives to discipline – to a disciplinary board. This body reviews the case and decides on possible sanctions which are then again subject to review by a court.

b Grounds for Discipline and General Requirements

Whatever the applicable lawyer code, violating rules of the governing code is always considered misconduct and a ground for discipline. Sanctionable offences are thus defined in reliance on the respective codes of conduct. This is broadened, however, by extending discipline to forms other than direct violation or by incorporating further standards outside the code as a base for discipline.[371] For this reason, professional discipline in the United States relies on general clauses, as identified from Germany, and which are also relevant to the ICC's regime.[372] The problem is not as exacerbate for US discipline as it would be for Germany, as the United States – unlike Germany – is not a quasi-criminal regime but more regulatory and therefore allows for relaxations of the applicable standards.[373]

Rule 8.4 of the ABA Model Rules of Professional Conduct and Rule 9.(A) of the ABA Model Rules of Lawyer Disciplinary Enforcement serve as good examples for the use of specific standards and more general clauses at the same time:

> Rule 8.4. Misconduct
>
> It is professional misconduct for a lawyer to:
>
> (a) violate or attempt to violate the Rules of Professional Conduct, knowingly assist or induce another to do so, or do so through the acts of another;
> (b) commit a criminal act that reflects adversely on the lawyer's honesty, trustworthiness or fitness as a lawyer in other respects;
> (c) engage in conduct involving dishonesty, fraud, deceit or misrepresentation;
> (d) engage in conduct that is prejudicial to the administration of justice;
> (e) state or imply an ability to influence improperly a government agency or official or to achieve results by means that violate the Rules of Professional Conduct or other law; or

[370] Disciplinary procedure will be dealt with in detail later, see below, III.C.i at 142–45.

[371] Restatement of the Law' (n 40) § 5. See also Arts 31, 32 ICC Code (ch 3, II.A.iv at 193–94) and Section 113 of the German BRAO (above, II.B.i.a at 62–63).

[372] See above, II.B.ia at 63–65, for Germany, and ch 3, II.A.iv.b at 194–201.

[373] Below, C.i at 144–45.

(f) knowingly assist a judge or judicial officer in conduct that is a violation of applicable rules of judicial conduct or other law.

Rule 9. Grounds For Discipline/Lesser Misconduct

1. Grounds for Discipline. It shall be a ground for discipline for a lawyer to:
   (1) violate or attempt to violate the [State Rules of Professional Conduct], or any other rules of this jurisdiction regarding professional conduct of lawyers;
   (2) engage in conduct violating applicable rules of professional conduct of another jurisdiction;
   (3) willfully violate a valid order of the court or the board imposing discipline, willfully fail to appear before disciplinary counsel for admonition pursuant to Rule 10(A)(5), willfully fail to comply with a subpoena validly issued under Rule 14, or knowingly fail to respond to a lawful demand from a disciplinary authority, except that this rule does not require disclosure of information otherwise protected by applicable rules relating to confidentiality.
2. Lesser Misconduct. Lesser misconduct is conduct that does not warrant a sanction restricting the respondent's license to practice law. Conduct shall not be considered lesser misconduct if any of the following considerations apply:
   (1) the misconduct involves the misappropriation of funds;
   (2) the misconduct results in or is likely to result in substantial prejudice to a client or other person;
   (3) the respondent has been publicly disciplined in the last three years;
   (4) the misconduct is of the same nature as misconduct for which the respondent has been disciplined in the last five years;
   (5) the misconduct involves dishonesty, deceit, fraud, or misrepresentation by the respondent;
   (6) the misconduct constitutes a 'serious crime' as defined in Rule 19(C); or
   (7) the misconduct is part of a pattern of similar misconduct.

As can be adduced from this, different sources of law can actually lead to disciplinany action. Today, the starting point will always be the pertinent code of professional conduct. Many provisions in these codes are relatively clear-cut, and it will thus be fairly simple to determine the necessary elements of an offence which have to be established to prove violation of the rule. On the other hand, this is much less clear for misconduct under sub-rules (b)–(d) of Rule 8.4 of the Models Rules of Professional Conduct ('criminal act that reflects adversely on the lawyer's honesty, trustworthiness or fitness as a lawyer in other respects', 'dishonesty, fraud, deceit or misrepresentation', 'prejudicial to the administration of justice').[374] Even single provisions within a code may contain rather general clauses which make them vague.

It needs to be stressed that the codifications in the United States have, however, seen a development towards more and more specific rules. The traditional standard for misconduct before the 1908 Canons had been simply 'unbecoming a

[374] See *Grievance Administrator v Fried*, 388 Mich 711 (Michigan Supreme Court, 1972) and *Grievance Administrator v Fried*, 456 Mich 234 (Michigan Supreme Court, 1997); SJ Ott, 'Professional Responsibility 1997–1998, Annual Survey of Michigan Law' (1999–2000) 45 *Wayne Law Review* 1127, 1143.

lawyer'.[375] Reliance on specific provisions began with these Canons. The Model Code of Professional Responsibility of 1969 explicitly drew a distinction between 'Disciplinable Rules' (DR) and 'Ethical Considerations' (EC).[376] Both sorts of provisions were grouped under nine Canons which were said – according to the Code's 'Preliminary Statement' – to 'embody the general concepts from which the Ethical Consideration and the Disciplinary Rules are derived'. The Model Code of Professional Responsibility goes on to say that

> [t]he Ethical Considerations are aspirational in character and represent the objectives toward which every member of the profession should strive. They constitute a body of principles upon which the lawyer can rely for guidance in many specific situations. The Disciplinary Rules, unlike the Ethical Considerations, are mandatory in character.

Despite this clear-cut scheme, the DR themselves contained provisions which can only be described as vague[377] (and which are repeated in the Model Code of Conduct):

> DR 1-102 Misconduct.
>
> (A) A lawyer shall not: . . .
> (5) Engage in conduct that is prejudicial to the administration of justice.
> (6) Engage in any other conduct that adversely reflects on his fitness to practice law.
>
> DR 7-106 Trial Conduct. . . .
>
> (C) In appearing in his professional capacity before a tribunal, a lawyer shall not: . . .
> (6) Engage in undignified or discourteous conduct which is degrading to a tribunal.

Occasionally, courts have even cited mere section titles within the Code, such as Canon 9 ('A Lawyer Should Avoid Even the Appearance of Impropriety') to establish a breach of professional standards.[378] This open-textured language in the codes in combination with lax construction has led to criticism by scholars but has withstood scrutiny on void for vagueness or due process challenges.[379] Among

[375] 'Restatement of the Law' (n 40) § 5, Comment c.

[376] American Bar Association, *Model Code of Professional Responsibility* (n 30) and above, III.A (n 315). See also JP Tomain and BG Watts, 'Between Law and Virtue' (2003) 71 *University of Cincinnati Law Review* 585, 589.

[377] Wolfram (n 322) 87.

[378] Rotunda and Dzienkowski (n 41) § 1-2(b), at 13, calls this phrase a 'favorite of some courts', in particular for conflicts of interests. See RD Rotunda, 'Alleged Conflicts of Interest because of the "Appearance of Impropriety"' (2005) 33 *Hofstra Law Review* 1141.

[379] Wolfram (n 322) 85–88; SJ Levine, 'Taking Ethics Codes Seriously: Broad Ethics Provisions and Unenumerated Ethical Obligations in a Comparative Hermeneutic Framework' (2003) 77 *Tulane Law Review* 527, 551, noting, inter alia, that courts often point to the specific legal skills of lawyers and use the standard of the 'reasonable attorney' to establish sufficient notice; 'Restatement of the Law' (n 40) § 5, Reporter's Note to Comment c; *In re West*, 805 P2d 351 (Supreme Court of Alaska, 1991); *In re Anderson*, 795 P2d 64 (Supreme Court of Kansas, 1990), cert. denied; *Anderson v Supreme Court of Kansas*, 498 US 1095, 111 SCt 985, 112 LEd2d 1069 (Supreme Court of the United States, 1991); *In re Stuhff*, 837 P2d 853 (Supreme Court of Nevada, 1992); *Matter of Holtzman*, 78 NY2d 184, 577 NE2d 30, 573 NYS2d 39 (Court of Appeals of New York, 1991), cert. Denied; *Holtzman v Grievance Committee*

the Rules in the current body of Model Rules itself, all are now in principle of a binding nature.[380] Some rules use 'may', though, which vests counsel with discretion. Finally, comments to the Rules are used to provide additional explanation and guidance, similar to the EC under the Model Code.

It has been noted by scholars that including permissive and aspirational rules in a code may be well justified, for the reasons of the general difficulty of only drafting bright-line rules in the first place and that professional decisions may often be of a controversial nature anyway, and should thus involve the exercise of discretion.[381] Stressing this need for general rules in professional regulation, it could even be argued that these are of normative and practical utility.[382] If discipline can only be based on disciplinable provisions which create actual obligations, there will always be the issue of distinguishing one from the other. Moreover, some provisions are more or less disciplinable according to their own wording but are general in a way that raises doubt as to whether they contain a clearly identifiable duty. Both seem to be common problems of all the disciplinary systems under examination.[383] As a rule of interpretation, general clauses or aspirational considerations cannot supersede more specific provisions.[384] In other words: a duty should be derived, and often can be derived from a disciplinary rule, even though the particular prohibition might be expressed better in one of the ethical considerations.[385]

Whatever the breached rule, it often contains a mental element. This is apparent from the wording of some of the specific provisions throughout the Model Rules as well as the definitions of misconduct and grounds of discipline in Rule 8.4 of the Model Rules and Rule 9 of the Model Rules of Disciplinary Enforcement. The categories used largely resemble those for criminal offences.[386] Some Rules explicitly require knowledge.[387] A similarly high mental threshold flows from wording such as 'dishonesty', 'fraud', 'deceit' in Rule 8.4(c) or 'wilfully' in Rule

For Tenth Judicial District, 502 US 1009, 112 SCt 648, 116 LEd2d 665 (Supreme Court of the United States, 1991). See also *In re Beaver*, 181 Wis2d 12, 510 NW2d 129, 58 ALR5th 855 (Supreme Court of Wisconsin, 1994); *In re Illuzzi*, 160 Vt 474, 632 A2d 346 (Supreme Court of Vermont, 1993); *In re Crossen*, 450 Mass 533, 880 NE2d 352 (Supreme Judicial Court of Massachusetts, 2008); see on this case MS Frisch, 'Zealousness Run Amok' (2007) 20 *Georgetown Journal of Legal Ethics* 1035; *In re Comfort*, 284 Kan 183, 159 P3d 1011 (Supreme Court of Kansas, 2007).

[380] The two exceptions would be Rule 1.5 (retainer preferably in writing, but not necessarily so) and Rule 6.1 (voluntary *pro bono*).

[381] BA Green and FC Zacharias, 'Permissive Rules of Professional Conduct' (2006) 91 *Minnesota Law Review* 265, 302.

[382] Levine (n 379) 530. See also SM Bundy and E Elhauge, 'Knowledge about Legal Sanctions' (1993) 92 *Michigan Law Review* 261, 271.

[383] See above, II.B.i.a at 63–65, on Germany and ch 3, II.A.iv.b at 194–201, on the ICC.

[384] 'Restatement of the Law' (n 40) § 5, Comment c, and Reporter's Note; *In re West* (n 379), but see also *Matter of Cohen*, 139 AD2d 221, 530 NYS2d 830 (Supreme Court of New York, 1988) and *State ex rel. Oklahoma Bar Ass'n v Hine*, 937 P2d 996 (Supreme Court of Oklahoma, 1997).

[385] Rotunda (n 312) 9.

[386] 'Restatement of the Law' (n 40) § 5, Comment d.

[387] See Rules 1.9.(b), 1.10.(a), 1.12.(c), 1,18.(c) on conflict of interest, see also Rule 1.13.(b); see Rules 3.3 and 3.4.(c), 4.1, 4.2 on relations and statements in particular to tribunal and other participants.

9.(3) of the Model Rules for Lawyer Disciplinary Enforcement. Rule 1.0 ('Terminology') of the Model Rules of Professional Conduct defines that

> (f) 'Knowingly,' 'known,' or 'knows' denotes actual knowledge of the fact in question. A person's knowledge may be inferred from circumstances.

Wilful blindness is therefore not included, and it has been argued that it should not be.[388] Others provisions make it clear that negligence is the minimum threshold to be met, by using language like 'reasonably should know' or 'reasonably should have known'.[389] A general fault requirement is not made explicit anywhere, however. It has been argued in scholarship that the degree of fault should be a key element in assessing misconduct and disciplining.[390] The Model Rules of Professional Conduct state in their 'Scope':

> [19] The Rules presuppose that disciplinary assessment of a lawyer's conduct will be made on the basis of the facts and circumstances as they existed at the time of the conduct in question and in recognition of the fact that a lawyer often has to act upon uncertain or incomplete evidence of the situation. Moreover, the Rules presuppose that whether or not discipline should be imposed for a violation, and the severity of a sanction, depend on all the circumstances, such as the willfulness [of] the violation.

Absent language in a provision, however, it is conceivable that some rules may be construed as ones of absolute liability.[391] In any case, the state of mind of counsel will be a factor in sanctioning.[392]

c Disciplinary Sanctions and the Nature of Professional Discipline

The available sanctions in disciplinary proceedings are usually disbarment, suspension for a fixed time, reprimand/public censure and admonition/private censure. Whereas these are clearly the primary sanctions, disciplinary systems may also provide for other measures to accompany these forms of discipline, such as probation, diversion programmes, settlement and mediation, imposition of the

[388] D Luban, 'Contrived Ignorance' (1998–99) 87 *Georgetown Law Journal* 957. But see *People v Rader*, 822 P2d 950 (Supreme Court of Colorado, 1992).

[389] See Rules 4.3, 4.4.

[390] Wolfram (n 322) 88–90; S Powell, 'Intent as an Element of Attorney Misconduct' (1993) 18 *Journal of the Legal Profession* 407. See also *State v Martin*, 231 Kan 481, 646 P2d 459 (Supreme Court of Kansas, 1982); *Louisiana State Bar Association v Ruiz*, 261 La 409, 259 So2d 895 (Supreme Court of Louisiana, 1972); *In re McCaffrey*, 275 Or 23, 549 P2d 666 (Supreme Court of Oregon, 1976); but on the other hand, *Committee on Professional Ethics and Conduct of Iowa State Bar Ass'n v Bitter*, 279 NW2d 521 (Supreme Court of Iowa, 1979).

[391] In particular in the areas of management of funds and conflict of interests, see *Office of Disciplinary Counsel v Davis*, 532 Pa 22, 614 A2d 1116 (Supreme Court of Pennsylvania, 1992). American Bar Association, *Minutes, Friday, September 15–Sunday, September 17, 2000* (Commission on Evaluation of the Rules of Professional Conduct).

[392] See American Bar Association, *Standards for Imposing Lawyer Sanctions*, 10; Powell (n 390). See *In re Anonymous*, 637 NE2d 131 (Supreme Court of Indiana, 1994); *In re Gygi*, 273 Or 443, 541 P2d 1392 (Supreme Court of Oregon, 1975).

costs of the proceedings and restitution.[393] The use of monetary fines has been suggested.[394] However, courts have only imposed fines on attorneys as disciplinary sanctions in isolated cases.[395] Provisions which allow disciplinary bodies to order restitution and fee forfeiture do not authorise the imposition of monetary fines.[396] Whenever courts have used fines in relation to breaches of professional rules, it was usually based on sources other than professional discipline, such as statute or contempt.[397] This reflects, or is explained by the purpose behind lawyer discipline.[398] In addition to being an administrative 'licensing regime', professional discipline does serve different purposes or orientations, taking into account the interest of clients, the individually concerned lawyer, the profession as a whole and the disciplinary process.[399] Courts have held almost unanimously, however, that professional discipline aims at protecting the public and maintain the integrity of the legal system, but does not have the purpose of punishing the lawyer.[400]

[393] Wolfram (n 322) 139–41; American Bar Association, *Model Rules for Lawyer Disciplinary Enforcement* (adopted by the American Bar Association House of Delegates on 8 August 1989 and amended on 11 August 1993, 5 August 1996, 8 February 1999 and 12 August, 2002) Rule 10.(A). (Types of Sanctions); American Bar Association, *Standards for Imposing Lawyer Sanctions* B.2.2–2.8; Kane et al (n 359) § 116; RM Kane, 'Attorneys at Law, Vol 7' in Lawyers Cooperative Publishing (ed), *American Jurisprudence*, 2nd edn (New York, Thomson/West, 1989) § 36 (Restitution). See ch 1, II.A (n 34), for Rev 3 ICTY Code, with new Art 47(D). It provides for restitution orders by the ICTY disciplinary bodies, albeit on a burden of proof beyond reasonable doubt.

[394] SG Bené, 'Why Not Fine Attorneys: An Economic Approach to Lawyer Disciplinary Sanctions' (1990–91) 43 *Stanford Law Review* 907.

[395] See *In re Hanratty*, 277 NW2d 373 (Supreme Court of Minnesota, 1979); *In re Discipline of Droz*, 123 Nev 20, 160 P3d 881 (Supreme Court of Nevada, 2007); *Matter of Reed*, 369 A2d 686 (Supreme Court of Delaware, 1977). A tradition of fines seems to exist in Kentucky, for continuing legal education requirements. See, eg, *Kentucky Bar Ass'n v Phebus*, 2008 WL 465380 (Supreme Court of Kentucky, 2008); *Kentucky Bar Ass'n v Fletcher*, 213 SW3d 691 (Supreme Court of Kentucky, 2007); *Kentucky Bar Ass'n v Nemer*, 198 SW3d 600 (Supreme Court of Kentucky, 2006); *Kentucky Bar Ass'n v Cook*, 188 SW3d 426 (Supreme Court of Kentucky, 2006).

[396] *The Florida Bar v St. Louis*, 967 So2d 108 (Supreme Court of Florida, 2007); *The Florida Bar v Frederick*, 756 So2d 79 (Supreme Court of Florida, 2000).

[397] *People v Dean*, 288 AD2d 636, 732 NYS2d 696 (Supreme Court of New York, 2001); *In re Bennett*, 301 AD2d 176, 754 NYS2d 789 (Supreme Court of New York, 2002); *In re Cochrane*, 92 Nev 253, 549 P2d 328 (Supreme Court of Nevada, 1976); *In re Contempt of Fox*, 796 NE2d 1186 (Supreme Court of Indiana, 2003); *Edwards v State*, 360 Ark 90, 199 SW3d 684 (Supreme Court of Arkansas, 2004); *In re Ladas*, 9 AD3d 234, 781 NYS2d 723 (Supreme Court of New York, 2004); *Welsh v Mounger*, 912 So2d 823 (Supreme Court of Mississippi, 2005).

[398] See explicitly *In re Laubenheimer*, 113 Wis2d 680, 335 NW2d 624 (Supreme Court of Wisconsin, 1983).

[399] FC Zacharias, 'The Purposes of Lawyer Discipline' (2003) 45 *William & Mary Law Review* 675, 678. Thus, goals within the same regime can be inconsistent. See also JC Ogando, 'Sanctioning Unfit Lawyers: The Need for Public Protection' (1991–92) 5 *Georgetown Journal of Legal Ethics* 459, 461.

[400] For federal jurisprudence, see *Ex parte Wall*, 107 US 265, 2 SCt 569, 27 LEd 552 (Supreme Court of the United States, 1883); *In re Rouss*, 221 NY 81, 116 NE 782 (Court of Appeals of New York, 1917); *In re Echeles*, 430 F2d 347 (United States Court of Appeals, Seventh Circuit, 1970). But see also *In re Ruffalo* (n 348) cited by some circuits: *Charlton v F. T. C.*, 543 F2d 903 (United States Court of Appeals, District of Columbia Circuit, 1976); *Erdmann v Stevens*, 458 F2d 1205 (United States Court of Appeals, Second Circuit, 1972). For state cases, see *Office of Disciplinary Counsel v Stern*, 515 Pa 68, 526 A2d 1180 (Supreme Court of Pennsylvania, 1987); *Office of Disciplinary Counsel v Costigan*, 526 Pa 16, 584 A2d 296 (Supreme Court of Pennsylvania, 1990); *Massameno v Statewide Grievance Committee*, 234 Conn 539, 663 A2d 317 (Supreme Court of Connecticut, 1995); *Bradpiece v State Bar*, 10 Cal3d 742, 518 P2d 337, 111 CalRptr 905 (Supreme Court of California, 1974); *State ex rel. Oklahoma Bar Ass'n v*

On the other hand, deterring future misconduct by concerned counsel and others within the community has been recognised as a principle underlying discipline.[401] At least one court opinion has recognised a dual purpose of discipline.[402] Nonetheless, very few authors argue that sanctions such as disbarment can be seen to fulfil purposes which are essentially similar to criminal punishment since disciplinary sanctions do express condemnation and aim at deterrence.[403] The nature of disciplinary proceedings also reflects in the procedure which is applied.[404]

ii Criminal Offences

As in Germany, criminal law has a regulatory function insofar as it imposes limits on attorney conduct. Quite a number of offences attach to the professional conduct of counsel, and accordingly to misconduct. Similar to the finding in Germany, few of them are truly counsel- specific.

Criminal offences are in principle applicable to defence attorneys.[405] In some cases, criminal conduct by defence lawyers may even draw harsher sentences than for other lawyers or non-professionals. The US Federal Sentencing Guidelines[406]

Raskin, 642 P2d 262 (Supreme Court of Oklahoma, 1982); *Attorney Grievance Com'n of Maryland v Powell*, 369 Md 462, 800 A2d 782 (Court of Appeals of Maryland, 2002); *In re Goldstaub*, 446 A2d 1192 (Supreme Court of New Jersey, 1982). See further Zacharias (n 400); JM Burkoff, *Criminal Defense Ethics, 2nd: Law and Liability*, 2005 edn (St Paul, Minn, West Group, 2005) § 1:7; JF Strength, 'Attorney Disciplinary Proceedings: Civil or Criminal in Nature?' (1994) 19 *Journal of the Legal Profession* 257.

[401] See *Louisiana State Bar Ass'n v Reis*, 513 So2d 1173 (Supreme Court of Louisiana, 1987) (disciplinary proceedings are designed to, inter alia, deter future misconduct); *Attorney Grievance Com'n of Maryland v Protokowicz*, 329 Md 252, 619 A2d 100 (Court of Appeals of Maryland, 1993) (purpose to protect the public rather than to punish, although concepts of general and specific deterrence consistent with that primary goal); *The Florida Bar v Lawless*, 640 So2d 1098 (Supreme Court of Florida, 1994) (Bar disciplinary action must, inter alia, be severe enough to deter other attorneys from similar misconduct).

[402] *Office of Disciplinary Counsel v Lucarini*, 504 Pa 271, 472 A2d 186 (Supreme Court of Pennsylvania, 1983).

[403] BA Green, 'The Criminal Regulation of Lawyers' (1998–99) 67 *Fordham Law Review* 327, fn 302, citing DM Kahan, 'Punishment Incommensurability' (1997–98) 1 *Buffalo Criminal Law Review* 691; DM Kahan, 'What do Alternative Sanctions Mean?' (1996) 63 *University of Chicago Law Review* 591.

[404] Below, III.C.i at 142–45.

[405] See 'Restatement of the Law' (n 40) § 8. This may be state or federal law, or both. Since a strict local forum rule is applied in criminal law (see Rensberger (n 358) 816), no choice of law arises. See also below at 158–61, 290, within the context of double jeopardy. Rule 18 of the Federal Rules of Criminal Procedure specifies which federal court may hear a particular criminal case: 'Unless a statute or these rules permit otherwise, the government must prosecute an offense in a district where the offense was committed. The court must set the place of trial within the district with due regard for the convenience of the defendant and the witnesses, and the prompt administration of justice'. *U.S. v Anderson*, 328 US 699, 66 SCt 1213, 90 LEd 1529, 703 (Supreme Court of the United States, 1946) holds: '[T]he locus delicti must be determined from the nature of the crime alleged and the location of the act or acts constituting it'.

[406] Under these Guidelines, offences carry a certain base level. Points are then added or deducted according to, inter alia, aggravating and mitigating factors, which eventually translates into a sentencing bracket for the applicable penalties (such as imprisonment or fines). See on the constitutionality *Blakely v Washington*, 542 US 296, 308–313 (Supreme Court of the United States, 2004). District judges are not strictly bound, though, as 18 U.S.C. § 3553(b)(1), requiring them to follow the Guidelines, has been struck down, *United States v Booker*, 543 US 220 (2005) (Supreme Court of the United States,

provide for an upward adjustment in sentencing for the abuse of position of trust or the use of special skill, for obstruction of justice, and also for the disruption of governmental functions.[407] Despite their professional role, counsel is barred from relying on it when he or she distorts the judicial process. Criminal laws thus figure more prominently in regulation than acknowledged by many scholars and even practising attorneys themselves.[408]

On the one hand, this comes down to very basic principles of general law. Defence lawyers represent or advise clients who have, or at least allegedly so, engaged in criminal conduct. When affiliating themselves too closely with this, they may incur accessorial and conspiracy liability.[409]

A number of crimes in US law address counsel in his or her professional capacity, however. This concerns in the first place those offences protecting against deliberate efforts to undermine the process.[410] Many of the relevant provisions are 'fairly open-textured',[411] and as 'professional crimes', are in tension with other professional norms. Among the most relevant in US law, which will be outlined below, are suborning perjury,[412] unduly influencing witnesses and evidence[413] and the catch-all offences of obstruction of justice.[414] The sources of these offences vary. Cited here are the federal statutes, but these are often similarly present at the state levels.[415]

Contempt is a federal criminal statute,[416] its basis is the courts' claimed inherent powers to regulate litigants rather than legislation.[417] Furthermore, a number of common law crimes will be left out.[418]

2005) (but upholding the remainder as functioning independently). State courts have been divided. The California Supreme Court denied that such a sentencing scheme affected the defendant's right to trial by jury, *People v Black*, 113 P3d 534 (Supreme Court of California, 2005) but was overruled by the US Supreme Court in *Cunningham v California*, 549 US 270 (Supreme Court of the United States, 2007).

[407] 'United States Sentencing Guidelines', *18 USCA Appx*, § 3B1.3, § 3C1.1, § 5K2.7; Hall (n 23) 27:4, 5, 6.

[408] Green (n 403) 330; Hall (n 23) § 1:17.

[409] See Hall (n 23) ch 24. For counsel before the international courts, this may bear importance with regard to issues such as witness intimidation (see JP Marx, 'Intimidation of Defense Witnesses at the International Criminal Tribunals: Commentary and Suggested Legal Remedies' (2007) 7 *Chicago Journal of International Law* 675) or collusive over-billing to the detriment of the court's legal aid scheme.

[410] Green (n 403) 361.

[411] ibid, 353.

[412] 18 U.S.C. § 1622. See Hall (n 23) chs 25 and 26.

[413] 18 U.S.C. 291(a)(3), § 1510(a), § 1512(b). See ibid, chs 23 and 24.

[414] § 18 U.S.C. §1503.

[415] See above, III.A at 106–07.

[416] § 18 U.S.C. § 402.

[417] See above, III.A at 109–13.

[418] Traditional common law crimes in relation to the administration of justice exist but can be neglected at this point. On the crimes of barratry, champerty and maintenance, see CE Torcia, *Wharton's Criminal Law*, 2007 Supplement, 15th edn (Deerfield, Ill, Clark Boardman Callaghan, 1993) § 563 (inciting litigation).

a Criminal Offences in Connection with the Criminal Trial as such

An important pillar as to trial-related crimes is the offence of obstruction of justice. It stems from the common law but is now codified in most jurisdictions, although some still recognise it as a common law offence.[419] The language of the main provisions under the US Code (U.S.C), 18 U.S.C § 1503 ('Influencing or injuring officer or juror generally') is very broad. Fleshing out the omnibus clause at the end[420] of sub-paragraph (a), though, it becomes more apparent how all-encompassing it can potentially be:

> Whoever . . . corruptly or by threats or force, or by any threatening letter or communication, influences, obstructs, or impedes, or endeavors to influence, obstruct, or impede, the due administration of justice, shall be [guilty of an offense].

Similar to contempt, it can be described to serve as a catch-all to curb misconduct by counsel, and it suffers from the same lack of contours. It has been said that it covers 'a variety limited only by the imagination of the criminally inclined'.[421] More specific provisions do exist. Of those, 18 U.S.C. § 1510 and § 1512 address the influencing of a court or a jury, destroying or concealing evidence, or unduly influencing witnesses. The relationship between those more specific provisions and the general clause § 1503 is controversial among circuits, thus leaving open the possibility of resorting to the latter as an residual clause, however close the alleged conduct may fall short of the requirements of the more specific offences.[422]

18 U.S.C. § 1503 has this wide scope as the protected legal interest – the 'due course of justice' – means not only the due conviction and punishment,[423] or respectively acquittal or discharge, but the course of proceedings in general.[424] At times, there may be an overlap with contempt since particular obstruction may

[419] See 18 U.S.C. § 1503 and the Model Penal Code § 242.1; EC Surette, 'Obstructing Justice, Vol 58' in Lawyers Cooperative Publishing (ed), *American Jurisprudence*, 2nd edn (New York, Thomson/West, 1989) § 1.

[420] As done by the Executive Office for US Attorneys (ed), *United States Attorneys' Manual, Title 9, Criminal* § 1724, Criminal Resource Manual.

[421] Surette (n 420) § 9. See also KR Taylor, 'The Obstruction of Justice Nexus Requirement after Arthur Andersen and the Sarbanes-Oxley Act' (2008) 93 *Cornell Law Review* 401. *U.S. v Aguilar*, 515 US 593, 599, 115 SCt 2357, 132 LEd2d 520 (Supreme Court of the United States, 1995) explicitly recognised the need to 'place metes and bounds on the very broad language of the catchall provision'. See also again Executive Office for US Attorneys (ed) (n 421) § 1724, Criminal Resource Manual. BM Haney, 'Contrasting the Prosecution of Witness Tampering Under 18 U.S.C. § 1503 and 18 U.S.C. § 1512: Why § 1512 Better Serves the Government at Trial' (2004) 9 *Suffolk Journal of Trial and Appellate Advocacy* 57; JK Fitzpatrick, 'Supreme Court Review: The Supreme Court's Bipolar Approach to the Interpretation of 18 U.S.C. 1503 and 18 U.S.C. Section 2232(c)' (1996) 86 *Journal of Criminal Law & Criminology* 1383, 1384; TA Pesce, 'Defining Witness Tampering Under 18 U.S.C. Section 1512' (1986) 86 *Columbia Law Review* 1417, 1426; TM Riley, 'Tampering With Witness Tampering: Resolving the Quandary Surrounding 18 U.S.C. §§ 1503, 1512' (1999) 77 *Washington University Law Quarterly* 249, 255.

[422] On the relationship between § 1503 and § 1512, see Haney (n 421).

[423] To which Section 258 German Criminal Code restricts the offence of *Strafvereitelung*. See above, II.B.ii.a at 68–69.

[424] Hall (n 23) § 22:1.

also constitute contempt of court if the elements of that offence are met.[425] Obstruction of justice may tend to punish 'contempts' outside of the presence of the court[426] whereas contempt would cover misconduct in the presence of the court. Furthermore, the use of summary contempt seems to be restricted and not be equated to general obstruction of justice under 18 U.S.C. § 1503.[427] However, parallel sanctioning is conceivable without double jeopardy. Summary contempt may require that the act has occurred in the presence of the court whereas this is an element unknown to witness retaliation; in exchange, however, the latter features the requirement of intent to retaliate which does not play a role in summary contempt.[428]

It seems fair to say that some elements of contempt and obstruction of justice are indeed similar. In both, the offender needs to act in knowledge of certain material elements, as will be outlined. Furthermore, both obstruction and contempt require a nexus, either to the court, or the existence of a judicial proceeding or investigation. For obstruction, proof is required that counsel acted with intent, and proof that 'the action had the natural and probable effect of interfering with the due administration of justice'.[429] It is an inchoate crime, however, since it suffices that the obstructive conduct 'endeavours' to do so: it need not be successful.[430] As far as the requisite intent is concerned, it has to be directed at impeding the administration of justice. This does not mean the specific purpose of obstructing justice, though, but only that it would precisely result as the natural and probable consequence.[431] The term 'corruptly' should probably not be overrated in this context. It can vary in meaning with the context of the prosecution, thus, many improper motives may allow the conclusion that the defendant acted with the necessary intent.[432]

Criminal law itself does not draw a line between proscribed and permissible conduct.[433] As 18 U.S.C. § 1515(c) explicitly put it: 'This chapter does not prohibit or punish the providing of lawful, bona fide, legal representation services in connection with or anticipation of an official proceeding'. Using the system's

[425] Torcia (n 418) § 562.

[426] *Nye v U.S.*, 313 US 33, 61 SCt 810, 85 LEd 1172 (Supreme Court of the United States, 1941).

[427] *U.S. v Williams*, 874 F2d 968, 58 USLW 2042 (United States Court of Appeals, Fifth Circuit, 1989).

[428] *U.S. v Ferrugia*, 604 FSupp 668 (United States District Court, E.D. New York, 1985), affirmed by *U.S. v Ferrugia*, 779 F2d 36 (United States Court of Appeals, Second Circuit, 1985).

[429] *In re Impounded*, 241 F3d 308 (United States Court of Appeals, Third Circuit, 2001); *U.S. v Cueto* 151 F3d 620 (United States Court of Appeals, Seventh Circuit, 1998).

[430] Green (n 403) 361; Surette (n 419) § 10 and § 15. It thus differs in concept from Germany. See above, II.B.ii.a at 69. On the other hand, the attempt is punishable under German law, thus in practice eradicating this theoretical divide.

[431] Surette (n 419) § 12, citing *U.S. v Bashaw*, 982 F2d 168 (United States Court of Appeals, Sixth Circuit, 1992); *U.S. v Guzzino and Ciarrochi*, 810 F2d 687; 22 FedREvidServ 473 (United States Court of Appeals, Seventh Circuit, 1987); *U.S. v Brenson*, 104 F3d 1267 (United States Court of Appeals, Eleventh Circuit, 1997).

[432] Surette (n 419) § 13. See *U.S. v Barfield*, 999 F2d 1520 (United States Court of Appeals, Eleventh Circuit, 1993).

[433] Green (n 403) 361. See above, II.B.ii.a at 69–70, on Germany, and below, III.B.iii.a at 132–33 on contempt.

tools of procedure can become a base for an obstruction of justice charge if carried by a 'corrupt purpose' on the lawyer's side.[434] The issue usually seen as closely connected would be whether ethics norms should be relied on in the interpretation of criminal offences. Some courts have done so, but such reliance seems to be far from general.[435] It might be less controversial when courts use ethics norms to limit the scope of criminal offence in order to accommodate professional ethics and other professional rules,[436] but more so if courts rely on professional duties on which to base criminal elements.[437]

It has been argued that judges should interpret restrictively, and prosecutors should prosecute restrictively and thus integrate the dual processes under criminal prosecutions and professional discipline, relying on the latter when in doubt.[438] Quintessentially, prosecuting defence lawyers for alleged criminal offences in connection with their work raises the same concerns that other measures do. As the criminal law is the harshest type of state control, criminal offences harbour the greatest potential of a 'chilling effect' on the defence. This always needs to be taken into account on constitutional grounds when assessing misconduct.[439]

b Criminal Offences on Specific Professional Duties

It has been shown in the section on Germany that criminal offences exist that attach to major professional duties, although they do not cover the full scope of the latter.[440] They seem to have no counterparts in US law.[441] Professional rules and discipline exist as a 'penumbra'[442] to criminal laws, but their scope is otherwise narrower. In the course of their work, attorneys will be more liable for prosecutions under certain provisions such as, for example, making false statements (18 U.S.C. § 1001) or wire and mail fraud,[443] or they may be targeted for legal advice.[444] Ultimately, however, these prosecutions are not legally counsel-specific.

[434] See PJ Henning, 'Overcriminalization: The Politics of Crimes Targeting Legal Advice' (2004–05) 54 *American University Law Review* 669, 680.

[435] Green (n 403) 377; BA Green, 'Zealous Representation Bound: The Intersection of the Ethical Codes and the Criminal Law' (1990–91) 69 *North Carolina Law Review* 687.

[436] See, eg, *People v Belge*, 50 AD2d 1088, 376 NYS2d 771 (Supreme Court of New York, 1975).

[437] See, eg, *U.S. v Bronston*, 658 F2d 920 (United States Court of Appeals, Second Circuit, 1981).

[438] Green (n 403) 388. See, however below, III.B.i.c at 122–24, on the purpose of discipline.

[439] See below, E at 163–64.

[440] See above, II.B.ii.b at 71.

[441] See Green (n 403) 321.

[442] ibid, 349, citing to JC Coffee, 'From Tort to Crime: Some Reflections on the Criminalization of Fiduciary Breaches and the Problematic Line Between Law and Ethics' (1981) 19 *American Criminal Law Review* 117, 137.

[443] Green (n 403) 342. See, cited by him, *U.S. v Bronston* (n 438). See also Henning (n 434) 689.

[444] Henning (n 434); Green (n 403) 359.

c Criminal Offences Pertaining to Financial Irregularities

Lastly, lawyers can be held criminally accountable for financial misdeeds under the US law on fraud, embezzlement and larceny.[445] Funds stemming from the client have also triggered money laundering issues.[446] It is a federal crime under 18 U.S.C. §§ 1956, 1957. It may result in forfeiture of attorney's fees, notwithstanding the problem of bona fide on counsel's part. This involves also more specific regulation on duties to report financial transactions.[447] Of course, money laundering goes beyond the issue of attorney fees. If in collusion with the client, counsel may just be held liable for his or her own crimes or as participant in the client's crime.[448]

d Legal Consequences of Criminal Offences

As to the consequences, imprisonment and fines can be handed down. Under the Sentencing Guidelines (§ 2J1.2(a)),[449] obstruction of justice carries a base offence level of 14 points. Without adjustments, this translates into imprisonment of between 15 and 21 months, and a fine of between $4,000 and $40,000. The sentence can be considerably higher with adjustments. Contempt, if analogous, draws the same under 18 U.S.C. § 401.[450] More flexibility may be said to follow for contempt, as courts have, based on their inherent powers, also reprimanded counsel or enjoined counsel from certain activities.[451]

Moreover, under the 2007 Federal Sentencing Guidelines, courts may in certain cases impose occupational restrictions.[452] Technically, courts can thus disbar, suspend, or disqualify for contempt and other crimes.[453] Courts seem to have been hesitant in that respect, however, rather leaving removal from the profession to the pertinent professional regimes.[454]

[445] Green (n 403) 331; Henning (n 434) 684 *et seq.*

[446] Hall (n 23) § 7:28–34; DM Morris, 'Attorney Fee Forfeiture' (1986) 86 *Columbia Law Review* 1021.

[447] Hall (n 23) § 8:1–42.

[448] ibid, § 8:43, 44.

[449] 'United States Sentencing Guidelines', *18 USCA Appx.*

[450] *U.S. v Remini*, 967 F2d 754 (United States Court of Appeals, Second Circuit, 1992).

[451] Hall (n 23) § 33:76

[452] Ch 5 – Part F – Sentencing Options, §5F1.5.

[453] Hall (n 23) § 33:12. Eg, Bruce Cutler, lawyer for mobster John Gotti, was suspended temporarily. *U.S. v Cutler*, 58 F3d 825, 838–840 (United States Court of Appeals, Second Circuit, 1995).

[454] *U.S. v Pastore*, 537 F2d 675 (United States Court of Appeals, Second Circuit, 1976); *U.S. v Sterber*, 846 F2d 842 (United States Court of Appeal, Second Circuit, 1988) (state pharmacy licence). See also BK Pinaire, MJ Heumann and J Lermann, 'Barred from the Bar: The Process, Politics, and Policy Implications of Discipline for Attorney Felony Offenders' (2005–06) 13 *Virginia Journal of Social Policy & the Law* 290.

iii Other Measures as Institutional Controls

All of the abovementioned measures have in common that they are indirect. They are controls which are only enforced after the fact. Moreover, they are applied by external actors. A number of measures exist in the United States, however, which are can be used by the institutions themselves before which attorneys practise. For criminal defence lawyers, these will essentially be the court system.[455] Courts have used statutory law, their contempt authority and inherent powers to sanction misconduct by litigants. The sheer record in terms of money – through a combination of all the available powers – has occured for discovery abuse in a product liability case: *In re E.I. du Pont de Nemours and Co.*[456]

The disctrict judge awarded US$6,843,837.53 to the other party for attorney fees and expenses and the same amount to be paid to the court for the conduct of DuPont and its lawyers during the protracted history of foregoing litigation. It reinstated a prior one million dollar order to force discovery and added to this another US$100 million should DuPont not meet the discovery obligations and publish a full-page advertisement in the *Wall Street Journal* and other newspapers in three states acknowledging the misconduct.

a Contempt of Court as a Direct Measure

A prominent creature of inherent powers is any court's authority to sanction for contempt.[457] It is now entrenched in federal statute (18 U.S.C. § 401), but is also grounded in inherent powers. Under those, irrespective of statute, courts can hold in contempt anyone whose conduct is disobedient, defiant, disruptive, or disorderly, and failure to react would compromise the integrity, authority and respect of the court and prevent it from administering justice.[458] It thus embraces a wide scope of conceivable misconduct which includes attorneys who can be held in contempt for a wide range of litigation-related activities.[459]

[455] See Wilkins (n 71) 807.

[456] *In re E.I. du Pont de Nemours and Co.*, 918 FSupp 1524 (United States District Court, M.D. Georgia, 1995), reversed for violation of due process and remanded, *In re E.I. DuPont De Nemours & Company-Benlate Litigation*, 99 F3d 363 (United States Court of Appeals, Eleventh Circuit, 1996), cert. denied *E.I. du Pont de Nemours and Co.v Bush Ranch, Inc.*, 522 US 906, 118 SCt 263, 139 LEd2d 190 (Supreme Court of the United States, 1997). On *Chambers v Nasco*, see above, III.A at 109–13.

[457] Ch 1, II.B.ii at 16–25, C.i and D at 28–37, for the ICTY relying on this concept. For annually reviewed US case law, see the Annual Review of Criminal Procedure, 'III. Trial, Authority of the Trial Judge' (2011) 40 *Georgetown Law Journal Annual Review of Criminal Procedure*, and previous issues. For scholarship in German, see Dueren (n 19); Lienert (n 19). On the United Kingdom, see JC Fox, *The History of Contempt of Court* (London, Professional Books, 1972).

[458] Torcia (n 418) § 608 and § 610 on witnesses; Executive Office for US Attorneys (ed) (n 420) Criminal Resource Manual 752 (General Definition of Contempt).

[459] See Torcia (n 418) § 609 (Acts of Attorneys); LH Dietz et al, 'Contempt, Vol 17' in Lawyers Cooperative Publishing (ed), *American Jurisprudence*, 2nd edn (New York, Thomson/West, 1989) §§ 63–79 (Conduct of and as Attorney); Hall (n 23) § 33:1-63; Executive Office for US Attorneys (ed) (n 420) chapter 9-39.000. For courts martial, see DA Anderson, 'Summary Contempt Power in the

Contempt defies a clear label as clearly criminal or civil.[460] [461] In its criminal dimension, however, it is simply a criminal offence, at least by having the consequences of the latter.[462] Criminal conduct can further be divided into two classes: direct contempt, occurring in the presence of the court, and indirect contempt, occurring outside it. Contempt cannot be equated with a general criminal offence on the administration of justice: it has the 'limited purpose of vindicating the authority of the court'.[463]

Criminal contempt is distinct from civil contempt, though, and both are possible alongside each other. Trial judges possess discretion in what to impose.[464] However, under the 'least possible power rule' the trial judge must at least consider obtaining compliance through civil contempt, albeit not actually imposing civil penalties before.[465]

Civil contempt has been described as remedial rather than punitive as it primarily aims at serving the purpose of other party litigants,[466] and is intended to coerce compliance with an order of the court or to compensate for losses or damages caused by noncompliance.[467] With civil contempt, the individual is held until he or she complies with the court's order and 'carries the keys of his prison in his own pocket'.[468] If a sentence is for a definite period of time and is not modifiable

Military: A Proposal to Amend Article 48, UCMJ' (1999) 160 *Military Law Review* 158. State law may vary, see *Ex parte Krupps*, 712 SW2d 144 (Texas Court of Criminal Appeals, 1986), cert. denied, *Krupps v Texas*, 479 US 1102, 107 SCt 1333, 94 LEd2d 184 (Supreme Court of the United States, 1987); *In re Daniels*, 219 NJ Super 550, 530 A2d 1260 (New Jersey Superior Court, 1987), affirmed, *In re Daniels*, 118 NJ 51, 570 A2d 416 (Superior Court of New Jersey, Appellate Division, 1990), cert. denied, *Daniels v Superior Court of New Jersey, Appellate Division*, 498 US 951, 111 S Ct 371, 112 L Ed 2d 333 (Supreme Court of the United States, 1990).

[460] It is recalled in this context that US American legal terminology usually uses 'civil' for all proceedings not of a criminal nature. *Zivil* in German legal doctrine, however, means private law and consequently only encompasses litigation among private parties. A number of 'civil' proceedings in the United States would be labelled 'administrative' (*verwaltungsrechtlich*) in Germany and other continental jurisdictions.

[461] *Young v U.S. ex rel. Vuitton et Fils S.A.* (n 339); *Myers v U.S.*, 264 US 95, 44 SCt 272 557 (Supreme Court of the United States, 1924).

[462] *Bloom v Illinois*, 391 US 194, 201 (Supreme Court of the United States, 1968) ('Criminal contempt is a crime in the ordinary sense'); Hall (n 23) citing *In re Long*, 276 GaApp 306, 623 SE2d 181 (Court of Appeals of Georgia, 2005). See likewise ch 1, II.C.i at 29, for the ICTY.

[463] *Young v U.S. ex rel. Vuitton et Fils S.A.* (n 339).

[464] *U.S. v North*, 621 F2d 1255 (United States Court of Appeals, Third Circuit, 1980).

[465] *Shillitani v United States*, 384 US 364 (Supreme Court of the United States, 1966); see Executive Office for US Attorneys (ed) (n 420) Criminal Resource Manual 784, for further case law.

[466] See, eg, *Citronelle-Mobile Gathering, Inc. v Watkins*, 943 F2d 1297, 1304 (United States Court of Appeals, Eleventh Circuit, 1991).

[467] See *Shillitani v United States* (n 465) 368–70; *Nye v U S.* (n 428); *Gompers v Buck's Stove & Range Co.*, 221 US 418, 31 SCt 492, 55 LEd 797 (Supreme Court of the United States, 1911); *Falstaff Brewing Corp. v Miller Brewing Co.*, 702 F2d 770 (United States Court of Appeals, Ninth Circuit 1983); *In re Rumaker*, 646 F2d 870 (United States Court of Appeals, Fifth Circuit 1980); *U.S. v Powers*, 629 F2d 619 (United States Court of Appeals, Ninth Circuit, 1980); *U.S. v North* (n 464) cert. denied; *Eyler v U.S.*, 449 US 866 (Supreme Court of the United States, 1981); *Carlson Fuel Co. v United Mine Workers*, 517 F2d 1348 (United States Court of Appeals, Fourth Circuit, 1975).

[468] *In re Nevitt*, 117 F 448 (United States Court of Appeals, Eighth Circuit, 1902); cited, among many others, by *Gompers v Buck's Stove & Range Co.*(n 467); *International Union, United Mine Workers of America v Bagwell*, 512 US 821, 114 SCt 2552, 129 LEd2d 642 (Supreme Court of the United States,

by the contemner and his subsequent compliance, the sentence is punitive and the contempt is criminal.[469] Most contempt proceedings involving counsel seem to be for criminal contempt;[470] however, it is stressed that both are possible in criminal trials. Some direct contempt may be punished summarily under Rule 42(b) of the Federal Rules of Criminal Procedure, but the majority of cases, ie, indirect contempt and all contempt occurring outside the presence of the court, requires notice and hearing under Rule 42(a).[471]

The prosecution must establish three elements for criminal contempt: (1) the existence of a reasonably specific lawful order; (2) that it has been violated; and (3) that this was done wilfully or intentionally.[472] Finally, to be contemptuous within the meaning of 18 U.S.C. § 401, the conduct must constitute 'an affront and in some way obstruct the proceedings or threaten the dispassionate administration of justice'.[473] This is an important threshold to criminal liability and is reflected in other case law. Courts have given examples to further help define the element of obstruction in contempt. It can happen by a delay of proceedings, causing additional work, inducing errors, or by imposing costs on parties.[474] Key is that the orderly process of the administration of justice is interrupted or the judicial process thwarted.[475] Courts have used a standard of material disruption or obstruction, but held that mere delay may suffice in this as long as it is carried by wrongful intent.[476] Inability to comply is a complete defence to a criminal contempt action, as contrasted with the mere refusal to do so.[477]

1994). In *Chadwick v Janecka*, 302 F3d 107 (United States Court of Appeals, Third Circuit, 2002), the Court held that Chadwick, the *habeas corpus* petitioner, could be imprisoned indefinitely under federal law for his failure to return about US$ 2.5 million he had hidden from his divorced wife. Eventually, he remained in prison for over 14 years.

[469] See *U.S. v Mathews*, 997 F2d 848, 851 (United States Court of Appeals, Eleventh Circuit, 1993).

[470] N Hollander and BE Bergman, *Everytrial Criminal Defense Resource Book* (St Paul, Minn, Thomson/West, 2007) § 70:3; Hall (n 23) § 33:1.

[471] See generally, *In re Gustafson*, 650 F2d 1017 (United States Court of Appeals, Ninth Circuit, 1981) and below, III.C.iii for details on the procedure for contempt.

[472] *U.S. v Paccione*, 964 F2d 1269, 1274–76 (United States Court of Appeals, Second Circuit, 1992); see also *U.S. v Turner*, 812 F2d 1552, 1565 (United States Court of Appeals, Eleventh Circuit, 1987); *In re Williams*, 509 F2d 949, 960 (United States Court of Appeals, Second Circuit, 1975). See for further discussion Executive Office for US Attorneys (ed) (n 420) Criminal Resource Manual 769.

[473] *Offutt v U.S.*, 348 US 11, 75 SCt 11, 99 LEd 11 (Supreme Court of the United States, 1954); *Gordon v U.S.*, 592 F2d 1215, 1217 (United States Court of Appeals, First Circuit, 1979).

[474] *U.S. v Oberhellmann*, 946 F2d 50 (United States Court of Appeals, Seventh Circuit, 1991).

[475] *U.S. v Warlick*, 742 F2d 113 (United States Court of Appeals, Fourth Circuit, 1984); *In re Dellinger*, 461 F2d 389 (United States Court of Appeals, Seventh Circuit, 1972).

[476] *U.S. v Seale*, 461 F2d 345 (United States Court of Appeals, Seventh Circuit, 1972). See also *In re Jefferson*, 657 SE2d 830, 283 Ga 216, at 8 (Supreme Court of Georgia, 2008), criticising the 'blurred and perhaps nonexistent distinction in the context of courtroom advocacy between a so-called "actual" obstruction and the "imminent threat" of one, we are persuaded that the "imminent threat" standard is the more cogent approach to defining the "act" element of contempt'.

[477] *U.S. v Joyce*, 498 F2d 592, 596 (United States Court of Appeals, Seventh Circuit, 1974), *U.S. v J. Myer Schine et al.*, 260 F2d 552, 555 (United States Court of Appeals, Second Circuit, 1958), cert. Denied; *U.S. v J. Myer Schine et al.*, 358 US 934 (Supreme Court of the United States, 1959); Executive Office for US Attorneys (ed) (n 420) Criminal Resource Manual 775.

There is a grey zone, though, which also raises constitutional considerations.[478] As other lawyer sanctions, it harbours the danger of chilling the requisite zealous advocacy.[479] Attorneys have often found themselves a target because,[480] for example, of disorderly conduct before the court during a trial, for submitting a false or fictitious document to the court, or for violating court orders, such as failing to limit cross-examination as court-directed.[481] The uncertainty is remedied in part by the required notice: failing a specific warning to spoken objections, defence counsel could not have known of the possibility of being held in contempt for such an objection.[482] In conclusion, contempt powers are a flexible and powerful element in safeguarding the conduct of proceedings.

b Other Procedural Measures

As part of the procedure they apply, courts have a range of other measures other than contempt at their disposal. There is always room for informal responses, such as a judicial rebuke.[483] Beyond this, however, courts can use their procedure to respond to misconduct. The Restatement list the following as 'the most familiar, applicable remedies and certain circumstances involved in their application to lawyers':[484]

(1) awarding a sum of money as damages;
(2) providing injunctive relief, including requiring specific performance of a contract or enjoining its nonperformance;
(3) requiring restoration of a specific thing or awarding a sum of money to prevent unjust enrichment;
(4) ordering cancellation or reformation of a contract, deed, or similar instrument;
(5) declaring the rights of the parties, such as determining that an obligation claimed by the lawyer to be owed to the lawyer is not enforceable;
(6) punishing the lawyer for contempt;
(7) enforcing an arbitration award;
(8) disqualifying a lawyer from a representation;
(9) forfeiting a lawyer's fee (see § 37);
(10) denying the admission of evidence wrongfully obtained;
(11) dismissing the claim or defense of a litigant represented by the lawyer;

[478] This is dealt with specifically below, III.E at 163–65. See also Hall (n 23) § 33:20, citing *Sacher v United States*, 343 US 1 (Supreme Court of the United States, 1952); *In re Little*, 404 US 553, 92 SCt 659, 30 LEd2d 708 (Supreme Court of the United States, 1972); *In re McConnell*, 370 US 230, 82 SCt 1288 (Supreme Court of the United States, 1962); *In re Dellinger* (n 475). See also the case of *In re Jefferson* (n 476).

[479] See below, III.E at 164, on balancing the need to ensure a fair and expeditious trial and the right to effective assistance under the Sixth Amendment.

[480] See the above-cited case law, and for further cases Torcia (n 418) § 631.

[481] *In re McDonald*, 819 F2d 1020 (United States Court of Appeals, Eleventh Circuit, 1987).

[482] *U.S. v Robinson*, 922 F2d 1531, 1534 (United States Court of Appeals, Eleventh Circuit, 1991).

[483] JD Fischer, 'Bareheaded and Barefaced Counsel: Courts React to Unprofessionalism in Lawyers' Papers' (1997) 31 *Suffolk University Law Review* 1, 9.

[484] 'Restatement of the Law' (n 40) § 6.

(12) granting a new trial; and
(13) entering a procedural or other sanction.

Not all of these can be ordered by the court experiencing the misconduct in the same proceeding. Moreover, some of these options will not be applicable in criminal proceedings or at least not as viable an option as in civil cases. Litigation in criminal cases – and arguably also not in many instances of civil litigation – does not involve a *res* which can be assessed in terms of damages. That criminal cases differ seems clear also from the 'lesser sanctions' argument which courts have invoked for their authority over litigants and their attorneys. As the Court of Appeals for the Eleventh Circuit framed it,

> [t]he authority of a court over officers of its bar is at least as great as its power over litigants. Since misconduct by a party courts the risk of outright dismissal, lesser sanctions undoubtedly attend the court's inherent power to discipline intentional attorney misconduct.[485]

In the criminal context, courts do decide about the admissibility of evidence and take into account whether it is tainted by misconduct.[486] The pursuit of criminal justice defies awarding the *res* to one side or the other, though.

Other remedies are nonetheless conceivable in the criminal context. It may advance the cause to grant injunctive relief, such as gag orders prohibiting the participants in a trial from releasing information about a case which may be prejudicial to the right to a fair trial.[487] Disqualifying a lawyer from the proceedings may be an avenue to remove counsel from the case in serious instances of misconduct. It needs to be taken into account, however, that this may cause substantial costs for clients and compromise the constitutional right to assistance by counsel which includes the choice of counsel.[488] This limits the use of disqualification to cases of affiliation with the client or where counsel is the 'target of investigation' in other respects, but makes it hard to use it on other grounds of misconduct.[489] Forfeiture of attorney fees addresses different kinds of misconduct.[490] One of the

[485] See, eg, *Kleiner v First Nat. Bank of Atlanta*, 751 F2d 1193 (United States Court of Appeals, Eleventh Circuit, 1985), relying on *Flaksa v Little River Marine Const. Co* (n 39) and *Roadway Express, Inc. v Piper*, 447 US 752, 100 SCt 2455, 65 LEd2d 488 (Supreme Court of the United States 1980) (pre-*Nasco*). *Fink v Gomez*, 239 F3d 989 (United States Court of Appeals, Ninth Circuit, 2001) stresses the requirement of bad faith.

[486] LM Morton, 'Seeking the Elusive Remedy for Prosecutorial Misconduct: Suppression, Dismissal, or Discipline' (1993–94) 7 *Georgetown Journal of Legal Ethics* 1083. On remedies for ineffective assistance by counsel, see Hall (n 23) § 10:2. Dismissal or reversal is only the last resort, though; *Bass v General Motors Corp.*, 150 F3d 842 (United States Court of Appeals, Eighth Circuit, 1998); *Diettrich v Northwest Airlines, Inc.*, 168 F3d 961 (United States Court of Appeals, Seventh Circuit, 1999); *State v Murray*, 443 So2d 955 (Supreme Court of Florida, 1984).

[487] *Sheppard v Maxwell*, 384 US 333, 86 SCt 1507, 16 LEd2d 600 (Supreme Court of the United States, 1966). Violation is punishable as contempt, Hall (n 23) § 12:26.

[488] *U.S. v Gonzalez-Lopez*, 548 US 140, 126 SCt 2557 (Supreme Court of the United States, 2006); 'Restatement of the Law' (n 40) § 6, Comment i, § 129.

[489] WG Phelps, 'Grounds for Disqualification of Criminal Defendant's Chosen and Preferred Attorney in Federal Prosecution' (1995) 127 *American Law Reports* 67. See also Green (n 403) 327, fn 72.

[490] 'Restatement of the Law' (n 40) § 37 and § 129; RL Rossi, 'Factors Affecting Right To Compensation' in *Attorneys' Fees*, 3rd edn (St Paul, Minn, Thomson/West, 2001) § 3:4; Kane, 'Attorneys at Law, Vol. 7' (n 393) § 262.

more exceptional – funds from illegal sources – has been mentioned before.[491] Fee forfeiture or annulment may also be ordered to compensate the client if counsel breaches duties to the client.[492] Thirdly, fee-related sanctions have been used in particular to address frivolous advocacy.[493]

The latter will be explained in more detail. Among the most direct measures against abusive litigation are sanctions against counsel. One of the flagship provisions for this is Rule 11 of the Federal Rules of Civil Procedure. This Rule envisages monetary sanctions but allows for other 'appropriate' measures as well.[494] It was introduced in 1983 and underwent substantial change in 1993.[495] Under the new provision, a sanction was not mandatory any more, and judges could handle the fine more flexibly. Parties moving for sanctions now had to do so separately. It could no longer be 'tagged on' as additional relief to another motion. Attorneys now had a continuing duty to correct a filing after signature but could now retreat to the 'safe harbour' of withdrawing a controversial filing. The new version also offered better procedural protections as there now has to be a warning before any sanction is imposed. Counterparts to Rule 11 can be found, albeit varying, in many US jurisdictions. Sanctions are sometimes mandatory, sometimes discretionary, some have a bad faith requirement, others not.[496] In essence, it needs to be stressed that Rule 11 has been used ever since and is still being used by courts. A number of authors describe it as the premier vehicle to enforce discipline, and their studies attest that it has changed the conduct and attitude of attorneys during litigation.[497]

The relevance of Rule 11 itself for the criminal defence is quite limited. As a rule of civil procedure it is not applicable to criminal trials[498] with the exception of

[491] See above, III.B.ii.c at 129.

[492] 'Restatement of the Law' (n 40) § 37.

[493] ibid, § 110 and in the following.

[494] See GP Joseph, *Sanctions: The Federal Law of Litigation Abuse*, 3rd edn (Albany, NY, Matthew Bender 2000) 256–86.

[495] ibid, 21–34. See also K Bunch, 'Taming the Fury: Do the 1991 Proposed Amendments to Rule 11 Go Far Enough?' (1991–92) 5 *Georgetown Journal of Legal Ethics* 957.

[496] RA Nolan, 'Ohio's Frivolous Conduct Statute: A Need for Stronger Deterrence' (1992) 21 *Capital University Law Review* 261, 261; E Schiller and JA Wertkin, 'Frivolous Filings and Vexatious Litigation' (2000–01) 14 *Georgetown Journal of Legal Ethics* 909 on California, Texas and Hawaii. See JW MacFarlane, 'Frivolous Conduct under Model Rule of Professional Conduct 3.1' (1997) 21 *Journal of the Legal Profession* 231 on objective/subjective standard.

[497] GN Vairo, 'Rule 11 and the Profession' (1998–99) 67 *Fordham Law Review* 589; GN Vairo, *Rule 11 Sanctions: Case Law, Perspectives and Preventive Measures*, 3rd edn (Chicago, American Bar Association, 2003) 41–54; LC Marshall, HM Kritzer and FK Zemans, 'Use and Impact of Rule 11' (1991–92) 86 *Northwestern University Law Review* 943; VH Kramer, 'Viewing Rule 11 as a Tool to Improve Professional Responsibility' (1990–91) 75 *Minnesota Law Review* 793; BC Keeling, 'A Prescription for Healing the Crisis in Professionalism: Shifting the Burden of Enforcing Professional Standards of Conduct' (1993) 25 *Texas Tech Law Review* 31 (critical of judicial punishment, argues for good faith standard and discipline outside court).

[498] *U.S. v White*, 980 F2d 836 (United States Court of Appeals, Second Circuit, 1992); Vairo, *Rule 11 Sanctions* (n 497) § 3.05[b] at 130–31. See also Hall (n 23) § 3:12; 'Restatement of the Law' (n 40) § 110, Comment f. An aberration would be *U.S. v Hawley*, 768 F2d 249 (United States Court of Appeals, Eighth Circuit, 1985).

habeas corpus proceedings, which are of a civil nature.[499] Using Rule 11 in criminal settings is not only problematic but unnecessary.[500] A string of other provisions exists which can produce results similar to Rule 11 as far as monetary sanctions and fee allocation are concerned. Appellate courts have Rule 38 of the Federal Rules of Appellate Procedure at hand which does not discriminate between civil and criminal procedure in that respect. Likewise, all federal courts can apply 28 U.S.C. § 1927 against attorneys. Failing that, it is inherent powers which can serve as a base for sanctions.[501] In conclusion, sanctions in direct response to litigation abuse by parties and their attorneys are possible through several avenues.[502] They are more common in civil litigation and their use may be controversial in criminal cases. Much criticism attaches to their procedural aspects and their effect on advocacy and this will be even more crucial in the criminal context. The procedure for these sanctions will be examined in detail later.[503] One essential finding can be made at this point, though: under codified rules, contempt and other inherent powers, US courts can sanction counsel directly during ongoing proceedings.

US criminal procedure also allows for addressing misconduct after the close of proceedings. Under the Federal Rules of Criminal Procedure, a defendant can move for a new trial (Rule 33). Breaches of professional duties by defence counsel can support a claim of ineffective assistance under the writ of habeas corpus.[504] Both new trial orders and review under habeas corpus disturb the findings on the merits. Courts have come to require a very high threshold for both. 'Ineffective assistance' has been understood to mean virtually no representation with a 'but for' causation test that there would have been a reasonable likelihood of a different outcome.[505] Similar high standards are required for a new

[499] See 28 U.S. Code, § 2254, Rule 11, § 2255, Rule 12 (rules of civil procedure apply 'to the extent that they are not inconsistent with these rules'); Vairo, *Rule 11 Sanctions* (n 497) § 3.05[b] at 131–34. Doubted by *U.S. ex rel. Potts v Chrans*, 700 FSupp 1505 (United States District Court, N.D. Illinois, 1988), vacated and remanded on other grounds by *Potts v Chrans*, 911 F2d 736 (Table), 1990 WL 124203 (Unpublished Disposition) (United States Court of Appeals, Seventh Circuit, 1990), but see *Mayle v Felix*, 545 US 644, 125 SCt 2562, 162 LEd2d 582 (Supreme Court of the United States, 2005); *Smith v Gilmore*, 111 F3d 55 (United States Court of Appeals, Seventh Circuit, 1997); *Anderson v Butler*, 886 F2d 111 (United States Court of Appeals, Fifth Circuit, 1989); *U.S. v Quin*, 836 F2d 654 (United States Court of Appeals, First Circuit, 1988).

[500] Vairo, *Rule 11 Sanctions* (n 497) § 3.05[a] at 131–32.

[501] Joseph, *Sanctions*, 3rd edn (n 494) 427–36; Vairo, *Rule 11 Sanctions* (n 497) § 12.03[b] at 764–70 citing *Chambers v Nasco* (above n 324), and stressing that it 'should be thought of as gap-filler'.

[502] Joseph, *Sanctions*, 3rd edn (n 494) 450–62, 477–78. He notes that sanctioning powers are, in comparison to civil litigation, used sparingly in criminal cases, though courts have used them. An often-cited case under Rule 38 of the Federal Rules of Appellate Procedure would be *In re Becraft*, 885 F2d 547 (United States Court of Appeals, Ninth Circuit, 1989).

[503] Below, III.C.iv at 151–53.

[504] 28 U.S. Code § 2241. See RB Gallagher et al, 'Habeas Corpus and Postconviction Remedies, Vol 39' in Lawyers Cooperative Publishing (ed), *American Jurisprudence*, 2nd edn (New York, Thomson/West, 1989) § 48.

[505] *Rompilla v Beard*, 125 SCt 2456 (Supreme Court of the United States, 2005); *Wiggins v Smith*, 123 SCt 2527 (Supreme Court of the United States, 2003); *Bell v Cone*, 122 SCt 1843 (Supreme Court of the United States, 2002); *Williams v Taylor*, 120 SCt 1495 (Supreme Court of the United States, 2000); *Roe*

trial.[506] In a civil context, it has been noted that misconduct must go quite beyond aggressive advocacy, and that the misconduct must be assessed in relation to the case in its totality.[507] Put differently, '[t]he purpose of a new trial . . . is not to punish . . . professional lapses but to obviate prejudice'.[508] A re-trial will thus only be appropriate for the gravest instances of misconduct which bear on the outcome of the proceedings. If it exhausts only a violation of the professional rules, the appropriate course is generally the referral to the disciplinary bodies and not a new trial.[509] This is reflected in the criteria which courts have developed for prosecutorial misconduct. To initiate a new trial, it must amount to unfairness affecting substantial rights thus denying the accused due process [510] Some circuits apply a two-step test in which they first clarify whether conduct was improper and then, if yes, decide whether a new trial is warranted. Under one approach, this is determined according to four factors:[511] whether the misconduct in question (1) prejudiced the defendant; whether it was (2) isolated or extensive; (3) deliberately or accidentally made; and whether (4) the evidence against the defendant was strong. Other circuits use the same factors but also explicitly take into account the 'curative actions taken by the trial court'.[512] Therefore, even misconduct with a notable effect on the proceedings will not be rectifiable through these post-conviction remedies as long as the proceedings are not tainted for the accused. It will clearly only cover those gravest instances but will not be a response to the bulk of misconduct which will be less then deliberate and not systematic. Factoring in previous curative measures and the strength of the evidence seem to be further arguments for courts to give priority to action during the proceedings and to upholding the outcome of the trial.

In conclusion, measures during the trial can address misconduct in a timely manner. They may help to rectify some of the effects on the process which misconduct may have caused. On the other hand, not all of them can be identified with counsel as can be seen with contempt.

v Flores-Ortega, 120 SCt 1029 (Supreme Court of the United States, 2000). See also *Smith v Robbins*, 120 SCt 746; 528 US 259 (Supreme Court of the United States, 2000). See Hall (n 23) § 10:8–13.

[506] See JR Kennel, 'New Trial, Vol 58' in Lawyers Cooperative Publishing (ed), *American Jurisprudence*, 2nd edn (New York, Thomson/West, 1989) § 124, § 125.

[507] *Aluminum Co. of Americav Aetna Cas. & Sur. Co.*, 140 Wash2d 517, 998 P2d 856 (Supreme Court of Washington, 2000).

[508] *Eklund v Lund*, 301 Minn 359, 222 NW2d 348 (Supreme Court of Minnesota, 1974).

[509] *First National Bank in Marlinton v Blackhurst*, 176 WVa 472, 345 SE2d 567 (Supreme Court of Appeals of West Virginia, 1986); *Gum v Dudley*, 202 WVa 477, 505 SE2d 391 (Supreme Court of Appeals of West Virginia, 1997).

[510] *U.S. v Scheetz*, 293 F3d 175 (United States Court of Appeals, Fourth Circuit, 2002); *U.S. v Tocco*, 200 F3d 401 (United States Court of Appeals, Sixth Circuit, 2000).

[511] *U.S. v Carter*, 236 F3d 777 (United States Court of Appeals, Sixth Circuit, 2001); *Slagle v Bagley*, 457 F3d 501 (United States Court of Appeals, Sixth Circuit, 2006).

[512] *U.S. v Beckman*, 222 F3d 512 (United States Court of Appeals, Eighth Circuit, 2000); *U.S .v Conrad*, 320 F3d 851 (United States Court of Appeals, Eighth Circuit, 2003); *U.S. v Hernandez-Guevara*, 162 F3d 863 (United States Court of Appeals, Fifth Circuit, 1998); *U.S. v Hasner*, 340 F3d 1261 (United States Court of Appeals, Eleventh Circuit, 2003); *U.S. v Shareef*, 190 F3d 71 (United States Court of Appeals, Second Circuit, 1999).

c Admission to the Bar as an Indirect Measure

The institutional controls described above are in response to specific instances of misconduct. Admission to the Bar serves as a filter before counsel can practice and commit misconduct in this function.[513] All US jurisdictions employ these kinds of entry controls.[514] The Supreme Court has held that it is possible to impose admission requirements in order to protect the public if the requirements show a 'rational connection with the applicant's fitness or capacity to practice law'.[515] This is understood to comprise educational requirements and other questions of competent rendition of legal services, but usually also extends to character and other personal qualities.[516] As part of this, the licensing bodies enquire, inter alia, into the prior criminal history of the candidate. Whereas an automatic disqualification followed for certain crimes and rebuttable presumptions were used, the trend now seems to go towards more flexible criteria and the use of specific factors.[517] Nonetheless, the current system has been assessed controversially in scholarship. The costs of excluding lawyers are said to be too high as the current schemes are more directed at the image of profession rather than being a control for quality services.[518] From a quite pragmatic level, commentators have noted that the resource constraints of Bars lead to unevenness in administering the evaluation, do not offer the requisite due process and cast a doubt on the reliability of the scheme.[519] The moral assessments in particular have been attacked fundamentally as being dangerous, due to their inevitable subjectivity and the lack of predictability.[520] Courts have, though, upheld the qualifications requirements, including the good moral character standard and defended them with the specificity of factors which are used today.[521]

[513] On unauthorised practice see above, III.B.i at 115.

[514] *In re Application of Oppenheim*, 141 NM 596, 159 P3d 245 (Supreme Court of New Mexico, 2007); *Law Students Civil Rights Research Council, Inc. v Wadmond*, 401 US 154, 91 SCt 720, 27 LEd2d 749 (Supreme Court of the United States, 1971).

[515] *Schware v Board of Bar Examiners of State of New Mexico*, 353 US 232, 77 SCt 752, 64 ALR2d 288, 1 LEd2d 796 (Supreme Court of the United States, 1957).

[516] 'Restatement of the Law' (n 40) § 2.

[517] MM Carr, 'The Effect of Prior Criminal Conduct on the Admission to Practice Law: The Move to More Flexible Admission Standards' (1994–95) 8 *Georgetown Journal of Legal Ethics* 367, 379; T Gallagher, 'Innocent until Proven Guilty – Not for Bar Applicants' (2007) 31 *Journal of the Legal Profession* 297, 300.

[518] Carr (n 517) 369.

[519] On due process see also Gallagher (n 517) 303. Schware, see above (n 515) was only arrested but never actually convicted.

[520] See the seminal paper by Rhode, 'Moral Character as a Professional Credential' (n 321); L Gunn, 'Past Crimes and Admission to the Bar' (1980) 5 *Journal of the Legal Profession* 179, and B McDowell, 'The Usefulness of "Good Moral Character"' (1994) 33 *Washburn Law Journal* 323.

[521] *In re Application of Oppenheim* (n 514); *Law Students Civil Rights Research Council, Inc.v Wadmond* (n 514).

d Ethics Committees

Ethics committees are not part of the formal disciplining system. Although they are in some way closely connected to professional discipline, they can be considered institutional since they do not engage in the actual prosecution of cases but provide advice on inquiry by attorneys. This also reveals the limitations of ethics opinions. Unscrupulous counsel will not heed it or bother to solicit one in first place. Their involvement has been advocated, though, in principle, and other actors, courts in particular, have shown their willingness to consider them.[522]

The benefit of ethics advice is easy to see. They provide education on the subject which can be tailored to the most pressing problems and compensate for deficits, they may indeed dissuade some attorneys in some hard cases or at least come up with a workable solution and they can prove the commitment to professional standards. The reality is removed from this ideal, though. The allegedly bad quality of opinions has drawn criticism[523] as well as the general stance of ethics committees: they have been described as displaying a great amount of self-interest in the profession on the one hand, but not recognising and addressing adequately issues particular to criminal defence work.[524] A number of suggestions have been made to improve ethics opinions.[525] Quite simply, experts sitting on these committees should be subject to more stringent credentials; outside comment from courts and non-lawyers has also been deemed to contribute; and the process of how ethics opinions are discussed and issued should be formalised.

iv Liability Controls

Liability specifically refers to claims pursued by injured clients or third parties.[526] It can be characterised as the principal type of private enforcement, in contrast to the public control in the other models.

As a starting point, malpractice litigation is generally a viable option for clients and others to pursue their claims.[527] Criminal lawyers are not exempt from this. Court-assigned attorneys owe the same duties as private attorneys and can be

[522] PA Joy, 'Making Ethics Opinions Meaningful: Toward More Effective Regulation of Lawyers' Conduct' (2001–02) 15 *Georgetown Journal of Legal Ethics* 313, 340.

[523] ibid, 345. See also LK Hellman, 'When Ethics Rules Don't Mean What They Say: The Implications of Strained ABA Ethics Opinions' (1996–97) 10 *Georgetown Journal of Legal Ethics* 317.

[524] DG Trager, 'Do Bar Association Ethics Committees Serve the Public or the Profession: An Argument for Process Change' (2006) 34 *Hofstra Law Review* 1129; Joy (n 522) 354.

[525] BA Green, 'Bar Association Ethics Committees: Are They Broken?' (2001–02) 30 *Hofstra Law Review* 731; CM Langford and DMM Bell, 'Finding a Voice: The Legal Ethics Committee' (2001–02) 30 *Hofstra Law Review* 855; WA McCaslin, 'Empowering Ethics Committees' (1995–96) 9 *Georgetown Journal of Legal Ethics* 959, 979; Joy (n 522) 372 (suggesting review by court).

[526] Above, Introduction, III at 4.

[527] Wilkins (n 71) 806; Leubsdorf (n 352).

sued for malpractise.[528] Only public defenders are sometimes given immunity by statute.[529]

Malpractice suits follow the normal procedure and requirements under tort and contract law.[530] Civil jurisdiction is generally in the realm of the states but it is conceivable that federal jurisdiction arises on the basis of a 'federal question' or 'diversity'.[531] Moreover, the federal district courts have 'original jurisdiction of any civil action by an alien for a tort only, committed in violation of the law of nations or a treaty of the United States'.[532] For most domestic misconduct involving that of a fiscal nature, state jurisdiction will be more likely. As to the substantive law, the respective law of conflicts determines the applicable content and will typically depend on an analyis of factors such as choice of law, the place where the contract is made or where services are performed, or where the lawyer acts otherwise.[533]

The details under state law vary, but professional negligence will generally follow under tort doctrine if the attorney has breached his or her duty to exercise the reasonable degree of skill and care. Some courts have held certified specialists to higher standards.[534] If all the elements are proven by the plaintiff, courts award damages which can include punitive damages.[535] No disbarment or other personal sanctions or recommendations result from these. The emphasis is thus on the 'making whole' aspect, including fee forfeiture and nullifying transactions.[536] For these reasons, malpractice litigation has never developed into a source of attorney conduct norms in the United States.[537] First, civil liability proceedings and professional discipline stand apart from each other. A breach of ethical rules does not suffice to establish negligence or, in particular, a violation of the standard of

[528] *Ferri v Ackerman*, 444 US 193, 100 SCt 402, 62 LEd2d 355 (Supreme Court of the United States, 1979).

[529] Leubsdorf (n 352) 137.

[530] Hall (n 23) § 31:3, 24.

[531] See E Chemerinsky, *Federal Jurisdiction*, 5th edn (New York, Aspen Publishers, 2007) 265–71; See *Tafflin* v *Levitt*, 493 U.S. 455, 459–60 (1990). 'Federal Question' can be invoked when the federal constitution, laws or US treaties are concerned. 'Diversity jurisdiction' becomes relevant, however, when citizens of different US states or foreign nationals are involved and the sum is over US$ 75,000 (28 U.S. Code §§ 1331, 1332).

[532] 28 U.S. Code §§ 1350.

[533] See 'Restatement of the Law, Second, Conflict of Laws' in American Law Institute (ed), (1971) particularly, §§ 4, 6, 145–148, 152, 155, 163, 186 to 188, 196.

[534] See BO Herring, 'Liability of Board Certified Specialists in a Legal Malpractice Action: Is there a Higher Standard?' (1998–99) 12 *Georgetown Journal of Legal Ethics* 67.

[535] See Leubsdorf (n 352) 136 *et seq* on criminal defence lawyers; and Hall (n 23) § 31:1–24. Four states (Michigan, Nebraska, New Hampshire and Washington) and Puerto Rico do not allow punitive damages, but the compensatory awards in Michigan and New Hampshire contain a punitive component. See RL Blatt, RW Hammesfahr and LS Nugent, *Punitive Damages: A State-By-State Guide To Law And Practice*, 2007 edn (Eagan, Minn, Thomson/West, 2007) § 3:2.

[536] TD Morgan, 'Sanctions and Remedies for Attorney Misconduct' (1994–95) 19 *Southern Illinois University Law Review* 343, 351

[537] JA McMorrow, 'Creating Norms of Attorney Conduct in International Tribunals: A Case Study of the ICTY' (2007) 30 *Boston College International & Comparative Law Review* 139, 156. See also MJ Duncan, 'Criminal Malpractice: A Lawyer's Holiday' (2003) 37 *Georgia Law Review* 1251.

care.[538] Moreover, the interests at stake in criminal litigation, such as the liberty of the defendant and the pursuit of justice on the other hand, are different from civil proceedings which result in a high threshold for causation and difficulties in assessing damages.

Therefore, the bearing of liability controls on criminal defence is limited but should not be fully discarded since it may be a tool well-suited to claim for specific types of misconduct, namely agency problems of a financial character, where the client needs to recover from his attorney as his acting agent. One of the clear advantages would be that the injured persons determine the process and tailor the remedies to their needs. On the other hand, this requires injured parties should have a quite high degree of legal sophistication, are well-funded and willing to engage in additional litigation.[539] This will typically not be the profile of most of the participants in criminal proceedings and, least of all, that of a convicted defendant.

v *Conclusion*

As seen above, the law governing counsel misconduct and allowing for sanctions and other responses has been explained. It can be noted that the scope of the various measures is different, although all of them, as institutional choices, are justifiable. The degree of viability and effectiveness varies, and so do the strengths and weaknesses. Legislative controls only cover a narrow slice of misconduct. The emphasis is on institutional controls, principally owing to the sanctioning powers of the courts, including their inherent powers. Professional discipline plays an important role but it is by far not the main type of discipline. Evidence suggests that judges prefer institutional controls over relying on discipline.[540] Nonetheless, the purpose and usefulness of 'professional codes' in the United States has been described as follows:

> What, then, is left for the professional codes to accomplish? Most commentators agree that, whatever legal ethics means, it has something to do with defining lawyers' roles in a system of resolving disputes. For particular situations that pose a dilemma, professional codes are supposed to help lawyers choose among two or more legal courses of conduct. At least part of the codes' function is to explain the parameters of the system and attempt to identify how, when, and why a lawyer should act differently than well-intentioned laypersons might act.
>
> Patently, however, the codes have subsidiary purposes. One is to provide a basis for sanctioning lawyer conduct that everyone agrees is wrongful, but which typically escapes punishment. Another is to create a fraternity, or 'profession', in which the

[538] See the case law cited by Hall (n 23) § 31:22; for a critical account see, A Peters, 'The Model Rules as a Guide for Legal Malpractice' (1992–93) 6 *Georgetown Journal of Legal Ethics* 609.

[539] Wilkins (n 71) 830.

[540] PA Joy, 'The Relationship between Civil Rule 11 and Lawyer Discipline: An Empirical Analysis Suggesting Institutional Choices in the Regulation of Lawyers' (2004) 37 *Loyola of Los Angeles Law Review* 765, 806.

> members perceive a norm in dealing with one another. The existence of this fraternity arguably facilitates the legal process. Finally, ethics codes provide standards to which courts can refer in adopting common law doctrine. Most codes accept, as a given, legal standards that pre-date the codes' adoption. However, when such standards are unclear or do not exist, drafters sometimes have attempted to supplement the substantive law.[541]

Therefore, professional codes may be useful as an overall frame and a catch-all net in relation to other controls and, in addition, they have served as more than just the vehicle for discipline. These functions implicate a vagueness problem in certain regards. On the one hand, professional codes are enforceable law. Even in these parts, the codified law oscillates between rules which seem clear and other, broader ones, the latter put in place to cater for all eventualities or simply reflect that professional decisions are often difficult and cannot be predicted along bright lines. Another source of vagueness is that codes, from the outset, tend to mesh up binding rules with aspirational considerations. Again, this may be deemed an advantage compared with the other controls, given the fact that a perfect code seems to be an illusion.[542] It may lead to confusion, however, if the issue is seen as the narrower one of actually sanctioning counsel.

C Comparison of the Procedure for the Various Measures

i Disciplinary Procedure

As could be seen, the harshest sanctions for counsel misconduct come with considerable procedural safeguards. Outside the core area of criminal sanctions, they decrease. An example of this would be the next tier – the disciplinary system.[543] It ultimately has a judicial component but is different from prosecutions and trials for criminal offences. The Model Rules of Disciplinary Enforcement can serve as the example. Whereas the ABA Model Rules of Professional Conduct set out the standards of professional conduct, these contain the rules of procedure.[544]

[541] FC Zacharias, 'Specificity in Professional Responsibility Codes: Theory, Practice, and the Paradigm of Prosecutorial Ethics' (1993) 69 *Notre Dame Law Review* 223, 229.

[542] FC Zacharias, 'The Quest for a Perfect Code' (1997–98) 11 *Georgetown Journal of Legal Ethics* 787.

[543] Above, III.B.i at 114–24.

[544] It is recalled again, that they are not as such applicable, as would hold true for all the Model Rules. Actual state rules vary even more than for the Model Rules of Professional Conduct: B Althoff, 'Lawyer Disciplinary Sanctions' (2001) *Professional Lawyer* 105, 105. For an overview on different states and courts of appeal, see A Rothrock, 'Attorney Discipline and Disability Process and Procedure – Part 1' (2007) 36 *Colorado Lawyer* 23 and A Rothrock, 'Attorney Discipline and Disability Process and Procedure – Part 2' (2007) 36 *Colorado Lawyer* 41; American Bar Association, *Report on the Lawyer Regulation System* (Massachusetts, October 2005); LH Averill, 'The Revised Lawyer Discipline Process in Arkansas: A Primer and Analysis' (1998) 21 *University of Arkansas at Little Rock Law Review* 13; *Rules of Attorney Disciplinary Enforcement* (Court of Appeals for the First Circuit, Effective August 1, 2002); Covington & Burling LLP, 'District of Columbia Legal Ethics: A Summary of the Law of Lawyering in the District of Columbia' (2007): www.dcbar.org/for_lawyers/resources/virtual_library/download.

Whereas professional discipline was once purely private and local, the adoption of the ABA model codifications and of the recommendations by reports such as the McKay Report later lead to more uniformity.[545] At present, professional discipline is administered in adjudicated proceedings under the auspices of the judicial branch, either directly by the highest state court or delegated to bodies within the Bar. Reprimands are issued as private or public ones. An attorney can be prohibited from practising by way of temporary suspension or disbarment and the latter sanctions, in particular, can be drastic. Disbarment follows automatically for some violations in a number of jurisdictions,[546] and is sometimes permanent.[547]

There has been recurring criticism that sanctioning under the existing disciplinary schemes is not very uniform and suffers from flaws.[548] As to general features, some can be identified which are common to the various attorney disciplinary systems. They are quite typical, as they set discipline apart from criminal justice and other mechanisms. Many features emulate the criminal process. The burden of proof rests with the disciplinary counsel which acts as the prosecutor in disciplinary matters. Before allegations formally go before an adjudicatory body, there is usually a screening and investigation process controlled by disciplinary counsel.[549] During this initial stage, an informal resolution can be reached, for which alternatives to formal discipline are often put in place.[550] Otherwise, the case will be filed and thus formally opened. It varies widely whether proceedings are conducted in private or publicly, and if so, from which point.[551] A case is either brought before a board which hands down a sanction or first before a hearing panel which recommends a sanction. Disciplinary systems then vary whether it is this board which actually imposes the sanction or whether this is done by the

cfml?filename=law_of_lawyering0707; JR Supple, 'Attorney Discipline in New York: A Nuts and Bolts Primer' in Practising Law Institute (ed), *18th Annual Elder Law Institute* (New York, 2006). See also American Bar Association, *Lawyer Regulation for A New Century. Report of the Commission on Evaluation of Disciplinary Enforcement* (McKay Report, February 1992).

545 Levin, 'The Case for Less Secrecy' (n 352) 16.

546 RR Caviedes, 'Remnants of an Attorney Disciplinary Sanction: Which Jurisdictions Impose Automatic Disbarment – What Offenses Warrant the Imposition of an Automatic Disciplinary Sanction?' (2002) 26 *Journal of the Legal Profession* 195.

547 B Finkelstein, 'Should Permanent Disbarment be Permanent?' (2007) 20 *The Georgetown Journal of Legal Ethics* 587.

548 Generally, Levin, 'The Emperor's Clothes' (n 352) 77 on fines; H Boyd and B Turetsky, 'Conversion and the Dilemma of Disciplinary Sanctions' (2000–01) 14 *Georgetown Journal of Legal Ethics* 1019; JD Fabian and B Reinthaler, 'An Examination of the Uniformity (or Lack Thereof) of Attorney Sanctions' (2000–01) 14 *Georgetown Journal of Legal Ethics* 1059; IGI Camarena, 'Domestically Violent Attorneys: Resuscitating and Transforming a Dusty, Old Punitive Approach to Attorney Discipline into a Viable Prescription for Rehabilitation' (2001) 31 *Golden Gate University Law Review* 155; CA Kelly, 'Lawyer Sanctions: Looking Back through the Looking-Glass' (1987–88) 1 *Georgetown Journal of Legal Ethics* 469; MM Petras, 'Survey Project: Attorney Sanctions: General Principles' (1989–90) 3 *Georgetown Journal of Legal Ethics* 57.

549 The standing of private persons in launching and pressing disciplinary complaint is limited to laying the information. See WB Woodall, 'Attorney Disciplinary Proceedings: Who Has Standing?' (2002) 26 *Journal of the Legal Profession* 279. See on the ICC Code, ch 3, II.A.v.c at 213–14.

550 See American Bar Association, *Model Rules for Lawyer Disciplinary Enforcement* (n 393) Rule 11(G)(1). See ch 3, II.A.v.d at 219, on the ICC.

551 Levin, 'The Case for Less Secrecy' (n 352).

highest court to which the board refers the matter for confirmation. In state disciplinary proceedings, the ultimate review power is with this highest court in the state.[552]

It is principally the nature of these disciplinary schemes which bears on the level of procedural protection. In the past, disciplinary proceedings were characterised as civil in nature, and accordingly no special procedural guarantees followed. The purported purpose was to ensure the fitness of the members of the profession to practice.[553] Over time, the procedure changed to a relatively formal administrative format. In particular – with the emergence of procedural protections in the 1960s – it became quasi-criminal.[554] This has, for example, lead courts to hold that disciplinary rules must be construed strictly, resolving any ambiguity in favour of the attorney.[555] Whereas courts have recognised that sanctions can amount to penalties in some way or another, they have firmly held that the principal purpose is the protection of the public and not punishment. Therefore, disciplinary proceedings have been categorised as *sui generis* but ultimately not been equated to criminal proceedings.[556]

Therefore, disciplinary proceedings come with considerable rights but not automatically with the full spectrum of criminal due process. Differences exist between minor grievances, serious but uncontested charges and serious contested charges.[557] A not too complicated procedure is seen as preferable for the minor cases and a hearing-type style procedure is afforded for the latter two. There is generally the benefit of a pre-charge screening by the disciplinary enforcement agency, the right to notice and to a statement of the charge or grievance as well as an opportunity to be heard by a neutral decision-maker. For the more advanced stages of the disciplinary process, more rights are generally afforded, such as: the right to formal or informal discovery; the right to assistance of counsel; the right to subpoena witnesses and evidence (although this is not absolute as to extend to every witness and every piece of evidence that the attorney wishes); the right to cross-examine adverse witnesses, to exclude evidence inadmissible under the rules of evidence, the requirement of proof by a preponderance of the evidence or, in some cases, by clear and convincing evidence and judicial review.[558]

By and large, this brings professional discipline into proximity with criminal justice. But marked differences do remain, however. Disciplinary proceedings

[552] Kane et al (n 359) § 109; Levin, 'The Case for Less Secrecy' (n 352) 19. It is recalled that the power to discipline, being an inherent judicial one, is usually held to originate with the courts, and in particular with the highest state court. See above, III.A at 109–13, and III.B.i.a at 114–15.

[553] *Ex parte Wall* (n 400); Strength (n 400) 260.

[554] *In re Ruffalo* (n 348); GC Hazard and C Beard, 'A Lawyer's Privilege Against Self-Incrimination in Professional Disciplinary Proceedings' (1987) 96 *Yale Law Journal* 1060, 1060; Strength (n 400) 260.

[555] *Matter of Thalheim*, 853 F2d 383 (United States Court of Appeals, Fifth Circuit, 1988); *U.S. v Brown*, 72 F3d 25 (United States Court of Appeals, Fifth Circuit, 1995); *In re Sealed Appellant*, 194 F3d 666 (United States Court of Appeals, Fifth Circuit, 1999).

[556] Strength (n 400) 261. See for case law above, at n 400.

[557] Hazard and Beard (n 554) 1061; ST Reaves, 'Procedural Due Process Violations in Bar Disciplinary Proceedings' (1998) 22 *Journal of the Legal Profession* 351.

[558] Hazard and Beard (n 554) 1061; Reaves (n 557) 362.

need not be public, and a jury trial is not required.[559] The attorney is usually under a duty to cooperate, of which a violation is relatively easy to punish.[560] Under the Model Rules of Professional Conduct, there is even a duty for attorneys to report violations.[561] This may be the most relevant area where the disciplinary scheme falls back and thus is in conflict with the higher criminal standards. This is likely for the significant number of cases in which the alleged misconduct also forms the subject of a genuinely criminal prosecution. The duty to cooperate in disciplinary proceedings may in particular compromise counsel's freedom from self-incrimination or his or her duty to confidentiality. In this respect, the different standards can be reconciled by conferring criminal immunity.[562]

ii *Procedure for Criminal Offences*

Criminal offences, such as the ones described above,[563] are prosecuted and tried in accordance with state criminal procedure, or in federal cases, the Federal Rules of Criminal Procedure and the Federal Rules of Appellate Procedure, respectively.[564] In addition, constitutional rights attaching to criminal proceedings are enshrined in the Bill of Rights, namely the Fourth, Fifth and Sixth Amendments to the Constitution.[565]

[559] Reaves (n 557) 361; KA Thompson, 'The Utilization of Juries in Lawyer Disciplinary Proceedings' (2000) 24 *Journal of the Legal Profession* 511.

[560] American Bar Association, *Model Rules of Professional Conduct* Rule 8.1(b) and Comment; JP Pewitt, 'Effective Self-Discipline: Non-Cooperation in the Disciplinary Process and Bar Association Response' (1989) 14 *Journal of the Legal Profession* 235; RV Speegle, 'Failure to Cooperate with a Disciplinary Proceeding' (1991) 16 *Journal of the Legal Profession* 325.

[561] Rule 8.3. See JL Hussey, 'Reporting Another Attorney for Violating the Rules of Professional Conduct: The Current Status of the Law in the States which have Adopted the Model Rules of Professional Conduct' (1999) 23 *Journal of the Legal Profession* 265. A much cited case is *In re Himmel*, 125 Ill2d 531, 533 NE2d 790, 127 IllDec 708, 57 USLW 2246 (Supreme Court of Illinois, 1988). It has been argued that this is important to justify self-regulation (DR Richmond, 'The Duty to Report Professional Misconduct: A Practical Analysis of Lawyer Self-Regulation' (1998–99) 12 *Georgetown Journal of Legal Ethics* 175) but also sparked advocation of reform (AF Greenbaum, 'The Attorney's Duty to Report Professional Misconduct: A Roadmap for Reform' (2002–03) 16 *Georgetown Journal of Legal Ethics* 259; NA Ott and HF Newton, 'A Current Look at Model Rule 8.3: How is it used and what are Courts doing about it?' (2002–03) 16 *Georgetown Journal of Legal Ethics* 747).

[562] In some jurisdictions, this may be done by the prosecutor: Hazard and Beard (n 554) 1070, but depending on the legislation, it is conceivable that the court itself may confer immunity. See Rule 12.(B.) of the Model Rules of Disciplinary Enforcement.

[563] Obstruction of justice, making false statements, fraud, money laundering, etc. Above, III.B.ii at 124–29.

[564] In addition to civilian justice, the Armed Forces hold courts martial under the Uniform Code of Military Justice (U.S. Code, Title 10, Ch. 47). On the courts martial system, see JB Roan and C Buxton, 'The American Military Justice System in the New Millennium' (2002) 52 *Air Force Law Review* 185; GD Henderson, 'Courts-Martial and the Constitution: The Original Understanding' (1957) 71 *Harvard Law Review* 293; KA Ruzic, 'Military Justice and the Supreme Court's Outdated Standard of Deference: Weiss v United States' (1994) 70 *Chicago-Kent Law Review* 265, 289; FA Gilligan and MD Wims, 'Civilian Justice v Military Justice' (1990) *Criminal Justice* 2.

[565] The Fourteenth Amendment makes these applicable to state proceedings and contains an independent due process guarantee. See WR LaFave, JH Israel and NJ King, *Criminal Procedure*, 4th edn (St Paul, Minn, Thomson/West, 2004) §§ 2.2–2.7.

Criminal prosecutions and trials against counsel are in principle no exception to this. This can become complicated to some extent, however, when counsel is prosecuted or tried for professional misconduct which is related to client-work. For these 'professional crimes', not only are the personal interests of counsel at stake, but also those of the client and this can create tension between the two. One example would be the right of counsel to reveal confidential client information in order to defend him or herself against allegations of wrongful conduct.[566] It is chiefly the client's right to assistance of counsel under the Sixth Amendment which is susceptible to being compromised by action against counsel. The role of counsel may also touch on rights under the other Amendments, such as the restrictions on search and seizure under the Fourth Amendment, or the freedom from self-incrimination and the right to due process under the Fifth Amendment. This risk is well-recognised, and a potential for it exists for all measures against counsel, not only in criminal proceedings against counsel. It will thus be revisited later as a general issue.[567] Since the criminal law harbours the harshest sanctions, the tension will be greatest here.

For federal cases, the United States Attorneys' Manual takes this tension into account and offers guidance on prosecutions against acting attorneys. Special attention is paid to the 'balance between an individual's right to the effective assistance of counsel and the public's interest in the fair administration of justice and effective law enforcement'.[568] Subpoenas as well as seizure and search warrants against counsel, irrespective of whether in criminal or civil matters, need authorisation by a presidentially appointed senior official, the Assistant Attorney General for the Criminal Division. Alternative means must be pursued first. The right to effective assistance does not render the attorney–client relationship impenetrable, however. For example, the United States has seen a series of cases on money laundering and attorney fees, and courts have held that the Sixth Amendment has a limit in that 'a criminal defendant may not use criminal proceeds to pay a fee to his defense counsel'.[569] While this always looms in the background, ordinary criminal procedure will generally be the yardstick for permissible defense conduct.

[566] Rule 1.6(b)(5) of the Model Rules, and Rotunda and Dzienkowski (n 41) § 1.6-12(d).

[567] Below, III.E, at 163–65.

[568] Executive Office for US Attorneys (ed) (n 420) 9-13.410 on subpoenas, 420 on warrants.

[569] See ibid, 9-105.600. Prosecution Standards – Bona Fide Fees Paid to Attorneys for Representation in a Criminal Matter); *Caplin & Drysdale, Chartered v U.S.*, 491 US 617, 109 SCt 2646, 105 LEd2d 528 (Supreme Court of the United States, 1989); *United States v Monsanto*, 491 US 600, 109 SCt 2657, 105 LEd2d 512 (Supreme Court of the United States, 1989); *In re Moffitt, Zwerling & Kemler, P.C.*, 846 F Supp 463 (United States District Court, E.D. Virginia, 1994), affirmed by *U.S. v Moffitt, Zwerling & Kemler, P.C.*, 83 F3d 660 (United States Court of Appeals, Fourth Circuit, 1996), cert. denied by *Moffitt, Zwerling & Kemler v U.S.*, 519 US 1101, 117 SCt 788, 136 LEd2d 730 (Supreme Court of the United States, 1997). See also above, at 129 (n 447); Morris (n 446).

iii Procedure for Contempt

It has been explained that different categories of contempt exist. The uniqueness of contempt is that it is a judicial power which can be qualified as institutional. All kinds of contempt actions have two distinctive features in common. First, contempt of court requires an act of disobedience or disrespect towards the judiciary or an interference with its orderly process, including against a person to whom the judicial functions have been delegated.[570] This includes, most characteristically, non-compliance with a prior court order.[571] Secondly, there will be a judicial certificate of contempt issued against the contemner as the centerpiece of the contempt action. The exact nature of this certificate may vary, as Rule 42 of the Federal Rules of Criminal Procedure shows: it can be an order to show cause why the attorney should not be held in contempt, an arrest order, or a contempt order imposing punishment right away.

The subsequent contempt proceedings open up an opportunity for purging the contempt, ie, demonstrating either complicance or the inability to follow the underlying order, but not to reconsider the legal or factual basis of the latter. An issue that could have been raised when the prior order was issued cannot be raised for the first time in the contempt proceedings.[572] In any event, it explains why contempt is an institutional control: it is the judges themselves who initiate the contempt action with the contempt order and subsequently administer the sanctions. This is notwithstanding that prosecutors will naturally apply for a show cause order under Rule 42(b), or that private participants for whose benefit the initial order has been issued will move for a contempt order, if the court does not initiate contempt proceedings *sua sponte*.[573]

As far as details are concerned, different substantive and procedural rules apply to civil and criminal contempts.[574] Contempt proceedings are criminal when aiming at punishment, such as a fine or imprisonment, with the goal of restoring the authority of the court.[575] Criminal contempt proceedings are usually handled separately and independently from the principal proceedings, with the public on

[570] Above, III.B.iii.a at 130 (n 459).

[571] See, eg, 18 U.S.C. 401, in particular sub-section (3). An attorney is not an 'officer' of the court for purposes of § 401(2), *In re Holloway*, 995 F2d 1080 (United States Court of Appeals, District of Columbia Circuit, 1993), cert. denied, *In re Holloway*, 114 SCt 1537, 128 LEd2d 190 (Supreme Court of the United States, 1994).

[572] *Maggio v Zietz*, 333 US 56, 69 (Supreme Court of the United States, 1948); *U.S. v Rylander*, 460 US 752, 103 SCt 1548, 75 LEd2d 521 (Supreme Court of the United States, 1983); *U.S. v First State Bank*, 691 F2d 332 (United States Court of Appeals, Seventh Circuit, 1982) (with dissent by J Doyle, on factual grounds); Executive Office for US Attorneys (ed) (n 420) Criminal Resource Manual 774.

[573] See Executive Office for US Attorneys (ed) (n 420) Criminal Resource Manual 768.

[574] ibid, Criminal Resource Manual 754. See also above, III.B.iii.a at 131, on the criminal/civil distinction in the law of contempt.

[575] ibid, Criminal Resource Manual 755, citing *Shillitani v United States* (n 465) 368–70; *Nye v U.S.* (n 426); *Gompers v Buck's Stove & Range Co.* (n 467) 442; *In re Rumaker* (n 467); *U.S. v Powers* (n 467); *U.S. v North* (n 465); *Carlson Fuel Co. v United Mine Workers* (n 467).

one side and the defendant on the other.[576] A trial court will enforce a public interest when enforcing its own orders, thus making a contempt action instituted by the court always criminal in nature.[577] On the other hand, a party can petition to hold someone in contempt, including the opposing party. This will often be the case for civil contempt that is remedial rather than punitive, serves only the purpose of the participant and is intended to coerce compliance with an order of the court or to compensate for losses or damages caused by non-compliance.[578] Proceedings in civil contempt are usually between the original parties; they are instituted and tried as part of the main cause or as a supplemental proceeding thereto.[579] A petition may seek civil and criminal contempt actions for the same acts at the same time.[580] When a contempt action is not clearly specified as criminal or civil and a single order is issued with both punitive and remedial sanctions, the criminal feature of the order dominates and the review will be for criminal contempt.[581]

An example of contempt proceedings would be Rule 42 of the Federal Rules of Criminal Procedure. It distinguishes two different methods of contempt proceedings: (1) on notice, with a separate trial; and (2), on summary disposition, without such a trial. For disposition on notice, the court must give notice and the defendant will be given time to prepare his or her defence in a separate trial, which may even come out as a full-blown jury trial.

In the majority of cases, the court's request to the United States Attorney for prosecution will be a formality, unless, private counsel may be more appropriate, for example, because the executive as a litigant has an interest of its own.[582] It needs to be emphasised for the understanding of contempt proceedings, though, that they differ from ordinary criminal prosecutions in that the court will not only initiate the contempt action as such but also launch the prosecution stage. The institution of criminal prosecutions would usually require a written accusation (either an indictment by a grand jury or information by a prosecutor).[583] Although a grand jury indictment may be used to institute a criminal contempt action, cases have indicated that it may even be objectionable to proceed in such a way because it might interfere with the judicial disposition of such matters.[584] Unless the

[576] Executive Office for US Attorneys (ed) (n 420) Criminal Resource Manual 755, citing to *Gompers v Buck's Stove & Range Co.* (n 467) 444–45.

[577] *MacNeil v U.S.*, 236 F2d 149 (United States Court of Appeals, First Circuit, 1956); Hall (n 23) § 33:2.

[578] See for references n 575.

[579] See for references n 576.

[580] It has been held the better practice is to file the petitions for such actions separately, Executive Office for US Attorneys (ed) (n 420) Criminal Resource Manual 765, citing to *Monroe Body Co. v Herzog*, 13 F2d 705, modified, 18 F2d 578 (United States Court of Appeals, Sixth Circuit, 1927).

[581] *Falstaff Brewing Corp. v Miller Brewing Co.* (n 467) 778; for further cases see Executive Office for US Attorneys (ed) (n 420) Criminal Resource Manual 758.

[582] Executive Office for US Attorneys (ed) (n 420) Criminal Resource Manual 768.

[583] ibid, Criminal Resource Manual 201 *et seq*, 207 (courts martial and contempt being the exception).

[584] Respectively *U.S. v Bukowski*, 435 F2d 1094, 1103 (United States Court of Appeals, Seventh Circuit, 1970); cert. denied, *U.S .v Bukowski*, 401 US 911 (Supreme Court of the United States, 1971);

alleged contempt 'involves disrespect toward or criticism of a judge' (paragraph (a)(3)), the same judge will rule as has issued the contempt order. However, the conviction in a criminal contempt action is a final judgment and is immediately appealable.[585]

On the other hand, there is a possibility of summary disposition for direct contempt which will be done if the contumacious conduct threatens to disrupt the trial or leads to a breakdown of the proceedings.[586] Thus, it will be the judge who tries the contemner immediately without further notice or hearing other than issuing the contempt order itself. In this case, no separate trial exists. However, the contempt order under Rule 42(b) must satisfy the basic requirements of 'fair notice' and must also state the 'essential facts' constituting the criminal contempt charged.[587] Proceeding under Rule 42(b) must allow a reasonable time for the preparation of a defence which will vary according to the circumstances of each case, and a short time may be sufficient.[588]

Civil contempt sanctions, ie, to compel future compliance with a court order, are imposed in an ordinary civil proceeding on notice by the judge and an opportunity to be heard.[589] Procedural guarantees are thus more limited than for criminal contempt.[590] For example, no right to jury trial exists for civil contempt.[591] The burden of proof to establish culpability is lower. Sometimes, a 'preponderance of evidence' standard is used, but mostly it is on 'clear and convincing' evidence.[592] Elements that must be proven may include: (1) that a court order was in effect; (2) that the order required certain conduct by the respondent; and (3) that the

and *U.S. v Levya*, 513 F2d 774, 775 (United States Court of Appeals, Fifth Circuit, 1975); Executive Office for US Attorneys (ed) (n 420) Criminal Resource Manual 766, with further references.

[585] *U.S. v Johnson*, 801 F2d 597, 599 (United States Court of Appeals, Second Circuit, 1986); *SEC v Simpson*, 885 F2d 390, 395 (United States Court of Appeals, Seventh Circuit, 1989); *Carlson Fuel Co v United Mine Workers* (n 467).

[586] See Hall (n 23) § 33:65, for details.

[587] Executive Office for US Attorneys (ed) (n 420) Criminal Resource Manual 762, 781, 782, citing to *U.S. v United Mine Workers*, 330 US 258, 298–300 (Supreme Court of the United States, 1947); *Myers v U.S.* (n 461).

[588] *U.S v Alter*, 482 F2d 1016, 1023 (United States Court of Appeals, Ninth Circuit, 1973); *U.S. v Hawkins* (United States Court of Appeals, Ninth Circuit, 1947), cert, denied, *U.S. v Hawkins*, 419 US 1079 (Supreme Court of the United States, 1974); see Executive Office for US Attorneys (ed) (n 420) Criminal Resource Manual 762, for details.

[589] *International Union, United Mine Workers of America v Bagwell* (n 468); *Blackmer v United States* 284 US 421, 52 SCt 252, 76 LEd 375, 440 (Supreme Court of the United States, 1932).

[590] EC Dudley, 'Getting beyond the Civil/Criminal Distinction: A New Approach to the Regulation of Indirect Contempts' (1993) 79 *Virginia Law Review* 1025, fn 23.

[591] *Shillitani v United States* (n 465); *International Union, United Mine Workers of America v Bagwell* (n 468) 2257; Executive Office for US Attorneys (ed) (n 420).

[592] P Coltoff et al, *Corpus Juris Secundum, Contempt* (St Paul, Minn, Thomson/West, 2008) § 88, 90; Dietz et al (n 459) § 183; *Federal Procedure, Lawyer's Edition*, vol 7A, Ch 17, Contempt (St Paul, Minn, Thomson/West, 2008) § 17:36. Using a preponderance of evidence *Hoffman v International Longshoremen's and Warehouse-men's Union, Local No. 10*, 492 F2d 929 (United States Court of Appeals, Ninth Circuit, 1974), affirmed on other grounds *sub nomine Muniz v Hoffman*, 422 US 454 (Supreme Court of the United States, 1975); but see also from the Ninth Circuit *Stone v City and County of San Francisco*, 968 F2d 850 (United States Court of Appeals, Ninth Circuit, 1992); *F.T.C. v Affordable Media*, 179 F3d 1228 (United States Court of Appeals, Ninth Circuit, 1999); *In re Dyer*, 322 F3d 1178 (United States Court of Appeals, Ninth Circuit, 2003).

respondent failed to comply with the court's order. The contemptuous action need not be wilful so long as the contemner actually failed to comply with the court's order.[593] Once contempt is so proven, the burden shifts to the alleged contemner to demonstrate why he or she was unable to comply with the court's order.[594]

It is recalled that contempt powers are very wide-reaching but at least for strictly criminal sanctions appropriate defence rights are in place. The presumption of innocence applies, proof beyond a reasonable doubt is required and the accused cannot be compelled to testify against himself.[595] The tendency to afford enhanced procedural protection follows the general effort to distinguish criminal from non-criminal proceedings. The distinction has drawn criticism, however.[596] It is said to create confusion, to be hard to delineate, that it does not remedy the flaws of the contempt procedure and that judges can craft their measures to minimise procedural protection. But the tendency is that some kind of measure that results in sanctions, or are punitive, are to be accompanied by procedural protection such as a notice of charges and the right to present a defence, freedom from self-incrimination, a certain burden of proof, right to legal assistance, an independent court and a jury trial and grand jury.[597] Summing up, the most drastic measures under the doctrine of contempt are also accompanied by the highest procedural safeguards. In criminal contempt, as well as the other criminal offences, the accused counsel can rely on a number of rights and procedures. On the other hand, this is relaxed for other kinds of contempt.

iv Other Procedures

In the previous two sections, the spotlight was on criminal and disciplinary proceedings. Both are ex post facto and thus separate from the immediate context within which the misconduct occurs. Morever, their sanctions provide more than just a strictly compensatory remedy for the immediate consequences of the incurred violation. All of this may explain why both apply enhanced procedural protections. A number of conduct controls, as could be seen above, are direct measures which are not administered in quite the same way. Put briefly, they do not generate separate fact-finding proceedings. Furthermore, they are much more stream-lined and as far as their details are concerned, it goes without saying that

[593] Dietz et al (n 459) § 183, citing *American Airlines, Inc. v Allied Pilots Association et al.*, 228 F3d 574 (United States Court of Appeals, Fifth Circuit, 2000), cert. denied, *Allied Pilots Assn et al. v American Airlines, Inc.*, 531 US 1191, 121 S Ct 1190, 149 L Ed 2d 106 (Supreme Court of the United States, 2001).

[594] Dietz et al (n 459) § 183, with *In re Bennett*, 298 F3d 1059 (United States Court of Appeals, Ninth Circuit, 2002) (appeal from bankruptcy court), and further references.

[595] *Michaelson v U.S. ex rel. Chicago, St. P., M. & O. Ry. Co.*, 266 US 42, 45 SCt 18, 69 LEd 162 (Supreme Court of the United States, 1924); Coltoff et al (n 592) § 88.

[596] Dudley (n 590) 1043. On the use of 'civil' and 'criminal' in US legal terminology, see above (n 460).

[597] ibid, 1082.

they again vary from each other. But fundamental issues surface again, such as the requirement to be heard or to have notice, and this is likely to be common to all the different procedures as will be shown below.[598] Of course, simply looking at 'other measures' in this section would unduly mesh together two different categories. Most of the other measures are conduct controls but there are also entry controls such as admission to the Bar.[599] It seems fair to say, however, that bar admission is closer to the procedures used for the other measures than criminal or disciplinary procedures. The latter are distinct because of the enhanced procedural standard that they afford to counsel.

Most relevant are conduct controls, though, and among them in particular litigation-related sanctions. Rule 11 of the Federal Rules of Civil Procedure[600] has been described above as an example of institutional control – thus as such a measure other than criminal or disciplinary. It is recalled that Rule 11 is not applicable in criminal proceedings but it is, inter alia, a good example for direct sanctions, along with its procedural framework. The procedural part of Rule 11 reads:

> Rule 11. Signing of Pleadings, Motions, and Other Papers; Representations to Court; Sanctions
>
> [. . .]
>
> (c) Sanctions.
>
> (1) In General. If, after notice and a reasonable opportunity to respond, the court determines that Rule 11(b) has been violated, the court may impose an appropriate sanction on any attorney, law firm, or party that violated the rule or is responsible for the violation. Absent exceptional circumstances, a law firm must be held jointly responsible for a violation committed by its partner, associate, or employee.
>
> (2) Motion for Sanctions. A motion for sanctions must be made separately from any other motion and must describe the specific conduct that allegedly violates Rule 11(b). The motion must be served under Rule 5, but it must not be filed or be presented to the court if the challenged paper, claim, defense, contention, or denial is withdrawn or appropriately corrected within 21 days after service or within another time the court sets. If warranted, the court may award to the prevailing party the reasonable expenses, including attorney's fees, incurred for the motion.
>
> (3) On the Court's Initiative. On its own, the court may order an attorney, law firm, or party to show cause why conduct specifically described in the order has not violated Rule 11(b).
>
> (4) Nature of a Sanction. A sanction imposed under this rule must be limited to what suffices to deter repetition of the conduct or comparable conduct by others similarly situated. The sanction may include nonmonetary directives; an order to pay a penalty into court; or, if imposed on motion and warranted for

[598] See, eg, *Fink v Gomez* (n 485) and *Goldin v Bartholow*, 166 F3d 710 (United States Court of Appeals, Fifth Circuit, 1999), which both stress the general requirement of bad faith, regardless of whether sanctions are based on Rule 11, § 1927, or on inherent powers.

[599] See below, at 153.

[600] See above, III.B.iii.b at 135–36.

effective deterrence, an order directing payment to the movant of part or all of the reasonable attorney's fees and other expenses directly resulting from the violation.

(5) Limitations on Monetary Sanctions. The court must not impose a monetary sanction:

(A) against a represented party for violating Rule11(b)(2); or

(B) on its own, unless it issued the show-cause orderunder Rule 11(c)(3) before voluntary dismissal or settlement of the claims made by or against the party that is, or whose attorneys are, to be sanctioned.

(6) Requirements for an Order. An order imposing a sanction must describe the sanctioned conduct and explain the basis for the sanction.

As can be seen from this, the court can act on its own initiative, or the other party can move for a sanction. Whether it is by that party's motion ((c)(2)), or or the court's order to show cause ((c)(3)), a sanction thus presupposes notice in any event. The concerned attorney will be given an opportunity to respond. Finally, the court has to make specific and reasoned findings, as flows from sub-rule (c)(6). Sanctions are subject to judicial review, even though this is usually only done as part of the final judgment.[601] Rule 11 has drawn a lot of criticism since 1983 most of this relating to procedure, namely due process concerns,[602] and the risk of additional collateral litigation.[603] As it stands now, this has been somewhat ameliorated.[604]

Similar procedural issues now follow for the sanctioning powers which explicitly apply to lawyers in criminal proceedings, such as 28 U.S.C. § 1927, civil contempt, or the concept of inherent powers. The procedure is not set out in as much detail, but a certain minimum of due process does apply here as well.[605] This is all the more important as using these alternative bases to Rule 11 may allow the court to undercut the more stringent requirements of, for example, Rule 11.[606] A heightened standard of proof – one of clear and convincing evidence – is used for inherent powers.[607] When used punitively, bad faith needs to be found.[608] Under § 1927, too, sanctions cannot be imposed on vicarious liability, although it is disputed

[601] Joseph, *Sanctions*, 3rd edn (n 494) 357–63. For Rule 37(a) of the Federal Rules of Civil Procedure (sanction for discovery abuse), see *Cunningham v Hamilton County*, 527 US 198; 119 SCt 1915; 144 LEd 2d 184 (Supreme Court of the United States, 1999). But (and this may be better fitting to criminal context) see *Transamerica Commercial Finance Corporationv Banton, Inc.*, 970 F2d 810, 815 (United States Court of Appeals, Eleventh Circuit, 1992) (sanctioned party severed from underlying case).

[602] M Stavis, ' Rule 11: Which is Worse – The Problem or the Cure?' (1991–92) 5 *Georgetown Journal of Legal Ethics* 597, 604. A need to provide notice and an opportunity to be heard had been assumed by courts before (*Tom Growney Equipment, Inc. v Shelley Irr. Development, Inc.*, 834 F2d 833, 56 USLW 2405, 10 FedRServ3d 215 (United States Court of Appeals, Ninth Circuit, 1987).

[603] S Lawshe, 'Survey Project: Attorney Sanctions, Rule 11' (1989–90) 3 *Georgetown Journal of Legal Ethics* 71, 75 *et seq*; F Woods, 'Sanctions – Stepchild or Natural Heir to Trial and Appellate Court Delay Reduction?' (1990) 17 *Pepperdine Law Review* 665.

[604] Vairo, *Rule 11 Sanctions* (n 497) § 7.02 at 400–02; Joseph, *Sanctions*, 4th edn (n 335) 342–51.

[605] Joseph, *Sanctions*, 3rd edn (n 494) 462–70; Joseph, *Sanctions*, 4th edn (n 335) § 29(A) at 427.

[606] Joseph, *Sanctions*, 4th edn (n 335) § 2(A)(4)(b) at 32.

[607] ibid, § 25(A)(3) at 396.

[608] ibid, § 27(A) at 409, citing *Roadway Express, Inc. v Piper* (n 485).

whether there is a subjective or an objective bad faith standard.[609] Sanctions under this provision are discretionary but the provision needs to be construed strictly.[610] Specific reasons for the sanction and how it was determined need to be given.[611] The exact due process requirements depend on the circumstances, though, and a hearing may not be necessary.[612] As holds true for the other institutional measures, § 1927 sanctions are not directly appealable.[613] As to non-punitive sanctions, courts can use civil contempt. It can be imposed regardless of the person's intent, as long as he or she can 'purge' him or herself by complying with the court order.[614] Although neither jury trial nor proof beyond a reasonable doubt is required, the concerned party or attorney needs to be afforded notice and an opportunity to be heard, but only in cases of criminal contempt, as discussed above, will this clearly include the right to counsel and to call witnesses.[615]

Finally, the procedure for Bar admission, ie to practise law, is distinct from ex post facto sanctioning.[616] Attaching specifically to the status of the attorney as a professional, it would have seemed equally fair to deal with it in the context of discipline. However, it is 'other procedure', since admission or non-admission is not in response to misconduct, as is covered by professional discipline. In order to be admitted, it is primarily educational requirements which need to be proven by the applicant. This is sometimes accompanied by much more controversial character requirements, the results of which can be questionable.[617] The applicant submits a questionnaire, other proof of good standing and official records. The extent of enquiry has been found by courts to be limited.[618] Although the scheme for these kinds of measures is by nature quite different from those attaching directly to misconduct, similar issues exist. The applicant has the burden of proof for the requirements, but due process is essentially required.[619] Decisions by the responsible board are subject to court review.[620]

[609] Vairo, *Rule 11 Sanctions* (n 497) § 12.08 at 760; Joseph, *Sanctions*, 3rd edn (n 494) 395–501.

[610] Joseph, *Sanctions*, 4th edn (n 335) § 22.

[611] ibid, § 25(C).

[612] ibid, § 25(B); *Cook v American Steamship Co.*, 134 F3d 771, 774–75 (United States Court of Appeals, Third Circuit, 1998).

[613] Joseph, *Sanctions*, 3rd edn (n 494) 417–26; Joseph, *Sanctions*, 4th edn (n 335) §25(D): *Cunningham* reasoning (above n 601) applies to all sanction powers, *Stanley v Woodford*, 449 F3d 1060 (United States Court of Appeals, Ninth Circuit, 2006).

[614] See *U.S. v Kouri-Perez* (n 340).

[615] *International Union, United Mine Workers of America v Bagwell* (n 468); 'Restatement of the Law' (n 40) § 105 (in particular e).

[616] See 'Restatement of the Law' (n 40) § 2.

[617] Recommendations on this by DH Stone, 'The Bar Admission Process, Gatekeeper or Big Brother: An Empirical Study' (1995) 15 *Northern Illinois University Law Review* 331, for fundamental critique see above, III.B.iii.c at n 520.

[618] 'Restatement of the Law' (n 40) § 2, Comment d.

[619] See ER Soeffing, 'Procedural due process requirements in proceedings involving applications for admission to bar' 2 *American Law Reports, 3d* 1266.

[620] See GA Noland, 'Court Review of Bar Examiners' Decision on Applicant's Examination' 39 *American Law Reports, 3rd* 719; Soeffing (n 619) § 6.

v *Analysis*

This short brush over the applicable procedures reveals similarities with Germany. As in Germany, the procedure for disciplinary measures is similar but at the same time distinct from criminal justice. Discipline has been described as an *aliud*. The US way to describe disciplinary proceedings as *sui generis* reflects this as well. Nonetheless, German professional discipline seems closer to criminal justice than its US counterparts. As a default rule, German discipline refers to criminal procedure in Section 116 BRAO.[621] [622] No such automatic reliance on criminal rules is known from US disciplinary schemes. To the contrary, the default position would be the rules of civil procedure. This illustrates how professional discipline has a tendency to follow criminal procedure in many respects, but that this is not necessarily the only conceivable model.

In the US context, Hazard and Beard have attempted to characterise disciplinary procedure and have distinguished different procedural models in this. They list criminal procedure, civil procedure, bilateral structures of an administrative type and unilateral/dispensatory justice.[623] The highest standards are definitely limited to genuinely criminal proceedings. Criminal procedure offers a range of constitutional guarantees and as far as such guarantees are concerned, these protections are punctuated in disciplinary proceedings, nudging them more to the civil side. This is quite obvious from the default reference to civil procedure, for example, by Rule 18(B) of the Model Rules for Lawyer Disciplinary Enforcement, but it is also that no lawyer is provided by public means or the lower burden of proof which deviate from the criminal standard. On the other hand, discipline does not fully follow the model of civil procedure. A pre-charge screening is conducted and, under Rule 15 of the Model Rules for Lawyer Disciplinary Enforcement, information is disclosed between the parties, although short of the full rules for discovery under civil procedure. Even though there is no jury trial, the procedure as such still emulates a trial, at least for more serious cases which are not dealt with as lesser misconduct. The issue of self-incrimination may serve as another example which demonstrates that discipline is middle ground between fully criminal and fully civil procedure. No freedom from self-incrimination as known in the framework of criminal proceedings is afforded to counsel. To the contrary, he or she is required to cooperate.[624] Under Rule 33(A) and (B) of the Model Rules for Lawyer Disciplinary Enforcement, a failure to answer or to appear is considered an admission of the factual allegations. Given that serious cases will often also constitute not just unethical but illegal, ie, criminal conduct, it poses a danger that attorneys' statements or documents may be used as evidence

[621] Above, II.B.i.b at 65–67 for the available sanctions.

[622] See above, II.C.i at 87 (n 189) on Section 116 BRAO.

[623] Hazard and Beard (n 554) 1064.

[624] Section 56 BRAO explicitly lists as grounds for refusing cooperation with the Bar Council the jeopardy of prosecution for criminal offences, lesser administrative infractions and for purely professional breaches.

against them. Here, the conferral of immunity by the prosecutor may be needed to ascertain constitutional mandates. It shows, however, that disciplinary proceedings are ultimately not criminal ones; this could already be seen from the substantive standards for professional breaches, which are more relaxed than criminal offences. Therefore, discipline is definitely middle ground between criminal and civil. It is a prosecution but in many respects leans more towards civil proceedings.

The authors' analysis also helps to understand how other sanctions come with minimum guarantees. Decision-making by authorities may be unilateral in a way that possibly affords opportunities but no enforceable participatory rights to affected actors. In the context of legal ethics, ethics committees come to mind. Virtually all sanctions under procedural models lumped together here as 'other procedure' concern private interests. These interests are, to use the words of Hazard and Beard, 'sensitive enough' to warrant 'a reasonably fair procedure'.[625] This would include as a minimum a right to notice of the charges, to a hearing or some other forum to present evidence and argument and to a review by an impartial body. This has been verified with litigation sanctions such as Rule 11 of the Federal Rules of Civil Procedure, 28 U.S.C. § 1927, and inherent powers, but also the non-criminal types of contempt, such as summary or civil. Warning and bad faith requirements ensure basic fairness.

What should be kept in mind for the later analysis of the ICC law is that different models of procedure exist but that a minimum of guarantees attaches to each of them.[626]

D The Relationship of the Various Measures

i *General Connections*

The previous section has shown again that measures against counsel misconduct can be taken on very different levels. Universalist claims in favour of one specific regulatory regime are unfounded,[627] as demonstrated by the findings for Germany and the United States. Since different sub-regimes exist and are justified, the question is what is the relationships between them.

An initial observation would be that there are general connections between the four regimes identified by Wilkins (criminal, disciplinary, institutional and liability). Some institutional controls are an immediate reaction serving a quite distinct purpose. Consequently, it seems less of a problem to align them since they simply deal with distinct issues. Similarly, compensatory measures seem to be less prone to conflict with other sanctions. Many of the measures outlined so far, though, are not strictly compensatory and ex post facto. Whether there is an overlap between

[625] Hazard and Beard (n 554) 1063.

[626] Ch 3, III.B at 278–79.

[627] Wilkins (n 71) 814.

sanctioning regimes depends on the purpose of measures attaching to the same factual conduct. The prime example of sanctioning regimes that interlock would be criminal law and professional discipline.

A direct connection between criminal law and discipline is created because criminal conduct is a ground for discipline. However, differences exist among states whether this is automatic or not, and for which criminal convictions additional discipline will or may be imposed.[628] A general guideline on this issue would be Rule 8.4 of the Model Rules of Professional Conduct which provides for additional discipline if the characteristics of the crime are relevant to the practice of law. This includes contempt citations, which may also be a base for discipline.[629] Since quite a number of offences are committed in private settings, discipline may follow for conduct which has no nexus to a lawyer's professional qualifications.[630] Essentially, disciplinary rules are phrased openly. The above-mentioned Rule 8.4 lists as grounds for discipline, beyond breaches of professional rules as such, if attorneys

> (b) commit a criminal act that reflects adversely on the lawyer's honesty, trustworthiness or fitness as a lawyer in other respects;
> (c) engage in conduct involving dishonesty, fraud, deceit or misrepresentation;
> (d) engage in conduct that is prejudicial to the administration of justice.

An even more inclusive approach had also been taken by the previous Model Code. Only parts of this Model Code have been retained in the above paragraphs (c) and (d). Moreover, additional discipline was seen as warranted for 'illegal conduct involving moral turpitude' but also – not restricted to criminal conduct – for 'any other conduct that adversely reflects on his fitness to practice law'.[631] These very broad clauses have been stricken from the Model Rules. Nonetheless, breaches of the regular law, be it criminal or institutionally sanctioned measures, will on a number of occasions give rise to disciplinary action.

Furthermore, a general connection between regular law, in particular criminal law, and professional rules is created by the fact that the former fills the spaces in the latter and provides the 'bounds of law' within which ethics operate. Ethical obligations may mandate zealous representation and thus be quite clear but may

[628] RK Dhanda, 'When Attorneys Become Convicted Felons: The Question of Discipline by the Bar' (1994–95) 8 *Georgetown Journal of Legal Ethics* 723.

[629] BW Hardison, 'Contempt Citation as Evidence of Unfitness to Practice Law' (1988) 13 *Journal of the Legal Profession* 271, 273.

[630] WZ Meadows, 'Attorney Conduct in the Operation of a Motor Vehicle as Grounds for Professional Discipline' (1993) 18 *Journal of the Legal Profession* 417; S McKay, 'Attorney Discipline for Failure to Pay Child Support' (1991) 16 *Journal of the Legal Profession* 289. It has been observed that it is the contempt towards justice which is sanctioned, rather than moral regulation, E Boykin, 'Lawyers' Non-Payment of Child Support as a Basis for Disciplinary Action' (1992) 17 *Journal of the Legal Profession* 193. See also *In re Kelley*, 52 Cal3d 487, 801 P2d 1126 (Supreme Court of California, 1990).

[631] DR 1-102. See J Wilson, 'The Definitional Problems with Moral Turpitude' (1991) 16 *Journal of the Legal Profession* 261; JT Burnett, 'Attorney Discipline under DR 1-102(A)(3): Imposing Sanctions Absent a Finding of Moral Turpitude' (1988) 13 *Journal of the Legal Profession* 245; CL Brown, 'Other Misconduct Warranting Discipline' (1992) 17 *Journal of the Legal Profession* 199.

have to be interpreted before the background of the pertinent offences, however ambiguous they are.[632]

On the other hand, professional rules may have an impact on the regular law. The Model Rules themselves stipulate that they do not determine further law, but 'lawyer's violation of a Rule may be evidence of breach of the applicable standard of conduct'.[633] Using ethical standards to determine the 'regular law' has drawn criticism, arguing that the two spheres of law are separate.[634] A less compelling agument for using ethics codes has been that the other regimes are flawed and more sophisticated guidance can be expected from ethics codes.[635] It remains open to doubt whether this is true, given the broad scope of some of the professional rules and the practical experience of how violations are sanctioned. On the other hand, they do try to identify all the important standards of care, whether owed to clients, non-clients and the profession. This concerns foremost civil liability, where courts have mostly declined to equate a disciplinary infraction with an actionable breach of the lawyer's fiduciary treaty.[636] Civil suits may not be pursuable before the ICC but this does not rule out the relevance of professional standards for other measures or in national forums. The emerging approaches in US scholarship can be summarised as follows: first, some contend that disciplinary violations constitute negligence per se; secondly, others see a rebuttable presumption that counsel acted negligently; and thirdly, it is seen as mere evidence of negligence. Some authors and courts refuse to take breaches of professional rules as such evidence.[637]

There may indeed be a case for using ethical standards in standards for malpractice, with certain qualifications.[638] Specific rules clearly articulate binding standards, and professional rules in general mirror general law. Furthermore, they identify a particular harm to the client and the rationales behind specific professional standards seem to be transferable to the other area of law. Courts have also used ethics to interpret criminal law.[639] This seems to be associated with

[632] Green (n 435).

[633] American Bar Association, *Model Rules of Professional Conduct* Scope, para 20.

[634] SE Kalish, 'How to Encourage Lawyers to be Ethical: Do Not Use the Ethics Codes as a Basis for Regular Law Decisions' (1999–2000) 13 *Georgetown Journal of Legal Ethics* 649, 669, arguing that ethics codes, even if adopted by the highest state court, are not true legislation (at 669), and that they are only research assistance (at 670), while conflicts between both systems are tolerable.

[635] GL Hampton, 'Toward an Expanded Use of the Model Rules of Professional Conduct' (1990–91) 4 *Georgetown Journal of Legal Ethics* 655, 660, and also in some way DL Draisen, 'The Model Rules of Professional Conduct and their Relationship to Legal Malpractice Actions: A Practical Approach to the Use of the Rules' (1997) 21 *Journal of the Legal Profession* 67.

[636] *Hizey v Carpenter*, 830 P2d 646; 119 Wn2d 251 (Supreme Court of Washington, 1992); *Miami International Realty Co. v Paynter*, 841 F2d 348 (United States Court of Appeals, Tenth Circuit, 1988). See further Green (n 403) 327, fn 52.

[637] Draisen (n 635) 69; GA Munneke and AE Davis, 'The Standard of Care in Legal Malpractice: Do the Model Rules of Professional Conduct Define it?' (1998) 22 *Journal of the Legal Profession* 33, 61.

[638] Munneke and Davis (n 637) 80. See also Leubsdorf (n 352) 117.

[639] *U.S. v Bronston* (n 437); see 'Restatement of the Law' (n 40) § 8, Comment c; ES Podgor, 'Criminal Misconduct: Ethical Rule Usage Leads to Regulation of the Legal Profession' (1988) 61 *Temple Law Review* 1323, 1336, and further *U.S. v Anderson*, 798 F2d 919 (United States Court of Appeal, Seventh Circuit, 1986); *U.S. v Machi*, 811 F2d 991 (United States Court of Appeal, Seventh Circuit, 1987);

further problems. Oftentimes, it will be quite easy to read any professional standard into the initially broad scope of the relevant criminal offences. The danger in this would be that it goes too far by entrenching professional rules as crimes, and resulting in to much regulation and relatively expensive criminal prosecution.[640] It seems accepted in modern criminal law that not every moral or ethical transgression or regulatory violation should be a crime.[641] It would be troubling because of the ensuing great discretion of prosecutors to prosecute criminally instead of relying on disciplinary system. A different issue may be, however, to resort to professional ethics for questions of procedure.[642]

ii Multiple Proceedings for the Same Facts within the Same Jurisdiction

As has been seen, the regimes are intertwined as far as the substantive law itself is concerned. But even independently thereof, relationships between the different regimes and within them exist because more than one sanction or measure can or will attach to the same set of facts. The Fifth Amendment to the US Constitution provides that 'nor shall any person be subject for the same offence to be twice put in jeopardy of life or limb'. This double jeopardy bar protects an accused not only from a second prosecution, but from multiple punishments for the same criminal conduct.[643] There is, however, a noted difference between the concepts of multiple punishment and successive prosecutions.[644] The crucial point for the former is whether the legislative intent covers convictions under more than one legal basis; the latter, on the other hand, raises issues of *res judicata.*

Going from there, it seems fair to say that parallel proceedings under all the different regimes identified so far are widely permissible. Typically, double jeopardy claims will fail because they only attach to criminal punishment. Proceedings under the other regimes are simply based on non-criminal and legislatively foreseen other footings. The prior issue is therefore whether the penalty in question is

People v Buster, 77 IllApp2d 224, 222 NE2d 31 (Illinois Appellate Court, 1966), using them on the one hand, and *Hefner v State*, 735 SW2d 608 (Texas Court of Appeals, 1987); *Pope v State*, 179 GaApp 739, 347 SE2d 703 (Georgia Court of Appeals, 1986) on the other.

[640] Podgor (n 639) 1346.

[641] Green (n 403) 338.

[642] FC Zacharias, 'Are Evidence-Related Ethics Provisions "Law"?' (2007) 76 *Fordham Law Review* 1315; JA Colquitt, 'Evidence and Ethics: Litigating in the Shadows of the Rules ' (2007) 76 *Fordham Law Review* 1641.

[643] Torcia (n 418) § 55; *U.S. v Benz*, 282 US 304, 51 SCt 113, 75 LEd 354 (Supreme Court of the United States, 1931); *U.S. v Halper*, 490 US 435, 109 SCt 1892, 104 LEd2d 487 (Supreme Court of the United States, 1989); *U.S. v Masters*, 978 F2d 281 (United States Court of Appeal, Seventh Circuit, 1992), rehearing *en banc* denied, *U.S. v Masters*, 1992 US App LEXIS 29076 (United States Court of Appeal, Seventh Circuit, 1992), cert. denied, *Masters v U.S.*, 508 US 906, 113 SCt 2333, 124 LEd2d 245 (Supreme Court of the United States, 1993), related proceeding *U.S. v Corbitt*, 13 F3d 207 (United States Court of Appeal, Seventh Circuit, 1993); *Arizona v Seats*, 638 P2d 1335, 131 Ariz 89 (Supreme Court of Arizona, 1981). But see the criticism by AB Poulin, 'Double Jeopardy and Multiple Punishment: Cutting the Gordian Knot' (2006) 77 *University of Colorado Law Review* 595.

[644] AB Poulin, 'Double Jeopardy Protection from Successive Prosecution: A Proposed Approach' (2004) 92 *Georgetown Law Journal* 1185, 1201.

punishment at all.[645] The pertinent test for determining whether concurrent criminal convictions are permissible is the one laid down by the Supreme Court in *Blockburger v U.S.*[646] To determine accordingly if multiplicity between criminal offences exists, a court must first look to 'whether Congress intended to punish each statutory violation separately'.[647] One example would be convictions for the same misconduct under a statutory criminal offence and contempt. *U.S. v Dixon*, reinstating *Blockburger*, summarises the law on this point as follows:

> We have held that constitutional protections for criminal defendants other than the double jeopardy provision apply in nonsummary criminal contempt prosecutions just as they do in other criminal prosecutions.... We think it obvious, and today hold, that the protection of the Double Jeopardy Clause likewise attaches.... In both the multiple punishment and multiple prosecution contexts, this Court has concluded that where the two offenses for which the defendant is punished or tried cannot survive the 'same-elements' test, the double jeopardy bar applies.... The same-elements test, sometimes referred to as the '*Blockburger*' test, inquires whether each offense contains an element not contained in the other; if not, they are the 'same offence' and double jeopardy bars additional punishment and successive prosecution. In a case such as *Yancy*, for example, in which the contempt prosecution was for disruption of judicial business, the same-elements test would not bar subsequent prosecution for the criminal assault that was part of the disruption, because the contempt offense did not require the element of criminal conduct, and the criminal offense did not require the element of disrupting judicial business. [note: *State v. Yancy*, 4 N.C. 133 (1814), it should be noted, involved what is today called summary contempt. We have not held, and do not mean by this example to decide, that the double jeopardy guarantee applies to such proceedings.] We recently held in *Grady* that in addition to passing the *Blockburger* test, a subsequent prosecution must satisfy a 'same-conduct' test to avoid the double jeopardy bar. The Grady test provides that, 'if, to establish an essential element of an offence charged in that prosecution, the government will prove conduct that constitutes an offense for which the defendant has already been prosecuted,' a second prosecution may not be had. . . . We have concluded, however, that Grady must be overruled. Unlike Blockburger analysis, whose definition of what prevents two crimes from being the 'same offence,' U.S. Const., Amdt. 5, has deep historical roots and has been accepted in numerous precedents of this Court, Grady lacks constitutional roots. The 'same-conduct' rule it announced is wholly inconsistent with earlier Supreme Court precedent and with the clear common-law understanding of double jeopardy. [648]

Consequently, sanctioning on the basis of truly criminal as well as non-summary contempt will usually be available alongside criminal prosecutions unless the

[645] This usually arises in a successive proceeding, rather than as whether multiple punishments are imposed in the same proceeding: Poulin (n 643) 595, fn 188.

[646] *Blockburger v U.S.*, 284 US 299, 52 SCt 180, 76 LEd 306 (Supreme Court of the United States, 1932).

[647] *Pandelli v United States*, 635 F2d 533 (United States Court of Appeals, Sixth Circuit, 1980), quoting *Jeffers v U.S.*, 432 US 137, 97 SCt 2207, 53 LEd2d 168 (Supreme Court of the United States, 1977).

[648] *U.S. v Dixon*, 509 US 688, 113 SCt 2849, 125 LEd2d 556 (Supreme Court of the United States, 1993). The *Blockburger* test had been briefly replaced by *Grady v Corbin*, 495 US 508, 110 SCt 2084, 109 LEd2d 548, 58 USLW 4599, 521–22 (Supreme Court of the United States, 1990).

latter exhausts the contempt charges.[649] This has drawn criticism and differentiated approaches have been suggested, such as focusing on a 'same transaction' test or balancing the specific government interests involved.[650]

As has been stressed, though, double jeopardy is a bar only within the framework of one or more criminal prosecutions. Besides criminal contempt, sanctions for attorney misconduct will not qualify as such. This has been demonstrated for contempt, and holds equally true for discipline.[651] In the same vein, additional discipline is not barred by other sanctions, for example, under Rule 11 sanctions[652] or contempt.[653]

Multiple proceedings hold a potential risk of burdening an individual twice with punishment for the same thing. Another issue would be the risk of reaching conflicting conclusions. From the perspective of the accused, the double jeopardy prohibition protects in this respect by establishing *res judicata.*[654] On the other hand, it can help in avoiding unnecessary litigation of settled issues. The problems of relitigation as well as the one of contrary outcomes are general ones.[655] Collateral estoppel is explained as when an issue of fact has once been determined by a valid and final judgment that issue cannot be litigated between the same parties in future lawsuits. It thus concerns the relationship of disciplinary cases to criminal prosecutions as well as those to civil malpractice suits or other administrative proceeings. Courts have tended to reject a defence of collateral estoppel by findings in other proceedings. Scholars have been more sympathetic to the concept but have conceded that the application of prior findings will often fail because of the differing standard of proof and adjudicated issues.[656] If the previous civil suit is litigated on a lower threshold it cannot be binding for disciplinary purpose. Even though

[649] Torcia (n 418) § 56. See, eg, *U.S. v Marquardo*, 149 F3d 36 (United States Court of Appeal, First Circuit, 1998); *U.S. v Mirra*, 220 FSupp 361 (United States District Court, S.D. New York, 1963); *People v Batey*, 228 Cal Rptr 787, 183 CalApp3d 1281 (California Court of Appeal, Fourth District, Division 1, 1986), cert. denied, *Batey v California*, 480 US 932, 107 SCt 1569, 94 LEd2d 761 (Supreme Court of the United States, 1987); *People v Totten*, 491 NE2d 924, 143 IllApp3d 132 (Appellate Court of Illinois, Second District, 1986), affirmed, *People v Totten*, 514 NE2d 959, 118 Ill2d 124 (Supreme Court of Illinois, 1987); *People v Rothman*, 808 NE2d 1018, 347 IllApp3d 587 (Appellate Court of Illinois, First District, 2004); *Commonwealth v Warrick*, 609 A2d 576 (Superior Court of Pennsylvania, 1992); but see *State v Dye*, 532 SE2d 574; 139 NC App 148 (North Carolina Court of Appeals, 2000); *State v Thompson* 659 P2d 383, 294 Ore 528 (Supreme Court of Oregon, 1983); *State v McIntyre*, 764 P2d 972, 94 Ore App 240 (Oregon Court of Appeals, 1988); *Ex parte Rhodes*, 974 SW2d 735 (Texas Court of Criminal Appeals, 1998).

[650] Poulin (n 644) 1277.

[651] *People v Artman*, 218 MichApp 236, 553 NW2d 673 (Court of Appeals of Michigan, 1996).

[652] See, eg, *In the Matter of Caranchini*, 160 F3d 420 (United States Court of Appeals, Eighth Circuit, 1998).

[653] Hardison (n 629) 273; Hall (n 23) § 33:6.

[654] Torcia (n 418) § 74.

[655] Hampton (n 635) 667.

[656] L Brickman and JM Bibona, 'Collateral Estoppel as a Basis for Attorney Discipline: The Next Step' (1991–92) 5 *Georgetown Journal of Legal Ethics* 1, 27; HR Lieberman, 'Use of Collateral Estoppel in Attorney Disciplinary Proceedings' (1998) *New York Law Journal* (27 July) discussing *Schwartz v Public Administrator*, 246 NE2d 725, 24 NY2d 65, 298 NYS2d 955 (Court of Appeals of New York, 1969). See also Wolfram (n 322) § 3.4.5 at 112–13.

the elements to be satisfied for establishing a breach often overlap in part, they may ultimately be different.

Both arguments have considerably less weight for the transfer from criminal findings to disciplinary cases. Here, the standard of proof is sufficient and stronger connections in substances are given. Nonetheless, Rule 18(G) of the Model Rules of Disciplinary Enforcement provides for pending litigation that a stay is possible but proceedings will not be automatically suspended to wait for the conclusion in the criminal proceedings. Furthermore, both are separate; the result in one does not dictate that in the other.[657] An attorney's acquittal or dismissal in a criminal prosecution is not necessarily a bar to disciplinary action against him or her.[658] Ordinarily, though, conviction from which an appeal is pending is a bar to another prosecution for the same offence,[659] an attorney's conviction from which an appeal is pending is not a bar to disciplinary action against him.[660] If a conviction is final the criminal evidence can be used in disciplinary proceedings, and it is seldom relitigated.[661] This is reflected by Rule 19 of the Model Rules of Disciplinary Enforcement, according to which a conviction serves as conclusive evidence, and only sentencing will be addressed.[662]

Summing up, findings within a certain regulatory regime will only prohibit a second sanctioning in quite limited circumstances. Essentially, it is only in a criminal case that a finding of guilt or no guilt may protect an attorney from repeated litigation for strictly the same charges. All other regimes operate independently, and contradicting findings are usually seen to pose no problem.

[657] Burkoff (n 400) § 1:8, and in particular fn 3, citing *In re Curtis*, 2003 WL 22187249 (CalBar Ct), 4 Cal State Bar Ct Rptr 601 (State Bar Court of California, 2003) 4–7, guided by *The Florida Bar v Hochman*, 815 So2d 624 (Supreme Court of Florida, 2002) and *In re Chastain*, 340 SC 356, 532 SE2d 264 (Supreme Court of South Carolina, 2000). See also *Attorney Grievance Com'n of Maryland v Childress* (n 660); *In re Segal*, 430 Mass 359, 719 NE2d 480 (Supreme Judicial Court of Massachusetts, 1999).

[658] 76 A.L.R. 3d 1028; Torcia (n 418) § 56, citing at fn 33 *In re Echeles* (n 400); *In re Segal*, 430 Mass 359, 719 NE2d 480 (Supreme Judicial Court of Massachusetts, 1999); *Office of Disciplinary Counselv Campbell*, 345 A2d 616, 463 Pa 472 (Supreme Court of Pennsylvania, 1975), cert. denied, *Campbellv Disciplinary Board of the Supreme Court of Pennsylvania*, 424 US 926, 96 SCt 1139, 47 LEd2d 336 (Supreme Court of the United States, 1976); *In re Discipline of Pendleton*, 11 P3d 284 (Supreme Court of Utah, 2000).

[659] Torcia (n 418) § 56, fn 34, citing *U.S.v Olson*, 57 F 579 (United States District Court, N.D. California, 1893); *Bustamantev People*, 317 P2d 885, 136 Colo 362 (Supreme Court of Colorado, 1957); *Statev Bockman* 124 SW2d 1205, 344 Mo 80 (Supreme Court of Missouri, 1939); *State v Biesemeyer*, 118 SW 1197, 136 MoApp 668 (Missouri Court of Appeals, 1909); *State v Glover*, 500 SW2d 271 (Missouri Court of Appeals, 1973).

[660] 76 A.L.R. 3d 1061; Torcia (n 418) § 56, fn 35: But see *Attorney Grievance Com'n of Maryland v Childress*, 360 Md 373, 758 A2d 117 (Court of Appeals of Maryland, 2000); *Re Ming*, 469 F2d 1352 (United States Court of Appeal, Seventh Circuit, 1972); *In re McDonald*, 296 So2d 141, 292 Ala 426 (Supreme Court of Alabama, 1974); *Grievance Administrator v Sauer*, 213 NW2d 102, 390 Mich 449 (Supreme Court of Michigan, 1973).

[661] JC Plaster, 'When Lawyers Go Bad: The Evidence Considered in the Disciplinary Proceedings of Convicted Attorneys' (2001) 25 *Journal of the Legal Profession* 219, 220.

[662] See, eg, for Minnesota *In re Disciplinary Action Against Dvorak*, 554 NW2d 399 (Supreme Court of Minnesota, 1996).

iii Proceedings in Separate Jurisdictions

In the previous section, multiple punishments or successive prosecutions were assumed to occur within the same jurisdiction. It is perfectly conceivable, given the reality of multiple bar admissions in the United States, that attorneys face proceedings in different jurisdictions.

In principle, proceedings in different jurisdictions in the same matter are permissible under the 'dual sovereign doctrine' if they are based on distinct sources of power.[663] Successive prosecutions for the same criminal conduct can be instituted by different governments as separate sovereigns, and they are possible even where the first trial already resulted in a conviction. Some exceptions have been acknowledged by courts, such as if one government acts as the agent of another, or where the second prosecution amounts to a sham to cover the first.[664] The general line would be, though, that in respect of the same crime, of which the respective governments have concurrent jurisdiction, a defendant may be prosecuted and convicted by the federal government and a state government, by a foreign country and a state, or by two states.[665] Per discretion, known as the 'Petite Policy', however, a federal prosecution will only be launched or pursued in the face of state proceedings if certain requirements are met.[666] Thus, an additional prosecution is warranted essentially in those cases only where the matter involves a substantial federal interest which the proceedings at state level have left 'demonstrably unvindicated'.

As far as non-criminal proceedings are concerned, the inherent powers doctrine explains in regard to contempt and discipline why these are likewise based on distinct sources.[667] Double jeopardy does not attach to discipline in first place, but even so, proceedings in different jurisdictions are no bar to multiple disciplining. Most disciplinary jurisdictions actually employ reciprocal discipline.[668] This is

[663] *Heath v Alabama*, 474 US 82, 88 (Supreme Court of the United States, 1985); see also JE Costa, 'Double Jeopardy and Non Bis In Idem: Principles of Fairness' (1998) 4 *UC Davis Journal of International Law and Policy* 181, citing *Bartkus v Illinois*, 359 US 121, 79 SCt 676, 3 LEd2d 684 (Supreme Court of the United States, 1959) (Black, J, dissenting). See on the history of the doctrine, MA Dawson, 'Popular Sovereignty, Double Jeopardy, and the Dual Sovereignty Doctrine' (1992) 102 *Yale Law Journal* 281, 292. See also AJ Colangelo, 'Double Jeopardy and Multiple Sovereigns: A Jurisdictional Theory' (2009) 86 *Washington University Law Review* 769, 778.

[664] *U.S. v Vanhoesen*, 529 FSupp2d 358 (United States District Court, N.D. New York, 2008); *U.S. v Moreno-Diaz*, 2007 WL 4426581 (United States Court of Appeals, Second Circuit, 2007).

[665] Torcia (n 418) § 73; *U.S. v Koon*, 34 F3d 1416 (United States Court of Appeals, Ninth Circuit, 1994), reversed in part but conviction affirmed by *Koon v U.S.*, 518 US 81, 116 SCt 2035 (Supreme Court of the United States, 1996), *People v Powell et al.*, No BA035498 (Superior Court of California, Los Angeles County, 1991), *Powell v Superior Court of Los Angeles County*, 232 Cal App3d 785, 283 Cal Rptr 777 (California Court of Appeal, Second District, Division 3, 1991), *People v Powell et al.*, (Superior Court of California, Ventura County, 1992).

[666] Executive Office for US Attorneys (ed) (n 420) Criminal Resource Manual, 9-2.031. Named after *Petite v U.S.*, 361 US 529, 80 SCt 450 (Supreme Court of the United States, 1960) (vacating a judgment at the request of the Justice Department made in accordance with its new policy).

[667] Above, III.A at 108–09.

[668] AM Colvin, 'Reciprocal Discipline: Double Jeopardy or a State's Right to Protect Its Citizens?' (2001) 25 *Journal of the Legal Profession* 143; *In re Lebbos*, 672 NE2d 517, 423 Mass 753 (Supreme Judicial Court of Massachusetts, 1996); *In re Dvorak*, 80 NW2d 586, 1998 ND 134 (Supreme Court of

not to say that reciprocal acceptance does not hinge on meeting certain requirements. Among these are usually that due process was afforded, that a firm burden of proof was used and that the elements of the breached professional standards do not differ substantially. Some states, such as North Dakota and Massachusetts, include a general 'grave injustice' qualifier. By and large, though, the emphasis is on preventing relitigation.[669] It seems fair to sum up that the problem lies less in the fact that counsel can be subject to proceedings in a number of jurisdictions and that some will adopt findings by other authorities for their own purposes, but rather how to coordinate reciprocal sanctions and ensure consistency.[670]

E Defence Rights and their Impact on the Regulation of Counsel

i Chilling Effect and Zealous Advocacy

That the different regimes intersect and influence each other has been amply demonstrated. The need for the various measures ro regulate counsel has become equally apparent. Just as in Germany, they sometimes harbour the potential to interfere with defence rights, which may also raise constitutional implications. On the one hand, due process rights of the concerned attorney attach to regulatory measures.[671] This has largely been the subject of the above section dealing with procedure. More generally, though, the regulation of counsel may also pose a risk of chilling zealous advocacy, which is of particular importance in criminal cases.[672] It is the attorney's duty of zealous advocacy which will usually be the primary source of friction between counsel's duties to the client and to the administration of justice. Moreover, the rights and interests of clients may clash directly with those of the lawyer. Both hold true of many measures regulating counsel, although contempt 'may well be the largest single constraint on the vigorousness of advocacy'.[673] This has been curbed by many courts by requiring a test of clear and present danger to the orderly administration of justice and of proportionality.[674] In the view of some courts, this still 'fails, in the context of courtroom advocacy, to adequately consider the represented party's rights to counsel and due process of law, the *raison d'etre* of such advocacy'.[675]

North Dakota, 1998) and *In re Disciplinary Action Against Dvorak*, 554 NW2d 399 (Supreme Court of Minnesota, 1996).

[669] *In re Edelstein*, 892 A2d 1153 (District of Columbia Court of Appeals, 2006).

[670] JA Parness, 'Enforcing Professional Norms for Federal Litigation Conduct: Achieving Reciprocal Cooperation' (1997) 60 *Albany Law Review* 303, 325 *et seq* in particular.

[671] See 'Comment, The Application of Criminal Contempt Procedures to Attorneys' (1973) 64 *The Journal of Criminal Law and Criminology* 300, 306; LS Raveson, 'Advocacy and Contempt: Constitutional Limitations on the Judicial Contempt Power, Part One: The Conflict between Advocacy and Contempt' (1990) 65 *Washington Law Review* 477, 487; *Ex parte Hudgings* (n 338).

[672] *State of Wisconsin v Glick*, 782 F2d 670, 673 (United States Court of Appeals, Seventh Circuit, 1986).

[673] Raveson (n 671) 483.

[674] *Young v U.S. ex rel. Vuitton et Fils S.A.* (n 339); *Ex parte Secombe* (n 39).

[675] *In re Jefferson* (n 476) at 5 citing *In re McConnell* (n 478) 236, overruling *Garland v Georgia*, 325 SE2d 131, 253 Ga 789 (Supreme Court of Georgia, 1985).

Therefore, courts, disciplinary bodies and other regulators in the United States need to consider various constitutional guarantees of the accused, in addition to those of the counsel who is allegedly in contempt. These guarantees of the client are the rights to effective counsel and zealous advocacy implicated or mandated by the Sixth Amendment, the more general the due process guarantees of the Fifth and Fourteenth Amendments and the First Amendment right to free speech.[676] The Supreme Court itself has highlighted the constitutional protection of advocacy while marking the limits as follows:

> It is the right of counsel for every litigant to press his claim, even if it appears far-fetched and untenable, to obtain the court's considered ruling, but if the ruling is adverse counsel's right is only respectfully to preserve his point for appeal. [677]

Although counsel's powers do not go unfettered, the Fifth and Sixth Amendments protect 'strenuous' and 'persistent' advocacy undertaken in good faith.[678] In particular, the Sixth Amendment is not confined to the courtroom. The client's rights can also be at stake when the attorney is targeted otherwise, be it by subpoenas, searches or gag orders.[679] Underlying this is that it is inappropriate to penalise an accused for the misconduct of his or her lawyer, or even that of a co-defendant's lawyer.[680] This is complemented by the First Amendment right of expression. Courts have held that in order to ensure this, the effect must be judged and not the content, and interference with free speech should be restricted to cases of an imminent – not merely a likely – threat to the administration of justice.[681] Language must thus obstruct the administration of justice before sanctions are deemed appropriate. This means forensic comments in and out of court, but also other regulatory aspects such as Bar admission or the solicitation of clients.[682]

[676] Raveson (n 671) 487. See also *Hawk v Cardoza*, 575 F2d 732, 735 (United States Court of Appeals, Ninth Circuit, 1978).

[677] *Sacher v United States* (n 478).

[678] *In re McConnell* (n 478) 236; *In re Dellinger* (n 475).

[679] See Hall (n 23) § 30:2 and § 30:11. In particular attorney–client privilege at stake, see USAM CRM 162 Federal Prosecution of Business Organizations, citing *Upjohn v United States*, 449 U.S. 383, 389 (1976). LS Yuan, 'Gag Order and the Ultimate Sanction' (1998) 18 *Loyola of Los Angeles Entertainment Law Journal* 629.

[680] *U.S. v Rogers*, 270 F3d 1076 (United States Court of Appeals, Seventh Circuit, 2001); *Hickey v State*, 484 So2d 1271 (District Court of Appeal of Florida, Fifth District, 1986). For conflicts among co-defendants, see *People v Hardy*, 2 Cal4th 86, 825 P2d 781, 5 CalRptr2d 796 (Supreme Court of California, 1992); *People v Estrada*, 63 CalApp4th 1090, 75 CalRptr2d 17 (California Court of Appeal, Fourth District, Division 1, 1998).

[681] *Eaton v City of Tulsa*, 415 US 697, 94 SCt 1228, 39 LEd2d 693 (Supreme Court of the United States, 1974); *In re Little* (n 478); *Holt v Virginia*, 381 US 131, 85 SCt 1375, 14 LEd2d 290 (Supreme Court of the United States, 1965); *Edmunds v Won Bae Chang*, 365 FSupp 941 (United States District Court, D. Hawaii, 1973).

[682] See generally WB Wendel, 'Free Speech for Lawyers' (2001) 28 *Hastings Constitutional Law Quarterly* 305; KM Sullivan, 'The Intersection of Free Speech and the Legal Profession: Constraints on Lawyers' First Amendment Rights' (1998–99) 67 *Fordham Law Review* 569; WS Croft, 'Free Speech and Fair Trials – Striking the Balance: A Case Comment and Analysis of the Maryland Publicity Rule as Applied in Attorney Grievance Commission of Maryland v Douglas F Gansler' (2006) 19 *Georgetown Journal of Legal Ethics* 345; JA Hinkie, 'Free Speech and Rule 3.6: How the Object of Attorney Speech Affects the Right to Make Public Criticism' (2007) 20 *Georgetown Journal of Legal Ethics* 695.

ii The Engrained Tension

The underlying dilemma is, of course, that attorneys pursue conflicting goals. This fits to any kind of advocacy, but particularly so to criminal defence. As one scholar puts it:

> Many of the rules, procedures, and accepted tactics of litigation in our system, in practice if not by design, not only fail to further the goal of accurate factfinding but actually impede it. The rules of evidence and trial practice arm advocates with devices to make witnesses who are telling the truth appear to be lying and witnesses who are lying appear to be telling the truth. These rules engender techniques for preventing the whole truth from reaching the factfinder, for filtering the truth, for limiting and qualifying the disclosures that are made. They permit attorneys to obfuscate the truth by presenting information that can mislead the trier.[683]

Quite plainly, this is simply owed to the design of the procedure. Within the framework of this existing procedure, lawyers can justify their actions based on what the processes of litigation permit and compel them to do on behalf of their clients.[684] In this, attorneys for both sides and judges are mutually dependent, and defence lawyers need to respect the authority of the court and fairness of the trial process. In the words of the above author, attorneys must accept the court's commands as the ultimate authority in a trial.[685]

Moreover, this procedure is the product of the outlined constitutional tenets. Since even those collide, the difficult question continues on this level as to how to treat conduct that is the core value of one goal while it impedes the other.[686] The degree and character of interference with the process which is required to amount to obstruction drawing sanctions, say, punishable by contempt, is thus a measurement of how the two interests are valued constitutionally. It has been argued that it is necessary, as a matter of constitutional rights, to value the weight of defence rights properly in face of the potentially broad and vague provisions against counsel misconduct.[687] This concerns contempt in particular, but also holds true of other measures. In this regard, it has been suggested prescribing narrowly the scope, the elements and the rationale of the pertinent measures.[688] It starts with whether the conduct in question is advocacy on a 'good faith' basis, whether it really constitutes a gross deviation from the norms of trial practice, or whether the nature or seriousness suffice to mark the issue or the case misconduct. All of

[683] Raveson (n 671) 529.

[684] ibid, 535. See also DL Rhode, 'Legal Ethics in an Adversary System: The Persistent Questions' (2005–06) 34 *Hofstra Law Review* 641, 643 and on 'moral activism' versus the standard conception of the lawyer's role, D Luban, 'Partisanship, Betrayal and Autonomy in the Lawyer–Client Relationship: A Reply to Stephen Ellmann' (1990) 90 *Columbia Law Review* 1004; Luban, *Lawyers and Justice* (n 26) 160–61, 169–74.

[685] See also *State of Wisconsin v Glick* (n 672) 670.

[686] Raveson (n 671) 538.

[687] ibid, 745.

[688] ibid, 786.

these criteria are somewhat malleable, but a general principle of proportionality behind them can be gathered from it. Stressing procedure and elements, it may help to allay the negative impact on attorneys by using notices and warning requirements, considering the effects on the deliberative process and taking into account the immediacy, patterns and persistence of conduct. Still other factors may arise from the context such as the participation or provocation by the judge or other participants to the proceedings or the inadequacy of rectifying the implications of misconduct only later during appellate review.

F Conclusion on the US Model

As could be seen from the previous section on the United States, measures against counsel misconduct are manifold there as well. Criminal offences attach to the more serious instances, and the more general background is a full-fledged regime of professional discipline. Contempt has been explained in detail, and is shown that it can be criminal or civil. Furthermore, contempt serves as one of the best examples for a particular feature, that of inherent powers. Understanding these inherent powers is also important in order to understand why courts in the United States generally tend to resort to institutional controls, which are consequently not limited to statutory bases. They make it possible for courts to react swiftly and conclusively. Many of these institutional controls are direct measures. Discipline, on the other hand, figures prominently but has been criticised as flawed.

Since various actors rely on different sources of power, they react to counsel misconduct quite independently from each other. Criminal proceedings and disciplinary ones can be instituted and conducted alongside each other. Within the federal system with its legal implications, attorneys can also be sanctioned multiply in and by different jurisdictions. They enjoy the protection of certain procedural guarantees, though to a varying degree, under the different kinds of procedures.

IV A Comparative Assessment

It has become apparent that counsel regulation on the national level can be quite impenetrable. It seems plain that international regimes cannot provide a framework that is as wide-ranging as on the national level. The international level would, for example, be hard-pressed to take care of all conceivable financial offences or to establish a sophisticated system of civil liability. Here, the conceivable optimum seems capturing this via disciplinary rules and moreover refer it to competent national jurisdictions. Civil liability is something, however, which may not be an effective sanctioning mechanism with respect to criminal litigation. This indicates that it will be even less relevant on the international level. Generally, it seems fair to conclude that the concentration on certain controls in the context of criminal litigation will be emulated by international criminal courts.

In any event, if no clear customary law exists other than different legal options, international courts have discretion to choose one of the methods in order to achieve the overall goal, which is 'the dispensing of international criminal justice'.[689] The national analysis demonstrates, though, the path dependencies arising from a criminal litigation system.

Starting with the common ground, the regulation of counsel both in Germany and the United States can be characterised by relying on an attorney-specific disciplinary regime. This does not preclude the applicability of criminal offences, though.[690] The disciplinary regime aims at being as conclusive as possible and incorporates criminal offences by either referring to them explicitly, or by otherwise making it possible to discipline for criminal acts. Although the details of the criminal offences and of the professional standards vary, they are surprisingly similar in many respects. The criminal laws in both countries only cover a slice of all conceivable misconduct. In contrast to the United States, the German Criminal Code does penalise some professional duties (Section 203, Section 353, Section 356). This addresses two core principles of professional ethics: the duty of confidentiality and freedom from conflicts of interests. As has been shown above, it in no way embrace the full spectrum of professional standards and it does not even cover all pertinent scenarios in the mentioned areas. It is usually a blanket provision such as *Strafvereitelung* (obstruction of justice) which provides a more general option.[691] It is, however, not specifically aimed at counsel misconduct, principally attaches to actual litigation and leaves many grey zones which do not help at all help to carve out professional standards and to sanction violations thereof precisely. Moreover, all the statutory criminal offences require intent, or the German variant of *dolus eventualis* which leaves out the many cases of mere negligent misconduct. Criminal law therefore does simply not amount to comprehensive regulation. In that regard, both the United States and Germany again are similar.[692] In both countries, the broad wording of the criminal offences and the exhaustive scope of disciplinary rule potentially conflict with counsels' duties as an advocate for their clients because it does not release them from their commitment to the administration of justice as the larger concept. In both countries, this calls for striking a balance between both, and particularly needs to be taken into account when prosecuting counsel or when establishing offences or breaches under the often broad provisions.

As far as the disciplinary controls are concerned, they are wide-ranging in substance, as has been just stressed. They typically provide for general clauses which

[689] *Prosecutor v Momčilo Krajišnik*, IT-00-39-A, Appeals Chamber, Decision (n 10) and para 3 of the Separate Opinion of Judge Shahabuddeen; see also K Zweigert and H Kötz, *An Introduction to Comparative Law*, 3rd edn (Oxford, Clarendon Press, 1998) A.3 at 46–47; K Zweigert and H Kötz, *Einführung in die Rechtsvergleichung*, 3rd edn (Tübingen, Mohr, 1996) § 3 VII at 46.

[690] Above, II.B.ii at 67–73, and III.B.ii at 124–30.

[691] Above, II.B.ii at 68–70, and III.Bii.a at 126–28.

[692] Above, II.B.ii at 73, and III.B.ii.a at 124.

bring about problems of defining permissible from impermissible conduct. Essentially emulating a criminal procedure, the disciplinary controls offer a sophisticated regime. One of the strengths of the German model seems to be the high level of legal safeguards.[693] In Germany, disciplinary judges as well as the prosecutors act independently from other institutions in prosecuting misconduct. This also hold true for their US counterparts, ie, the disciplinary bodies including Bar Councils. Marked differences of the US model exist, of course, and stem from the classification of discipline as decidedly non-criminal.[694] Both in Germany and the United States, the *sui generis* nature of disciplinary proceedings has been pointed out. Essentially, *sui generis* principally helps to explain what discipline is not. In direct comparison, it can be seen that *sui generis* thus in both cases denotes a model somewhere in between criminal procedure on the one hand and civil or administrative procedure on the other. In this, current German discipline leans much more towards the criminal model than does the US counterpart. Consequently, the German procedure offers higher procedural protections. Needless to say, the degree and manner of state and counsel involvement are also different in Germany and the Umited States. In spite of all these variations they both still fit Wilkins' definition of disciplinary controls which are undertaken on an ex post facto basis and emulate a criminal prosecution. In neither case does it really seem to hurt that the disciplinary bodies do not have the direct inside knowledge of the institution before which misconduct occurs. Furthermore, they arguably both share the same weaknesses. It seems disputable whether these sanctions under the disciplinary procedures are truly effective. The disciplinary regimes tend to appear underused in both countries.

Regarding other legislative controls, executive bodies do not seem have much of an impact on criminal defence lawyers. In both countries, most criminal defence work will be litigation-related and thus happen before criminal courts and not executive authorities. The relevance of legislative controls other than criminal law seems limited in both cases. Similarly, civil liability can be discarded as a control mechanism with respect to the criminal law context.[695] A theoretical explanation has been given by Wilkins.[696] Neither German nor American alleged or convicted criminals will ever have the resources, the legal sophistication, or the numbers to reach a critical lobby which would allow speaking of a scheme of regulation of counsel. Secondly, the legal thresholds make it considerably complicated to establish all the elements for malpractice of criminal defence attorneys. The duties to be breached or the applicable standard of care are not as clear as in other legal practices. Damages for wrongful conviction or the appropriate compensation for sentences or fines are hard to assess in any jurisdiction. All of this is not to say that there will not be misconduct that can be grasped quite easily in

[693] Above, II.C.iv at 92–93.
[694] Above, III.B.i.c at 122–24, and III.C.i at 144–45.
[695] Above, II.B.iv at 85 and III.B.iv at 139–41.
[696] Wilkins (n 71) 830.

terms of civil liability. This will then be conduct that could attach to any lawyer, but is not characteristic of the international criminal defence lawyer.

As to highly relevant controls where both systems differ much more markedly, the German model features relatively weak powers by affected courts.[697] The options of criminal courts to deal with counsel misconduct are primarily directed at excluding counsel or restricting evidence, thus intra-procedural measures. As far as institutional controls are concerned, this seems to be a quite defence-friendly role model. The exclusion of counsel cannot be effectuated easily but is an option in rather extreme cases.[698] The other major option is the doctrine of *Rechtsmißbrauch* (abuse of process),[699] allowing the court to impose restrictions on counsel's trial strategy. Restrictions on evidence have been used to curb *Konfliktverteidigung* (confrontational defence). It is one of the above-mentioned intra-procedural measures, of which the benefit has to be weighed against the costs for participants. Taking into account the jurisprudence of the European Court of Human Rights,[700] Germany could probably not introduce contempt proceedings administered by the same bench before it was committed. But whatever examples of institutional controls exist allowing for direct responses is not systematic, offers only limited means and, probably most important, does not flow from inherent powers. This stands in stark contrast to the United States. Here, contempt and other inherent powers, along with statutory institutional controls are in place and are actually used.[701]

[697] Above, II.B.iii.a at 75, 78.

[698] Above, II.B.iii.a at 79–81.

[699] Above, II.B.iii.a at 75–79.

[700] *Kyprianou v Cyprus*, application no 73797/01, Grand Chamber, 15 December 2005, case note by OR Kissel, 'Ungebühr vor Gericht (§ 178 GVG) – vorbei?' (2007) *Neue Juristische Wochenschrift* 1109. The Court acknowledges, however, the need for swift reactions by judges which appears to leave room for the possibility of summary procedures.

[701] Above, III.B.iii at 130–39.

3

The International Criminal Court's System

I The General Layout of the ICC System of the Regulation of Counsel

A Introduction to the ICC's Legal Instruments in General

The ICC is governed by the Rome Statute as the primary body of rules.[1] On the one hand, it sets out the organisational framework and the substantive criminal law of the Court. Furthermore, it contains large parts of the procedure, though this is not exhaustive.[2]

The Rules of Procedure and Evidence (RPE)[3] were finalised in negotiations of the Preparatory Commission for the ICC in 2000.[4] The RPE constitute a secondary set of rules, foremost on procedure, with no clear-cut criteria whether specific provisions were incorporated into the Statute and others left to the RPE.[5] The RPE elaborate on the procedure but go beyond what is mandated by the Statute in a number of respects.[6] Article 51(5) of the Statute makes it clear, though, that the Statute shall prevail over the RPE if both conflict. The RPE may thus be subordinate and subject to this rule on conflicts, but they are nonetheless binding legislation for the Court on.[7]

[1] Text of the Rome Statute circulated as document A/CONF.183/9 of 17 July 1998 and corrected by procès-verbaux of 10 November 1998, 12 July 1999, 30 November 1999, 8 May 2000, 17 January 2001 and 16 January 2002. The Statute entered into force on 1 July 2002. ICC-ASP/4/Res.1, 2 December 2005.

[2] For a further overview on the procedural instruments see C Kreß, 'The Procedural Texts of the International Criminal Court' (2007) 5 *Journal of International Criminal Justice* 537, and C Kreß, 'Die strafprozessualen Texte des Internationalen Strafgerichtshofs' (2006) 153 *Goltdammer's Archiv* 528. See further WA Schabas, *The International Criminal Court. A Commentary on the Rome Statute* (Oxford, Oxford University Press, 2010) 386–90, and G Bitti, 'Article 21 of the Statute of the International Criminal Court and the Treatment of Sources of Law in the Jurisprudence of the ICC' in C Stahn and G Sluiter (eds), *The Emerging Practice of the International Criminal Court* (Leiden, Martinus Nijhoff, 2009) 288–92.

[3] ICC-ASP/1/3 (part II-A).

[4] Preparatory Commission for the ICC, *Finalized draft text of the Rules of Procedure and Evidence* (PCNICC/2000/1/Add.1, 2 November 2000), and before that Preparatory Commission for the ICC, *Finalized draft text of the Rules of Procedure and Evidence* (PCNICC/2000/INF/3/Add.1, 12 July 2000). See also below at n 392.

[5] Kreß, 'The Procedural Texts' (n 2) 539.

[6] eg, Rules 44–62 RPE.

[7] Schabas (n 2) 386, citing some first case law, *Situation in the Democratic Republic of Congo*, ICC-01/04-101, Pre-Trial Chamber I, Decision on the Applications for Participation in the Proceedings of

Thereafter, the Regulations of the Court (RoC) were enacted by the judges, pursuant to Article 52 of the Statute.[8] This tertiary tier of rules shows that some rule-making powers remain with the judges under the ICC's legal framework.[9] All of the RoC 'shall be read subject to the Statute and the Rules' (Regulation 1(1)), which settles their tertiary rank. According to Article 52(1), they are meant to direct the necessary routine functioning of the Court. It is noted, however, that the RoC should not be underestimated as merely internal rules of lesser importance.[10] For example, they govern the admission of defence counsel (Regulation 21(2)), a whole range of procedural issues in chapter 3 entitled 'Proceedings before the Court' (Regulations 20–66) and further issues regarding counsel and legal assistance in chapter 4 (Regulations 67–85).

The Regulations of the Registry (RoR), envisaged in Rule 14(1) RPE, followed in 2006 after they had been approved by the Presidency.[11] According to their Regulation 1(1), they shall be read subject to the Statute, the RPE and the RoC. This follows the same scheme again, creating a quaternary level which once more contains all but trivial rules.[12]

Moreover, ancillary instruments of a varying nature add to the ICC's legal framework.[13] Among them are some which also contribute to the Court's procedural set-up, such as the Agreement on the Privileges and Immunities of the International Criminal Court,[14] the Headquarters Agreement with the Netherlands[15] and the Code of Conduct for counsel.

All of the outlined legal instruments are the bases for the Court's administration of justice, forming 'a beautiful pyramid, composed of at least four different layers which represent a sum of 702 articles, rules and regulations'.[16] Within this pyramid, the supremacy of the Statute and of the RPE trumps the other instruments.[17] Remaining ambiguities will need to be settled along the 'general principles of interpretation of legal texts, such as *lex specialis derogat legi generali* and *lex posterior derogat priori*, and with reference to the authority of the body responsible for adopting the text'.[18]

VPRS 1, VPRS 2, VPRS 3, VPRS 4, VPRS 5 and VPRS6, 17 January 2006, para 47, and *The Prosecutor v Omar Hassan Ahmad Al Bashir*, ICC-02/05-01/09-3, Pre-Trial Chamber I, Decision on the Prosecution's Application for a Warrant of Arrest against Omar Hassan Ahmad Al Bashir, 4 March 2009, para 28.

[8] ICC-BD/01-01-04, adopted by the judges of the Court on 26 May 2004, Fifth Plenary Session, 17–28 May 2004. Amended 9 March 2005 (ICC-BD/01-01-04/Rev.01-05) and 14 June/14 November 2007 (ICC-BD/01-02-07).

[9] Kreß, 'The Procedural Texts' (n 2) 540.

[10] ibid.

[11] Regulations of the Registry, ICC-BD/03-01-06, date of entry into force: 6 March 2006.

[12] Kreß, 'The Procedural Texts' (n 2) 541 and below at 176–77.

[13] ibid.

[14] ICC, *Agreement on the Privileges and Immunities of the International Criminal Court* (ICC-ASP/1/3, ICC-ASP/1/3, 3–10 September 2002).

[15] ICC, *Headquarters Agreement between the International Criminal Court and the host State* (ICC-BD/04-01-08, 7 June 2007).

[16] Bitti (n 2) 291.

[17] ibid, 289–92.

[18] Schabas (n 2) 387.

The Code of Conduct has been said to be silent on its exact place within the hierarchy of the ICC's instruments.[19] In some way, it will interact with other ICC instruments and even be determinative: whenever these use general clauses, for example, 'obstructing' in Article 70(1)(c) or 'misconduct' in Article 71(1), the more specific Code provision may come in to fill the blank. More generally, though, the Code fits in after the Statute, the RPE, the RoC and the RoR. Article 2(1) of the Code points to them for defining the terms used in it. Moreover, Article 7(3) and Article 31(a) indicate that the four major instruments must be considered when interpreting the Code.

At a first glance, the ICC system is from the very outset more advanced compared with the International Criminal Tribunal for the former Yugoslavia (ICTY) or the International Criminal Tribunal for Rwanda (ICTR). Some gaps may remain, but generally, however, it seems to aim at a more civil law codification approach, under which control over conduct is based solely on Statute and the RPE, both adopted by the full authority of the Assembly of States Parties. Where the judges come in, for the Regulations of the Court, this is explicitly deemed to be only for the routine functioning and subject to the superior two instruments. The Code of Conduct for counsel, as the most counsel-specific disciplining instrument, was adopted by the Assembly of States Parties as well.

This stands in contrast with what has been called a common law approach, according to which control of proceedings is an inherent power of the Court.[20] This may be labelled the 'Vujin polarisation'. The ICTY Appeals Chamber stated in its first judgment in this contempt case:

> Although the law of contempt has now been partially codified in the United Kingdom, the power to deal with contempt at common law has essentially remained one which is part of the inherent jurisdiction of the superior courts of record, rather than based upon statute. On the other hand, the analogous control exercised in the civil law systems over conduct which interferes with the administration of justice is based solely upon statute, and the statutory provisions, in general, enact narrow offences dealing with precisely defined conduct where the jurisdiction of the courts has been or would be frustrated by that conduct.[21]

It is noted that the statutory foundation of the ICC is quite different from that of the ICTY and the ICTR. It is the Assembly of States Parties which adopts the instruments of the Court. In contrast, the judges had a much greater legislative role at the ICTY and ICTR, and a lot of the instruments were added when needed. The ICTY and ICTR Codes of Conduct serve as another example. Pursuant to Rule 46(C) and (D), respectively, of the RPE, the Codes are promulgated by the

[19] Bitti (n 2) 291; Schabas (n 2) 387.

[20] Ch 1, II. B.ii at 17–18, C at 28–32, and ch 2, III.A at 109–13. In the meantime, see *The Prosecutor v Thomas Lubanga Dyilo*, ICC-01/04-01/06-2705, Trial Chamber I, Decision on the defence request to reconsider the 'Order on the numbering of evidence' of 12 May 2010, 30 March 2011, paras 16–18, and the Separate Opinion by Judge Blattmann.

[21] *Prosecutor v Duško Tadić*, IT-94-1-A-R77, Appeals Chamber, Judgment on Allegations of Contempt against Prior Counsel, Milan Vujin, 31 January 2000, para 17. See in detail ch 1, II.ii.a at 16–19.

Registrar after approval by the President or the plenary of the judges. In contrast, the ICC Code of Conduct was adopted by the Assembly of States Parties.[22]

For the ICC, there will arguably be less need to resort to unwritten powers since lengthy conferences of the state parties took place to adopt the legal instruments, and there is a more complete statutory framework from the very beginning. Although the ICC system seems to resemble a more civil law approach, this is not entirely clear. The ICC may still rely on unwritten powers in some regards. If counsel regulation is understood to constitute an essential and inherent competence of the Court, it is conceivable that it will be invoked. This will possibly not happen for contempt or other criminal proceedings, but perhaps for lesser measures.

B The Bases for Disciplining Counsel in Particular

i The Statute and the Rules of Procedure and Evidence

The Rome Statute itself remains silent on the professional conduct of defence counsel. The right of suspects and accused to legal assistance is enshrined in Article 55(2)(c) and (d) and Article 67(1)(b) and (d).[23] This guarantees rights of the defence to the extent that measures infringe the right to legal assistance. Furthermore, some guidance may be drawn from the general procedural features enshrined in the Statute. The pertinent provisions have an impact on the conduct of participants, including counsel. Articles 70 and 71 come to mind here. The Statute, however, does not mention more specific regulation, let alone the enactment of professional rules for counsel.

This is done by Rule 8 RPE, which provides for a code of conduct for counsel. Rule 21(2) is the basis for the list system for counsel. Rule 22(1) is more specific as it touches on the minimum qualifications. Lastly, Rule 22(3) is quite generic as it declares all of the Court's law as pertinent to counsel. Apart from this, the RPE provide little more than general guidance.

ii The Code of Conduct for Counsel and the Rules of Procedure and Evidence of the Disciplinary Board and the Disciplinary Appeals Board

Counsel in this context denotes lawyers for defendants, witnesses, victims and other participants besides Court organs. Additional codes or rules address the conduct of lawyers for Court organs, ie, judges,[24] prosecutors[25] and other

[22] Below at 174.

[23] See also below, IV at 280–81.

[24] ICC, *Code of Judicial Ethics* (ICC-BD/02-01-05, 9 March 2005), based on Arts 45–47 of the Statute, Rules 23–32 RPE. The rules of that Code are only intended as 'guidelines on the essential ethical standards' and 'advisory in nature' (Rule 11).

[25] See Arts 45–47 of the Statute, Rules 23–32 RPE, for the Prosecutor and his or her deputies. See for members of the OTP in general ICC, *Regulations of the Office of the Prosecutor* (ICC-BD/05-01-09, 23

staff.[26] Although a need for oversight exists for them as well,[27] it constitutes a fully distinct regime.

The ICC Code of Professional Conduct for counsel was adopted on 2 December 2005 as Resolution ICC-AP/4/Res.1, when the Assembly at its fourth meeting took note of the report of the Working Group on the draft Code of Professional Conduct for counsel[28] and adopted the Code of Professional Conduct for counsel during the third plenary meeting.[29] It needs to be emphasised that the Code is eventually a product of the Assembly, although the influence of the judges in the drafting process is prominent.[30] It has been expressly noted that the influence of the legal profession was limited.[31]

The Assembly of States Parties passed the Code by consensus. It should not be misconstrued from this fact that no disputes existed. The final version of the Code deviated from the previous draft prepared by the Registry in consultation with the Office of the Prosecutor (OTP) (the Proposal)[32] and another draft by the Registrar after meetings with representatives of several associations of lawyers (the Draft Code of May 2004).[33] Further, another draft Code report was submitted by the Bureau.[34] However, the various drafts seemed to constitute an agreement in principle on the content of the Code.

Various comments and criticism were advanced by non-governmental organisations, Bar associations and other groups, mostly with regard to the Proposal or the Draft Code. The efforts to codify professional duties have, by and large, met

April 2009), with Regulation 17 pointing to the Staff rules of the ICC (see next footnote), and Regulation 51 on 'Relations with the defence'. In the drafting process, the ICTY judges had suggested having a common Code for defence and prosecution counsel (Preparatory Commission for the ICC, *Contributions of the Chambers of the International Criminal Tribunal for the former Yugoslavia* (PCNICC1999WGRPEDP.38, 13 August 1999 (26 July 1999)), para 26).

[26] ICC, *Staff Rules of the International Criminal Court* (Annex to ICC/AI/2005/003, ICC-ASP/4/3, 25 August 2005, adopted 3 December 2005, entry into force 21 April 2005). See in particular chapter I ('Duties, Obligations and Privileges', Rules 101.1-9) thereof, at 9–13, and chs X ('Disciplinary Measures', Rules 110.1-8) and XI ('Appeals', Rules 111.1-5) of the Staff Rules, at 64–72 thereof.

[27] See Assembly of States Parties to the ICC, *Establishment of an independent oversight mechanism* (ICC-ASP/8/Res.1, 26 November 2009).

[28] ICC-ASP/4/WGCPC/1, chaired by Michèle Dubrocard of France (Assembly of States Parties to the ICC, *Fourth session, The Hague, 28 November to 3 December 2005, Official Records* (ICC-ASP/4/32), para 16, at 5).

[29] ibid, para 32, at 8; see pt III of the report.

[30] For the ICTY, the norms of the Code of Conduct have been said to be crucially influenced by the judges, see JA McMorrow, 'Creating Norms of Attorney Conduct in International Tribunals: A Case Study of the ICTY' (2007) 30 *Boston College International & Comparative Law Review* 139, 159.

[31] S Kay and B Swart, 'The Role of the Defence' in A Cassese, P Gaeta and JRWD Jones (eds), *The Rome Statute of the International Criminal Court: A Commentary* (Oxford, Oxford University Press, 2002) 1435.

[32] ICC, *Proposal for a draft Code of Professional Conduct for counsel before the International Criminal Court (August 2004)* (ICC-ASP/3/11/Rev.1).

[33] ICC, *Draft Code of Conduct for Counsel before the ICC* (Registry, May 2004).

[34] ICC, *Report of the Bureau on the draft Code of Professional Conduct for Counsel* (ICC-ASP/4/21, 10 October 2005). See also ICC, *Overview of the efforts of the Registrar in relation to the defence, the legal participation of victims, and the consultation process followed – report pursuant to paragraph 4 of the statement of the focal point on the establishment of an international criminal bar* (ICC-ASP/3/7, 9 July 2004).

with approval. However, specific provisions have encountered opposition. It is understood that these comments were influenced by the respective missions and mandates of the cited organisations.

The International Criminal Bar (ICB) acknowledged the significance of codes of conduct.[35] It suggested a number of changes of which many have been incorporated into the new Code of December 2005. Whereas the ICB seemed to approve of the drafts as such, substantial criticism was ultimately not considered, particularly in respect to the secrecy of the lawyer–client bond[36], counsel's independence[37] and a more limited role of the Registrar.[38]

The Association of Defence Counsel Practising before the ICTY (ADC-ICTY)[39] stressed the need for a common set of rules for international lawyers and held the Draft Code to 'provide a solid basis'.[40] It lobbied for a clearer division of professional duties on the one hand, and purely procedural or formal duties on the other. It argued that the latter should be banned from a code of conduct. In general, it also strove for a stronger and more independent position of the defence towards the Court and other participants.[41]

On behalf of the American Bar Association (ABA), its Center of Professional Responsibility furnished a comprehensive assessment of the Draft Code.[42] Whereas it 'commended [the Bureau] for its diligent work', it suggested 'areas for improvement'.[43] As expected, it lodged criticism with respect to particular rules. Moreover, it drew the attention to the ABA Model Rules of Professional Conduct, the Model Rules for Lawyer Disciplinary Enforcement and the Report of the Commission on Evaluation of Disciplinary Enforcement.[44]

[35] International Criminal Bar (Ethics Committee), *Commentary on the ICC Draft Code of Professional Conduct for Counsel Before the International Criminal Court submitted at the last ASP session in The Hague, 6-10 September, 2004* and also International Criminal Bar (Ethics Committee), *General Observations by the Committee on Ethics of the International Criminal Bar on the Draft Code of Conduct for Counsel before the ICC prepared by the Registrar of the ICC* (9 February 2004); International Criminal Bar (Ethics Committee), 'Proposed Code of Conduct and Disciplinary Procedure Applicable to Counsel Appearing before the International Criminal Court' (2005) 11 *Law and Business Review of the Americas* 83.

[36] See, eg, International Criminal Bar (Ethics Committee), *Commentary on the ICC Draft Code of Professional Conduct for Counsel* (n 35) on Art 9 (Counsel–client relationship).

[37] See, eg, ibid, on Art 15 (Conflict of interest), or on Art 29 (Relations with witnesses and victims).

[38] eg, ibid, on Arts 18, 34, 37 and 39.

[39] On the ADC-ICTY, see ch 1, II.B.v at 27–28.

[40] S Kirsch, *Draft Code of Conduct for Counsel before the ICC* (Association of Defence Counsel practising before the International Criminal Tribunal for the Former Yugoslavia, 15 September 2004) at 2, who also authored the position paper of the *Bundesrechtsanwaltskammer* (S Kirsch, *Stellungnahme der Bundesrechtsanwaltskammer zum Entwurf eines Verhaltenskodexes für Verteidiger vor dem Internationalen Strafgerichtshof (Draft Code of Conduct for Counsel before the ICC)* (BRAK-Stellungnahme-Nr. 1/2004)).

[41] Kirsch, *Draft Code of Conduct for Counsel* (n 40) at 4.

[42] ES Rosen and GA Kuhlman, *Comments on the October 10, 2005 Draft Code of Professional Conduct for Counsel Before the International Court* (American Bar Association, 10 October 2005).

[43] D Stoelting, *ABA Representative to the International Criminal Bar, Letter to the Fourth Session of the Assembly of States Parties* (10 November 2005) 1.

[44] Rosen and Kuhlman (n 42) 2–3. See ch 2, III.A at 107–08, and III.C.i at 142–45, on disciplinary enforcement.

Finally, various non-governmental organisations have issued their views on the defence before international courts. These statements are usually limited to specific topics. Among the most contentious issues was, inter alia, the fee-splitting prohibition and ensuing reporting duties by counsel.[45]

The members of the boards have adopted provisional Rules of Procedure and Evidence of the Disciplinary Board and the Disciplinary Appeals Board.[46] Whereas they commendably provide additional guidance, the members' authority to adopt such an instrument is questionable. Article 2(2) clarifies, however, that the provisions of the Code prevail over those of the Disciplinary RPE in case of incompatibility. In any event, some of the provisions merely point to the Code and other law of the Court which govern disciplinary issue (for example, Arts 2, 5, 6, 7(1), 15(1), 16(2) Disciplinary RPE).

iii The Regulations of the Court and the Registry

As has already been noted,[47] the judge-made RoC and the RoR are lower in the hierarchy than the Statute and the RPE but are important as they concretise them and interact with them. As can be discerned from Rule 22(3) RPE, the RoC and the RoR are determinative for counsel's conduct.

Section 1 of chapter 4 of the RoC provides the details on the list of counsel in Regulations 67–73. Thereby, the RoC entrench the entire law of admission as list counsel, removal from the list and judicial review. This goes beyond what Rule 21(2) of the RPE merely hints at when it tasks the Registrar to 'create and maintain a list of counsel' and adds substance to the qualification criteria mentioned in Rule 22(1) RPE. Furthermore, the remaining part of chapter 4 of the RoC contains a wide range of additional provisions on counsel issues in Section 2 (Defence through counsel, Regulations 74–78), Section 3 (Legal representatives of victims, Regulations 79–82) and Section 4 (Legal assistance paid by the Court, Regulations 83–85). Many of these provisions touch on vital interests of counsel and relate to good practice and misconduct.

The same can be said of the RoR. Their chapter 4 (Counsel issues and legal assistance) again picks up on the appointment of counsel (Section 2, Regulations 122–29) and legal assistance paid by the Court (Section 3, Regulations 130–39). The training of counsel (Section 4, Regulations 140–42) may help to prevent misconduct. Last but not least, Regulations 147–49 in Section 6 contain the

[45] Coalition for the International Criminal Court, *Legal Representation Team, Submission to the 4th session of the Assembly of the State Parties, Comments on Article 22 of the Draft Code of Professional Conduct for Counsel acting before the ICC* (November 2005) 2–6; KD Hurwitz, *Comments on the Draft Code of Conduct for Counsel before the International Criminal Court* (Human Rights First, 26 November 2005) 1–2; B MacPhee, *Defending Atrocity Crimes, The Requirements of Defense Counsel before the ICC* (The American Non-Governmental Organizations Coalition for the International Criminal Court, 30 August 2005) 20.

[46] Disciplinary Committees, *Rules and Procedures of the Disciplinary Board and the Disciplinary Appeals Board* (15 November 2010).

[47] Above I.A at 171.

provisions relating to Articles 36 and 44 of the Code. Again, this is highly relevant to the topic.

II Specific Measures against Counsel Misconduct

A The Disciplinary System of the ICC

The Code of Professional Conduct aims specifically at regulating misconduct. It was adopted in 2005, and elections took place in 2006 and again in 2010 when the mandate of the first elected members of the disciplinary boards expired, to fill the positions at the two adjudicating bodies – the Disciplinary Board and the Disciplinary Appeals Board.[48] The Commissioner responsible for investigating complaints was appointed by the Presidency in 2007.[49]

In March 2010 the first case was heard.[50] Counsel Hervé Diakiese of the Democratic Republic of Congo had not reported a domestic disciplinary procedure resulting in a one-year suspension in 2009. The Commissioner argued this to be in breach of Regulation 69(3) of the RoC and counsel's undertaking (presumably the one under Art 5 of the Code), ie, to inform the Court of any change in his circumstances including the initiation of a domestic disciplinary procedure.[51] The Board eventually imposed a public reprimand.[52] In October 2010 another case was referred to the disciplinary bodies by Trial Chamber I.[53] It saw prima facie evidence that a counsel for victims had disregarded his duty of confidentiality under Article 8 of the Code. Counsel was reported to have given his passwords to some of the ICC's computer systems to third parties. This may have been beyond the four members of counsel's team, including another law firm and an NGO, granting access to confidential material.

[48] Registry, Results of the election of members of the ICC Disciplinary Board and Disciplinary Appeals Board, 8 December 2006; Registry, Results of the 2010 election of members of the ICC Disciplinary Board and Disciplinary Appeals Board, 6 December 2010. The pertinent provisions are Rules 36 and 44(5) ICC Code, and Regulations 147 and 148 RoR. On the one hand, this strengthens the autonomy of the international criminal Bar, in accordance with domestic practice (ch 2, II.A. and B.i.b at 60 and 86, respectively, for Germany, and III.A and C.i at 108–09 and 142–45, respectively, for the United States). On the other hand, it may be less fortunate as it opens the gates to bar politics, Rosen and Kuhlman (n 42) Comment 7, 7.

[49] Presidency, Results of the selection of the Commissioner by the Presidency, 21 June 2007.

[50] *The Registrar v Hervé Diakiese*, Complaint 01/09, Disciplinary Board, Transcript, 12 March 2010.

[51] *The Registrar v Hervé Diakiese*, DO-01-2010, Disciplinary Board, Decision of the Disciplinary Board, 9 July 2010, para 17.

[52] ibid, paras 52–53.

[53] *The Prosecutor v Thomas Lubanga Dyilo*, ICC-01/04-01/06-2383-RED, Trial Chamber I, Redacted Submission by Trial Chamber I to the Registry pursuant to Article 34(l)(a) of the Code of Professional Conduct for counsel, 11 October 2010.

i An Overview of the ICC Code

The Code was preceded by three similar drafts.[54] With regard to its substance, the Code entrenches a range of duties which are similar to what can be found in other national and international codes.[55] In drafting it, the working groups of the Bureau of the Assembly considered submissions from state parties, non-governmental organisations and lawyers' associations.[56] Among the basic duties that can be identified are many which are common to a lot of national codes of conduct: the conscientious exercise of the profession (Art 5), independence (Art 6), the duty to objectivity and truth (Art 7), secrecy (Art 8) and avoiding conflict of interests (Art 16). Broadly, it follows the traditional lines of professional ethics.

The majority of the professional obligations in the Code seem to affirm general principles pertaining to the entire profession rather than denoting particular ethical pitfalls foremost encountered by criminal defence lawyers.[57] Of course, the Code makes explicit reference to the ICC's very own legal framework, and it has incorporated a number of rules to address some of the difficulties experienced by the other international criminal courts, such as fee-splitting (Art 22) and witness protection (Art 8(4)). As far as it also lays down rather general values of the legal profession, it can be said to be anchored in the 'general principles governing the practice and ethics of the legal profession', as they are expressly recognised in the preamble. Altogether, the substantial scope of the Code does arguably not constitute an immense departure from many known national and international models.

Some provisions relate to the applicability of the Code. This concerns principally the actual reach of the disciplinary regime, ie, the scope of the jurisdiction under the Code. Article 1 declares it applicable to 'defence counsel, counsel acting for States, amici curiae and counsel or legal representatives for victims and witnesses practicing at the International Criminal Court' and thus provides for the personal jurisdiction. With respect to the subject-matter, Article 4 establishes the primacy of the ICC Code over other professional standards 'in respect of the practice and professional ethics of counsel when practicing before the Court'. Article 45 provides for the entry into force, and hence temporal jurisdiction, of

[54] See above, I.B.ii at 174.

[55] A Harting, *Berufspflichten des Strafverteidigers und Sanktionierung pflichtwidrigen Verhaltens* (Bonn, Deutscher Anwaltverlag, 2008) 275–84; JT Tuinstra, *Defence Counsel in International Criminal Law* (Cambridge, Cambridge University Press, 2009) 198–216. See also comparatively on conflict of interest, C Deckenbrock, *Strafrechtlicher Parteiverrat und berufsrechtliches Verbot der Vertretung widerstreitender Interessen* (Bonn, Deutscher Anwaltverlag, 2009) 204–17 on the United States, and throughout on Germany.

[56] ICC, *Report of the Bureau on the draft Code of Professional Conduct for Counsel* (n 34) 3.

[57] See D Luban, 'Are Criminal Defenders Different?' (1992–93) 91 *Michigan Law Review* 1729; M Blake and A Ashworth, 'Ethics and the Criminal Defense Lawyer' (2004) 7 *Legal Ethics* 167. For a brief comparative account of case scenarios in criminal defense: C Lüdtcke, A Harting and S Haumer, 'Rechtsvergleichende Lösung der praktischen Fälle' in T Weigend, S Walther and B Grunewald (eds), *Strafverteidigung vor neuen Herausforderungen – Denkanstöße aus sieben Rechtsordnungen* (Berlin, Duncker & Humblot, 2008) 323–26.

the Code and subsequent amendments 30 days after their adoption by the Assembly of States Parties.[58]

Lastly, chapter 4, entitled 'Disciplinary regime', contains in Articles 30–44 the procedural and evidentiary rules for disciplinary proceedings under the Code. This includes issues of admissibility and the organisation of the disciplinary procedure before the ICC bodies. Misconduct allegations are investigated and prosecuted by the Commissioner and adjudicated before the Disciplinary Board.[59] Article 39 provides for the details on the proceedings, which can take different outcomes.[60] The available sanctions are listed in Article 42: admonishment, public reprimand, a fine, suspension of up to two years and a permanent ban. Counsel or the Commissioner can appeal to the Disciplinary Appeals Board.[61] Furthermore, Articles 30 and 38 contain important statements on the admissibility of a disciplinary case. Article 30 clarifies that the disciplinary regime of the ICC does not preclude any other bodies with regulatory powers to exercise their functions. Article 38 provides that the disciplinary procedure before the ICC bodies is complementary to pending national procedures, though.[62]

Summing up, the Code seems to provide a comprehensive framework for the disciplinary regime. Its scope aims at covering all kinds of conceivable misconduct. The procedural portion of the Code sets forth comprehensive rules on proceedings under the ICC disciplinary regime.

ii The Nature of Professional Discipline under the ICC Code and the Burden of Proof in particular

In the first case under the ICC Code, the Commissioner has argued that the ICC disciplinary proceedings 'are not in the nature of a criminal trial, they are an inquiry into conduct'.[63] This is in agreement with domestic systems as far as they create professional discipline to be an additional system to criminal justice, therefore non-criminal system.[64] The fully non-criminal nature is uncontroversial with respect to rules pertaining on the more administrative aspects of licensing lawyers and managing appointment or assigment, as entrenched in the RPE, the RoC and the RoR.[65] Accordingly, they follow the rules and more general characteristics of civil or administrative procedure.[66]

[58] The ICC Code, adopted on 2 December 2005 (above, I.B.ii at 174), therefore initially entered into force on 1 January 2006.

[59] In detail below, II.A.v.c–e at 212–25.

[60] On the conclusion of the procedure, see below, II.A.v.f at 225–27.

[61] Below, II.A.v.h at 230–34, on the appeals procedure.

[62] On both issues, see ch 4, II.A at 291–97, and C at 298–300.

[63] *The Registrar v Hervé Diakiese*, Complaint 01/09, Transcript (n 50) 6. See also *The Registrar v Hervé Diakiese*, DO-01-2010, Decision (n 51) para 17.

[64] Ch 2, II.C.iv at 92, for Germany, and III.C.v at 154, for the United States.

[65] Above, I.B.i at 173, and I.B.iii at 176.

[66] Ch 2, II.C.iii at 89–92 and III.C.iv at 150–53.

Apart from that, however, considerable differences remain on how closely the actual disciplinary sanctioning scheme as contained in chapter 4 of the Code resembles criminal justice. It is noted that a number of rights known from the criminal process are afforded in professional discipline, although it is frequently stressed that 'differences between the two proceedings can be justified, inter alia, by the specific nature of the offence or by purpose of simplification'.[67] On the other hand, it cannot be ignored that some of the sanctions under disciplinary law are similar. Although imprisonment is not an option, fines and disbarment are similar to what may follow from criminal convictions.[68]

Sanctions under the Code should not automatically be equated with criminal punishment. It is typically argued that criminal or quasi-criminal measures put the citizen at a risk of loss of limb or liberty and therefore warrant certain safeguards. Disbarment is not much of a deprivation of liberty if it only prohibits counsel from practising at the ICC, and neither will an average fine infringe liberty or property interests substantially. On the other hand, it can be seen from the United States that disbarment from the Bar of a single court may nonetheless lead to reciprocal discipline and consequently the loss of the state Bar membership and thus the licence to practise at all.[69] Even when they retain their home licence, some of the attorneys in international criminal defence may have no domestic practice to fall back on. As far as a monetary fine is concerned, the maximum of €30,000 can have similar devastating implications for the attorney's business, in particular for those who do not hail from North America or Western Europe.

The nature of professional discipline bears on practical questions. Depending on the nature of the discipline, taking recourse to general criminal procedure will make more sense if the more specific rules of procedure for professional discipline fail to yield an answer, rather than to rely on the general rules of civil or administrative procedure. The first is more appropriate for quasi-criminal systems, such as in Germany,[70] whereas the latter may fit in better with a *sui generis* system more removed from criminal justice such as in the United States.[71] This is most prominently illustrated by the burden of proof for a finding of misconduct. The Code is silent on the burden of proof but the Disciplinary RPE, in Article 16(1), hold it to be 'clear and convincing evidence', in line with the pertinent standard in the United States. In Germany, Section 116 BRAO declares the Code of Criminal Procedure applicable mutatis mutandis, unless the BRAO's own provisisons are

[67] Association internationale de droit pénal, 'Principles of Criminal Procedure and their Application in Disciplinary Procedures, Draft Resolution' (2003) 74 *Revue internationale de droit pénal* 1103. See also the dispute in the framework of the European Convention whether Art 6(1) applies to professional disciplinary proceedings, CJF Kidd, 'Disciplinary Proceedings and the Right to a Fair Criminal Trial under the European Convention on Human Rights' (1987) 36 *The International and Comparative Law Quarterly* 856; B Lang, J Herberg and C Weir, 'The Duty to Act fairly' (Liberty Focus on Public Law and Human Rights (18 November 2005) para 8.

[68] See below, II.B.iii at 244–48. From a comparative perspective, monetary fines are uncommon, Harting (n 55) 340–41.

[69] Ch 2, III.D.iii at 162–63.

[70] Ch 2, II.C.iv at 92.

[71] Ch 2, III.C.v at 154.

more specific.[72] The burden of proof for sanctions under Section 114 BRAO is 'beyond a reasonable doubt'.[73] The ABA Model Rules for Lawyer Disciplinary Enforcement provide in Rule 18 (Additional Rules Of Procedure) that:

> A. Nature of Proceedings. Disciplinary proceedings are neither civil nor criminal but are sui generis.
> B. Proceedings Governed by Rules of Civil Procedure and Evidence. Except as otherwise provided in these rules, the [state rules of civil procedure] and the [state rules of evidence in civil nonjury matters] apply in discipline and disability cases.
> C. Standard of Proof. Formal charges of misconduct, lesser misconduct, petitions for reinstatement and readmission, and petitions for transfer to and from disability inactive status shall be established by clear and convincing evidence.[74]

The pertinent Commentary to cited Rule 18 of the ABA Model Rules for Lawyer Disciplinary Enforcement explains that '[t]he standard of proof for misconduct is higher than 'preponderance of the weight of credible evidence' which is usually deemed sufficient in civil proceedings, yet not as stringent as 'beyond a reasonable doubt' required in criminal cases'. Much depends therefore on how the character of disciplinary proceedings is to be understood. A quasi-criminal nature will tend to support the view that, just as in criminal proceedings, 'proof beyond reasonable doubt' is required. In litigation between equals a burden of preponderance seems more appropriate as both parties' fate is equally at stake. A compromise, owing to the in-between *sui generis* character, may be 'clear and convincing evidence', as indicated in the Disciplinary RPE (Art 16(1)).

However, in the ICC's context, the methodology set forth in Article 21(1) is foremost determinative, though, for settling the standard of proof and therefore the character of professional discipline. This is (a) in the first place, the Statute, the EoC and the RPE, (b) in the second place, applicable treaties and the principles and rules of international law and (c) failing that the general principles of law derived by the Court from national laws of legal systems of the world including, as appropriate, the national laws of states that would normally exercise jurisdiction.[75] The Court's primary law is silent on the issue. The Statute as well as the RPE is, of course, in full conformity with the 'beyond a reasonable doubt' threshold. It can also be gathered from those sets of rules that they aim at a high due process standard.

The wording of Article 21(1)(a) of the Statute does not clearly settle the rank of the Code in terms of methodology. It can nevertheless be presumed that the by-instruments need to be compatible with the superior ones, that they should be interpreted to emulate those in doubt, or that they at least should breathe their spirit.[76] This is not compelling, however. Differences in the character and scope of rules beyond the Court's main instruments can justify a different conclusion if the

[72] Ch 2, II.B.i.b at 67.
[73] Ch 2, II.C.i. at 87.
[74] Ch 2, III.C.v at 154 (n 189).
[75] See in detail, Bitti (n 2).
[76] Above, I.A at 172.

underlying rationales and circumstances warrant a departure from solutions found there.

The Code itself speaks of 'Sanctions' in Article 42. This may be understood to denote a rather punitive character. There are, though, a number of conceivable civil sanctions, such as punitive and multiple damages, fines, forfeitures and deprivations of a vested right to conduct a business.[77] This moniker of 'sanctions' does not solve the problem but contributes to creating it in first place. It needs to be recalled that the civil/criminal divide is not settled easily and may very well be altogether delusive.[78] Whether the drafters of the ICC Code had an inclination towards one or the other seems, put frankly, unanswerable, in spite of the title of Article 42 of the Code, and Article 16(1) of the Disciplinary RPE.

However, many indicators within the Code as it stands point to the criminal – or at least the quasi-criminal side. The label may be of limited guidance, but an analysis into the effects created by the sanctions under the Code and how the disciplinary bodies arrive at them is more reliable. Injured persons do not have standing in the disciplinary procedure. Neither is directly remedial action possible under the Code. If tangible harm occurs to the client or others, this can possibly be addressed by other remedies available in the ICC legal framework.[79] Unlike the ICTY, the disciplinary boards do not award restitution or bind organs of the Court with their decision.[80] All of this marks differences from civil proceedings as far as genuinely private litigation is concerned. In that respect, the analysis of how the ICC disciplinary bodies arrive at their decisions leads away from seeing them as civil proceedings.

It seems undisputable that the disciplinary process is a public regime, not private litigation.[81] It has been pointed out that it is at odds with a purely remedial approach to sanction attempts to breach a rule, which arguably also applies to acts of inducement (see Art 31(a) and (b) of the Code).[82] On the other hand, adminis-

[77] AX Fellmeth, 'Civil and Criminal Sanctions in the Constitution and Courts' (2005) 94 *Georgetown Law Journal* 1, 40.

[78] ibid. US courts have used a number of factors to determine the character of sanctions, and which protections they need to afford. In doing this, they have tended to give deference to the legislator. See *Kennedy v Mendoza-Martinez*, 372 US 144, 83 SCt 554, 9 LEd2d 644 (Supreme Court of the United States, 1963) (using a seven-factor test); *Hudson v U.S.*, 522 US 93, 118 SCt 488, 139 LEd2d 450 (Supreme Court of the United States, 1997), reversing *U.S. v Halper*, 490 US 435, 109 SCt 1892, 104 LEd2d 487, 448–49 (Supreme Court of the United States, 1989); Fellmeth (n 77) 3.

[79] eg, intra-procedural measures (below, II.C.iii at 263–66).

[80] The opposite was proposed by Rosen and Kuhlman (n 42) Comments 11, 9. It proves all the more that ICC discipline is quasi-criminal. See also on the one hand, *Prosecutor v Momčilo Krajišnik*, IT-00-39-A, Disciplinary Board, Decision in the Appeal by the Disciplinary Board in the Matter of Mr Deyan Ranko Brashich, Attorney at Law from the United States, 22 May 2007, paras 43–49, below v.h., n 318. On the other hand, the ICTY Code has been amended in the meantime, see ch 1, II.A at (n 34). It now provides for restitution orders by the ICTY disciplinary bodies, see Rev 3, Art 47(D).

[81] See GC Hazard and C Beard, 'A Lawyer's Privilege Against Self-Incrimination in Professional Disciplinary Proceedings' (1987) 96 *Yale Law Journal* 1060, 1066, speaking of discipline as 'a relatively formal version of administrative law procedure'. On the different terminology, see ch 2, III.B.iii (n 460).

[82] Fellmeth (n 77) 62.

trative law which implements policies may base an assessment on an overall assessment which may take into account rather general point such as 'moral character', 'good standing' or *Würdigkeit* (worthiness). Attempts or other involvement in illicit acts thus constitute a breach because they are as much against a certain policy as the actual breach and similarly trigger action under the administrative structure. However, an administrative structure per se does not necessarily call for enhanced protection. US courts have acknowledged the specific character of disciplinary controls, distinguished them from civil and criminal procedure but described them as *sui generis*. Nonetheless, they have found that the purpose of professional discipline is to protect the public and to maintain the integrity of the legal system.[83] Therefore, the nature of discipline is said to assess and licence attorneys, it is preventive and not punitive. It is accompanied by somewhat enhanced protections but not criminal due process. The question would thus still be whether the ICC disciplinary procedure demands more then these somewhat enhanced protections, how enhanced they need to be and whether the current protections afforded under the Code satisfy this.

In an attempt to answer this, a look at the sanctions may not be conclusive, but it does arguably reveal more similarities of the ICC regime with the ICTY or Germany than the United States. On the other hand, the punitive or non-punitive character of the sanctions under Article 42(1) will also depend on how the ICC bodies interpret the relevant provisions of the Code. Although a fine of up to €30,000 can be quite high, this cap cannot be explained by a conceivable maximum of possibly incurred harm which is remedied through the fine. This can be taken as another indicator of it being punitive.[84] It will be the case all the more if the Boards allocate the fine to the Court and not to the harmed individuals, and if they do not tie the amount of the fine to such identifiable harm. A ban under Article 42(1)(e) is permanent and results in removal from the list of eligible counsel. How punitive this truly is will also depend on whether and when counsel is granted reinstatement.[85] Disbarment may be remedial if it only restores a rightful state.[86] A fitting example would be Regulation 71 RoC. The Registrar will remove counsel from the list if they do not satisfy the requirements necessary for originally being included on the list. Thus, once counsel proves that the criteria are met again, he or she will be re-admitted to the list. This would be a genuine licensing regime. If the ban under the Code is indeed permanent and the striking of the

[83] See ch 2, II.B.i.c at 144.

[84] Unlike criminal fines (see Rule 166(5) RPE for Art 70 sentences), unpaid disciplinary fines are usually not commuted into imprisonment (see Section 204(3) BRAO for Germany). In the ICC context, this would also, of course, involve questions of how to enforce disciplinary sanctions, which will be with dealt later (see ch 4, II.B at 97–98). The ICC would mainly request having the fine enforced in monies and presumably not seek substitute imprisonment. Refusal to pay a fine could constitute a separate violation under Art 31(c) of the Code and may consequently result in disbarment from the ICC.

[85] See Art 20 Disciplinary RPE.

[86] AX Fellmeth, 'Challenges and Implications of a Systemic Social Effect Theory' (2006) *University of Illinois Law Review* 691, 740.

list is for good without any subsequent reassessment, it is punitive.[87] The latter is also reinforced by the adoption of limitation periods.[88]

It seems fair to conclude that the Code's sanctions are not remedial. One of the reasons put forward why procedural protections are unnecessary in remedial proceedings is that they set in opposition two equal parties.[89] What one party loses, the other wins and vice versa. Procedural protections are equally awarded to both parties. The exercise of a procedural right by one party is often results in a disadvantage for the other party, but it is simply necessary in order to enable both parties to participate in the proceedings. It is different from the kind of one-sided enhanced protection which is typical of criminal procedure and other punitive proceedings. Discipline under the Code is one-sided, though, and the Code itself consequently assumes the need for some rights under Article 40.[90]

The same conclusion to a quasi-criminal system with a burden of proof beyond a reasonable doubt can be discerned from the sources provided for under Article 21(1)(b) and (c). The UN Basic Principles on the Role of Lawyers as an enunciation of international law within the UN framework are inconclusive.[91] On the other hand, the ICTY Code[92] in Article 47(C) and the Code of Professional Conduct for Counsel with the Right of Audience before the Special Court for Sierra Leone[93] in its Article 33(F), adopt the criminal standard of beyond a reasonable doubt.[94]

International precedents thus support the quasi-criminal approach so far, although it is of course not automatically binding on the ICC.[95] The existing rules and practice may not allow only one conclusive resolution as customary law but ultimately reflect general principles derived from international systems. The ICC bodies are certainly not prevented from relying on international bodies. From this angle, it seems that the issue can be resolved in favour of the quasi-criminal standard.

In addition, general principles from national law, as provided by Article 21(1)(c) of the ICC Statute, can to be discerned. In this respect, the US Model Rules only provide a cornerstone. Germany and many other systems would point to the quasi-criminal nature of their disciplinary systems. Finally, it should be taken into account that national models seem to be based on differing premises, but both the

[87] See again, Rosen and Kuhlman (n 42) Comments 12, 9, which propose adopting the opposite.

[88] Because, as ABA commentators argued (ibid, Comment 6, at 6), the fitness of counsel to practise may still be in question in spite of a lapse of the statute of limitations. Regulatory law indeed does not know them.

[89] Fellmeth (n 77) 34.

[90] K Rogall, 'Germany: Principles of Criminal Procedure and their Application in Disciplinary Procedures' (2003) 74 *Revue internationale de droit pénal* 925, has pointed out that legislators are to some degree free to develop disciplinary procedure.

[91] *Basic Principles on the Role of Lawyers, Adopted by the Eighth United Nations Congress on the Prevention of Crime and the Treatment of Offenders* (UN Doc. A/CONF.144/28/Rev.1, at 118 (27 August to 7 September 1990)) Rules 26–29.

[92] See *Prosecutor v Momčilo Krajišnik*, IT-00-39-A, Decision in the Appeal (n 80) paras 18–19.

[93] See ch 1, IV at 46.

[94] The ICTR Code does not contain a disciplinary procedure, ch 1, III.A at 37.

[95] See above, Introduction (n 4).

German and the US system can be based on punitive authority. It rather seems to be this determination of the purpose of the proceedings which allows a conclusion as to the appropriate standard of proof. The ICC Code does rely on punitive measures, such as the monetary fine, which is hard to explain by administrative, protective, or compensatory considerations.[96] In that respect, discipline under the ICC Code goes beyond the purview of 'licensing proceedings'.[97]

Taken together, the ICC Code seems to have taken more from national systems which understand lawyer discipline as a quasi-criminal process. The general principle for that model should be the 'beyond a reasonable doubt' standard as far as the burden of proof for actual sanctions is concerned,[98] in contrast to Article 16(1) of the Disciplinary RPE.

Consequently, the proximity to criminal proceedings should also show in related respects whenever the nature of proceedings is concerned. The burden of proof has been used foremost at this point as it illustrates a very practical aspect.[99] The same considerations apply, though, for a number of other issues discussed in the further course of this chapter on discipline, for example, the use of general clauses,[100] a potential fault requirement,[101] the procedural rights of counsel[102] and sentencing.[103]

iii The Jurisdictional Scope of the Code and other Issues of Applicability

a Personal Jurisdiction

Article 1 clarifies the applicability of the Code. In short, it binds all counsel before the ICC other than counsel for Court organs.[104] It specifically lists 'defence counsel, counsel acting for States, *amici curiae* and counsel or legal representatives for

[96] L Haller, ' Disciplinary Fines: Deterrence or Retribution?' (2002) 5 *Legal Ethics* 152, 162.

[97] American Bar Association, *Lawyer Regulation for A New Century. Report of the Commission on Evaluation of Disciplinary Enforcement* (McKay Report, February 1992) Recommendation 9, at 35. See also American Bar Association, *Standards for Imposing Lawyer Sanctions,* 13: 'Purpose of Lawyer Discipline Proceedings. The purpose of lawyer discipline proceedings is to protect the public and the administration of justice from lawyers who have not discharged, will not discharge, or are unlikely properly to discharge their professional duties to clients, the public, the legal system, and the legal profession'.

[98] M Chiavario, 'Principles of Criminal Procedure and their Application in Disciplinary Proceedings – General Report' (2004) 74 *Revue internationale de droit pénal* 707, 728, shows that countries are split on the issue. The trend seems to be, though, to apply 'beyond a reasonable doubt' if proceedings are punitive. See also JW Hall, 'Comparison of the Proffered Ethical Codes of the International Criminal Bar and the International Bar Association for Practice Before the International Criminal Court' (17th International Conference of the International Society for the Reform of Criminal Law, The Hague, 24–28 August 2003) 45, fn 8, indicating that a similar standard exists in Quebec.

[99] See also below, II.A.v.f at 227.

[100] Below, II.A.iv.b at 195–201.

[101] Below, II.A.iv.d at 206–08.

[102] Below, II.A.v.b at 210–12, and II.A.v.e at 220–26.

[103] Below, II.A.v.g at 228–30.

[104] ie Chambers (and the Presidency), the Registry or the Office of the Prosecutor (Arts 34 and 39 ICC Statute).

victims and witnesses'. This should cover all relevant persons who are not subordinate to Court organs as such. The latter hold their own disciplinary powers.[105] Since counsel from the Office of Public Counsel for the defence[106] and the Office of Public Counsel for victims[107] act independently from the Court, they should fall within the ambit of Article 1 of the Code as defence counsel and counsel for victims, respectively.

It could be criticised that counsel for the defence and for the OTP do not act on a level playing field, ie, making them subject to similar professional standards.[108] However, the particular need for the regulation of counsel is apparent. Thus, most actors being legal representatives for participants are covered by the same set of ethics and the adjoining enforcement mechanisms. Defence counsel should perhaps be interpreted liberally, given that new forms of legal assistance – if not of representation – have emerged. Standby counsel, for example, essentially fulfill the same functions as officially assigned defence counsel, and they should be held to the same standards.[109] The Code of Conduct aims at regulating professionals who are involved in the Court's administration of justice and this applies likewise to standby counsel.

Article 1 is also relevant to the scope of the Code when referring to counsel 'practising at the International Criminal Court'. Read together with Article 4,[110] it becomes clear that the Code is meant to apply to lawyers when they actually exercise their functions in relation to the Court. The effect of Article 4 is only that the Code's rule prevails whenever counsel practises in a Court matter. It does arguably not claim to fully govern counsel's practice, including domestic matters. Not all counsel will always act in matters which are relevant to the Court. Most counsel will presumably retain their domestic practice while representing clients before the ICC. Even if they work at the Court in The Hague for what may in fact turn out to be full-time for a period, they will necessarily still be admitted domestically, retain any membership of a law firm and consequently deal with existing and new clients together. Mere inclusion in the list of counsel is therefore not a conclusive criterion for a specific case.

As a result, counsel should not be subject to the Code when not handling ICC business. On the other hand, even conduct that does not arise from Court-related

105 Above, I.B.ii at 173. Amicus curiae prosecutors for contempt proceedings before the ICTY have been held to be bound by the ICTY Code (*Prosecutor v Radoslav Brđanin, Concerning Allegations against Milka Maglov*, IT-99-36-R77, Registry, Decision, 29 October 2003, on this case see ch 1, II.B.ii.d at 23).

106 Regulation 77 RoC, see in particular sub-regulation (2).

107 Regulation 81 RoC, and again, its sub-regulation (2).

108 On their criminal liability, see below II.B at 237, with n 329.

109 On cases from the UN tribunals, see G Boas, 'The Right to Self-Representation in International and Domestic Criminal Law – Limitations and Qualifications on that Right' in H Abthai and G Boas (eds), *The Dynamics of International Criminal Justice* (Leiden, Martinus Nijhoff, 2005) 60–67, 90; *Prosecutor v Momčilo Krajišnik*, IT-00-39-A, Appeals Chamber, Decision on Momčilo Krajišnik's Request to Self-Represent, on Counsel's Motion in Relation to Appointment of Amicus Curiae, and on the Prosecution Motion of 16 February 2007, 11 May 2007.

110 Even a bright-line rule on conflicts such as Art 4 ICC Code requires criteria to declare the Code applicable in first place. See OL Knöfel, 'Anwalts-Kollisionsrecht' (2003) *Anwaltsblatt* 3, 7.

proceedings may potentially lead to disciplinary measures. It is a generally accepted principle that private misconduct may form a base for professional discipline in certain circumstances.[111] Article 4 would be rendered meaningless, though, if it were possible to assess all non-ICC related conduct as private, yet disciplinable as private misconduct. Apart from this, it needs further clarification whether and to what extent extra-professional conduct is covered by the Code and sanctionable under it.[112] Therefore, 'practising at the Court' and 'when practising before the Court' need to be aligned and to be interpreted more narrowly. Distinctive criteria need to be found to define these elements.

First, purely formal criteria are not convincing. Simply being physically present at the Court would be a clear and objective criterion, but presence may not be in relation to any official functions of the ICC. It seems to make sense, however, to apply the Code to counsel as soon as they enter into a professional relationship with the Court. This is clearly the case when counsel formally accept assignment to a suspect or accused before the ICC on request from a Chamber (see Art 11 of the Code). By accepting the assignment, they express their consent to be included on the list of counsel, or to be added if not listed, and subject themselves to the governing regulations accordingly. Similarly, the ICTY Code provides that counsel is to be understood to encompass a person 'who is or has been assigned by the Registrar to represent a client'.[113]

If counsel is retained privately, the representation agreement is established when counsel, whether listed or not, accepts representation of a client. In some way that marks the beginning of a professional exchange for counsel with the Court's organs and individuals involved in ICC proceedings, if the case is handled by the ICC under its own jurisdiction and after the declaration of admissibility, or in the process thereof. The ICTY Code also mentions counsel who 'is or has been engaged by a client and has filed a power of attorney with the Registrar' or who 'is in communication with a prospective client'. The ICTR Code, in contrast, seems to be more lenient. Other than through assignment, counsel only comes within the scope of the Code if her or she '[h]as filed his or her power of attorney with the Registrar'. The filing of a power of attorney as the equivalent of assignment by a court seems to be an equally suitable threshold marking counsel's entering into a particular professional relationship with a court. The ICTY Code has a point, though, when it also declares counsel subject to the Code before they are officially retained. If they engage in communication that is likely to result in representing a client before the ICC, a link to the ICC's administration of justice is already established. The actual conclusion of a representation agreement does mark an important step, and many professional obligations arise from it.

[111] Ch 2, II.B.i.a at 62, for Germany, and III.B.i.b at 118, III.D.i at 155, for the United States. See also the first case of counsel Diakiese, above at 177.

[112] On private misconduct by counsel and the ICC Code, see below, II.A.iv.a at 194.

[113] See Art 1(A). The only difference here, albeit again of a quite formal character, is that counsel is assigned by a Chamber in the case of the ICC (Regulation 76 RoC), and the Registry in the case of the ICTY or the ICTR (see Art 1(A) ICTR Code with similar wording).

But there are also pre-contractual duties; and other ones seem to arise from sources other than the counsel-client agreement in the first place. The establishment of a representation agreement may therefore be a sufficient precondition for subjecting counsel to the Code in some cases, but not always a necessary one. Sometimes therefore 'practising at the Court' and 'when practising before the Court' must also be determined along substantive criteria if the conclusion of a representation agreement does not allow an unmistakable conclusion that counsel is now practising before the ICC. In the same vein, representation of *any* client will not suffice; a client has to be represented in particular in relation to ICC proceedings.

Materially speaking, counsel is therefore subject to the ICC's regime if practising in relation to a matter over which the ICC has jurisdiction or if misconduct otherwise relates to the specific capacity of being an ICC-listed counsel. With regard to the former, however, it seems to go too far to cover all cases over which the Court has jurisdiction. This would not take into account that complementarity is a guiding principle of the Statute. Consequently, many cases over which the ICC has jurisdiction as a back-up judiciary are expected not to go before the ICC, but instead they will hopefully be tried in a domestic forum. Those cases may in some way be linked to the ICC's mission but they are not integral to the Court's administration of justice. Therefore, it does not suffice that the Court's jurisdiction extends to a certain case or suspect. A case involving a suspect and his or her counsel is of relevance to the Court, however, if it has been declared admissible since it has then become the Court's work. This is similar to the formal criterion that counsel is assigned in a case already declared admissible or in the official procedure of being decided.

In addition, it may make sense to link counsel and client to the Court if there is a substantial likelihood that a case will be declared admissible. If counsel is already admitted to the ICC List of Counsel,[114] this seems clear since counsel has then been warned. The only conceivable scenario not yet discussed would be that counsel is not formally admitted, but clearly eligible, and takes on a case before the ICC as de facto counsel. Should counsel then be subject to the Code and the procedure under it even before formal admission because he or she is in the ICC's jurisdiction after concluding an agreement vis-a-vis a client? US model rules[115] seem to support such an approach, whereas other countries, such as Germany[116]

[114] See Rule 21 RPE.

[115] Even foreign attorneys who are not specifically licensed are subject to discipline. See Rule 6 of the *Model Rules for Lawyer Disciplinary Enforcement*: '[A]ny lawyer not admitted in this jurisdiction who practices law or renders or offers to render any legal services in this jurisdiction is subject to the disciplinary jurisdiction of this court and the board'. No reasoning is given in the ABA's Commentary on these rules. Discipline is also applied for acts after leaving the Bar. The argumentation for cases of special admission reads: 'Commentary: In the same way that the motorist has given his implied consent to be bound by the traffic laws of the states he travels, the lawyer admitted for a limited purpose subjects himself or herself to the rules of conduct in the jurisdiction'. See ch 2, III.B.i.a at 115.

[116] Counsel only becomes subject to professional discipline after formal admission to the Bar, and no procedure can be instituted after counsel has left it: M Kleine-Cosack, *Bundesrechtsanwaltsordnung*, 6th edn (Munich, Beck, 2009) § 113, mn 2; T Dittmann in M Henssler and H Prütting (eds), *Bundesrechtsanwaltsordnung*, 3rd edn (Munich, Beck, 2010) § 113, mn 16. See ch 2, II.B.i.a at 65.

or England and Wales[117] tend to make formal admission a prerequisite to professional discipline. Of course, the ICC rules are paramount here. Regulation 75 (to which Rule 21(1) of the RPE points) distinguishes between list counsel in sub-regulation (1) and non-list counsel under sub-regulation (2). At the end of sub-regulation (2), it clarifies that the duty counsel will act for a suspect or an accused until the permanent counsel is admitted and has filed a power of attorney. In other words, counsel cannot exercise defence rights until this has happened. Conversely, he or she should not be considered as practising before the Court. It could, of course, be argued that this is not a question of rights, and that it is duties which are concerned. These may well extend to before, as is the case with Article 12 ('Impediments to representation') and address de facto counsel as well. At least, this is an argument for extending the substantial scope to also cover counsel and their conduct before they are admitted to the list. Furthermore, Rule 22(3) sets out that counsel for the defence shall be subject to the Code, inter alia, in the performance of their duties; this is not limited to actual admission.

It remains ambiguous whether current admission is a prerequisite to exercising professional discipline, leaving out counsel before being called to the Bar via the list, or after leaving the list of counsel. Quintessentially, though, counsel may only act for a client in proceedings and thus enter into a professional discourse with the Court if he or she has been added to the list. No professional relationship automatically arises from mere eligibility, unlike current admission.[118] Expressing the will towards the Court to represent a client is a first step towards this professional relationship. Likewise, Rule 22 relates the performance of duties to the Code's regime in sub-rule (3), and, in sub-rule (2), obliges counsel to file a power of attorney at the earliest possibility. Regulation 75 of the RoC directs the Registrar to other Regulations which set out the criteria for eligibility to be included on the list, subsequent to which counsel will be able to practise before the Court. Discipline should therefore only run from the moment that counsel is included on the list. Misconduct prior to admission should be addressed by way of the prior eligibility check by the Registrar. Articles 1 and 4 of the Code should thus be construed restrictively. Likewise, personal jurisdiction under the Code should cease with membership in the list. If counsel cannot presently act, he or she should not any longer be considered practising . Since the relationship with the Court is then defunct, the Court loses that jurisdiction. Taking critical cases into consideration, it is reiterated that withdrawal from the list is dependent on the Registrar doing that in accordance with Regulation 71 of the RoC.

Summing up, a two-pronged test should be used to establish the personal jurisdiction of the Code over counsel. Under the first prong, current inclusion in the ICC List of Counsel is needed, as personal disciplinary jurisdiction only encompasses counsel who are currently admitted. Under the second prong, it needs to

[117] See the Code of Conduct, Part X – Definitions, Rule 1001: '"[B]arrister" means an individual who has been called to the Bar by one of the Inns of Court and who has not ceased to be a member of the Bar'.

[118] See the case of counsel Diakiese, above at 177.

be tested whether the allegations either (a) relate to the status of counsel if they arise irrespective of a handled case,[119] or (b) for case-related misconduct, if they stem from a matter that is material to the ICC's administration of justice, because counsel is either representing a client before the Court, because he or she is otherwise advising in a matter which falls under the ICC's jurisdiction which has been declared admissible or is in the process of being declared so, or which carries a substantial likelihood of qualifying as admissible.[120]

b Temporal Jurisdiction

Personal jurisdiction under the Code includes some temporal aspects such as the period before and after formal admission. Apart from whether an individual is subject to discipline, the points in time may generally restrict the authority of a court to deal with certain conduct. Jurisdiction *ratione temporis*, however, must be distinguished from the prohibition of retroactivity.[121] The *nullum crimen* maxim just bars ex post facto criminalisation but not the retroactive assumption of jurisdiction.

The ICTY did find itself in the situation of retroactively applying a disciplinary procedure to conduct that had occurred before the disciplinary portion of the Code had been enacted. Apparently, it was argued that no ex post facto offences were thus created by the ICTY, but only jurisdiction was assumed retroactively (which was foreseen by a provision). The ICTY did not have a problem as to the subject-matter; it was rather the lack of a procedure.[122] The same seems conceivable for the ICTR.[123] There may be arguments in favour of and against the retroactive application of procedural law. A strict interpretation of this strives for certainty in terms of the applicable law. As to the principle of legality, the ICTY has in essence held that the subject-matter jurisdiction had legitimately been conferred on the disciplinary bodies, and that this jurisdiction was just assumed later. It is remarked in respect to the reasoning of the ICTY that legal certainty as to the existence of a prohibition may also extend to the punishment of a crime, and that the ICTY's retroactive assumption of jurisdiction may therefore be questionable.

[119] ibid.

[120] There may still be a dilemma owing to the ICC's Art 17 complementarity scheme. It tells the Court to exercise deference to national proceedings before declaring a case admissible and thus making it pending. Imagine that counsel has been retained by a client for the national proceedings, and that he or she will continue to do so in the subsequent ICC proceedings as well. The problem here would be that the ICC Code can either be construed to become applicable only after admissibility has been declared, or it could be interpreted to subject counsel to it as soon as conduct falls under the ICC's jurisdiction. In the first case, covering counsel only after the case is taken on by the ICC, we would have to live with prior unethical conduct. In the alternative, if the ICC Code prevails early on, we force counsel to potentially breach domestic law.

[121] See SA Williams in O Triffterer (ed), *Commentary on the Rome Statute of the International Criminal Court*, 2nd edn (Munich, Beck, 2008) art 11, mn 2.

[122] Ch 1, II.B.i.b at 14–15.

[123] Ch 1, II.iv. at 38.

Presumably, no such retroactivity dilemma exists for the ICC in practical terms. The substantive duties, the definition of misconduct and the legal consequences of finding a violation, along with the procedure to establish it, have all been enacted at the same time. The Code entered into force on 1 January 2006, according to Article 45, and was subsequently published in the Court's Official Journal pursuant to Article 46.[124] The Code and the disciplinary procedure apply from that date. Before that point, no case of an accused individual had commenced. This means that virtually no defence counsel were involved in the Court's proceedings, and therefore presumably no occasions for misconduct have existed.[125] What may happen is that amendments to procedure and substantive provisions are added. Purely procedural changes also apply to running proceedings and, of course, prior conduct. Substantive changes should be exempt from retroactive application since discipline is a quasi-criminal regime.[126] This may even be moot if prior conduct can be covered through a general clause.[127]

c Other Requirements for the Applicability of the Code

Once counsel is practising before the Court within the confines of Articles 1 and 4, the Code applies to counsel's conduct in relation to the ICC. This therefore refers to any counsel who advises in a matter over which the Court has jurisdiction which has been declared admissible (or is likely to be) and who is admitted to the list. This is notwithstanding other professional standards, as made clear in Article 4. Thus, the Code enjoys primacy in substance. Put another way, other rules do not have an effect on the applicability of the Code. Article 4 is a clear-cut provision which makes sense, as it helps to avoid 'double deontology dilemmas'.[128] [129] Its thrust is comprehensive as it relegates all which counsel is otherwise 'bound to honour'. Article 4 does not differentiate whether these rules are mandatory –

[124] This should apply to amendments (see Art 45 of the Draft Code) as well, pursuant to Regulation 7(1)(g) RoC, strengthening legal certainty. Art 3 ('Amendment procedure') provides for the procedure of amending the Code. It remains to be seen whether the anticipated procedure permits all concerned actors to duly voice their input.

[125] If the example of the ICTY is invoked, jurisdiction might only be assumed by reliance on the RPE, which were finalised on 2 November 2000. Rule 8 provides for the drafting of a Code of Professional Conduct. The Statute does not address counsel misconduct.

[126] On the nature of the ICC disciplinary regime, see above, II.A.ii at 179–85. If discipline is quasi-criminal, it should entail protection from retroactivity. This will arguably then flow from the broader *nullum crimen* principle under international law, if not from Art 22 of the Statute (see B Broomhall in O Triffterer (ed), *Commentary on the Rome Statute of the International Criminal Court*, 2nd edn (Munich, Beck, 2008) art 22, mn 17).

[127] The use of general clauses will be discussed below, II.A.iv.b at 194–201.

[128] M Walsh, 'The International Bar Association Proposal for a Code of Professional Conduct for Counsel Before the ICC' (2003) 1 *Journal of International Criminal Justice* 490, 499.

[129] This solves the conflict of laws from the ICC perspective but not for the domestic regime. For the actual admissibility of concurrent proceedings, in particular with a view to Art 38 of the Code, see ch 4, II.A, C at 291–97 and 298–300, respectively.

usually as a consequence of being licensed nationally – or voluntary – as would be the case for non-governmental professional associations and interest groups.[130]

This seems uncontestable for private associations which counsel adheres to voluntarily, and it should be equally so at least in relation to Member States, all of which have adopted the Code by consensus.[131] This is considerably less clear for counsel licensed by non-member States, such as US lawyers. The doctrine of privity in contract law, or of *pacta tertiis nec nocent nec prosunt*, comes to mind.[132] However, counsel choose voluntarily and in person to act in relation to the ICC. US sovereignty, or that of any other nation, is not affected by this. It may also be considered part of customary international law that state or international bodies have the power to regulate counsel regardless of nationality within what is in principle their jurisdiction.[133] Cooperation, in particular the enforcement of decisions, may then be a different story.[134]

Finally, the applicability of a legal regime can be hindered by immunities and other exemptions from the exercise of jurisdiction. Immunities and privileges can either be claimed by the ICC, or by states and other international organisations in their relationship with the ICC.[135]

As far as the former is concerned, the Agreement on the Privileges and Immunities of the International Criminal Court[136] as well as the Headquarters Agreement with the Netherlands[137] provides for immunities of counsel. They can be formally lifted by the Presidency.[138] Such a formal waiver is not needed, though, when applying the ICC disciplinary procedure, and should also not constitute an obstacle for other ICC measures: the mentioned immunities and privileges are intended to prevent other national and international jurisdictions from impinging on ICC sovereignty and not to create the requirement of authorisation by the Presidency.[139]

[130] Rosen and Kuhlman (n 42) 5, have pointed out that US Supreme Courts usually claim inherent powers to regulate counsel (see on this ch 2, III.A at 109–13). Presumably, any nationally competent regulatory body, be it courts or administrative agencies, will retain its competence with regard to national regulation. ICC disciplinary decisions only have effects before the ICC. Arts 4, 30, and 38 cannot be construed as limiting the powers of US Supreme Courts or any other national regulatory body. Whether national bodies recognise ICC decisions, and thus give ICC discipline effects within their own jurisdiction, rather concerns reciprocal discipline (see ch 4, II.C at 298–300).

[131] See above, I.B.ii at 174.

[132] See Arts 33, 34, *Vienna Convention on the Law of Treaties* (UN Treaty Series, vol 1155, at 33) (23 May 1969, entered into force on 27 January 1980). The ICTY and ICTR are not affected since they are created under ch VII of the UN Charter.

[133] DF Vagts, 'The International Legal Profession: A Need for More Governance?' (1996) 90 *American Journal of International Law* 250, 253. See also from the ICTY context, ch 1, II.D at 35–36.

[134] See ch 4, II.B at 297–98.

[135] On the effect of ICC immunities and privileges on proceedings in other jurisdictions, see ch 4, II.C at 298–300, and III.C at 307, including on the arrest of ICTR defence counsel Peter Erlinder in Rwanda (nn 73 and 111).

[136] ICC, *Agreement on the Privileges and Immunities of the International Criminal Court* (n 14) Art 18.

[137] ICC, *Headquarters Agreement between the International Criminal Court and the host State* (ICC-BD/04-01-08, 7 June 2007) Art 25 (with a similar wording to the above-mentioned Agreement).

[138] By the Presidency, see Art 26(2)(f) and Art 30 (2)(b)(ii), respectively.

[139] Immunities may be relevant, however, with regard to prosecution or disciplining in other jurisdictions and thus have repercussions on the ICC procedure, eg, the complementarity element under Art 38 of the Code. See ch 4, II.A at 291–97.

Should immunities and privileges be claimed by states or other entities, on the other hand, they can only be relevant to the ICC if they conform to the applicable international law. Again, state parties are a priori estopped since they unanimously adopted the Code. With respect to ordinary counsel, it is noted that they choose freely to submit themselves to the ICC's disciplinary authority. As long as they are only affected in their personal capacity, the purpose of immunities, ie, safeguarding the sovereignty of a state or other international subjects, is not concerned. This might differ for counsel who are officially acting for states and may therefore enjoy, despite the Court's inherent power, the status of a diplomatic agent with the pertinent immunities.[140] However conceivable, this will typically not be the case if states are only participants in the ICC's proceedings.

iv The Definition of Misconduct for the Purpose of Disciplinary Proceedings

a The Breach of an Applicable Rule

Article 31 is entitled 'Misconduct' and defines what constitutes disciplinable misconduct (or 'grounds for discipline', to use term from the ABA's Model Rules, or 'breach of duty', in the terminology of the BRAO). Similar to other disciplinary codes, some general as well as a number of more specific duties are identified in the Code but actual discipline is anchored in one generic provision.[141] Such provisions usually point to the applicable professional rules and stipulate that a breach of these rules may or will draw sanctions. Whether there has been an actual breach or not is a question of the substantive law.[142]

Pursuant to Article 31(a), these relevant rules are in the ICC's case 'any provisions of this Code, the Statute, the Rules of Procedure and Evidence and the Regulations of the Court or of the Registry in force'. Other codes tend to contain such a general reference clause as well, although the extent varies.[143] For the ICC, it can be said to be the minimum to include the Code itself, and other legal obligations from the listed instruments.

The ICTY counterpart (Art 35 ICTY Code) points to such instruments but also 'any other applicable law' and only declares it misconduct 'inter alia'. Article 20

[140] See Arts 31 and 32, *Vienna Convention on Diplomatic Relations* (UN Treaty Series, vol. 500, at 95) (18 April 1961, entered into force on 24 April 1964). It is uncertain how far customary law extends immunity beyond acting heads of state and whether it could be argued that if state representatives are not immune from truly international jurisdiction for their private acts, this includes lesser jurisdiction, such as discipline.

[141] Section 113 BRAO, for Germany; American Bar Association, *Model Rules for Lawyer Disciplinary Enforcement* (adopted by the American Bar Association House of Delegates on August 8, 1989 and amended on 11August 1993, 5 August 1996, 8 February 1999 and 12 August 2002) Rule 9; Harting (n 55) 291–95, 303, 312.

[142] See in detail, Harting (n 55) 69–284; KS Gallant, 'The International Criminal Court' in M Bohlander, R Boed and RJ Wilson (eds), *Defense in International Criminal Proceedings* (Ardsley, NY, Transnational Publishers, 2006) 457–78.

[143] Ch 2, II.B.i at 62 (for Germany), III.B.i.b at 118–19 (for the United States) and for the ICTY and the ICTR in the following.

ICTR Code does the latter as well. Otherwise, it only mentions the Code, but in Article 12, reference is made to the Rules, and in addition, to Tribunal rulings. Similarly, according to Article 7(3) ICC Code, the law with which counsel shall comply at the ICC is that of the Statute, the Rules, the Regulations of the Court, but also any further 'rulings as to conduct and procedure as may be made by the Court'. Lastly, Article 5 on the solemn undertaking by counsel establishes another very general reference as well. It can be seen that the scope of disciplinable rules can easily be widened by holding these channelling provisions to be genuine obligations under the Code. It would ultimately soften considerably the listing of statutory instruments in Article 31(a). If Articles 5 or 7(3) were held to constitute a discrete obligation, many simple court rulings could create professional standards which are subject to discipline under the Code.

This would definitely mean a departure from a duty-based approach towards a general clause. The permissibility of such an approach is still to be discussed below (under the next heading). From a more general perspective, it is common for professional codes to include in the misconduct provision more categories of relevant rules than just from the Code itself and other professional standards. First, criminal acts tend to draw discipline, sometimes limited to those which reflect on counsel's integrity as a lawyer. This is done in Germany, whereas the ABA Model Rules and the ICTY/ICTR Code include this and go even further and take disciplinable standards from a second category, ie, other acts, including non-criminal acts in relation to dishonesty.[144] This is, again, sometimes limited to professional settings, for example, when mentioning another act in relation to administration of justice, or an attempt to influence the course of court business in an improper manner.[145]

In conclusion, it is a common feature to refer to conduct beyond the immediate scope of the Code. If beyond the Code, it is sometimes restricted to professional settings, or to criminal acts, or otherwise within the framework of profession regulation. As far as Article 31 is concerned, it explicitly refers to rules imposing 'ethical or professional' obligations. If the former is understood to denote non-professional obligations and not just professional ethics, this would set it apart from other regimes at first blush, which limit discipline to professional issues. This difference could be bridged by construing it as private misconduct.[146] The other particularity is that it has a much shorter listing of applicable statutes, and that it per se does not include non-statutory standards. This is confusing insofar as provisions other than this central misconduct provision, for example Articles 6 and 7(3) of the ICC Code, address other rules, and the misconduct provision then points to those.

[144] Ch 1, II.A at 12 (for the ICTY), III.A at 37 (for the ICTR), ch 2, II.B.i at 63–65 (for Germany), III.B.i.b at 118–19 (for the United States).

[145] See ibid.

[146] On the grasp of disciplinary codes over private misconduct in Germany and the United States, see ch 2, II.B.i.a at 62, for Germany, and III.B.i.b at 118, D.i at 155, for the United States.

b The Use and Significance of General Clauses in the Code

This demonstrates that the issue of the applicable standards cannot be separated from that of the use of non-determined clauses. It is understood that all legal norms are undetermined to some degree. Real problems of legality arise where rules – here those of professional conduct – are not simply interpreted but created. The problem of general clauses should not be brushed away easily for quasi-criminal systems such as the ICC disciplinary procedure.[147] The use of general clauses can raise concerns, in particular where discipline is understood to constitute quasi-criminal sanctioning, as in Germany, but less so in a more regulatory *sui generis* regime as in the United States.[148] Even though general clauses can indeed be problematic with respect to the principle of legality, it will be argued in this section that even in a quasi-criminal system as the ICC's, general clauses can be useful and can constitute at least a base for minor sanctions, namely admonishment pursuant to Article 42(1)(a) of the Code.

This argument unfolds more fully in three steps. First, through a comparison with the ad hoc Tribunals and the national models. National practice tends to declare the use of general clauses permissible, particularly those in disciplinary proceedings. General clauses are indeed used in some way or another in Germany,[149] Spain,[150] the Netherlands[151] and the United States.[152] It might not be too useful to interpret the ICC Code in a way that departs from the 'general principles governing the practice and ethics of the legal profession', to which the preamble refers.

Secondly, by a query into the principle of legality, more precisely the rationales of fair notice, of the separation of powers and of the rule of law. It can be demonstrated that none of them per se disallow the use of general clauses in professional discipline. There is a legitimate interest in greater flexibility in the context of professional rules since these are different in purpose and substance from criminal law.

The third step considers the various factors as far as actually imposing sanctions on the basis of general clauses is concerned. By weighing the protected freedoms of the individual against the public interests in disciplining and how they differ those behind criminal law, admonishment will be identified as the permissible sanction.

From the beginning, it needs to be emphasised that general clauses are indeed widely used and are part of the terminology employed in legal ethics because they

[147] See above, II.A.ii at 179–85, for the arguably quasi-criminal nature of the ICC disciplinary proceedings.

[148] See ch 2, II.B.i at 62–65 (for Germany), III.B.i.b at 118–21 (for the United States).

[149] Ch 2, II.B.i.a at 63–65. See also in detail Harting (n 55) 85–110, 291–94, 429–30.

[150] Not entirely clear in that respect: Harting, ibid, 189–97.

[151] See the general clause of Art 46 of the *Advocatenwet* (Lawyer's Act) ibid, 206. See also, eg, *Steur v The Netherlands*, Application no 39657/98, Second Section, Judgment, 28 January 2004, para 15.

[152] Ch 2, III.B.i.b at 118–22.

are useful to describe the desirable best practice of counsel.[153] The ICC Code does this in Article 5, Article 6(1),[154] Article 7(1) and (3). Similarly, the German Code, the BRAO, contains Section 43, in addition to Section 113; the ABA Model Rules contain Rule 8.4 (c), exceeding the literal scope of Rule 9 of the Model Rules for Lawyer Disciplinary Enforcement. That a violation of mandatory rules can be disciplined goes without saying. Apart from that, one may also encounter general clauses that contain aspirational rules, ie, what the ideal lawyer should aspire to do. In such a case, the aspirational rule does in itself not constitute the binding minimum of good practice, but describes best practice.[155] If such aspirational rules are cited in the context of a general rule during sanctioning, it may look like discipline is actually administered for the breach of that aspirational rule. This raises no concern, though, if sanctioning is truly based on some other rule of a binding nature, and the aspirational, non-binding rule is only cited in support and explanation of that binding standard derived from some other rule. In essence, counsel is then sanctioned for breaching the binding rule, not the aspirational one. Put differently, the real problems arise if sanctioning builds solely on the breach of a rule which is on the one hand openly worded and commands mandatory adherence at the same time.

The ICTY and the ICTR regimes can be understood to be very comprehensive in this regard.[156] For misconduct, Article 35(iii) of the ICTY Code lets any 'conduct involving dishonesty' suffice. Article 10 of the ICTY and Article 5 of the ICTR Code oblige counsel, inter alia, to 'preserve their own integrity and that of the legal profession as a whole'. Article17(1) of the ICTR Code requires counsel to 'act fairly, honestly and courteously towards all persons with whom they have professional contact'. Article 20(b) and (c) of the ICTR Code have already been cited, making it disciplinable to engage in dishonest conduct, or such one being prejudicial to the proper administration of justice before the Tribunal. Further, in Articles 1(C) and 1(6) respectively, the ICTY and the ICTR Codes provide that the '[g]eneral provisions of this Code should not be read or applied in a restrictive way by reason of any particular or illustrative provisions'. All of this tends to lead to a very wide and indeterminate base for discipline. The same is conceivable under the ICC Code if the disciplinary bodies use one of the more general provi-

[153] RD Rotunda, *Legal Ethics in a Nutshell*, 3rd edn (Eagan, Minn, Thomson/West, 2007) 8–10; Preparatory Commission for the ICC, *Contributions of the Chambers of the International Criminal Tribunal for the former Yugoslavia* (13 March 2000) fn 43 (on ICTY Code). See also foregoing n 144 for the provision of the ICTY, ICTR, German and US-American codes.

[154] See, however, Harting (n 55) 272: 'lediglich Appellcharakter' (only of an aspirational character).

[155] See ch 2, III.B.i.b at 120–21, on the differentiation of aspirational ethical rules and binding professional standards in the United States. See also the proposal by JI Turner, 'Legal Ethics in International Criminal Defense' (2010) 10 *Chicago Journal of International Law* 1, 57, to develop 'nonbinding guidelines'.

[156] It could be added that Art 38 ICTY Code and Art 1(4) ICTR Code recall the Tribunal's inherent jurisdiction which is claimed to be unaffected by the Code. It becomes clear from this that the ICTY and the ICTR regimes adhere to a different approach anyway, as far as the first limb of the principle of legality is affected, that of statutory entrenchment or the separation of powers (on this, see also Harting (n 55) 103–10, 183–85, 200–02, 431). On the other hand, these provisions address the Tribunal's general powers rather than the disciplinary powers in particular.

sions like Article 5, Article 6(1), Article 7(1) or 7(3) to base unwritten standards on them.[157]

The principle of legality is therefore relevant to professional discipline by the ICC. As to this principle, it has been argued that several rationales underlie it. These are the separation of powers, fair notice and the rule of law.[158] First, the principle of legality mandates that the law itself, not the administering judge, sufficiently clearly sets out what the applicable standard is in substance. This would be the *Bestimmtheitsgrundsatz* (principle of certainty) in German or the notions of fair notice and void for vagueness in US American doctrine. Secondly, that creating law is the prerogative of the legislative. This is expressed by the *Vorbehalt des Gesetzes* (requirement of statutory authorisation) in German constitutional doctrine but also aptly resonates in the US Supreme Court's jurisprudence, namely in Scalia's dissent to *Nasco v Chambers*, with regard to the separation of powers.[159] Finally, the rule of law aims at limiting arbitrary application of a rule.

The most eminent underlying issue is whether such clauses award counsel the requisite fair notice before punishment. Fair notice ideally achieves an *ex ante* function of announcing the rules of conduct.[160] Factually, the exact content will often be inaccessible. Moreover, a search for precedents will usually be needed. The crucial fairness issue here is – if we go along the lines of Jeffries – that liability should be permitted if a law-abiding person, ie, counsel, would have known better. But this can be achieved by general clauses which can give sufficient guidance for a legal debate.[161] Certainly, it is disturbing to inflict punishment on an honest person. This is what fair notice is about, protecting those who attempt to abide by the rules. On the other hand, many legal systems adhere to the rule of *ignorantia juris neminem excusat.*[162] However, this can and should be cured by allowing a warning and using a fault requirement. There is reason – in particular taking into account the nature of professional discipline – to admonish mischievous counsel. In many cases, counsel themselves will suspect their conduct to be bordering on the fringes of permissible practice. On the other hand, fair notice fails when a law-abiding person in the actor's situation might have had no reason to avoid the proscribed behaviour. If unawareness of illegality is itself the wrong, the actor is at fault, but this is not a problem inherent to the general clause. The fault is less when not complying with a general clause which contains unwritten standards if those standards are unclear or just emerging. On the other hand, the facts may be

[157] In the first case to be heard (above at 177, n 50), the Commissioner seems to have relied on both Art 5, where he speaks of the oath or the undertaking, and Art 7(3). The latter does not amount to using a general clause because Regulation 69(3) RoC clearly establishes information duties.

[158] See for a detailed analysis see JC Jeffries, 'Legality, Vagueness, and the Construction of Penal Statutes' (1985) 71 *Virginia Law Review* 189 and PH Robinson, 'Fair Notice and Fair Adjudication: Two Kinds of Legality' (2005) 154 *University of Pennsylvania Law Review* 335, the latter also distinguishing different principles of legality, by what he calls 'rules legality' and 'adjudication legality'.

[159] *Chambers v Nasco*, 501 US 32, 111 SCt 2123, 115 LEd2d 27, 59 USLW 4595, 19 FedRServ3d 817, 63–67 (Supreme Court of the United States, 1991) and also ch 2, III.A at 109–13.

[160] See Robinson (n 158).

[161] For this test, see *Ontario v Canadian Pacific Ltd.*, 2 SCR 1031 (Supreme Court of Canada, 1995).

[162] On this maxim (ignorance of the law is no excuse), see Jeffries (n 158) 208.

that the actor was well aware of the possibility of illegality even though it was not laid down in the exact phrasing. It remains with the court, though, to prove that an established standard existed and how it was accessible to the actor; in other words, that a law-abiding person would indeed have known better. Therefore, it seems more preferable to include a culpability requirement than disallow a general clause on the grounds of a lack of fair notice.

The separation of powers has been dealt with above.[163] In essence, it attempts to prevent judges from usurping the domain of the legislative by judicial lawmaking. Article 7(3), and in particular its reference to 'rulings as to conduct and procedure as may be made by the Court', should not be understood as empowering judges to create professional standards in substance.[164] This has been highlighted already during the drafting stage of the Code. It is the disciplinary bodies' responsibility 'to differentiate and to define material violations that may require sanctions' under the Code. But not all Court rulings should have this power. Secondly, it must be emphasised that 'the simple failure to comply with administrative rules cannot lead to disciplinary sanctions or penalties for ethical misconduct'. In many instances, however, judicial creation of law is inevitable. The work of judges is a necessary instrument complementing the legislative process. In other words, it will often be undeniable and inevitable that judges create law. They do this by applying legislation when interpreting it which often involves an element of discretion or choice. The issue is rather how wide a margin we give to judges. If the margin is too wide, this may, of course, provoke concerns of fair notice or arbitrariness, the other two rationales. But as far as the separation of powers argument goes, it chiefly prohibits judicial lawmaking to be inconsistent with legislative choice. General clauses, however, thoroughly lay down legislative intent in a manner similar to detailed provisions. Judges need to respect these choices, of course. The separation of powers argument is therefore unfounded if the general clauses as such are a product of legislation. Consequently, the disciplinary bodies should not be categorically barred from basing discipline on general clauses in the ICC Code, such as Articles 6(1) or 7(1), or Article 24(1).[165]

Finally, the rule of law intends to restrict arbitrariness by ensuring 'adjudication legality'.[166] The goal herein is regularity and evenhandedness in the administration of justice and accountability in the use of government power.[167] It is still possible to reconcile this with having a general clause. Decisions by the disciplinary bodies are reasoned, and hearings are public. Furthermore, they can be appealed. The Boards are thus obliged to justify their decisions and demonstrate how their finding of a breach is linked to the applicable professional standards. It

[163] Ch 1, I.A at 8; ch 2, on Germany, II.A at 60, II.B.i.a at 64, II.C.iii at 90–91 and on the United States, III.A at 112.

[164] Kirsch, *Draft Code of Conduct for Counsel* (n 40) at 5–6.

[165] Doing this, they would have to prove that the legislative did not remain deliberately silent and thus negated the existence of a duty. General clauses will therefore always be residual clauses. See Kleine-Cosack (n 116) § 43, mns 11–13. See also ch 2, II.B.i.a at 63–65, and III.B.i.b at 118–21.

[166] Robinson (n 158).

[167] Jeffries (n 158) 212.

does not seem to advance regularity and evenhandedness if courts place a breach under a specific provision due to the lack of a residual clause, if this results in clouding the uncertainty of a breach in just the same way. To the contrary, it may even enhance regularity and evenhandedness if courts pronounce on unclear rules and relate their findings to other case law. The potential to abuse powers can also be successfully limited by only allowing particular sanctions, such as simple warnings carrying no further implications.[168]

Overall, a strict approach would surely be beneficial to the rule of law from counsel's perspective. However, we cannot ignore the need for flexibility in the context of professional rules. Professional rules are different in purpose and substance from criminal law. The latter only covers the small fraction of reprehensible behaviour that is held to necessitate constant state control and intervention. Bluntly, the state lets no one opt out from this. The lawyer's profession, however, is a scheme which counsel has deliberately and voluntarily opted into. Professional standards should aim at fully regulating counsel conduct. Arguably, no other regulatory regime can or should do this better. Moreover, the purpose of such a regime is precisely to provide full and authoritative guidance. It is simply impossible to exhaust the range of conceivable misconduct in detail through statutory entrenchment. For full guidance, the pertinent authorities should be placed in a position to pronounce on it if the circumstances warrant so.

In conclusion, the use of general clauses to define the limits of professional conduct should be permissible. However, a discrepancy is still discernable between defining the limits of professional conduct along a permissible degree of indeterminacy on the one hand, and actually imposing a sanction for a finding of misconduct in the individual case on the other. Put differently, when would it be really inappropriate for a general clause to trigger a certain sanction?

From a formal position, it could be argued that it is a different thing whether something is declared misconduct by statute (see Rule 8.4 ABA Model Rules) or whether it is explicitly disciplinable (see Rule 9 ABA Model Rules for Lawyer Disciplinary Enforcement). This is not about the fact that guiding principles are used, but whether discipline can be based on such clauses. Therefore, it could be argued that general terms should, of course, be used to outline the limits to permissible conduct. These are perhaps rather policy-oriented norms than legal norms. The rule of strict construction should not apply as strictly. Actual discipline, it is logically argued, is a different matter. This does not confuse that legal norms are to some extent defined by their enforceability.[169] At least actual enforcement based on indeterminate clauses would probably overstretch the requirements to statutory entrenchment, or the rule of law, respectively, as a consequence.

In a material sense, it has been suggested that such an inquiry requires the consideration of various factors: the protected freedoms; the nature of governmental interest; the feasibility of being more precise; and whether uncertainty affects the

[168] As to this conclusion in the German scheme, see ch 2, II.B.i.a at 64–65.

[169] See HLA Hart, *The Concept of Law*, 2nd edn (Oxford, Oxford University Press, 1994) 20–25.

fact or merely the grade of liability. This reflects that discretion, as desirable as it is, is a trade-off between the individual interests of being spared from a sanction and the public interest in denouncing misconduct.[170]

The protected freedom behind criminal law due process is usually the right to liberty as far as imprisonment is concerned. For monetary fines, it would have to be understood as a right to protection of property. Since many more consequences may result from criminal convictions, more abstract concepts have been used in domestic jurisdictions, such as a right to privacy.[171] If we examine more closely the sanctions under the professional procedure, a fine may be imposed, which certainly affects the monetary interests of counsel. All the other sanctions primarily affect the professional freedom of counsel. Bans to practise deprive counsel of the right to exercise the profession in total, whereas a reprimand or admonishments are lighter sanctions. In particular, those two only affect quite abstract freedoms of counsel. Even the harsher ones only deprive counsel of protected freedoms which he or she has acquired by gaining standing before the Court. The freedoms are privileges. Bans may indeed translate into losses that are more than just symbolic. Admonishment and reprimands entail first and foremost intra-professional effects.[172] Even though all of these measures may have in common with criminal sanctions that an individual is publicly rebuked for his or her behaviour, the protected freedoms which are affected differ considerably. The physical liberty of the person is never at stake in disciplinary proceedings. Fines are a sanction also found in the criminal law. The protection of property rights is in some way comparable to safeguarding the personal interest in liberty. Similarly of a personal nature is the interest in being allowed to exercise a profession. Banning a lawyer from the profession is highly intrusive. As far as the protected interest is concerned, it is a delicate one. Simple admonishment, on the other hand, does not take away this privilege. In conclusion, it needs to be recognised that a quite differentiated assessment can be made here. Not all disciplinary measures affect the same freedoms or are equally intrusive, and at least in the case of admonishment, it shows that freedoms may actually only be minimally impaired. Even the attaching costs are at the discretion of the Board and can be handled accordingly within this margin of discretion if a general clause is used.[173]

Among the other factors mentioned are the governmental interest in prosecuting misconduct and the feasibility of being more precise. It is a valid interest to supervise and control counsel, and to react appropriately to cases of abuse. There is a strong interest in pronouncing on unclear cases. Professional standards make

[170] Jeffries (n 158) 196 and 213 respectively.

[171] A classic text would be S Warren and L Brandeis, 'The Right to Privacy' (1890) 4 *Harvard Law Review* 193. See also *Olmstead v United States*, 277 US 438 (1928) (Supreme Court of the United States, 1928).

[172] See also below, II.A.v.g at 227–28, on the difference between those two sanctions and their symbolic nature.

[173] Art 42(3) of the Code. As has been stressed, 'the obligation to bear the costs of the procedure should not be excessive in comparison to the actual sanction itself'; Kirsch, *Draft Code of Conduct for Counsel* (n 40) at 21.

it apparent how it can become infeasible to reach perfect precision. The profession shares common principles which are by definition clear in their thrust, albeit not precise in detail. It is acknowledged that precision is desirable but should be weighed against the other factors. Again, a balance can be achieved here by only allowing the lightest sanction, that of admonishment. Lastly, it makes a difference whether the fact of liability is at stake when invoking a general clause, or whether it affects the grade of sanctioning only. It cannot be denied that the fact of liability or not is a crucial question. But again, this can be alleviated by only allowing warnings which are a relatively limited, symbolic kind of liability. This is why basic admonishment pursuant to Article 42(1)(a) should be permissible.

c The Substantiality Threshold

The foregoing sketched out the scope of the central misconduct provision, Article 31, in various regards. The range of the relevant rules has been dealt with under (i), the foregoing section has addressed the use of general clauses.

Article 31 raises one more debatable point. Paragraph (a), as well as paragraph (b) referring to it, provide for a breach of a 'substantial ethical or professional duty' as an element of misconduct. It thus establishes a substantiality threshold. The Code does not contain concrete criteria to define this any further, neither does it give us any other hint. Exceptions that clearly contain disciplinable misconduct would be Article 22(5) and Article 31(c). The explicit stipulations contained therein should not be misconstrued as implying that none of the other provisions are substantial. This would actually render most of the Code meaningless. Article 22(5) seems to be merely a supplementary appeal.

What can be discerned from the mere wording is that it is not the breach itself that needs to reach a certain threshold, but the relevant duty. This seems an oddity, to say the least. A systematic and a purpose interpretation support an approach that the substantiality requirement should be read into connection to the the breach rather than the duty itself, against the immediate wording of the provision, already *de lege lata.*

It is common for professional ethics to distinguish between graver and lesser instances of misconduct.[174] At the same time, however, counsel is usually bound by the entire canon, irrespective of the gravity of the single rule. Commentators have therefore suggested deleting the term 'substantial'.[175] It seems commendable to do this in relation to the duties. First, such a clear departure from domestic models should be avoided if there is no cogent reason to do so. Secondly and more importantly, counsel should indeed obey all rules; this is not contradicted by the fact that some duties may be more important than others, and a breach of them may typically be graver than that of others. However, the outcome may also be graver if a conceivably less significant duty is violated in a particularly

[174] Ch 2, II.B.i.b at 65–66, III.B.i.b at 119.

[175] Rosen and Kuhlman (n 42) 5.

persistent manner, rather than if a duty is only concerned peripherally, even though it is somewhat more central. How significant an obligation is will have to be assessed on a case-by-case basis.[176] It seems impossible, however, to declare a professional rule as such insignificant.

Therefore, the substantiality requirement for the duty should be ignored *contra legem scripta* but in line with the *ratione legis*. In order to rectify the wording *de lege ferenda*, the substantiality requirement should be shifted to the breach.[177] A conceivable alternative wording of Article 31(a) would therefore be (emphasis added for clarification): 'Counsel commits misconduct when he or she: (a) **Substantially** violates or attempts to **substiantially** violate any provisions of this Code'.

This would make clear that only reasonably serious breaches of professional standards amount to disciplinable misconduct under (a). No need is discernable to qualify misconduct under (b) and (c) in the same manner, for example, by adding 'substantially' after 'when he or she' in the first line of Article 31, with the effect of reading it with all three paragraphs. The participatory modes in (b) have misconduct pursuant to (a) as a prerequisite, anyway. Furthermore, (b) covers knowing violations only, and (c) necessitates a preceding disciplinary decision. Knowledge and non-compliance in spite of an explicit decision both per se indicate a sufficiently substantial breach.

The comparative background of adding the substantiality requirement would be that it is indeed more common to distinguish substantial from lesser misconduct, rather than the types of duties. Section 74 of the German BRAO or Rule 9 of the ABA Model Rules for Lawyer Disciplinary Enforcement can serve as examples from national systems.[178] The ICC regime itself does so in relation to judges, the Prosecutor and Deputies and the Registrar and Deputies. Rules 24 and 25 ICC RPE[179] set out criteria to help distinguish definitions of serious misconduct and a serious breach of duty from one of a less serious nature; they do not differentiate according to more and less substantial duties. Rule 24 indicates that serious misconduct can be characterised by particular harm (see sub-rule (1)(a)(i), disclosing facts or information, when this is seriously prejudicial to the judicial proceedings or to any person). Confidentiality is an example of a substantial duty, but it also

[176] See also Rule 25(2) RPE (Definition of misconduct of a less serious nature) in the context of judicial and prosecutorial misconduct.

[177] Thus contributing to a fault requirement, below, II.A.iv.d at 206. Even when simply striking 'substantial', the substantiality requirement could be read in as a general principle of professional ethics.

[178] Ch 2, II.B.i.b at 66, III.B.i.b at 119. The Spanish *Estatuto General de la Abogacía Española* (Spanish Lawyers' General Statute, see Harting (n 55) 303–05) also distinguishes variously grave infractions, Arts 83–86. It lists specific duties of which the breach is deemed grave or particularly grave. In some way, a ranking of duties could thus be attempted for the ICC as well. On the other hand, it appears rather to be a sentencing scheme.

[179] See R Dixon and KAA Khan (eds), *Archbold International Criminal Courts*, 2nd edn (London, Sweet & Maxwell, 2005) §16-66 to §16-68; D Tolbert and B Benoit in O Triffterer (ed), *Commentary on the Rome Statute of the International Criminal Court*, 2nd edn (Munich, Beck, 2008) art 46, mns 7–10. For *travaux prêparatoires*, see, Preparatory Commission for the ICC, *Proposal submitted by Spain and Venezuela concerning the Rules of Procedure and Evidence, Disciplinary measures (Development of articles 46 and 47 of the Statute)* (PCNICC/1999/WGRPE/DP.12, 16 July 1999).

features the concept of prejudice or harm. Sub-rule (2)(b) qualifies repeating conduct as a serious breach. Furthermore, sub-rule (1)(a)(iii) refers to the abuse of office for personal reasons, and sub-rule (2)(a) mentions acting knowingly. Rule 25 gives examples of misconduct of a lesser nature. It is deemed less serious (sub-rule (1)(a) of the Rule) to fail to comply with or to ignore requests made by the presiding judge or by the Presidency in the exercise of their lawful authority, even if doing this repeatedly. Sub-rule (1)(b) mentions conduct outside the course of official duties, even though this causes or is likely to cause harm to the standing of the Court.

It flows from this that typical and well-known arguments from through all domestic jurisdictions are used within the ICC regime itself. They can thus be used as indicators. Misconduct is more substantial if it causes or may cause actual harm or prejudice to the proceedings or a person, if it involves a pattern of repetitions, or if it occurs knowingly. Mitigating factors, so to speak, are if the misconduct constitutes mere disobedience or disrespect rather than a real violation, or if the standing of the Court is affected, in contrast to an identifiable victim. It would be advisable to take up these leads in the application of the ICC Code. The listed examples from the RPE are, of course, only guidelines. Ultimately, the assessment is dependent on the facts of the case (see the 'inter alia' clauses). The same should apply to the counsel disciplinary regime.

As an alternative to the suggested approach, criteria would have to be settled on in order to distinguish substantial from unsubstantial duties. Under the suggested approach, the following analysis can be of use as well, namely, to indicate the substantiality of the breach and therefore misconduct. If a duty is of more substantial significance, the likelihood of substantial misconduct is greater. It needs to be remarked that substantial ethical duties are also disciplinable pursuant to Article 31(a). The duties flowing from the present Code of Professional Conduct seem to be professional duties by definition. The following overview does thus not address what could be understood to comprise the said ethical duties. The Code does not elaborate on the definition of ethical duties but seems to assume, as the reference is made in Article 31(a) itself, that such duties are contained in the ICC's statutory instruments.[180]

'Substantial' certainly requires a duty of some importance. It seems feasible to transfer the criteria set out above for these purposes. Of course, duties protecting identifiable personal interests or the core values of the proceedings are more important. Assuming a modern understanding of the criminal process and professional rules, protecting the standing of a court and the legal profession as its own value seems not a substantial priority.[181] Therefore, abstract guiding principles and the standing of the profession should not rank as relevant as the more specifically defined interests lying at the heart of the Court's mission and the

[180] Whether private misconduct is disciplinable is a separate issue. See above at 194. In short, some jurisdictions discipline private misconduct but require some link to the profession, ch 2, II.B.i.a at 62, for Germany, and III.B.i.b at 118, III.D.i at 155, for the United States.

[181] Ch 1, II.ii.b at 25, ch 2, II.D at 95, III.E at 164–66. See also below n 187.

proceedings to achieve them. It has also been suggested in relation to the Code at the drafting stage that it intermeshes real professional and ethical duties with those pertaining rather to the conditions of admission to practice and formal procedural obligations.[182] The number of such provisions seems to have been greatly reduced, though. From the current Code, Article 5 ('Solemn undertaking'), Article 7(3) (general compliance with rules of procedure),[183] Article 11 ('Establishment of the representation agreement')[184] and Article 22(3) (signing an undertaking to respect the fee-splitting prohibitions) can all be discarded. They govern various aspects of the profession but they do not contain specific duties. This still leaves most of the Code. It is reiterated that each rule will have to be assessed individually and in light of the facts of the case. Generally, a duty seems more substantial if it has the protections of interests of an identifiable victim at its core, or if it has a direct connection to the purpose of the proceedings. It may also be an indication of substantiality if a duty is explicitly elaborated in the Code.

From the general provisions in Chapter 1 of the Code, Article 6(1) lists general principles of the profession rather than specific duties. Others may be personally affected by a lawyer who does not act honourably, independently and freely. It does not provide for more detailed, clear-cut professional duties. Because Article 6(1) is so vague and contains general principles rather than precise rules, it should not be resorted to it as a general clause for defining disciplinable misconduct.[185] Similarly, Article 6(2) only seems to become substantial if it concerns the current case of counsel, because the individual interest is concerned, and not just the profession *in abstracto*. Articles 12 and 16 are more specific and thus arguably more substantial in this regard.

Article 7(1) requiring respect and courtesy also appears too general to be called substantial. Neither do paragraphs (2) and (3) contain self-standing duties. Respect and courtesy can be important because they safeguard the interests and the participation of individuals, but this seems rather specifically entrenched in Articles 9, 14 and 15 in relation to clients, in Article 24 in relation to the Court and in Article 29 in relation to witnesses and victims.

Article 8 (professional secrecy and confidentiality) clearly contains one of the core values of the profession. It helps in protecting the client's interests and also the integrity of the proceedings and safety of the participants.

Article 10 seems more regulatory and therefore less substantial. It pays reverence to professional ethics worldwide and may help to establish and maintain trust in the profession. But individual interests such as financial indemnity of the client and the quality of representation are protected by more specific provisions (see Articless 14 and 15), and those are thus relatively more important.

[182] See Kirsch, *Draft Code of Conduct for Counsel* (n 40) at 3–4.

[183] See ibid, 5.

[184] ibid, 7. It is a professional obligation, though, to represent a client until withdrawal or replacement with a sufficient cause has been granted, *Prosecutor v Vidoje Blagojević and Dragan Jokić*, IT-02-60-A, Appeals Chamber, Judgement, 9 May 2007, para 17.

[185] Above, II.A.iv.b at 194–201.

Summing up, it could be argued that few of the provision from the first chapter prescribe substantial duties as required by Article 31(a). Only Article 8 appears to be a clear candidate.

Chapter 2 deals with the representation of a client by counsel and therefore contains a number of provisions protecting clients' interest in effective legal assistance. This holds true for all of Article 12 and Articles 14–19. Article 20 protects the financial interests of the client. Articles 21 and 22 are devoted to problems identified from the fee-splitting controversies before the other international criminal courts and in particular the UN tribunals.[186] There, it is usually not the client's property interests which are compromised, quite in the contrary, but counsel's independence as an officer of the court. Given the elaborateness of the Code in this respect and the practice of the other courts, there can be little doubt that it is a substantial duty for counsel to refrain from fee-splitting or other arrangements undermining his or her independence through financial considerations.

In chapter 3, the Code turns to counsel's relations with the Court and others. Article 23 seems primarily a question of procedure since a violation in itself does not carry a potential of harm. Substantial duties in this regard should rather be seen arising from Articles 24 and 25. Article 24(1) is commendable for taking prejudice as a criterion for misconduct. It would be very questionable, however, to impose on counsel a general substantial duty to safeguard the Court's reputation.[187] The remainders of Articles 24 and 25 are more oriented at the proceedings themselves and the potential harm that may be caused for participants thereof. These are substantial concerns in the management of any court proceedings, and should therefore rank as substantial duties under the purview of Article 31(a).

In contrast, the wording of Article 26 indicates concrete duties. They do not venture substantially beyond what is provided by the other provisions on confidentiality and against conflicts of interests. Article 27(1) is also just another general clause, and Articles 27(2) and 27(3) are of a procedural nature. The same applies to Article 28, which can be characterised as parallel to Article 23. Finally, Article 29 does address individual interests of participants and should therefore rank as a substantial duty.

Summing up, a range of provisions from the Code can be argued to have the potential for a substantial duty. This can particularly be said of Articles 8, 12, 14–21, 24, 25 and 29. However, it is recalled that the substantiality of misconduct must more persuasively attach to the breach, not the abstract professional duty.[188] This should be made explicit *de lege ferenda*, and it ought to be read this way already *de lege lata*. The substantiality of the duty is merely indicative of the substantiality of the misconduct in question.

[186] See *Follow-up investigation into possible fee-splitting arrangements between defence counsel and indigent detainees at the International Tribunal for Rwanda and the International Tribunal for the Former Yugoslavia* (UN Doc. A/56/836, 26 February 2002) 9.

[187] At least, progress has been made from the May 2004 draft Code, which also listed the 'dignity and decorum of the Court', see Kirsch, *Draft Code of Conduct for Counsel* (n 40) at 17.

[188] Above at 202.

d Fault Requirement

Irrespective of whether the duty or the breach is concerned, the need to distinguish differently grave instances of misconduct is apparent. It is common for domestic disciplinary regimes to take into account the extent of fault or culpability for discipline. Some do this as an element of misconduct,[189] whereas others mention it as a factor in sanctioning.[190] Where fault is a constitutive element for misconduct, negligence typically suffices. Since criminal offences against the administration of justice, including Article 70 of the Statute, usually require intent, this is a sensible approach suited to the disciplinary regime in its purpose of complementing the criminal law. Given the harsh disciplinary penalties that may follow in some instances, it seems fair, however, to at least permit a defence of honest and reasonable mistake, or make the degree of culpability a binding consideration in sanctioning.

The ICTY and ICTR Codes are silent on the matter of fault, although Article 47(D) of the ICTY Code requires that: 'In determining the sentence imposed, the Disciplinary Panel must take into account any mitigating factors it considers relevant . . . A sentence must be proportionate in view of the misconduct'.

Although fault can, of course, always be factored in through the sanctioning discretion of the Disciplinary Board under Article 41,[191] intervention seems most appropriate if *mala fides*, ie, some kind of fault, is attributable to counsel. This also serves to protect those peers who have bona fides because '[n]o court can function efficiently without a relationship of trust between counsel and the judges'.[192] No clear precedents exist, though, which would mandate including fault as a general element or requirement of misconduct but it is definitely a factor in sentencing.

Whereas the Code and the RPE use concepts of fault in various instances, neither of them rule out the existence of no-fault liability. Within the framework of disciplinary measures for certain officials of the Court, Rule 24(2) of the RPE presumes it to be a serious breach of duties for judges and others if they act knowingly or grossly negligently. Nothing, however, precludes the possibility of categorising faultless conduct as a less serious kind of misconduct, but still constituting misconduct after all.

[189] eg, Germany (Section 113(1) BRAO, see ch 2, II.B.i.a at 63–65) and Kleine-Cosack (n 116) § 113, mn 17. For the Netherlands, see Harting (n 55) 312, and in particular Art 46 of the *Advocatenwet* ('*in strijd met de zorg die zij als advocaat behoren te betrachten*').

[190] eg, the ABA *Model Rules for Lawyer Disciplinary Enforcement*, Rule 10(C) (Factors to be Considered in Imposing Sanctions). See also, *Standards for Imposing Lawyer Sanctions* (n 97) at 13, for further definitions of the terms. This is discussed in more detail in ch 2, III.B.i.b at 121–22.

[191] On sentencing, see below, II.A.v.f at 227–30.

[192] *Prosecutor v Zlatko Aleksovski*, IT-95-14/1-AR77, Appeals Chamber, Judgement on Appeal by Anto Nobilo Against Finding of Contempt, 30 May 2001, para 2 of Judge Robinson's Separate Opinion.

Notwithstanding the conclusion that no-fault liability is in theory possible under the Code, at the very least negligence, or even more, may sometimes be required. For example, Article 22(3) provides that counsel 'shall not deceive or knowingly mislead the Court'. Article 26(3) imposes the duty to refrain from contact with an unrepresented person '[i]f counsel becomes aware of a potential conflict of interest'. All of these breaches must be committed at least with knowledge of the relevant facts. Furthermore, the concept of attempt, which typically calls for intent, [193] can be found in Article 31(a) of the Code. Article 32 provides that counsel shall be liable for the misconduct of assistants and other staff if he or she orders or approves it (which would have to be classified as intent under Art 30 of the Statute), knows of it (presumably knowledge pursuant to Art 30 of the Statute), or has information suggesting (ie, at least some form of negligence). On the one hand, this seems to rule out no-fault liability for supervising counsel, but on the other, Article 32 may just be some form of superior responsibility. Since counsel is held responsible for the conduct of others, it could be argued, the comparatively higher threshold is appropriate here. However, the provision as such should be read as being confined to command responsibility, rather than making general statements about fault requirements in discipline as such. Strict liability under Article 31 would thus still be conceivable.

In theory, strict or absolute liability is therefore conceivable for breaches of the Code if provisions have the purpose of leading counsel to take precautions irrespective of individual fault.[194] As a policy instrument, no-fault liability is purely result-based. A failure to take due precautionary measures would certainly in itself amount to negligent behaviour if reasonable counsel would have been aware of the pertinent risk. The notion behind strict liability would, however, be a matter of policy – guiding future conduct by counsel and others – and not to require fault and hold counsel accountable who, notwithstanding all due diligence, had no reason to initiate precautions. For example, Articles 21 and 22 aim at preventing certain financial arrangements and connections. With no-fault liability, the mixing of funds in contravention of Article 21(3) would be considered misconduct, even though no scrupulous counsel would have had reason to put the money into a trust account. The client or third parties may attempt to involve counsel in money laundering or fee-splitting schemes without even raising reasonable suspicions. On a fault-based approach, the disciplinary bodies would have to establish counsel's departure from reasonable diligence.

This remaining theoretical possibility of no-fault liability for a limited number of instances is, notwithstanding the substantiality test for assessing the alleged misconduct at large, as outlined above.[195] Ordinarily, breaches without fault on

[193] See Art 25(3)(f) of the ICC Statute. Since misconduct is defined along general clauses and without using specific offences, it has been disputed that general doctrines of criminal law, more specifically ones of attributing individual responsibility, have a role in the disciplinary regime. See Rogall (n 90) 934. Consequently, attempt is not mentioned in the German BRAO.

[194] See ch 2, III.B.i.c at 122, with fn 391.

[195] Above, II.A.iv.c at 201–05.

counsel's side will not qualify as substantial misconduct. This is still conceivable, though, if the effects as such make a breach substantial. From a policy perspective, an argument can be made that the possibility of no-fault liability is justified and should be retained. The utility of professional rules as comprehensive guidelines could be seen when discussing the use of general clauses.[196] The same can be achieved with no-fault liability. In any event, international precedents make the existence of fault a binding factor in sentencing. Analogous to the advocated limited use of general clauses, namely to shape professional standards but not to impose negative consequences on unsuspecting counsel,[197] no-fault liability is permissible when issuing an admonishment according to Article 40(1)(a) of the Code. Fault is to be required and proven for the punitive sanctions under (b) to (e), ie, public reprimand, a fine, suspension and a ban.

v The Disciplinary Procedure

a Overview and General Features

The ICC Code of Professional Conduct not only sets out the professional standards, but contains its own disciplinary procedure.[198] These rules of procedure can be found in Articles 33–44 of the Code. They do not appear to constitute a complete system of procedural rules. In the meantime, the members of the disciplinary bodies have adopted their own Rules of Procedure and Evidence.[199]

Domestic systems usually do not fully map out rules of procedure and evidence either; instead, they may point to other sets of rules to complement that of the respective disciplinary procedure. The German BRAO declares criminal procedure applicable,[200] whereas the ABA Model Rules for Lawyer Disciplinary Enforcement refer to civil procedure.[201] No such residual clause can be found in the ICC Code. Article 2(1) only provides for reliance on the Statute, the RPE and the RoC for the definitions of terminology. However, Article 4 Disciplinary RPE[202] ('Situations Not Covered') allows for any 'necessary interim or any other appropriate measure' and suggests taking amendments. Similarly unclear, Article 14(1) Disciplinary RPE ('Non-compliance with these Rules'), and Article 19(5), permit 'any decision or take any measure that is necessary in the interests of the proper administration of justice', which is said to be 'without prejudice to the inherent

[196] Above, II.A.iv.b at 195–201.

[197] Above, II.A.iv.b at 199–201.

[198] A disciplinary procedure was introduced into the ICTY Code only by Rev1. The ICTR Code only features the generic provision which the ICTY Code had initially. See ch 1, II.A at 12, and III.A at 37, respectively.

[199] See above, I.B.ii at 176.

[200] Section 116 BRAO, ch 2, II.B.i.b at 67.

[201] Rule 18(B.): 'Except as otherwise provided in these rules, the [state rules of civil procedure] and the [state rules of evidence in civil nonjury matters] apply in discipline and disability cases'. See also above, II.A.ii at 181.

[202] See above, I.B.ii (n 46).

powers of the Disciplinary Board' (see also Art 19(6.)). The first is impractical, and both fail to provide clear guidance to the boards.

In contrast, Article 21 of the Statute states that '[t]he Court shall apply: (a) In the first place, this Statute, Elements of Crimes and its Rules of Procedure and Evidence'. For the purpose of the applicable law, an argument can be made that the disciplinary organs are part of the Court and therefore should be guided by Article 21. Accordingly, they should adopt the same sources of law to complement the Code of Conduct. The disciplinary regime is after all a part of the Court because it aims at safeguarding the administration of justice by this very Court. The defence may never have been pursued as a separate Court organ.[203] Nonetheless, the disciplinary authorities should not be confused with an independent entity, such as a freely constituted counsel association, despite ensuring elements of self-governance for counsel. The Code mandatorily covers all types of private counsel, not only defence lawyers, and binds them to all of the Court's law.[204] Moreover, the embedment in the the Court is demonstrated by the majority of the members of the Disciplinary Appeals Board being judges of the Court.[205] Throughout the disciplinary procedure, the disciplinary bodies rely on the Registry for secretariat services.

Furthermore, it should be deemed a sensible solution since this is the body of law that all participants will be more familiar with more than any other and whose administration the Code aims to serve. It would thus appear that the general ICC procedure and evidence is to be applied by the Disciplinary Boards, should the Code fail to address a specific issue. Typically, domestic regimes include an express or implicit reservation that the applicability of the other rules needs to be compatible with the nature of disciplinary proceedings. Therefore, coercive measures available under criminal procedure may not be available in the context of professional discipline. This applicability of a rule will have to be determined on a case-by-case basis. While this concededly does not yield very concise instructions, it is hoped that it can be a starting point to align the disciplinary procedure with the ICC law as such. Peculiarities of professional discipline can be taken into account through (b) and (c) of Article 21(1) of the Statute.[206] That a default reference is useful can easily be demonstrated by the issue of the language of proceedings. The Code does not address the working language of the disciplinary proceedings, although Article 12(4) Disciplinary RPE now elaborate on this.

By way of a default reference to the Statute and the RPE, English and French could easily be declared the applicable languages. That this is not inconsistent with the Code can be seen by its Article 3(1). It presupposes that counsel communicates in one of the two working languages, English or French,[207] when proposing amendments. Furthermore, counsel must be fluent in at least one of the

203 Schabas (n 2) 518–19.
204 See above, II.A.iii.a at 185.
205 Art 44(4)(a) Code of Conduct.
206 See also above, ch 2, II.C.i at 87 (n 189).
207 Art 50(2) of the Statute, Rule 41 RPE.

two to become listed.[208] Out of fairness considerations, counsel should be able to give a preference as soon as he or she becomes involved according to Article 37(1).[209]

b Procedural Guarantees

In general, Article 40 sets out a catalogue of rights which apply to counsel during the disciplinary procedure,[210] presumably including during the preliminary investigatory period. At least, Article 15(1) Diciplinary RPE emphasises the Disciplinary Boards' obligation to 'ensure due process throughout the procedure'.

The first of these is the right to legal assistance. 'Entitled to assistance' is not to be read as vesting counsel with a right to a court-remunerated duty counsel in minor cases.[211] Assignment by the Board may be advisable in more serious cases, though, or when counsel cannot defend himself or herself, for example, when detained.[212] Of course, concerned counsel may be assisted by other counsel retained privately. Taking into consideration the use of terms in Article 1 and throughout the Code, it appears that this is meant to denote a counsel practising at the Court, ie, a counsel from the list. Of course, non-listed counsel could always be added to the list in appropriate circumstances in order represent a case.[213] A teleological interpretation would argue against confining to counsel on the list, and rather supports the *pro hac vice* admission of non-list counsel as well. Different expertise is needed in disciplinary proceedings than that in war crimes trials. The lawyer–client relationship does not need the same degree of quality control when retaining and instructing counsel, and therefore depends considerably less on the quality control by list admission. Lastly, requiring list admission could prolong and complicate the proceedings which should benefit from their flexibility and quickness.

The second right contained in paragraph (2) is the one to remain silent. This was only added to the Draft Code of May 2004.[214] As can be gathered from Articles 37 and 38, this right to silence cannot be understood as an absolute right against self-incrimination, however. Counsel is required to cooperate in several respects, such as giving information on national proceedings. It could be said that

[208] Rule 22(1) RPE.

[209] See also *In re Florence Hartmann*, IT-02-54-R77.5, Decision on Defence Motion Requesting the Provision of Supporting Materials in the French Language, 1 December 2008; *In re Florence Hartmann*, IT-02-54-R77.5, Order to Registry to Translate Filings into the French Language, 1 December 2008.

[210] See in general, the *Basic Principles on the Role of Lawyers* (n 91) 123, Principles 26–29.

[211] Tuinstra (n 55) 29–30.

[212] See for Germany, Kleine-Cosack (n 116) § 116, mn 4, § 117, mn 1, on the applicability mutatis mutandis of Section 140(1), (2) of the Code of Criminal Procedure. On assignment of counsel under these provisions, see ch 2, I.A at 53, on Germany.

[213] Although there may be limitations on the right to choose a specific counsel, the international courts tend to follow personal preferences, including adding non-listed counsel, Tuinstra (n 55) 32–33, 52–64.

[214] See Kirsch, *Draft Code of Conduct for Counsel* (n 40) at 20.

Article 40(2) needs to be read to the effect that there exists a right not to testify against oneself, but that this is with emphasis 'before the Disciplinary Board', and that this does not rule out cooperation duties, in particular outside the actual hearing before the Board.[215]

The third right under paragraph (3) is the right to full disclosure of the report of the Commissioner and the evidence as such gathered by the Commissioner. Given that there appears to be no formally filed indictment (such as the document containing the charges under Art 61 of the Statute for trials under the Statute) besides the Commissioner's report, this should be handled in a manner which is sufficient to acquaint concerned counsel with the exact disciplinary charges.[216]

The fourth due process right under the Code is time to prepare the defence. The notification of charges, as flows from paragraph (4), therefore needs to be timely, along with the time afforded to consult with other counsel.

Lastly, paragraph (5) contains the right of counsel to question witnesses. This fifth right to confront witnesses seems to pertain to the hearings stage of the disciplinary procedure rather then the entire procedure.

On the national level, Hazard and Beard have identified the following as necessary for minimum guarantees, which also would be a minimum for quasi-criminal justice.[217] First, concerned counsel needs be given notice and needs a precise statement of the charge or grievance; secondly, the right to present evidence and argument; thirdly, the right to assistance of counsel; fourthly the right to appellate or to judicial review; fifthly, the right to some kind of pretrial discovery; and lastly, as a particular feature of criminal justice, the privilege against self-incrimination. They contrast this with the prevailing US model which they describe as 'a relatively formal version of administrative law procedure'.[218] The latter includes a screening by the disciplinary enforcement agency; again notice and a statement of the charge or grievance; formal or informal discovery; right to assistance of counsel; the rights to subpoena witnesses and evidence, to cross-examine adverse witnesses, and to exclude evidence inadmissible under the rules of evidence; a standard of proof by a preponderance of the evidence or, mostly, by clear and convincing evidence; and the right to judicial review.

German law provides for all of this because of the default reference in Section 116 of the BRAO, pointing to criminal procedure. The right to assistance to counsel applies as it would there. The *Anschuldigungsschrift* serves as an indictment. *Akteneinsicht* makes it possible for counsel and his lawyer to consult the available evidence before the hearing. *Beschwerde*, *Berufung* and *Revision* are different means of appeal against decisions in disciplinary matters. The privilege against self-incrimination is the same as in criminal matters. The only substantial difference is the somewhat relaxed rules of evidence.

[215] See below, II.A.v.e at 224–26.

[216] See below, II.A.v.e at 221–22, From the first case before the ICC disciplinary bodies, see *The Registrar v Hervé Diakiese*, Complaint 01/09, Transcript (n 50) 11–12, 42–43.

[217] Hazard and Beard (n 81) 1063.

[218] ibid, 1066.

The ICC largely lives up to a similar procedural standard in Article 40. Counsel has an unfettered right to assistance from other counsel. The right to silence is intact, albeit the Board's possibility of drawing adverse inferences. In spite of counsel's duty to cooperate in identifying pending domestic procedures, the ICC thus comes closer to the position in Germany than the United States where counsel's duties are usually more extensive.[219] A similar high standard is illustrated by counsel's right to pre-trial discovery and his or her right to confront witnesses.

In two respects, though, the ICC Code curiously flops from this high quasi-criminal standard. As to the first, counsel can confront witnesses once they have been called under Article 39(7), but there is no clearly entrenched right of counsel to call witnesses on his or her own, or to otherwise present evidence. Of course, this paragraph (7) could be interpreted in a way which allows for that. Counsel's right to be heard would then not be limited to legal arguments but extend to the tendering of evidence. Likewise, the second sentence could be interpreted that the Disciplinary Board should usually follow a motion by counsel to call additional witnesses.[220] It is not only the defendant-counsel who calls witnesses in support of his or her case but also the Commissioner, who needs to buttress the formal charges with evidence at the hearing. To be in line with domestic models, the ICC disciplinary procedure should be interpreted as an adversarial proceeding. How this is achieved in technical terms is of secondary importance. It could be done by giving the parties the right and the responsibility to call witnesses and evidence.[221] Requiring the parties to move to the judges who then call witnesses and evidence is another option which would have the advantage to possibly conform more to the wording of Article 39(7) and the general procedure of the ICC.

The second point concerns the requirement of a precise statement of the charge. Prior to a case going before the Board for the hearing, the Commissioner submits a report, (Art 39(5)) which is disclosed to the counsel (Art 40(3)) in which the precise charge should be clearly set out.[222] The Commissioner's report should not be understood to present the evidence only, but rather as a formal accusation because the Commissioner effectively acts as the prosecutor.

Both issues – that of presenting evidence and providing sufficient notice of the legal claims and their alleged factual basis – are not even unique to criminal due process. It is simply what a fair trial requires, even in non-criminal proceedings. The ICC disciplinary bodies should handle both accordingly.

[219] See for Germany on the one hand Section 56(1) BRAO, and on the other for the United States, American Bar Association, *Model Rules for Lawyer Disciplinary Enforcement* (n 141) Rule 9(a)(2), Rule 14; Rosen and Kuhlman (n 42) 5.

[220] Under German criminal procedure, parties generally introduce evidence by such motions to the court. See Section 244 Code of Criminal Procedure, ch 2, II.B.iii.a at 75 (n 132).

[221] As it is suggested by Rosen and Kuhlman (n 42) 8.

[222] ibid.

c Launching and Course of Disciplinary Proceedings

The Code provides for a formal filing of a complaint. In principle, the disciplinary procedure is thus tailored to deal with individual misconduct from the past or the present. No duty of automatic oversight is on the Commissioner. This seems advisable as he is not constantly present at the seat of the Court, or otherwise involved in the ICC as an institution.[223] Breaches of professional rules will often be linked to litigation, though this need not be the case.[224] For active ICC counsel who are involved in pending litigation, though, judges observing counsel in court or otherwise during the proceedings are most likely to notice misconduct.[225]

The Code contains no mechanism to rule on an issue of professional standards preventively. During the drafting stage, it had been suggested establishing a body with the competence to issue advisory opinions on legal ethics.[226] Unlike the ICTY, where the Disciplinary Board has been used for Advisory Opinions,[227] the ICC professional bodies have not been vested with such tasks. Counsel only participate in the general Advisory Committee on Legal Texts.[228] This committee's primary role is to consider and report on proposals concerning the Rules, the Elements of Crimes and the Regulations of the Court, which seems to exclude broader issues of legal ethics.[229] Matters of professional ethics may be brought before other organs of the ICC, though, as part of procedural issues, as the case of counsel Jens Dieckmann has shown.[230]

On filing the complaint, the Commissioner takes over and decides whether to proceed with the case to the Disciplinary Board. Article 34 sets out the applicable procedure for lodging a complaint. The concerned Chamber and the Prosecutor (presumably also any subordinate staff at the OTP through him or her) may file

[223] It has, however, been suggested (ibid, 4, see also, n 256) that the Commissioner should be able to hire his or her own permanent staff in order to achieve full independence from the Court's organs, most notably the Registry. Otherwise, the Registry is most likely to assume an oversight role, which may fit ill within the regulatory framework. See below (n 231).

[224] See above, II.A at 177, for the first two cases.

[225] See Tuinstra (n 55) 234. An example would be the first referral to the disciplinary bodies, *The Prosecutor v Thomas Lubanga Dyilo*, ICC-01/04-01/06-2383-RED, Trial Chamber I, Redacted Submission (n 53).

[226] Inter alia, by Kirsch, *Draft Code of Conduct for Counsel* (n 40) at 5.

[227] See, eg, *Prosecutor v Gotovina et al*, IT-06-90-AR7.1, Appeals Chamber, Decision on Miroslav Šeparović's interlocutory appeal against Trial Chamber's decisions on conflict of interest and finding of misconduct, 4 May 2007, and *Prosecutor v Gotovina et al*, IT-06-90-AR73.2, Appeals Chamber, Decision on Ivan Čermak's interlocutory appeal against Trial Chamber's decision on conflict of interest of attorneys Čedo Prodanović and Jadranka Sloković, 29 June 2007.

[228] See Regulation 3 RoR.

[229] Regulation 4 RoC.

[230] See *The Prosecutor v Joseph Kony et al*, ICC-02/04-01/05-378, Presidency, Reasons for the Decision on the Application of Mr Jens Dieckmann of 28 October 2008 for judicial review of his appointment by the Registrar as defence counsel, in accordance with the decision of the Pre-Trial Chamber II of 21 October 2008, 10 March 2009, paras 15–18, 25–28, 32–33 (appeal to the Presidency within the context of counsel's assignment by the Registrar, and the scope thereof). See also below at 115, and in detail below, II.C.v at 269–72, on institutional ethical advice under the framework of the Registry, including a discussion of the Dieckmann case.

such complaints. This may also be done by any other 'person or group of persons whose rights or interests may have been affected by the alleged misconduct'. Finally, the Registrar has this right.[231] A discernable difference here is that the former have to channel complaints through the Registry, which is, of course, not required by the Registrar.

Paragraph (1)(a) provides for Chambers 'dealing with the case' to submit complaints. This should cover all misconduct arising from all the proceedings which are before this specific Pre-Trial, Trial, or Appeals Chamber. Going from a functional interpretation of the term 'Chamber', it makes sense to vest with this right any judge who is ultimately responsible for governing the exact proceedings from which, or in relation to which, counsel's 'case' of misconduct arises, including the Presidency or single judges.[232] No such prior relationship to counsel is needed for the Prosecutor (para (1)(b)) or the Registrar (para (4)). Since complaints have to be channelled through the heads of these two organs, it could be argued that those organs are affected in their own interests, and accordingly have a supervisory function including over counsel who are not involved in any identifiable pending cases.

Much more interesting than the rights of the Court's chambers seems to be the curtailed right of all other complainants, including counsel, to lodge a complaint. Paragraph (1)(c) requires that their rights or interests may have been affected by the conduct in question. They need to claim a potential violation of rights or interest of their own. The Commissioner should not impose too strict standards in this.[233] According to the wording, the mere possibility, ie, arguably even less then a prima facie case, suffices that pertinent rights or interests may have been affected. Commendably, there is no substantiality threshold as in Article 41(1) of the ICTY Code. Interpreting this liberally may indeed help to bring cases before the disciplinary bodies. The Code can particularly serve as a basis of identifying pertinent protected rights and interests, as it clearly imposes on counsel with duties towards certain clients, witnesses and other individuals. It should not be taken to be conclusive, however. The current scheme does not provide for other counsel who are not affected to file complaints, unless that such other counsel could be argued to hold a vested interest in the profession's reputation – albeit that being a very questionable concept. There are a fortiori no whistle-blowing

[231] Giving such powers to the Registry may not be entirely consistent with its neutral role (see also Rosen and Kuhlman, n 42), since it is otherwise supposed to be restricted to secretariat services. However, it is subsequently the responsibility of the Commissioner to probe into the substance and thus undertake a pre-charge screening. As far as the handling of complaints is concerned, the Registry's role should indeed be restricted to transmitting the complaint.

[232] It is therefore argued that the Presidency could submit the matter to the disciplinary authorities in the case of *The Prosecutor v Joseph Kony et al*, ICC-02/04-01/05-378, Presidency (n 230) or to the Advisory Committee on Legal Texts (see below, II.C.v at 270–72).

[233] See also Rosen and Kuhlman (n 42) Comment 5, at 6: '[T]he Commissioner should evaluate all information coming to his or her attention, whether by complaints or other sources, alleging misconduct by counsel. Given the nature of the crimes to be prosecuted before the International Criminal Court, the source of complaints should not be limited'.

obligations on counsel.[234] However, this does not preclude the possibility of bringing misconduct to the attention of a Chamber, the Prosecutor or the Registrar, who can then file the complaint.

No right to file a complaint exists for counsel or for the Commissioner. Neither are included in the listing in Article 34(1).[235] A self-purging procedure is, for example, an option expressly provided for by the German BRAO (see Section 123). As far as counsel is concerned, it could be argued that he or she is affected in his or her own interests, primarily professional reputation, by allegations of misconduct. However, the wording of Article 34(1)(c) argues against such a right. Counsel is not strictly speaking affected in his or her rights or interests by the misconduct if committed by himself or herself, but only by the allegations thereof. Apart from this, the provision speaks of interests that may have been affected in the past. This rules out using the complaint procedure under Article 34(1) for preventive advice on an imminent or a general ethics issue on counsel's initiative. Going from what the Presidency has so far held, no other mechanism for counsel to solicit ethics advice on professional matters or to achieve a pertinent authoritative ruling by a Court body is readily apparent.[236] As a matter of policy, it would seem desirable, though, to have such options. Both counsel and Commissioner can turn to one of the Court organs to follow-up with a complaint, in any event. Even though the Code does not contain a self-purging or ethics advice procedure, the Court organs should use the opportunity to file a complaint in appropriate circumstances to award certainty to counsel, particularly if counsel supports this.[237]

The ICC Code does not provide for the withdrawal of a complaint, as does Article 43 of the ICTY Code. Therefore, pending complaints are unaffected by later statements of the complainant. The Registrar to whom the complaint was submitted will be in a position to proceed with the complaint or not on his or her initiative.

Article 35 renders counsel's misconduct subject to a statute of limitations. At least, the right to file such a complaint lapses at that point. But as the Commissioner cannot act on his or her own initiative and can only investigate a matter following a complaint (see Art 39), practically it comes down to a statutory bar. On the other hand, pending complaints are not affected. The ABA has argued against any form of limitations, arguing that 'the conduct of a lawyer, no matter when it occurs, is relevant to fitness of practice'.[238] Statutes of limitations are known in

[234] See Art 36 ICTY Code; Art 21 ICTR Code; American Bar Association, *Model Rules of Professional Conduct*, Rule 8.3.

[235] See above at 213, and in detail below II.C.v at 270–72, on the question of institutional ethical advice under the framework of the Registry, including a discussion of the Dieckmann case, mentioned in the following note.

[236] *The Prosecutor v Joseph Kony et al*, ICC-02/04-01/05-378, Presidency (n 230) para 33.

[237] See in detail below, II.C.v at 270–72.

[238] Rosen and Kuhlman (n 42) Comment 6, at 6; American Bar Association, *Model Rules for Lawyer Disciplinary Enforcement* (n 141) Commentary to Rule 18. Nonetheless, it thus can and should at least be a factor in sentencing and the assessment of evidence.

some jurisdictions, though, and reflect a permissible policy choice. Furthermore, the fitness to practice in general can still be assessed by the Registrar under Regulation 71 of the Regulations of the Court, and by any Chamber when appointing counsel under Regulation 76.

The limitation period runs from the end of the representation agreement which counsel has with a client or the Court (see Art 11). Of course, many professional duties attach to such an agreement and to how counsel discharges his or her functions under the agreement. However, this fails to address violations of post-contractual duties. Counsel may still substantially violate professional duties after ending a case.[239] Confidentiality obligations, among others, come to mind. Moreover, there may be a need to discipline counsel who have not been representing under a specific agreement at all.

This would be better served by a provision along the lines of Article 41(3) ICTY Code, which itself provides that the Disciplinary Panel may pursue complaints after the 12-month deadline if the matter is of general importance or in the interests of justice in a pending case. This is a relative approach which is independent of a specific case. Of course, 12 months from the point when the complainant has known or should have reasonably known may be considered too short a period and a longer period, such as two years, may be advisable.

Moreover, the possibility of taking up a case later 'in the interests of justice' is questionable and does not buttress legal certainty. To avoid this, an absolute limitation period could still be retained by the ICC, for example, stipulating that it expires five years from the time of the alleged misconduct, irrespective of the knowledge of others of it, or that it runs from the time of removal off the list of counsel.[240]

Summing up, it could be said that complaints can only be filed by a select group and are then channelled through an independent prosecuting agent, in the person of the Commissioner. This launching of a procedure is similar to that of other regimes,[241] and to that effect commendable. Some regimes may provide for automatic oversight by a central body.[242] In practice, this should have little significance if others may also file complaints and if the handling body may well dismiss a complaint. It should be seen as an improvement over the ICTY Code that the Registry, ie, a Court organ, may file complaints but holds only an administrative role beyond that and plays no active role in the disciplinary procedure itself.[243] Under the ICTY procedure, the Disciplinary Panel handles complaints and may also act on its own initiative (see Arts 40 and 41). Whereas it deserves criticism that the Disciplinary Panel of the ICTY is the investigatory and the judicial body

[239] MB Nelson, 'When Clients Become Ex-Clients: The Duties Owed after Discharge' (2002) 26 *Journal of the Legal Profession* 233.

[240] Rule 164 RPE provides for a limitation period of five years for prosecuting Art 70 crimes by the Court, and of 10 years for the enforcement of sentences (below, II.B.iv at 249). It is argued that the disciplinary system should not be harsher than the criminal laws in that respect.

[241] Ch 2, II.C.i at 86.

[242] ibid.

[243] Above n 231.

at the same time, and that findings are in consultation with the duty judge of the Tribunal, this is somewhat remedied by the fact that findings can be appealed to a Disciplinary Board (see Art 48 ICTY Code). However, the Registrar comes into play here as he or she may file an appeal.

The ICC procedure is closer to the German and US model. In Germany, mutual notification by the Bar and the Prosecutor takes place (see Section 120a BRAO). The latter then submits a writ of accusation to a court (Section 121 BRAO). It features a stricter, civil law understanding of the principle of legality, ie, the duty to investigate, but the Prosecutor may stay proceedings. In the United States, according to Rule 11(A) of the ABA Model Rules for Lawyer Disciplinary Enforcement, '[t]he disciplinary counsel shall evaluate all information coming to his or her attention by complaint or from other sources alleging lawyer misconduct or incapacity'. Investigations are then conducted by disciplinary counsel, who subsequently has discretion to dismiss a case or formally proceed with it (see Rules 4(B) and 11).

Similarly, the ICC Commissioner may, pursuant to Article 39, dismiss a complaint or investigate and then submit it to the disciplinary authorities.[244] Those are the Disciplinary Board and the Disciplinary Appeals Board. Article 36 elaborates further on the disciplining bodies. Two permanent and one ad hoc member sit on the bench of the Disciplinary Board. A case may then go before the Appeals Boards which is staffed by three judges of the Court and two elected list counsel.

Whereas this course of proceedings has a lot in common with national procedures, there is one peculiarity owing to the ICC's special nature. The disciplinary procedure is subject to the principle of complementarity (Art 38). In essence, this gives national regimes priority over that of the ICC.[245] It also explains the role of the ad hoc member on the Disciplinary Board. This member is 'appointed by the national authority competent to regulate and control the activities of counsel'.

The Code does not define any further what this national authority is, what competence to regulate means in this context, or what to do with competing authorities,[246] in particular if counsel is licensed in more than one jurisdiction which can be considered the exclusive home jurisdiction for disciplinary purposes. The most pragmatic solution might be to assign this role to the Bar association or the other controlling administrative authority which has issued the certificate that counsel submitted under Regulation 69(2)(b) RoC when seeking inclusion on the list of counsel, in order to confirm the necessary qualifications. If

[244] One purpose of whether to dismiss the complaint or not will also be a 'sufficiency test' (see Hazard and Beard (n 81) 1066). Beyond that, the Disciplinary Board does not engage in a 'probable cause' test of its own. See below, II.A.v.e at 220–21. On the other hand, Art 39(4), providing for the Commissioner to seek an amicable settlement in appropriate circumstance but notwithstanding the assessment of the Board, offers an opportunity to filter out baseless or light allegations prior to any formal procedure.

[245] See on this complementarity regime under Art 38 of the Code the detailed analysis, ch 4, II.A at 291–97.

[246] Rosen and Kuhlman (n 42) Comment 7, at 6. For Germany, Harting (n 55) 336, fn 1575, suggests the Bar Council of the Regional Bar (*Rechtsanwaltskammer*). The issue has no implications for Regulation 123 RoR, as it can be read to notify appointment of counsel to all of the conceivable authorities.

more than one institution is competent and consequently claims to be the national authority to appoint the ad hoc member under Article 36(5), then the ICC would have to choose. Only one representative can sit as the requisite third ad hoc member on the bench according to Article 35(1) of the Code. The need to choose between competing requests is not unknown to the ICC legal framework, though. The interests of more than one state are at stake, for example, by competing requests to have a person surrendered (Art 90 of the Statute), and thus to exercise control over a person. Similarly, the ICC could choose the disciplinary authority according to criteria which govern competing surrender requests (Arts 90(6) and (7) of the Statute: time of the appointments; nationality or residence of counsel; relative nature and gravity of the conduct in question). From the idea underlying Article 90(2) of the Statute, it would follow that the priority of deciding on the responsible state rests with the ICC so far as state parties are concerned. Regardless of, for example, the complementarity test under Article 38 of the Code later, the Disciplinary Board would need to staff its full bench in the first place.

The composition follows from Article 36(1) and (5) of the Code if the competence of one out of several conceivable national authorities remains uncontested. If contested, the two permanent members and with them the alternate member if needed should decide on the competent national authority. Article 36(1) governs the unavailability of a permanent member. It should apply mutatis mutandis to determine the ad hoc member, rather than allowing a deadlock between the two permanent members. Article 36 also leaves unanswered the question of who serves on the Board if the competent national authority does not adequately respond to the notification by the Board or for some other reasons fails to appoint an ad hoc member in a satisfactory manner. Paragraph (10) only states that the alternate member will replace one of the permanent members if the latter is unavailable.[247] The same should happen mutatis mutandis to make up for the ad hoc member.

In summary, the disciplinary procedure of the ICC is launched by a complaint which is transmitted from the Registrar to the Commissioner. This will then either be aligned with a national authority, or fully investigated by the Commissioner in order to determine whether to bring it before the Disciplinary Board.

d The Investigation of Misconduct Allegations

Article 33 vests the Commissioner with investigatory powers while Article 37 maps out the procedure on receipt of a complaint. The Commissioner forwards the complaint to concerned counsel. Counsel is then obliged under the ICC procedure to respond to the Commissioner. As part of this response, counsel is called on to indicate whether domestic proceedings have been instituted. This includes

[247] Rosen and Kuhlman (n 42) Comment 7, at 7, rightly observe that the Code is silent on the exact circumstances which would render one of the permanent members unable to sit.

statements about which institution is doing this, what the alleged facts are in the respective case and other detailed information about the domestic procedure (Art 38 (3) and (6)). Whereas some basic cooperation duties sometimes exist in professional discipline,[248] it is noted that counsel may be compelled to incriminate him or herself through this.[249] It could be contemplated *de lege ferenda* whether the Registry, along with a domestic liaison person, such as the prospective ad hoc Board member, may even be in a better position to arrange for this exchange of information. Pursuant to Article 38(2), it is this ad hoc member in any case who is tasked to 'serve as the contact point with the relevant national authority for all communication and consultation regarding the procedure'. It would then simply be the right of counsel to invoke domestic proceedings as a preliminary procedural bar to ICC disciplinary action.

As far as the investigation itself is concerned, Article 39(2) provides that the Commissioner shall promptly investigate a case of misconduct if it is not dismissed. The rules of evidence are not as refined as those for truly criminal proceedings under the Statute and the RPE. Paragraph (3) allows, or points the Commissioner to, respectively, 'all evidence, whether oral, written or any other form, which is relevant and has probative value'. This is an appropriate evidentiary threshold for discipline.

Apart from this, only a few details are provided for the investigatory phase. There is a general confidentiality requirement.[250] The Commissioner may attempt an amicable settlement, but this does not preclude a decision by the Board, which is ultimately called on to establish the truth (para (7)). However, settlements may have great merit if a minor issue is concerned that is within the parties' disposal, such as fee disputes between the client and the lawyer.[251] From a theoretical perspective,[252] it can be generalised that settlements tend to make sense where agency problems are concerned, ie, they arise from within the principal-agent relationship between a client and his or her lawyer. There, the dispute impacts the relationship negatively, and both parties are typically inclined to achieve an efficient outcome in order to pursue other goals. Consensual settlements are less suited where duties have been violated that are external to the client–lawyer relationship. Often, the client and the laywer collude in the violation, or one of them is at least indifferent to the matter and thus unlikely to push for settling it.

The Code also provides for urgent motions (para (8)) to a Chamber in the exceptional case that a temporary suspension seems warranted.[253] In presumably

[248] Ch 2, II.C.iii at 91, III.C.i at 145.

[249] On the right to silence under Art 40(2) of the Code, see above, II.A.v.b at 210–11.

[250] Pre-trial confidentiality is also the rule nationally, in the United States (Rosen and Kuhlman (n 42) Comment 5, at 6, and ch 2, III.C.i at 44–45, as well as in Germany, see ch 2, II.C.i at 87.

[251] See M Martínez, 'ICTY' in M Bohlander, R Boed and RJ Wilson (eds), *Defense in International Criminal Proceedings* (Ardsley, NY, Transnational Publishers, 2006) 130; see also Rosen and Kuhlman (n 42) 8. On the duty of disciplinary authorities to investigate the facts including good faith of counsel, see *Steur v The Netherlands* (n 151) para 42.

[252] DB Wilkins, 'Who Should Regulate Lawyers?' (1992) 105 *Harvard Law Review* 801, 832.

[253] The same is possible on appeal above, II.A.v.h at 230.

the majority of cases, the concerned counsel's misconduct will be linked to litigation, and it will then be possible to identify an individual client or other participant in this or a specific part of proceedings to which it relates. It will then be usually clear which Chamber holds competence in the matter. This does not rule out, though, that a counsel appears before more than one Chamber at the same time and that his or her misconduct affects all of them. In this case, a Chamber may, of course, ban counsel from its own proceedings, respectively. Regarding a different scenario, it could be that counsel is not formally appearing before any Chamber but, for example, represents a client before the Registry or another Court organ. As long as the misconduct affects pending proceedings, it will still be possible to conclude to a competent Chamber. Lastly, it is also conceivable that counsel engages in misconduct that is not litigation-related at all, such as the first case heard, of counsel Diakiese.[254] Article 39(8) does not provide for this. It is suggested that such a case should be assigned to the Presidency which could deal with it as an issue of the proper administration of the Court under Article 38(3)(a), rather than assigning it to a non-judicial organ such as the Registry. Presumably, however, misconduct by non-active counsel will seldom warrant immediate exclusion from the Bar of the ICC.

Pertaining to a general matter of investigations, it is unclear whether the Commissioner can make use of ICC investigation resources. The Commissioner is part of the institution at large, however.[255] The Code itself also does not prohibit cooperation from the Office of the Prosecutor and it may even seem preferable in order to safeguard the Registry's neutrality in the disciplining process.[256]

Lastly, investigations by the Commissioner may involve witnesses or other evidence beyond documents of the Court. This makes it necessary for the Commissioner to request the assistance of states. This would supposedly then be dealt with as with any cooperation request by the Court under Article 93(1) of the Statute.[257]

The formal end of an investigation is the report to the Board pursuant to Article 39(5) Code of Conduct and Article 7 Disciplinary RPE, which has to be disclosed to concerned counsel, pursuant to Article 9 Disciplinary RPE. The Commissioner has no power to admonish counsel for lesser misconduct.

e Disciplinary Hearings

Not every case of misconduct under the Code will necessarily be heard by the Disciplinary Board after the Commissioner's initial investigation. A case can be inadmissible because the statute of limitations has lapsed, as discussed above

[254] See *The Registrar v Hervé Diakiese*, Complaint 01/09, Transcript (n 50) discussed in more detail, above at 177.

[255] Above, II.A.v.c (n 223).

[256] Rosen and Kuhlman (n 42) 4, have suggested that the Commissioner should be enabled to hire his or her own, independent staff. See also McKay Report (n 97) Recommendation 15, at 46.

[257] On cooperation, see ch 4, II.B at 297–98.

under c. Another issue of admissibility is that of complementarity. It is linked with the *ne bis in idem* principle.[258] Both are similar to the effect that they deal with a possible multiplicity of proceedings. This is, of course, important for the relationship with national proceedings, and is examined in detail in a later chapter.[259] At this point, only the effect of national procedures to render a disciplinary case at the ICC inadmissible needs to be emphasised.

If a procedure is continued pursuant to Article 38, the Commissioner will eventually submit a report to the Disciplinary Board (Art 39(5)). Based on this, the Board will then hold a hearing in the matter, with the details spelt out in Articles 8, 10 and 11 Disciplinary RPE. Pursuant to Article 43(4), hearings before the Appeals Board in principle follow the same rules.[260]

The concerned counsel has the right to have the evidence against him or her disclosed as well as the report itself (Art 40(3)). Since counsel also has to be afforded sufficient time to prepare a defence (Art 40(4)), this should guarantee that counsel is made familiar with the allegations in time. The Board should schedule the hearing accordingly. The Code procedure does not provide for consultations between counsel and the Board before the hearing except those set out in Article 38.[261] The Board can, however, take into consideration the settlement attempts by the Commissioner – as Article 39(4) indicates – as well as the Report itself. In addition, the disclosure right of Article 40(3) will lead to the exchange of statements and filings to the Board before the hearing, pursuant to Articles 8 and 12 Disciplinary RPE.[262]

No confirmation of the allegations is strictly needed, though, before a case is heard by the Board. If a final decision has been handed down nationally, the Board declares, pursuant to Article 38(5), to what extent that national decision covers the misconduct or not. It thus exercises some form of control over the complaint and gives exact contours to the allegations before the case is actually heard. Of course, the Commissioner does this himself, too. On investigation, he has the power to narrow down the subject of the complaint (which may initially be broad and unfounded) into the report. He or she will then let counsel know the result. If Article 38(4) applies, a continuation declaration by the Board and its

[258] Which under customary international law only applies within the same legal system, see J Stigen, *The Relationship between the International Criminal Court and National Jurisdictions – The Principle of Complementarity* (Leiden, Martinus Nijhoff, 2008) 206–08.

[259] For the relationship and a possible *ne bis in idem* between criminal and disciplinary proceedings, see ch 2, II.D.i and ii at 93–100, on Germany, and III.D.ii and iii at 158–63, on the United States. On general aspects of the the relationship of the ICC disciplinary procedure to national jurisdictions, see ch 4, II.A at 291–97.

[260] Appeals are discussed in more detail below, II.A.v.h at 230–34.

[261] The ABA *Model Rules for Lawyer Disciplinary Enforcement* provide for a 'Prehearing Conference', see Rule 18(E). Rule 18(H.) features a simplified hearing for lesser misconduct.

[262] The comments by Rosen and Kuhlman (n 42) hold merit for the trial stage as well: The Code could use some more elaboration on what briefs are filed by the participants, or how this is done. In the meantime, the Disciplinary RPE (above, I.B.ii, n 46.) have allayed this lacuna to some extent. The alternative would be a generic referral to use, eg, the Rules mutatis mutandis. See above, II.A.v.a at 208, and ch 2, II.B.i.b at 67, for Germany, and above, II.A.ii at 181 for the United States.

reasons can achieve this as well. It is hoped that decisions under Article 38[263] help to state the allegations precisely.

In any event, no equivalent to an indictment exists, whereas a determination that probable cause exists to believe that misconduct occurred forms part of domestic procedures and the ICTY procedure.[264] It is conceivable that neither paragraphs (4) nor (5) are applicable *stricto sensu* because no domestic proceedings take place at all. If the Disciplinary Board is informed through counsel[265] that no domestic proceedings are pending, Article 38(4) and (5) are strictly speaking not applicable. Consequently, the Board could proceed to a hearing after having received the Commissioner's report but without having to confirm it in any way. It would be desirable, therefore, in any event that the report states the scope forming subject of the hearing as exactly as possible.[266]

As far as the actual hearing itself is concerned, the Code does not prescribe many details. There is probably not that great a need as disciplinary hearings are traditionally handled more flexibly than true criminal trials. The Disciplinary RPE now give some more guidance in Article 15.

Hearings are public (Art 39(6)).[267] They can be fully or partially held in closed session. The Code mentions explicitly the protection of victims and witnesses, as well as confidential information in the Commissioner's report. The counterpart of the Statute would be Article 64(7), which includes a reference to the victims and witness protection provision of Article 68.[268] Article 72 of the Statute elaborates on national security.[269] In line with this, the Disciplinary RPE address confidentiality concerns in Articles 8(1)(c), 9(4)and 15(2).

Article 39(7) of the Code states that the Commissioner and counsel shall be called and heard by the Board. This is quite rudimentary but it quintessentially

[263] Any decision based on it can be appealed to the Disciplinary Appeals Board. However, this can evidently not lead to a decision on the merits of the complaint. This is the purpose of the hearing before the Disciplinary Board. Art 38(7) appeals are there to review complementarity issues. For a discussion on who has the right to appeal, see below, II.A.v.h at 230.

[264] For the setting out of charges in the ICC's first case, see above at 177, on *The Registrar v Hervé Diakiese*, Complaint 01/09, Transcript (n 50) 6–8, 53. From other jurisdictions, see Rule 11(E) and (F) of the ABA *Model Rules for Lawyer Disciplinary Enforcement* (review of Commissioner's decision by Board and subsequently by the Court), Rule 16(A) and (C) of the ABA *Model Rules for Lawyer Disciplinary Enforcement* (from that moment, proceedings are public) and Section 131 BRAO for Germany. From the ICTY Code, see Art 46.

[265] In itself, this could be held to be a questionable arrangement for considerations of freedom from self-incrimination. On the right to silence under Art 40(2) of the Code, see below at 224 (n 281). It has been suggested (above, II.A.v.d at 219) using the ad hoc member of the Disciplinary Board as a liaison with domestic authorities.

[266] A written statement for that purpose is guaranteed in the disciplinary process for judges and other court officials. See Rule 27(1) RPE. For the first ICC disciplinary case, see *The Registrar v Hervé Diakiese*, Complaint 01/09, Transcript (n 50) 6–7, 42–43.

[267] For the United States, see Rule 16(C) of the ABA *Model Rules for Lawyer Disciplinary Enforcement.* German hearings are non-public unless counsel selects public hearings, see Section 135 BRAO, and the criticism by M Kleine-Cosack, *Bundesrechtsanwaltsordnung*, 5th edn (Munich, Beck, 2008) § 135.

[268] See also Arts 57(3)(c), 64(2) and (6)(c), (e) of the Statute) for Chambers' obligations to protective measures.

[269] National security issues are probably less relevant for defence counsel. But the Code also applies to counsel acting for states, Art 1 of the Code (above, II.A.iii.a at 185).

reflects the practice of court proceedings worldwide to hear the plaintiff first and then the defendant. The first case in March 2010 gives a taste.[270] Again, the Disciplinary RPE now offer more detail on procedure in Article 15.

This layout is compatible with the general procedural elements under the ICC framework in Article 64(8)(a) and (b) of the Statute. Pursuant to those two paragraphs, the confirmed charges are first read out. The accused then has the opportunity to make a statement which is followed by submissions of evidence by the parties. Article 39(7) is much briefer, but provides, in particular as refined in Article 15 Disciplinary RPE, essentially for the same structure. When the Commissioner is heard, he or she should read out the charges. The right to be informed of the charges and the possible sanction does not explicitly apply to disciplinary proceedings by virtue of the Statute or comparable international human rights standards such as the ICCPR or the ECHR, because those are foremost confined to criminal trials. It seems vital, though, to make the proceedings fair.[271] Moreover, clearly establishing the subject of the allegations will usually help in speeding up the proceedings. It is reiterated that the counsel has the right to remain silent, under Article 40(2). An admission of guilt, as with Article 65 of the Statute, will also expedite and facilitate disciplinary proceedings.

The criminal procedure under the Statute is, of course, much more formalised than the disciplinary procedure. Article 39(7) provides for the taking of evidence that the Disciplinary Board 'may also call and hear any person deemed useful for the establishment of the truth'. Therefore, the Board can take evidence on its own Board's initiative in addition to the parties, as specified in more detail in Article 15(7) and (8) Disciplinary RPE. Testimony will be valuable in this. This presumably does not rule out that the Board can also rely on documentary evidence, and order its production, as entrenched in Article 15(8) Disciplinary RPE. Documents may easily be available, including those from other proceedings in the same matter, whether criminal or otherwise and it will typically be easier to simply tender those as documents, rather than oral testimony.

Evidence seems widely admissible. For the investigation, Article 39(3) provides that '[t]he Commissioner shall take into consideration all evidence, whether oral, written or any other form, which is relevant and has probative value'. The same must consequently apply for the Disciplinary Board. There is no point the Commissioner gathering evidence that will be inadmissible at a later stage of the proceedings. Regarding evidence, disciplinary procedures tend to enjoy relaxations from criminal law standards.[272] This does not rule out that the Board may

[270] *The Registrar v Hervé Diakiese*, Complaint 01/09, Transcript (n 50).

[271] See also Hazard and Beard (n 81) 1066, speaking of disciplinary procedure in the United States as a 'relatively formal version of administrative law procedure'.

[272] See Art 46(D) ICTY Code. For Germany, see Sections 137 and 138 BRAO (derogating Section 250 of the Code of Criminal Procedure): Witnesses can be interrogated by Court outside the hearing (but on request of one of the parties, they have to be heard in the hearing). The ABA *Model Rules for Lawyer Disciplinary Enforcement* declare that '[d]isciplinary proceedings are neither civil nor criminal but are sui generis' and suggest that the 'state rules of civil procedure' apply (see Rule 18 (A), (B)). This may have a similar effect. It is noted, however, that the divide between 'criminal evidence' and 'civil

rely on the Statute,[273] the Rules of Procedure and Evidence[274] and any other rules of the ICC mutatis mutandis, as appropriate.[275] Modifications of the law of procedure and evidence may also imply modifications of the Court's power to issue certain orders. It is noted that, for example, the ABA Model Rules for Lawyer Disciplinary Enforcement and the German disciplinary procedure, respectively, provide for subpoenas[276] and the compellation of witnesses and documents.[277] This is notwithstanding the question of enforceability through the ICC's cooperation regime.[278]

Although the law of evidence may be relaxed in comparison with the criminal law of evidence, fundamental due process rights do apply. Article 40 lists the rights afforded to counsel, paragraphs (1), (2) and (3) being of particular importance for the hearings. Pursuant to paragraph (1), counsel may thus rely on representation and assistance by other counsel and both counsel and assisting counsel may examine witnesses (para (3)).

Strictly speaking, this is only a right to confront 'any person called by the Disciplinary Board to testify before it'. On a simple reading, this does not allow for counsel to call his or her own witnesses, as is the the right to 'present witnesses' under Article 15(8) of the Disciplinary RPE. The full right to 'obtain the attendance and examination of witnesses on his or her behalf under the same conditions as witnesses against him or her' is indeed enshrined in Article 67(1)(e) of the ICC Statute, and in particular for removal proceedings in Article 46(4). The rights of counsel should not fall behind the due process rules for judges and other ICC personnel, [279]as reflected in Article 46. Counsel should be afforded equivalent defence rights. Therefore, the right to call witnesses, along with the right to submit other evidence, should already be read into Article 39(7) as part of the calling and hearing of counsel, or into Article 40(4), ie, counsel's right to prepare his or her defence.[280]

Paragraph (2) makes it clear that counsel cannot be compelled to testify, at least during the Board hearing.[281] On the other hand, it also clearly states that the Board

evidence' may be wider in the European legal traditions than in the United States, there rather treated as 'a single set of doctrines'. See DA Sklanzky and SC Yeazell, 'Comparative Law Without Leaving Home: What Civil Procedure Can Teach Criminal Procedure, and Vice Versa' (2006) 94 *Georgetown Law Journal* 683, 686.

[273] See Art 69 therof.

[274] See Rules 63–103 thereof.

[275] See for this fundamental issue, above II.A.v.a at 208.

[276] American Bar Association, *Model Rules for Lawyer Disciplinary Enforcement* (n 141) Rule 14.

[277] Via the applicability of criminal procedure, see Kleine-Cosack (n 116) § 116, mn 4, § 117, mn 1.

[278] See ch 4, II.B at 297–98.

[279] The rights enjoyed by them are also contained in Rule 27 RPE, see in particular sub-rule (2). On further details, see Tolbert and Benoit (n 179) art 46, mns 19–21.

[280] See for further discussion, see above, II.A.v.b at 211.

[281] The right to silence does arguably not invalidate the use of documents and other non-personal evidence produced by counsel or ordered from him or her. See Hazard and Beard (n 81) 1072. See also above, II.A.v.d at 210–11, on counsel's duty to give information on national proceedings. From the national level, the McKay Report also views the right 'to present evidence and confront witnesses' as essential, even for expedited procedures: McKay Report (n 97) Recommendation 9, at 35.

can draw inferences from counsel's silence. Although this does not go as far as the right to silence under the Statute,[282] it is presumably consonant with existing professional discipline. This limited right to silence – but not absolute freedom of non-incrimination – is also reflected in the cooperations duties under Article 44(B)(ii) and (D) ICTY Code, the latter even providing for a penalty of up to €10,000 for failing to produce documents or cooperate on the order of the panel. It is a clear improvement of the ICC Code that non-compliance is not fined separately.

The Code is silent on hearings in the absence of concerned counsel, although under Article 11 Disciplinary RPE counsel will be cited or summoned to appear by notice of the Secretariat. Pursuant to Article 15(6), the matter can be heard in the absence of counsel, in the presence of counsel's representative, or the matter can be adjourned. Absent counsel can apply for reinstatement under Article 18 Disciplinary RPE.

The commentary on Rule 33 of the ABA Model Rules for Lawyer Disciplinary Enforcement states that '[f]ailure by respondents to answer or to appear in disciplinary matters is a significant problem'. The disciplinary authorities of the ICC may not be safe from this, either. In criminal trials, it is a recognised principle that hearings cannot be held *in absentia*.[283] Criminal courts usually hold the power, though, to summon and arrest the accused in order to compel presence. Those powers are usually not available to disciplinary bodies. Under German law, the BRAO provides that counsel will be summoned but cannot be arrested for the purpose of the disciplinary proceedings.[284] To a similar effect, the ABA Model Rules for Lawyer Disciplinary Enforcement point to the Rules of Civil Procedure applicable in the pertinent jurisdiction (Rule 18 (B.)). This should rule out arrests as well. Domestic disciplinary procedure usually compensates for this by adopting a default rule. Rule 33 of the ABA Model Rules for Lawyer Disciplinary Enforcement equates the failure to answer charges to be an admission of the

[282] Art 67(1)(h), according to which the accused has the right '[n]ot to be compelled to testify or to confess guilt and to remain silent', but with the addendum 'without such silence being a consideration in the determination of guilt or innocence'. On the right to silence and negative inferences, should counsel choose to testify, in German disciplinary proceedings, see *Bundesgerichtshof*, 12 February 2001, AnwSt (R) 15/00, para 13 *Bundesgerichtshof*, 12 February 2001, AnwSt (R) 15/00, para 13 (author's translation): 'At least if the disciplinary measure may turn out to be a threat to the professional existence of counsel (which is insofar oftentimes graver than the criminal punishment) the conflict of counsel must be taken into account, and mere denial (contrary to the truth) cannot be held against him. Otherwise, counsel would indirectly be pressured into a confession, just to escape negative implications from his defence, if he chooses to mount a defence in first place'. From a US perspective, Hazard and Beard (n 81) 1069, write: 'Most states regard disciplinary proceedings as quasi-criminal and consequently disallow an adverse inference where a defendant has invoked the privilege against self-incrimination. Some courts, however, consider disciplinary proceedings to be civil in nature for almost all purposes, and therefore allow an adverse inference to be drawn even where the defendant has invoked the privilege'. The issue becomes even more complex if counsel is given immunity for criminal proceedings, which may then allow using counsel's silence against him again, after all, within the framework of professional discipline.

[283] See Art 63 ICC Statute and the commentary by WA Schabas in O Triffterer (ed), *Commentary on the Rome Statute of the International Criminal Court*, 2nd edn (Munich, Beck, 2008) art 63, mns 1–10.

[284] Section 133, Section 134 and Section 117 BRAO.

factual allegations, and the failure to appear to be concession to any motion or recommendations to be considered.

In a similar vein, the ICC's Board may, under Article 40, 'draw any inferences it deems appropriate and reasonable', but such a non-contestation of the facts should only be assumed after a repeated failure to appear. This also presumes that the charges are clear and counsel has been summoned. On showing of good cause, the case should be continued and counsel rehabilitated.

In conclusion, the Code provides the participants with the necessary statutory framework to conduct hearings in a disciplinary matter. This framework may seem underdeveloped in parts which is not untypical for disciplinary regimes, as other sets of rules of procedure and evidence usually supplement the former. It seems most advisable to return to the ICC procedure and evidence, as appropriate,[285] although the Disciplinary RPE do offer improvement, despite their obscure source.

f Termination of the Disciplinary Procedure

The procedure is terminated if a complaint is dismissed by the Commissioner under Article 39(1) (which cannot be appealed). If it continues, it is reported to the Board, which can suspend the procedure temporarily or close it on grounds of inadmissibility. Such decisions under Article 38 are appealable (para (7)) thereof. Otherwise, the procedure will be terminated on a hearing before the Board, pursuant to Article 15 Disciplinary RPE. Based on this hearing, the Board may under Article 41 either enter a finding of no misconduct, ie, an acquittal, or one of misconduct, ie, a conviction, as set out in Article 16 Disciplinary RPE.

The wording of Article 41 of the Code indicates that the Board can undertake a summary finding, rather than entering convictions for individual counts.[286] This would be similar to the predominant approach in Germany.[287] Other national systems vary, but it seems a general principle that a finding of misconduct can be based on a summary assessment rather than proving discrete counts or charges.[288]

A sanction is not mandatory, though. Article 42(1) provides merely that the Board 'may impose one or more of the following sanctions'. Even if a finding of misconduct has been made, it thus need not necessarily impose formal admonishment.[289] The wording of Article 41(1) ('one or more of the following') makes it clear that measures can be accumulated, but that the list is exhaustive, as is agreed for Article 77 of the Statute.[290] The Board is vested with greater flexibility, how-

[285] See above, II.A.v.a at 208.

[286] See on the other hand Arts 46, 47 and 48 ICTY Code.

[287] Kleine-Cosack (n 116) § 113, mns 22–37.

[288] For a comparative account, see Harting (n 55) 294–96, 309, 316–17, 326–27, 331–35.

[289] However, the mere finding of misconduct, thus finding counsel at fault, may be said to be of a sanctioning effect. See the European Court of Human Rights, *Steur v The Netherlands* (n 151) paras 29, 44.

[290] See RE Fife in O Triffterer (ed), *Commentary on the Rome Statute of the International Criminal Court*, 2nd edn (Munich, Beck, 2008) art 77, mns 1, 7.

ever, by virtue of paragraph (2) which allows recommendations by the Disciplinary Board along with admonishment. A problem with the regulation of counsel seems to be minor misconduct which does not require a sophisticated proceeding or sanction.[291] In that respect, the power of the Board to establish facts and issue recommendations – but without a sanction – could prove valuable. Furthermore, recommendations form part of admonishment as a sanction and along with the latter, they are therefore part of the disciplinary decision under Article 41. Being such a decision pursuant to Article 31(c), a breach of these recommendations becomes disciplinable misconduct in itself.

All of this presupposes a finding of misconduct. It remains unclear from the wording of the Code which burden of proof has to be met before the Board can enter a finding of misconduct.[292] 'Beyond reasonable doubt' has been argued to be the fitting standard of proof in that respect.[293] Article 16(1) Disciplinary RPE has, however, settled the standard at 'clear and convincing evidence'.

On a side note, it needs to be remarked that the required elements to be established have an impact on the general issue of standard of proof. An allegation of misconduct may, for example, be based on a general clause and the mere appearance of unethical behaviour. The burden of proof is then much lower as a matter of principle than that for establishing the breach of a specific rule, in particular if it requires proving a result.[294]

g Sanctions and Sentencing

In the case of a finding of more than lesser misconduct, the termination of proceedings will often be followed by a sanction. Article 42 provides for the permissible sanctions against counsel. Relatively few sentencing considerations seem necessary for admonishment and recommendations, but even in those instances, the Board will not be safe from deciding whether they still suffice, or whether the misconduct warrants a stiffer response as the provision does not contain further technical details.

Concerning the two sanctions – admonishment and reprimand – it is not quite clear what the difference between them is. Where discipline is in principle non-public, such as the ICTY or some US states, admonishment tends to be the lighter sanction because is not made generally known (thus sometimes called private censure). Reprimands, in contrast, are published. The ICC disciplinary hearings are public anyway, any final decision will be made public and they are, furthermore, published in the Official Journal of the Court. This raises the question of how admonishment and reprimand under Article 42 are different. It is suggested that reprimands are to be communicated to the broader public in addition to the

[291] See the McKay Report (n 97) Recommendation 9, at 31.
[292] See Rosen and Kuhlman (n 42) 8.
[293] See above, II.A.ii at 179–85.
[294] See also n 291.

publication in the Official Journal. Moreover, the entry in the counsel's personal file may be of import. In Germany, both *Warnung* and *Verweis* are not publicised, but the latter goes into counsel's file and implies consequences. Thus sanctioned counsel are, for example, banned from running for office within the Bar or at a disciplinary court. This would constitute a plausible distinction between admonishment under Article 42(1)(a) and reprimand under Article 42(1)(b) by giving the former no effect beyond the disciplinary procedure itself, whereas the latter can be held against counsel, for example, by the Registrar when considering assignment of counsel.

Moreover, failure to adhere to decisions by the Board constitutes a ground for discipline in itself under Article 31(c), although this necessitates a new proceeding and does not enable the disciplinary bodies to enforce a suspended sanction right away. A different issue would be the enforcement of an actually imposed sanction. Other courts have, for example, allowed convicted contemner to pay fines in instalments.[295] This could be taken up by the ICC by applying Rule 146 of the RPE mutatis mutandis.

Article 42 does not include an option to suspend a sanction on probation, as has been done by the other international courts for contempt.[296] Counsel can apply for reinstatement, however (Art 20 Disciplinary RPE), with no discernible minimum period of disbarment.

Probation as used for criminal sentences probably does not fit or is at least unnecessary in the context of professional discipline, and is indeed unknown for disciplinary measures in Germany. In the United States, it is used to describe a sanction 'that allows a lawyer to practice law under specified conditions'.[297] If a disciplinary body intends to impose a sanction that expressly stops short of tangible consequences, admonishment or reprimand are the options which are specifically in place for this in professional discipline. A specified condition can be achieved by combining admonishment or a reprimand with recommendations under Article 41(2); a breach of the latter will then constitute misconduct under Article 31(c) of the Code, thus being sanctionable.[298]

No sanctioning objective, let alone specific sentencing guidelines can, however, be gathered from the Code. In the hearing in the first case Commissioner Hampton elaborated on some guiding principles: accountability; public denunciation; deterrence, both specific and general; rehabilitation and redemption.[299]

[295] *Prosecutor v Vidoje Blagojević and Dragan Jokić* IT-02-60-A, Appeals Chamber, Judgement (n 184).

[296] *Prosecutor v Slobodan Milošević, Contempt Proceedings Against Kosta Bulatović*, IT-02-54-R77.4, Trial Chamber, Decision on Contempt of the Tribunal, 13 May 2005 (four months' sentence suspended for two years); *Prosecutor v Zlatko Aleksovski*, IT-95-14/1-AR77, Appeals Chamber, Judgement on Appeal (n 192) (monetary fine partially suspended). A conditional discharge was handed down in *Independent Counsel v Margaret Fomba Brima, Neneh Bah Jalloh, Esther Kamara, Anifa Kamara*, SCSL-2005-02 and SCSL-2005-03, Trial Chamber I, Sentencing Judgement in Contempt Proceedings, 21 September 2005.

[297] *Standards for Imposing Lawyer Sanctions* (n 97) B.2.7.

[298] See above, II.A.v.f at 227, on recommendations under Art 42(2) of the Code.

[299] *The Registrar v Hervé Diakiese*, Complaint 01/09, Transcript (n 50) 11–12; see also *The Registrar v Hervé Diakiese*, DO-01-2010, Decision (n 51) para 17.

These principles may be familiar from domestic practice, but no explicit reference in the ICC's legal framework can be identified. Deriving such principles, again, necessary to take recourse to the methodology under Article 21(1) of the Court's Statute. Just as in relation to other issues of procedure, the Statute and the RPE contain rules which could serve as a starting point in one way or another.[300] It would be fallacious to expect full guidance from them since disciplinary matters are, after all, simply not criminal proceedings. The Statute, in Article 78, points to the gravity of the crime and the individual circumstances of the convicted person. This is elaborated in more detail in Rule 145, and for monetary fines, in Rule 146. It is obvious that some of the mentioned factors, such as duress, defencelessness of victims or cruel commission, are not really applicable in the framework of professional discipline. For Article 70 offences, Rule 162 indicates that seriousness of the offence, however malleable a term, is a factor in deciding whether to intervene. The factor of an existing link with a pending case seems useful as it directs the judges to whether actual or potential harm was caused. In conclusion, some factors, such as the gravity of the wrong or of the result, seem common to all kinds of sanctioning. Other points seem less characteristic for disciplinary sentencing. Customary law has never developed for sentencing which means turning to the national level.

The ABA Model Rules, in Rule 10(C) provide for 'Factors to be Considered in Imposing Sanctions':

(1) whether the lawyer has violated a duty owed to a client, to the public, to the legal system, or to the profession;
(2) whether the lawyer acted intentionally, knowingly, or negligently;
(3) the amount of the actual or potential injury caused by the lawyer's misconduct; and
(4) the existence of any aggravating or mitigating factors.

Paragraphs (2)–(4) are well known from criminal sentencing.[301] Otherwise, as German law indicates, the stress is more on the professional dimension and less on guilt.[302] This is expressed, in the ABA Model Rules, in paragraph (1). The professional dimension is set out by listing different beneficiaries of duties owed by counsel. It also implies a ranking – putting first duties to the client and last, duties to the profession.[303] Similar views are reflected in German scholarship. The

[300] Above, II.A.v.a at 208.

[301] See *Standards for Imposing Lawyer Sanctions* (n 97) 10, 11, for further details on them. In *Prosecutor v Issa Hassan Sesay*, SCSL-04-15-T-CCC32-485, President, Decision on complaint pursuant to Article 32 of the Code of Professional Conduct for Counsel With the Right of Audience Before the Special Court for Sierra Leone, 20 February 2006, 7, the SCSL stresses that counsel who was found to have slapped a female court staff member 'was well aware that he was intimidating'. It also weighed aggravation and mitigation factors, where they consider the profession's integrity on the one hand, and counsel's apology on the other.

[302] Kleine-Cosack (n 116) § 114, mns 26–27; Dittmann (n 116) §114, mns 5, 6; G Gribbohm, 'Die ehrengerichtlichen Berufs- und Vertretungsverbote in der Rechtsprechung des Senats für Anwaltssachen des Bundesgerichtshofs' in OF von Gamm, P Raisch and K Tiedemann (eds), *Festschrift für Gerd Pfeiffer* (Cologne, Heymanns, 1988) 916–18.

[303] *Standards for Imposing Lawyer Sanctions* (n 97) 10, 11, for further details.

standing of the profession is held to be of lesser or almost no concern.[304] Similar guidelines should be developed for the ICC disciplinary regime.

h Disciplinary Appeals Procedure

The Code provides for the possibility of appellate review. Appeals of final decisions by the Board are governed by Articles 43 and 44 of the Code. Apart from this, Article 38 also allows for complementarity appeals. As to the first, the Code entitles the disciplined counsel as well as the Commissioner to appeal the findings by the Disciplinary Board within 30 days of the delivery of the impugned decision.[305] Article 43 sets out the ensuing appeals procedure, which are elaborated on by Articles 19 and 22 Disciplinary RPE. Presumably, delivery means the notification of the fully reasoned and written decision to the concerned counsel according to Article 41(2) and (3) and to the Commissioner, via the Secretariat, respectively, pursuant to Article 17 Disciplinary RPE.[306]

Article 44 contains the rules for the more general set-up of the appeals body.[307] Whereas Article 43(1), using the singular, means the final decision of the Disciplinary Board, Article 44(1) uses the plural and comprises the other category of appealable decisions under the Code, those under Article 38. It could probably be read in a broader fashion as including appeals against any 'decision' of the board other than the two mentioned categories. This would then allow for further kinds of appeals of an interlocutory nature.[308] Whether to allow this or not ultimately also affects the efficiency of disciplinary proceedings. As it stands, the explicit mention of the complementarity appeals in Article 38(7) argues for a more streamlined appeals apparatus. Besides this, errors can thus only be challenged as part and parcel of the Article 42 appeal. The issue of temporary suspension of counsel may arise fairly early in the proceedings and such a decision is not made by the Board or Appeals Board but by a Chamber.[309] Appeals against it should, accordingly, be possible under Article 82(1)(d) of the Statute.

The exact scope and standard of review on appeal is unclear from the wording of Articles 43 and 44.[310] Article 44(1) is specific in the respect that the appellant

[304] R Zuck in R Gaier, C Wolf and S Göcken (eds), *Anwaltliches Berufsrecht* (Cologne, Heymanns, 2010) § 115b BRAO, mn 13; Kleine-Cosack (n 116) § 115b, mn 8; Dittmann (n 116) § 114, mn 5.

[305] The ICTY Code provides for a 14-day deadline, and later 'if the matter is of general importance for the Tribunal or in the interests of justice in a pending case' (Art 46(3)).

[306] The ICTY Code of Conduct is preferable in this respect, see Art 48. The appeal in *Prosecutor v Momčilo Krajišnik*, IT-00-39-A, Decision in the Appeal (n 80) was heard, though not filed in a timely manner (see paras 7–17). The Board further held that the appeals brief, not only the notice of appeal, must be filed within the time-limit (para 7).

[307] There is a clerical error in para (6) of Art 44, where it should read 'Appeals Board' in both instances.

[308] It would, of course, make sense to require additional criteria as it is for interlocutory appeals for core crime proceedings. See C Staker in O Triffterer (ed), *Commentary on the Rome Statute of the International Criminal Court*, 2nd edn (Munich, Beck, 2008) art 82, mn 11.

[309] It will not always be entirely clear which Chamber this will be. See above, II.A.d. at 219–20.

[310] See also Rosen and Kuhlman (n 42) Comment 13, at 9, on Art 44 of the 2005 Draft Code: 'Any rule relating to the appellate process for the disciplinary mechanism should set forth the standard of

can challenge issues of fact and issues of law. Accordingly, the Disciplinary Appeals Board can presumably affirm or reverse the Disciplinary Board's findings of fact as well as those on the law. This in itself is not exhaustive, though, and raises the general point that 'appeal' in itself is not a clear concept.[311] Appellate bodies usually settle issues of law more or less freely from the finding at first instance. Factual findings, on the other hand, will not necessarily be so easily disturbed and could possibly lead to a new trial with new evidence, irrespective of the use of the former findings as evidence.

Much more often, however, the standard of review is restricted to an appeal on the record where new evidence is widely precluded. The appellant must prove a reversible error from the established trial record. This is also the model followed by the ICTY Code of Conduct, where Article 48(F) provides that the Appeals Panel 'shall not receive or consider any evidence that was not presented to the Disciplinary Panel, unless it considers that the interests of justice so require'. Appeal courts may also give significant deference to the initial trier of fact. In some cases, they keep themselves to an 'abuse of discretion' standard of review, and consequently appellate judges do not easily substitute their own assessment of facts which can be illustrated, for example, by the 'reasonableness standard' for factual issues employed by the ICTY and the ICTR Appeals Chambers.[312]

Without referring to the the latter explicitly, the ICTY President has used such a standard, ie, upholding the finding in first instance as 'reasonable'.[313] However, the appeals decisions do not elaborate on the exact standard of appellate review.[314] They mainly deal with errors of law which they find in effect to be freely reviewable.[315] With reference to the sentencing stage, the disciplinary appeals do not yield claritiy on the standard of appellate review either. In the first appeal, counsel was suspended from practice in first instance.[316] Since the President saw no error in the finding of misconduct, supposedly no need existed to disturb the Disciplinary Panel's decision. Furthermore, counsel had not challenged the

review and any requirements for briefing and/or oral argument. If briefing and/or oral argument are to conducted pursuant to other existing rules, this should be noted'.

[311] Staker (n 308) art 81, mns 18–22; R Roth and M Henzelin, 'The Appeal Procedure of the ICC' in A Cassese, P Gaeta and JRWD Jones (eds), *The Rome Statute of the International Criminal Court: A Commentary* (Oxford, Oxford University Press, 2002) 1538–441.

[312] Inter alia, *Prosecutor v Ramush Haradinaj et al*, IT-04-84-A, Appeal Chamber, Judgement, 19 July 2010, paras 12–13; *Prosecutor v Naser Orić*, IT-03-68-A, Appeals Chamber, Judgement, 3 July 2008, paras 9–12; *Simon Bikindi v Prosecutor*, ICTR-01-72-A, Appeals Chamber, Judgement, 18 March 2010, paras 12, 13; *The Prosecutor v Athanase Seromba*, ICTR-2001-66-A, Appeals Chamber, Judgement, 12 March 2008, paras 10–13; *Sylvestre Gacumbitsi v Prosecutor*, ICTR-2001-64-A, Judgement, 7 July 2006, paras 7–9.

[313] *Prosecutor v Mitar Raševć*, IT-97-25/1-PT, President, Decision on Appeal Against Disciplinary Panel Decision, 5 November 2003, para 4.

[314] In the other case heard by the Disciplinary Board the factual finding was based on the respondent's submissions, see *Prosecutor v Momčilo Krajišnik*, IT-00-39-A, Decision in the Appeal (n 80) para 33. In any event, no trial *de novo* took place. On both cases, see ch 1, II.B.i.a and b at 14–16.

[315] ibid, paras 31, 32, 34, 37–39. See also *Prosecutor v Mitar Rašević*, IT-97-25/1-PT, President, Decision on Appeal (n 313) paras 3, 6.

[316] *Prosecutor v Mitar Rašević*, IT-97-25/1-PT, President, Decision on Appeal (n 313) para 1.

sanction in terms of sentencing. Consequently, it could be argued, no error in this respect was claimed on appeal and therefore no remedy warranted. In the other case, the complaint had been dismissed in first instance by the Disciplinary Panel.[317] Thus, the Disciplinary Board now considered the appropriateness of the sanction for the first time and not in an appellate function.[318]

What has been outlined in the foregoing stems mostly from the context of genuinely criminal proceedings, but the issue remains the same for professional discipline. The standard of judicial review of recommendations of disciplinary agencies differs in the United States. As Wolfram writes:

> Three standards of review are commonly encountered, the first one much more than the others. (1) De novo review permits the reviewing court to substitute its own judgment on matters of credibility and inference and freely to reach conclusions different from those of the hearing panel. (2) Under the 'substantial evidence on the whole record' test, the court will normally accept factual determinations but will override them in compelling instances and in most cases will more freely draw its own conclusions on matters of inference. And (3) under the 'any competent evidence' standard, findings and conclusions will be accepted if they have any evidentiary support in the record made before the hearing panel. The second and third standards obviously place at an intended disadvantage a lawyer or bar counsel who attempts to overturn an adverse finding; such a party bears the burden of demonstrating error.
>
> Choice of the standard involves a balance of fairness and consistency in rule application on the one hand and efficiency and similar considerations of judicial administration on the other. Practicalities also play a part and are at the base of the common attitude that findings of a disciplinary body based on conflicting testimony will normally not be disturbed because of the hearing panel's more advantageous position from which to determine the accuracy and veracity of testimony. That superiority follows from the fact that whatever the standard of review, the appellate procedure in all states are similar and consist if review of the record made before the hearing panel without the reviewing court's hearing any live testimony on its own.[319]

This aptly illustrates the options. Just to contrast this with Germany, the BRAO also features different modes of appeal.[320] Decisions of the first-instance Lawyers' Disciplinary Court will be reviewed by *Berufung* (Section 143). This means basically a second trial before the Higher Lawyers' Court where all the evidence can potentially be recalled. After this, *Revision* (Section 145) allows for another review, this one by the Federal Supreme Court. The Federal Supreme Court hears cases

[317] *Prosecutor v Momčilo Krajišnik*, IT-00-39-A, Decision in the Appeal (n 80) para 1.

[318] ibid, paras 40–42, 51. The rest of the passage deals with a legal issue again, whether *restitutio in integrum* is available as a sanction to the disciplinary bodies, with the Board advocating it, *Prosecutor v Momčilo Krajišnik*, IT-00-39-A, Decision in the Appeal (n 80) paras 43–49.

[319] CW Wolfram, *Modern Legal Ethics* (St Paul, Minn, West, 1986) § 3.4.5, 111–12 (citations omitted). See also American Bar Association, *Model Rules for Lawyer Disciplinary Enforcement* (n 141) Rule 11 E and F; McKay Report (n 97) Recommendation 11, at 36 (usually appellate review, not *de novo*); *Disciplinary Proceedings against Gamino*, 206 Wi 32, para 18 (Wisconsin Supreme Court, 2006) (referee's findings of fact on a disciplinary matter will not be set aside unless clearly erroneous).

[320] See Kleine-Cosack (n 116) § 142, § 143, mns 3–5, § 145, mns 1–2; F Johnigk in R Gaier, C Wolf and S Göcken (eds), *Anwaltliches Berufsrecht* (Cologne, Heymanns, 2010) § 142, mns 1–2, § 143, mns 1–4, § 145, mns 1–25.

where disbarment or a practice restriction has been handed down. In all other cases, leave to appeal is needed and the latter is only to be granted for settling questions of principle on points of law or of professional standards.[321]

Consequently, the Disciplinary Appeals Board will have to develop its standard when the first cases come before it. As a starting point, the wording of paragraph (1) of Article 43 indicates that the appellant can address specific factual or legal grounds and does not just identify issues. Thus, the trial record and the findings thereupon would be saved as long as they are not specifically challenged. Such an understanding would argue against a full further scrutiny. On the other hand, Article 43(4) provides that the Disciplinary Appeals Board follows the same procedure as the Disciplinary Board. The governing articles would thus chiefly be Article 39; Articles 37 and 38 concern stages that are before the actual disciplinary procedure. The subsequent provision, Article 40, lists procedural safeguards for the concerned counsel which should be simply equally applicable before the Disciplinary Appeals Board, in order not to undermine their validity during the first instance. It is also easily conceivable how Articles 40 and 41 operate before the Appeals Board.

It is the disciplinary procedure itself, as laid out in Article 39, and its significance for appeals which is the trickier part. Sticking to the phrasing of Article 43(4), this would mean that the Disciplinary Appeals Board in principle observes all the procedural steps contained in Article 39, unless they are clearly tailored for trial proceedings. Of those steps, the first three paragraphs thus seem inapplicable. As to paragraphs (1) and (2), it is not, of course, within the Commissioner's discretion whether to pursue the proceedings. On appeal, it will either be the Commissioner himself who has lodged the appeal or concerned counsel, in which case the Commissioner cannot simply end the procedure. Similarly, paragraph (3) is only an evidentiary rule which governs the stage before a case formally goes before the Board. Therefore, paragraphs (1)–(3) seem to characterise more or less a pre-hearing stage, and they should consequently be considered trumped by the more pertinent pre-appeals provisions of Article 43(1) to 43(3).

The remainder of Article 39, paragraphs (4)–(8), can be fitted to the appellate level in one way or another, although there remains some doubt about paragraph (4). A settlement is in principle conceivable on appeal as well. It is understood that the Commissioner does not have the powers to conclude a settlement binding the Disciplinary Boards, and that this would be the same for the Disciplinary Appeals Board; both would be free to take effects flowing from an agreement into consideration but could ultimately reject it. The obstacle here would rather lie in the fact that the trial record would be expanded by such a post-trial settlement. Whether paragraph (4) is applicable may therefore depend on the overall concept behind the disciplinary appeals structure. Under a *de novo* approach, it may even make sense to allow a new settlement attempt. If the

[321] This makes particular sense because the Federal Court has a role of ensuring uniformity among the 28 Bars in Germany.

Disciplinary Appeals Board restricts itself to a more summary review it would be more consistent to forego a settlement stage on appeal and proceed directly to an appeals hearing.

Applying Article 39(5) to 39(8) to this appeals hearing stage mutatis mutandis, the procedure would come out as follows, along with the protections of Article 40. The Commissioner submits a new report to the Disciplinary which functions as appeals brief and is disclosed to counsel sufficiently prior to the appeals hearing. Article 43(2) and (3) only speak of a notification of the appeal to the secretariat of the Disciplinary Board and subsequent transmission to the Disciplinary Appeals Board's secretariat. If the procedure on appeal is supposed to emulate the procedure before the Disciplinary Board, a pre-appeals hearing disclosure can be gathered from Article 39(2) and Article 40(3), again mutatis mutandis. Apparently, no statutory right to file his or her own brief-in-reply exists for counsel on first instance or on appeal. During the ensuing, normally public hearing however, the Commissioner as well as counsel will be called and heard. In first instance, the Disciplinary Board may call and hear witnesses and other persons. Correspondingly, the Disciplinary Appeals Board does the same. Whether it calls such evidence, to what extent it sticks to the existing record of the proceedings and how it evaluates newly-gathered evidence, will then again depend on the standard of appellate review it adopts ultimately. Again, the Commissioner can move to a Chamber to have counsel temporarily suspended.[322]

Summing up, a number of details of the appeals procedure are still open. The most important item would be the exact standard of appellate review. Under a *de novo* standard, the Appeals Board would not have to adhere to the prior record of the proceedings at all. On the other hand, this is not desirable and is certainly not legally warranted. The procedure before the Disciplinary Board has all the attributes of a formal judicial trial. It is therefore recommended that the Disciplinary Appeals Board arrives at an approach which provides sufficient flexibility to rectify aberrations and helps to develop the law on the one hand, but also on the other, does not burden the disciplinary system's efficiency with double-work and redundancies. The appropriate approach therefore is one along the lines of the 'reasonableness' standard of the ICTY and ICTY Chambers, coming out similar to the 'substantial evidence on the whole record' standard used in some US disciplinary regimes.[323]

vi Conclusion

This part of the chapter has given an overview of the ICC's disciplinary system *stricto sensu*. The centerpiece is the Code of Professional Conduct for counsel which entered into force on 2 January 2006 and hence catches practically all defence counsel conduct before the ICC so far. It is the legal basis setting out the professional standards for attorneys in relation to the ICC. In this regard, a broad

[322] See above, II.A.v.d at 219.

[323] See above, 231–32 (nn 312 and 319).

interpretation of the scope of 'practising at the International Criminal Court' has been recommended. This encompasses those attorneys who are currently admitted to the ICC list of counsel, among them of course those who are representing a client in a current pending matter, and one that has been declared admissible, is in the process of being so, or carries a substantial likelihood of qualifying as admissible. It has been argued against reading into this clause lawyers who are not formally admitted but can be said to be practising before the Court nonetheless because they factually advise in a matter which falls under the ICC's jurisdiction. It is the ICC Code, in any event, that claims primacy over other rules and will therefore govern counsel's conduct in substance once he or she falls under the personal jurisdiction, rather than other codes.

The substantive scope of the Code is exhaustive; it incorporates many of the established principles underlying the legal profession. Besides the professional standards it specifically spells out, it also refers to conduct beyond the immediate scope of the Code, which other codes do as well. As can be gathered from reference in Article 31 to 'ethical obligations', it also extends to extra-professional misconduct, again as others do. Just as other codes, the ICC Code also contains several general clauses, including Article 7(3). It has been argued that resorting to this should, in certain circumstances, be permissible. It is also worth highlighting that Article 31(a) requires, for a disciplinable breach, that a 'substantial' duty has been violated. It is known from national professional discipline that lesser breaches are not automatically disciplinable. Usually, however, the criterion is how substantial the breach is, making it therefore not the abstract content of the rule that counts, but rather a kind of fault requirement.

Much of the disciplinary procedure is, again, similar to what exists nationally. The facts are investigated by a Commissioner appointed by the Presidency. This bears more resemblance to the role of many Bar Councils in the United States – different from Germany – where the regional Bars handle complaints but ultimately the regional Attorney-General's Office bring disciplinary matters before a court. Both models, however, have in common that an independent official is in charge of investigations and has some discretion to screen out cases. Furthermore, proceedings in both systems then go before a quasi-judicial panel staffed by lawyers for an adversarial hearing. The first board conducts an adversarial hearing, and its findings may then be appealed. It is also a commonality that disciplinary bodies are composed of attorneys in first instance. Whereas the exact nature of the appeal may vary, the appeal bench often features professional judges along with attorney, or is entirely composed of such judges; so does the ICC Disciplinary Appeals Board. This at least stands in contrast to, for example, how disciplinary matters are prosecuted under the ICTY Code. There, the hearing panel investigates as well as tries the case. Moreover, it consults with the duty judge. This may remind the reader of some US states where the hearing panel's recommendations need confirmation by the highest state court.[324]

[324] See ch 2, III.C.i at 143–44.

Sanctioning thus takes place according to a formalised procedure. The available sanctions, again, largely reflect the practice at the national level. Specifically professional sanctions such as admonishment and reprimand are supposed to send clear signals to the lawyer, and grave cases are catered for by the possibility of suspension for a fixed time and ultimately for an indefinite time. It is quite noteworthy, though, that the ICC Code provides for a monetary fine. Fines may be unusual in some domestic systems but they do exist in a number of jurisdictions, including Germany und the ICTY.[325]

A number of details of the ICC's disciplinary procedure are still shrouded in some mystery. But worldwide quite different models exist, as referred to above, and this may be the reason why the newly-created international code is, in some respects, ambivalent. Two such examples would be the standard of proof and the need for concise charges to be filed by the Commissioner. Professional discipline is placed somewhere between general administrative procedures and criminal proceedings. The ICC disciplinary regime is eventually closer to the quasi-criminal model.[326]

In conclusion, it is reiterated that the ICC disciplinary procedure in many respects follows along the same lines of identified from national systems of attorney professional discipline. It affords due process, even though it is not quite what would apply in genuinely criminal cases. The exceptions to the enhanced criminal standard can be justified by the specific needs of professional discipline. Evidence is admissible more freely. Counsel is under more duties to cooperate than the ordinary accused. Both are sensible restrictions. Relaxed evidence and some cooperation help considerably in making discipline more flexible and easier to administer efficiently; it nonetheless still allows counsel to launch a full defence. The freedom from self-incrimination seems intertwined with the presumption of innocence. Maintaining this presumption rigidly seems a characteristic of truly criminal proceedings and their substantial accusations, their potential sanctions and the ensuing stigma.

Lastly, another debatable relaxation would indeed be lowering the burden of proof. Unlike the previous two points, however, it would not in any way make investigations or proceeding in general more efficient. The allocation of the burden of proof should therefore rather depend on material reasons. Having said this, the overall similarity of the ICC's procedure to the quasi-criminal model, the comparison to the ICTY and the nature of the actual sanctions would argue leaving it at the criminal 'beyond a reasonable doubt', in conformity with the mirrored rights under Article 40 and the Disciplinary Board's mandate to establish the truth. The broad wording of many professional standards, among them general clauses, will keep the threshold low.

[325] It is certainly not the oddity assumed by Harting (n 55) 341, 432. See also *Prosecutor v Momčilo Krajišnik*, IT-00-39-A, Decision in the Appeal (n 80) para 45, fn 50.

[326] See above, II.A.ii at 179–85, for the arguably quasi-criminal nature of the ICC disciplinary proceedings.

B Criminal Offences under the ICC Statute

i Offences in Connection with the Administration of Justice

As with any other court, the ICC needs to safeguard in particular the reliability of the evidence before it, but also the impartiality of its decision-makers in all other respects, whether it is in connection with judicial proceedings or other more mundane, administrative purposes.[327] It can be seen from the national models that criminal offences play an important role in regulating counsel. The ICC Statute itself contains such criminal offences with relevance to the work of counsel. During the years of drafting the Court's Statute, the states progressed from simply extending their domestic perjury crimes to a more sophisticated set of offences.[328] These offences cover much, albeit not all, counsel misconduct recognised from the past and conceivable for the future of the ICC. Moreover, counsel is not rendered immune from them, though this is not made explicit by the phrasing of the relevant provisions.[329] Lastly, it is noted how Schabas rightly cautions against equating the criminal offences under the ICC Statute with the criminal offence of contempt identified from the UN tribunals:

> This jurisprudence [of the ad hoc tribunals] provides some authority to judges at the International Criminal Court, should they confront situations not expressly covered by Articles 70 and 71. But they will have to bear in mind that there is an important distinction between the law applicable to the International Criminal Court and that of the *ad hoc* tribunal. In the latter, the judged themselves chose to codify the contempt powers in the Rules of Procedure and Evidence that they had adopted. At the International Criminal Court, however, the comparable provisions are found in the *Statute* itself. It would be a bold interpretation for the Court to deem that, whatever the terms of the *Statute*, judges are free to go beyond because of an 'inherent power'.[330]

The principal criminal provision safeguarding this would be Article 70, much of which directly pertains to the criminal process.[331]

[327] See F Terrier, 'Powers of the Trial Chamber' in A Cassese, P Gaeta and JRWD Jones (eds), *The Rome Statute of the International Criminal Court: A Commentary* (Oxford, Oxford University Press, 2002) 1309; DK Piragoff in O Triffterer (ed), *Commentary on the Rome Statute of the International Criminal Court*, 2nd edn (Munich, Beck, 2008) art 70, mn 5. K Ambos, *Internationales Strafrecht*, 2nd edn (Munich, Beck, 2008) § 7, mns 262–63, speaks of Art 70(1) as *Rechtspflegedelikte* (offences against the administration of justice), which seems under-inclusive, though he later also recognises that it pertains to bribery offences (fn 1036 there). See further (n 342).

[328] See for a brief summary, Piragoff (n 327) art 70, mns 3–4; Schabas (n 2) 854. See also the other preparatory documents pertaining to the creation of what is now Art 70 and 71, below at 241–42.

[329] See on Art 71, O Triffterer in O Triffterer (ed), *Commentary on the Rome Statute of the International Criminal Court*, 2nd edn (Munich, Beck, Nomos, 2008) art 71, mns 13–15. Likewise, for ICC officials 'there is nothing that would prevent their prosecution' (Dixon and Khan (n 179) §16–69).

[330] Schabas (n 2) 855.

[331] The final text of Art 70 and Art 71 was developed in Rome Conference for the ICC, *Working Paper on Article 70* (A/CONF.183/C.1/WGPM/L.68, 9 July 1998), and subsequent Revs 1 and 2 of 10 and 11 July, respectively (see also below at 242).

As a starting point, the provision explicitly vests the Court with its own statutory jurisdiction over conduct jeopardising proceedings. In contrast to national systems, there exists no *omnibus* clause of 'obstruction of justice' or *Strafvereitelung* along the lines of 18 U.S.C. § 1503 or Section 258 German Criminal Code.[332] Instead, the ICC Statute lists six distinct offences.

The first offence under Article 70(1)(a) is a perjury provision.[333] This is a standard staple on the domestic level.[334] It has been argued that this provision not only applies to trial proceedings, but all the other phases of procedure as well.[335] This extension beyond the principal trial has merit. Another indication in its favour is the mention of the 'investigative' along with the 'judicial process' in Article 70(4)(a). Strictly speaking, however, the mention of 'proceedings before all Chambers' in Rule 63(1) suggests that investigation and other phases, where the case is not before a Chamber, are not covered by (a). The result would be that perjury can only be committed in judicial proceedings but not by statements to the OTP/investigators or any other organ of the Court. Such statements to non-judicial organs may fall under (b) for participants to the proceeding or (c) for non-participants.

As this offence governs witness testimony, the wording of Article 70(1)(a) limits its relevance to counsel. Given his or her function as defence attorney and thus in view of the confidentiality duties and privileges,[336] instances will seldom arise, if at all, where counsel is called as a witness. Since the accused technically does not count as a witness either,[337] counsel will hardly incur liability as a party to client perjury.[338] Involvement in the perjured testimony of others will tend to fall under (d). This first clause is therefore not a primary measure against counsel misconduct.

The second and the third offences pertain much more to counsel in his or her role as advocate and are likely to be applicable. Highly relevant, they make it criminal to present false or forged evidence at all stages as well as otherwise influencing a witness or other evidence in an impermissible manner. Among the two, paragraph (1)(b) may be considered as the more counsel-specific. Tendering evidence goes to the heart of counsel's work. Paragraph (c) also addresses evidence but does encompass acts by non-participants.

The fourth, fifth and the sixth offences move away from protecting the criminal trial per se. They still aim at ensuring the Court will properly discharge of all its tasks, although this is, in contrast, not limited to pending judicial proceedings. Reaching beyond, they can relate to all kinds of conceivable duties which officials of the Court have to discharge. Besides their judicial functions, this could encompass anything from the wide range of everyday operations of the Court. An exam-

[332] See ch 2, II.B.ii.a at 68, and III.B.ii.a at 126, respectively. See also Schabas (n 2) 855.

[333] Piragoff (n 327) art 70, mn 6.

[334] See ch 2, II. B.ii at 68, and III.B.ii.a at 125.

[335] Piragoff (n 327) mn 6, fns 17 and 18, and mn 5, fn 14, citing Rule 63.

[336] Art 69(5) of the Statute and Rule 73(1) RPE.

[337] Art 47(1)(h) gives the accused to right to make an unsworn oral or written statement. He or she does thus not fall under the purview of Art 69(1).

[338] Similar to Germany and different from the United States (ch 2, III.B.ii.a at 125).

ple could be procurement: an ICC procurement officer discharges of official duties towards the Court in a tendering process, and it may constitute one of the offences under Article 70 of the State if he or she is bribed for the purpose of retaining a lucrative contract in violation of those duties.[339] Consequently, such offences can address more general aspects of good governance. The 'corruptly influencing' clause in (d) and 'soliciting or accepting a bribe' in (f) complement each other in that respect, as the latter covers the receiving end, a Court insider,[340] and the other the giving counterpart who will typically be the outside the Court (though not necessarily so). The first two limbs of the fourth in (d) – 'impeding' and 'intimidating' – on the other hand seem to have more in common with the fifth offence of retaliation under (e). They are less about the good governance by the Court but rather concern one-sided efforts to compromise the Court's work.

Summing up, three categories of offences under Article 70(1) exist which should cover most of what is needed. It is criminal under (a) and (b) to contribute false testimony or evidence to the trial. Furthermore, as contained in (c), it is criminal to otherwise influence the collection or rendition of evidence.[341] Lastly, (d), (e) and (f) can be grouped together as attacks against the good governance of the Court, beyond the criminal trial itself.[342] Some of the offences use more specific language, others are quite wide ('corruptly influencing', 'obstructing', 'interfering'). Strict construction is the key here. The use of the special mental element of 'corruptly' denotes a case of 'otherwise' provided from Article 30 and will come into play for this. As far as all the other offences are concerned, the intent element of the chapeau is simply the one under Article 30.[343] Negligence has been left out.

[339] See Schabas (n 2) 856.

[340] Such a clause was not included until the Rome Conference. See Rome Conference for the ICC, *Proposal submitted by Japan on Article 70, Offenses or Acts Against the Integrity of the Court* (A/CONF.183/C.1/WGPM/L.13, 26 June 1998). Counsel supposedly do not count as such officials of the Court. See, eg, Rule 171(2) RPE, distinguishing 'official of the Court' from 'defence counsel' and 'legal representative of victims'. No elaborate definition exists but it presumably means representatives of all four Court organs (Piragoff (n 327) art 70, mn 10. Preparatory Commission for the ICC, *Unofficial Proposal by Italy: Atteintes à l'administration de la justice. Proposition de règles de droit pénal (article 70.2)* (1 June 1999) fn 2, contemplates regarding counsel as officials for the purpose to award them the same amount of protection from reprisals as other representatives of the Court.

[341] Terrier (n 327) 1310, points out that the first portion of (c) serves to protect witnesses, whereas the last one is said to have more in common with the protection and reliability of evidence. It seems helpful, though, to also divide along the proposed lines, ie, immediate production of tainted evidence or testimony before the Court in contrast to the previous phases. Piragoff (n 327) art 70, mn 1, calls it 'efforts to otherwise interfere with the evidence gathering process'.

[342] Terrier (n 327) 1310, speaks of (d) and (e) as protecting officials, and of (f) as protecting the Court from officials. This is correct. Emphasising the proper discharge of duties more generally, it seems fair to lump them together. Piragoff (n 327) art 70, mn 1, very succinctly summarises them as 'efforts to influence the judicial process'. Strictly speaking, this would limit the offences to those against the administration of justice *strictu sensu* and leave out corrupting non-judicial operations (as described above). Schweizerischer Bundesrat, *00.090, Botschaft über das Römer Statut des Internationalen Strafgerichtshofs, das Bundesgesetz über die Zusammenarbeit mit dem Internationalen Strafgerichtshof und eine Revision des Strafrechts vom 15. November 2000* (Bundesblatt Nr. 7, 391–570, 20 February 2001) 561, mentions *aktive und passive Bestechung* (active and passive corruption).

[343] Piragoff (n 327) art 70, mn 5. Art 30(1) speaks of 'intent and knowledge', whereas 'knowledge' is left out in the chapeau of Art 70. It will nonetheless have to be read in since 'one cannot perform an action or cause a consequence intentionally unless one has also knowledge of the circumstances in

There is, furthermore, no element of special intent to interfere with the governance of the Court or its administration of justice in particular. Such an interpretation would at least bring the ICC in line with the existing jurisprudence.[344]

Article 70 does not contain a catch-all criminal offence of obstructing criminal justice.[345] Such a general thrust is inherent in Article 71, ie, to cover simply any imaginable 'misconduct, including disruption of its proceedings or deliberate refusal to comply with its directions'. However, Article 71 is not a criminal offence. It can be concluded that the Statute does not know an *omnibus* criminal offence comparable to obstruction of justice under the US Code or German Section 258, *Strafvereitelung*. In itself, this is probably not too remarkable. Paragraphs (a) and (c) cover much of what has the potential to thwart the adjudication of a case before the Court. Nonetheless, it does leave lacunae, in particular in respect to conceivable acts by defence counsel in connection with the trial. One example would be counsel helping his or her client to evade arrest, or hindering the enforcement of court orders. This is not directly related to evidence and thus fails to fall under the Article 70 offences and arguably also holds true for other defence-related misconduct such as, suborning perjury from the client or a tactical delay of the proceedings.

Summing up, no general clause is apparent from the wording of Article 70, but some of the existing wording can be interpreted broadly, in particular the third and the fourth offences, and commentators suggest doing so.[346] Paragraph (c) has an *omnibus* function to some extent and indeed uses the language of '[c]orruptly influencing . . . , obstructing or interfering'. On the other hand, this is linked to the 'attendance or testimony of a witness' and the 'collection of evidence'. Both are quite specific aspects of the criminal process. It is not to be equated with obstructing or interfering with the criminal process in general. Paragraph (d) 'parallels'[347] some of the crimes in paragraph (c), and its scope is also widened by the use of '[i]mpeding, intimidating or corruptly influencing' to describe the criminal acts. It need to be stressed, however, that it is indeed a 'parallel' only because it shifts the focus away from safeguarding the judicial process to the Court's works on all other levels. The duties of officials presumably denote the

which that action or consequence was committed' (DK Piragoff and D Robinson in O Triffterer (ed), *Commentary on the Rome Statute of the International Criminal Court*, 2nd edn (Munich, Beck, 2008) art 30, mn 10).

[344] From the ICTY, see *Prosecutor v Zlatko Aleksovski*, IT-95-14/1-AR77, Appeals Chamber, Judgement on Appeal (n 192) 53–54; *Prosecutor v Slobodan Milošević*, IT-02-54-T, Trial Chamber, Trial Chamber Finding in the Matter of Witness K12, 21 November 2002, with Judge Kwon's Dissenting Opinion to Oral Decision on K12; *Prosecutor v Slobodan Milošević*, Trial Chamber, Decision on Contempt of the Tribunal (n 296) para 17; *Prosecutor v Vidoje Blagojević and Dragan Jokić* , IT-02-60-A, Appeals Chamber, Judgement (n 184) paras 25–28. See on Germany and the United States, ch 2, II.B.ii.a at 69, and III.B.ii.a at 127.

[345] M Bohlander, *Gerichtliche Sanktionen gegen Anwälte wegen Mißbrauchs von Verfahrensrechten* (Aachen, Shaker, 2001) 91.

[346] Piragoff (n 327) art 70, mn 5.

[347] ibid, art 70, mn 10. See also Preparatory Commission for the ICC, *Proposal by Italy concerning article 70 of the Rome Statute* (PCNICC/1999/WGRPE/DP.17, 26 July 1999) (broad interpretation of offences, ie, no actual effect needed, still possible after the termination of a certain case, at 2 and 3).

general ones but not the conduct of proceedings itself. Consequently, Paragraphs (a) to (c) should not be understood to be *leges speciales* to paragraph (d). A *Blocksburger* test and a *Rechtsgut* (legal interest) analysis[348] should yield the result that, for example, giving false testimony is not a more specific instance of 'impeding . . . an official for the purpose of forcing . . . the official to perform . . . improperly'. Paragaph (d) is, therefore, not a residual clause for what is not covered by paragraphs (a) to (c).

The drafting history of Article 70 also corroborates that paragraph (d) should not be read broadly to function as an *omnibus* clause of obstruction of justice; rather it lends support to the notion that the provision pertains to the administration of justice in a wider sense, ie, operating and managing the Court. Extending national laws on perjury to cover the ICC was the starting point for the ILC in 1994 but was soon deemed insufficient.[349] One of the earliest proposals, by the United States in 1996, used broad language but kept apart the two concepts of obstruction of adjudication on the one hand, and of interference with the governance of a court, on the other.[350] Also in 1996, the Preparatory Committee considered the issue of offences against the integrity of the Court.[351] During this, the concept of contempt as used by the ICTY and other, broad concepts of obstruction were put on the record (but never substantially used again). A similar approach including contempt and obstruction can be found in a subsequent draft of late 1997,[352] which listed the same four offences featured in the US proposal of 1996. The Zutphen draft of early 1998 continued along exactly the same lines with changing the number of the Article but it did note expressly that '[t]here was a view that these offences required further definition in the Statute . . . Additional discussions are needed on this article'.[353] Even the Preparatory Committee's draft Statute of April 1998[354] still contained contempt like clauses but it is the first indication of the spin-off of what later became Article 71. The broad obstruction clause and the contempt clause had been confined to the immediate proximity to

[348] Ch 2, II.B.ii.a at 70, and III.D.ii at 144–45.

[349] International Law Commission, *Report of the International Law Commission on the work of its forty-sixth session (2 May–22 July 1994)* (A/49/10, 4 August 1997) 58–59.

[350] See Preparatory Committee for the ICC, *Proposal Submitted by the United States of America, Offenses against the Integrity of the Court* (A/AC.249/WP.41, 23 August 1996) (suggesting four distinct articles: 'Perjury', 'Influencing, impeding or retaliating against officials of the Court', 'Obstructing the functions of the Court' and 'Contempt').

[351] Preparatory Committee for the ICC, *Report of the Preparatory Committee on the Establishment of an International Criminal Court, Volume II (Compilation of Proposals)* (A/51/22[VOL.II](SUPP), 13 September 1996) 210–13. No modifications to this occurred in August 1997 (Piragoff (n 327) art 70, fn 5), see Preparatory Committee for the ICC, *Abbreviated Compilation of Proposals on Procedural Matters* (A/AC.249/1997/WG.4/IP, 4 August 1997) 44–46.

[352] Preparatory Committee for the ICC, *Decisions taken by the Preparatory Committee at its Session held from 1 to 12 December 1997* (A/AC.249/1997/L.9/Rev.1, 18 December 1997), Annex III, Report of the Working Group on Procedural Matters, at 31.

[353] Preparatory Committee for the ICC, *Report of the Inter-Sessional Meeting from 19 to 30 January 1998 in Zutphen, The Netherlands* (A/AC.249/1998/L.13, 4 February 1998) 119, in fns 217 and 219.

[354] Preparatory Committee for the ICC, *Report of the Preparatory Committee on the Establishment of an International Criminal Court* (A/CONF.183/2/Add.1, 14 April 1998), 111 (Part One. Draft Statute for the International Criminal Court).

trial action. In all other respects, the more trial-specific acts had been separated from the more remote ones, relating to the general management of Court business only. An unofficial working paper first removed contempt-like misconduct from the criminal provision of Article 70, thus disposing of the options in that respect and introduced the non-criminal provision of Article 70bis.[355]

During the Rome Conference, the drafting of Article 70 started on 16 June 1998, when the Committee of the Whole referred it to the Working Group on Procedural Matters.[356] Whereas this Working Group first focused on the many other issues of procedure under its remit,[357] the working paper of June was twice revised.[358] Article 70 was thus put into shape with addendum 7 to the working paper on 13 July and transmitted.[359] As it then stood, it was included in the Report of the Drafting Committee and the Draft Statute therein and consequently the Report of the Committee of the Whole.[360] Deliberations in the plenary meetings only concerned the statute of limitations,[361] which can primarily be explained by their quite different nature from the core crimes.

It emerges thus as the conclusion from the drafting that the ICC's criminal offences are different from the ICTY and the ICTR, but likewise differ in comparison from the national models. First and most markedly, they do not entrench the concept of contempt of court. Concededly, the ICTY only pronounced on contempt for the first time in late 1998 in the case of *Nobilo*, and the more groundbreaking appeals decisions were handed down in 2000 and 2001,[362] ie, after the

[355] Rome Conference for the ICC, *Unofficial Working Paper on Article 70, Offences against the Integrity of the Court and Article 70 bis, Sanctions for Misconduct before the Court* (15 June 1998) see the bracketed text in the chapeau of Art 70(1).

[356] Rome Conference for the ICC, *Report of the Working Group on Procedural Matters* (A/CONF.183/C.1/WGPM/L.2, 24 June 1998) 1 (para 1), reprinted as well in Rome Conference for the ICC, *Official Records, Volume III: Reports and other documents* (A/CONF.183/13(Vol.III)) 277, 288.

[357] See Add. 1, Add.l/Corr.l, Add.2, Add.2/Corr. 1 and 2, Add.3, Add.4, Add.5, Add.5/Corr.l, Add.6, Add.6/Corr.l.

[358] Rome Conference for the ICC, *Working Paper on Article 70* (n 331) (still bracketed: [before it]; sentence not fixed); Rome Conference for the ICC, *Working Paper on Article 70, Rev. 1* (A/CONF.183/C.1/WGPM/L.68/Rev.1, 10 July 1998) (punishment fixed, paras straightened out); Rome Conference for the ICC, *Working Paper on Article 70, Rev. 2* (A/CONF.183/C.1/WGPM/L.68/Rev.2, 11 July 1998) (finalised: brackets in first para taken out, punishment shifted to para 3, brackets around para removed), also reprinted in Rome Conference for the ICC, *Official Records, Volume III* (n 356) 299.

[359] Rome Conference for the ICC, *Official Records, Volume III* (n 356) 278 (Report of the WGPM, para 9) and 288. The final wording can be found in Rome Conference for the ICC, *Report of the Working Group on Procedural Matters, Addendum 7* (A/CONF.183/C.1/WGPM/L.2/Add.7, 13 July 1998) 1, 3-4. No more changes were transmitted by Rome Conference for the ICC, *Report of the Working Group on Procedural Matters, Addendum 8* (A/CONF.183/C.1/WGPM/L.2/Add.8, 15 July 1998). The previous addendums incorporated other draft articles of Part 6.

[360] Rome Conference for the ICC, *Official Records, Volume III* (n 356) 140 (with Art 70 and 70bis at 166–67) and at 93 (with Art 70 and 70bis at 118) respectively.

[361] See Rome Conference for the ICC, *Official Records, Volume II: Summary records of the plenary meetings and of the meetings of the Committee of the Whole* (A/CONF.183/13(Vol.II)) 142–43 (2nd meeting, 16 June 1998, at 3.20 pm, paras 48, 63, 74).

[362] *Prosecutor v Zlatko Aleksovski*, IT-95-14/1-T, Trial Chamber, Finding of Contempt of the Tribunal, 11 December 1998; *Prosecutor v Duško Tadić*, IT-94-1-A-R77, Appeals Chamber, Judgment (n 21); *Prosecutor v Duško Tadić*, IT-94-1-A-AR77, Appeals Chamber, Appeal Judgement on Allegations

adoption of the Rome Statute. It still seems fair to assume from the various proposals and other pertinent documents that the drafters were generally cognisant of the broader concept underlying the ICTY law as well as, say, the US doctrine of contempt. The ICTY RPE were amended in October and November 1997, Revision 12, to explicitly refer to the inherent nature of these powers.[363]

Likewise for obstruction of justice offences, various alternatives had all been tabled during the drafting but eventually were not adopted. Whatever exists as contempt powers was 'split'[364] from Article 70 and made into Article 71.[365] At this point – and as far as the analysis of the criminal offences under Article 70 is concerned – Article 71 is remedial in comparison and contains other qualifiers. It is by no way the same as the broad common law contempt powers, encompassing criminal contempt, and it is certainly not as broad as the powers held by the ad hoc Tribunals. Even comparing with civil law countries and the obstruction offences identified there, it seems fair to conclude that various clauses had been proposed but rejected. Such content should consequently not be read into the current wording, and in particular under paragraph (d).

ii Offences on Specific Professional Duties or Pertaining to Financial Irregularities

Article 70 focuses on offences against the administration of justice from several angles. The ICC Statute does not address specific professional duties by way of criminal offences, as could be found in Germany.[366] The German approach seemed rather unusual from a comparative perspective in the first place. Moreover, the ICC's criminal jurisdiction simply focuses on the important core crimes. The Code of Conduct will supposedly serve the purpose of prosecuting those wrongs which are of a specifically professional nature. The relevance of more general criminal laws in the regulation of criminal defence attorneys should not be underestimated, however. A considerable number of the prosecutions of attorneys are for financial crimes such as fraud, embezzlement or money laundering.[367] This is not to say that they will occur frequently in connection with the Court, or that the Statute should have incorporated such offences; it simply illustrates that the need to address misconduct in terms of criminal law may in some respect go beyond what is contained in the statute. To have those instances

of Contempt Against Prior Counsel, Milan Vujin, 27 February 2001; *Prosecutor v Zlatko Aleksovski*, IT-95-14/1-AR77, Appeals Chamber, Judgement on Appeal (n 192). See in detail ch 1, II.B.ii at 20–22.

[363] For the ICTR, this extension was only effectuated on 27 May 2003, though. The pending contempt cases and the inherent contempt powers were brought to the drafters' attention for the RPE, inter alia, through Preparatory Commission for the ICC, *Contributions of the Chambers* (n 153) 14.

[364] Piragoff (n 327) art 70, mn 4. But see also above at 238 on the scope of the perjury provision under Art 70(1)(a).

[365] See below, II.C.ii at 256–63.

[366] Ch 2, II.B.ii.b at 71.

[367] Ch 2, II.B.ii.c at 71–72, III.B.ii.c at 129.

prosecuted on the national level will therefore be of importance. The optimal use of cooperation and assistance to the states by the Court may play a role here, but the extent to which this will actually be possible is not certain, as the Court's legal framework may not allow for what is in principle desirable.[368]

iii Legal Consequences of Criminal Offences

a Criminal Punishment

Punishment is the primary consequence of a conviction for an Article 70 offence. Pursuant to paragraph (3), this can mean imprisonment of up to five years or a fine. Both can also be accumulated. Along with punishment there may also be further consequences such as the removal from the list of counsel by the Registrar, or in the appropriate circumstances, forfeiture of proceeds or the award of reparations. Lastly, acts punishable under Article 70 will usually appear to constitute professional misconduct under the Code of Conduct for counsel.

As far as criminal punishment is concerned, the provisions on the sentences for the core crimes are either not applicable or they are modified. Rule 166 RPE specifically addresses sanctioning under Article 70. It can be gathered from sub-rules (1) and (2) that forfeiture is the only measure to be imposed according to the general provisions of the Statute and the Rules.

For the two more important penalties of imprisonment and fines, Rule 166 is supposed to give guidance. Sub-rules (3)–(5) elaborate on fines and result in a scheme slightly varying from what Rule 146 generally decrees for fines.[369] First, a difference lies in the amount of the fine. Article 70 fines have a limit of 50 per cent of the convicted person's assets, pursuant to Rule 166(3). Rule 146(2), for the core crimes, sets this maximum at 75 per cent. Secondly, Rule 146(4) contains an option to calculate the fine according to a *per diem* system. Rule 166(3), on the other hand, simply provides that offences may be separately fined and that fines may be cumulative. This is rather unrefined. The other method is only an option,

[368] See on Art 93(10), C Kreß and K Prost in O Triffterer (ed), *Commentary on the Rome Statute of the International Criminal Court*, 2nd edn (Munich, Beck, 2008) art 93, mns 61–69. See also ch 4, III.B at 302–06.

[369] See Fife (n 290) art 77, mns 26–28. On the *travaux préparatoires* for Rule 146, in particular the feasibility of a fixed cap for the core crimes: Preparatory Commission for the ICC, *Proposal submitted by France concerning part 7 of the Rome Statute of the International Criminal Court, on penalties* (PCNICC/1999/WGRPE(7)/DP.1, 19 November 1999) at 2–3; Preparatory Commission for the ICC, *Discussion paper submitted by the Coordinator concerning Part 7 of the Rome Statute of the International Criminal Court, on penalties* (PCNICC/1999/WGRPE(7)/RT.2, 9 December 1999). The 50% maximum for Art 70 fines first appears in Preparatory Commission for the ICC, *Discussion paper proposed by the Coordinator regarding rules of procedures and evidence relating to Part 6 of the Rome Statute, concerning the trial* (PCNICC/2000/WGRPE(6)/RT.10, 23 June 2000). Before, a fixed-amount cap had been considered, see Preparatory Commission for the ICC, *Proceedings of the Preparatory Commission at its second session (26 July–13 August 1999)* (PCNICC/1999/L.4/Rev.1, 18 August 1999) Rule 6.36 (Penalties), sub-rule (a); Preparatory Commission for the ICC, *Discussion paper submitted by the Coordinator concerning Part 7 of the Rome Statute* (n 369).

though, which leaves room for a bulk assessment. Vice versa, judges are not precluded from adopting such a system for Article 70 fines if they consider it helpful.

Sub-rules (4) and (5) of Rule 166 correspond more closely to sub-rules (3) and (5) of Rule 146. The former two, with the same wording, provide on the modalities that fines are not necessarily enforced with immediate effect but that payment plans are to be considered.[370] Sub-rules (5) – under Rule 146 as well as the Rule 166 counterpart – deal with cases if enforcement proves fruitless. They allow commuting into imprisonment fines that cannot be enforced due to 'continued wilful non-payment'.

There are two slight discrepancies between them, though. First, in the case of Article 77 fines, it is explicitly the Presidency which determines whether all available enforcement measures have been exhausted. For Article 70 fines, the same is done by 'the Court'. This is somewhat ambiguous as the term is not defined conclusively in the RPE.[371] Aligning both rules as well as the Presidency's generally strong role in the enforcement process both argue the case for having the Presidency do this for Article 70 fines as well.[372]

The other difference is the maximum length of the substitute prison sentence. From one angle, Article 77 fines for core crimes are in principle harsher. It has already been mentioned above that the fines imposed under Article 70 may not exceed 50 per cent of the convicted person's assets while this maximum is 75 per cent for the core crimes.[373] In regard to substitute imprisonment, though, Rule 146(5) is more lenient than Rule 166(5). The former contains a maximum of five years, but it is also limited to a quarter of the principal prison sentence imposed and it may not lift the total imprisonment to more than 30 years. This basically means that it will result in less than five years for Article 77(1) sentences under 20 years, and that it will have no effect at all for sentences of 25 years and more. For offences against the administration of justice, on the other hand, the available maximum is five years in any event. This appears strange, but may be explained by the fact that Article 77 fines will always be punishment in addition to imprisonment, whereas fines serve as a self-standing purpose within the context of Article 70.

Apart from those enforcement issues relating to monetary fines, Rule 166 is regrettably silent on actual sentencing issues. The general reference in Rule 163(1) would potentially lead to Articles 77 and 78. Article 77 and the Rules thereunder

[370] Above, II.A.v.g at 228 (n 295).

[371] Pursuant to Art 34 of the Statute itself, it comprises as organs the Presidency, the three judicial Divisions, the Office of the Prosecutor and the Registry. It could thus mean the Trial Chamber or Appeals Chamber that has imposed the fine to supervise its enforcement (see the interplay of Rules 163(1) and 166(1) RPE with Arts 61(11) and 83(1) mutatis mutandis).

[372] See Rule 217, to which Rule 166(5) itself refers. See also Rule 199 (Organ responsible under Part 10): 'Unless provided otherwise in the Rules, the functions of the Court under Part 10 shall be exercised by the Presidency'.

[373] This difference seems justified, given the presumably much greater heinousness of the core crimes. See also above (n 369).

are, however, disallowed by Rule 166(2).[374] Other than that, Part 7 and with it Articles 78–80 are not expressly excluded. Therefore, it seems possible and advisable to resort to Article 78 on sentencing, and with it Rule 145(1) and (2), notwithstanding the references to Article 77 therein. All the named factors are in principle transferable to offences against the Court's administration of justice.[375] This seems also true for Rule 146(2), listing 'damage and injuries caused as well as the proportionate gains derived from the crime by the perpetrator' as a guiding factor. Direct reliance on this is impossible, however unfortunate, because it is one of the Rules under Article 77.

The pertinent prior case law of the other international courts has largely evolved along entrenched lines of sentencing.[376] The individual harm caused, the gravity of the conduct as well as the abstract interest at stake, ie, safeguarding criminal justice, have been stressed. The purposes identified have been those of deterrence and also of retribution. Exemplary for this, the ICTY Appeals Chamber highlighted the following points in the contempt proceedings against attorney Milan Vujin:

> [T]he Respondent's conduct has been *against* the interests of his client . . . The conduct of the Respondent in this case strikes at the very heart of the criminal justice system . . . The contempt requires punishment which serves not only as retribution for what has been done but also as deterrence of others who may be tempted to act in the same way.[377]

Similar factors have been used in the other contempt cases, albeit not all of them concerning lawyers. The judges have returned to the gravity of conduct and to deterrence.[378] This has been said to pertain directly to the administration of jus-

[374] Some certainty in respect to the applicable sanction is warranted by the principle of *nulla poena sine lege*, Fife (n 290) art 77, mn 19. More specific guidance than upper and lower limits is arguably not strictly required by the *nulla poena* principle, though highly advisable. It is noted that Art 70(3) sets a clear sentencing range. This is less so for fines. The German Federal Constitutional Court has struck down Section 43a of the German Criminal Code (providing for fines limited by the existing assets of the offender) as void for vagueness (*Bundesverfassungsgericht*, 20 March 2002, 2 BvR 794/95, BVerfGE 105, 135 (*Vermögensstrafe*)).

[375] Triffterer (n 329) art 71, mn 28, appears to draw a similar conclusion for Art 71 sanctions. See generally on sentencing by the ICC, M Jennings in O Triffterer (ed), *Commentary on the Rome Statute of the International Criminal Court*, 2nd edn (Munich, Beck, 2008) art 78, mns 9–11, and 16; JC Nemitz, *Strafzumessung im Völkerstrafrecht. Ein Beitrag zur Strafzwecklehre und zur Strafzumessungsmethode unter besonderer Berücksichtigung des Römischen Statuts* (Freiburg, edition iuscrim, 2002).

[376] S D'Ascoli, 'Sentencing Contempt of Court in International Criminal Justice' (2007) 5 *Journal of International Criminal Justice* 735, 749.

[377] *Prosecutor v Duško Tadić*, IT-94-1-A-R77, Appeals Chamber, Judgment (n 21) paras 167–68. The appeal in the matter was decided on written briefs and did not address sentencing (*Prosecutor v Duško Tadić*, IT-94-1-A-AR77, Appeals Chamber, Appeal Judgement (n 362).

[378] *Prosecutor v Ivica Marijačić and Markica Rebić*, IT-95-14-R77.2, Trial Chamber, Judgement, 10 March 2006; *Prosecutor v Josip Jović*, IT-95-14 and IT-95-14/2-R77, Trial Chamber III, Judgement, 30 August 2006, para 26; *Prosecutor v Domagoj Margetić*, IT-95-14-R77.6, Trial Chamber I, Judgement on Allegations of Contempt, 7 February 2007, paras 84–87. On the gravity of the offence, see also from the SCSL, *Independent Counsel V Margaret Fomba Brima, Neneh Bah Jalloh, Esther Kamara, Anifa Kamara*, SCSL-2005-02 and SCSL-2005-03, Trial Chamber I, Sentencing Judgement (n 296) paras 21–29.

tice[379] and includes elements of retribution.[380] Reference has also been made to the vulnerability of victims.[381] Furthermore, the personality of the offender and other individual factors, such as the offender's mental state during commission,[382] their personal circumstances[383] and any prior criminal record have been considered.[384] Cooperation[385] and remorse[386] have been cited as post-conduct factors. That the trust vested in counsel by his office can be an aggravating factor flows from the gravity of the crime as directed against the administration of justice.[387] Altogether, uniformity in sentencing will make it advisable to take into consideration other, in due course forthcoming, case law for Articles 6, 7 and 8 convictions.

The enforcement of sentences is usually governed by Part 10 of the Statute. Rule 163(3) RPE declares only select provisions of that Part applicable. Those four are Articles 103, 107, 109 and 111. Article 103 provides that imprisonment takes places in a willing state. Article 107 specifies what happens thereafter. Article 111 addresses the escape from the state of enforcement and subsequent extradition or surrender if apprehended again. Article 109 governs both fines and forfeiture, with both essentially enforced pursuant to national procedures.

These provisions still leave enough of the necessary basic enforcement framework. The remaining, inapplicable Articles concern details on how prison sentences will be enforced, which may arguably be of equal importance. It is to some extent understandable that states possibly did not feel ready to commit themselves to the same enforcement regime as for the core crimes. Consequently, the issues of when and how a change of the enforcement state can occur (Art 104), how the supervisory powers over enforcement and the conditions of imprisonment are allocated between the ICC and states (Arts 105 and 106), which specialty clauses will be permissible (Art 108) and which body can review a sentence (Art 110) are left unregulated.

On the other hand, the established international law in that field for horizontal cooperation will arguably produce similar results in any event.[388] As the sending

[379] *Prosecutor v Beqa Beqaj*, IT-03-66-T-R77, Trial Chamber I, Judgement on Contempt Allegations, 27 May 2005, para 60.

[380] ibid, para 58.

[381] ibid, paras 61–62.

[382] *Prosecutor v Domagoj Margetić*, IT-95-14-R77.6, Trial Chamber I, Judgement (n 378) para 88; *Independent Counsel v Margaret Fomba Brima, Neneh Bah Jalloh, Esther Kamara, Anifa Kamara*, SCSL-2005-02 & SCSL-2005-03, Trial Chamber I, Sentencing Judgement (n 296) para 30.

[383] *Prosecutor v Domagoj Margetić*, IT-95-14-R77.6, Trial Chamber I, Judgement (n 378) para 89.

[384] *Independent Counsel v Margaret Fomba Brima, Neneh Bah Jalloh, Esther Kamara, Anifa Kamara*, SCSL-2005-02 and SCSL-2005-03, Trial Chamber I, Sentencing Judgement (n 296) para 31; *Prosecutor v Beqa Beqaj*, IT-03-66-T-R77, Trial Chamber I, Judgement on Contempt Allegations (n 379) para 63.

[385] *Independent Counsel v Margaret Fomba Brima, Neneh Bah Jalloh, Esther Kamara, Anifa Kamara*, SCSL-2005-02 and SCSL-2005-03, Trial Chamber I, Sentencing Judgement (n 296) paras 32–33.

[386] ibid, para 34.

[387] See Preparatory Commission for the ICC, *Proposal by Italy* (n 347) at 2, though not adopted, suggested harsher penalties for any person who is entrusted with special functions at the Court.

[388] See C Nicholls, C Montgomery and JB Knowles, *The Law of Extradition and Mutual Assistance*, 2nd edn (Oxford, Oxford University Press, 2007) 189–204, 229–37; MC Bassiouni, *International Extradition, United States Law and Practice*, 5th edn (Oxford, Oxford University Press, 2007) 537–603;

entity, the Court would generally prescribe the principal sentence and be able to add specialty reservations, whereas the custody state uses its national laws during the enforcement process. The crucial differences weakening the Court's position would be, however, that it is unable to freely transfer the detained person to a third state and to override the rules of the custody state on early release and other reductions of actual imprisonment.

b Other Consequences

Among the non-criminal consequences are three which presuppose a conviction: forfeiture, reparations and automatic disbarment by the Registrar. Disciplinary proceedings may attach, but to some degree independently of the outcome of the criminal trial.

Any conviction under Article 70 will automatically result in removal from the list of counsel by the Registrar.[389] Forfeiture and reparations are within the discretion of the Chamber. Rule 166(2) RPE clarifies that non-criminal forfeiture may also attach to convictions under Article 70(3). The general reference to the Articles of the Statute and the RPE in Rule 163(1) leads to the option to award reparations pursuant to Article 75. Both are noteworthy because such recovery is not available under the disciplinary procedure. Given the lack of a general jurisdiction for malpractice, it may also be attractive to make up for a civil remedy.[390]

Article 70 offences will usually be professional misconduct under Article 31(a) or (b), ie, violation of a Statute provision imposing a substantial ethical or professional duty. Article 70 is arguably the one provision of the Statute that imposes the most substantial professional duty on counsel, ie, to respect the administration of justice of the ICC by refraining from committing criminal offences against it. Criminal proceedings do not automatically entail disciplinary proceedings, let alone make them redundant. By and large, the criminal and the disciplinary regime complement each other but to a certain degree operate independently.[391]

G Gilbert, *Transnational Fugitive Offenders in International Law, Extradition and Other Mechanisms* (The Hague, Martinus Nijhoff, 1998) 195–99; W Schomburg et al, *Internationale Rechtshilfe in Strafsachen*, 4th edn (Munich, Beck, 2006) Einleitung, mn 74; Council of Europe, *Convention on the Transfer of Sentenced Persons* (CETS no 112, 21 March 1983), Arts 8–14.

[389] Regulation 71(1)(c) RoC. Similar provisions can be found in the RoR: Regulation 126 (for assistants to counsel) and Regulation 138 (for investigators).

[390] See below, II.D at 272–74.

[391] On the relationship of criminal and disciplinary measures, see ch 4, IV.C at 272–74. On Art 70 and discipline for judges, see Preparatory Commission for the ICC, *Proposal submitted by Spain and Venezuela* (n 179) at 1.

iv The Procedure for Criminal Offences

a Mutatis mutandis application of the Statute and the RPE

The procedure for Article 70 proceedings is, mutatis mutandis, the same as for the core crimes (Rule 163(1)).[392] As the Statute explicitly distinguished 'offences' under Article 70 and 'crimes within the jurisdiction of the Court' under Article 5, not necessarily all of the procedural provisions for the latter will apply.[393] Aligning the procedure to the extent possible makes sense, though, as it promises to lead to uniformity and efficiency. Such a boilerplate reference should also be adopted for the disciplinary procedure.[394]

Pursuant to Rule 165, the Office of the Prosecutor investigates allegations of criminal misconduct. According to Rule 171 RPE, criminal offences under Article 70 (and accompanying Rules 162–69) take preponderance over Article 71 (with Rules 170–71 RPE). They are, moreover, subject to a statute of limitations, as set out in Rule 164 RPE.[395]

In several respects, the procedure is somewhat leaner than what is done for the core crimes. In comparison to those, a number of points during pre-trial are more relaxed and, more importantly and rightly so, result in a procedure that is more suited to ordinary crimes. No extended pre-trial phase takes place before the confirmation of charges. Rule 165(3) allows for deciding the confirmation on written submissions instead of a full-blown hearing. There is less prosecutorial discretion on political grounds than Article 53 would normally provide for core crimes, and arrests are not mandatory as they would be under Article 59. Prosecutions are handled separately from the case in connection with which they might have

[392] See on the drafting of the corresponding Rules of Procedure and Evidence the subsequent notes, and Preparatory Commission for the ICC, *Discussion paper proposed by the Coordinator Part 6 of the Rome Statute: The Trial* (PCNICC/1999/WGRPE/RT.5, 1 July 1999) 8–11 (setting forth most of what exists now); Preparatory Commission for the ICC, *Comments made to document PCNICC/1999/ WGRPE/RT.5* (6 August 1999) at 15–18 (listing the various comments by states on the procedure in relation to Art 70). See before that, Preparatory Commission for the ICC, *Revised discussion paper proposed by the Coordinator Rules of Procedure and Evidence related to Part 6 of the Statute* (PCNICC/1999/WGRPE/RT.5/Rev.1, 11 August 1999); Preparatory Commission for the ICC, *Rules of Procedure and Evidence* (PCNICC/1999/L.5/Rev.1/Add.1, 22 December 1999), Preparatory Commission for the ICC, *Rules of Procedure and Evidence* (PCNICC/2000/L.1/Rev.1/Add.1, 10 April 2000); Preparatory Commission for the ICC, *Draft Rules of Procedure and Evidence as they emerged from the Mont Tremblant Intersessional Meeting* (PCNICC/2000/WGRPE/INF/1, 24 May 2000); Preparatory Commission for the ICC, *Discussion paper proposed by the Coordinator regarding rules of procedures and evidence relating to Part 6 of the Rome Statute, concerning the trial* (n 369); Preparatory Commission for the ICC, *Finalized draft text of the Rules of Procedure and Evidence* (PCNICC/2000/L.2/ Add.1, 29 June 2000) referring to Preparatory Commission for the ICC, *Report of the Working Group, Chapter 10, Offences and misconduct against the Court* (PCNICC/2000/WGRPE/L.10, 27 June 2000).

[393] Schabas (n 2) 856.

[394] Above, II.A.v.a at 208.

[395] Different from the core crimes (Art 29 of the Statute). See from the drafting history, Preparatory Commission for the ICC, *Proposal submitted by Austria concerning the Rules of Procedure and Evidence, Rule 6.29. Statute of limitations (as contained in document WGRPE/RT.5)* (PCNICC/1999/WGRPE/ DP.25, 29 July 1999) (proposal for a plain statute of limitations).

arisen. It needs to be noted that they can be joined with a core crime case (Rule 165(4)). This could create something similar in effect to a summary procedure.[396]

In principle, all of these features are commendable. By and large, the same procedure applies with which the Court organs are familiar from the core crimes, but it is more streamlined where necessary and possible. For example, assignment of counsel need not follow as automatically as for core crimes if allegations under Article 70 are relatively minor.[397]

Special concern should be paid to the impartiality of the judges where a case is joined with a pending core crime case. In addition, it might then happen that a case is tried before an Appeals Chamber as the bench of first instance. This creates the same dilemma that the ICTY encountered and which led it to amend Rule 77 RPE.[398]

Finally, Rule 168 establishes a bar of *ne bis in idem* for cases of criminal misconduct. Moreover, Rule 162 makes the availability and the effectiveness of prosecutions factors for delegating them to national states.[399]

b Jurisdiction

Other than procedural aspects, it is principally such issues of the Court's jurisdiction where the regimes of core crimes and offences against the administration of justice differ. Unlike earlier proposals jurisdiction for the offences under Article 70 is universal.[400] The admissibility requirements under Part 2, do not apply, though, as Rule 163(2) provides. This fits in with the picture of original powers.[401] Whereas at one point it was contemplated taking into account local statutes of limitation,[402] such links to national jurisdiction were eventually removed.

What remains as traces of complementarity under Article 70(4) of the Statute is somewhat different in principle from Article 17 of the Statute.[403] Article 70

[396] For summary adjudication of criminal contempt in US federal law, see ch 2, III.C.iii at 149.

[397] See Tuinstra (n 55) 29–30, and above II.A.v. at 210, for legal assistance in disciplinary proceedings.

[398] *Prosecutor v Duško Tadić*, IT-94-1-A-AR77, Appeals Chamber, Appeal Judgement (n 362) with a dissent by Judge Wald; now Rule 77(K), as amended by Rev 23, 12 July 2002.

[399] For more details on both *ne bis in idem* and national prosecutions, see ch 4, III.A at 302.

[400] Rome Conference for the ICC, *Proposal submitted by The Netherlands, Article 70* (A/CONF.183/C.1/WGPM/L.65, 9 July 1998) (ICC's jurisdiction by the rule of territoriality; referral by ICC to the territorial state with preferent jurisdiction); with a different approach: Preparatory Commission for the ICC, *Proposal submitted by the Netherlands in connection with document PCNICC/1999/WGRPE/RT.5* (PCNICC/1999/WGRPE/DP.27, 30 July 1999) (primary jurisdiction of the ICC, at 1; applicability of Arts 103 and 109).

[401] See also Schweizerischer Bundesrat, *00.090, Botschaft über das Römer Statut des Internationalen Strafgerichtshofs* (n 342) 561.

[402] Preparatory Commission for the ICC, *Rules of Procedure and Evidence* (PCNICC/1999/L.5/Rev.1/Add.1, 22 December 1999) fn 11; Preparatory Commission for the ICC, *Proposal submitted by Colombia, Comments on the discussion paper proposed by the Coordinator (PCNICC/1999/WGRPE/RT.5)* (PCNICC/1999/WGRPE/DP.36, 6 August 1999) (stressing conflict of jurisdiction but with a tilt towards complementarity, para 1; speaking out against statutory limitation but with mistaken belief that this would bar revision of ICC core crimes cases, para 2).

[403] Ch 4, III.A at 300–02, for more details.

offences are explicitly exempted from the complementarity requirement.[404] Rule 162 speaks of the availability and moreover of the effectiveness of prosecutions. The named factors are known from conflicts of criminal jurisdictions.[405] This should be, properly speaking, understood to constitute mere guidance whether to actually adjudicate, but not an admissibility threshold or anything similar which needs to be surpassed before prosecutions can be launched.[406]

v *Conclusion on Criminal Offences*

In conclusion, the ICC regime relies on criminal offences to safeguard the administration of justice, contained in Article 70 of the Statute. They directly concern the administration of justice *stricto sensu*, and arguably beyond that the general governance of the Court. Counsel are not exempt from criminal liability. The procedure is the ordinary one under the Statute and the RPE, save some variations. It offers due process in these respects and is thus a clear improvement over the occasionally murky procedure for contempt under Rules 77 of the ICTY and ICTR RPE.[407] There, the patchy statutory framework left open essential issues on procedural safeguards, such as the right to appeal or even the characterisation of contempt as a criminal offence.[408]

Article 70 proves that the ICC also subscribes to a elaborate scheme of criminal offences in the area of misconduct. Consequently, it can be assumed to figure importantly in the regulation of counsel. The approach is distinctly different from the ad hoc Tribunals, though which adopted a very broad provision modelled on the doctrine of contempt. The ICC on the other hand uses codified offences; and to that effect, the civil law approach has prevailed.[409] In spite of the ICC's *Kompetenz-Kompetenz* authority as an international court to interpret its own instruments,[410] there is an agreement to the contrary effect of assuming inherent

[404] Pursuant to Rule 163(2), Part 2 shall not apply to them. This includes Art 17.

[405] The catalogue seems to stem from Preparatory Commission for the ICC, *Proposal submitted by Poland concerning the Rules of Procedure and Evidence, Article 70, Rule 6.26* (PCNICC/1999/WGRPE/DP.29, 2 August 1999) (catalogue of factors for consideration of whether to defer to another jurisdiction), and was then amalgamated with the proposal DP.27 by the Netherlands into Preparatory Commission for the ICC, *Proposal submitted by the Netherlands and Poland concerning the Rules of Procedure and Evidence, Article 70, Rule 6.26* (PCNICC/1999/WGRPE/DP.31, 3 August 1999).

[406] In a similar vein, Schabas (n 2) 856, who calls the exercise of jurisdiction by the ICC under Art 70(4) 'discretionary'.

[407] G Sluiter, 'The ICTY and Offences against the Administration of Justice' (2004) 2 *Journal of International Criminal Justice* 631; M Bohlander, 'International Criminal Tribunals and their Power to Punish Contempt and False Testimony' (2001) 12 *Criminal Law Forum* 91, and (more on ECHR and Kyprianou case) AC Emilianides, 'Contempt in the Face of the Court and the Right to a Fair Trial' (2005) 13 *European Journal of Crime, Criminal Law & Criminal Justice* 401.

[408] *Prosecutor v Duško Tadić*, IT-94-1-A-AR77, Appeals Chamber, Appeal Judgement (n 362), Separate Opinion Judge Wald Dissenting From the Finding of Jurisdiction, at 3–4.

[409] D'Ascoli (n 376) 755; Bohlander (n 407) 111.

[410] See with regard to deciding on the admissibility of a criminal case under the complementarity scheme of Art 17: *The Prosecutor v Joseph Kony et al*, ICC-02/04-01/05-377, Pre-Trial Chamber II, Decision on the admissibility of the case under article 19(1) of the Statute, 10 March 2009, para 46.

criminal powers. It would be erroneous, however, to underestimate the vagueness issues that statutory obstruction of justice offences entails.

As to the consequences of criminal convictions, the available sanctions appear sufficient to address even grave instances of misconduct. The Court thus has the necessary tools to react swiftly and on this its own, sovereign initiative. Some features may be appealing, such as the possibility of recovering damages, which is not the case under the disciplinary procedure or by way of civil jurisdiction.

C Other Measures as Institutional Controls

i Institutional Controls and Inherent Powers

It could be seen from national practice that measures other than professional discipline or criminal prosecutions figure prominently in the regulation of counsel. This is due to the fact that they aim at misconduct which is not addressable through those two regimes and that they provide courts with directly available reactions. These measures have been grouped together and explained as institutional controls: they limit actors to their institutional responsibility – for example, judges to what occurs during litigation before the respective bench – but have indeed played out to be the most suitable measures for litigation-based misconduct and offer a great variety of embedded weapons.[411] To some extent, the experience of the ad hoc Tribunals can be cited as additional evidence to that effect. Chambers there, in particular of the ICTY, have made use of the possibility to launch contempt proceedings themselves with orders *in lieu* of indictments and not to rely on the OTP.[412] They have also frequently resorted to denying fees to counsel.[413]

With Article 71, the ICC Statute explicitly vests judges with powers to react to misconduct immediately. In addition to this, the ICC's procedure in its entirety makes many more measures available to the judges and the Registry. Within the context of a stay of proceedings in the *Lubanga* case, the ICC Appeals Chamber has elaborated on the concept underlying Article 71 in its judgment of 8 October 2010.[414] Apart from situating Article 71 within the Court's procedural framework,

[411] See Wilkins (n 252) 807.

[412] Inter alia, *Prosecutor v Radoslav Brđanin, Concerning Allegations against Milka Maglov*, IT-99-36-R77, Order Instigating Proceedings against Milka Maglov, 8 May 2003; *Prosecutor v Milan Milutinović et al (Protić Contempt)*, IT-05-87-R77.1, Trial Chamber, Order to Vacate Warrant of Arrest and Order In Lieu of Indictment, 9 March 2007; *Proscutor v Mom ilo Krajišnik*, IT-00-39-R77.1, Trial Chamber I, Order in Lieu of Indictment on Contempt concerning Branko Đerić, 27 June 2006; *Prosecutor v Ramush Haradinaj et al (Kabashi Contempt)*, IT-04-84-R77.1, Trial Chamber, Order In Lieu of Indictment for Contempt Concerning Shefqet Kabashi, 5 June 2007; *In re Florence Hartmann*, IT-02-54-R77.5, Specially Appointed Trial Chamber, Order in lieu of an Indictment on Contempt, 27 August 2007; *Prosecutor v Vojislav Šešelj*, IT-03-67-T, Trial Chamber III, Order in Lieu of an Indictment for Contempt against Ljubiša Petković, 13 May 2008.

[413] Ch 1, III.B.iii at 41, for fee-denial by the ICTR.

[414] *The Prosecutor v Thomas Lubanga Dyilo*, ICC-01/04-01/06-2582 (OA 18), Appeals Chamber, Judgment on the appeal of the Prosecutor against the decision of Trial Chamber I of 8 July 2010 enti-

this judgment seems noteworthy because it deals with the issue of judicial powers in broader terms, affirming some earlier holdings of the Court. In particular, the Appeals Chamber contends the ultimate authority of the Chambers of the Court over the trial:

> 47. Under the Statute, the Trial Chamber, subject only to the powers of the Appeals Chamber, is the ultimate guardian of a fair and expeditious trial. Article 64 (2) of the Statute provides that it is the Trial Chamber which shall ensure that the trial is conducted fairly, expeditiously and with full respect for the rights of the accused. As correctly noted in the Impugned Decision, the Appeals Chamber has previously confirmed that '[t]he ultimate responsibility for securing justice and ensuring fairness has been given to the Chamber (Article 64(2) of the Statute) and these responsibilities cannot be delegated by, or removed from, the judges'.[415]

This is argued to flow from the fundamental responsibility of the Chambers to ensure a fair and expeditious trial, leading the Appeals Chamber to its key findings 1 and 2 of the judgment:

> 1. Orders of the Chambers are binding and should be treated as such by all parties and participants unless and until they are suspended, reversed or amended by the Appeals Chamber or their legal effects are otherwise modified by an appropriate decision of a relevant Chamber.
> 2. Even if there is a conflict between the orders of a Chamber and the Prosecutor's perception of his duties, the Prosecutor is obliged to comply with the orders of the Chamber.[416]

The Appeals Chamber places great weight on court orders and compliance with them. These key findings are important as they stress the supreme position of the judges within the process. Moreover, the Appeals Chamber construes an intrinsic link between judicial orders and the responsibility of the judges to safeguard the trial:

> [W]hen there is a conflict between the Prosecutor's perception of his duties and the orders of the Trial Chamber, the Trial Chamber's orders must prevail. This is a fundamental criterion for any trial to be fair. The Appeals Chamber fully endorses the statement of the Trial Chamber that '[n]o criminal court can operate on the basis that

tled 'Decision on the Prosecutor's Urgent Request for Variation of the Time-Limit to Disclose the Identity of Intermediary 143 or Alternatively to Stay Proceedings Pending Further Consultations with the VWU', 8 October 2010. See also below II.C.iii at 263–65, III.A at 275.

415 ibid, para 47. Omitted fn 122 cites to *The Prosecutor v Thomas Lubanga Dyilo*, ICC-01/04-01/06-1401, Trial Chamber I, Decision on the consequences of non-disclosure of exculpatory materials covered by Article 54(3)(e) agreements and the application to stay the prosecution of the accused, together with certain other issues raised at the Status Conference on 10 June 2008, 13 June 2008, para 88, with the mentioned confirmation contained in *Prosecutor v Thomas Lubanga Dyilo*, ICC-01/04-01/06-1486 (OA 13), Appeals Chamber, Judgment on the appeal of the Prosecutor against the decision of Trial Chamber I entitled 'Decision on the consequences of non-disclosure of exculpatory materials covered by Article 54(3)(e) agreements and the application to stay the prosecution of the accused, together with certain other issues raised at the Status Conference on 10 June 2008', 21 October 2008, para 76.

416 *The Prosecutor v Thomas Lubanga Dyilo*, ICC-01/04-01/06-2582 (OA 18), Appeals Chamber, Judgment (n 414) paras 1, 2, fully developed in paras 47–48 and 49–54, respectively.

whenever it makes an order in a particular area, it is for the Prosecutor to elect whether or not to implement it, depending on his interpretation of his obligations'.[417]

Read together, this is an important statement on the interpretation of the judicial powers within the ICC's framework. It is noted that the Appeals Chamber expressly refers to Article 64(2) of the Statute. Paragraphs (1) and (2) of that Article stand somewhat in contrast. Paragraph (1) ties the judges to the statutory framework; on the other hand, this is juxtaposed with their supreme responsibilities as laid out in paragraph (2). It could even be said that these neighbouring paragraphs aptly illustrate the tension between formal statutory authorisation, as spelled out in paragraph (1), and the material objective, ie, a fair and expeditious trial, contained in paragraph (2). As to the issue at hand, the Appeals Chamber could have limited the essence of paragraph (2) to describing a general maxim that governs the interpretation of the judicial powers foremost given to the judges under paragraph(1), ie, the legislated base of the Statute and the Rules. Interestingly enough, the Appeals Chamber did not do this; instead, it read into paragraph (2) what it calls '[t]he ultimate responsibility for securing justice and ensuring fairness'.[418] Of this it claims to 'ha[ve] been given to the Chamber (Article 64(2) of the Statute) and these responsibilities cannot be delegated by, or removed from, the judges'. The Appeals Chamber did not confine the inherent judicial responsibility under paragraph (2) to constitute merely an interpretative principle or a goal of the criminal process. What is more, this responsibility is viewed as a complementary and arguably to some degree a corrective function to those under the Statute and the RPE mentioned in paragraph (1). Both the emanation of such powers from the judges and the existence in addition to what has been legislatively endowed are two hallmarks of inherent powers.

In conclusion, it seems fair to say that the Appeals Chamber has affirmed the existence of inherent powers under the ICC's legal framework by this, exemplified by the unwritten competence to even order a complete stay of the proceedings. However, the assumption of the judges' ultimate authority needs to be read in conjunction with the Appeals Chamber's key finding 3. It is instructive on the relationship between the undeniable inherent powers and the statutory powers, or put differently, the relationship between paragraphs (1) and (2) of Article 64 of the Statute. According to the Chamber, Article 71 constitutes the primary tool to achieve compliance by the participants and to exercise control over the proceedings.[419] The Appeals Chamber seems to explicitly acknowledge the relevance of statutory entrenchment:

> [A]rticle 71 of the Statute provides Trial Chambers with a **specific tool** to maintain control of proceedings . . . Given their **specific inclusion in the Statute and Rules of Procedure and Evidence**, sanctions under article 71 and rule 171 are the normal and

[417] ibid, para 48. The omitted fn 144 cites to para 27 of the impugned decision.

[418] Already cited above at 253. See also *The Prosecutor v Thomas Lubanga Dyilo*, ICC-01/04-01/06-2705, Trial Chamber I, Decision (n 20), para 13.

[419] See *The Prosecutor v Thomas Lubanga Dyilo*, ICC-01/04-01/06-2582 (OA 18), Appeals Chamber, Judgment (n 414) paras 3, 55–61.

> proper means to bring about compliance in the face of refusals to follow the orders of a Chamber (emphasis added).[420]

This appears to favour a more civil law statutory approach to judicial powers. The notion of unwritten powers is affirmed, not ruling them out, as the Chamber is cautious to add in a footnote that

> [t]he Appeals Chamber does not preclude the possibility that, in some situations, a fair trial may have become irreparably impossible, including for reasons unrelated to the refusal of a party to comply with its orders, and that a stay would be justified before the imposition of sanctions.[421]

This snippet in a footnote certainly offers no comprehensive clarification on the relationship between explicit statutory and unwritten inherent judicial powers. It would presumably overstate what the Chamber hand in mind in the specific case of the *Lubanga* stay of proceedings to draw general conclusions from just this footnote. However, it needs to be read in the context of the Appeals Chamber's further reasoning on the application of the doctrine of abuse of process in paragraphs 59–61 of the judgment. There, the Appeals Chamber could have confined itself to arguing how the Trial Chamber had not yet lost control over the proceedings, thus resolving the issue as a matter of proportionality. Instead, it argues as a decisive point that the Statute has vested Chambers with a specific tool, according the latter priority.

In consequence, the approach by the Appeals Chamber would come out to establish a priority of using the statutory powers over general inherent powers, and in particular with a view to Article 71, the conclusion would be that it or other statutory provisions do not rule out the remaining unwritten powers. But at the same time, the Chamber's emphasis of specific statutory authorisation and the priority over unwritten powers is striking. Inherent powers exist but not parallel to statutory ones, as seen for the United States.[422] Moreover, unwritten powers would seem permissible as a last resort. The threshold for invoking them comes out as rather high under what the Appeals Chamber has put forward as the appropriate standard for a stay of proceedings (exceptional remedy,[423] losing control,[424] irreparable damage to the trial).[425] If taking the priority of statutorily authorised tools seriously, the applicable standard for other procedural measures than a stay of proceedings would have to be similarly high. Chambers cannot base unwritten procedural measures on purely inherent powers unless they have demonstrated a

420 ibid, para 59.

421 ibid, para 60, fn 135.

422 See ch 2, III.A at 109–13, inter alia, with a discussion of *Nasco v Chambers*. In the meantime, see, however, *The Prosecutor v Thomas Lubanga Dyilo*, ICC-01/04-01/06-2705, Trial Chamber I, Decision on the defence request to reconsider the 'Order on the numbering of evidence' of 12 May 2010, 30 March June 2011, paras 16–18, and the Separate Opinion by Judge Blattmann.

423 *The Prosecutor v Thomas Lubanga Dyilo*, ICC-01/04-01/06-2582 (OA 18), Appeals Chamber, Judgment (n 414) para 55.

424 See ibid, paras 59–61.

425 See ibid, para 60, with fn 135, and para 61. See also 'frustration of the object of the judicial process', para 55.

pertinent lacunae in the ICC's statutory legal framework that leaves the problem which arises unaddressable and threatens to compromise the proceedings irreparably.

Overall, this trend to a civil law approach is commendable; it is in line with the *travaux préparatoires* and thus arguably reflects best what the states had in mind for the Court's constituent legal set-up. During the drafting of the RPE, a broad proposal by was tabled by Australia.[426] It was modelled after Rule 5 of the ICTY RPE and would have explicitly given judges a leeway to grant relief as they see fit. This was not adopted and it left the basic question of how to fill gaps, for example, by using customary law.[427]

In essence, the Appeals Chamber judgment has now shown the ICC to rely on a statutory base for judicial functions and powers, unlike what actually lies at the heart of the competing concept of contempt in the common law. It resembles more the civil law tradition. Even there, courts are vested with a certain base of unwritten powers, thus inherent, *qua* the function of the criminal process and their judicial authority therein.[428] These are not as far-reaching as in the common law[429] and – given the Chamber's emphasis on Article 71 as the central sanctioning tool – do not comprise sanctioning powers. But just as their common law counterparts, they employ procedures and measures other than sanctioning to safeguard the judicial process and to address gaps.[430]

ii Article 71 of the Statute

a The Nature of Article 71

Article 71 may play out to be one of the most useful among the Court's institutional controls. It could be seen under the preceding heading that the Appeals Chamber has advocated using sanctions available to it under its powers. Contempt-like powers have widely been resorted to for disciplining counsel with non-criminal sanctions, although there has occasionally been a very fine line

[426] Preparatory Commission for the ICC, *Proposal submitted by Australia, Draft Rules of Procedure and Evidence of the International Criminal Court* (PCNICC/1999/DP.1, 26 January 1999).

[427] J Cockayne, 'Commentary' in A Klip and G Sluiter (eds), *Annotated Leading Cases of International Criminal Tribunals, vol 4, The International Criminal Tribunal for the former Yugoslavia 1999–2000* (Antwerp, Intersentia, 2002) 199; Bohlander (n 407) 116 (on the compellability of witnesses, though this seems to have been resolved by Rule 65(1) RPE).

[428] See in the context of *Rechtsmissbrauch* (ch 2, II.B.iii.a at 75–79) H Kudlich, *Strafprozeß und allgemeines Mißbrauchsverbot. Anwendbarkeit und Konsequenzen eines ungeschriebenen Mißbrauchsverbots für die Ausübung strafprozessualer Verteidigungsbefugnisse* (Berlin, Duncker & Humblot, 1998) 60–112, 175–77, 199–227, 249–58; T Abdallah, *Die Problematik des Rechtsmißbrauchs im Strafverfahren. Eine Untersuchung unter besonderer Berücksichtigung der verfassungsrechtlichen Bezüge des Strafprozeßrechts* (Berlin, Duncker & Humblot, 2002) 85–87, 141–45, and in particular 150–58; C Fahl, *Rechtsmißbrauch im Strafprozeß* (Heidelberg, C. F. Müller 2003) 75–124.

[429] See ch 2, III.A at 109–13, and L Symons, 'The Inherent Powers of the ICTY and ICTR' (2003) 3 *International Criminal Law Review* 369, 373, on English law.

[430] Cockayne (n 427) 199–200. See below, II.C.iii at 263–66 on the other measures by Chambers.

between criminal and non-criminal measures.[431] Article 71 is the option which complements the Court's criminal laws under Article 70 of the Statute, but which itself stops short of a criminal measure.

Commentators have likened this to contempt as we know it from common law jurisdictions and as it emerged in the practice of the UN tribunals as well.[432] Indeed, in the *Lubanga* case the Prosecutor referred to Article 71 as 'contempt'. Although the Appeals Chamber did not follow in terminology, it acknowledged a punitive and a coercive dimension of Article 71.[433] By this, the judges can be said to have distanced themselves – whether consciously or not – from understanding Article 71 as contempt or affirming the doctrine of contempt as the underlying base. The further analysis by the Chamber demonstrates that Article 71 is a specific tool under statutory law enjoying priority over unwritten powers – all of this differs from the concept of contempt. But the Chamber correctly highlights the function of Article 71 as a control tool with both punitive and coercive elements. This is what Article 71 has in common with criminal and civil contempt.[434]

The concept of contempt in the common law tradition features two striking characteristics. First, it is based on the courts' inherent powers. Secondly, its purpose is to ensure the authority of the court and the integrity of the criminal process. It is broad and builds on the wider notion of misbehaviour and non-compliance with orders as a particular subset. Out of these two features, Article 71 shares the latter but arguably not the basis in inherent powers. The wording of Article 71(1) is itself quite vague. Although it is located in Part 6 of the Statute ('The Trial'), it empowers any judge of the Court presiding over one of its proceedings to react directly to misconduct.[435] Such a wide scope is now indicated by the cited Appeals Chamber decision.[436] Chambers are hailed as the 'guardian of a fair and expeditious trial'.[437] Consequently, the purpose of the powers under

[431] C Gane, 'Commentary' in A Klip and G Sluiter (eds), *Annotated Leading Cases of International Criminal Tribunals, vol 5, The International Criminal Tribunal for the former Yugoslavia 2000–2001* (Antwerp, Intersentia, 2003) 240–41, referring to the ECHR cases of *Ravnsborg v Sweden*, application no 14220/88, 2 July 1988, paras 31–35 thereof, and *Putz v Austria*, application no 18892/91, 26 January 1996, see paras 32–37 there, with dissents from Judge De Meyer and Judge Jungwiert.

[432] Schabas (n 2) 859. See on the Tribunals T Spronken, 'Commentary' in A Klip and G Sluiter (eds), *Annotated Leading Cases of International Criminal Tribunals, vol 7, The International Criminal Tribunal for the former Yugoslavia 2001* (Antwerp, Intersentia, 2005) 226–27; C Brants, 'Commentary' in A Klip and G Sluiter (eds), *Annotated Leading Cases of International Criminal Tribunals, vol 6, The International Criminal Tribunal for Rwanda 2000–2001* (Antwerp, Intersentia, 2003) 458–67; Cockayne (n 427); M Veldt, 'Commentary' in A Klip and G Sluiter (eds), *Annotated Leading Cases of International Criminal Tribunals, vol 3, The International Criminal Tribunal for the former Yugoslavia 1997–1999* (Antwerp, Intersentia, 2001) 57–62. On contempt, see also N Keijzer, *Contempt of Court* (Gouda, Quint, 2000); CJ Miller, *Contempt of Court*, 3rd edn (Oxford, Oxford University Press, 2000). See also Section 178 of the Courts Constitution Act in Germany, ch 2, II.B.iii.a at 74.

[433] *The Prosecutor v Thomas Lubanga Dyilo*, ICC-01/04-01/06-2582 (OA 18), Appeals Chamber, Judgment (n 414) paras 34, 59.

[434] See also below at 262.

[435] Triffterer (n 329) art 71, mn 10; Schabas (n 2) 859–60. The latter emphasises the French wording '*Sanctions en cas d'inconduite à l'audience*' and notes the marked contrast to the ICTY and the ICTY.

[436] See *The Prosecutor v Thomas Lubanga Dyilo*, ICC-01/04-01/06-2582 (OA 18), Appeals Chamber, Judgment (n 414) paras 59–60.

[437] See ibid, para 47. For a further analysis, see above II.C.i at 253.

Article 71 is to buttress this role of the Chamber, just as would be the rationale underlying the concept of contempt. Another striking parallel would that Article 71 is seen as the principal tool in ensuring non-compliance with orders. This is corroborated by the Chamber's key findings 1 and 2.[438] A seeming counterpart in German law – Section 178 of the Courts Constitution Act – differs crucially. It has no general thrust but is a rather isolated tool for handling disruptions of the proceedings in the courtroom by non-participants. In particular, it does not apply to counsel.[439]

Similar to contempt, the procedure for Article 71 is typically a summary one.[440] This should not be confused with summary disposition for contempt, as distinguished from disposition on notice.[441] The summary character stems from what Rules 170 and 171(1), (5) provide: a warning and a hearing are necessary before the imposition of a sanction but that no separate fact-finding process need take place.

In conclusion, Article 71 is an institutional control that shares some important features of contempt, ie, being a general tool in the hands of the judges, with a punitive and a coercive function. It differs, though, from contempt by being a statutory instrument, endowed to the judges by the ICC legislative, not an enunciation of an inherent judicial power. This it has in common with Section 178 of the Courts Constitution Act in Germany. It is also different from Rule 77 RPE of the ad hoc Tribunals in the regard that the latter only embodies criminal contempt. Article 71 has a punitive element, as a fine can be unconditional. This punitive element sets it apart from civil contempt. Thus, Article 71 encompasses some functions of coercive civil contempt but not compensatory civil contempt.[442] However, Rule 171 RPE requires the deliberate refusal to follow judicial directions. Proving intent would usually not be an element of civil contempt in the United States.[443]

b The Scope of Article 71

An important qualifier in the wording of Article 71 would be that only persons who are present before the Court can thus be sanctioned. A narrow interpretation of this is advanced by Triffterer,[444] as well as presumably by Schabas.[445] Consequently, all of Article 71 would be restricted to sessions of the Court. This effectively reduces its scope to persons while they are physically present, as with Section 178 Courts Constitution Act in Germany. With respect to counsel, it would thus exclude all other acts taking place outside the courtroom as well as

[438] Above, II.C.i at 253.

[439] Ch 2, II.B.iii.a at 74.

[440] Schabas (n 2) 860.

[441] See ch 2, III.C.iii at 148.

[442] See also ch 2, III.C.iii at 147.

[443] JW Hall, *Professional Responsibility in Criminal Defense Practice*, 3rd edn (St Paul, Minn, Thomson/West, 2005) § 33:8, fn 3. For more details, ch 2, III.C.iii at 150.

[444] Triffterer (n 329) art 71, mn 11–12, 19–20.

[445] Schabas (n 2) 859–60.

filings. Such a view has been rejected by the Appeals Chamber's broad understanding of Article 71 as a general sanctioning tool to safeguard a fair and expeditious trial. In the pertinent judgment, Article 71 was held to be applicable and even to be the most appropriate tool to address the OTP's failure to comply with orders in respect of proceedings which definitely were outside the courtroom.[446]

The Appeals Chamber's reasoning does not specifically deal with the presence requirement. It only engages in a rather slim conceptual analysis of Article 71 by emphasising the coercive component under Rule 171(4) RPE.[447] Although this observation quite aptly grasps a crucial point about the concept of Article 71, as shown in the preceding section, the Appeals Chamber leaves undiscussed the single elements. As will be shown below, however, the broad understanding of Article 71 by the Appeals Chamber can be bolstered by way of an comparative and purpose analysis.

In principle, it is quite correct to stress the presence requirement in Article 71; it is clearly a required element and should not be brushed aside too quickly when resorting in particular to Rule 171.[448] However, it constitutes a serious bottleneck in this provision. Under the strictly literal interpretation advocated by Triffterer, and probably by Schabas as well, there would be no vast difference between the scope of Rules 170 and 171. Whereas Rule 170 is aimed at unruly behaviour and the control over the courtroom,[449] the latter would simply address misconduct that cannot be cured by excluding a person from being physically at the place of the court session because it impinges on the legal and not just the factual dimension of what unfolds.[450] Its scope, too, would still be limited to the courtroom.

Much more misconduct is conceivable, though, that can take place out of the Court's sight, and contempt powers have indeed reached beyond the doors of the Court.[451] Violations of protective measures for witnesses or of other confidentiality obligations may happen during a court session, for example, as was the case of Nobilo.[452] The allegations in another case, that of Vujin,[453] show that such occurrences can take place outside the courtroom and that they may relate to pending litigation.[454] Vujin was indicted for contempt on a count of tendering

[446] See above, II.C.i at 252.

[447] *The Prosecutor v Thomas Lubanga Dyilo*, ICC-01/04-01/06-2582 (OA 18), Appeals Chamber, Judgment (n 414) para 59.

[448] Conflicts in interpretation need to be resolved in favour of the Statute. See Art 51(5) of the Statute.

[449] As counterparts, compare Rule 80 ICTY/ICTR RPE; Section 178 of the German Courts Constitution Act.

[450] eg, a witness' refusal to testify, see Rule 65(2) RPE.

[451] As is noted by Schabas (n 2) 860.

[452] Ch 1, II.B.ii.b at 20–22.

[453] Ch 1, II.B.ii.a at 16–19.

[454] From the SCSL, see also the cases of *Independent Counsel v Brima Samura*, SCSL-2005-01, Trial Chamber I, Judgement in Contempt Proceedings, 26 October 2005, paras 54, 77 (disclosing confidential information in the premises but not in the courtroom); *Independent Counsel v Margaret Fomba Brima, Neneh Bah Jalloh, Esther Kamara, Anifa Kamara*, SCSL-2005-02 and SCSL-2005-03, Trial Chamber I, Sentencing Judgement (n 296) paras 23–29 (witness intimidation on the way to the court). See also JP Marx, 'Intimidation of Defense Witnesses at the International Criminal Tribunals: Commentary and Suggested Legal Remedies' (2007) 7 *Chicago Journal of International Law* 675.

false evidence, but also on one of manipulating witnesses in the field. From this perspective, the crucial point would be how far Rule 171 reaches. Fathoming this may be the key to answering the question of how akin to contempt Article 71 really is. Of course, it remains to be seen how the Court will interpret the phrasing of Article 71 when applying Rule 171.[455] This interpretation will determine its relevance, including but not limited to the regulation of counsel. If the Court were to effectively confine it to courtroom behaviour, this would then leave out the bulk of counsel's work.

Interpreting Article 71 and Rule 171 as strictly may not be necessarily warranted. Quite the contrary, good reasons are conceivable for a wider understanding of when persons are present before the Court. The narrow approach to Article 71 could perhaps be justified if this provision had never been intended to reach beyond the courtroom. To conclude so from the sparse materials seems far-fetched.[456] Other arguments tend to support a wider interpretation of presence before the Court and consequently a wider scope of Rule 171.

The section entitled 'Misconduct before the Court' or 'Inconduite à l'audience' can be read as going beyond physical presence. 'Before the court', 'devant la cour', 'audience' and similar expressions are routinely used to describe a state where persons enter into a relationship with the Court and, to that effect, figuratively speaking, go before the Court.[457] Presence before the Court would thus potentially include all persons who conduct acts having a nexus to court proceedings. Functional arguments distinguish when a bench is in session from the time before and after on the one hand, and on the other, extends the scope to onsite visits by judges and to judicial deliberations.[458] It is more coherent to read 'present before the Court' as requiring a current procedural nexus between the Court and the sanctioned person. This nexus can be the physical presence in the courtroom during an ongoing session, as is the case with Rule 170 RPE. It is also created, though, by a judge aiming a direction pursuant to Article 171 at a person who is otherwise interacting with the Court within the framework of its proceedings.

[455] See above (n 448).

[456] The ABA tabled proposals to the Preparatory Commission for the RPE, which would have made Art 71 a fully fledged contempt provision US and ICTY style, to which reference is made explicitly, American Bar Association (Section of International Law and Practice), *Draft Rules of Procedure and Evidence of the International Criminal Court: Parts 7 (Evidence) and 10 (Offences Against the Administration of Justice)* (1 June 1999) at 9–10; American Bar Association (Section of International Law and Practice), *Draft Rules of Procedure and Evidence for the International Criminal Court* (10 February 1999), Rule 35 (Misconduct of Counsel) and Rule 107 (Contempt of the Court). This was not adopted, but Art 71 essentially was the result of a 'compromise . . . achieved rather quickly', Triffterer (n 329) art 71, mn 5.

[457] See ICC Code of Conduct, Art 2; Art 4. In the Code's context of professional ethics, it is undeniable that the term connotes more than just a physical relationship of counsel to the Court and its dealings. See above, II.A.iii.a at 186–90. See also Rule 46(A) ICTY RPE, speaking of 'le bon déroulement de l'audience' and 'entendre ce conseil' in French, whereas the English version uses 'the proper conduct of the proceedings' and 'the proper conduct of the proceedings'. See Rule 46(C.) of the ICTR RPE for 'refusant de l'entendre'/'refusing audience'. All of this shows how 'audience' and similar terms are used interchangeably for a wider scope of the proceedings.

[458] Triffterer (n 329) art 71, mns 11–13, 19–20.

A systematic comparison of Rules 170 and 171 provides further argument for extending the latter in such a fashion. The sanction under Rule 170 is the interdiction to attend physically, whereas Rule 171 speaks of the interdiction of a person from the proceedings in sub-rule (1), and of the interdiction from exercising specific functions in sub-rule (2). Both show that it is the participation in the proceedings at large which is at the core of the sanction, rather than merely excluding someone physically. Further, sub-rule (4) provides that fines can accumulate on a daily basis for continuing misconduct. It is, therefore, not an essential element of Rule 171 misconduct that it is contemporaneous with a currently ongoing session inside the courtroom.

In respect to the purpose of sanctioning misconduct and irrespective of the pertinent criminal offences and the other regulatory mechanisms, Article 71 fits into the overall scheme by providing judges with a tool to respond to misconduct summarily. Reducing it to courtroom occurrences is at odds with the goal of wholly protecting the administration of justice. Giving such powers to judges can be ambivalent because of their involvement in the pertinent incidents, how it affects them and the resulting bias. This is not cured, however, by restricting the applicability of Article 71 to the courtroom. It is ultimately under-inclusive in those regards which really matter. Harmful influences can just as well develop from outside the courtroom, and it may often be the more serious kind of misconduct.

Even when guided by the wording, presence can encompass more than immediate presence, as can be seen from the law of contempt from a comparative view. The presence element is often essential in direct contempt and even then, 'actual presence' is sometimes used. Much more common is a different, wider concept of 'presence', as in contempt 'in the face of the court'. In the United Kingdom, for example, it comprises contempt

> in the courtroom itself (for example, interrupting or interfering with the proceedings); or in the court building where it has been reported to the judge (for example, threatening a witness waiting to give evidence); or beyond the courtroom and the court's precincts, when it is reported to the judge and it relates to proceedings whether in progress or pending (for example, improper approaches to witnesses or jurors).[459]

Similarly, federal law in the United States emphasises that the link with the formal exercise of a judicial function makes contempt direct.[460] The key element here is arguably not physical presence, but whether the judges concerned can observe the contumacious act, and that no formal fact-finding process is needed. This sets 'direct' contempt apart from 'constructive' or 'indirect' contempt.[461] The UN tribunals have not distinguished along these lines but extended the scope of Rule 77 RPE

[459] See Crown Prosecution Service, 'Legal Guidance on Contempt of Court', www.cps.gov.uk/legal/a_to_c/contempt_of_court/#a10.

[460] Executive Office for US Attorneys (ed), *United States Attorneys' Manual, Title 9, Criminal)* Criminal Resource Manual 759.

[461] See ch 2, III.B.iii.a at 31–32, and EC Dudley, 'Getting beyond the Civil/Criminal Distinction: A New Approach to the Regulation of Indirect Contempts' (1993) 79 *Virginia Law Review* 1025, 1030.

to include the latter. They have, for example, cited for contempt foreign journalists publishing confidential information and otherwise endangering the integrity of the criminal process, who were surely far from the tribunal's premises geographically.[462]

In light of this, the scope and character of Article 71 comes out to a general misconduct provision. It is applicable to counsel as a person who is in principle always present before the court when handling a case, including filings. In regard to the non-punitive element of Article 71,[463] it does not in principle need to be construed as strictly mandated as for a criminal provision. The warning requirement under both Rules 170 and 171 will, if handled properly, guarantee a fair notice to counsel. Moreover, Rule 171 requires the deliberate refusal to follow judicial directions.[464]

c Procedure for Article 71

The legal framework on the procedure and the enforcement of sanctions under Article 71 was, owing to compromise, left unregulated in Rome.[465] With the RPE, it is lean indeed but this should be less surprising if we recall the character of Article 71 as an institutional control. Other sanctions do not yet exist since the sanctions are those 'provided for in the Rules of Procedure and Evidence' and the residual clause for 'similar measures' has not been used so far.

Similar to contempt, the procedure is somewhat summary.[466] Rules 170 and 171(1), (5) are quite specific that a person must be warned and heard before a sanction can be imposed. Rule 171(3), ie, prolonged or permanent interdiction from exercising functions, is the only instance where a matter must be referred to an additional hearing by the Presidency. This can be explained by the gravity of that sanction. Generally, though, judges do not enter into a fact-finding process before imposing a sanction. This is in line with the thrust of institutional controls to react swiftly. This does not preclude a more stretched-out procedure if appropriate, as the Appeals Chamber has indicated.[467]

The Statute and the Rules are silent on how sanctions under Article 71 can be reviewed. Allowing an appeal under Article 81 of the Statute similar to criminal convictions would potentially undermine the promise of a rapid sanction because of ensuing satellite litigation. Accordingly, there is fittingly no automatic right to appeal. Similar to US procedure,[468] it is appealable as part of the principal appeal or, if necessary, under Article 82(d) of the Statute as an interlocutory appeal.[469]

[462] See ch 1, II.B.ii at 24.

[463] See Rule 171(4), and above at 258.

[464] Proving intent would usually not be an element of civil contempt in the United States, Hall (n 443) § 33:8, fn 3.

[465] Triffterer (n 329) art 71, mn 37.

[466] See above, II.C.ii.a at 258.

[467] *The Prosecutor v Thomas Lubanga Dyilo*, ICC-01/04-01/06-2582 (OA 18), Appeals Chamber, Judgment (n 414) paras 59–60.

[468] Ch 2, III.C.iii at 149, in particular, n 585.

[469] Gallant (n 142) 477–78 (arguing for a liberal use of the discretionary review powers).

Regarding enforcement, direct measures are less of a problem as they are enforced immediately, such as the expulsion from the courtroom or the interdiction from appearing before the Court. With fines, the uncertainty is the same as exists for fines under Article 70. State parties are not obliged to enforce such fines and non-state parties even less so.[470]

iii Other Measures by Chambers

The foregoing on Article 71 demonstrated how the ICC relies primarily on statutorily entrenched bases, unlike, for example, the broader concept of inherent powers that lies truly at the heart of the concept of contempt in the common law. Even in the civil tradition, though, courts can be said to be vested with a certain base of unwritten powers due to their margin of appreciation in applying the available criminal procedure.[471] Just as their common law counterparts, they employ procedures and measures other than sanctioning to safeguard the judicial process and to address gaps.[472] To some degree, it is known in all jurisdictions and the ICC itself has already taken up the notion of inherent powers.[473] It has already made reference to the concepts of abuse of process or procedure.[474]

Precedents by international courts can be cited from within the practice of the ICTY and ICTR where measures were not provided for but nonetheless adopted as available under the judges' procedural authority.[475] Among those were ordering an apology and compensation for the violation of accused's rights,[476] cessation orders,[477] plea-bargaining,[478] appellate review[479] and broad powers to assign counsel.[480] These powers can be summarised along the lines of 'regulating proceedings and preventing abuse of process', 'controlling and supervising officers of the court' and 'supervising inferior courts'.[481] Although a statutory power, Rule 46 RPE, and with it the possibility of withholding fees, is recalled.[482]

[470] See M Bohlander, 'International Criminal Defence Ethics: The Law of Professional Conduct for Defence Counsel Appearing before International Criminal Tribunals' (2000) 1 *San Diego International Law Journal* 75, 88; Cockayne (n 427) 200. See also ch 4, II.B at 297–98.

[471] Above, II.C.i at 255.

[472] Cockayne (n 427) 199–200.

[473] On the *Lubanga* case: n 488.

[474] See on abuse of process before the ICC, Schabas (n 283) art 67, mn 59.

[475] Symons (n 429) 376.

[476] *André Rwamakuba v Prosecutor*, ICTR-98-44C-A, Appeals Chamber, Decision on Appeal against Decision on Appropriate Remedy, 13 September 2007, para 24 (and with a Partly Dissenting Opinion of Judge Shahabuddeen).

[477] See ch 1, n 108.

[478] See GP Lombardi, 'Legitimacy and the Expanding Power of the ICTY' (2003) 37 *New England Law Review* 887, 898.

[479] *Prosecutor v Duško Tadić*, IT-94-1-AR72, Appeals Chamber, Decision on the Defence Motion for Interlocutory Appeal on Jurisdiction, 2 October 1995, para 18.

[480] See *Prosecutor v Pauline Nyiramasuhuko and Arsène Ntahobali*, ICTR-97-21-T, Decision on Ntahobali's Motion for Withdrawal of Counsel, 22 June 2001, para 20.

[481] Symons (n 429), 401.

[482] See ch 1, II.A at 11, III.A and B.iii at 37, 41–42.

The ICC has already seen a fee dispute, concerning counsel Hadi Shalluf in the *Situation in Darfur*. The Registry refused to pay fees because, in its view, counsel had not acted within the prescribed mandate under Rule 103 RPE. As it was the Registry itself rather than the Chamber, it can be said to pertain to the Registry's competence.[483] It needs to be stressed, however, that the Pre-Trial Chamber affirmed the Registry's denial. It assessed the 'filings of the *ad hoc* Counsel . . . frivolous and vexatious' and considered them 'an abuse of procedure'.[484] This is exactly what underlies the fee denial at the UN tribunals. It only leaves the question whether fee denial could be imposed originally by a Chamber. None of the legal instruments of the Court provides for the possibility of specifically withholding fees.

From a general perspective, it seems conceivable to be able to address the underlying issue of frivolous litigation through Article 71, albeit not with fee denial as the sanction. As argued above, Article 71(1) contains two elements. The first is the commission of misconduct as the central element. A wide notion of misconduct underlies the nature of Article 71.[485] The wording does not pose an obstacle as counsel who engages in frivolous litigation can be said to 'commit misconduct'. Secondly, Article 71 requires some form of presence before the Court. Filings would meet the presence requirement and therefore be within the scope of Article 71.[486] As a consequence, a fine can be imposed by the Court if, pursuant to Article 71 (2), the procedure under Rule 171 RPE is met. Rule 171(1) RPE requires for a fine first a warning by the Chamber, a deliberate refusal and another hearing. This appears to rule out a summary fee denial similar to what happened before the ICTR. Moreover, the priority of Article 71 to achieve control over proceedings would have to be considered.[487] The Appeals Chamber has hailed compliance with court orders as the centerpiece of a fair trial – in the interest of all participants. In consequence, any Chamber would presumably have to give directions and use Article 71 before imposing other sanctions on the basis of inherent powers.

The ICC has furthermore resorted to the concept of abuse of process in the *Lubanga* case for stays of proceedings.[488] These stays were ordered for prosecution

[483] See below, II.C.iv.c at 268.

[484] *Situation in Darfur*, ICC-02/05-60, Registry, Réponse du Greffier au 'Recours à l'encontre de la décision du Greffe du 13 février 2007' déposé le 27 février 2007 par Me. Hadi Shalluf, 6 March 2007, at 7, with paras 19 and 20

[485] See above, II.C.ii.a at 256–58.

[486] See above, II.C.ii.b at 258–62.

[487] Above, II.C.i at 253.

[488] The first stay dates back to 2006 (see *The Prosecutor v Thomas Lubanga Dyilo*, ICC-01/04-01/06-772, Appeals Chamber, Judgment on the Appeal of Mr Thomas Lubanga Dyilo against the Decision on the Defence Challenge to the Jurisdiction of the Court pursuant to article 19 (2) (a) of the Statute of 3 October 2006, 14 December 2006, paras 36, 39), repeating in 2008 (*The Prosecutor v Thomas Lubanga Dyilo*, ICC-01/04-01/06-1486 (OA 13), Appeals Chamber, Judgment on the appeal (n 415) paras 74–100, with Separate Opinion by Judge Pikis). The year 2010 witnessed a new edition of this (*The Prosecutor v Thomas Lubanga Dyilo*, ICC-01/04-01/06-2582 (OA 18), Appeals Chamber, Judgment (n 414) and *The Prosecutor v Thomas Lubanga Dyilo*, ICC-01/04-01/06-2583 (OA 17), Appeals Chamber, Judgment on the appeal of Prosecutor against the oral decision of Trial Chamber I of 15 July 2010 to release Thomas Lubanga Dyilo, 8 October 2010, paras 22–25.

misconduct, ie, chiefly not disclosing exculpatory material to the defence and on the prosecution's use of intermediaries. Although the stays were later reversed, the *Lubanga* case entrenches the abuse of process doctrine in the ICC's jurisprudence.

Misconduct may therefore result in curtailing procedural rights of the defence, by claiming unwritten powers but also by using one of the above categories. The abuse of trial powers may lead to a forfeiture of the right to, for example, tender evidence.[489] Within the context of Article 71 and a stay of proceedings in *Lubanga*, the Appeals Chamber puts forward some material arguments for according priority to a statutory tool, at least concerning the said stay of proceedings) The interests of all affected do not only comprise the interest of the public, ie, that of international community, in the outcome of the case, but include those of the accused and the victims:

> 60. Recourse to sanctions enables a Trial Chamber, using the tools available within the trial process itself, to cure the underlying obstacles to a fair trial, thereby allowing the trial to proceed speedily to a conclusion on its merits. Doing so, rather than resorting to the significantly more drastic remedy of a stay of proceedings, is in the interests, not only of the victims and of the international community as a whole who wish to see justice done, but also of the accused, who is potentially left in limbo, awaiting a decision on the merits of the case against him by the International Criminal Court or another court. Accordingly, the Appeals Chamber finds that, to the extent possible, a Trial Chamber faced with a deliberate refusal of a party to comply with its orders which threatens the fairness of the trial should seek to bring about that party's compliance through the imposition of sanctions under article 71 before resorting to imposition of a stay of proceedings.
> 61. [B]efore ordering the stay of proceedings, the Trial Chamber should have imposed sanctions and given such sanctions a reasonable time to bring about their intended effects.[490]

In short, the participants in proceedings hold reasonable expectations that the case is resolved on the merits rather than on procedural considerations. Furthermore, procedural measures must be proportional. In passing, the Appeals Chamber also touches on the point of how curtailing procedural rights of the defence can be balanced against the rights of the accused to effective legal representation and assistance.[491]

[489] See also Art 69(7)(b). From the ICTY case law, see ch 1, II.B.iii at 25 (n 111), on an order by an ICTY trial chamber regarding the organisation of the proceedings in the *Šešelj* case. For Germany, see ch1, IIB.iii.a at 76, on setting deadlines for the presentation of evidence.

[490] See *The Prosecutor v Thomas Lubanga Dyilo*, ICC-01/04-01/06-2582 (OA 18), Appeals Chamber, Judgment (n 414) paras 47, 59–61. See also below, III.A at 275.

[491] See in more detail below, IV at 279–83.

iv Registry Measures against Misconduct

a Admission of Counsel

Under the ICTY and ICTR framework, the Registries also have a task in the regulation of counsel. They exercise control over the entry to the Bar of the Tribunals and thus powers under 'soft law'.[492] Similarly, the ICC Registrar also has powers to address counsel misconduct.[493]

The Registry first plays a crucial role in the process of counsel being admitted to practise before the Court in first place.[494] Secondly, assignment to a specific case will in practice be crucial in determining whether and how counsel will be able to act before the Court. Both issues, including the one of assignment, have tended to become an important domain of the Registries.[495] However, it is prone to doubt whether the Registrar can base measures on 'disciplinary factors'.[496]

Regulation 67 RoC sets out the 'Criteria to be met by counsel'. One of these criteria would be that counsel has not been convicted of a 'serious criminal or disciplinary offence considered being incompatible with the nature of the office of counsel before the Court'. This offers some latitude to define the exact requirements, which is the original task of the Registry, as Regulations 69 and 70(2) illustrate. The Registry has less discretion once counsel has made it to the list, as can be seen from Regulation 71 on the 'Removal and suspension from the list of counsel'. In most of these scenarios, the Registry implements decisions by other bodies of the Court, such as convictions by Chambers or by the Disciplinary Boards. The criteria for initial inclusion reflect, however, again in sub-regulation (1)(a). It appears that there is some discretion under (a), but reinstatement should follow once counsel proves that he or she meets the criteria again. This makes the removal by the Registry a somewhat administrative measure.

Any of these decisions by the Registry are subject to review by the Presidency under Regulation 72 which reins in the powers of the Registry somewhat. It is, though, an entry control rather than a tool for pending proceedings. In this context, it is not quite clear what the scope of a review of the removal by the Registry is if it follows under Regulation 71(1) or (2). It seems to be of an executing nature only. The Presidency should consequently not interfere with the original decision of Chambers or disciplinary bodies to disbar or suspend counsel. Another related problem exists if the removal concerns a permanent interdiction under Article 71 of the Statute and Rule 171(3) of the RPE (see Regulation 71(1)(d) RoC). Here, the interdiction as such has been handed down by the Presidency, which now is

[492] McMorrow (n 30) 166.

[493] Tuinstra (n 55) 81–82.

[494] Generally on the competence and qualifications of counsels, see ibid, 38–49. See also S Starr, 'Ensuring Defense Counsel Competence at International Criminal Tribunals' (2009) 14 *University of California at Los Angeles Journal of International Law and Foreign Affairs* 169.

[495] See Dixon and Khan (n 179) §§ 20–77 to 81.

[496] Schabas (n 283) art 67, mn 31.

supposed to review itself. A sensible solution would be that the review of the Presidency under Regulation 72 usually only extends to how the removal was executed but cannot reverse the principal decision as the basis for the removal. A material review makes sense, though, for a refusal of inclusion in the list under Regulation 70 RoC, ie, review under Regulation 72(1)(a) RoC.

b Appointment of Counsel

Section 2 appears more relevant for running trials, but it is again primarily the Chambers of the Court deciding on the fate of counsel. Under Regulation 76, the Registry will be consulted before counsel is appointed. The ultimate decisions is with the Chamber, though, as is the case for allowing counsel to withdraw under Regulation 78.[497] The ICC has held already in its early case law that the right to representation by a lawyer and to choose one's counsel is not absolute and that it is subject to limitations.[498] In this context, it seems worthwhile to draw attention to the assignment of legal assistance under the Rules and the Regulations. It is effectively the Registry ruling on the issue of indigence as well as authorising payments to counsel under the Court's legal aid framework. Review is guaranteed by the Presidency for the refusal of the assignment of counsel (Rule 21(3) RPE).[499]

c The Scope of Legal Assistance and Fee Issues

Disputes may also arise over the scope of the legal assistance by the Court (Regulations 83(4) and 85(5) RoC) and over specific fee payments (Regulation 135 RoR).[500] For those, judicial review is effectuated by the pertinent Chamber. Nonetheless, the Registry is an actor in reacting to counsel conduct through this avenue. It is noted that the non-payment of fees has garnered quite some popularity in particular with the ICTY when reacting to counsel misconduct linked to actual litigation.[501] In cases of fee denials under Rules 73(D) and 73(F) of the ICTY and the ICTR RPE, respectively, fees are withheld by the Registry on a finding of frivolousness by a Chamber. Under Regulations 133–35 RoR, it is conceivable that the ICC Registry may deny fees on its own initiative.

[497] See Tuinstra (n 55) 49–52 on the ICTY's and the ICTR's efforts to deal with incomepetent representation.

[498] *The Prosecutor v Thomas Lubanga Dyilo*, ICC-01/04-01/06-931, Presidency, Decision on the 'Demande urgente en vertu de la Règle 21-3 du Règlement de procédure et de preuve' and on the 'Urgent Request for the Appointment of a Duty Counsel' filed by Thomas Lubanga Dyilo before the Presidency on 7 May 2007 and 10 May 2007, respectively, 29 June 2007, para 25, fn 26, with references to the pertinent case law of the ICTR, the ICTY and the ECHR. See also Tuinstra (n 55) 32–33, 52–64.

[499] See *The Prosecutor v Joseph Kony et al*, ICC-02/04-01/05-378, Presidency (n 230).

[500] On counsel remuneration by the international courts, see Tuinstra (n 55) 33–38.

[501] Ch 1, III.B.iii at 41, for the ICTR's case law.

The *Shalluf* case may have given a foretaste of this.[502] Hadi Shalluf was appointed ad hoc counsel for the purpose of representing and protecting the general interests of the defence in the Situation in Darfur, Sudan, during the proceedings pursuant to Rule 103 RPE.[503] When he claimed fees for certain work, the Registry refused them as unlinked to counsel's mandate.[504] Counsel then moved to the Pre-Trial Chamber to have this decision reviewed. The Registry contended that there was no fee dispute in the first place since any work outside the mandate was simply not remunerable. Accordingly, it had not acted under Regulation 135.[505] As to the formal argument of the existence of a Regulation 135 decision, the Pre-Trial Chamber correctly pointed out that the Registrar had at least through his response of 6 March 2007 taken a decision on the payment of fees. In substance, however, the Chamber sided with the Registry. It first dismissed counsel's motion to review the Registry decision to not pay fees for December 2006 to February 2007 by holding the 'legal scope of the mandate of the ad hoc Counsel as being strictly limited' and described counsel's filings as 'vexatious and frivolous claims'.[506] This was reiterated on the second review decision for the November 2006 fees.[507] Eventually, the Chamber held the fee denial to constitute primarily a administrative decision by the Registrar. It refused leave to appeal because 'counsel did not bring any elements showing to which extent the issue of the payment of his fees of November 2006 would significantly affect the fair and expeditious conduct of the proceedings or the outcome of a trial'.[508]

The possibility of judicial review via Regulation 135 RoR is an improvement over fee denial as applied by the ICTR. Nonetheless, the Registry's and the Chamber's reasoning is problematic; instead of giving prior guidance to counsel, a sanction was imposed. Counsel is faced with the duty to discharge of his responsibilities on the one hand and grappling with overstepping the unclear mandate on the other, without a possibility of clarifying the contours.[509] This approach by the Registry and Chamber harbours a significant potential to undermine professional judgement of how to conduct the defence. This problem has surfaced in other contexts where permissible zealous defence needs to be delineated from impermissible abuse. The German case of *Zündel* is instructive in this regard.[510] In

[502] Tuinstra (n 55) 239–41. For fee-denial by the ICTY and ICTR, see the references above n 482.

[503] *Situation in Darfur, Sudan*, ICC-02/05-10, Pre-Trial Chamber I, Decision Inviting Observations in Application of Rule 103 of the Rules of Procedure and Evidence, 24 July 2006.

[504] *Situation in Darfur*, ICC-02/05-60, Registry, Réponse du Greffier au 'Recours à l'encontre de la décision du Greffe du 13 février 2007' déposé le 27 février 2007 par Me. Hadi Shalluf, 6 March 2007, Annex 1 (letter of 24 January 2007) and Annex 3 (letter of 13 February 2007).

[505] ibid, paras 15–17, and Annex 3 (the letter to counsel of 13 February 2007).

[506] *Situation in Darfur, Sudan*, ICC-02/05-66, Pre-Trial Chamber I, Decision on the Request for Review of the Registry's decision of 13 February 2007, 15 March 2007, at 6–7.

[507] *Situation in Darfur, Sudan*, ICC-02/05-100, Pre-Trial Chamber I, Decision on the Request for Review Pursuant to Regulation 135(2) of the Regulations of the Registry Submitted by the Former Ad hoc Counsel for the Defence on 27 July 2007, 18 September 2007.

[508] *Situation in Darfur, Sudan*, ICC-02/05-109, Pre-Trial Chamber I, Decision on the Request for Leave to Appeal to the Decision Issued on 23 September 2007, 31 October 2007.

[509] See below at 270, on Jens Dieckmann, ad hoc counsel for the defence in the *Situation in Uganda*.

[510] Ch 2, II.E.ii at 102–05.

short, the reasoning of the Karlsruhe Higher Regional Court deserves laudable mention: it showed due concern not to encroach on determining the appropriate defence strategy, but to rather anchor the misconduct by counsel in the non-compliance with court orders. This seems preferable as it helps in safeguarding the function of the defence by delineating the bounds of the permissible and not overdeterring permissible defence conduct in first place.[511] Institutional actors should use the primary procedural tools by issuing orders and if those are not complied with, subsequent sanctions become appropriate.

d Disciplinary Authority of the Registrar

The Registry does not have a general competence to sanction misconduct of participants. It has been seen so far that most measures by the Registry chiefly execute judicial decisions from within the ICC framework. In this, the Registrar does not hold truly autonomous disciplining powers.[512] Furthermore, this becomes apparent from Regulation 9 RoR, under which the onus is on the Registrar to inform the handling Chamber, which will then take the necessary steps.

Thus, the Registry holds a secondary role in reacting to instances of non-compliance, leaving the primary responsibility to the Chambers of the Court. This is a tribute to the Registry's neutral role. On the other hand, the Registry is the organ responsible for running the administration of the Court and will be directly confronted with counsel misconduct in this respect. In spite of formal powers, the Registry will arguably develop policies and be in a position to implement them in one way or another. Issuing internal guidelines governing, for example, admission to the list and the actual assignment of counsel or remuneration comes to mind. For all of this, mechanisms of judicial review are in place, however. Quite laudably, this removes some of the uncertainties under the ICTY's and the ICTR's regime[513] and brings them in conformity with basic due process under administrative law.[514]

v *General Ethics Advice*

More generally, the Registry can act in its role as a neutral adviser when it comes to professional standards and ethics issues. It was also contemplated at one point anchoring such tasks in the RPE, with the establishment of a defence unit,

[511] See below, IV at 281–82.

[512] Save the disciplinary regime o over detainees (Regulations 207–12 RoR).

[513] C Rohde, 'Are Administrative Decisions from the Registry Appealable?' in R May et al (eds), *Essays on ICTY Procedure and Evidence in Honour of Gabrielle Kirk McDonald* (The Hague, Kluwer, 2001) 509–29.

[514] Hazard and Beard (n 81) 1062.

under the auspices of the Registry but independent in content matter.[515] In the meantime, counsel Jens Dieckmann has pointed to the need for counsel to achieve clarity on professional obligations. He was appointed as ad hoc counsel 'to represent persons under arrest warrants' in the case of *The Prosecutor v Joseph Kony et al* within the *Situation in Uganda*.[516] The Presidency has explicitly requested the Registry to look into the issue as it found that no professional ethics committee or the like existed under the ICC framework.[517] In that, the Presidency drew particular attention to Rules 16 and 20 RPE.

The Trial Chamber and the Appeals Chamber[518] failed to shed further light on mechanisms to settle issues of professional ethics, though. What is more, the Appeals Chamber even created more potential for ethics dilemmas by holding that

> [t]he mandate of 'counsel to attend and represent the interests of the defence' is of a *sui generis nature* and must be understood differently from the mandate of counsel who has been appointed to represent suspects as individuals. In circumstances where the suspects are at large and counsel is appointed to represent their interests generally in proceedings, such counsel cannot speak on their behalf. A client and counsel relationship does not exist between them, and counsel does not act for or as agent of the suspects. Counsel's mandate is limited to merely assuming the defence perspective, with a view to safeguarding the interests of the suspects in so far as counsel can, in the circumstances, identify them. The provisions of the Code of Conduct regarding representation are therefore not directly applicable to such counsel.[519]

What flows from this for professional ethics? Since the Registry is indeed vested with broad responsibilities towards counsel – in particular in the area of professional regulation – it makes sense that counsel turns to the Registry. In addition to Rules 16 and 20 RPE, mentioned above, quite specific provisions can even be

[515] Preparatory Commission for the ICC, *Proposal submitted by Canada, France, Germany and the Netherlands in connection with article 43 of the Rome Statute of the International Criminal Court concerning the Rules of Procedure and Evidence as regards document PCNICC/1999/DP.1* (PCNICC/1999/WGRPE(4)/DP.2, 6 August 1999), providing for the establishment of a separate defence unit, but then again allotted to the Registrar in Rev 1.

[516] For the wider context, see the main string of proceedings, ie, the Pre-Trial Chamber's decision on the admissibility challenge by the defence, which also deals with the mandate of *ad hoc* counsel for the defence and potential conflicts of interest for him, *The Prosecutor v Joseph Kony et al*, ICC-02/04-01/05-377, Pre-Trial Chamber II, Decision (n 410) paras 30–32. Meanwhile, this decision has been upheld on appeal, *The Prosecutor v Joseph Kony et al*, ICC-02/04-01/05-408, Appeals Chamber, Judgment on the appeal of the Defence against the 'Decision on the admissibility of the case under article 19 (1) of the Statute' of 10 March 2009, 16 September 2009. The appeals decision again elaborates on, inter alia, the role of *ad hoc* counsel (*The Prosecutor v Joseph Kony et al*, ICC-02/04-01/05-408, Appeals Chamber, Judgment on the appeal (n 516) paras 52–62) and the scope of representation, ibid, paras 53–68). For his own account, see J Dieckmann and C Kerll, 'Representing the "General Interests of the Defence": Boon or Bane? – A Stocktaking of the System of *ad hoc* Counsel at the ICC' (2011) 11 *International Criminal Law Review* 105.

[517] *The Prosecutor v Joseph Kony et al*, ICC-02/04-01/05-378, Presidency (n 230) para 33. See also above, II.A.v.c at 215.

[518] See above (n 516).

[519] *The Prosecutor v Joseph Kony et al*, ICC-02/04-01/05-408, Appeals Chamber, Judgment on the appeal (n 516) para 56.

found in the RoC – namely Regulations 77 and 81 – on which these responsibilities can easily be based.[520] Moreover, the Advisory Committee on Legal Texts comes to mind.[521] Instead of requesting the Registry to enquire into the matter, the Presidency could also have turned to the Advisory Committee, as it could task this Committee with ethics questions on an ad hoc basis. Furthermore, any Chamber, arguably including the Presidency, can file a case with the ICC disciplinary bodies. This is what should have been done, in view of the absence of the possibility for counsel to launch a self-purging procedure.[522]

The Appeals Chamber in some way did settle the concrete ethics issue by declaring the pertinent provisions of the Code not 'directly applicable' to counsel Dieckmann. This should suffice to approve his conduct and shield him from disciplinary consequences. From a more general perspective, it sadly leaves open many questions. If the provisions are not directly applicable to counsel, could they become indirectly applicable in other scenarios? What would be those constellations? Which provisions do apply to ad hoc counsels for the defence, and which do not? How will counsel know? What is the way to find out? Arguably all of this can be ameliorated by fleshing out a clear mechanism on gathering preventive ethics advice, as outlined in the foregoing.

In the aftermath, a working paper has been provided by the Registry, in response to the Presidency's request.[523] It considers four mechanisms: (1) enlarging the mandate of the Commissioner responsible for investigating complaints of misconduct; (2) appointment of one or several former elected members of the disciplinary organs or commissioners; (3) appointment of advisers solely from those admitted to the List of Counsel; and (4) appointment of advisers from among individuals proposed by Counsel on the List and by associations of lawyers.

Whereas all of these options seem more or less suitable for the purpose of rendering preventive ethics advice, it is submitted that none of them is fully persuasive. Tasking the disciplinary boards provided for by the ICC Code promises a more efficient solution.

Option 1 has merit in making use of the existing disciplinary system and the attaching structures and expertise. However, the working paper identifies disadvantages of the advisory role of the Commissioner, in particular harbouring the potential for conflict if the Commissioner investigates later.[524] Moreover, structural amendments to the Code's procedures would be necessary.

The need for amendments would also result from option 2. On the one hand, setting up an ethics committee from former members would build on synergies

[520] See sub-regulation (5) of Regulation 77 RoC, and the similar provision in Regulation 81(4)(a) and (b) for counsels for victims.

[521] See Regulation 4 RoC, with sub-regulation (4). On the Advisory Panels of the ICTY and the ICTR see Tuinstra (n 55) 87–88.

[522] Above, II.A.v.c at 215.

[523] ICC, *Working document on potential mechanisms that can furnish advice to counsel on professional ethics* (May 2010) paras 9–20. See also International Criminal Bar, *Newsletter* (June 2010) 11.

[524] ICC, *Working document* (n 523) paras 11–12.

with the existing structures,[525] but on the other, it would still come out as a double structure.

The peer system envisaged under option 3 raises serious doubts, as acknowledged by the working paper itself: counsel would have to confront colleagues with ethical problems, without a non-defence counsel perspective.[526] Again, another clear disadvantage would be the creation of an additional and thus a double structure.

Option 4 suggests a panel of external advisers. It may indeed bring in experts on professional ethics from a broader background than the Court.[527] However, this seems unnecessary as the existing members of the ICC disciplinary scheme already have the required competence, and eventually the result would again only be double structures.

As discussed before the most sensible proposal could therefore be a self-purging procedure for counsel, not available yet under the triggering scheme of Article 34 of the Code.[528] Such a self-purging procedure could be introduced simply by granting the right to file a complaint to counsel, by adding (d), 'Counsel him or herself' to paragraph (1). (As consequential revision, 'Filing a complaint of misconduct' etc could be rephrased into 'Filing a case of misconduct'.) This would bring the issue before the disciplinary bodies, just like any allegations of professional misconduct under the Code. This would make optimal use of the existing and competent structures of the ICC disciplinary scheme. Furthermore, the preliminary procedure would also draw on the expertise of the Commissioner. Conflicts of interests will not as easily materialise for the members of the disciplinary boards as for the Commissioner. Unlike the Commissioner, they would not act in an advisory capacity first and as a prosecutor later, but as a ruling authority throughout. Prior ethics advice would, of course, bind the Boards later in their judicial function. Moreover, both the Disciplinary Boards as well as the Disciplinary Appeals Board can resort to their alternate members if necessary. Lastly, it could be contemplated that the Appeals Board could directly hear a case of self-purging which would prevent exclusive peer control by defence counsel and employ a broader participatory base.

D Liability Controls: Individual Action against Misconduct

In some cases, misconduct of counsel acting before the ICC may directly affect clients or other individuals. Some may then wish to bring action against counsel for breach of professional duties. This can be achieved under national laws governing the relationship between the lawyer and the client. Effectively, clients will sue in contract or tort (or similar contractual or non-contractual concepts). In

525 ibid, paras 14–15.
526 ibid, para 18.
527 ibid, paras 19–20.
528 Above, II.A.v.c at 215.

some settings – and in particular for certain classes of clients – holding lawyers thus liable is a viable option.[529] Most importantly, it allows affected individuals to recover damages. Liability controls therefore make it possible to pursue individual needs under a readily available routine procedure.

As has been seen above, the significance and the efficacy of civil claims depends on several factors.[530] In particular in the criminal context, civil lawsuits are only likely to succeed to a fairly limited degree. The sustained loss and causation are specific elements that need to be proven by the plaintiff. Moreover, lawyers benefit from a certain margin of professional discretion. All of this should substantially lower the expectations when it comes to liability controls to generally set and enforce professional standards for the ICC. They may nonetheless be useful in particular cases, such as those involving financial irregularities to the client's detriment. In conclusion, liability controls should not be seen as market shaping or as a tool available to the Court as are the others. It would be wrong, however, to discard them entirely.

A general civil jurisdiction is unknown to the ICC's legal framework. Injured individuals can file complaints pursuant to Article 34(1)(c) of the ICC Code's disciplinary scheme, but the Code does not provide for material or immaterial recovery.[531] Article 85 and Rules 173–75 RPE only award compensation for wrongful acts by the ICC – such as arrests, detention, convictions or acquittals.[532] In theory, Article 70 convictions may yield reparations but presume that the misconduct is criminal. Furthermore, it will then be the Office of the Prosecutor and not the concerned individual who enforces these controls. On the whole, it is safe to say that the ICC's regulatory scheme does not contain liability controls.

Unless the Court adopts unlikely compensatory authority based on inherent powers,[533] plaintiffs will accordingly have to file suits before national courts. Which national forum to choose will be decide on a case-by-case basis and cannot be analysed in depth here.[534] There may exist explicit forum agreements between the client and the lawyer, which would then be the prime guiding factor. Usually, this will result in the laws of the jurisdiction where the lawyer and client come from or reside, where they conclude the representation agreement, or that of the place where the services are performed or a wrongful act has been committed. Given that the the seat of the ICC is in the Netherlands, legal action may often lead to Dutch courts and Dutch law.[535]

[529] Wilkins (n 252) 806.

[530] See ch 2, II.B.i at 84–85, for Germany, and III.B.iv at 135–41, for the United States.

[531] Above, II.A.vi at 140.

[532] Staker (n 308) art 85, in particular margin notes 6–8.

[533] See above, II.C.iii at 263.

[534] See ch 2, III.B.iv at 263, for the United States, and for Germany, R Zuck, 'Internationales Anwaltsrecht' (1987) *Neue Juristische Wochenschrift* 3033, 2033, and the statutory provisions of German private international law in the *Einführungsgesetz zum Bürgerlichen Gesetzbuch* (Introductory Act to the Civil Code, in particular Arts 27, 28(2), 40).

[535] See above, II.A.iii.c at 192, and ch 4, II.C at 299–300, on the immunity of counsel under the Agreement on the Privileges and Immunities and the Headquarters Agreement, which would need to be waived by the Presidency.

E Self-governing Professional Bodies

In addition to the legal framework of the ICC itself, counsel may be subject to rules set by international professional bodies, in particular Bar associations or associations equivalent to national Bars. Membership of those associations may be on a voluntary basis; sometimes it is a requisite before being admitted to act before a court, as it is the case for the ICTY.[536] Other organisations such as the International Criminal Bar (ICB) do not have such a mandatory membership base. However, they serve as dialogue partners in the development of the ICC regime and bind their members to their own standards.[537]

It is acknowledged that professional bodies can certainly contribute to the regulation of counsel as far as the concept as a whole is concerned. They are furthermore a central element of self-governance, thus vital to the underlying, often-cited creed of the independence of the lawyer as a free profession.[538] To the extent that they are not formally incorporated into the ICC's regime, however, they do this as private actors.[539] From the Court's perspective, their activities therefore represent informal and sometimes non-legal regulation.[540] This is, of course, notwithstanding that the pertinent professional bodies and their actitivies may fall under specific jurisdictions. Those are not part of the ICC's original legal framework, though; rather they are on the national level.[541]

It can be concluded that self-governing professional bodies cannot issue binding acts. As a matter of substance, Article 4 of the ICC Code would in effect trump other rulemaking bodies,[542] be they national or international, self-governing or not and not exercising direct regulation.

III A Comparison and Analysis of the Various Measures

A The Available Measures and their Scope with regard to Counsel Misconduct

It has emerged from the previous chapters how proceedings against counsel depend on the nature of the alleged misconduct as well as the persons and institu-

[536] See ch 1, II.B.v at 28.

[537] International Criminal Bar, *Code of Conduct and Disciplinary Procedure* (Sub-committee on Ethics, 2003). See also International Criminal Bar, *Constitution* (June 2008).

[538] Tuinstra (n 55) 88–100.

[539] Two examples where counsel are formally involved would be as members of the Board and the Appeals Board in the ICC disciplinary procedure (see Arts 36 and 44 of the ICC Code) and the Advisory Committee for Legal Texts (above II.A.v.c at 213).

[540] On informal and non-legal regulation, see Introduction, II at 3.

[541] See International Criminal Bar, *Constitution* (June 2008) Art 2.

[542] Above, II.A.iii.c at 191–92, and ch 4, I.B at 287–89.

tions concerned. The measures within the ICC's legal framework are in essence those which also exist in the other jurisdictions under scrutiny. The ICC features a special set of professional rules aimed at the private attorneys appearing before it. Its Statute also prescribes criminal offences. In the other jurisdictions, these two offer the most drastic sanctions for the gravest examples. In day-to-day business, though, discipline in the broader sense rests on other pillars as well, all of which can be found in the ICC's framework.

Measures belonging to three out of the four conceivable enforcement controls can be found in the ICC's regime, all of which can fulfil their own specific purposes:[543] the disciplinary procedure under the ICC Code as a means of professional discipline *stricto sensu*; criminal prosecutions under Article 70 of the Statute with its basis in a quasi-legislative act; and non-criminal sanctions under Article 71 along with a wide array of conceivable procedural measures which are directly triggered by those court organs witnessing misconduct.

Liability controls are the only type of responses clearly missing from the ICC framework, but this should not come as a great surprise. The other international criminal courts are not equipped with civil jurisdiction either and several reasons are likely for this. First, they are after all criminal courts which focus on criminal trials. Apart from that, they are simply not entrenched in a similarly comprehensive jurisdiction as their national counterparts. Even on the national level, malpractice claims are understood as civil litigation and are accordingly handled by civil courts. In consequence, it does not constitute an oddity that malpractice claims may have to be filed in such national civil jurisdictions. Moreover, civil malpractice has tended to play a considerably lesser role in creating norms for attorney conduct, due to factors which carry even more weight in international criminal cases.[544] The conclusion would be that liability controls are effectively irrelevant.

As far as measures by Chambers are concerned, they extend to cover whatever is imaginable in terms of the Court's procedure.[545] It is therefore impossible to sketch out fully what is available as a sanctioning measure. It seems important, though, to stress that national courts have made ample use of sanctions available to them under their procedures, starting with formalised sanctions like contempt and other such measures,[546] but extending to general concepts such as abuse of process and the law of evidence.[547] In some way, the ICC might already have picked up on the latter when threatening a stay of proceedings in the *Lubanga* case when the OTP failed to disclose crucial evidence.[548] This may be turned against counsel, too, by restricting defence evidence or otherwise curtailing defence rights.

[543] See Wilkins (n 252) 812, 819–20, 847–48.

[544] See ch 2, I.B.iv at 84–85, and III.B.iv at 139–41.

[545] On the open-endedness of procedural measures, G Bitti in O Triffterer (ed), *Commentary on the Rome Statute of the International Criminal Court* 2nd edn (Munich, Beck, 2008) art 64, mns 1 and 7.

[546] See ch 2, III.B.iii.a at 130–33.

[547] See ch 2, II.B.iii.a at 75–79, III.B.iii.b at 134.

[548] Above, II.C.iv at 264 (n 488).

Given the Appeals Chamber's stance in the judgment of 8 October 2010, the threshold for resorting to unwritten inherent powers is rather high, and the latter are consequently limited. The Chamber's approach featured in the judgment builds on two elements: the significance of statutory authorisation and priority of statutory law over inherent powers.[549] The standard for invoking inherent powers therefore seems to be that the specifically included procedural instruments under the Statute and the RPE have been used to no avail, that the integrity of the process is damaged and cannot be vindicated otherwise, or to use the words of the Appeals Chamber, that a loss of control of the proceedings has taken place and that, consequently, a fair trial has become impossible.[550] The Appeals Chamber expressly emphasised that foremost reliance on Article 71 is in the interests of all those affected, ie, the international community, also including accused and victims.

It has been repeatedly pointed out that the ICC's disciplinary system is quite sophisticated. As with other regimes of professional discipline, it aims to comprehensively cover and regulate the conduct of counsel.[551] It covers all facets of counsel's activities. Moreover, it is not limited as far as the exact setting of misconduct is concerned. Misconduct in private capacity may also be addressed.[552] A crucial difference between criminal convictions and discipline is that the latter is not bound to limitations of strict constructions and wider concerns as is the criminal law. Owing to the international setup, it remains debatable for a number of scenarios whether the Code will be applicable in terms of personal jurisdiction.[553] Apart from these fringe issues, this sub-regime's scope seems exhaustive. The obstacles in sanctioning misconduct by counsel will rather be rooted in the general weaknesses of professional discipline.[554]

On the other hand, it reflects clearly from the ICC's criminal provisions that the scope may be considerably narrower for other kinds of controls. Article 70 is not specifically tailored towards counsel or towards acts which they commit in their professional capacity. Of course, some of the offences pertain closely to the criminal trial. As has been shown in the analysis of Article 70, 'presenting false evidence' (para (1)(d)), or 'influencing a witness' (para (1)(c)), would constitute such examples. In general, however, none of the offences attaches directly to the status of counsel. With regard to the criminal acts, Article 70 of the Statute does not contain a general clause to address misconduct by counsel. This leaves open to doubt whether Article 70, and thus the criminal offences at a whole, will have a wide-ranging regulatory effect.

It is observed that the interpretation of the elements of the offences under Article 70 will ultimately have an effect on this assessment.[555] There may be enough

[549] See above, II.C.i at 254–56.

[550] See *The Prosecutor v Thomas Lubanga Dyilo*, ICC-01/04-01/06-2582 (OA 18), Appeals Chamber, Judgment (n 414) paras 47, 59–61.

[551] Above, II.A.i at 178.

[552] Above, II.A.iv.a at 194.

[553] See above, II.A.iii.a at 185–90.

[554] See ch 2, II.B.i at 61, III.B.i at 115.

[555] Above, II.B.i at 240–43.

latitude in the 'corruptly influencing' clauses of paragraphs (1)(c) and (d) to nudge it more towards an *omnibus* offence. The comparative analysis of the ICTY has indicated that broad criminal provisions exist and are indeed used. The concepts underlying these offences may vary. Criminal contempt has been discussed for the ad hoc Tribunals and within US law. Statutory offences against the administration of justice have been highlighted against the background of German law. Irrespective of the conceptual differences, they have in common their broad scope which allows for addressing defence counsel misconduct flexibly and comprehensively.

This holds primarily true for misconduct which is related to litigation. A nexus to ongoing proceedings typically constitutes an element of the respective crime. Although the scope of the ICC criminal law may fall back behind what is covered by *omnibus* clauses in national law, it does in principle provide for criminal prosecutions of misconduct of this kind. Furthermore, it has already been elaborated that misconduct may also occur unrelated to specific proceedings, for example, when counsel breaches duties which he or she may have generally in the relationship with the client. The scope is again narrower here as the ICC Statute does not include criminal offences beyond the core of the administration of justice.

All of this permits us to draw the following inferences. The ICC features considerably fewer criminal controls than would typically be available in other jurisdictions. Prosecutions on the national level may help to catch some kinds of criminal misconduct which evades the ICC but this, on the other hand, may bring about difficult issues of reciprocity and cooperation. Furthermore, it is not immediate regulation by ICC organs. Conceptually, the ICC's executive/legislative controls seem unlikely to contribute to the regulation of counsel.

It is, finally, the scope of the institutional measures which promises the widest umbrella for misconduct. Similar to the criminal law, the focus here will be on litigation-related misconduct, but as emphasised before, it is impossible to outline the contours of this. The institutional measures derive from the entire spectrum of powers which the different organs and bodies of the Court hold. In its current state and with a growing case load, the Court is only starting to explore and to investigate them. From a conceptual angle, however, institutional controls have been the kind that courts in particular have most explicitly resorted to. Due to their nature, they offer the widest scope and are the most dynamic and do not need to be construed as strictly as punitive provisions. They can also often be adapted to the given situation and are immediately available to judges and other actors within the institution.

In the latter regard, it remains to be seen to what extent the ICC, and in particular the Chambers in their case law, will ascribe itself inherent powers. These are the source of contempt powers on the common law jurisdictions, as has been outlined. Even though the ICC is unlikely to claim such sanctioning powers – as indicated by what is now only the first case in *Lubanga*[556] but might emerge as a trend –its focus will be on procedural measures.

[556] See above, II.C.i at 275.

B The Differences in Procedure

The different purposes of the various measures reflect in the applicable procedures. In this, the ICC's regime largely follows what is known from the national jurisdictions. By and large, it features a high degree of procedural guarantees. In particular, the criminal and the disciplinary procedures offer the necessary due process.[557] In relation to some of the administrative measures, a number of details seem less clear. This is most likely explained by the drafting history of the Statute and the other legal documents of the Court. Central aspects of the administration of the Court are, of course, addressed in detail; whereas others were more on the periphery and are therefore more prone to contain minor oddities. However, sufficient procedural rights also exist for them.[558]

The most sophisticated procedure exists, of course, for criminal offences, owing to the general reference that it is, mutatis mutandis, the same as for the core crimes.[559] Within this context, offences against the administration of justice may have received relatively little attention, in comparison with the Court's principal mandate of codifying the substance and the prosecution of the major crimes under international law. The procedure still comes out quite manageably as it emulates the general procedure of the Court. Select provisions are declared inapplicable. This is sometimes, for example, in respect of the complementarity scheme envisaged for the core crimes, grounded in the very specific characteristics that set apart international crimes from ordinary crimes. The inapplicability of the said provisions concerns principally features which are unique to international crimes. In spite of their link to the ICC, the offences against the administration of justice have more in common conceptually with their counterparts safeguarding the national administration of justice. In conclusion, prosecutions for Article 70 offence share the principal character of the ICC procedure.

In the context of the regulation of counsel, this also means that the OTP is responsible for handling prosecutions, including their initiation and investigation.[560] Chambers cannot trigger criminal prosecutions. This stands in contrast to common law jurisdiction, where criminal contempt may be an option. Similarly, the ICTY's regime differs. Although contempt can also be prosecuted by its OTP or an amicus curiae prosecutor, issuing an order *in lieu* of indictment offers the advantage of reacting directly to counsel misconduct. This advantage is missing from the ICC regime, save under Article 71.

The same categorisation of indirect sanctioning also holds true for the disciplinary regime. As is common for national regimes, it follows a quasi-criminal procedure. The procedure as such offers a high due process standard, though it is

[557] Above, II.A.v.b and e at 210–11, 221–26, B.iv at 249–51.

[558] See above, II.C.ii.c at 262.

[559] Rule 163(1) RPE, in detail above, II.B.iv.a at 249.

[560] Rule 165(1) RPE; see also above, II.C at 252, with n 412.

not free of minor ambiguities.[561] Prosecutions are handled by an independent commissioner; the case is then heard by a panel. Herewith, it can clearly be distinguished from the ICTY precedent where the Tribunal's organs are involved to a much greater degree. Most notably for the practical use in the regulation of counsel before the ICC, a complementarity clause can be found in the ICC Code. It has been argued that this kind of complementarity should be interpreted to relieve the disciplinary authorities of the ICC from double work, thus ensuring effective proceedings, rather than safeguarding national sovereignty.

With respect to the issue of effectiveness of the regulation of counsel through this set of controls, the ICC disciplinary system may possibly encounter the same limitations that plague national regimes. As a matter of regulatory policy, this should curtail the expectations in professional discipline, but most importantly, it will arguably not replace the need for judges to deal with immediate sanctions. The impact will also depend on what resources will actually be accorded to disciplinary investigations and how actively Chambers or other Court organs file complaints arising from their domain.

Finally, the procedure for administrative and procedural measures constitutes the contrasting model to the criminal and disciplinary prosecutions. Whereas some procedural protections apply herein as well, they generally allow more direct reactions. Procedural measures can be taken immediately by Chambers as part of the proceedings in which misconduct is encountered. Similarly, the procedure for administrative measures is not as protracted as for the judicial and quasi-judicial proceedings in the case of criminal and disciplinable acts.

Nonetheless, procedural protections exist. Measures are judicially reviewed by the acting Trial or Appeals Chamber, or sometimes by Presidency. The persons concerned need to be heard and are to be notified of the reasons for decisions.[562] These requirements promise to ensure sufficient due process by administrative standards. It is noted that some procedural measures many not afford an opportunity of immediate appellate review, and in those cases it should be possible to achieve a review as part and parcel of the full judgment.[563]

IV Defence Rights and their Impact on the Regulation of Counsel

The ICC has so far been restricted to a small number of active proceedings. It therefore goes without saying that many issues and occasionally problems which are central to the criminal trial have not in practice unfolded fully. Defence rights have gained some attention, though, from the very outset. The provision of

561 Above, II.A.vi at 266.

562 eg, Regulations 70(2), 71(3), 72, 83(4), 85(1) RoC. See above, II.C.iv at 266, 268, for details.

563 Gallant (n 142) 477.

sufficient funds for the defence has been a recurring theme before the international criminal courts.[564] It resurfaced for the ICC when the *Lubanga* case was launched in 2007.[565] While these issues do not pertain to counsel misconduct, they highlight the importance of defence rights to the international criminal process.[566] A whole range of provisions contain defence rights or otherwise touch on the status of defence counsel.[567] Some of these provisions relating to defence have been mentioned and analysed in the earlier part of this chapter. They reflect that the Statute entrenches rights of the defence, the clearest enunciation of this being Article 67(1)(d) and (e) which contain several aspects of the right to defence.[568]

To varying extents, defence rights are constitutionally mandated in national criminal jurisdictions and to that effect, Article 67 builds on domestic constitutional precedents. A draft resembling more closely the US Constitution was not adopted.[569] The final outcome at the Rome Conference was rather modelled on the ICCPR.[570] Irrespective of the origin, it has been noted that the significance of the rights contained therein may trump other law of the Statute or ICC law. Schabas describes it as having a 'hierarchically superior status within the *Statute*',[571] which also extends to other substantive as well as procedural matters.[572] Consequently, it should also have such an effect on the regulation of counsel beyond the Statute. The ICC should not fall back behind the established standards of the ad hoc Tribunals.[573]

[564] KS Gallant, 'The Role and Powers of Defense Counsel in the ICC Statute' (2000) 34 *The International Lawyer* 21, 36.

[565] See CA Müller, 'The Work of the International Criminal Court in 2007' (2008) 50 *German Yearbook of International Law* 679, 686. The International Criminal Bar and the *Ordre des Avocats de Paris* filed amicus curiae briefs: *The Prosecutor v Thomas Lubanga Dyilo*, ICC-01/04-01/06-918, Motion and proposed Amicus Brief in relation to the *pro se* request for review of the Registry decision of 14 May 2007 by Thomas Lubanga Dyilo on behalf of the International Criminal Bar pursuant to Rule 103 of the Rules of Procedure and Evidence, 5 June 2007; *The Prosecutor v Thomas Lubanga Dyilo*, Motion for Leave to File proposed Amicus Curiae Submission of the International Criminal Bar Pursuant to Rule 103 of the Rules of Procedure and Evidence, 10 April 2008; *The Prosecutor v Thomas Lubanga Dyilo*, ICC-01/04-01/06-917, Application for intervention in the proceedings as amicus curiae by the Ordre des Avocats de Paris under rule 103 of the Rules of Procedure and Evidence, 29 May 2007.

[566] See from a comparative perspective A Eser, 'Verteidigung in der internationalen Strafgerichtsbarkeit' in H Schöch (ed), *Strafverteidigung, Revision und die gesamten Strafrechtswissenschaften: Festschrift für Gunter Widmaier zum 70. Geburtstag* (Cologne, Heymann, 2008) 147–76, and W Schomburg, 'The Role of International Criminal Tribunals in Promoting Respect for Fair Trial Rights' (2009) 8 *Northwestern University Journal of International Human Rights* 1.

[567] For an overview, see Gallant (n 142) 437–45; Gallant (n 564).

[568] Schabas (n 283) art 67, mns 28, 37–41; Gallant (n 142) 445–55; S Kirsch, 'The International Criminal Court' in M Bohlander, R Boed and RJ Wilson (eds), *Defense in International Criminal Proceedings* (Ardsley, NY, Transnational Publishers, 2006) 455–75.

[569] Schabas (n 283) art 67, mn 57. See ch 2, III.E at 164, on US constitutional guarantees.

[570] ibid, art 67, mns 28, 58–61; A Converti, 'The Rights of the Accused' in F Lattanzi (ed), *The International Criminal Court, Comments on the Draft Statute* (Naples, Editoriale Scientifica, 1998) 234–36.

[571] Schabas (n 283) art 67, mn 61 (emphasis in original).

[572] ibid, art 67, mn 62.

[573] S Beresford and H Lahiouel, 'The Right to be Defended in Person or Through Legal Assistance and the International Criminal Court' (2000) 13 *Leiden Journal of International Law* 949. See on the ICTR, SM Meisenberg, 'The Right to Legal Assistance at the International Criminal Tribunal for Rwanda: A Review of its Jurisprudence' in E Decaux, A Dieng and M Sow (eds), *From Human Rights to*

The resulting due process rights need to be respected during any criminal prosecutions of counsel themselves, of course. This concerns counsel's right to defence; however, defence rights have a second dimension, that of the client's right to defence. Within the ICC legal framework, Article 67(1)(d) guarantees the right to choice of and to assistance by counsel. Sub-paragraph (e) contains other specific rights, such as the right to have witnesses examined and to raise defences. All of this is part of the overarching right to a fair trial.[574] Along with the right to equality,[575] fair trial therefore prohibits the arbitrary targeting of counsel.

As has been shown earlier, measures against counsel may have the potential to interfere with these defence rights and in particular the counsel's right and duty to advocacy. Since the ICC follows the same procedural model of free advocacy as does the United States[576] and Germany,[577] the same structural tension also exists for the ICC. Providing justice and a fair trial may at times create conflicting goals. Even though the ICC Code does not use the same terminology, it flows from its Articles 6, 14 and 24(2), inter alia, that counsel are awarded some latitude in professional judgement when representing a client before the ICC. Furthermore, some provisions against counsel misconduct tend to be potentially broad and vague. This is a common feature at the national level, and is the same for the ICC as has been implied before. Whereas most criminal offences under Article 70 are commendably clearcut, '[c]orruptly influencing a witness' under (c), or '[i]mpeding'/'corruptly influencing an official of the Court' under (d) leave much more room for interpretation. It is even more apparent for professional discipline, where counsel can be disciplined for violating 'any provisions of this Code, the Statute, the Rules of Procedure and Evidence and the Regulations of the Court or of the Registry in force imposing a substantial ethical or professional duty on him or her' (Art 31(a) ICC Code). Furthermore, procedural measures may not always have clearly defined statutory requirements. As to the example of abuse of process, they may not be based on written powers at all. Even if they are statutorily codified, malleable terms such as 'frivolous motion' are used.[578] This calls for striking a sound balance which reconciles all the competing interests.

To avoid a negative chilling effect on counsel, respecting defence rights must be accorded an appropriate rank in the interpretation of the pertinent sources of the regulation of counsel. First, the principle of proportionality has been recognised as a stake in counsel regulation.[579] It should reflect that the consequences and

International Criminal Law Studies in Honour of an African Jurist, the Late Judge Laïty Kama (Leiden, Martinus Nijhoff, 2007) 125–57.

[574] Schabas (n 283) art 67, mn 41.

[575] ibid, art 67, mn 18.

[576] See ch 2, I.C and D at 55–58.

[577] See ch 2, I.A and B at 51–55.

[578] See Rule 46 ICTY and ICTR RPE, and above, II.C.iv at 268 for the Shalluf case.

[579] M Scharf, 'Chaos in the Courtroom: Controlling Disruptive Defendants and Contumacious Counsel in War Crimes Trials' (Guest Lecture Series of the Office of the Prosecutor, The Hague, 25 September 2006) 6, fn 52, citing *Prosecutor v Slobodan Milošević*, IT-02-54-R73.7, Appeals Chamber, Decision on Interlocutory Appeal of the Trial Chamber's Decision on the Assignment of Defense Counsel, 1 November 2004, paras 17–18.

disadvantages to the client must not outweigh the benefits seemingly derived from the disciplinary measure. For example, convictions under Article 70 result in automatic removal from the list. However minor the gravity of the crime, it thus has the potential to deprive the client of his or her counsel of faith and seriously undermine his ability to present a defence. In the context of prosecution misconduct, the Appeals Chamber has held that using less intrusive sanctions under Article 71 are mandated before resorting to drastic ones such as a stay of proceedings.[580]

Furthermore, the attorney's corresponding duty to zealous advocacy should be protected as long as it is advocacy undertaken in good faith. This has been acknowledged in the domestic context and by international courts.[581] Defence lawyers are vested with rights for the good of their client, but at the same time for the good of the system of criminal justice. The latter builds on the idea of a fair trial where the conflicting interests of defence rights and effective administration of justice interact again. The typical phrasing found in US legal ethics would be that it is the defence lawyer's professional duty to represent his or her client 'within the bounds of law'.[582] In other words, the ICC instruments employ the same concept. The ICC Code lets counsel act within his or her professional judgement which nonetheless needs to respect the law of the Court and its procedure, as is shown, for example, in Articless 7(3), 14(2)(a), 24(1), (4) and (5). In the same vein, other international courts have held that the choice of counsel can be duly limited if counsel fails to follow generally accepted standards of professional ethics.[583] Similarly with this example of an entry control, the function of counsel as an officer of the court or agent in the administration of justice imposes limits on what counsel can or cannot do.

Along with the duties of an officer of the court, counsel must be given the room to enjoy the rights flowing from this role as only then will counsel be afforded the opportunity to fully discharge of his or her responsibilities. This needs to take into account that counsel's responsibities are by their very nature twofold. Counsel needs to represent his or her client's case while reconciling this with the overall objective of the criminal process. All other participants therefore need to recognise this dual and sometimes awkward role.

Therefore, any regulatory measure should take into consideration whether acts by counsel ever reach the sufficient threshold to properly be treated as misconduct; whether the appropriate reaction should actually result in a sanction against counsel; and whether immediate action is justified.[584]

[580] *The Prosecutor v Thomas Lubanga Dyilo*, ICC-01/04-01/06-2582 (OA 18), Appeals Chamber, Judgment (n 414) para 60, fn 135. See above, II.C.i at 255.

[581] Ch 1, II.B.ii.b at 21–22, ch 2, I.D at 56–57.

[582] See above at ch 2, ibid.

[583] Schabas (n 283) art 67, mn 31, referring to *Ensslin, Baader and Raspe v Federal Republic of Germany*, application nos 7572/76, 7586/76, 7587/76, 1978, Decision on the admissibility of the applications, 8 July 1978, and *X and Y v Federal Republic of Germany*, application nos 5217/71 and 5367/72, Commission, 20 July 1972 (refusal to wear a gown).

[584] Adopted from the US context, see ch 2, III.E at 165–66.

From the very outset, it should be remembered that respect for advocacy entails recognising a 'good faith' basis. Misconduct will usually be the exception to the rule, which begs the necessity of a finding: that the acts in question really deviated in a discernable manner from the norms of trial practice, that the nature or seriousness of the acts mark the issue or the case misconduct, taking into account the immediacy, patterns, persistence and the effect on the deliberative process.

The primary framework employed to handle conflicts during the trial should be the general rules and elements of procedure as the engine of the trial, not sanctions against participants. By putting the trial and achieving its goals first, the negative impact on attorneys should be allayed by using notices and warnings requirements, priority should be given to sanctions, or alternatives to them, which have the least effect on the deliberative process and the participation or provocation by other participants to the proceedings should to be taken into consideration.

V Assessment of the ICC Regime

Summing up, the ICC's system of regulation of counsel can be described as a multi-tiered system. In that respect, it resembles the domestic systems which have been studied in the earlier part of this chapter. All of the systems examined consist of several layers and, in nearly all of them, distinct professional standards along with a disciplinary procedure govern the conduct of counsel. Further, criminal law competes with this and shapes the rules of permissible conduct. The scope and source of criminal offences varies considerably, though. Finally, all the courts have institutional powers. That no liability controls exist is due to the courts' nature as criminal courts, rather than as a deliberate omission.

In all of this, the ICC regime resembles what is known from the other international courts and also domestic criminal justice. More particularly, though, the mere existence of certain regulatory mechanisms is not necessarily determinative of what will effectively be applied. It therefore remains somewhat clouded as to how this will play out, or rather how it is played by the relevant actors. This in particular concerns how the different sets of controls within the ICC's system can be aligned. This chapter's purpose has been examining the character and the substance of the various enforcement mechanisms as well as the application of measures under them. What has been left out so far is a scrutiny of the relationships between each of them.[585] Suffice it to set out the problem by one illustrative example – disbarment for grave misconduct. Disbarring a lawyer from the ICC can be achieved by disciplinary disbarment under the Code or removal according to Regulation 71(1)(c) RoC as a consequence from an Article 70 conviction, but also by interdicting counsel to exercise his or her functions pursuant to Article 71

[585] See ch 4, IV at 307–10.

and Rule 171(2) and (3) RPE. The latter may tend to be more attractive to judges of the ICC who are observing counsel misconduct at first hand. This is not to say that disbarment via the disciplinary regime or as a consequence of a criminal conviction will not happen; but they are certainly the more unwieldy options, however, just as would be disciplinary or criminal sanctions compared with institutional measures in the other jurisdictions, Germany and the United States. What this simply means in the ICC context is that often more than one of the available sets of controls will be capable of achieving the desired sanctioning goals. How they relate to each other is a more general issue arising in each of the multi-tiered disciplining systems in this study, not just that of the ICC. Therefore, the questions of relationships will be reserved for the following chapter.

As has been shown all through this chapter, the ICC has been vested with a comprehensive and potentially powerful disciplinary system, at least in theory. The criminal controls under the ICC legal framework are conceptually much more limited. Lastly, institutional and more specifically procedural controls are part of this same framework. Practically speaking, as has been argued throughout this study, the focus in the regulation of counsel may practically differ from what it may seem to be according to the rules. All the existing controls have their own justification in the theoretical model, but with differences as to their practical application. Therefore, it is open to doubt whether the ICC disciplinary regime will live up to more than has its other international and national counterparts. The ICC criminal offences may suffer from a somewhat limited scope, but will arguably still be the tool of choice for the gravest instances of misconduct. The most viable tool to regulate counsel will arguably be procedural measures by the judges. National as well as international courts have turned to this, and no compelling reason can be conceived why the ICC bodies should not follow.

Applying the perspective of institutional choice,[586] certain patterns can be observed. The Assembly of States Parties, ie, the ICC legislative body, has set rules on the regulation of counsel. It has done so in a quite extensive manner, in comparison with the American model. The strongest regulatory instruments, the Statute, the RPE and in particular, the Code, have been adopted by the Assembly itself. This does include, along with the criminal offences, controls such as under Article 71 which are exercised by the judges. It needs to be emphasised, though, that judges do not promulgate the content of the rules, albeit through their practice. The arguably most attractive institutional actors, the judges, are in contrast relegated to the Regulations of the Court. With these, the judges have laid down rules chiefly on controlling the admission of counsel to the Court and other institutional issues. This constitutes an entry control but does not pertain to the ongoing business. In other words, the existing regulatory setup deprives the judges of considerable powers. Similarly, the Registry as the Court's administrative agency has only been granted limited powers. Furthermore, the Regulations of the

[586] See J Mehta, 'The Development of Federal Professional Responsibility Rules: The Effect of Institutional Choice on Rule Outcomes' (2007) 6 *Cardozo Public Law, Policy and Ethics Journal* 57, 97.

Registry effectively need to be approved by the Presidency, ie, again judges.[587] Self-governance of the profession has so far not played out as a major factor. Bar associations have not drafted up the rules nor are they entrusted with enforcing discipline themselves.

Summing up, the ICC's model can be likened in many aspects to the German model: it is built primarily on a legislatively based foundation. Judges operate within this legislatively circumscribed framework. The most extensive powers of sanctioning misconduct are not accorded to the judges; moreover, it does not provide for inherent judicial sanctioning powers. The concept of contempt is not entrenched in the Statute or the RPE. The possibility and scope of inherent powers still need to be worked out in practice. Nonetheless, it seems fair to predict that the eventual case law will deal with extending the allotted statutory powers and developing sanctioning mechanisms alongside them.

[587] See Rule 14 RPE.

4

The Relationships between the Different Regimes

I The Concurrence of the ICC and National Jurisdictions

A The Multiplicity of Applicable Regimes

As holds true for many other issues in international criminal law, the national and the international level are intertwined in the matter at hand. The ICC Code does not establish an exclusive set of rules for lawyers practising in the international arena. This raises the question of the relationship between applicable regimes. In the majority of cases, counsel will be bound by national codes of conduct. Lawyers receive their training and their principal admission domestically. Even though some may devote themselves to a primary practice before international courts, it makes sense to view counsel as bound to a specific country.[1] This reflects that fact that counsel have their professional home there, as well as the fact that domestic enforcement mechanisms may be more apposite and effective than those available to the ICC. As a consequence, multiple sanctioning may occur in a vertical dimension: bodies of the ICC sanction counsel misconduct, but so do domestic authorities on the national level as well. These multiple proceedings in different states along with the ICC can be explained by the fact that all of them are sovereign subjects under international law.

Furthermore, sanctions from different sets of controls may attach to the same set of allegations of misconduct. This is most evident for professional discipline and criminal offences. A lawyer who commits a crime in the course of his professional activities will typically also breach professional obligations. Another example would be procedural responses to counsel misconduct, such as disqualifying or withdrawing counsel. These immediate measures do not preclude additional sanctions, ie, criminal offences and professional discipline. Thus, it is possible and

[1] Due to this, Dutch counsel van der Spoel was brought before domestic bodies by the accused, *Prosecutor v Vojislav Šešelj*, IT-03-67-PT, Registry, Professor Vojislav Šešelj submits a request to be visited by his Legal Counsels representing him before the Bar Association of the Netherlands in the disciplinary proceedings instituted against attorney-at-law van der Spoel, 19 May 2006.

often highly likely that multiple measures are taken within the same legal forum, in other words on a horizontal plane.

However, since institutional controls seem bound to the affected institution itself, there seems little room for overlap. Institutional measures by the ICC will typically have no counterparts or repercussions as such on the national level. They will henceforth be disregarded in this chapter, and the focus will be on disciplinary and criminal sanctions.

B The Conflict of Professional Rules in particular

Multiple regulation is most apparent for professional rules. As has been pointed out before, most defence counsel before the ICC will be admitted domestically, which makes them subject to national codes of conduct. By this, counsel is subject to the ICC's professional standards and at the same time to those of his or her home jurisdiction – or even many more, given the example of the United States where membership of more than one Bar is not unusual. Moreover, any other state where counsel works, including travel for professional purposes such as site visits and private investigations, may claim its code of professional conduct to be applicable for activities on its territory.[2] Having said this, the potential of conflicts between professional rules can easily be grasped.[3] No conflict exists at all, though, if rules are either uniform in substance or if rules of conflict determine that a specific set of rules prevails.[4] Traditionally, the most advanced efforts of this kind have been made in private international law. Therefore, legal malpractice claims should follow the established rules of that regime.[5] Strictly speaking, a conflict of laws in that field is inconceivable since the ICC does not hold any pertinent jurisdiction.

In respect to professional discipline, the ICC Code sets uniform standards for counsel appearing before that Court, as the ad hoc Tribunals have done. Such a uniform set is still a relative novelty for international institutions,[6] and certainly

[2] On the Netherlands as the Host State, see the immunity provision under Art 25 of the ICC, *Headquarters Agreement between the International Criminal Court and the host State* (ICC-BD/04-01-08, 7 June 2007). Being a state party, any Dutch professional rules would be trumped by the supremacy clause of Art 4 ICC Code of Conduct.

[3] For the earlier days of the ICTR when the pertinent Code lacked a conflict rule, see *Prosecutor v Jean-Bosco Barayagwiza*, ICTR-97-19-T, Decision on Defence Counsel Motion to Withdraw, 2 November 2000; JT Tuinstra, *Defence Counsel in International Criminal Law* (Cambridge, Cambridge University Press, 2009) 236.

[4] See OL Knöfel, *Grundfragen der internationalen Berufsausübung von Rechtsanwälten* (Bonn, Deutscher Anwaltverlag, 2005) 444–51; JL Krystinik, 'The Complex Web of Conflicting Disciplinary Standards in International Litigation' (2003) 38 *Texas International Law Journal* 815, 826.

[5] See DF Vagts, 'Professional Responsibility in Transborder Practice: Conflict and Resolution' (1999–2000) 13 *Georgetown Journal of Legal Ethics* 677, 694, and ch 2, II.B.i at iv at 84, and III.B.iv at 263. It is noted that counsel may enjoy immunity under the Agreement on the Privileges and Immunities of the ICC, unless they are waived. See below, II.C at 299–300.

[6] See DF Vagts, 'The International Legal Profession: A Need for More Governance?' (1996) 90 *American Journal of International Law* 250, 260 (on arbitration tribunals, the ICJ and the ECJ).

given the complexity and conclusiveness of the ICC Code. It does not resolve all conflicts through uniformity, however, since this would presuppose that the competing rules, ie, national codes, are all harmonised as to be uniform in substance.[7] To a large extent, the ICC Code does mirror established professional standards which are likewise enshrined in the other codes binding counsel. Thus, in many instances no conflict will arise.

The hard cases are those, however, where professional standards diverge or even contradict each other. Counsel will not be able to comply with all of them unless resolved by rules of conflict. Such a priority rule on the conflict of law is provided in the ICC Code. Article 4 establishes supremacy of the ICC Code over other applicable regulations 'when [counsel is] practising before the court'.[8] With regard to state parties, this should resolve any conflict of laws in favour of the ICC Code, as state parties are bound to honour the Code as are their licensing and oversight bodies as well. It is noted, though, that this only resolves conflicts of substantive law. It thus at least settles the issue of the applicable standards but, in respect to adjudication, leaves room for multiple disciplinary procedures in different jurisdictions.[9]

Counsel from non-state parties will run the risk of facing diverging standards.[10] The ICC's prescriptive jurisdiction can generally be based, in particular in regard to non-state parties, on the ICC's inherent power to regulate counsel. Further, professional discipline is an opt-in system that does not engage concerns of state sovereignty. Both the ICC as well as the home jurisdiction may thus prescribe professional standards and enforce them. Article 30 of the Code expressly allows for sanctioning by other disciplining bodies irrespective of the ICC substantive rules or its disciplinary procedure.[11] The principle of *ne bis in idem* does not explicitly apply.[12] To the extent that membership to a Bar association is based on voluntary adhesion and the sanctions are not of a penal nature, this seems justifiable.

[7] Traditionally, the aim and scope of professional rules has been very diverse (eg, within the European Community: RJ Goebel, 'Lawyers in the European Community: Progress towards Community-Wide Rights of Practice' (1991–92) 15 *Fordham International Law Journal* 556, 626), which leaves a long way to go before harmonisation can be achieved.

[8] See ch 3, II.A.iii.a at 186–90. It seems unclear, inter alia, to what extent the standards set by the Code apply in proceedings – such as extradition – before national courts which may still have a clear link to the ICC. They may be also binding for legal action of that kind of proceedings on the national level. See, eg, the ICB Commentary (ch 3, I.B.ii at 175, n 35) on Art 1, suggesting adding 'or counselling in matters related to the ICC'. This still leaves the need to establish clear criteria to determine when a matter is related to the ICC but acknowledges the fact that a lawyer may also be retained for general consulting purposes and not only litigious matters.

[9] See below, II.A at 291–97, and C at 298–300, on multiple enforcement.

[10] On the cumulation of applicable rules of professional conduct, see also Knöfel (n 4) 449.

[11] Before the ICTY, at least one lawyer has cited 'an unexpected professional obligation in his national jurisdiction' and requested his replacement. The ICTY Registry granted the request, *Prosecutor v Bruno Stojić*, IT-04-74-PT, Deputy Registrar, Decision, 24 February 2006 (counsel was Tomislav Kuzmanović, the home jurisdiction presumably Wisconsin).

[12] eg, the ICTY Code contains a double jeopardy safeguard for proceedings before the ICTY Disciplinary Board (Art 50).

Strictly speaking, the underlying problem of vertical multiplicity is less a problem of conflict of laws but rather of jurisdiction, and then essentially of double jeopardy. In respect to both of these points, it can be argued that counsel has waived jurisdictional and even double jeopardy protections by appearing before the ICC.[13] Nonetheless, a reasonable domestic choice of law clause is preferable as counsel then ideally has guidance and is relieved of ethical dilemmas. An example for a suitable clause would seem to be Rule 8.5(b) of the ABA's Model Rules of Professional Conduct, despite its shortcomings.[14] It puts just weight on the forum of the Court in pending matters. An analysis of a similar effect has been attempted above for Articles 1 and 4 of the ICC Code.[15]

In the absence of such a clear clause, a conflict will simply be impossible to resolve. Even quite advanced efforts to create uniform rules, such as by the Council of Bars and Law Societies of Europe (CCBE), have failed so far.[16] It harmonises but does not really solve the still remaining conflict of laws. Instead, it just declares all conceivable disciplinary regimes applicable.[17] Practically, it is indeed likely that many jurisdictions will hold their own professional standards applicable by membership in the respective Bar or by the principle of territoriality.[18] This is illustrated by Germany, where no satisfactory answer has therefore been found for these double deontology dilemmas.[19]

C Criminal Offences

Furthermore, the ICC has prescriptive jurisdiction for criminal offences. This poses no problem in respect to state parties as they explicitly vested the ICC with these powers in the Statute. With regard to non-state parties, such as the United States, the protective principle should justify Article 70 of the ICC Statute. In prosecuting offences against the administration of justice, the ICC does not act as

[13] What remains is an issue of due process; see ch 2, III.D.iii at 162–63, and below, II.C at 298–99. On the protection from unfair assertions of jurisdiction and waivers thereof, see from the United States, *Asahi Metal Industry Co. v Superior Court*, 480 US 102, 107 SCt 1026, 94 LEd2d 92 (Supreme Court of the United States, 1987); *Burger King v Rudzewicz*, 471 US 462, 105 SCt 2174, 85 LEd2d 528 (Supreme Court of the United States, 1985).

[14] See ch 2, III.B.i.a at 115–17, and D.iii at 162–63. On the United States, see moreover, Knöfel (n 4) 483–546.

[15] Ch 3, II.A.iii.a at 186–90.

[16] Goebel (n 7) 625; Knöfel (n 4) 451–54. See also JY Whitaker, 'Remedying Ethical Conflicts in a Global Legal Market' (2006) 19 *Georgetown Journal of Legal Ethics* 1079.

[17] See Art 2.4 with Commentary, *Code of Conduct for European Lawyers* (originally adopted at the CCBE Plenary Session held on 28 October 1988, subsequently amended during the CCBE Plenary Sessions on 28 November 1998, 6 December 2002 and 19 May 2006) German version reprinted by M Kleine-Cosack, *Bundesrechtsanwaltsordnung*, 5th edn (Munich, Beck, 2008) 742–54. See also ch 2, II.D.ii at 98–99. On the CCBE see LS Terry, 'An Introduction to the European Community's Legal Ethics Code – Part II: Applying the CCBE Code of Conduct' (1993–94) 7 *Georgetown Journal of Legal Ethics* 345, 373.

[18] Knöfel (n 4) 444–82.

[19] ibid, 449, 462, 545.

a proxy for the community of nations but in its own right, and in this regard it has primary powers.[20]

As far as adjudicative jurisdiction is concerned, the complementarity principle of the Statute is not applicable. The ICC, and along with it other states, may thus embark on proceedings if their administration of justice is affected.[21] Concurrence seems to be less of a problem as far as the content of the law is concerned. As long as jurisdictions only safeguard the domestic administration of justice (be it by principle, or because they require a pending domestic proceeding), there is no conflict with ICC offences; the ICC, on the other hand, does not prescribe general criminal offences. All of this makes an overlap less likely.

Taking into consideration the obligations of states under Article 70(4)(a)[22] to extend the scope of their domestic offences, there may very well be additional jurisdiction, however. Conflicts of criminal jurisdictions represent an unsolved problem in transnational proceedings.[23] Generally speaking, no clear ranking of jurisdictional principles or an authoritative settling mechanism have emerged.

By whatever state, such parallel criminal proceedings of the ICC along with states may result in double jeopardy, which is simply the status quo in international customary law.[24] The *ne bis in idem* bar in Rule 168 of the Rules of Procedure and Evidence (RPE) protects from multiple conviction by the ICC but not necessarily vice versa. Article 20 of the ICC Statute only applies to the 'core crimes' such as genocide but does not extend to Article 70 'offences'. It would be desirable if jurisdictions could be aligned, but it will have to be seen how this plays out. The scenario of multiple criminal proceedings is a well known issue in international law which is certainly not a peculiarity of prosecutions before international courts. Criminal double jeopardy will most effectively be countered by consultation mechanisms.[25] The RPE take a sensible approach in Rule 162 by ensuring both such a consultation mechanism in sub-rule (1) and giving further guidance in sub-rules (2)–(4).[26]

[20] See in particular Art 70(4)(b), below III.A at 300–02.

[21] Again, see in detail below, III.A.

[22] Below, III.C at 306–07.

[23] See C Warbrick and K Brookson-Morris, 'Conflicts of Criminal Jurisdiction' (2007) 56 *International and Comparative Law Quarterly* 659; A Klip, *European Criminal Law. An Integrative Approach* (Antwerp, Intersentia, 2009) 363–67.

[24] See H Kreicker, 'Deutschland' in A Eser and H Kreicker (eds), *National Prosecution of International Crimes*, vol 1 (Freiburg, edition iuscrim, 2003) 395–98.

[25] AJ Colangelo, 'Double Jeopardy and Multiple Sovereigns: A Jurisdictional Theory' (2009) 86 *Washington University Law Review* 769, 848.

[26] In detail below, III.A at 300–01.

II Enforcing Professional Discipline

A The ICC Disciplinary Procedure vis-a-vis National Disciplinary Procedures

i The Nature of Article 38 Complementarity

The ICC's prescriptive jurisdiction over matters of professional discipline does not necessarily mean that the disciplinary bodies will exercise discipline. Article 38 of the Code has been likened to Article 17 complementarity.[27] The title of the provision indeed recalls Article 17 of the Statute, where the principle of complementarity is enshrined as a striking feature of the ICC's setup.[28] This principle can be summarised by saying that the Court may have jurisdiction but does not exercise it for reasons of inadmissibility when an able and willing state prosecutes the matter domestically.

Similar restraints seemingly follow for the disciplinary regime from Article 38 of the Code. It will be shown, however, that the rationale underlying the complementarity of Article 38 should not be likened to that of Article 17. Interestingly enough, though quite fitting, Article 70 offences are exempted from the complementarity requirement.[29] Professional discipline is a particularised, albeit softened sanctioning mechanism which relates to the administration of justice of the Court itself just as much as those criminal offences. Both of them are based on the Court's own inherent powers. A binding admissibility threshold based on complementarity would be fundamentally at odds with this objective for both sub-regimes.

There are several purposes and reasons behind the principle of complementarity as known from Article 17. Only some of them are convincing in the context of Article 38 of the Code (and Art 70(4) of the Statute for criminal offences).[30]

[27] Tuinstra (n 3) 219, 238. She concedes that counsel may not be safe from double intervention and senses that the ICC disciplinary bodies may be more appropriate to determine whether misconduct has occurred and to rule on it (see in the following, at 291–98). Her assessment of the Dutch disciplinary organs adopting the ICTY's pronouncement (Tuinstra, ibid, 237, with fns 349–51, and 238) fails to highlight a crucial point: reciprocal discipline as such makes sense and may be warranted, Contrary to Tuinstra's view, reciprocal discipline is not simply 'interfering'. See in more detail below C at 298–300. She is right, though, in stressing that there may be concerns of disproportionality and heterogeneity.

[28] For literature on Art 17 of the Statute, see JK Kleffner and G Kor (eds), *Complementary Views on Complementarity* (The Hague, T.M.C. Asser, 2006); C Cárdenas, *Die Zulässigkeitsprüfung vor dem Internationalen Strafgerichtshof* (Berlin, Berliner Wissenschafts-Verlag, 2005); L Lafleur, *Der Grundsatz der Komplementarität, Der Internationale Strafgerichtshof im Spannungsfeld zwischen Effektivität und Staatensouveränität* (Baden-Baden, Nomos, 2011); JT Holmes, 'Complementarity: National Courts versus the ICC' in A Cassese, P Gaeta and JRWD Jones (eds), *The Rome Statute of the International Criminal Court: A Commentary* (Oxford, Oxford University Press, 2002); SA Williams and WA Schabas in O Triffterer (ed), *Commentary on the Rome Statute of the International Criminal Court*, 2nd edn (Munich, Beck, 2008) art 17; WA Schabas, *The International Criminal Court. A Commentary on the Rome Statute* (Oxford, Oxford University Press, 2010) 335–52.

[29] Pursuant to Rule 163(2), Part 2 shall not apply to them. This includes Art 17. On the procedure for Art 70 offences, see below, III.A at 300–02.

[30] See below, III.A at 300–02.

First, the arguably best-known purpose explains why the ICC is given supplementary jurisdiction along with national forums: as a 'back-up'. It aims at preventing the abuse of judicial proceedings, as well as guaranteeing sanctioning which is fair and effective. At least with respect to the international crimes under the Court's jurisdiction by virtue of Article 5 of the Statute, the historical record has it that states have too often not prosecuted those presumably responsible. If national prosecutions take place, political factors may mar the proceedings, or the internationally accepted standards of due process and the rule of law are not met as would be desirable. In any event, most commentators would easily agree that complementarity has merit for its supervisory function. In a similar vein, it goes without saying that national prosecutions can, of course, only claim primacy if they are genuine. While all of this seems undisputed, 'back-up arguments' do not exhaustively explain why national jurisdiction is seen as preferable over an international one, and why an according complementarity scheme was chosen in first place.[31] Or, slightly re-phrased: what exactly qualifies a national forum as the in principle primary jurisdiction, rather than an international one, if both are available? It is noted at this point that clear differences exist between prosecuting the core crimes on the one hand and professional misconduct within a disciplinary framework on the other. This may lead to different conclusions for resolving complementarity issues – general as well as specific ones.

The first group of arguments clusters around the notions of the 'natural judge' and 'sovereignty'. Throughout history, mention has been made of the 'inherent, fundamental idea of national jurisdiction'.[32] This is often intertwined with the notion of state sovereignty.[33] Whereas these sovereignty considerations indeed carry weight as far as basic legitimacy questions are concerned, arguments based solely on them 'have little value for determining whether national jurisdictions are *better suited* to deal with international crimes'.[34] Other arguments bear more relevance for assessing what complementarity of ICC disciplinary proceedings towards those of counsel's home jurisdiction means.

A second cluster of arguments is about the particular 'local effects' of national proceedings.[35] The legitimacy and credibility of proceedings may be enhanced through them. They are also said to contribute better to establishing the historical record. On the other hand, these arguments are controversial at best. It may sometimes be that international courts operate more independently and without the taint of a victor's regime. Many of the 'local effects arguments', moreover,

[31] See J Stigen, *The Relationship between the International Criminal Court and National Jurisdictions – The Principle of Complementarity* (Leiden, Martinus Nijhoff, 2008) 20–21.

[32] MM El Zeidy, 'The Principle of Complementarity: A New Machinery to Implement International Criminal Law' (2002) 23 *Michigan Journal of International Law* 869, 873, in the context of the Versailles Treaty of the Allies and Germany after the First World War and with a further history of the principle.

[33] Stigen (n 31) 15–18.

[34] ibid, 20. One of the differences between crimes and professional discipline is that the latter features no universal jurisdiction, therefore the question whether really 'any State' is preferable (see Stigen (n 31) 21) is moot.

[35] Stigen (n 31) 21–23; JI Turner, 'Nationalizing International Criminal Law' (2005) 41 *Stanford Journal of International Law* 1, 25.

have less merit within the framework of professional discipline. Professional ethics and their enforcement address misconduct which is highly individual and concerns professional standards, not those of the general public and broader social life. It is not aimed at, and does not directly deal with, societal structures as is done by criminal law.

For similar reasons, a third group of arguments seems less significant in the present context. 'Compliance arguments' recognise the assets of national proceedings but help to identify some of the particular strengths of international criminal justice, ie, encouraging as well as helping national counterparts to comply. Accordingly, use should be made of both national and international prosecutions, but the latter mainly serves as incentive to act and help, and thus act as a catalyst for compliance.[36] At the same time, it is presumed to make the ICC focus on the appropriate selection of cases.[37] The purpose behind complementarity can thus be summarised that international courts have an important flagship function; they should take on a limited number of the most important cases, but otherwise rather focus on their important supervisory role.

All of this may not quite fit in with main characteristics of professional discipline, however. Article 17 complementarity will usually award a certain margin of discretion and deviance to national authorities.[38] States do not need to apply the exact body of ICC law or handle a case just as the ICC would do, as long as overall they act genuinely. The Code of Professional Conduct, on the other hand, provides in Article 4 that the law of the ICC shall prevail over the domestic professional standards. The ICC regime is supreme rather than just supervisory. Moreover, a supervisory role presupposes that the ICC can interfere effectively in case of non-compliance.[39] This is apparently not the case since states are under no duty to cooperate, nor do they need to adopt professional standards similar to those of the ICC.[40] The particular effects of international justice, namely that it is hoped to lead to internal changes on the domestic level, are not pursued for discipline. Misconduct is not like systemic crime in violation of international human rights. Malpractice may cause substantial problems, but it is more an issue of the ICC's administration of justice and of the international setting, rather than of the entire legal profession within a country. Neither is there probably a need to take on an appropriate selection of cases only. The limited number of instances and their extent before the other international courts tend to suggest that the ICC disciplinary bodies can handle all pertinent allegations.

[36] Stigen (n 31) 18, 27–28; Kleffner and Kor (eds) 79–104 (ch 3); Turner (n 35) 31, who also points out that the ICC can assist national courts in various ways.

[37] Stigen (n 31) 3–7, 19. Contrary to Art 17 of the Statute, Art 38 of the Code does not contain a sufficient gravity requirement.

[38] ibid, 18; Holmes (n 28) 673–74. See also Turner (n 35) 32, who also refers to the model of the ECHR giving states 'some leeway in interpreting and applying the European Convention on Human Rights'.

[39] Stigen (n 31) 19.

[40] See below, B at 297–98, on the scope of Art 86 for cooperation; in contrast, compare the duties to harmonise domestic law and to cooperate under Art 70(4)(a) and (b) concerning the offences against the administration of justice.

Finally, there is a fourth basket containing what could be called 'pragmatic arguments' in favour of complementarity. Because of the '[g]iven physical proximity, local courts often have the best access to information, evidence, and testimony about the alleged events'.[41] This is supposed to result in more effectiveness and higher quality.[42] Again, these arguments have arisen in the debate concerning complementarity under Article 17 of the Statute. At the same time, though, they seem to be the arguments that are the least context-specific, ie, they are equally applicable to criminal and disciplinary proceedings. It seems indeed true that the lack of language barriers or the ready availability of documents and witnesses can expedite and facilitate proceedings, irrespective of the nature of the proceedings. It appears less clear that this will always be the case with ICC-related misconduct. Counsel will not necessarily use the domestic language when practising before the Court. Domestic disciplinary bodies may not be familiar with the ICC legal framework at all and all of this will tend to create linguistic and legal barriers for domestic proceedings after all. Furthermore, the pertinent documents will often be in ICC custody, and witnesses may even be ICC staff. This necessitates international cooperation, which proceedings in the home jurisdiction are theoretically supposed to evade. All of these are factors which suggest that the ICC will be the better suited forum in many cases. In conclusion, all of the 'pragmatic arguments' definitely need to be taken into consideration. Unlike with Article 17 complementarity, they do not necessarily argue in favour of national trials. Although they are important factors in assessing whether it is advisable for the ICC to engage its complementary jurisdiction, there should in no way be the automatic presumption of the preference of national proceedings.

Any activities of the ICC affect sovereignty and national interests. The disciplinary regime does this, too. For the complementarity assessment under Article 38 of the Code, compliance and local effects arguments are of little weight within the disciplinary framework. The disciplinary regime serves to protect chiefly the administration of justice of the ICC. Herein, the ICC does not act as an agent of the international community[43] and does not need a triggering mechanism for professional proceedings, but it is concerned per se. No Article 38 complementarity test is discernible from the transcript or the decision in the first disciplinary case at the ICC. This may not have been deliberate but taking on the case eventually had merit because the ICC's own interests were concerned there.[44]

The existence of international and national mechanisms alongside each other is more of a dilemma firstly of multiple jurisdiction, ie, which of several regimes are applicable at the same time, and secondly of reciprocal discipline, ie, whether and how counsel should be sanctioned multiply. This is different from complemen-

[41] WW Burke-White, 'A Community of Courts: Toward a System of International Criminal Law Enforcement' (2003) 24 *Michigan Journal of International Law* 1, 15. See also Stigen (n 31) 20, citing the pertinent OTP Policy Paper in fn 42.

[42] Stigen (n 31) 21–25.

[43] As is often argued for the Art 5 crimes, ibid, 26.

[44] Ch 3, II.A at 177 (n 51).

tarity as known from Article 17 of the Statute. Article 38 of the Code governs a horizontal relationship rather than a vertical one, which is the case for Article 17 of the Statute. This will have to be kept in mind when determining whether information by national authorities is satisfactory or adequate pursuant to Article 38.

ii The Application of Article 38 Complementarity

As far as specific disciplinary measures are concerned, they are admissible if either letter (a), (b) or (c) of paragraph (4) is met (if no domestic decision has been handed down yet), or paragraph (5)(a) or (b) (if such a decision has been made). Article 38 thus enshrines a form of complementarity before national decisions have been made as well as afterwards (the latter meaning a *ne bis in idem*). These provisions express a tendency to leave cases to domestic authorities. In both cases, the crucial issue seems to be, though, whether the national procedure addresses the allegations as adequately as would and should be done by the ICC disciplinary bodies. Based on the foregoing, pragmatic reasons should count foremost for answering this.[45]

The clearest case in favour of proceeding before the ICC appears to be paragraph (4)(c). Very similar in wording to Article 17 of the Statute, it provides that the procedure before the ICC Disciplinary Board may continue if the Board considers that the national authorities are 'unable or unwilling' to conclude their procedure. 'Genuinely' is not used in Article 38, but the idea would presumably be the same. Inability[46] has been described as 'a gap in State jurisdictions, a gap created by the lack of repression'.[47] This can be caused by poor administration of justice, a breakdown of state institutions, or widespread anarchy. It is also conceivable that simply no disciplinary system is in place at all. Unwillingness is effectively a test of the good faith of national authorities.[48] Article 17(2) makes mention of certain factors to be considered in this test.[49] A state could be held to be unwilling if the procedures were meant to shield the person, happened with an unjustified delay, or were not conducted independently or impartially.

National inaction results in automatic admissibility under (a) if there is no pertinent communication at all within a reasonable time.[50] Fixing a certain time period for this seems impossible. Waiting becomes unreasonable, however, if it becomes foreseeable that an ICC procedure could be conducted but would be delayed. As has been shown, the ICC has an equal interest in a speedy and

[45] eg, the availability of evidence.
[46] See Stigen (n 31) 313–30; El Zeidy (n 32) 902; Williams and Schabas (n 28) art 17, mn 24.
[47] El Zeidy (n 32) 903.
[48] ibid, 899; Stigen (n 31) 251–53.
[49] See for details Stigen (n 31) 257–308.
[50] ibid, 199–202. The Code is silent on what happens if national authorities do not communicate and do not even appoint an *ad hoc* member to the Disciplinary Board within reasonable time. Art 36(10) could be applied mutatis mutandis, allowing the alternate member to sit in for the unavailable *ad hoc* member.

effective procedure, and no primacy of the national system warrants national proceedings the same way as do Article 5 crimes.

Alternatively, all these considerations could be taken in account when determining whether the information received is 'unsatisfactory' pursuant to letter (b) of Article 38(4). In some way, (b) may be used as a residual clause if national authorities are not evidently unable or unwilling, but there is a probability that the outcome of prospective proceedings will not be adequate under ICC Code standards. Proof of ongoing national proceedings, as well as simple statements that an investigation will take place technically constitutes a response pursuant to (a), and this may neither meet the higher unwillingness or inability threshold pursuant to (c).[51] They may thus escape both the (a) and (c) test, but would then be covered by (b). This is essentially an adequacy test, which is also the critical issue under paragraph (5). It is recalled that the purpose behind Article 38 is to align the ICC's system with national ones. With the foregoing in mind, this should not be interpreted to the same effect as Article 17 of the Statute. A decentralised system is not needed in the disciplinary context in the same way. Compliance is certainly welcome but not as required. Local effects are probably not needed at all. Altogether, there seems to be more flexibility in the disciplinary context than with Article 17 complementarity. Article 38 complementarity basically boils down to establishing a consultation mechanism.[52]

Paragraph (5) of Article 38 is applicable if a final decision has been reached on the national level. If it adequately addresses the misconduct in question, the ICC Disciplinary Board has to close its case. On the other hand, there will be no need to continue the case if the national proceedings fully covered what its ICC counterparts would have done. Put differently, if the professional ethics of the ICC have been genuinely enforced by another body, the ICC does not need to repeat the same exercise (ie, *ne bis in idem* should apply). But a complaint may not have been addressed adequately in factual or legal respects. This is more obvious with regard to facts. The Pre-Trial Chamber has stressed that national proceedings must 'encompass both the person and the conduct which is the subject of the case before the Court'.[53] It should be held the same for questions of law, however. Article 4 of the ICC Code provides that it prevails over national standards. Consequently, a decision is only adequate if it mirrors the ICC standards to a high degree. This is a notable difference from the model of complementarity under Article 17. In the latter, the ICC is not supposed to review national decisions which is possible for disciplinary decisions, and even necessary. If national decisions are not a full substitute for ICC decisions, the ICC needs to hand down its own decision. The procedure will thus be continued according to Article 38(5)(b).

[51] ibid, 202–13, for examples and details.

[52] Similar to Rule 162 RPE for Art 70 offences, where no admissibility threshold exists (above, n 29). Further on the procedure for Art 70 offences, see ch 3, II.B.iv at 249–51.

[53] *The Prosecutor v Thomas Lubanga Dyilo*, ICC-01-04-01-06, Pre-Trial Chamber I, Decision on the Prosecutor's Application for a warrant of arrest, 10 February 2006, para 31.

In conclusion, the Code's model of complementarity is different from that under Article 17 of the Statute. The threshold of admissibility should be seen as considerably lower, due to the different purpose of Article 38 complementarity. The Disciplinary Board has wide scope for declaring a case admissible and continuing the procedure. However, both types of complementarity share the same idea. There should be 'interaction' and 'procedural dialogue'[54] between the ICC Disciplinary Board and national authorities to avoid duplicate proceedings, as for both administering criminal justice and professional discipline, each forms a 'community of courts'.[55]

B International Cooperation for ICC Disciplinary Proceedings

Once the ICC launches disciplinary proceedings, it may depend on states for assistance, including enforcement measures.[56] The ICC equivalent to disbarment (permanent ban on practising before the Court and striking off the List of Counsel) and other sanctions need not be enforced externally. At least with respect to fines and the reimbursement of costs of the disciplinary procedure, the Court has to rely on cooperation by states. Assistance may furthermore be necessary during investigations by the Commissioner or for summoning witnesses. Article 87(1) of the Statute provides for requests to state parties, and paragraph (5) for those to non-state parties, be it ad hoc, treaty-based or otherwise. Article 93(1) of the Statute lists a wide array of specific cooperation requests to state parties by the Court other than for arrest and surrender of a person. Whereas the latter two are inconceivable within the context of professional discipline, it may remain of relevance for prosecuting criminal offences, notably under Article 70 of the Statute. Generally speaking, Article 93(1) serves as a broad legal base for international cooperation request, in particular in light of the general clause of subparagraph (l).

It is, however, observed that no cooperation duties for states in the field of professional discipline exist. The existing general duty to cooperate pursuant to Article 86 does arguably not extend to Article 70 offences,[57] and a fortiori even less so to disciplinary measures. This does, of course, not rule out that states will nonetheless cooperate in disciplinary proceedings on an ad hoc basis.

Even then, domestic law will usually not make explicit mention of disciplinary proceedings and may therefore not serve as a base for assistance in disciplinary matters. In the case of Germany's Law on Cooperation with the International Criminal Court (ICC Act),[58] Section 47(1) contains a limiting clause, as assistance is to be given only 'in accordance with the Rome Statute and this law'. Since the

[54] Kleffner and Kor (eds) (n 28) 108.
[55] Burke-White (n 41) 75.
[56] On the cooperation of individual countries with the ICC for crimes, see below, III.C (n 85).
[57] See in detail also below, III.B at 300–05.
[58] Below, III.B at 305–06 (in particular n 102).

Act's scope appears clearly limited to strictly criminal proceedings, assistance for the purpose of professional discipline has no legal base, nor has the enforcement of disciplinary fines under the ICC Code. Given Germany's strict approach, according to which statutory authorisation is needed,[59] disciplinary fines handed down by the ICC bodies would effectively be unenforceable in Germany. Neither would German authorities be able to assist the Court in pending disciplinary matters.

It is hoped that this has illustrated that a number of issues remain unclear where cooperation is concerned which is not encompassed by Article 86. For obvious reasons, the clear focus in drafting had been on the core crimes. The ICC Code of Conduct was a latecomer in the Court's legal framework. Nonetheless, effective cooperation is conceivable because states have their own vital interest in regulating and, if necessary, sanctioning the activities of lawyers from private practice.

C Reciprocal Discipline

The need to respond adequately to a lawyer's unfitness to practise is why domestic authorities are likely to exercise discipline themselves and in cooperation with the ICC, irrespective of the limited duty to cooperate with the ICC. The US Model Rules for Lawyer Disciplinary Enforcement, for example, encourage Bars to adopt foreign disciplinary findings on a routine basis, in order to prevent relitigation of principally the same issue and to guarantee the effectiveness of sanctions.[60] The same is commendable for the ICC in relation to national Bars and vice versa.

Some form of reciprocal discipline by the ICC is explicitly recognised in the Court's own law. Violations of professional standards with no link to the ICC do not constitute misconduct pursuant to Article 31 of the Code and are therefore not disciplinable by the ICC disciplinary bodies. However, reciprocity is achieved through Regulation 71(1)(a) of the Regulations of the Court. Once counsel has been convicted of a serious criminal or disciplinary offence on the national level, he or she no longer meets the criteria required for the inclusion in the List of Counsel.[61] He or she will consequently be disbarred from the ICC.

A reciprocal adoption by state disciplinary bodies may often be the appropriate course. Scenarios are conceivable, though, where additional measures may be warranted and others where this is not the case at all. For example, only the domestic disciplinary bodies will ultimately be in a position to decide whether additional sanctions, such as domestic disbarment, additional practice restrictions within the domestic framework, or a higher fine are necessary on top of an

[59] Ch 2, II.B.i at 64.

[60] Bundesregierung, *Entwurf eines Gesetzes zur Ausführung des Römischen Statuts des Internationalen Strafgerichtshofes vom 17. Juli 1998* (BT-Drs. 14/8527, 13 February 2002) at 40; American Bar Association, *Model Rules for Lawyer Disciplinary Enforcement* (adopted by the American Bar Association House of Delegates on 8 August 1989 and amended on 11 August 1993, 5 August, 8 February 1999 and 12 August 2002) Rule 22. See also ch 2, III.D.iii at 162–63.

[61] Regulation 67(2) RoC. See further ch 3, II.C.iv.a at 266.

ICC disciplinary sanction. There is nothing wrong with such reciprocal measures as long as they respect the primacy of Article 4 (whenever the state is bound by the Code). The ICC disciplinary bodies are accorded primary jurisdiction by Article 4 and Article 38 but this should not be misconstrued as exclusive jurisdiction.[62]

This is notwithstanding the fact that some elements of the domestic disciplinary process may be of a more punitive nature. If several sanctions of a criminal or a quasi-criminal purpose accumulate, the need to acknowledge that counsel is sanctioned more than once in some way will be greater, even if multiple punishment is not inflicted *stricto sensu.* Therefore, domestic disciplinary authorities should take into account punitive elements contained in foreign sanctions at least as mitigating, should there remain the need to hand down an additional sanction.[63]

When administering professional discipline, national authorities have to attain a waiver in respect of counsel's immunity.[64] According to Article 18(1)(b) of the Agreement on the Privileges and Immunities of the International Criminal Court,[65] counsel enjoys '[i]mmunity from legal process of every kind in respect of words spoken or written and all acts performed by him or her in official capacity . . . even after he or she has ceased to exercise his or her functions'. This provision speaks of 'legal process of every kind', not only criminal prosecutions or civil suits. Consequently, this encompasses all legal proceedings, including formal discipline, which attach to counsel's official capacity as an ICC-listed counsel.

The Agreement binds all states who have ratified it,[66] also in respect to their own nationals.[67] This immunity can be waived or invoked by the Presidency of the ICC.[68] A similar immunity applies in respect of the Netherlands as the host state, under the Headquarters Agreement,[69] which again can be waived by the Presidency.[70] The arrest of ICTR counsel Peter Erlinder, albeit in a criminal

[62] See Tuinstra (n 3) 238, but also the pertinent critique, above II.A.i at 291–97.

[63] See also ch 2, II.D.i at 95–97, on Germany.

[64] See also ch 3, II.A.iii.c at 192–93, on immunities. On Art 48 of the Statute, see Schabas (n 28) 620–26, with 624 on counsel in particular.

[65] ICC, *Agreement on the Privileges and Immunities of the International Criminal Court* (ICC-ASP/1/3, ICC-ASP/1/3, 3–10 September 2002).

[66] Art 35.

[67] Art 23(b)(2).

[68] Art 26(2)(f).

[69] ICC, *Headquarters Agreement* (n 2). The ICTY Host Agreement (ICC, *Headquarters Agreement* (n 2) Art 25) which had also been adopted provisionally for the ICC before the entering into force of the former (ICTY, *Headquarter Agreement between the United Nations and the Kingdom of the Netherlands* (S/1994/848, S/1994/848)), only awards immunity to counsel for criminal proceedings, not for professional discipline, Art XIX(3). See also ICC, *Temporary Headquarters Agreement* (19 November 2002); ICC, *Report on the draft headquarters agreement between the International Criminal Court and the host State* (ICC-ASP/5/25, ICC-ASP/5/25, 9 November 2006); JJE Schutte, 'Legal and Practical Implications, from the Perspective of the Host Country, Relating to the Establishment of the International Tribunal for the Former Yugoslavia' (1994) 5 *Criminal Law Forum* 423, 430; S Muller, 'Immunities of ICTY Staff Members, Assets and Archives before the ICTY' in R May et al (eds), *Essays on ICTY Procedure and Evidence in Honour of Gabrielle Kirk McDonald* (The Hague, Kluwer, 2001) 439–54. The permanent Headquarter Agreement also applies to Dutch nationals or residents, Art (4)(b).

[70] Art 30(2)(b)(ii).

case,[71] demonstrates that counsel do run the risk of facing serious allegations of violating national laws in the course of their work. More generally, immunity serves as a bar to protect counsel from frivolous interference by national authorities.[72]

III Criminal Proceedings

A ICC Proceedings for Offences under Article 70 of the Statute

The procedure under Article 70(2) has already been sketched out.[73] If it seems fit under Article 70(4), the case may be referred to national jurisdictions. Rule 162 RPE speaks only of 'the Court' deciding on the exercise of jurisdiction. Since 'the Court' encompasses both the judges and the Office of the Prosecutor (OTP) (Article 34 (a) and (b)), the OTP may already refer a case during the investigation phase (Rule 165(1) RPE). Having the Court dealing with Article 70 offences itself, on the other hand, is particularly conceivable if the suspect or accused is an official of the Court with no specific ties to a state party. This may particularly be the case for counsel misconduct.

Apart from this, both the Court and states can embark on prosecutions. For the ICC, the referral of a case in accordance with Article 70(4)(b) is an option. As flows from Rule 162 RPE, the ICC holds some sort of primary – although not exclusive – jurisdiction: the Court may consult with state parties (1), but must engage in a decision not to exercise jurisdiction of its own before requesting a state party to proceed.

What remains as a trace of complementarity under Article 70(4) of the Statute and Rule 162 RPE differs somewhat in principle from Article 17 of the Statute. Article 70 offences are explicitly exempted from the complementarity requirement.[74] Rule 162 speaks of the availability and moreover of the effectiveness of prosecutions. The named factors are known from conflicts of criminal jurisdictions.[75] This should be, properly speaking, understood to constitute mere

[71] Below III.C at 307. On a motion to ascertain functional immunity for defence counsel and staff from the ICTY case law, see *Prosecutor v Gotovina et al*, IT-06-90-T, Trial Chamber, Decision on Defendant Ante Gotovina's Motion for a Restraining Order against the Republic of Croatia, 23 July 2009, paras 18–21 (motion denied).

[72] On the potential of national disciplinary authorities to interfere, see Tuinstra (n 3) 234. Her interpretation of Art 38 complementarity deserves criticism, though, above II.A.i at 291–97.

[73] Ch 3, II.B.iv.a at 249–60.

[74] Pursuant to Rule 163(2), Part 2 shall not apply to them. This includes Art 17.

[75] The catalogue stems from Preparatory Commission for the ICC, *Proposal submitted by Poland concerning the Rules of Procedure and Evidence, Article 70, Rule 6.26* (PCNICC/1999/WGRPE/DP.29, 2 August 1999) (catalogue of factors for consideration of whether to defer to another jurisdiction) and was then amalgamated with the proposal DP.27 by the Netherlands into Preparatory Commission for the ICC, *Proposal submitted by the Netherlands and Poland concerning the Rules of Procedure and Evidence, Article 70, Rule 6.26* (PCNICC/1999/WGRPE/DP.31, 3 August 1999).

guidance whether to actually adjudicate but not an admissibility threshold or anything similar which needs to be surpassed before prosecutions can be mounted.[76]

The setup serves to decide and justify where to delegate cases, over which the Court naturally has jurisdiction, rather than a bar to the latter (as holds true for Article 38 complementarity in disciplinary proceedings).[77] The crucial difference would be that a case is inadmissible by virtue of Article 17 if a state is willing and able to prosecute it at the national level. In the affirmative, the ICC cannot override national jurisdiction.

To the contrary, Article 70(4) and Rule 162 do not provide for such a mechanism on the same principle. The desirability of encouraging states to prosecute the respective counterparts of Article 70 offences nationally[78] certainly does underlie paragraph (4)(b) and the pertinent Rule 162(2) RPE. Unlike Article 17, though, it does not operate as a bar to ICC prosecutions. Article 70(4)(b) even comes out to the contrary; even though prosecutions do not hinge on authorisation by the ICC, they can be made subject to a request by the ICC, according to whether the ICC itself deems it proper. Consequently, the objective of Article 70(4)(b) is not to achieve a bottom-to-top complementarity with the ICC at the top as the court of last resort. In prosecuting offences against the administration of justice, the ICC does not act as a proxy for the community of nations but in its own right. It is indicative that Rule 162(2) lists not only pragmatic points of the evidentiary situation and expediting proceedings, but a range of separate jurisdictional considerations which highlight the significance of the administration of justice by the ICC as sovereign interest. As flows from (a), the availability and effectiveness of prosecution in a state party, the quality of domestic proceedings can be assessed by the ICC before the backdrop of its own protected interests in the administration of justice; (b), the seriousness of the offence, hints at the fact that the conduct in question may transgress national jurisdictions; (c), the possible joinder to core crimes, demonstrates the possible proximity to the crimes under the Court's own jurisdiction. Lastly, (e), entrenches the notion that exercise of jurisdiction by the ICC may be warranted because the conduct pertains foremost to the ICC's own proceedings.

Furthermore, Article 70(4)(b) read together with Rule 162 RPE presupposes for the concrete case that the Court has jurisdiction and likewise at least one other state party. When the Court has no jurisdiction in the first place, there is nothing for the ICC to decide about exercising it pursuant to Rule 162(1). If no state has jurisdiction, this makes a decision on a Rule 162(4) moot. Put differently, Article 70(4)(b) and Rule 162 govern the scenario that both the ICC and at least one state party have jurisdiction. Accordingly, they aim at settling a conflict of

[76] In a similar vein, Schabas (n 28) 856, calling the exercise of jurisdiction by the ICC under Art 70(4) 'discretionary'.

[77] Above, II.A at 291–97.

[78] Schabas (n 28) 857.

jurisdictions authoritatively by the ICC rather than this Court jumping in because national courts fail to prosecute.[79]

Therefore, Article 70(4)(b) should be understood as a top-to-bottom rule, encouraging referring cases to the national level similar to Rule 11bis ICTY and ICTR RPE. This once more reinforces the assessment that the Court has primary, ie, inherent powers.[80] Inherent does not mean unwritten, however. This clearly distinguishes the ICC's regime from the those of the United Nations International Criminal Tribunal for the former Yugoslavia (ICTY) and the International Criminal Tribunal for Rwanda (ICTR).[81] What inherent boils down to in this context (and again similar to Art 38 complementarity), is that it needs to be considered whether the ICC, rather than the national level, constitutes the more appropriate forum.

Finally, Rule 168 establishes a bar of *ne bis in idem* for cases of criminal misconduct, at least for the ICC with regard to foreign decisions.[82] The Rule does not contain a sham trial or fair trial qualifier as does the corresponding Article 20 of the Statute. The latter cannot simply be invoked mutatis mutandis, since Rule 163(2) decidedly rules out Part 2 of the Statute (save Art 21). Instead, the availability and in particular the effectiveness of domestic proceedings can be taken into account by the ICC prior to deciding, under Article 70(4)(b) and Rule 162 RPE, on which jurisdiction should be exercised or requested to prosecute.

B International Cooperation for ICC Criminal Proceedings

For its own criminal proceedings under Article 70 of the Statute, the ICC may again depend on states for assistance and enforcement measures.[83] The pertinent provision would in principle be Article 87(1) of the Statute for requests to state parties and paragraph (5) for those to non-state parties as long as the core crimes are involved. For those, Article 89 governs surrender to the Court, Article 92 provisional arrest by a state and Article 93(1) lists other available measures. Notwithstanding the applicability of national procedures pursuant to Article 88 of the Statute, this raises in the first place the question of cooperation duties of states. Rule 167 RPE specifically addresses international cooperation and judicial

[79] See Klip (n 23) 367, and *Council Framework Decision 2009/948/JHA of 30 November 2009 on prevention and settlement of conflicts of exercise of jurisdiction in criminal proceedings*, for the attempts within the European Union to solve or reduce pertinent conflicts.

[80] See Preparatory Commission for the ICC, *Rules of Procedure and Evidence* (PCNICC/1999/L.5/Rev.1/Add.1, 22 December 1999), Rule 6.32(a); Preparatory Commission for the ICC, *Proposal submitted by the Netherlands in connection with document PCNICC/1999/WGRPE/RT.5* (PCNICC/1999/WGRPE/DP.27, 30 July 1999) at 1.

[81] Ch 1, II.B.i.a at 17–18, D at 33, 36–37, III.B.ii at 39–40, D at 45.

[82] Above, I.C at 290.

[83] On individual countries, see R Cryer and O Bekou, 'International Crimes and ICC Cooperation in England and Wales' (2007) 5 *Journal of International Criminal Justice* 441 and ibid, 449 ; P Wilkitzki, 'The German Law on Cooperation with the ICC' (2005) 76 *Revue internationale de droit pénal* 97; P Wilkitzki, 'The German Law on Cooperation with the ICC' (2002) 2 *International Criminal Law Review* 195.

assistance. No duty to cooperate flows from this, as sub-rule (2) only makes reference to the conditions under Article 70(2) of the Statute.[84] According to this, the domestic laws of the requested state govern the request.

It does not seem permissible to conclude to such cooperation duties simply *a maiore ad minus* from states obligations under Article 70(a) and (b). The adaptation of national legislation under (a) views at prosecutions and trials in a domestic forum. It therefore does not address cooperation for international proceedings at all. The same holds true for a state's duties after an Article 70(b) referral from the ICC. In that case, duties to prosecute effectively ensue, but again only within the national framework. It does not trigger cooperation duties. Those are an *aliud* to prosecution, although the latter may cause more extensive efforts.

It is noted that the duty of states to cooperate under Article 86 only extends to 'crimes within the jurisdiction of the Court'.[85] This is the exact phrasing of the title of Article 5 of the Statute used to circumscribe the Court's jurisdiction over the core crimes of genocide, crimes against humanity, war crimes and the crime of aggression. Similarly, Article 93(1)(l) appears to speak of those 'crimes' only. In contrast to Part 9 of the Statute, Article 70 of the Statute speaks of 'offences', and it its paragraph (4) merely recognises two duties of a state party to assist the Court in prosecuting offences against its administration of justice.[86] The first is (a), to make its own offences applicable to offences committed on its one territory or by a national. The second (b), would be to handle such cases in domestic courts at the request of the ICC.

This casts serious doubt on whether the 'offences' under Article 70 of the Statute are covered, let alone disciplinary investigations and prosecutions.[87] The Code of Professional Conduct and its procedures were definitely unknown when the Statute was drafted and adopted. In addition to the clear textual distinction between 'crimes' and 'offences' under the Statute, an argument can be made from the drafting history of what is now Part 9. It appears that a number of options were presented to the drafting bodies, among which were broad ones that did not limit states' obligations the core crimes. Initially, the Ad hoc Committee focused on cooperation for the core crimes only.[88] Similarly, the Preparatory Committee

[84] Schabas (n 28) 858.

[85] C Kreß and K Prost in O Triffterer (ed), *Commentary on the Rome Statute of the International Criminal Court*, 2nd edn (Munich, Beck, 2008) art 86, mn 15, note that a coherent interpretation with Part 2 is needed for Art 86. Accordingly, the Court has the competence to rule on the issue of whether it has jurisdiction in a particular case. Part 2, however, only concerns the issue of jurisdiction for core crimes in first place.

[86] See DK Piragoff in O Triffterer (ed), *Commentary on the Rome Statute of the International Criminal Court*, 2nd edn (Munich, Beck, 2008) art 70, mn 20.

[87] See also from a more general stance, A Zahar, 'International Court and Private Citizen' (2009) 12 *New Criminal Law Review* 569, 578.

[88] See, eg, Ad Hoc Committee for the ICC, *General Issues Relating to States' Cooperation with ICC; Proposal by the Coordinator* (UD/A/AC.244/IP, 16 August 1995), and Preparatory Committee for the ICC, *Unofficial Discussion Draft, Part 7: International Cooperation, United States* (7 April 1996) at 1 (both 'crimes under this Statute').

faced mostly proposals addressed at cooperation for the core crimes.[89] Even with regard to the scope of cooperation duties in this narrow area, it was observed that

> all basic elements of the required cooperation between the court and States should be laid down explicitly in the statute itself, while the list of such elements need not be exhaustive. It was suggested that a State would need to have a clear understanding of the types of assistance required to qualify their obligations in accordance with its domestic law, or to make provisions in their law for specific forms of assistance to be available.[90]

This needs to be contrasted with other proposals aiming at a much broader area of cooperation, namely the duty to cooperate 'in connection with any investigations and proceedings under this Statute'.[91] In a similar vein, some states suggested that the pertinent Article could list the core areas of cooperation but without being exhaustive or otherwise limited to the core crimes.[92]

At the end of 1997, the Preparatory Committee's Working Group on International Cooperation and Judicial Assistance still carried with it some of the different proposals with regard to the rigidity of the cooperation duty. As to the substantive matter, it seems to have limited it by having settled on the use of the phrase 'crimes under the Statute', which was said to be derived from Article 51(1) of the ILC Draft of 1994.[93] This paragraph reads: 'States Parties shall cooperate with the Court in connection with criminal investigations and proceedings under

[89] See Preparatory Committee for the ICC, *Part 7, International Cooperation: Proposal, Submitted by the United States of America* (A/AC.249/WP.15, 19 August 1996).

[90] Preparatory Committee for the ICC, *Draft Summary of the Proceedings of the Preparatory Committee During the Period 25 March–12 April: VI. Cooperation between States and the International Criminal Court* (A/AC.249/CRP.6, 10 April 1996) 2, paras 4 and further 5–6.

[91] Preparatory Committee for the ICC, *International Cooperation and Judicial (Mutual) Assistance: Working Paper, Submitted by South Africa and Lesotho* (A/AC.249/L.5, 7 August 1996) at 5.

[92] See Preparatory Committee for the ICC, *Compilation of Proposals on Judicial Cooperation and Enforcement Submitted to August 1996 Phase of the Preparatory Committee on the Establishment of an International Criminal Court* (UD/A/AC.249/1996/WG.5/IP, 22 August 1996) at 7, 8; Preparatory Committee for the ICC, *Tentative Draft on International Cooperation and Judicial Assistance, Japan* (A/AC.249/WP.14, 19 August 1996) ('matters including but not limited to'); Preparatory Committee for the ICC, *Unofficial Tentative Draft on International Cooperation and Judicial Assistance, Japan* (4 April 1996), Preparatory Committee for the ICC, *Report of the Informal Group on Judicial Cooperation and Enforcement* (A/AC.249/CRP.17, 27 August 1996); Preparatory Committee for the ICC, *State Proposals on Part 7. International Cooperation and Judicial [Mutual] Assistance* (UD/A/AC.249/1996/WG.5/IP, 21 August 1996); Preparatory Committee for the ICC, *Legal Experts Project: Working Group on Compliance with Requests by the Court, Annex II, Part 7. International Cooperation and Judicial Assistance* (UD/A/AC.249/1996/WG.5/IP, 13 September 1996) ('the widest possible measure of mutual assistance').

[93] Preparatory Committee for the ICC, *Legal Experts Project: Working Group on Compliance with Requests by the Court, Annex III. Working Paper prepared by interested delegations regarding Part 7 (International Cooperation and Judicial Assistance)* (UD/A/AC.249/1996/WG.5/IP, 13 September 1996). At that stage, a negative definition of cooperation duties had been tabled as well (see the bracketed clause in Art 51(1): '[A State Party shall not deny a request for cooperation except as specifically provided in this Part.]'). Fn 6 remarks on such an approach that '[t]he need for and the propriety of this sentence was questioned. It could be reconsidered in the light of the other provisions on cooperation'. (Both are repeated in Preparatory Committee for the ICC, *Abbreviated Compilation of Proposals on International Cooperation and Judicial Assistance (ILC Statute Part 7) and Enforcement (ILC Statute Part 8)* (A/AC.249/1997/WG.5/CRP.1, 25 November 1997) at 2, fn 5).

this Statute'.[94] It should not be misconstrued as a broad approach embracing all kinds of criminal proceedings because offences on the administration of justice within the Court's own jurisdiction were unknown.[95] Moreover, the Commentary to Article 51 makes it clear that there had been no consensus about a general duty to cooperate on all matters which could potentially come before the Court.[96] During the decisive stages of the drafting of the Statute at the Rome Conference in 1998, the Working Group reduced the Rolling Text for Article 85 (what is now Art 86) to 'crimes under this statute'.[97] The Drafting Committee then came up with the final phrasing of 'crimes within the jurisdiction of the Court',[98] at a point when Article 70 and the 'offences' under it had already been clearly juxtaposed to the 'crimes' under Article 5 of the Statute.[99]

Given all of this, the drafting history supports a narrow interpretation of the general duty to cooperate pursuant to Article 86. It is restricted to Article 5 crimes and does not cover cooperation for investigations and prosecutions under Article 70 or the ICC Code of Conduct.[100] Unlike the contended lack of cooperation duties towards the ICTY or the ICTR for contempt proceedings,[101] the matter would not have been ultra vires for the Assembly of States Parties. The ambit of the cooperation regime could have been drawn out a lot further but ultimately it was not.

Again, this does not preclude that states will nonetheless cooperate in Article 70 proceedings. Duties may follow from domestic legislation, if not the Statute. For example, Germany does not discriminate between core 'crimes' and other 'offences' in its implementing legislation.[102] Section 1(2) ICC Act defines 'Court' with whom Germany cooperates as the 'International Criminal Court established

[94] Preparatory Committee for the ICC, *Unofficial Abbreviated Compilation of Proposals on International Cooperation and Judicial Assistance (ILC Statute Part 7) and Enforcement (ILC Statute Part 8)* (UD/A/AC.249/1997/WG.1/IP, 1 December 1997).

[95] Instead, only Art 44(2) of the ILC Draft obligated states to extend their own perjury laws. See ch 3, II.B.i at 241 (in particular in n 349).

[96] International Law Commission, *Report of the International Law Commission on the work of its forty-sixth session (2 May-22 July 1994)* (A/49/10, 4 August 1997) 62–63.

[97] ibid, 63, Commentary (3); Rome Conference for the ICC, *Report of the Working Group on International Cooperation and Assistance* (A/CONF.183/C.1/WGIC/L.11, 1 July 1998).

[98] Rome Conference for the ICC, *Rolling Text of Articles 85 and 86* (A/CONF.183/C.1/WGIC/L.10, 1 July 1998); Rome Conference for the ICC, *Texts Adopted on Second Reading* (A/CONF.183/DC/R.77, 6 July 1998).

[99] Ch 3, II.B.i at 242 (nn 356–60).

[100] Rome Conference for the ICC, *Report of the Drafting Committee to the Committee of the Whole, Part 9. International Cooperation and Judicial Assistance* (A/CONF.183/C.1/L.68, 13 July 1998); M Bohlander, 'International Criminal Defence Ethics: The Law of Professional Conduct for Defence Counsel Appearing before International Criminal Tribunals' (2000) 1 *San Diego International Law Journal* 75, 88.

[101] Ch 1, II.D at 35–36 (n 190).

[102] *Law on Cooperation with the International Criminal Court* (ICC Act), Gesetz über die Zusammenarbeit mit dem Internationalen Strafgerichtshof (IStGH-Gesetz – IStGHG) of 21 June 2002, BGBl. I2144. See J Cockayne, 'Commentary' in A Klip and G Sluiter (eds), *Annotated Leading Cases of International Criminal Tribunals, vol 4, The International Criminal Tribunal for the former Yugoslavia 1999–2000* (Antwerp, Intersentia, 2002) 200; Bundesregierung, *Entwurf eines Gesetzes zur Ausführung des Römischen Statuts des Internationalen Strafgerichtshofes vom 17. Juli 1998* (n 60).

by the Rome Statute, including its Presidency, its Chambers, its Office of the Prosecutor, its Registry and staff of these Organs'. It does not list the disciplinary bodies but it clearly does cover Article 70 offences which are prosecuted by the Prosecutor and tried before Chambers.[103] Section 2 provides for the surrender of persons for the purpose of all criminal prosecutions and enforcement of sentences pursuant to the Rome Statute; Sections 29 and 30 address search and seizure; Section 40 the enforcement of sentences imposed under the Statute; and Section 43 monetary fines. The latter expressly speaks of sentences for 'a criminal act in Article 5 of the Rome Statute' along with a 'criminal act as set forth in Article 70 para 1 of the Rome Statute'. Section 54 on temporary surrender mentions Article 70 as well. Lastly, Section 63 specifically addresses domestic German prosecutions under Article 70(4) of the Statute and provides that 'the Court shall be informed as soon as possible of the activities undertaken based upon the request.' Section 47 further provides for other mutual legal assistance (*sonstige Rechtshilfe*) to the Court, such as summoning witnesses (Section 53), the service of documents (Section 57) and the disclosure of official documents and information by German courts and authorities to the Court (Section 58). Consequently, Germany would be under a domestic legal duty to cooperate fully in all criminal proceedings before the ICC, including those under Article 70 of the Statute (but arguably not for disciplinary proceedings).[104]

C National Criminal Prosecutions

It is conceivable that states prosecute misconduct if it falls under their jurisdiction and amounts to a domestic criminal offence. State parties are under particular obligations to extend their criminal laws in such a way and to prosecute pursuant to Article 70 of the Statute.[105]

As it stands, the double jeopardy bar in Rule 168 RPE only bars the ICC from a new trial. States are not bound by either Rule 168 or Article 20 of the Statute from prosecuting and entering a conviction.[106]

[103] The draft legislation rejects a duty of cooperation for other than criminal proceedings. See Wilkitzki (2005) (n 85); Wilkitzki (2002) (n 85).

[104] On non-cooperation in disciplinary matters, see above II.B at 297–98.

[105] Under German law, the pertinent offences with the administration of justice as the protected legal interest were usually understood to mean the administration of justice by German authorities (see P Cramer in W Joecks and K Miebach (eds), *Münchener Kommentar zum StGB*, vol 3 [§§ 185–262] (Munich, Beck, 2003) § 258, fn 4). Statutory amendments have been enacted with regard to bribing judges and other officials as well as the perjury offences under Section 153 of the Criminal Code. See Section 2 of the *Gesetz über das Ruhen der Verfolgungsverjährung und die Gleichstellung der Richter und Bediensteten des Internationalen Strafgerichtshofs* (published in BGBl. I 2002, 2144, 2162), declaring judges and other officials of the ICC equivalent to German judges and officials for the purposes of Sections 331–36 and 338 of the StGB. No such provision exists for Section 258. For perjury offences, see Art 1 of the *Gesetz zur Umsetzung des Rahmenbeschlusses des Rates der Europäischen Union zur Bekämpfung der sexuellen Ausbeutung von Kindern und der Kinderpornographie* (published in BGBl. I 2008, 2149), introducing new Section 162 of the Criminal Code; A Sinn, 'Die Einbeziehung der internationalen Rechtspflege in den Anwendungsbereich der Aussagedelikte' (2008) *Neue Juristische Wochenschrift* 3526.

[106] Above, I.C at 290.

For criminal prosecution in relation to counsel's official capacity as an ICC-listed counsel, the possible immunity under Article 18(1) of the Agreement on the Privileges and Immunities of the International Criminal Court or Article 25 of the Headquarters Agreement is emphasised.[107] Again, the Agreement on the Privileges and Immunities in this respect binds all states having ratified it. National authorities consequently need to attain a waiver by the Presidency of the ICC.[108] A waiver is unnecessary, though, if a case is referred to a state party under Article 70(4). In respect to such a case, the Court can be said to waive the applicable immunities implicitly.

The need for such protection from national criminal proceedings can be illustrated by the arrest of ICTR counsel Peter Erlinder in Rwanda. His arrest was based on charges of 'denying and minimizing' the Rwandan Genocide for statements that he made in the context of defending a client before the ICTR, and which were deemed by Rwandan authorities in violation of their domestic criminal laws.[109]

IV The Relationships of Sanctions within the ICC Regime

A Concurrence Issues between the ICC's Enforcement Mechanisms

Finally, multiplicity problems occur in horizontal relations. This seems less of an issue under international law but rather within the respective legal order. The relationship of different measures within the same forum basically depends on the different purposes underlying them and needs to be aligned within this system. The purpose and character of institutional and liability controls on the one hand, and the criminal law on the other, are obviously distinct. Therefore, multiple proceedings in the same factual matter are plainly permissible. Professional discipline

[107] Above, II.C at 300, including n 71 on a motion to ascertain functional immunity for defence counsel and their staff in the ICTY case of *Gotovina*. See also ch 3, II.A.iii.c at 192–93.

[108] Art 26(2)(f).

[109] See the Registrar's *note verbale* to Rwanda of 15 June 2010, annexed to *Théoneste Bagosora et al v Prosecutor*, 98-41-A, Registry, Further Registrar's Submissions under Rule 33 (B) of the Rules of Procedure and Evidence in Respect of the Appeals Chamber Order to the Registrar dated 9 June 2010, 15 June 2010. The Appeals Chamber held that his visit to Rwanda was not in his official capacity and that he would not enjoy immunity in regard to these acts there. Immunity does attach to words and acts undertaken as part of his defence work at the ICTR before and after (*Théoneste Bagosora et al v The Prosecutor*, ICTR-98-41-A, Appeals Chamber, Decision on Aloys Ntabakuzes's Motion for Injunctions Against the Government of Rwanda Regarding the Arrest and Investigation of Lead Counsel Peter Erlinder, 6 October 2010, paras 27–30). He was later banned from the ICTR for refusing to travel to Rwanda and further appearing in the case (see *Aloys Ntabakuze v The Prosecutor*, ICTR-98-41A-A, Appeals Chamber, Order Imposing Sanctions on Ntabakuze's Lead Counsel, 21 April 2011).

is more difficult in this respect as its relationship will depend on how the character, the content and its closeness to criminal proceedings are assessed. Moreover, Article 71 merits a few words as it is an institutional control but does provide for the possibility of a fine, in furtherance of purely procedural measures. This embraces overlaps with the punitive elements of the retrospective sanctioning systems, Article 70 and professional discipline.

B The Relationship of Article 70 Proceedings to Article 71

Rule 172 RPE expounds explicitly on the relationship of criminal law to the non-criminal sanctions under Article 71: 'If conduct covered by article 71 also constitutes one of the offences defined in article 70, the Court shall proceed in accordance with article 70 and rules 162 to 169'. Such a clear priority rule is laudable and removes concurrence issues between the two.

From a policy perspective, giving priority to criminal prosecutions for Article 70 offences over the institutional measures under Article 71 seems a sound choice. In respect of fines or other retributive elements of Article 71 sanctions, the possible imposition of a criminal sentence pursuant to Article 70(3) of the Statute serves the sanctioning purpose. In consequence, no need for an Article 71 fine will exist. If necessary, temporary interdiction under Article 71 and temporary suspension under Rule 71(2)(b) of the Regulations of the Court (RoC) could be ordered in the interim. As long as it is made subject to decisions later in the criminal investigation, this seems reconcilable with the notion underlying cited Rule 172. It would at least be more proportional than, say, ordering immediate arrest under Rule 169 RPE. It could be argued that foregoing Article 71 deprives the judges of the coercive functions of a repeating cumulative fines for continuing misconduct as prescribed in Rule 171(3) RPE. However, this is only seemingly so. If the continuing misconduct constitutes a criminal act, be it the same as the original or a new one, the prospect of the criminal sentence for it can exercise the coercive function. Should the continuing misconduct not be criminal, the judges will simply be in a position to proceed in accordance with Article 71, Rules 170 and 171 for that distinct instance of misconduct.

Measures and findings taken for the purposes of Article 71 may be of evidentiary use in subsequent criminal proceedings for Article 70. As Rules 163 and 165 make clear, a full trial will take place for them in any event. Since the standard for criminal convictions is beyond reasonable doubt, prior findings on a lower threshold will of course not be binding in any respect.

C The Relationship of Professional Discipline towards Article 70 and Article 71 Sanctions

No such clear-cut rule can be found for professional discipline. Allegations of misconduct may also constitute the base for charges under Article 70 and 71 of the ICC Statute.[110] Although it could be argued that those Articles are genuine criminal offences and sanctioning thus serves a different purpose than imposing disciplinary measures, it needs to be clarified how they might affect each other.[111] As far as professional discipline is concerned, adherence to professional rules may argue in favour of counsel under criminal prosecution but is usually not considered binding for criminal law. Criminal conduct, on the other hand, is generally understood to be a foundation for professional discipline.

In Germany, disciplinary proceedings need to be suspended if criminal prosecutions are instituted, and professional discipline can only be imposed in addition to a criminal conviction if professional aspects warrant it.[112] Findings in the previous criminal trial are binding for the disciplinary case. The rationale seems to be that professional discipline is viewed as quasi-criminal. It follows criminal procedure and, for example, provides for monetary fines.

Under US law, no fixed relationship seems to exist in terms of procedure.[113] Criminal charges, contempt proceedings and professional discipline can all be pursued alongside each other. The purposes underlying those different measures are seen as vastly different. Professional discipline is argued to be a measure *sui generis* which carries a lower standard of proof, refers to civil procedure as applicable and does not recognise fines. The Model Rules for Lawyer Disciplinary Enforcement reject a suspension of the disciplinary proceedings in the case of concurrent pending criminal or civil trials.[114]

In this study, it has been argued that the ICC is closer to the German model, ie, taking a quasi-criminal approach.[115] The defendant counsel is awarded a number of rights under Article 40 of the ICC Code which are typically awarded as criminal due process rights. The fine as a sanction under Article 41 is punitive. Furthermore, Regulation 71(1) establishes a link between criminal proceedings in relationship to professional misconduct and professional regulation. Pursuant to subregulation (1)(c), removal from the list of counsel necessarily results from any criminal conviction, whereas this is not the case in the disciplinary procedure.

In consequence, it is suggested that discipline by the ICC authorities should be aligned with criminal proceedings by giving the lead to the latter. After the criminal procedure is closed, it can be concluded by discipline. Using the findings of the criminal procedure is appropriate because it increases the efficiency of the disciplinary procedure and because it is in line with what is usually done domestically.[116] If the burden of proof is the same for criminal convictions and

[110] See ch 3, II.A.iv.a at 193.

[111] eg, with regard to the enforcement of sanctions or the admissibility of evidence obtained within the course of other proceedings. See also Art 38 ICTY Code.

[112] Ch 2, II.D.i at 95–97.

[113] Ch 2, III.D.ii at 158–61.

[114] JM Burkoff, *Criminal Defense Ethics, 2nd: Law and Liability*, 2005 edn (St Paul, Minn, West Group, 2005) §1:8, with pertinent case law in fn 3, and § 2:9. See also American Bar Association, *Model Rules for Lawyer Disciplinary Enforcement* (n 60) Rule 18(G).

[115] See ch 3, II.A.ii at 179–85.

[116] See ch 2, II.D.i at 95, and III.D.ii at 160–61.

professional discipline, the ICC disciplinary bodies should recognise a defence of collateral estoppel, ie, exonerating prior findings. Finally, when imposing disciplinary sanctions it should be taken into consideration whether and to what extent an additional response, through the avenue of professional discipline, is warranted. This could again follow along the lines of the German model, making a second sanction appropriate if warranted as disciplinary *addendum*.[117] This would be a consequence of assessing discipline under the ICC Code as a quasi-criminal control, rather than a *sui generis* system fully detached from criminal law as in the United States.[118] This would do justice to the concept of professional discipline as a sanctioning format addressing counsel in his specific professional capacity.

As far as Article 71 sanctions are concerned, it is stressed that their purpose is rather administrative. It shares with civil contempt and other institutional measures that the primary function will often be coercive (*Beugungsfunktion* in German), not punitive.[119] Moreover it is different as it is an immediate measure, with the disciplinary regime under the Code and Article 70 criminal proceedings being retrospective. Therefore, Article 71 serves a different purpose. Consequently, pertinent parallel sanctions will be permissible. Of course, proportionality in administering professional discipline as well as in criminal sentencing would require considering the effects of Article 71 sanctions.[120] Findings under the procedure for Article 71 will not binding since they will follow from a lower burden of proof. Again, they may be used as relevant evidence.

[117] Ch 2, II.D.i at 95.
[118] Ch 2, III.D.ii at 160.
[119] Ch 3, II.C.ii.a at 258.
[120] Ch 2, II.D.i at 97.

Conclusions on International Counsel and Misconduct

I A Summary of the Study

This study started out based firstly on the assumption that codes of conduct and other instruments prescribe professional standards for lawyers, and that this is a common phenomenon. Such standards serve to regulate the profession. Most particularly, they help in establishing rules for what constitutes the desirable good practice of lawyers on the one hand, and misconduct on the other. It has been a second premise of the study that misconduct does occur. Identifying the exact limits of the permissible can be hard, and it is sometimes impossible. Professional standards are often of a guiding nature, rather than being bright-line rules. This is also owing to the role of defence lawyers in the modern criminal process. They are supposed to act as advocates for their clients and they are at the same time entrusted with special duties towards the administration of justice. This interdependence between two fundamentally conflicting ends creates a tension that reflects in the regulation of counsel. It seems beyond dispute, though, that many instances of misconduct clearly fall below what is acceptable. Going from this premise, the focus throughout the study has been on answering the question of which measures are available to courts and the other actors in the administration of justice in response to misconduct.

In chapter one, the International Criminal Tribunal for the former Yugoslavia (ICTY), the International Criminal Tribunal for Rwanda (ICTR) and the Special Court for Sierra Leone (SCSL) were examined as the exemplars of the modern generation of international criminal courts leading up to the ICC. It was outlined how Chambers and other organs of the Tribunals sanctioned misconduct, foremost disclosure of protected information, fee issues, frivolous litigation and interferences with witnesses or evidence. Although a disciplinary framework was in place for the ICTY and the SCSL, the three UN tribunals have mostly pursued other avenues for sanctioning misconduct. Defence counsel were held in criminal contempt for the graver occurrences of misconduct, whereas less serious forms have drawn warnings, suspensions and fee denial. In this, the tribunals have not built on provisions that were entrenched in their Statutes, Rules of Procedure and Evidence, and other instruments, but they have enlarged their powers gradually in order to adapt to the needs, namely those in respect of the doctrine of contempt. As a side effect, the applicable procedure has lacked or still lacks corresponding safeguards.

This was contrasted, in chapter two, with the national models of Germany and the United States. The chapter thus demonstrated how the regulation, and as part of its sanctioning mechanisms, rests on a number of distinct bases. At the outset, regulation of lawyers in both countries is provided for by systems of professional discipline. In both countries, professional discipline helps set standards, but the system is ultimately underused and does not capture all the conceivable forms of misconduct as effectively as other measures can. Thus, sanctioning builds on a pool of measures, which would make it short-sighted to limit a study into reactions against misconduct to professional discipline. In general, this pool on the whole is the same for criminal defence lawyers as for other lawyers, all of them being members of the same, integrated profession. However, criminal defence brings about particular types of misconduct which tend to draw specific kinds of reactions. Civil malpractice claims, or 'liability controls', are practically irrelevant for criminal defence. This is due to a number of factors of the criminal trial but also the client structure. An essential finding was made that the main focus of reactions in both countries is on 'institutional controls', typically measures by the affected courts, and the criminal laws, as 'legislative controls'. The reason for reliance on the former, in both countries, has been explained by the fact that firstly a large portion of misconduct by defence lawyers is litigation-related, and secondly that these controls are immediately available to the affected actors. Consequently, this results in preferring them over more protracted ex post facto reactions. However, criminal prosecutions do figure prominently, as they carry the harshest sanctions. It could be observed for both countries how the most pertinent offences against the administration of justice are usually framed along general clauses and that they intertwine substantively with other professional standards. The emphasis on institutional controls and the criminal law was similarly strong in both countries. This again corroborates the major finding in relation to the Tribunals in chapter one. However, it also helped to discern a fundamental distinction between the common law approach of the United States, and with it also the Tribunals, and the civil law approach represented by Germany. The concept of inherent powers in general and of contempt in particular was explained and analysed for the United States and the Tribunals. It constitutes a fundamentally different footing for reacting to counsel misconduct than what the German approach builds on – that of statutory entrenchment. Germany has shown, though, that courts still resort to unwritten powers, though these appear much more limited.

Chapter three then turned to the ICC. The offences against the administration of justice in Article 70 of the Statute constitute an equivalent to legislative controls in the national model. An attempt was also made to identify institutional actors within the ICC's framework, which lead to examining the procedural powers of Chambers and powers of the Registry.

Finally, chapter four put the various reaction mechanisms into relationship with each other. Multiple admission and consequently multiple regulation is recognised from the United States, but it also follows for most lawyers in international criminal defence. Generally, this leads to competition among international and national jurisdictions on the one hand, and among the different sets of sanctions on the other. The vertical concurrence between different jurisdictions may bring about conflicts of law and multiple proceedings for the same instance of misconduct. This is less of a problem for institutional controls but can be more challenging for professional controls. In its Articles 4 and 38, the ICC Code offers solutions for both, with the devil being in the detail. As to the second type of multiplicity of sanctions – horizontal concurrence – it is foremost criminal sanctions and disciplinary measures which need to be reconciled, in particular if discipline is quasi-criminal.

II Sanctioning Counsel and the Various Types of Enforcement Mechanisms

The ICC's legal framework vests the Court with a sound foundation for regulating the activities of counsel and if necessary sanctioning counsel.

So far, the ICC has put an emphasis on institutional measures. It does not hold contempt powers, as the UN tribunals do, but has made use of other institutional mechanisms when, for example, denying fees to counsel Hadi Shalluf.[1] This fits in with the model outlined by Wilkins. The Chamber and the Registry certainly used the information advantages as they would as the relevant institutions predictably do.[2] Other advantages over discipline can also easily be illustrated. [3] Withholding fees was faster and less complicated than having the issues of the scope of the mandate settled by the disciplinary bodies.[4] However, at the same time the danger of over-deterring lawful conduct materialised.[5] On the one hand, this may have lead Shalluf refrain from filing some unnecessary pleadings. On the other hand, it may well kept him from pursuing more valid points for which he feared to go unremunerated again. The reluctance to act as defence counsel in the view of such institutional sanctions can be understood from the Dieckmann case.[6] Finally, the possibly weak position of the affected individual[7], the suspect or accused, becomes apparent. Institutional measures such as fee denial have had the advantage of expediting the proceedings in some way, but with little say from possible defendants thus potentially causing a disadvantage to them. In conclusion, referring such ad hoc defence issues and alleged or potential misconduct arising from them to a disciplinary mechanism, promises that they should be resolved more advantageously.

[1] Ch 3, II.C.iv at 268, for the *Shalluf* case.

[2] DB Wilkins, 'Who Should Regulate Lawyers?' (1992) 105 *Harvard Law Review* 801, 835.

[3] See ibid, 843.

[4] See JT Tuinstra, *Defence Counsel in International Criminal Law* (Cambridge, Cambridge University Press, 2009) 233.

[5] Wilkins (n 2) 837.

[6] Ch 3, II.C.v at 270–71.

[7] Wilkins (n 2) 839.

Institutional controls will predictably form the bulk of sanctions, and judging from the very early case law of the ICC, this would appear to be the case. Institutional controls are administered by the judges, and therefore prove the fastest and often most effective controls. Throughout this study I have attempted to demonstrate how this is prone to compromising defence rights and for this reason, the ICC should take a cautious position in relation to it. Of course, it still needs to be seen how the availability and reality of sanctions will play out before the ICC. The Tribunals and the national models have given certain leads. The ICC may arguably not be as free as it would like to adopt these leads. Whereas any court will always have some inherent powers flowing from its procedural authority, the ICC definitely appears to lack the broad scope of inherent powers that it ingrained for the Tribunals and common law courts. Ultimately, it remains open whether the ICC is more of a civil law court. But counsel regulation may at least point in this direction.

Disciplinary measures have been used, however, to address other problems. The first two ICC disciplinary cases dealt with counsel not reporting relevant personal circumstances (the imposition of a domestic disciplinary sanction) and breaching confidentiality duties (passing on a password to protected information).[8] Using the disciplinary system made sense for both and having caused no tangible harm so far, both instances can be described as low level misconduct involving a more abstract breach of professional norms.[9] It needs to be stressed, however, that disciplinary controls have structural limitations.[10] For example, once the leak of protected information affects the proceedings, an additional stronger institutional, ie, procedural measure may become necessary to safeguard the progress of the proceedings.[11] Furthermore, personal liability – though not provided under the ICC regime –may be needed to compensate the affected individuals.

Disciplinary controls are easily the most specific tools in counsel regulation. This holds true again for the ICC, with its scheme of professional discipline based on the ICC Code. However, the experience of the International Tribunal as well as the national models of the United States and Germany have shown that in many cases they do not provide us with the most immediate and most effective sanctions. Professional discipline offers the foundation for the regulation of the profession, but it has tended to be underused in all of the considered jurisdictions. It therefore seems safe to assume the same for the ICC in the long run. This is not to say that professional discipline should be neglected; to the contrary, it is easily the most versatile form of sanctioning but in order to achieve this, sufficient funding and support from within the profession are needed.

[8] Ch 3, II.A at 177.

[9] See for both Wilkins (n 2) 848. See also Tuinstra (n 4) 234. Negligence may be an important indicator that it is indeed a minor case not warranting a fully-fledged trial. But the state of mind does not seem to be the key. Rather, the issue is rather whether discipline is preferable because it produces less transaction costs and is equally effective. The judge dealing with negligence by way of institutional measures may be more advisable in other circumstances.

[10] Wilkins (n 2) 822.

[11] Discipline can also be beneficial if knowledgeable lawyers participate. See Tuinstra (n 4) 233. But judges may, or even should be, equally familiar with the issues involved in professional ethics.

Whereas a legislative *stricto sensu* does not exist for international organisations, a number of measures can still be identified which would be legislative controls in the national model because they are external, and because they are exercised by a non-judicial authority that can be held accountable politically. Criminal offences are the prime example of this, on the national level as well as in the international arena as they are typically used to hold counsel responsible for intentional misconduct of a serious nature. Their scope is narrower than that of any of the other sets of controls.

Article 70 offences are in place as the ICC's legislative-style controls with external regulators.[12] They have not been used yet. As in the national models, criminal offences are reserved for addressing the most serious instances of misconduct. This is in line with the theoretical model. External regulators are not necessarily more vigilant.[13] Moreover, the costs of legislative controls in terms of administrative, participants and third-party costs tends to be higher than for others.[14] This can also be said of Article 70 offences, prosecutions for which require a much more protracted procedure and the involvement of more participants than would any of the other ICC sanctioning mechanisms.

Finally, it is reiterated that liability controls are the only true lacuna of the ICC's regime. However, international criminal justice in general does not provide for liability controls. This does not seem a fundamental flaw, though, as civil liability is not an effective sanctioning mechanism in criminal defence. Whatever turns out to be necessary needs to be regulated on the national level. It does therefore not seem a great loss, given the costs and benefits of litigation for weak individual clients.[15] This is not to say that recourse to liability may not become necessary in isolated instances which will have to be catered for by national jurisdictions, which will presumably be an acceptable forum.

Altogether, the ICC's system is quite sophisticated and seems up to the challenge of offering the 'appropriate disciplinary enforcement mechanisms'.[16] It features what is needed most in criminal justice, as a litigation-dominated area of legal practice: the two fitting main pillars would be a comprehensive system of discipline on the one hand, with a wide range of institutional controls including the Chambers and the Registrar, on the other.[17] Both pillars would help to achieve compliance in the various fields of counsel misconduct. These are complemented

[12] See Wilkins (n 2) 846.
[13] ibid, 844.
[14] See ibid, 847.
[15] ibid, 830.
[16] See Tuinstra (n 4) 232–35.
[17] Tuinstra probably underestimates the usefulness and the role of the Registrar. See ibid, 235. On her note that 'the Registrar, not necessarily being a legally trained person, may not be competent to assess whether or not counsel's misconduct has been unprofessional' it is remarked that it is, of course, usually not the Registrar in person who deals with the nitty-gritty routine of counsel issues. Rather, he or she will benefit from trained legal staff, as would be the case for other areas such as witness protection. On the independence, it depends on what the Registrar does, and if he or she acts at arm's length in appropriate circumstances. Entry controls should be less problematic than withdrawing assignment in a pending case.

by some external, legislative-style controls which quite sensibly have a narrow scope to cover only the most serious criminal instances of misconduct.

As has been noted also by Tuinstra,[18] such a combination is needed, due to the relative advantages and disadvantages of each sets of controls. Concluding, as Tuinstra does, that simultaneous sanctions should not apply seems unconvincing in this respect. [19] As the various measures by the ICC serve different purposes, applying some of them at the same time may be needed and permissible as long as they are aligned.[20] Lastly, the ICC measures come with procedural safeguards and thus promise to ensure the necessary independence of counsel.

III Misconduct and the Double Role of Counsel

In both international and domestic criminal law, allegations of misconduct as well as debating it as a more abstract phenomenon inevitably raise the issue of the role of counsel. Of course, the view will often be influenced by the personal role and experience of the interlocutor. From a more theoretical perspective, the question has been put forward whether the nature of international criminal proceedings – as they have formed the subject of this study – explain the difficulties and challenges encountered by defence counsel.[21] The foregoing findings before the backdrop of the theoretical model are notwithstanding that the role of the defence in international criminal proceedings as well as the overall nature of the latter still need further clarification and refinement.[22]

However, international criminal law – whether trials before international courts or international crimes before national courts – in the end boils down to criminal law. In many ways, such international criminal law is markedly different from what springs to mind as the typical substance-matter of domestic criminal law. The factual background is vastly different, and with it the surrounding criminological phenomena and political dimension. On the other hand, although the crimes may differ from most ordinary offences, international criminal trials share with trivial national ones the essential purpose, that of holding individuals accountable for their respective deeds. Be it international or national, criminal law is about meting out justice by handing down a verdict over personal conduct and imposing a sentence on that person if found guilty. In other words, the purpose behind criminal law at its very core is to publicly denounce instances of wrongdoing, to put an individual in the dock and either put him or her into jail for it if found guilty or to restore innocence. It goes without saying that there may

[18] ibid.

[19] ibid.

[20] See ch 3, III.A at 276–77.

[21] Tuinstra (n 4) 104; JI Turner, 'Legal Ethics in International Criminal Defense' (2010) 10 *Chicago Journal of International Law* 1, 1.

[22] Tuinstra (n 4) 5, 7–8 and 103–50.

be additional and starkly different objectives and dimensions to international criminal justice.[23] But these objectives attach to the larger question of how much sense it makes and what can be achieved by threatening to put perpetrators of international crimes into jail. The corresponding questions can already be hard to answer for ordinary domestic criminal justice; for international criminal justice, they become still more complex and answering them becomes even harder. However, the centrepiece of criminal law remains what it is – attributing individual accountability: singling out, marking, and punishing the wrongdoer.

In a similar vein, such an essential commonality between international and national law can also be found in respect to the administration of criminal justice, particularly criminal procedure with its fundamental features and the roles of the participants therein. International criminal trials eventually have the same goal as the conducting of domestic trials: gathering and discussing evidence on the facts in question with a view to proving or unravelling them, with the suspect or accused presumed innocent in the interim. The nature of criminal proceedings on the international level may be different and novel in certain criminological, political and even many legal regards. Even though the exact role of counsel within the international proceedings may therefore differ from what each of us has become familiar with,[24] the principal purpose – and with it the position of a defence lawyer – comes as no surprise and stays the same: that of defending his or her client.

It is this very task, entrusted to counsel, that circumscribes the role but surely does not settle all the resulting ambiguities; rather it creates additional challenges by casting defence lawyers in a double role. This consequence is, however, not to be viewed primarily as an ambiguity just waiting to be resolved intellectually; it may indeed be that it is not even capable of a solution. The tension between counsel being the advocate for the client on the one hand, and being at the same time an officer of the court, constitutes defence counsel's perennial burden.[25] It certainly calls for explanation as a matter of philosophy.[26] Moreover, the defence tension creates real dilemmas in the courtroom which can affect counsel and other participants and may then become the breeding-ground for misconduct, or at least what is perceived as misconduct without necessarily being so. In short, the role of counsel and its imminent tension which creates friction though it is inevitably engrained in the system of modern criminal justice, will often surface when

[23] Turner (n 21) 7.

[24] See ibid, 13 (examining the inquisitorial and the adversarial trial tradition in the international criminal context).

[25] See ibid, 1.

[26] See, inter alia, R Wasserstrom, 'Lawyers as Professionals: Some Moral Issues' (1975) 5 *Human Rights* 1; C Fried, 'The Lawyer as Friend: The Moral Foundations of the Lawyer–Client Relation' (1976) 85 *Yale Law Journal* 1060; GJ Postema, 'Moral Responsibility in Professional Ethics' (1980) 55 *New York University Law Review* 63; SL Pepper, 'The Lawyer's Amoral Ethical Role: A Defense, A Problem, and Some Possibilities' (1986) *American Bar Foundation Research Journal* 613; WH Simon, 'Ethical Discretion in Lawyering' (1988) 101 *Harvard Law Review* 1083; D Luban, *Legal Ethics and Human Dignity* (Cambridge, Cambridge University Press, 2007) 65–95; T Dare, *The Counsel of Rogues? A Defence of the Standard Conception of the Lawyer's Role* (Farnham, Ashgate, 2009) 1–14.

one has to deal with misconduct. This is not to say that the role and task of counsel in any way justifies misconduct but it is precisely this role of the defender that causes the intrinsic tendency for counsel to push the boundaries of the permissible. At the same time it is this same tension behind the defence role that reins in the range of the permissible. Counsel's task is to defend without crossing over into the black. However, what about all the shades of grey? Stretching the boundaries on behalf and in favour of the accused by straying into darker grey happens as part of the function of the defender. Seeking to avoid any area of dark grey would run into conflict with this function. This is why such professional zeal must be respected and ought not to be equated with misconduct.[27]

For the time being, the ICC will take on more cases, which will possibly experience and substantially suffer from misconduct. No legal mechanism will guarantee or produce what is probably needed most in the administration of justice – personal integrity. The administration of justice may be indeed be affected by unruly counsel, but a successful trial also depends on more general factors in the management of the case and the perception of the other participants of their role.[28] As has been noted, 'judicial timidity and prosecutorial bullishness is exactly the area in which international criminal courts and tribunals must mature'.[29] Ethical defence lawyers should help in countering both and thus contribute their share to their role.

[27] See also Tuinstra (n 4) 233–35, 242–43.

[28] G Boas, *The Milošević Trial: Lessons for the Conduct of Complex International Proceedings* (Cambridge, Cambridge University Press, 2007) 153–70 for the Milošević Trial, and 170–204 for a comparative analysis. See again Tuinstra, (n 4) 108–50, with a particular focus in the ICTY, ICTR, and the ICC.

[29] Boas (n 28) 201.

Bibliography

'III. Trial, Authority of the Trial Judge' (2011) 40 *Georgetown Law Journal Annual Review of Criminal Procedure*.

'Comment, The Application of Criminal Contempt Procedures to Attorneys' (1973) 64 *The Journal of Criminal Law and Criminology* 300.

Federal Procedure, Lawyer's Edition (St Paul, Minn, Thomson/West, 2008).

Abdallah, T, *Die Problematik des Rechtsmißbrauchs im Strafverfahren. Eine Untersuchung unter besonderer Berücksichtigung der verfassungsrechtlichen Bezüge des Strafprozeßrechts* (Berlin, Duncker & Humblot, 2002) 236.

Adams, GB, 'Reflections on the Reaction to Proposed Rule 8.5: Consensus of Failure' (1995) 36 *South Texas Law Review* 1101.

Althoff, B, 'Lawyer Disciplinary Sanctions' (2001) *Professional Lawyer* 105.

Alvarez, JE, *International Organizations as Law-Makers* (Oxford, Oxford University Press, 2006) XLVIII, 660.

Ambos, K, *Internationales Strafrecht*, 2nd edn (Munich, Beck, 2008) XLVIII, 555.

American Bar Association, *Canons of Professional Ethics*, Appendix B of the 1907 Report of the Association's Committee on Canons of Ethics (A.B.A. Reports XXXI, 685–713).

—— *Lawyer Regulation for A New Century. Report of the Commission on Evaluation of Disciplinary Enforcement* (McKay Report, February 1992).

—— *California Report on the Lawyer Regulation System* (2001).

—— *Client Representation in the 21st Century. Report of the Commission on Multijurisdictional Practice* (12 August 2002)

—— *Report on the Lawyer Regulation System* (Massachusetts, October 2005.

—— *Standing Committee on Professional Discipline, Survey on Lawyer Discipline Systems* (2007).

Anderson, DA, 'Summary Contempt Power in the Military: A Proposal to Amend Article 48, UCMJ' (1999) 160 *Military Law Review* 158.

Arbour, L, 'Legal Professionalism and International Criminal Proceedings' (2006) 4 *Journal of International Criminal Justice* 674.

Association internationale de droit pénal, 'Principles of Criminal Procedure and their Application in Disciplinary Procedures, Draft Resolution' (2003) 74 *Revue internationale de droit pénal* 1103.

Aultman, MH, 'A Post Conference Reflection: Does Amended Model Rule 8.5 Help Anyone?' (1995) 36 *South Texas Law Review* 1055.

Averill, LH, 'The Revised Lawyer Discipline Process in Arkansas: A Primer and Analysis' (1998) 21 *University of Arkansas at Little Rock Law Review* 13.

Azarnia, G, 'Commentary' in A Klip and G Sluiter (eds), *Annotated Leading Cases of International Criminal Tribunals, vol 21, The Special Court for Sierra Leone 2004–2006* (Antwerp, Intersentia, 2010) 638–46.

Barton, BH, 'Why Do We Regulate Lawyers?: An Economic Analysis of the Justifications for Entry and Conduct Regulation' (2001) 33 *Arizona State Law Journal* 429.

Barton, BH, 'An Institutional Analysis of Lawyer Regulation: Who Should Control Lawyer Regulation – Courts, Legislatures or the Market?' (2003) 37 *Georgia Law Review* 1167.

Barton, S, 'Zivilrechtliche Risiken' in G Widmaier (ed), *Münchener Anwaltshandbuch Strafverteidigung* (Munich, Beck, 2006) 2098–115.

Bassiouni, MC, *International Extradition, United States Law and Practice*, 5th edn (Oxford, Oxford University Press, 2007) XXV, 1166.

Bauer, W, 'Der Ablehnungsgrund der Prozessverschleppungsabsicht' (2008) *Neue Zeitschrift für Strafrecht* 542.

Beale, SS, 'Reconsidering Supervisory Power in Criminal Cases: Constitutional and Statutory Limits on the Authority of the Federal Courts' (1984) 84 *Columbia Law Review* 1433.

Bené, SG, 'Why Not Fine Attorneys: An Economic Approach to Lawyer Disciplinary Sanctions' (1990–91) 43 *Stanford Law Review* 907.

Beresford, S and Lahiouel, H, 'The Right to be Defended in Person or Through Legal Assistance and the International Criminal Court' (2000) 13 *Leiden Journal of International Law* 949.

Beulke, W, 'Kleider machen Strafverteidiger!?, – oder: sitzungspolizeiliche Maßnahmen und die Mär vom "T-Shirt-Verteidiger" in R Michalke et al (eds), *Festschrift für Rainer Hamm* (Berlin, De Gruyter, 2008) 21–40.

—— 'Missbrauch von Verteidigerrechten – eine kritische Würdigung der jüngsten Rechtsprechung' in M Böse and D Sternberg-Lieben (eds), *Grundlagen des Straf- und Strafverfahrensrechts, Festschrift für Knut Amelung zum 70. Geburtstag* (Berlin, Duncker & Humblot, 2009) 543–64.

Beulke, W and Ruhmannseder, F, 'Beweisantrag in Prozessverschleppungsabsicht, Anmerkung zu BGH, Beschl. v. 9.5.2007 – 1 StR 32/07' (2008) *Neue Zeitschrift für Strafrecht* 300.

—— *Die Strafbarkeit des Verteidigers*, 2nd edn (Heidelberg, C.F. Müller, 2010) XXVIII, 462.

Bitti, G, 'Article 21 of the Statute of the International Criminal Court and the Treatment of Sources of Law in the Jurisprudence of the ICC' in C Stahn and G Sluiter (eds), *The Emerging Practice of the International Criminal Court* (Leiden, Martinus Nijhoff, 2009) 285–304.

Blake, M and Ashworth, A, 'Ethics and the Criminal Defense Lawyer' (2004) 7 *Legal Ethics* 16.

Blankenburg, E and Schultz, U, 'German Advocates: A Highly Regulated Profession' in R Abel and P Lewis (eds), *Lawyers in Society* (Berkeley, University of California Press, 1995) 92–127.

Blatt, RL, Hammesfahr, RW and Nugent, LS, *Punitive Damages: A State-By-State Guide To Law And Practice*, 2007 edn (Eagan, Minn, Thomson/West, 2007) xxiii, 863.

Boas, G, 'The Right to Self-Representation in International and Domestic Criminal Law – Limitations and Qualifications on that Right' in H Abthai and G Boas (eds), *The Dynamics of International Criminal Justice*, (Leiden, Martinus Nijhoff, 2005).

—— *The Milošević Trial: Lessons for the Conduct of Complex International Proceedings* (Cambridge, Cambridge University Press, 2007) 306.

—— 'Commentary' in A Klip and G Sluiter (eds), *Annotated Leading Cases of International Criminal Tribunals, vol 21, The Special Court for Sierra Leone 2004–2006* (Antwerp, Intersentia, 2010) 676–82.

Bockemühl, J, 'Anmerkung zu OLG Düsseldorf StV 2004, 62' (2004) *Strafverteidiger* 63.

Bohlander, M, 'A Silly Question? Court Sanctions Against Defence Counsel for Trial Misconduct' (1999) 10 *Criminal Law Forum* 467.

—— *Gerichtliche Sanktionen gegen Anwälte wegen Mißbrauchs von Verfahrensrechten* (Aachen, Shaker, 2001) VIII, 111, A1–A 226.

—— 'International Criminal Defence Ethics: The Law of Professional Conduct for Defence Counsel Appearing before International Criminal Tribunals' (2000) 1 *San Diego International Law Journal* 75.

—— 'International Criminal Tribunals and their Power to Punish Contempt and False Testimony' (2001) 12 *Criminal Law Forum* 91.

—— 'The Defence' in G Boas and WA Schabas (eds), *International Criminal Law Developments in the Case Law of the ICTY* (Leiden, Martinus Nijhoff, 2003) 35–74.

—— *The German Criminal Code, A Modern English Translation* (Oxford, Hart, 2008) 216.

Bohlander, M, Boed R and Wilson, RJ (eds), *Defense in International Criminal Proceedings* (Ardsley, NY, Transnational Publishers, 2006).

Böhm, KM, '"Verteidigerfremdes Verhalten" – Neue Wege zur Ausschließung lästiger Strafverteidiger?' (2006) *Neue Juristische Wochenschrift* 2371.

Boyd, H and Turetsky, B, 'Conversion and the Dilemma of Disciplinary Sanctions' (2000–01) 14 *Georgetown Journal of Legal Ethics* 1019.

Boykin, E, 'Lawyers' Non-Payment of Child Support as a Basis for Disciplinary Action' (1992) 17 *Journal of the Legal Profession* 193.

Brady, HJ and Nemitz, JC, 'The Offence of Perjury under International Law: The False Testimony of Witness L' (1998) 11 *Journal of International Law of Peace and Armed Conflict/Humanitäres Völkerrecht – Informationsschriften* 162.

Brand, RA, 'Professional Responsibility in a Transnational Transactions Practice' (1997–98) 17 *Journal of Law and Commerce* 301.

Brants, C, 'Commentary' in A Klip and G Sluiter (eds), *Annotated Leading Cases of International Criminal Tribunals, vol 6, The International Criminal Tribunal for Rwanda 2000–2001* (Antwerp, Intersentia, 2003) 458–67.

Breucker, H, *Verteidigungsfremdes Verhalten* (Berlin, Duncker & Humblot, 1993) 224.

Brickman, L and Bibona, JM, 'Collateral Estoppel as a Basis for Attorney Discipline: The Next Step' (1991–92) 5 *Georgetown Journal of Legal Ethics* 1.

Brown, CL, 'Other Misconduct Warranting Discipline' (1992) 17 *Journal of the Legal Profession* 199.

Browne, MN, Williamson, CL and Barkacs, LL, 'Purported Rigidity of an Attorney's Personality: Can Legal Ethics Be Acquired?' (2005–06) 30 *Journal of the Legal Profession* 55.

Bunch, K, 'Taming the Fury: Do the 1991 Proposed Amendments to Rule 11 Go Far Enough?' (1991–92) 5 *Georgetown Journal of Legal Ethics* 957.

Bundy, SM and Elhauge, E, 'Knowledge about Legal Sanctions' (1993) 92 *Michigan Law Review* 261.

Burke-White, WW, 'A Community of Courts: Toward a System of International Criminal Law Enforcement' (2003) 24 *Michigan Journal of International Law* 1.

Burkoff, JM, *Criminal Defense Ethics, 2nd: Law and Liability*, 2005 edn (St Paul, Minn, West Group, 2005).

Burnett, JT, 'Attorney Discipline under DR 1-102(A)(3): Imposing Sanctions Absent a Finding of Moral Turpitude' (1988) 13 *Journal of the Legal Profession* 245.

Busse, F, *Deutsche Anwälte. Geschichte der deutschen Anwaltschaft 1945-2009, Entwicklungen in West und Ost* (Bonn, Deutscher Anwaltverlag, 2010) 677.

Bussenius, A, *Geldwäsche und Strafverteidigerhonorar* (Baden-Baden, Nomos, 2004) 204.

Camarena, IGI, 'Domestically Violent Attorneys: Resuscitating and Transforming a Dusty, Old Punitive Approach to Attorney Discipline into a Viable Prescription for Rehabilitation' (2001) 31 *Golden Gate University Law Review* 155.

Cárdenas, C, *Die Zulässigkeitsprüfung vor dem Internationalen Strafgerichtshof* (Berlin, Berliner Wissenschafts-Verlag, 2005) 248.

Carr, EA and Van Fleet, A, 'Professional Responsibility Law in Multijurisdictional Litigation: Across the Country and across the Street ' (1995) 36 *South Texas Law Review* 859.

Carr, MM, 'The Effect of Prior Criminal Conduct on the Admission to Practice Law: The Move to More Flexible Admission Standards' (1994–95) 8 *Georgetown Journal of Legal Ethics* 367.

Cassese, A, Gaeta P and Jones, JRWD (eds), *The Rome Statute of the International Criminal Court: A Commentary* (Oxford, Oxford University Press, 2002).

Caviedes, RR, 'Remnants of an Attorney Disciplinary Sanction: Which Jurisdictions Impose Automatic Disbarment – What Offenses Warrant the Imposition of an Automatic Disciplinary Sanction?' (2002) 26 *Journal of the Legal Profession* 195.

Cedarbaum, JG, 'Restrictions on U.S. Attorneys Practicing before International Criminal Tribunals' (2004) 98 *American Journal of International Law* 141.

Chemerinsky, E, *Federal Jurisdiction*, 5th edn (New York, Aspen Publishers, 2007) 1128.

Chiavario, M, 'Principles of Criminal Procedure and their Application in Disciplinary Proceedings – General Report' (2004) 74 *Revue internationale de droit pénal* 707.

Cockayne, J, 'Commentary' in A Klip and G Sluiter (eds), *Annotated Leading Cases of International Criminal Tribunals, vol 4, The International Criminal Tribunal for the former Yugoslavia 1999–2000* (Antwerp, Intersentia, 2002) 191–200.

Coffee, JC, 'From Tort to Crime: Some Reflections on the Criminalization of Fiduciary Breaches and the Problematic Line Between Law and Ethics' (1981) 19 *American Criminal Law Review* 117.

Colangelo, AJ, 'Double Jeopardy and Multiple Sovereigns: A Jurisdictional Theory' (2009) 86 *Washington University Law Review* 769.

Colquitt, JA, 'Evidence and Ethics: Litigating in the Shadows of the Rules' (2007) 76 *Fordham Law Review* 1641.

Coltoff, P, Kennell, J, Martin, L and Muskus, T, *Corpus Juris Secundum, Contempt* (St Paul, Minn, Thomson/West, 2008).

Colvin, AM, 'Reciprocal Discipline: Double Jeopardy or a State's Right to Protect Its Citizens?' (2001) 25 *Journal of the Legal Profession* 143.

Converti, A, 'The Rights of the Accused' in F Lattanzi (ed), *The International Criminal Court, Comments on the Draft Statute* (Naples, Editoriale Scientifica, 1998) 219–50.

Costa, JE, 'Double Jeopardy and Non Bis In Idem: Principles of Fairness' (1998) 4 *UC Davis Journal of International Law and Policy* 181.

Cramton, RC, 'Furthering Justice by Improving the Adversary System and Making Lawyers More Accountable' (2001–02) 70 *Fordham Law Review* 1599.

Croft, WS, 'Free Speech and Fair Trials – Striking the Balance: A Case Comment and Analysis of the Maryland Publicity Rule as Applied in Attorney Grievance Commission of Maryland v Douglas F Gansler' (2006) 19 *Georgetown Journal of Legal Ethics* 345.

Cryer, R and Bekou, O, 'International Crimes and ICC Cooperation in England and Wales' (2007) 5 *Journal of International Criminal Justice* 441.

D'Ascoli, S, 'Sentencing Contempt of Court in International Criminal Justice' (2007) 5 *Journal of International Criminal Justice* 735.

Dahns, C, 'Die kleine BRAO-Reform – Änderungen durch das Gesetz zur Stärkung der Selbstverwaltung der Rechtsanwaltschaft' (2007) *Neue Juristische Wochenschrift* 1553.

Dahs, H, 'Berufsgerichtliche Verfahren' in G Widmaier (ed), *Münchener Anwaltshandbuch Strafverteidigung* (Munich, Beck, 2006) 1969–91.

Daly, MC, 'Resolving Ethical Conflicts in Multijurisdictional Practice – Is Model Rule 8.5 the Answer, an Answer, or No Answer at All?' (1995) 36 *South Texas Law Review* 715.

Dare, T, *The Counsel of Rogues? A Defence of the Standard Conception of the Lawyer's Role* (Farnham, Ashgate, 2009) 182.

Dawson, MA, 'Popular Sovereignty, Double Jeopardy, and the Dual Sovereignty Doctrine' (1992) 102 *Yale Law Journal* 281.

De Groot-Van Leeuwen, LE and De Groot, WT, 'Studying Codes of Conduct: A Descriptive Framework for Comparative Research' (1998) 1 *Legal Ethics* 155.

Deckenbrock, C, *Strafrechtlicher Parteiverrat und berufsrechtliches Verbot der Vertretung widerstreitender Interessen* (Bonn, Deutscher Anwaltverlag, 2009).

Devlin, MM, 'Development of Lawyer Disciplinary Procedures in the United States' (1993–1994) 7 *Georgetown Journal of Legal Ethics* 911.

Dhanda, RK, 'When Attorneys Become Convicted Felons: The Question of Discipline by the Bar' (1994–95) 8 *Georgetown Journal of Legal Ethics* 723.

Dieckmann, J and Kerll, C, 'Representing the "General Interests of the Defence": Boon or Bane? – A Stocktaking of the System of *ad hoc* Counsel at the ICC' (2011) 11 *International Criminal Law Review* 105.

Dietz, LH, Gregor, R, Jacobs, A and Kane, R, 'Contempt, Vol. 17' in Lawyers Cooperative Publishing (ed), *American Jurisprudence, 2d* (New York, Thomson/West, 1989).

Dixon, R and Khan, KAA (eds), *Archbold International Criminal Courts*, 1st edn (London, Sweet & Maxwell, 2003).

—— (eds), *Archbold International Criminal Courts*, 2nd edn (London, Sweet & Maxwell, 2005).

Dolovich, S, 'Ethical Lawyering and the Possibility of Integrity' (2002) 70 *Fordham Law Review* 1629.

Draisen, DL, 'The Model Rules of Professional Conduct and their Relationship to Legal Malpractice Actions: A Practical Approach to the Use of the Rules' (1997) 21 *Journal of the Legal Profession* 67.

Dudley, EC, 'Getting beyond the Civil/Criminal Distinction: A New Approach to the Regulation of Indirect Contempts' (1993) 79 *Virginia Law Review* 1025.

Dueren, W, *Contempt – das Rechtsinstitut des Contempt in der politischen Realität der USA* (Munich, de Smet, 1974) 216.

Duncan, MJ, 'Criminal Malpractice: A Lawyer's Holiday' (2003) 37 *Georgia Law Review* 1251.

Dungan, CP, 'Avoiding "Catch-22s": Approaches to Resolve Conflicts Between Military and State Bar Rules of Professional Responsibility' (2005–06) 30 *Journal of the Legal Profession* 31.

Edelkötter, F, *Der Anwalt in Deutschland und in England* (Münster, Lit, 2005).

El Zeidy, MM, 'The Principle of Complementarity: A New Machinery to Implement International Criminal Law' (2002) 23 *Michigan Journal of International Law* 869.

Elbs, H and Klemke, O, 'Leitfaden zum anwaltsgerichtlichen Verfahren' (2005) *Anwaltsblatt* 56.

Ellis, MS, 'Achieving Justice before the International War Crimes Tribunal: Challenges for the Defense Counsel' (1997) 7 *Duke Journal of Comparative & International Law* 519.

—— 'The Evolution of Defense Counsel Appearing Before the International Criminal Tribunal for the Former Yugoslavia' (2003) 37 *New England Law Review* 949.

Ellmann, S, 'Lawyers and Clients' (1987) 34 *University of California at Los Angeles Law Review* 717.

Emilianides, AC, 'Contempt in the Face of the Court and the Right to a Fair Trial' (2005) 13 *European Journal of Crime, Criminal Law & Criminal Justice* 401.

Eser, A, 'Verteidigung in der internationalen Strafgerichtsbarkeit' in H Schöch (ed), *Strafverteidigung, Revision und die gesamten Strafrechtswissenschaften: Festschrift für Gunter Widmaier zum 70. Geburtstag* (Cologne, Heymann, 2008) 147–76.

Eser, A and Kreicker, H (eds), *National Prosecution of International Crimes*, vol 1 (Freiburg, edition iuscrim, 2003).

Fabian, JD and Reinthaler, B, 'An Examination of the Uniformity (or Lack Thereof) of Attorney Sanctions' (2000–01) 14 *Georgetown Journal of Legal Ethics* 1059.

Fahl, C, *Rechtsmißbrauch im Strafprozeß* (Heidelberg, C. F. Müller 2003) XII, 796.

Feldman, HL, 'Beyond the Model Rules: The Place of Examples in Legal Ethics' (1998–1999) 12 *Georgetown Journal of Legal Ethics* 409.

Felleman, S, 'Ethical Dilemmas and the Multistate Lawyer: A Proposed Amendment to the Choice-of-Law Rule in the Model Rules of Professional Conduct' (1995) 95 *Columbia Law Review* 1500.

Fellmeth, AX, 'Civil and Criminal Sanctions in the Constitution and Courts' (2005) 94 *Georgetown Law Journal* 1.

—— 'Challenges and Implications of a Systemic Social Effect Theory' (2006) *University of Illinois Law Review* 691.

Feuerich, WE and Weyland, D (eds), *Bundesrechtsanwaltsordnung*, 7th edn (Munich, Vahlen, 2008) XVII, 1688

Finkelstein, B, 'Should Permanent Disbarment be Permanent?' (2007) 20 *The Georgetown Journal of Legal Ethics* 587.

Fischer, JD, 'Bareheaded and Barefaced Counsel: Courts React to Unprofessionalism in Lawyers' Papers' (1997) 31 *Suffolk University Law Review* 1.

Fischer, T, *Strafgesetzbuch und Nebengesetze*, 58th edn (Munich, Beck, 2011) LX, 2548.

Fitzpatrick, JK, 'Supreme Court Review: The Supreme Court's Bipolar Approach to the Interpretation of 18 U.S.C. 1503 and 18 U.S.C. Section 2232(c)' (1996) 86 *Journal of Criminal Law & Criminology* 1383.

Foth, E, 'Zur ehrengerichtlichen Ahndung des Ungehorsams eines Rechtsanwalts gegenüber einer die Ordnung in der Sitzung betreffenden Anordnung des Vorsitzenden' (1997) *Neue Zeitschrift für Strafrecht* 36.

Fox, JC, *The History of Contempt of Court* (London, Professional Books, 1972) XXIII, 252.

Freedman, MH, 'Are the Model Rules Unconstitutional?' (1981) 35 *University of Miami Law Review* 685.

—— 'Professionalism in the American Adversary System' (1992) 41 *Emory Law Journal* 467.

—— 'Henry Lord Brougham and Zeal' (2006) 34 *Hofstra Law Review* 1319.

—— 'Henry Lord Brougham, Written by Himself' (2006) 19 *Georgetown Journal of Legal Ethics* 1213.

—— 'In Praise of Overzealous Representation – Lying to Judges, Deceiving Third Parties, and Other Ethical Conduct' (2006) 34 *Hofstra Law Review* 771.

Fried, C, 'The Lawyer as Friend: The Moral Foundations of the Lawyer–Client Relation' (1976) 85 *Yale Law Journal* 1060.

Frisch, MS, 'No Stone Left Unturned: The Failure of Attorney Self-Regulation in the District of Columbia' (2004–2005) 18 *Georgetown Journal of Legal Ethics* 325.

—— 'Zealousness Run Amok' (2007) 20 *Georgetown Journal of Legal Ethics* 1035.

Gaede, K, 'Schlechtverteidigung – Tabus und Präklusionen zum Schutz vor dem Recht auf wirksame Verteidigung?' (2007) *Höchstrichterliche Rechtsprechung im Strafrecht* 402.

Gaetke, ER, 'Lawyers as Officers of the Court' (1989) 42 *Vanderbilt Law Review* 39.

Gaier, R, Wolf, C and Göcken S (eds), *Anwaltliches Berufsrecht* (Cologne, Heymanns, 2010) XXXVI, 2268.

Gallagher, RB, Hall, TM, Harrison, DB et al, 'Habeas Corpus and Postconviction Remedies, Vol 39' in Lawyers Cooperative Publishing (ed), *American Jurisprudence*, 2nd edn (New York, Thomson/West, 1989).

Gallagher, T, 'Innocent until Proven Guilty – Not for Bar Applicants' (2007) 31 *Journal of the Legal Profession* 297.

Gallant, KS, 'The Role and Powers of Defense Counsel in the ICC Statute' (2000) 34 *The International Lawyer* 21.

Gane, C, 'Commentary' in A Klip and G Sluiter (eds), *Annotated Leading Cases of International Criminal Tribunals, vol 5, The International Criminal Tribunal for the former Yugoslavia 2000-2001* (Antwerp, Intersentia, 2003) 236–44.

Gier, K, 'Prosecuting Injustice: Consequences of Misconduct' (2006) 33 *American Journal of Criminal Law* 191.

Gilbert, G, *Transnational Fugitive Offenders in International Law, Extradition and Other Mechanisms* (The Hague, Martinus Nijhoff, 1998) XXXI, 486.

Gilligan, FA and Wims, MD, 'Civilian Justice v Military Justice' (1990) *Criminal Justice* 2.

Göddeke, D, *Die Einschränkung der Strafverteidigung* (Köln, Pahl-Rugenstein, 1980) 303.

Goebel, RJ, 'Lawyers in the European Community: Progress towards Community-Wide Rights of Practice' (1991–92) 15 *Fordham International Law Journal* 556.

Green, BA, 'Zealous Representation Bound: The Intersection of the Ethical Codes and the Criminal Law' (1990–91) 69 *North Carolina Law Review* 687.

—— 'The Criminal Regulation of Lawyers' (1998–99) 67 *Fordham Law Review* 327.

—— 'Bar Association Ethics Committees: Are They Broken?' (2001–02) 30 *Hofstra Law Review* 731.

Green, BA and Zacharias, FC, 'Permissive Rules of Professional Conduct' (2006) 91 *Minnesota Law Review* 265.

Greenbaum, AF, 'The Attorney's Duty to Report Professional Misconduct: A Roadmap for Reform' (2002–03) 16 *Georgetown Journal of Legal Ethics* 259.

Gribbohm, G, 'Die ehrengerichtlichen Berufs- und Vertretungsverbote in der Rechtsprechung des Senats für Anwaltssachen des Bundesgerichtshofs' in OF von Gamm, P Raisch and K Tiedemann (eds), *Festschrift für Gerd Pfeiffer* (Cologne, Heymanns, 1988) 911–27.

Griffin, L, 'The Lawyer's Dirty Hands' (1994–95) 8 *Georgetown Journal of Legal Ethics* 219.

Gröner, K, *Strafverteidiger und Sitzungspolizei* (Berlin, Duncker & Humblot, 1998) 221.

Grunewald, B and Piepenstock, K, 'Anwaltliche Berufspflichten – Verstöße gegen § 43 BRAO und anwaltsgerichtliche Maßnahmen' (2000) *Monatschrift für Deutsches Recht* 869.

Gunn, L, 'Past Crimes and Admission to the Bar' (1980) 5 *Journal of the Legal Profession* 179.

Hall, JW, 'Comparison of the Proffered Ethical Codes of the International Criminal Bar and the International Bar Association for Practice Before the International Criminal Court' (17th International Conference of the International Society for the Reform of Criminal Law, The Hague, 24–28 August 2003).

Hall, JW, *Professional Responsibility in Criminal Defense Practice*, 3rd edn (St Paul, Minn, Thomson/West, 2005).

Haller, L, ' Disciplinary Fines: Deterrence or Retribution?' (2002) 5 *Legal Ethics* 152.

Hamm, R, 'Fristenregelung für Beweisanträge?' in F Herzog and U Neumann (eds), *Festschrift für Winfried Hassemer* (Heidelberg, CF Müller, 2010) 1017–28.

Hampton, GL, 'Toward an Expanded Use of the Model Rules of Professional Conduct' (1990–91) 4 *Georgetown Journal of Legal Ethics* 655.

Haney, BM, 'Contrasting the Prosecution of Witness Tampering Under 18 U.S.C. § 1503 and 18 U.S.C. § 1512: Why § 1512 Better Serves the Government at Trial' (2004) 9 *Suffolk Journal of Trial and Appellate Advocacy* 57.

Hardison, BW, 'Contempt Citation as Evidence of Unfitness to Practice Law' (1988) 13 *Journal of the Legal Profession* 271.

Harlow, CW, *Defense Counsel in Criminal Cases* (Bureau of Justice Statistics, NCJ 179023, 2000).

Hart, HLA, *The Concept of Law*, 2nd edn (Oxford, Oxford University Press, 1994) X, 263.

Harting, A, *Berufspflichten des Strafverteidigers und Sanktionierung pflichtwidrigen Verhaltens* (Bonn, Deutscher Anwaltverlag, 2008) 436.

Hartung, W and Römermann, V (eds), *Berufs- und Fachanwaltsordnung*, 4th edn (Munich, Beck, 2008) XXIV, 1263.

Hazard, GC and Beard, C, 'A Lawyer's Privilege Against Self-Incrimination in Professional Disciplinary Proceedings' (1987) 96 *Yale Law Journal* 1060.

Hellman, LK, 'When Ethics Rules Don't Mean What They Say: The Implications of Strained ABA Ethics Opinions' (1996–97) 10 *Georgetown Journal of Legal Ethics* 317.

Henderson, GD, 'Courts-Martial and the Constitution: The Original Understanding' (1957) 71 *Harvard Law Review* 293.

Henning, PJ, 'Overcriminalization: The Politics of Crimes Targeting Legal Advice' (2004–05) 54 *American University Law Review* 669.

Henssler, M, 'Der lange Weg zur EU-Niederlassungsrichtlinie für die Anwaltschaft' (1999) *Zeitschrift für Europäisches Privatrecht* 689.

Henssler, M and Prütting H (eds), *Bundesrechtsanwaltsordnung*, 1st edn (Munich, Beck, 1997) 1479.

—— *Bundesrechtsanwaltsordnung*, 2nd edn (Munich, Beck, 2004) 2295.

—— *Bundesrechtsanwaltsordnung*, 3rd edn (Munich, Beck, 2010) 2010.

Herring, BO, 'Liability of Board Certified Specialists in a Legal Malpractice Action: Is there a Higher Standard?' (1998–99) 12 *Georgetown Journal of Legal Ethics* 67.

Herrmann, J, 'Die Strafprozeßreform vom 1.1.1975' (1976) *Juristische Schulung* 413.

Hinkie, JA, 'Free Speech and Rule 3.6: How the Object of Attorney Speech Affects the Right to Make Public Criticism' (2007) 20 *Georgetown Journal of Legal Ethics* 695.

Hodgson, J, 'The Role of the Criminal Defence Lawyer in an Inquisitorial Procedure: Legal and Ethical Constraints' (2006) 9 *Legal Ethics* 125.

—— 'The Role of the Criminal Defence Lawyer in Adversarial and Inquisitorial Procedure' in T Weigend, S Walther and B Grunewald (eds), *Strafverteidigung vor neuen Herausforderungen – Denkanstöße aus sieben Rechtsordnungen* (Berlin, Duncker & Humblot, 2008) 45–59.

Hollander, N and Bergman, BE, *Everytrial Criminal Defense Resource Book*, (St Paul, Minn, Thomson/West, 2007).

Hricik, D and Ellis, J, 'Disparities in Legal Ethical Standards between State and Federal Judicial Systems: An Analysis and a Critique' (1999–2000) 13 *Georgetown Journal of Legal Ethics* 577.

Hülk, F, *Chancen und Grenzen einer unmittelbaren Sanktionierung anwaltlichen Fehlverhaltens in den USA und Deutschland* (Osnabrück, Rasch, 2001) 112.

Hurwitz, KD, *Comments on the Draft Code of Conduct for Counsel before the International Criminal Court* (Human Rights First, 26 November 2005).

Husmann, JH, *Freie Advokatur im Zwangsverband? Eine Untersuchung über die Erziehungsbedürftigkeit des Rechtsanwalts* (Würzburg, Libertas, 1970) 44.

Hussey, JL, 'Reporting Another Attorney for Violating the Rules of Professional Conduct: The Current Status of the Law in the States which have Adopted the Model Rules of Professional Conduct' (1999) 23 *Journal of the Legal Profession* 265.

Israel, JH, 'Free-Standing Due Process and Criminal Procedure: The Supreme Court's Search for Interpretive Guidelines' (2001) 34 *Saint Louis University Law Journal* 303.

Jahn, M, 'Sitzungspolizei contra "Konfliktverteidigung"? Zur Anwendbarkeit der §§ 176ff. GVG auf den Strafverteidiger' (1998) *Neue Zeitschrift für Strafrecht* 389.

—— 'Keine Anwendung der sitzungspolizeilichen Vorschriften auf Strafverteidiger' (2004) *Juristenzeitung* 207.

—— 'Anmerkung zu BGH NJW 2006, 2421' (2006) *Juristenzeitung* 1134.

Jarvis, RM, 'Cross-Border Legal Practice and Ethics Rule 4-8.5 Why Greater Guidance Is Needed' (1998) 72 *Florida Bar Journal* 59.

Jeffries, JC, 'Legality, Vagueness, and the Construction of Penal Statutes' (1985) 71 *Virginia Law Review* 189.

Joecks, W and Miebach K (eds), *Münchener Kommentar zum StGB*, 6 vols (Munich, Beck, 2003).

Joseph, GP, *Sanctions: The Federal Law of Litigation Abuse*, 3rd edn (Albany, NY, Matthew Bender 2000).

—— *Sanctions: The Federal Law of Litigation Abuse*, 4th edn (Albany, NY, Matthew Bender, 2008).

Joy, PA, 'Making Ethics Opinions Meaningful: Toward More Effective Regulation of Lawyers' Conduct' (2001–02) 15 *Georgetown Journal of Legal Ethics* 313.

—— 'The Relationship between Civil Rule 11 and Lawyer Discipline: An Empirical Analysis Suggesting Institutional Choices in the Regulation of Lawyers' (2004) 37 *Loyola of Los Angeles Law Review* 765.

Jungk, A, 'Gesteigerte Haftung des Fachanwalts?' (2007) *Anwaltsblatt* 227.

Kahan, DM, 'What do Alternative Sanctions Mean?' (1996) 63 *University of Chicago Law Review* 591.

—— 'Punishment Incommensurability' (1997–1998) 1 *Buffalo Criminal Law Review* 691.

Kalish, SE, 'How to Encourage Lawyers to be Ethical: Do Not Use the Ethics Codes as a Basis for Regular Law Decisions' (1999–2000) 13 *Georgetown Journal of Legal Ethics* 649.

Kane, RM, 'Attorneys at Law, Vol 7' in Lawyers Cooperative Publishing (ed), *American Jurisprudence*, 2nd edn (New York, Thomson/West, 1989).

Kane, R, Kennel, JR, Martin, L et al, *Corpus Juris Secundum, Attorney & Client* (St Paul, Minn, Thomson/West, 2008).

Kappelmann, T, *Die Strafbarkeit des Strafverteidigers. Zur Abgrenzung von strafbewehrten und straffreien Prozesshandlungen durch zweckorientierte Auslegung prozessualer Befugnisse* (Baden-Baden, Nomos, 2006) 138.

Kargl, W, 'Das Unrecht der Strafvereitelung – insbesondere zu den strafrechtlichen Grenzen der Strafverteidigung' in R Michalke et al (eds), *Festschrift für Rainer Hamm* (Berlin, De Gruyter, 2008) 235–54.

Kastenberg, JE, 'The Right to Assistance of Counsel in Military and War Crimes Tribunals: An International and Domestic Law Analysis' (2003) 14 *Indiana International & Comparative Law Review* 175.

Keeling, BC, 'A Prescription for Healing the Crisis of Professionalism: Shifting the Burden of Enforcing Professional Standards of Conduct' (1993) 25 *Texas Tech Law Review* 31.

Keijzer, N, *Contempt of Court* (Gouda, Quint, 2000) 35.

Kelly, CA, 'Lawyer Sanctions: Looking Back through the Looking-Glass' (1987–88) 1 *Georgetown Journal of Legal Ethics* 469.

Kempf, E, 'Der zu (späte) Beweisantrag' (2010) *Strafverteidiger Forum* 316.

—— 'Missbrauch im Strafprozess – Peccatur intra et extra muros' in F Herzog and U Neumann (eds), *Festschrift für Winfried Hassemer* (Heidelberg, CF Müller, 2010) 1041–53.

Kennel, JR, 'New Trial, Vol 58' in Lawyers Cooperative Publishing (ed), *American Jurisprudence*, 2nd edn (New York, Thomson/West, 1989).

Kidd, CJF, 'Disciplinary Proceedings and the Right to a Fair Criminal Trial under the European Convention on Human Rights' (1987) 36 *The International and Comparative Law Quarterly* 856.

Kilian, M, 'Organisationsformen internationaler Tätigkeit von Anwaltsgesellschaften' in M Henssler and M Streck (eds), *Handbuch des Sozietätsrechts* (Cologne, Otto Schmidt, 2001) 893–1011.

—— 'Berufsrechtliche Verantwortlichkeit von Strafverteidigern' in T Weigend, S Walther and B Grunewald (eds), *Strafverteidigung vor neuen Herausforderungen – Denkanstöße aus sieben Rechtsordnungen* (Berlin, Duncker & Humblot, 2008) 113–56.

Kirsch, S, 'The Trial Proceedings before the ICC' (2006) 6 *International Criminal Law Review* 275.

Kissel, OR, 'Ungebühr vor Gericht (§ 178 GVG) – vorbei?' (2007) *Neue Juristische Wochenschrift* 1109.

Klabbers, J, *An Introduction to International Institutional Law* (Cambridge, Cambridge University Press, 2002) 399.

Kleffner, JK and Kor, G (eds), *Complementary Views on Complementarity* (The Hague, T.M.C. Asser, 2006) XVI, 181.

Kleine-Cosack, M, 'Verfassungswidriges Standesrecht – Notwendigkeit einer Ersetzung der Standesrichtlinien durch ein grundgesetzkonformes Berufsrecht' (1988) *Neue Juristische Wochenschrift* 164.

—— *Bundesrechtsanwaltsordnung*, 3rd edn (Munich, Beck, 1997) XXXVI, 826.

—— *Bundesrechtsanwaltsordnung*, 4th edn (Munich, Beck, 2003) XXXIV, 922.

—— 'Berufsrechtliche Risiken' in G Widmaier (ed), *Münchener Anwaltshandbuch Strafverteidigung* (Munich, Beck, 2006) 2078–97.

—— 'Anfang von Ende der Satzungsversammlung' (2007) *Anwaltsblatt* 409.

—— *Bundesrechtsanwaltsordnung*, 5th edn (Munich, Beck, 2008) XXIX, 773.

—— *Bundesrechtsanwaltsordnung*, 6th edn (Munich, Beck, 2009) XXV, 776.

Klip, A, 'Commentary' in A Klip and G Sluiter (eds), *Annotated Leading Cases of International Criminal Tribunals, vol 1, The International Criminal Tribunal for the former Yugoslavia 1993–1998* (Antwerp, Intersentia, 1999) 214–15.

—— *European Criminal Law. An Integrative Approach* (Antwerp, Intersentia, 2009) XV, 531.

Knauer, C and Wolf, C, '20 Jahre "Bastille-Entscheidungen" des Bundesverfassungsgerichts – Von der Liberalisierung und Kommerzialisierung des Anwaltsberufs' (2007) *BRAK-Mitteilungen* 142.

Knierim, TC, 'Die zivilrechtliche Haftung des Strafverteidigers' in W Beulke and E Müller (eds), *Festschrift zu Ehren des Strafrechtsauschusses der Bundesrechtsanwaltskammer* (Neuwied, Luchterhand, 2006) 115–48.

Knöfel, OL, 'Anwalts-Kollisionsrecht' (2003) *Anwaltsblatt* 3.

—— *Grundfragen der internationalen Berufsausübung von Rechtsanwälten* (Bonn, Deutscher Anwaltverlag, 2005) 1050.

Koch, L and Kilian, M, *Anwaltliches Berufsrecht* (Munich, Beck, 2007).

Kölbel, R, 'Strafrechtliche Haftung für prozessbedingte sekundäre Viktimisierung' (2007) 119 *Zeitschrift für die gesamte Strafrechtswissenschaft* 334.

Krach, T, '130 Jahre "Grundgesetz der Anwaltschaft"' (2008) *Neue Juristische Online Zeitschrift* 2628.

Kramer, VH, 'Viewing Rule 11 as a Tool to Improve Professional Responsibility' (1990–91) 75 *Minnesota Law Review* 793.

Kraus, JM, 'Attorney Discipline Systems: Improving Public Perception and Increasing Efficacy' (2000–01) 84 *Marquette Law Review* 273.

Krehl, C, 'Der verfassungsrechtliche Schutz rechtlichen Gehörs im Strafverfahren' in F Herzog and U Neumann (eds), *Festschrift für Winfried Hassemer* (Heidelberg, C.F. Müller, 2010) 1055–71.

Krekeler, W, 'Strafrechtliche Risiken des anwaltlichen Berufs' in B Binnewies and R Spatscheck (eds), *Festschrift für Michael Streck* (Cologne, Otto Schmidt, 2011) 717.

Kreß, C, 'Commentary' in A Klip and G Sluiter (eds), *Annotated Leading Cases of International Criminal Tribunals, vol 9, The Special Court for Sierra Leone 2003–2004* (Antwerp, Intersentia, 2006) 202–08.

—— 'Die strafprozessualen Texte des Internationalen Strafgerichtshofs' (2006) 153 *Goltdammer's Archiv* 528.

—— 'The Procedural Texts of the International Criminal Court' (2007) 5 *Journal of International Criminal Justice* 537.

Krystinik, JL, 'The Complex Web of Conflicting Disciplinary Standards in International Litigation' (2003) 38 *Texas International Law Journal* 815.

Kudlich, H, *Strafprozeß und allgemeines Mißbrauchsverbot. Anwendbarkeit und Konsequenzen eines ungeschriebenen Mißbrauchsverbots für die Ausübung strafprozessualer Verteidigungsbefugnisse* (Berlin, Duncker & Humblot, 1998) 389.

Kühne, H-H, 'Rechtsmißbrauch des Strafverteidigers?' (1998) *Neue Juristische Wochenschrift* 3027.

Künzel, M, 'Erfahrungen eines Zwangsverteidigers' (1981) *Strafverteidiger* 464.

Kutak, RJ, *Model Rules of Professional Conduct, Proposed Final Draft of May 30, 1981* (Commission on Evaluation of Professional Standards, May 30, 1981).

LaFave, WR, Israel, JH and King, NJ, *Criminal Procedure*, 4th edn (St Paul, Minn, Thomson/West, 2004).

Lafleur, L, *Der Grundsatz der Komplementarität, Der Internationale Strafgerichtshof im Spannungsfeld zwischen Effektivität und Staatensouveränität* (Baden-Baden, Nomos, 2011) 396.

Lambrecht, U, *Strafrecht und Disziplinarrecht* (Frankfurt a.M., Lang, 1997) 247.

Lang, B, Herberg, J and Weir, C, 'The Duty to Act fairly' (Liberty Focus on Public Law and Human Rights (18 November 2005).

Langford, CM and Bell, DMM, 'Finding a Voice: The Legal Ethics Committee' (2001–02) 30 *Hofstra Law Review* 855.

Lawshe, S, 'Survey Project: Attorney Sanctions, Rule 11' (1989–90) 3 *Georgetown Journal of Legal Ethics* 71.
LeDonne, GB, 'Revisiting the McDade Amendment: Finding the Appropriate Solution for the Federal Government Lawyer' (2007) 44 *Harvard Journal on Legislation* 231.
Leipold, K, *Anwaltsvergütung in Strafsachen* (Munich, Beck, 2004) XXII, 223.
Leitner, W, 'Anmerkung zu LG Mannheim NJW 2009, 1096' (2009) *Neue Juristische Wochenschrift* 1096.
Leubsdorf, J, 'Legal Malpractice and Professional Responsibility' (1995) 84 *Rutgers Law Review* 101.
Levin, LC, 'The Emperor's Clothes and Other Tales about the Standards for Imposing Lawyer Discipline Sanctions' (1998–99) 48 *American University Law Review* 1.
—— 'The Case for Less Secrecy in Lawyer Discipline' (2007) 20 *The Georgetown Journal of Legal Ethics* 1.
Levine, SJ, 'Taking Ethics Codes Seriously: Broad Ethics Provisions and Unenumerated Ethical Obligations in a Comparative Hermeneutic Framework' (2003) 77 *Tulane Law Review* 527.
Lieberman, HR, 'Use of Collateral Estoppel in Attorney Disciplinary Proceedings' (1998) *New York Law Journal* (27 July).
Lienert, H, *Der Contempt of Court im anglo-amerikanischen Recht* (University of Freiburg, unpublished doctoral thesis, 1956) XVI, 169.
Little, DC, 'The Potential Impact of the Restatement (Third) of the Law Governing Lawyers' (1996) 25 *Colorado Lawyer* 83.
Lombardi, GP, 'Legitimacy and the Expanding Power of the ICTY' (2003) 37 *New England Law Review* 887.
Louven, C, 'Die Haftung des deutschen Rechtsanwalts im internationalen Mandat' (1997) *Versicherungsrecht* 1050.
Love, MC, 'The Revised ABA Model Rules of Professional Conduct: Summary of the Work of Ethics 2000' (2002) 15 *Georgetown Journal of Legal Ethics* 441.
Luban, D, *The Good Lawyer: Lawyers' Roles and Lawyers' Ethics* (Totowa, Rowman & Allanheld, 1983) viii, 368.
—— 'The Sources of Legal Ethics: A German–American Comparison of Lawyers' Professional Duties' (1984) 48 *Rabels Zeitschrift für ausländisches und internationales Privatrecht* 245.
—— *Lawyers and Justice, An Ethical Study* (Princeton, Princeton University Press, 1988) 472.
—— 'Partisanship, Betrayal and Autonomy in the Lawyer–Client Relationship: A Reply to Stephen Ellmann' (1990) 90 *Columbia Law Review* 1004.
—— 'Are Criminal Defenders Different?' (1992–93) 91 *Michigan Law Review* 1729.
—— 'Friendly Amendment to Model Rule 8.5' (1995) 36 *South Texas Law Review* 1015.
—— 'Contrived Ignorance' (1998–99) 87 *Georgetown Law Journal* 957.
—— *Legal Ethics and Human Dignity* (Cambridge, Cambridge University Press, 2007) 337.
Lüdtcke, C, Harting, A and Haumer, S, 'Rechtsvergleichende Lösung der praktischen Fälle' in T Weigend, S Walther and B Grunewald (eds), *Strafverteidigung vor neuen Herausforderungen – Denkanstöße aus sieben Rechtsordnungen* (Berlin, Duncker & Humblot, 2008) 323–26.
MacFarlane, JW, 'Frivolous Conduct under Model Rule of Professional Conduct 3.1' (1997) 21 *Journal of the Legal Profession* 231.
MacPhee, B, *Defending Atrocity Crimes, The Requirements of Defense Counsel before the ICC* (The American Non-Governmental Organizations Coalition for the International Criminal Court, 30 August 2005).

Majumdar, M, 'Ethics in the International Arena: The Need for Clarification' (1995) 8 *Georgetown Journal of Legal Ethics* 439.

Malmendier, B, '"Konfliktverteidigung" – ein neues Prozeßhindernis?" (1997) *Neue Juristische Wochenschrift* 227.

Marshall, LC, Kritzer, HM and Zemans, FK, 'Use and Impact of Rule 11' (1991–92) 86 *Northwestern University Law Review* 943.

Martineau, RJ, 'The Attorney as an Officer of the Court: Time to take the Gown off the Bar' (1984) 35 *South Carolina Law Review* 541.

Martyn, S, 'Judicial Reliance on the Restatement (3d) of the Law Governing Lawyers' (1995) 2 *Professional Lawyer* 8.

Marx, JP, 'Intimidation of Defense Witnesses at the International Criminal Tribunals: Commentary and Suggested Legal Remedies' (2007) 7 *Chicago Journal of International Law* 675.

Mashburn, AR, 'A Clockwork Orange Approach to Legal Ethics: A Conflicts Perspective on the Regulation of Lawyers by Federal Courts' (1994–95) 8 *Georgetown Journal of Legal Ethics* 473.

McCaslin, WA, 'Empowering Ethics Committees' (1995–96) 9 *Georgetown Journal of Legal Ethics* 959.

McDowell, B, 'The Usefulness of "Good Moral Character"' (1994) 33 *Washburn Law Journal* 323.

McKay, S, 'Attorney Discipline for Failure to Pay Child Support' (1991) 16 *Journal of the Legal Profession* 289.

McMorrow, JA, 'The (F)Utility of Rules: Regulating Attorney Conduct in Federal Court Practice' (2005) 58 *Southern Methodist University Law Review* 3.

—— 'Creating Norms of Attorney Conduct in International Tribunals: A Case Study of the ICTY' (2007) 30 *Boston College International & Comparative Law Review* 139.

Meadows, WZ, 'Attorney Conduct in the Operation of a Motor Vehicle as Grounds for Professional Discipline' (1993) 18 *Journal of the Legal Profession* 417.

Mehle, V, 'Einschränkung der Strafverteidigung durch das Berufsrecht?' in E-W Hanack et al (eds), *Festschrift für Peter Rieß* (Berlin/New York, de Gruyter, 2002) 317–29.

Mehta, J, 'The Development of Federal Professional Responsibility Rules: The Effect of Institutional Choice on Rule Outcomes' (2007) 6 *Cardozo Public Law, Policy and Ethics Journal* 57.

Meisenberg, SM, 'The Right to Legal Assistance at the International Criminal Tribunal for Rwanda: A Review of Its Jurisprudence' in E Decaux, A Dieng and M Sow (eds), *From Human Rights to International Criminal Law Studies in Honour of an African Jurist, the Late Judge Laïty Kama* (Leiden, Martinus Nijhoff, 2007) 125–57.

Mettraux, G, 'Commentary' in A Klip and G Sluiter (eds), *Annotated Leading Cases of International Criminal Tribunals, vol 9, The Special Court for Sierra Leone 2003–2004* (Antwerp, Intersentia, 2006) 572–74.

Meyer-Goßner, L, *Strafprozessordnung*, 53rd edn (Munich, Beck, 2010) LXVIII, 2328.

Michalke, R, 'Anmerkung zu BGH, Beschl. v. 9.5.2007 – 1 StR 32/07' (2008) *Strafverteidiger* 228.

Miller, CJ, *Contempt of Court*, 3rd edn (Oxford, Oxford University Press, 2000).

Morgan, TD, 'The Evolving Concept of Professional Responsibility' (1976–77) 90 *Harvard Law Review* 702.

—— 'Sanctions and Remedies for Attorney Misconduct' (1994–95) 19 *Southern Illinois University Law Review* 343.

Morris, DM, 'Attorney Fee Forfeiture' (1986) 86 *Columbia Law Review* 1021.

Morton, LM, 'Seeking the Elusive Remedy for Prosecutorial Misconduct: Suppression, Dismissal, or Discipline' (1993–94) 7 *Georgetown Journal of Legal Ethics* 1083.

Mullenix, LS, 'Multiforum Federal Practice: Ethics and *Erie*' (1995–96) 9 *Georgetown Journal of Legal Ethics* 89.

Müller, CA, 'The Work of the International Criminal Court in 2007' (2008) 50 *German Yearbook of International Law* 679.

Müller, E, 'Strafrechtliche Risiken' in G Widmaier (ed), *Münchener Anwaltshandbuch Strafverteidigung* (Munich, Beck, 2006) 2041–77.

—— 'Berufsbild und Berufsethos des Strafverteidigers' (2009) *Neue Juristische Wochenschrift* 3745.

—— 'Von der Verantwortung des Verteidigers – Ein Bericht – III' in F Herzog and U Neumann (eds), *Festschrift für Winfried Hassemer* (Heidelberg, C.F. Müller, 2010) 1089–101.

Müller, E and Gussmann, K, *Berufsrisiken des Strafverteidigers* (Munich, Beck, 2007) XXII, 157.

Müller, I, 'Pflichtverteidiger – Verteidiger wessen Vertrauens?' (1981) *Strafverteidiger* 570.

Muller, S, 'Immunities of ICTY Staff Members, Assets and Archives before the ICTY' in R May et al (eds), *Essays on ICTY Procedure and Evidence in Honour of Gabrielle Kirk McDonald* (The Hague, Kluwer, 2001) 439–54.

Munneke, GA and Davis, AE, 'The Standard of Care in Legal Malpractice: Do the Model Rules of Professional Conduct Define it?' (1998) 22 *Journal of the Legal Profession* 33.

Needham, CA, 'Multijurisdictional Practice Regulations Governing Attorneys Conducting a Transactional Practice' (2003) *University of Illinois Law Review* 1331.

Nehm, K and Senge, L, 'Ursachen langer Hauptverhandlungen – dargestellt am Beispiel von 3 Strafverfahren' (1998) *Neue Zeitschrift für Strafrecht* 377.

Nelson, MB, 'When Clients Become Ex-Clients: The Duties Owed after Discharge' (2002) 26 *Journal of the Legal Profession* 233.

Nemitz, JC, *Strafzumessung im Völkerstrafrecht. Ein Beitrag zur Strafzwecklehre und zur Strafzumessungsmethode unter besonderer Berücksichtigung des Römischen Statuts* (Freiburg, edition iuscrim, 2002) XVI, 312.

Nicholls, C, Montgomery, C and Knowles, JB, *The Law of Extradition and Mutual Assistance*, 2nd edn (Oxford, Oxford University Press, 2007) lxviii, 807.

Niemöller, M, 'Prozessverschleppung – die Absicht genügt' (2008) *Neue Zeitschrift für Strafrecht* 181.

—— 'Nochmals: Prozessverschleppung –Entgegnung auf Bauer' (2009) *Neue Zeitschrift für Strafrecht* 129.

—— 'Zum exzessiven Gebrauch des Beweisantragsrechts' (2010) *Juristische Rundschau* 332.

Nolan, RA, 'Ohio's Frivolous Conduct Statute: A Need for Stronger Deterrence' (1992) 21 *Capital University Law Review* 261.

Noland, GA, 'Court Review of Bar Examiners' Decision on Applicant's Examination' 39 *American Law Reports, 3rd* 719.

Nsereko, DDN, 'Commentary' in A Klip and G Sluiter (eds), *Annotated Leading Cases of International Criminal Tribunals, vol 8, The International Criminal Tribunal for the former Yugoslavia 2001–2002* (Antwerp, Intersentia, 2005) 375–86.

Ogando, JC, 'Sanctioning Unfit Lawyers: The Need for Public Protection' (1991–92) 5 *Georgetown Journal of Legal Ethics* 459.

Oosthuizen, GH, 'Of Misconduct, Contempt, False Testimony, Rule Mutations and other Interesting Powers: A Potpourri of Questions and Notes' in R May et al (eds), *Essays on ICTY Procedure and Evidence in Honour of Gabrielle Kirk McDonald* (The Hague/London/Boston, Kluwer, 2001) 387–402.

Ostler, F, '100 Jahre Rechtsanwaltsordnung' (1979) *Neue Juristische Wochenschrift* 1959.

Ott, NA and Newton, HF, 'A Current Look at Model Rule 8.3: How is it used and what are Courts doing about it?' (2002–03) 16 *Georgetown Journal of Legal Ethics* 747.

Ott, SJ, 'Professional Responsibility 1997-1998, Annual Survey of Michigan Law' (1999–2000) 45 *Wayne Law Review* 1127.

Paepcke, P, 'Die Grenzen anwaltschaftlicher Ehrengerichtsbarkeit' in OF von Gamm, P Raisch and K Tiedemann (eds), *Festschrift für Gerd Pfeiffer* (Cologne, Heymanns, 1988) 985–96.

Parness, JA, 'Enforcing Professional Norms for Federal Litigation Conduct: Achieving Reciprocal Cooperation' (1997) 60 *Albany Law Review* 303.

Patterson, LR and Metzloff, TB, *Legal Ethics: The Law of Professional Responsibility*, 3rd edn (New York, Matthew Bender & Co, 1989) xx, 822.

Pepper, SL, 'The Lawyer's Amoral Ethical Role: A Defense, A Problem, and Some Possibilities' (1986) *American Bar Foundation Research Journal* 613.

Pesce, TA, 'Defining Witness Tampering Under 18 U.S.C. Section 1512' (1986) 86 *Columbia Law Review* 1417.

Peters, A, 'The Model Rules as a Guide for Legal Malpractice' (1992–93) 6 *Georgetown Journal of Legal Ethics* 609.

Petras, MM, 'Survey Project: Attorney Sanctions: General Principles' (1989–90) 3 *Georgetown Journal of Legal Ethics* 57.

Pewitt, JP, 'Effective Self-Discipline: Non-Cooperation in the Disciplinary Process and Bar Association Response' (1989) 14 *Journal of the Legal Profession* 235.

Phelps, WG, 'Grounds for Disqualification of Criminal Defendant's Chosen and Preferred Attorney in Federal Prosecution' (1995) 127 *American Law Reports* 67.

Pinaire, BK, Heumann, MJ and Lermann, J, 'Barred from the Bar: The Process, Politics, and Policy Implications of Discipline for Attorney Felony Offenders' (2005–06) 13 *Virginia Journal of Social Policy & the Law* 290.

Plaster, JC, 'When Lawyers Go Bad: The Evidence Considered in the Disciplinary Proceedings of Convicted Attorneys' (2001) 25 *Journal of the Legal Profession* 219.

Podgor, ES, 'Criminal Misconduct: Ethical Rule Usage Leads to Regulation of the Legal Profession' (1988) 61 *Temple Law Review* 1323.

Poser, S, 'Multijurisdictional Practice for a Multijurisdictional Profession' (2002–03) 81 *Nebraska Law Review* 1379.

Postema, GJ, 'Moral Responsibility in Professional Ethics' (1980) 55 *New York University Law Review* 63,

Poulin, AB, 'Double Jeopardy Protection from Successive Prosecution: A Proposed Approach' (2004) 92 *Georgetown Law Journal* 1185.

—— 'Double Jeopardy and Multiple Punishment: Cutting the Gordian Knot' (2006) 77 *University of Colorado Law Review* 595.

Powell, MJ, 'Professional Divestiture: The Cession of Responsibility for Lawyer Discipline' (1986) *American Bar Foundation Research Journal* 31.

Powell, S, 'Intent as an Element of Attorney Misconduct' (1993) 18 *Journal of the Legal Profession* 407.

Pushaw, RJ, 'The Inherent Powers of Federal Courts and the Structural Constitution' (2001) 86 *Iowa Law Review* 735.

Raveson, LS, 'Advocacy and Contempt: Constitutional Limitations on the Judicial Contempt Power, Part One: The Conflict between Advocacy and Contempt' (1990) 65 *Washington Law Review* 477.

Reaves, ST, 'Procedural Due Process Violations in Bar Disciplinary Proceedings' (1998) 22 *Journal of the Legal Profession* 351.

Remagen-Kemmerling, M, *Der Ausschluß des Strafverteidigers in Theorie und Praxis* (Berlin, Duncker & Humblot, 1992) 217.

Rensberger, JL, 'Jurisdiction, Choice of Law, and the Multistate Attorney' (1995) 36 *South Texas Law Review* 799.

Rhode, DL, 'Moral Character as a Professional Credential' (1985) 94 *Yale Law Journal* 491.

—— *In the Interests of Justice: Reforming the Legal Profession* (Oxford, Oxford University Press, 2000) 268.

—— 'Legal Ethics in an Adversary System: The Persistent Questions' (2005–06) 34 *Hofstra Law Review* 641.

Richmond, DR, 'The Duty to Report Professional Misconduct: A Practical Analysis of Lawyer Self-Regulation' (1998–99) 12 *Georgetown Journal of Legal Ethics* 175.

Rick, MB, *Die verfassungsrechtliche Stellung des Rechtsanwalts* (Bonn, Deutscher Anwaltverlag, 1998) 271.

Riley, TM, 'Tampering With Witness Tampering: Resolving the Quandary Surrounding 18 U.S.C. §§ 1503, 1512' (1999) 77 *Washington University Law Quarterly* 249.

Ritts, GJ, 'Professional Responsibility and the Conflict of Laws' (1993) 18 *Journal of the Legal Profession* 17.

Roach, AE, 'The Virtues of Clarity: The ABA's New Choice of Law Rule for Legal Ethics' (1995) 36 *South Texas Law Review* 907.

Roan, JB and Buxton, C, 'The American Military Justice System in the New Millennium' (2002) 52 *Air Force Law Review* 185.

Robinson, D, 'The Identity Crisis of International Criminal Law' (2008) 21 *Leiden Journal of International Law* 925.

Robinson, PH, 'Fair Notice and Fair Adjudication: Two Kinds of Legality' (2005) 154 *University of Pennsylvania Law Review* 335.

Rogall, K, 'Germany: Principles of Criminal Procedure and their Application in Disciplinary Procedures' (2003) 74 *Revue internationale de droit pénal* 925.

—— 'Die Vorkolloquien und Resolutionsentwürfe zur Vorbereitung des XVII. Internationalen Strafrechtskongresses der AIDP vom 12–19. September 2004 in Peking, Thema III: Die Prinzipien des Strafprozesses und ihre Anwendung im Disziplinarverfahren (Santiago de Chile, 21–26.9.2003)' (2004) 116 *Zeitschrift für die gesamte Strafrechtswissenschaft* 251.

Rogers, CA, 'Context and Institutional Structure in Attorney Regulation: Constructing an Enforcement Regime for International Arbitration' (2003) 39 *Stanford Journal of International Law* 1.

Rohde, C, 'Are Administrative Decisions from the Registry Appealable?' in R May et al (eds), *Essays on ICTY Procedure and Evidence in Honour of Gabrielle Kirk McDonald* (The Hague, Kluwer, 2001) 509–29.

Römermann, V and Hartung, W, *Anwaltliches Berufsrecht* (Munich, Beck, 2002) XVIII, 368.

Rosen, ES and Kuhlman, GA, *Comments on the October 10, 2005 Draft Code of Professional Conduct for Counsel Before the International Court* (American Bar Association, 10 October 2005).

Rossi, RL, 'Factors Affecting Right To Compensation' in *Attorneys' Fees*, 3rd edn (St Paul, Minn, Thomson/West, 2001).

Rothrock, A, 'Attorney Discipline and Disability Process and Procedure – Part 1' (2007) 36 *Colorado Lawyer* 23.

—— 'Attorney Discipline and Disability Process and Procedure – Part 2' (2007) 36 *Colorado Lawyer* 41.

Rotunda, RD, 'Gauging the Impact of the Proposed Restatement of the Law Governing Lawyers' (1998) 9 *Professional Lawyer* 2.

—— 'Alleged Conflicts of Interest because of the "Appearance of Impropriety"' (2005) 33 *Hofstra Law Review* 1141.

—— *Legal Ethics in a Nutshell*, 3rd edn (Eagan, Minn, Thomson/West, 2007) xxxv, 492.

Rotunda, RD and Dzienkowski, JS, *Legal Ethics: The Lawyer's Deskbook on Professional Responsibility*, 2007–08 edn (St Paul, Thomson/West, 2007) xxxi, 2044.

Rueschemeyer, D, *Lawyers and their Society, A Comparative Study of the Legal Profession in Germany and in the United States* (Cambridge, Mass, Harvard University Press, 1973) IX, 254.

Ruzic, KA, 'Military Justice and the Supreme Court's Outdated Standard of Deference: Weiss v United States' (1994) 70 *Chicago-Kent Law Review* 265.

Salditt, F, 'Zur Stellung des Strafverteidigers' in G Widmaier (ed), *Münchener Anwaltshandbuch Strafverteidigung* (Munich, Beck, 2006) 1–26.

Schabas, WA, 'Le Règlement de preuve et de procédure du Tribunal international chargé de poursuivre les personnes présumées responsables de violations graves du droit international humanitaire commises sur le territoire de l'ex-Yougoslavie depuis 1991' (1993–94) 8.1 *Revue québécoise de droit international* 112.

—— *The UN International Criminal Tribunals: the former Yugoslavia, Rwanda and Sierra Leone* (Cambridge, Cambridge University Press, 2006) 766.

—— *The International Criminal Court. A Commentary on the Rome Statute* (Oxford, Oxford University Press, 2010) LXX, 1259.

Scharf, M, 'Chaos in the Courtroom: Controlling Disruptive Defendants and Contumacious Counsel in War Crimes Trials' (Guest Lecture Series of the Office of the Prosecutor, The Hague, 25 September 2006).

Schautz, W, *Strafrechtliche Grenzen des Verteidigerhandelns, insbesondere im Hinblick auf die Strafvereitelung, § 258 StGB* (University of Würzburg, unpublished doctoral thesis, 1988) XXII, 156.

Schellenberg, F, 'Notwendige Verteidigung' (1996) *Strafverteidiger* 641.

Schiller, E and Wertkin, JA, 'Frivolous Filings and Vexatious Litigation' (2000–01) 14 *Georgetown Journal of Legal Ethics* 909.

Schlecht, K, *Die zivilrechtliche Haftung des Strafverteidigers. Zugleich eine Darstellung seines Pflichtprogramms* (Tübingen, Mohr Siebeck, 2006) XI, 270.

Schneider, B, 'Probleme der Auswahl des Pflichtverteidigers und sog. Ersatzverteidigers' (1985) *Zeitschrift für Rechtspolitik* 209.

Schönke, A and Schröder, H (eds), *Strafgesetzbuch, Kommentar*, 28th edn (Munich, Beck, 2010) XXXVII, 3042.

Schomburg, W, 'The Role of International Criminal Tribunals in Promoting Respect for Fair Trial Rights' (2009) 8 *Northwestern University Journal of International Human Rights* 1.

Schomburg, W, Lagodny, O, Gleß, S and Hackner, T, *Internationale Rechtshilfe in Strafsachen*, 4th edn (Munich, Beck, 2006) LXXVII, 2450.

Schultz, U, 'Legal Ethics in Germany' (1997) 4 *International Journal of the Legal Profession* 55.

Schutte, JJE, 'Legal and Practical Implications, from the Perspective of the Host Country, Relating to the Establishment of the International Tribunal for the Former Yugoslavia' (1994) 5 *Criminal Law Forum* 423.

Senge, L, 'Missbräuchliche Inanspruchnahme verfahrensrechtlicher Gestaltungsmöglichkeiten – wesentliches Merkmal der Konfliktverteidigung? Abwehr der Konfliktverteidigung' (2002) *Neue Zeitschrift für Strafrecht* 225.

Seyersted, F, *United Nations Forces in the Law of Peace and War* (Leiden, Sijthoff, 1966) 447.

Simon, WH, 'Ethical Discretion in Lawyering' (1988) 101 *Harvard Law Review* 1083.

—— 'Who Needs the Bar?: Professionalism without Monopoly' (2003) 30 *Florida State University Law Review* 639.

Sinn, A, 'Die Einbeziehung der internationalen Rechtspflege in den Anwendungsbereich der Aussagedelikte' (2008) *Neue Juristische Wochenschrift* 3526.

Sklanzky, DA and Yeazell, SC, 'Comparative Law Without Leaving Home: What Civil Procedure Can Teach Criminal Procedure, and Vice Versa' (2006) 94 *Georgetown Law Journal* 683.

Sluiter, G, 'The ICTY and Offences against the Administration of Justice' (2004) 2 *Journal of International Criminal Justice* 631.

Smith, A, 'The Difference in Criminal Defense and the Difference it Makes' (2003) 11 *Washington University Journal of Law and Policy* 83.

Soeffing, ER, 'Procedural due process requirements in proceedings involving applications for admission to bar' 2 *American Law Reports, 3d* 1266.

Speegle, RV, 'Failure to Cooperate with a Disciplinary Proceeding' (1991) 16 *Journal of the Legal Profession* 325.

Spronken, T, 'Commentary' in A Klip and G Sluiter (eds), *Annotated Leading Cases of International Criminal Tribunals, vol 7, The International Criminal Tribunal for the former Yugoslavia 2001* (Antwerp, Intersentia, 2005) 225–33.

Starr, S, 'Ensuring Defense Counsel Competence at International Criminal Tribunals' (2009) 14 *University of California at Los Angeles Journal of International Law and Foreign Affairs* 169.

Stavis, M, ' Rule 11: Which is Worse – The Problem or the Cure?' (1991–92) 5 *Georgetown Journal of Legal Ethics* 597.

Stigen, J, *The Relationship between the International Criminal Court and National Jurisdictions – The Principle of Complementarity* (Leiden, Martinus Nijhoff, 2008) XII, 533.

Stone, DH, 'The Bar Admission Process, Gatekeeper or Big Brother: An Empirical Study' (1995) 15 *Northern Illinois University Law Review* 331.

Strength, JF, 'Attorney Disciplinary Proceedings: Civil or Criminal in Nature?' (1994) 19 *Journal of the Legal Profession* 257.

Sue, I, *Rechtsstaatliche Probleme des anwaltlichen Standesrechts* (University of Göttingen, unpublished doctoral thesis, 1986) 225.

Sullivan, KM, 'The Intersection of Free Speech and the Legal Profession: Constraints on Lawyers' First Amendment Rights' (1998–99) 67 *Fordham Law Review* 569.

Supple, JR, 'Attorney Discipline in New York: A Nuts and Bolts Primer' in Practising Law Institute (ed), *18th Annual Elder Law Institute* (New York, 2006) 199–210.

Surette, EC, 'Obstructing Justice, Vol 58' in Lawyers Cooperative Publishing (ed), *American Jurisprudence*, 2nd edn (New York, Thomson/West, 1989).

Sward, EE, 'Values, Ideology, and the Evolution of the Adversary System' (1989) 64 *Indiana Law Journal* 301.

Symons, L, 'The Inherent Powers of the ICTY and ICTR' (2003) 3 *International Criminal Law Review* 369.

Taupitz, J, *Die Standesordnungen der freien Berufe: geschichtliche Entwicklung, Funktionen, Stellung im Rechtssystem* (Berlin, de Gruyter, 1991) XXVIII, 1640.

Taylor, KR, 'The Obstruction of Justice Nexus Requirement after Arthur Andersen and the Sarbanes-Oxley Act' (2008) 93 *Cornell Law Review* 401.

Terry, LS, 'An Introduction to the European Community's Legal Ethics Code – Part II: Applying the CCBE Code of Conduct' (1993–94) 7 *Georgetown Journal of Legal Ethics* 345.

Thompson, KA, 'The Utilization of Juries in Lawyer Disciplinary Proceedings' (2000) 24 *Journal of the Legal Profession* 511.

Tolbert, D, 'The ICTY and Defense Counsel: A Troubled Relationship' (2003) 37 *New England Law Review* 975.

Tomain, JP and Watts, BG, 'Between Law and Virtue' (2003) 71 *University of Cincinnati Law Review* 585.

Torcia, CE, *Wharton's Criminal Law*, 4 vols, 2007 Supplement, 15th edn (Deerfield, Ill, Clark Boardman Callaghan, 1993).

Trager, DG, 'Do Bar Association Ethics Committees Serve the Public or the Profession: An Argument for Process Change' (2006) 34 *Hofstra Law Review* 1129.

Triffterer, O (ed), *Commentary on the Rome Statute of the International Criminal Court*, 2nd edn (Munich, Beck, 2008).

Tuinstra, JT, *Defence Counsel in International Criminal Law* (Cambridge, Cambridge University Press, 2009) 323.

Turner, JI, 'Nationalizing International Criminal Law' (2005) 41 *Stanford Journal of International Law* 1.

—— 'Legal Ethics in International Criminal Defense' (2010) 10 *Chicago Journal of International Law* 1.

—— *Plea Bargaining Across Borders* (New York, Aspen Publishers, 2010) XVI, 294.

Uphoff, RJ, 'The Role of the Criminal Defense Lawyer in Representing the Mentally Impaired Defendant: Zealous Advocate or Officer of the Court?' (1988) 1988 *Wisconsin Law Review* 65.

Vagts, DF, 'The International Legal Profession: A Need for More Governance?' (1996) 90 *American Journal of International Law* 250.

—— 'Professional Responsibility in Transborder Practice: Conflict and Resolution' (1999–2000) 13 *Georgetown Journal of Legal Ethics* 677.

Vairo, GN, 'Rule 11 and the Profession' (1998–99) 67 *Fordham Law Review* 589.

—— *Rule 11 Sanctions: Case Law, Perspectives and Preventive Measures*, 3rd edn (Chicago, American Bar Association, 2003).

Veldt, M, 'Commentary' in A Klip and G Sluiter (eds), *Annotated Leading Cases of International Criminal Tribunals, vol 3, The International Criminal Tribunal for the former Yugoslavia 1997-1999* (Antwerp, Intersentia, 2001) 357–62.

Vogel, M, *Versagung, Rücknahme und Widerruf der Anwaltszulassung wegen Unwürdigkeit der Person* (Bonn, Deutscher Anwaltverlag, 1995) 150.

von Münch, I, *Legal Education and the Legal Profession in Germany* (Baden-Baden, Nomos, 2002) 97.

Wagner, T, *Die Konkurrenz zwischen dem Strafverfahren und dem anwaltsgerichtlichen Verfahren in gleicher Sache* (Berlin, Duncker & Humblot, 2005) 188.

Waldhorn, G, *Das Verhältnis von Strafverteidigung und Begünstigung* (University of Würzburg, unpublished doctoral thesis, 1967) V, 95.

Walsh, M, 'The International Bar Association Proposal for a Code of Professional Conduct for Counsel Before the ICC' (2003) 1 *Journal of International Criminal Justice* 490.
Warbrick, C and Brookson-Morris, K, 'Conflicts of Criminal Jurisdiction' (2007) 56 *International and Comparative Law Quarterly* 659.
Ward, CC, 'Law of Choice: Implementation of ABA Model Rule 8.5' (2005–06) 30 *Journal of the Legal Profession* 173.
Warren, S and Brandeis, L, 'The Right to Privacy' (1890) 4 *Harvard Law Review* 193.
Wasserstrom, R, 'Lawyers as Professionals: Some Moral Issues' (1975) 5 *Human Rights* 1.
Wassmann, H-J, *Strafverteidigung und Strafvereitelung* (University of Hamburg, unpublished doctoral thesis, 1982) XII, 276.
Weigend, T, 'Anmerkung zu BGH NStZ 1997, 46' (1997) *Neue Zeitschrift für Strafrecht* 47.
—— 'Germany' in CM Bradley (ed), *Criminal Procedure A Worldwide Study*, 2nd edn (Durham, Carolina Academic Press, 2007) 243–72.
Wendel, WB, 'Free Speech for Lawyers' (2001) 28 *Hastings Constitutional Law Quarterly* 305.
—— 'Nonlegal Regulation of the Legal Profession: Social Norms in Professional Communities' (2001) 54 *Vanderbilt Journal of Transnational Law* 1955.
—— 'Busting the Professional Trust: A Comment on William Simon's Ladd Lecture' (2002–03) 30 *Florida State University Law Review* 659.
Whelan, CJ, 'Ethics Beyond the Horizon: Why Regulate the Global Practice of Law?' (2001) 34 *Vanderbilt Journal of Transnational Law* 931.
Whitaker, JY, 'Remedying Ethical Conflicts in a Global Legal Market' (2006) 19 *Georgetown Journal of Legal Ethics* 1079.
Widmaier, G (ed), *Münchener Anwaltshandbuch Strafverteidigung* (Munich, Beck, 2006) XXXVI, 2768.
Wilkins, DB, 'Legal Realism for Lawyers' (1990) 104 *Harvard Law Review* 468.
—— 'Who Should Regulate Lawyers?' (1992) 105 *Harvard Law Review* 801.
—— 'Afterword: How Should We Determine Who Should Regulate Lawyers? – Managing Conflict and Context in Professional Regulation' (1996) 65 *Fordham Law Review* 465.
Wilkitzki, P, 'The German law on Cooperation with the ICC' (2002) 2 *International Criminal Law Review* 195.
—— 'The German Law on Cooperation with the ICC' (2005) 76 *Revue internationale de droit pénal* 97.
Wilson, J, 'The Definitional Problems with Moral Turpitude' (1991) 16 *Journal of the Legal Profession* 261.
Winkler, K, *Die Strafbarkeit des Strafverteidigers jenseits der Strafvereitelung – zugleich ein Beitrag zur Auslegung des § 261 StGB* (Hamburg, Kovač 2005) XXI, 478.
Wippman, D, 'The Costs of International Justice' (2006) 100 *American Journal of International Law* 861.
Wirtz, M, *Die Regelungskompetenz der Satzungsversammlung* (Bonn, Deutscher Anwaltverlag, 2004) 343.
Wolfram, CW, *Modern Legal Ethics* (St Paul, Minn, West, 1986) xxiv, 1114.
—— 'The Concept of a Restatement of the Law Governing Lawyers' (1987) 1 *Georgetown Journal of Legal Ethics* 195.
—— 'Lawyer Turf and Lawyer Regulation – The Role of the Inherent-Powers Doctrine' (1989–90) 12 *University of Arkansas at Little Rock Law Journal* 1.
—— 'Toward a History of the Legalization of American Legal Ethics – I. Origins' (2001) 8 *University of Chicago Law School Roundtable* 469.

—— 'Expanding State Jurisdiction to Regulate Out-of-State Lawyers' (2001–02) 30 *Hofstra Law Review* 1015.
—— 'Toward a History of the Legalization of American Legal Ethics – II. The Modern Era' (2001–02) 15 *Georgetown Journal of Legal Ethics* 205.
Woodall, WB, 'Attorney Disciplinary Proceedings: Who Has Standing' (2002) 26 *Journal of the Legal Profession* 279.
Woods, F, 'Sanctions – Stepchild or Natural Heir to Trial and Appellate Court Delay Reduction?' (1990) 17 *Pepperdine Law Review* 665.
Yuan, LS, 'Gag Order and the Ultimate Sanction' (1998) 18 *Loyola of Los Angeles Entertainment Law Journal* 629.
Zacharias, FC, 'Specificity in Professional Responsibility Codes: Theory, Practice, and the Paradigm of Prosecutorial Ethics' (1993) 69 *Notre Dame Law Review* 223.
—— 'Federalizing Legal Ethics' (1994) 73 *Texas Law Review* 335.
—— 'A Nouveau Realist's View of Interjurisdictional Practice Rules' (1995) 36 *South Texas Law Review* 1037.
—— 'Reconceptualizing Ethical Roles' (1997) 65 *George Washington Law Review* 169.
—— 'The Quest for a Perfect Code' (1997–98) 11 *Georgetown Journal of Legal Ethics* 787.
—— 'The Purposes of Lawyer Discipline' (2003) 45 *William & Mary Law Review* 675.
—— 'Are Evidence-Related Ethics Provisions "Law"?' (2007) 76 *Fordham Law Review* 1315.
Zacharias, FC and Green, BA, 'Federal Court Authority to Regulate Lawyers: A Practice in Search of a Theory' (2003) 56 *Vanderbilt Law Review* 1303.
—— '"Anything Rather than a Deliberate and Well-Considered Opinion" – Henry Lord Brougham, Written by Himself' (2006) 19 *Georgetown Journal of Legal Ethics* 1221.
Zahar, A, 'International Court and Private Citizen' (2009) 12 *New Criminal Law Review* 569.
Zitrin, R and Langford, CM, *Legal Ethics in the Practice of Law*, 2nd edn (New York, Matthew Bender & Co, 2001).
Zuck, R, 'Internationales Anwaltsrecht' (1987) *Neue Juristische Wochenschrift* 3033.
—— 'Die notwendige Reform des anwaltlichen Berufs- und Standesrechts' (1988) *Neue Juristische Wochenschrift* 175.
—— 'Standesrecht und Verfassungsrecht' in OF von Gamm, P Raisch and K Tiedemann (eds), *Festschrift für Gerd Pfeiffer* (Cologne, Heymanns, 1988) 985–96.
Zweigert, K and Kötz, H, *Einführung in die Rechtsvergleichung*, 3rd edn (Tübingen, Mohr, 1996) 729.
—— *An Introduction to Comparative Law*, 3rd edn (Oxford, Clarendon Press, 1998) XXVI, 714.
Zwiehoff, G, 'Haftung des Strafverteidigers?' (1999) *Strafverteidiger* 555.

INDEX

Index

Index

Index

CPSIA information can be obtained
at www.ICGtesting.com
Printed in the USA
LVHW081924060420
652384LV00007B/51

9 781849 463171